D0440721

A HISTORY OF THE SOUTH

VOLUMES IN THE SERIES

Volume I

THE SOUTHERN COLONIES
IN THE
SEVENTEENTH CENTURY
1607–1689

A HISTORY

OF

THE SOUTH

Volume I

EDITORS

WENDELL HOLMES STEPHENSON

E. MERTON COULTER

The
Southern Colonies
in the Seventeenth
Century
1607-1689

BY WESLEY FRANK CRAVEN

LOUISIANA STATE UNIVERSITY PRESS

THE LITTLEFIELD FUND FOR SOUTHERN
HISTORY OF THE UNIVERSITY OF TEXAS

1970 PRINTING

ISBN 0–8071–0001–3 (cloth)

ISBN 0–8071–0011–0 (paper)

COPYRIGHT © 1949 AND 1970 BY

LOUISIANA STATE UNIVERSITY PRESS

AND THE LITTLEFIELD FUND

FOR SOUTHERN HISTORY

THE UNIVERSITY OF TEXAS

Designed by Robert Josephy

PUBLISHERS' PREFACE

A HISTORY OF THE SOUTH is sponsored by Louisiana State University and the Trustees of the Littlefield Fund for Southern History at The University of Texas. More remotely, it is the outgrowth of the vision of Major George W. Littlefield, C.S.A., who established a fund at The University of Texas in 1914 for the collection of materials on Southern history and the publication of a "full and impartial study of the South and its part in American history." Trustees of the Littlefield Fund began preparations in 1937 for the writing of the history that Major Littlefield contemplated. Meanwhile, a plan had been conceived at Louisiana State University for a history of the South as a part of that institution's comprehensive program to promote interest, research, and writing in the field of Southern history.

As the two undertakings harmonized in essentials, the planning groups united to become joint sponsors of *A History of the South*. Wendell Holmes Stephenson, then professor of American history at Louisiana State University, and the late Charles W. Ramsdell, professor of American history at The University of Texas, were chosen to edit the series. They had been primarily interested in initiating the plans, and it was appropriate that they should be selected to edit the work. Upon the death of Professor Ramsdell in 1942, E. Merton Coulter, professor of history at the University of Georgia, was named his successor.

Volumes of the series are being published as the manuscripts are received. This is the third published volume; it follows Volume V. When completed, the ten-volume set will represent about twelve years of historical planning and research.

EDITORS' PREFACE

THE PROJECT for a multivolume co-operative history of the South had its inception a dozen years ago. In 1936 one of the present editors drafted a plan for a ten-volume work to be published by the Louisiana State University Press, and early in November of the following year sent invitations to some of the scholars selected to contribute to it. Among them was Charles W. Ramsdell, who had, meanwhile, outlined a similar project for six volumes, to be published by the Littlefield Fund for Southern History of The University of Texas and to be written by some of the historians chosen for the Louisiana State University series. One comprehensive history of the South was indispensable; competing projects would be prejudicial to the success of either. Negotiations to merge the two began immediately, with the happy result that the Littlefield Fund for Southern History and the Louisiana State University Press would co-operate in sponsoring the history, the two originators of rival plans would co-operate in editing it, and ten scholars would co-operate in writing it. *A History of the South,* two volumes of which have already appeared, is therefore in several senses a co-operative work.

The death of Dr. Ramsdell in 1942 was a serious misfortune for the project. He was to have contributed the volume on the Southern Confederacy, and the present editors have often felt the need of his broad learning, critical judgment, and sound scholarship. If the format of the work permitted, they would dedicate the series to his memory. Appreciated for his sense of honor and genial spirit, respected for his scholarly contributions, he was also esteemed for his wealth of information on the Confederacy. His habit of perfection did not wholly prevent him from putting in print his vast knowledge of the Confederacy, but it did impede its fullest exploitation.

The contributors to *A History of the South* have predicated their volumes largely upon contemporary records, whether printed or manuscript. They have gone to the original materials of their periods, not only to discover authentic data but also to recapture the spirit of the times. They have utilized the findings of other scholars, but while these have been helpful they have not obviated the necessity for the drudgery of discovery and exploration in a field which until recently was largely virgin soil. The gaps have often been wider than established verities. Particularly has this been true of the early and recent periods of Southern history.

Yet the accumulated heritage of scholarly books and monographs has been impressive. The Critical Essays on Authorities are a tribute not only to the industry of the authors for painstaking research in the documents, but also to the scores of scholars, who, during the past fifty years, have labored to investigate minute segments of Southern history. The present work is a logical culmination of the pioneering efforts of historians whose labors began in the closing years of the nineteenth century.

Professionally trained historians have been at the task of recording the South's past since the decade of the 1880's. Herbert B. Adams attracted a score of young Southern scholars to the Johns Hopkins University, directed their dissertations on Southern subjects, inspired them with ambition to continue research on the history of their region, to inaugurate courses in state and regional history, to build collections of Southern materials, and to establish media for the publication of the results of their research. After the turn of the century, William A. Dunning at Columbia University carried forward the work begun by Adams, instilled in Southern scholars an interest in the War for Southern Independence and in the Reconstruction period, inspired research and publication, and encouraged the teaching of courses in Southern history.

From that early day to this, the momentum has steadily increased. In 1900 some fifteen or twenty books on Southern history were published; a generation later the annual output reached seventy-five to one hundred. Meanwhile, most of the states of the South inaugurated or continued state historical society publications which, by the 1930's, were printing annually a couple of hundred monographs in Southern history. The first systematic course in the history of the region was established at the Johns Hopkins University in 1898; by the 1930's nearly a hundred colleges and universities from New

England to the Rio Grande were offering one or more courses in the history of the South.

This growing interest in the teaching and writing of Southern history led to the formation of the Southern Historical Association in 1934 and to the inauguration of its official publication, the *Journal of Southern History*. Within a few years the Association's membership reached a thousand; its existence served to promote a sense of common problems and purposes among historians interested in the South. It also served to stimulate interest in productivity and to emphasize the need for a comprehensive history of the region. The time seemed propitious for launching a project for a multivolume co-operative history of the South.

The present series is not the first co-operative venture in writing a comprehensive history of the South. Forty years ago a larger group of associated scholars united in producing in twelve volumes *The South in the Building of the Nation* (Richmond, 1909). It served a useful purpose, and parts of it have not been entirely superseded. But the intervening generation has brought to light a voluminous mass of original material, and the researches of scores of scholars have eased the path of present-day historians. A chief deficiency of the earlier work was a lack of integration in organization, for it treated separately the history of the several Southern states, the political, economic, social, and intellectual history of the South, and Southern biography. Each volume of *A History of the South* provides a continuous narrative of a definite period.

It remains to be said that each contributor to *A History of the South* has been left free, within the limits of his period, to present his material and interpret the results of his findings as he pleases. The editors have not provided a central theme or pattern of history, nor have they, except in a general way, attempted to define the South, geographically or otherwise. Authors of early volumes in the series are writing, in fact, about periods which antedated a Southern consciousness. How the physical and human resources of a region, bounded by a zone rather than a line, became welded into a conscious unity and yet remained a part of American society may find expression in the volumes which follow. It is hoped that the layman as well as the student of history may find them a profitable experience.

THE EDITORS

AUTHOR'S PREFACE

TO WRITE of the South when there was no South is a task not without difficulties. The men and women whose story is recounted in the following pages were not Southerners; in fact, they did not think of themselves even as Americans. They were Europeans and, for the most part, Englishmen. The sectional prides and prejudices which found expression in their lives bespoke principally the ancient ethnological and political divisions of Britain, and only gradually did they have occasion to substitute feelings born of their special position in America. It thus has been necessary for the author to write with an eye to geographical limits which as yet had acquired no particular social or political significance, and to do this without reading back concepts that would be out of place and could only distort the picture. An attempt has been made to tell the story in its fullest context, without doing violence to the limits set. It is hoped that the narrative will contribute to a better understanding no less of our national than of our sectional origins, for regional history must find its ultimate justification in the light it brings to a study of the nation itself.

At the same time the assignment carried certain advantages. Just what of the sixteenth and seventeenth centuries belongs to a history of the South? The answer depends to some extent upon one's definition of the South, and since a definition in exact geographical or political terms is difficult to achieve, the emphasis naturally tends to fall on the peculiar qualities of Southern society. It is pertinent to inquire how early the distinguishing features of that society appeared and to re-examine those assumptions about his past which have helped to shape the Southerner's understanding of himself. The author has felt a certain freedom to write, as one born and reared in North Carolina, of those things especially which have acquired importance in the tradition of the South. To cover events and developments in all those areas which at one time or another may have been identified with a Southern attitude has not seemed so important as to trace anew the course of a history to which all Southerners have looked back as on their beginnings.

Such an approach necessarily gives to the Virginia colony a place of special prominence. Not only was it the first of the Southern colonies, but it remained the largest and the most influential. Like Massachusetts, Virginia served as a mother colony from which, after the middle of the seventeenth century, there moved out for the occupation of neighboring areas an increasing stream of emigrants who carried with them social and political habits of enduring influence upon the Southern way of life. A study of the development of local government in seventeenth-century Virginia contributes to an understanding of the political structure of nineteenth-century Kentucky or Tennessee.

As will have been gathered from the foregoing statements, English settlement has been emphasized. Spaniard and Frenchman had pioneered in the original discovery of much of the area that would be divided among the Southern states, but the people who overran the region for the most part traced their origins back to the English settlements of the Eastern seaboard. Here and there a New Orleans or a St. Augustine recalls to mind the empires they once graced, but such relics are valued chiefly for their uniqueness and as pleasant reminders of things now past and gone. An effort has been made to include, in their most significant context, all parts of the story, but the author has sought to avoid byways that would serve chiefly to impose upon the reader new and unfamiliar names that would be noted only to be quickly forgotten.

The footnotes and the appended essay on authorities will indicate the author's heavy indebtedness to other scholars and the points on which it has been necessary to seek guidance from primary sources. In quotations taken from contemporary writings the original spellings have been followed, partly to preserve something of the flavor of the period. But, for the sake of a more readable text, I have made such changes as the use of *u* in place of the interchangeable *u* and *v* at the beginning of a word, and I have not hesitated to write out those abbreviations and symbols which chiefly reflect the limitations of a quill pen and which leave no question as to meaning. Special acknowledgment for helpful suggestions is due Charles S. Sydnor of Duke University, David B. Quinn of the University College of Swansea, and my colleague, Bayrd Still of New York University. Another colleague, Ralph B. Flanders, has been good enough to read the entire manuscript and to place at my disposal his wide knowledge of Southern history. Floyd Holloway, Clerk of Court, York County, Virginia, extended many courtesies to me during a visit to Yorktown for the purpose of studying the York County records. I am also glad to acknowledge courtesies extended by the Duke University Library, by William J. Van Schreeven of the Virginia State Library, and by H. J. Eckenrode of the Virginia Conservation Commission. Especially heavy is my indebtedness to Theodore F. Jones and William A. Finn of the New York University Library and to the staff of the New York Public Library.

W. F. C.

CONTENTS

ILLUSTRATIONS

CHAPTER I

SPAIN'S ROUTE TO THE
NEW WORLD

TO TRAVEL through the South with knowledge of its history is to hearken to the echoing footsteps of men of many nations and races who have passed that way. Through much of its history the region was divided among three contending European empires, each of which has left its imprint. In this contest the superior strength and ultimate triumph of the British stand among the more significant facts of Southern history. But it must not be forgotten that the French settlements at Port Royal and on the St. Johns predated the initial English effort at Roanoke Island by almost a quarter of a century, that the oldest city of the South was Spanish in its origins, that France's challenge from the lower Mississippi to expanding interests of the English colonies along the Eastern seaboard still stood almost on the eve of the American Revolution, and that the final extinction of Spain's title in Florida and in Texas was postponed until the nineteenth century. One must turn back to the earliest days of Europe's interest in America to pick up the story at the beginning.

And in the beginning the story is that of a southern approach to North America by way of the sailing route across the Atlantic that was first made known by Christopher Columbus in the service of Spain. For it was by use of Spain's route to the New World that the settlement not only of Spanish Florida but of the English in Virginia, Maryland, and the Carolinas was initially accomplished. Upon the historian of the South falls thus at the outset an obligation to point up the antiquity of those influences which joined in a common and significant chronicle the development of European imperialism in Africa, in the West Indies, and in the southeastern part of what is now the United States.

It was off Africa, upon whose people there was destined to be imposed so much of the burden of a new world's conquest, that Europeans found their point of departure for the discovery of America. Conveniently situated islands have frequently served as steppingstones for imperialists, and so it was with the Azores, Madeira, the Canaries, and Cape Verde Islands as the Portuguese and Spaniards inaugurated the modern age of maritime adventure. Their route of advance carried down the West African coast into the Gulf of Guinea, past the Grain, Ivory, and Gold Coasts to the Slave Coast. For the Portuguese the West African hump pointed southward toward the Cape of Good Hope and beyond to the fabulous riches of the East Indies. It proved for the Spaniards, however, a barrier turning their attention westward.

In a developing rivalry between the two peoples, political as well as maritime interests were involved. Portugal and Castile were leading competitors for mastery of the Iberian Peninsula, and, when possession of the Canaries had become a principal bone of contention, they entered into the Treaty of Alcacovas in 1479. By its provisions Portugal was effectively excluded from the politics of the rest of the peninsula, receiving in return a recognition of the priority of her claim to the Azores, Madeira, and the Cape Verde Islands and to the exploration and trade of Guinea to the East Indies, while Castile secured the Canaries. Papal sanction, the highest international sanction of the day, confirmed a bargain which so limited Spain's rights in the West African sphere as to cause her to look westward for further opportunities of expansion.[1] And so it was that Christopher Columbus secured from Ferdinand and Isabella backing for his voyage. His primary objective as he set sail from the Canaries on September 6, 1492, will probably remain a favored subject of debate.[2] But controversy over the man's motivation can in no way detract from the importance of his achievement, for it was he who first charted the way to a new world and in so doing fixed one of the decisive dates of history.

[1] For the effect on the American story of successive European rivalries from this point forward, the most suggestive single study is Arthur P. Newton, *The European Nations in the West Indies, 1493–1688* (London, 1933).

[2] It should be noted that Samuel E. Morison, *Admiral of the Ocean Sea; A Life of Christopher Columbus* (Boston, 1942), restores the traditional view that Columbus sailed in quest of the Indies.

The America of his discovery was destined long to be known among Europeans as simply the West Indies. In common usage this designation served chiefly to distinguish the expanding area of Spain's trans-Atlantic activity from the East Indies of Portugal, but however broad the connotation, the name focuses attention on the central importance of those islands to which it was finally limited. For a brief interval after Columbus' first voyage uncertainty existed both as to the achievement that should be credited to him and as to the objectives that should thereafter be followed. But decisive action came with the sailing of Nicolas de Ovando in 1502 with 32 ships and 2,500 settlers for the purpose of converting a feeble outpost, established on the island of Hispaniola by Columbus, into a serious colonizing venture.[3] By the time of Ovando's retirement from command in 1509, his success had provided a solid foundation for further effort. Already, Ponce de León had undertaken, in 1508, the conquest of Puerto Rico. Jamaica's settlement dates from 1509. Two years later Diego Velasquez de Cuellar began the occupation of Cuba. In the Greater Antilles, Spain had added to the Canaries a second outpost of empire.

Upon these West Indian communities, as later upon other such outposts, fell the obligation to press forward with the initial task of geographic exploration. Columbus' voyage of 1492 had posed a problem not yet solved. What lands were these? What was their position in relation to the Indies? What was the answer to many other questions raised by tentative conclusions regarding these two? Columbus had taken up the quest of a solution in his later voyages, and when he was forced to yield the leadership others carried on the search. While one group of adventurers consolidated the Spanish position in the Greater Antilles, another charted much of the South and Central American coast in an attempt to find a way through or around the barrier there revealed. The year

[3] For the following rapid survey of the founding of the Spanish Empire, chief reliance has been placed on Woodbury Lowery, *The Spanish Settlements within the Present Limits of the United States, 1513-1561* (New York, 1901); J. Bartlet Brebner, *The Explorers of North America, 1492-1806* (New York, 1933); Edward G. Bourne, *Spain in America, 1450-1580* (New York, 1904); John N. L. Baker, *A History of Geographical Discovery and Exploration* (London, 1931); Herbert E. Bolton and Thomas M. Marshall, *The Colonization of North America, 1492-1783* (New York, 1920).

3

1513 acquired special significance when Balboa crossed the Isthmus of Panama, and Ponce de León sailed from Puerto Rico to explore the coast of Florida.[4]

Sailing by way of the Bahamas, Ponce landed on the eastern coast of the mainland at Eastertide, by happy inspiration christened his discovery Florida, and coasted down the peninsula into the Gulf of Mexico. Within four years explorers licensed by Velasquez in Cuba were following the shores of Yucatán, from where the work was carried forward to approximately the site of Vera Cruz. The year 1519 saw a Jamaican-based expedition under the command of Alonzo de Pineda complete the initial survey of the Gulf shores. This was the year Magellan found the straits leading to the East in the far south. With information regarding his discovery available after 1522, there remained the possibility of a more inviting passage north of Florida. The test was undertaken by Estevan Gómez in a voyage of 1524–1525 southward from Newfoundland along the Atlantic coast.

In these several enterprises there had been, of course, more than one interest involved. Among others, the prospects for colonization had not been overlooked. In 1514 Ponce de León secured a patent to Florida and in 1521 made an abortive attempt at settlement that cost him his life. Governor Francisco de Garay of Jamaica followed up Pineda's exploration by securing a patent to the northern shores of the Gulf of Mexico. After Gómez came Lucas Vásquez de Ayllon, a man who had combined exploration with slave trading northward along the Atlantic coast from Florida for several years past, to establish in 1526 a colony of short endurance on the Carolina coast. Though elsewhere traders and pearl hunters had been more successful, the real accomplishment of these early years had been the delineation of the eastern bounds of America, or the taking, as it were, of those observations necessary to determine the Spaniard's position in relation to the ultimate goal of successful imperialism.

Let us look briefly at the reading. To the extreme south and around the South American continent was a way to the Orient, but one presenting difficulties that for the time outmeasured its

---

[4] For the possibility of earlier knowledge of Florida, see Lowery, *Spanish Settlements*, 123 ff.

advantages. To the north lay a temperate zone promising pro- ductivity comparable to that of Europe, but as Peter Martyr de- clared, in a passage worth recalling in all attempts to explain the frequent inclination of European imperialists toward southern regions, "what need have we of what is found everywhere in Eu- rope?" "It is towards the south," he continued, "not towards the frozen north, that those who seek fortune should bend their way; for everything at the equator is rich." [5] And along the equatorial coasts of Central America there were men who had reason to be- lieve that this was true. Reports of populous and wealthy com- munities beyond had already brought into position the forces Francisco Pizarro was to lead to the conquest of Peru by 1533, while Mexico City had fallen to Cortes as early as 1521 and the conquest of Mexico was approaching an early conclusion.

The Mexican and Peruvian conquests, together with the estab- lishment of Spanish hegemony over Central America, mark a shift of emphasis from the occupation of island plantations and the pursuit of coastal exploration to the exploitation of continental interiors. Islands previously occupied were not to be abandoned, with the single exception for a short interval in the case of Puerto Rico. Efforts to chart the coastlines more exactly continued, but such ventures took second place to the great overland marches. Drawn on by the hope of duplicating the success of Cortes and Pizarro, and by the familiar Indian trick of reporting gold beyond, the men of Spain marched inland, often with amazing endurance and at times with no more reward than an honorable death and posthumous fame.

Thus to Florida came Pánfilo de Narváez in 1528 with a patent embracing areas formerly granted Ponce de León and Garay. Land- ing on the peninsula enclosing Tampa Bay, he and his settlers marched northward to Appalachee, a small and disappointing Indian village in present-day Alabama. Misfortune turned their footsteps back to the coast near St. Marks Bay, where a loss of shipping led them to an attempt in crudely fashioned vessels to coast their way to Mexico. Misfortune still attended them as they landed, or were wrecked, on the coasts of what would later be known as Texas. Nearly all of the survivors soon succumbed to

[5] Quoted by Brebner, *Explorers of North America*, 32.

inhospitable surroundings, but eight years later Spaniards on the far side of Mexico were astonished to meet with Cabeza de Vaca, treasurer of the expedition. From a point in the neighborhood of the Trinity and Sabine rivers he had worked his painful way across Texas and much of northern Mexico, where, having reached the Pacific slope, he turned southeast to effect a reunion with his fellow countrymen. There was little in his experience, or the account he provided of it, to encourage others to follow in his footsteps.[6] Yet, when he returned to Spain in 1537 the information he brought seemed rather to encourage, than to discourage, Hernando de Soto in plans for another expedition to Florida.

To undertake to retrace de Soto's steps exactly is to attempt the impossible and invite attack from those specialists whose function it is to preserve the vested interest of local tradition. Disembarking on the western coast of the Florida peninsula in 1539, he moved northward to winter at Appalachee. From there a rough approximation of his route carries northeastward across the Savannah, northward through western South Carolina possibly to the headwaters of the Broad River in North Carolina. Then turning southward, he seems to have skirted the Appalachians through upper Georgia into Alabama and continued to a point above Mobile Bay. From there he moved in a northwesterly direction across the present-day state of Mississippi to winter (1540–1541) within a few days' march of the great river. Below the site of modern Memphis he crossed the Mississippi, moved northward a way, then back and westward to the Ozarks. The next winter (1541–1542) seems to have been spent along the Arkansas River, at the mouth of which the leader of this now ragged and desperate band died the following spring. Luis Moscoso de Alvarado, succeeding to the command, persuaded his men to attempt an overland march for New Spain. Their route carried southwestward as far possibly as Texas, and then with apprehension as to what lay ahead strengthened by some knowledge of Cabeza de Vaca's experience, they turned back to the Mississippi. Down it they floated in 1543. By

---

[6] His account, along with original narratives of the expeditions of Hernando de Soto and Francisco Vásquez de Coronado, will be found in Frederick W. Hodge and Theodore H. Lewis, *Spanish Explorers in the Southern United States, 1528–1543* (New York, 1907).

6

September 311 of the original 600 and more had found their way after four remarkable years to the safety of Mexico.

This is an oft-told story of courage and endurance; but it is far more than that. The immediate results for Spanish imperialism were negative, but in the long run for the larger movement of European expansion decidedly positive. Such overland journeys are properly classified with the efforts at sea of Martin Frobisher or John Davis, whose search for the Northwest Passage brought no immediate reward. Where the initial task was one of discovery, each and all who made the venture contributed to the sum of knowledge upon which the ultimate achievement would depend. De Soto and his men had passed through or touched upon perhaps ten of the modern states forming the region to which this history is devoted. Some knowledge of its topography, climate, inhabitants, flora, and fauna, yea even of the humble opossum and the unsociable polecat, had passed into the experience of Europeans.[7]

After 1543 the main force of the Spanish legions in North America marched on in another direction—to the mines of northern Mexico and along a route that carried in time to New Mexico. Elsewhere energies were absorbed in the penetration of South America, or in the adventure across the Pacific leading ultimately to an extension of Spain's empire as far west as the Philippine Islands.

Yet, for a while some were reluctant to yield all hopes of Florida. To it in 1549 came the Dominican Fray Luis Cancer to achieve martyrdom on the very shore upon which he landed. The quest of a more worldly empire was undertaken anew in 1559, when from Mexico came an expedition of some 1,500 colonists and soldiers under command of Don Tristan de Luna y Arellano. The plan called for two settlements: one in the Gulf region and another on the Carolina coast at Santa Elena. Vessels sent forward for preliminary investigation at this second point miscarried, but a base was established at Pensacola Bay. The main body marched inland to occupy a deserted Indian village situated in all probability on the Alabama River. A smaller force pushed on to the province of

---

[7] Note Richard Hakluyt's publication, at a crucial point in the Virginia experiment, of an account of de Soto's experience as *Virginia richly valued* (London, 1609).

Coca in the northeastern part of what is now Alabama. Misfortune and disappointment had dogged the expedition from the first. Withdrawn in 1560 to the coast, its command passed to Angel de Villafañe, whose attention was directed principally to Santa Elena. The search for a suitable location was pressed along the coast as far north perhaps as Cape Hatteras, but the end was unsatisfactory and no settlement was made. The entire project was abandoned in 1561. In this year it was officially decided to leave Florida, for a time at least, to its native inhabitants.

A half century had repeatedly witnessed abortive attempts to exploit the region that is now the southeastern part of the United States. Though the area was not without its attractions nor its yet unexplored possibilities, the immediate rewards that elsewhere so frequently helped the Spaniard over the inevitably difficult first years had here eluded him. It was not so much the advantage in holding Florida as it was the disadvantage of having another hold it that would shortly bring him back to a renewal of the effort.

The same observation may be made of regions west of Florida. After Cabeza de Vaca, de Soto, and Moscoso had come, in 1541, Coronado, who had discovered New Mexico the preceding year. From there he moved into upper Texas, turned northward through Oklahoma into Kansas, and then completed the triangle. But though New Mexico was to be settled by the close of the sixteenth century and Santa Fe, destined to become its most famous community, early in the next, it required a much later French threat on the lower Mississippi to bring Spain to a full awareness of the advantage in occupying Texas. The Spanish occupation of Florida and of Texas falls in a chapter of the empire's history to which the key is imperial rivalry.

First to present a serious challenge to the Portuguese and Spanish monopolies were the French. From 1530, through years known best to Americans for Jacques Cartier's voyages to Canada, French corsairs and interlopers forced Portugal to assume an increasingly burdensome charge in defense of her West African trade. By the middle of the century, when the English made a serious bid to share, the French adventurers had virtually broken the monopoly.[8] In these initial years of transoceanic sailing, as in the present age

[8] John W. Blake, *European Beginnings in West Africa, 1454-1578* (London, 1937).

of air transport, Africa lay close to America, where as early as 1555 a French attempt at settlement was made on the coast of Brazil. Already a hardy band of *filibustiers,* whose names would be better known had there been in France a Richard Hakluyt to record their exploits, had caused the Spaniard to give thought to the protection of his shipping and towns. Among them Huguenots were especially prominent, and it was the Huguenot Jean Ribaut who in 1562 coasted the shore of Florida to establish a short-lived settlement at Port Royal, within the present limits of South Carolina. Two years later a more serious effort was made under the command of René Laudonnière, best known to students of American settlement for his account of Florida which afterward was closely studied by the English colonizers of Virginia. This time the French selected a site farther south, and there on the St. Johns River they built Fort Caroline.[9]

In 1565 the infant community at Fort Caroline entertained briefly Captain John Hawkins, on the way home from the second of his famous slave-trading expeditions. If his hosts received him with a measure of caution, as the record indicates, they may be pardoned, for he represented a development in English policy of hardly less interest to the French than to the Spanish.

The beginnings of England's golden age of adventure, though usually stamped Elizabethan, predated Elizabeth's reign by several years. Initial moves were consequently shaped by political considerations arising from the Catholic reaction under Queen Mary and her marriage to Philip II of Spain. The obvious necessity, in the circumstances, of avoiding a conflict with Spanish interests was reinforced by economic considerations directing attention to possibilities lying outside the areas of Spanish endeavor. England's staple was woolen cloth, and the need to expand its market, which

---

[9] See René Laudonnière's account in Richard Hakluyt, *The Principal Navigations, Voyages, Traffiques & Discoveries of the English Nation* (Glasgow, 1903–1905), VIII, 439–86; IX, 1–100; Jean Ribaut, *The Whole & True Discouerye of Terra Florida; A facsimile reprint of the London edition of 1563, together with a transcript of an English version in the British Museum with notes by H. M. Biggar, and a biography by Jeannette Thurber Connor* (De Land, 1927); Henry P. Biggar, "Jean Ribaut's Discouerye of Terra Florida," in *English Historical Review* (London), XXXII (1917), 253–70; Woodbury Lowery, *The Spanish Settlements within the Present Limits of the United States. Florida, 1562–1574* (New York, 1905).

underlies so much of English adventure through the second half of the sixteenth century, made of Cathay (northern China) with its temperate climate and its reputed wealth an object of special interest.[10] In effect, Elizabeth's accession in 1558 altered the situation but slowly. Her position, to say the least, was for a time precarious, and dictated the caution in foreign affairs which seems to have been suited to her temperament. Maritime adventure was marked, therefore, by an initial focus on the search for a northern passage to the East, a line of action calculated not to join the issue with Spain and at the same time to serve best the economic needs of the community.

As early as 1553 a company of gentlemen and merchants had sent an expedition around the Scandinavian peninsula in search of a northeast passage. The English ships failed to make Cathay, but one of the three reached the White Sea and the territories of Ivan of Russia. The company, originally chartered by Edward VI, was rechartered in 1555 by Philip and Mary in an action implying a limited though not insignificant sanction by Philip of English maritime ambitions. Known best as the Muscovy Company, it prosecuted a valuable trade with the Russians and through the early years of Elizabeth's reign sought an overland trade by way of Russia with Cathay and Persia.[11] Though the results in this latter effort proved disappointing, the Muscovy Company stands first among the great corporate agencies of Elizabethan adventure. Its primacy emphasizes the weight of those influences which at the outset worked for what has been described as a peaceful program of expansion.

Hawkins' voyages were by no means altogether out of line with such a program. Since the days of Henry VII and the marriage of Catherine of Aragon to Henry VIII Englishmen had traded profitably with Spain. And though new difficulties were now appearing, English merchants were still admitted to the Canaries as well as to Spanish ports. The possibility that these concessions might be broadened to include a trade with the West Indies ap-

---

[10] See particularly, Sir William Foster, *England's Quest of Eastern Trade* (London, 1933).

[11] *Ibid.*; James A. Williamson, *Maritime Enterprise, 1485–1558* (Oxford, 1913), 307–37.

peared worth testing. It is well to recall that for a time after Elizabeth's accession the danger to her position revolving around the person of Mary Queen of Scots was joined to a French, rather than a Spanish, championship of Mary's claim to the English throne. French influence at the Scottish court carried a threat, from the Spanish point of view, that English sea power might soon be allied with that of France in challenging Spain's supremacy, and at a time when as yet the defense of her imperial interests was imperfectly prepared. In the circumstances it was reasonable to assume that Spain might not be indifferent to suggestions of mutual assistance from the English. Perhaps, in return for aid in policing seas overrun by French corsairs, she would allow suitable trade concessions in West Indian ports. It was true that Philip, in loyalty to treaties with Portugal, had early opposed the English trade to Africa which Hawkins now sought to join with a trade to the West Indies, but princes had been known before to take a selfish view of their interests.

With the purpose of testing the possibilities and demonstrating a mutual advantage, with care to maintain the appearance of a legitimate trade, and with the aid of Spanish subjects at several points, Hawkins made his first voyage in 1562, the very year of Ribaut's settlement at Port Royal.[12] A cargo, chiefly of West African Negroes, was exchanged in the Spanish plantations, principally for sugar and hides. The result justified a second venture in 1564. By the time of his arrival in America early in 1565, Spanish colonial officials had been instructed to forbid the trade—an official ruling which gave warning of a determination, in keeping with established policy, to maintain an exclusive monopoly. But attention was directed first to expulsion of the French, and Hawkins, though with more difficulty than before, disposed of his cargo.

The French challenge, indeed, presented a far more serious problem than did Hawkins. Fort Caroline's position on the St. Johns commanded the homeward route of the Spanish ships, for

---

[12] The authority of course is James A. Williamson, *Sir John Hawkins, the Time and the Man* (Oxford, 1927). See also, and especially for the situation in the Spanish colonies that made the trade possible, Irene A. Wright (ed.), *Spanish Documents Concerning English Voyages to the Caribbean, 1527–1568* (London, 1929).

the winds and currents of the Caribbean area offered no satisfactory alternative to the Florida channel and a course running with the Gulf Stream northward past Bermuda. Philip II committed the task to his ablest seaman, Pedro Menéndez de Avilés, an incorruptible servant of his king and a man possessed of so fanatical a devotion to the Catholic faith as to make of him a doubly strong instrument for the expulsion of intruders who were at the same time Protestants. At the head of an expedition sent from Spain for the purpose, he reached Florida on August 28, 1565. On the same day, Ribaut arrived off Fort Caroline with reinforcements and instructions to supersede Laudonnière in the command. The issue was quickly joined. South of Fort Caroline, Menéndez fortified a position to which he gave the name of St. Augustine. Ribaut unwisely moved by sea with most of his force to attack the new fortification. Menéndez struck overland to capture, on September 20, Fort Caroline, which had been left with a depleted garrison. Ribaut and his men suffered shipwreck to the south of St. Augustine, and had no choice but to surrender and throw themselves on Menéndez's mercy. As is well known, there was no mercy. Save for a handful who professed Catholicism, they were put to the sword. And so ended the French colony.[13]

The task of advancing French interests in America had fallen largely to the Huguenots, and France was now almost on the eve of the St. Bartholomew's Day Massacre. Except for the continued activity of *filibustiers,* renewal of the French challenge awaited the seventeenth century. On our maps today only the name of Port Royal survives to remind us of this earlier defiance.

Hawkins' turn came at San Juan de Ulua, off Vera Cruz, in 1568. He had set sail on the third of his voyages the preceding year. Though realist enough to appreciate the trend of events, he had not entirely surrendered his earlier hopes and had departed with assurances to the Queen of a peaceful trade. To these assurances he had been faithful, according to his lights. Force had been used, but it was trade and not plunder on which he insisted. When attacked by a fleet newly arrived from Spain to which he probably

[13] In addition to authorities already cited, see Jeannette T. Connor (ed. and trans.), *Pedro Menendez de Aviles, Adelantado, Governor and Captain-General of Florida, Memorial by Gonzalo Solis de Meras* (De Land, 1923).

could have denied admittance to the harbor where his own vessels lay at anchor, he regarded it as the rankest sort of treachery. Escaping with only two ships and a few of his men, Francis Drake among them, he returned home to carry the word that all hope of collaboration in America between England and Spain was ended. It was now clear that Englishmen, like Frenchmen, must prepare for an open defiance of Spain's pretensions or else be excluded from America.

The date itself is significant, for it marks a turning point in Europe no less than in America. By 1568 the Catholic Counter Reformation had gained momentum in its effort to stem the growth of Protestantism, and the line between the contending ideologies of the day had been more sharply defined. Religious wars in France had been renewed in 1567, with a consequent reduction of her power both on the Continent and abroad. Almost simultaneously a Protestant rebellion in Scotland, expressive partly of the dislike of French influence in the Scottish government, led in 1568 to Mary's expulsion from the country and her long imprisonment at the hands of Elizabeth. The Queen of the Scots thus became at last a convenient instrument of Spanish policy, her claims to England's throne a ready means to effect the removal of Elizabeth, who in 1570 was belatedly excommunicated by the Pope. With Mary substituted for Elizabeth, not only would it be possible to restore the leading Protestant power to the Catholic fold but her increasingly troublesome seamen might be brought under effective control. The threat of such a move to England's political, religious, and economic independence required, of course, no underscoring for loyal Englishmen. Hawkins turned his attention to preparation of the navy for the seemingly inevitable conflict, while Drake, his former lieutenant, moved to an immediate acceptance of the challenge by plundering in 1573 the Peruvian treasure as it passed through Panama.[14] Soon the Elizabethan "sea dogs" were as great a scourge along the Spanish Main as had ever been the *filibustiers*. And to them were added the "sea beggars" of Holland, proudly wearing, as have so many men, a term of derision. In the Netherlands the Protestant subjects

[14] See James A. Williamson, *The Age of Drake* (London, 1938), in addition to his study of Hawkins.

13

of Philip II had given him trouble as early as 1566. Three years later they were pressing an organized rebellion for independence. To them, as with the English, the breaking of Spanish power in Europe involved its reduction in America. Rarely have circumstances so combined to permit men, on both sides of the conflict, to serve God and country with such equal devotion.

The contest was partly, of course, diplomatic. Spain insisted upon monopolistic rights in America except insofar as she shared them with Portugal under the treaty of demarcation, and upon a doctrine of mare clausum for the defense of all approaches to her territories. In justification of her position she advanced the principle of title by right of discovery. Her opponents replied, first, in kind. John Cabot acquired for this generation of Englishmen an importance he had not been accorded for half a century. His explorations of the North Atlantic had been close in point of time to the voyages of Columbus, and though the discoveries made had encouraged little of the further effort that might have provided a direct link with Elizabethan adventure, they offered a useful basis for England's claim to a share in the New World. Right of discovery, however, could not carry Englishmen everywhere in America that they wished to go; especially would they find themselves handicapped in entering some of its more southern regions. Consequently, a more useful argument, and one that has repeatedly done service since, was found in the doctrine of effective occupation. According to that doctrine, Spain could properly claim an exclusive title only to areas she had actually occupied. As for the question of control over seaway approaches to her territories, circumstances lent favor in the eyes of Spain's opponents to doctrines regarding freedom of the seas that were subsequently summed up by the Dutch student Hugo Grotius in his *Mare Liberum*.[15]

A century would pass before Spain's agreement to either of these principles had been won. Meanwhile, in preference to surrender of the advantages of a European peace because of inabilty to agree on questions outside Europe, it became the custom to recognize

[15] The best discussion of the diplomatic side of the story is in Newton, *European Nations in the West Indies*. See also, Blake, *European Beginnings in West Africa;* Eva G. R. Taylor (ed.), *The Original Writings & Correspondence of the Two Richard Hakluyts* (London, 1935), II, 290–313, 420–25; and note the younger Hakluyt's later translation, *ibid.,* I, 62; II, 497–99, of the *Mare Liberum.*

that the peace of Europe did not extend beyond the "lines of amity"—the Tropic of Cancer to the south and the prime meridian to the west. From this virtual agreement to disagree came the colorful and all too frequently accurate phrase, "No peace beyond the line."

In the continuing contest, England enjoyed a certain advantage because Philip II's support of the early efforts of the Muscovy Company had by implication excepted the Arctic regions from the monopolies claimed under the treaty between Spain and Portugal.[16] Having thus yielded on the point of a literal interpretation of where the line ran, it was the more difficult to say just where it should be finally drawn. With Sir Humphrey Gilbert and Sir Walter Raleigh succeeding Ribaut and Laudonnière, with the English in the seventeenth century acquiring footholds along the Chesapeake and Massachusetts bays, the French in the St. Lawrence basin, the Dutch at the mouth and up the valley of the Hudson, and all of the three in the Lesser Antilles, the line for practical purposes was drawn so as increasingly to restrict Spain's pretensions. Ultimately, her original position became even diplomatically untenable.

Yet it was only her pretensions to a monopoly that she actually surrendered. Save for the relatively unimportant colony of Jamaica, seized by Oliver Cromwell in 1655, the solid achievement of a century of empire building remained intact. Internal revolution rather than conquest by European rivals was to bring about the empire's eventual disruption, and not until the nineteenth century. The fact testifies to the effectiveness of defensive plans drawn originally in no small part by Menéndez and thereafter gradually perfected. An answer to the depredations of privateers and pirates was found in the organization of the famous treasure fleets and a system of convoys, to which was added fortification of coastal cities. Havana emerged as a city of first importance because of its strategic location as a fortified point of concentration for the Panamanian and Mexican fleets on the way home. She thus became the key to control of the homeward route, her capture the dream of every pirate who roamed American seas. In supplement to her defenses stood those of St. Augustine. The fortifications begun

16 Williamson, *Maritime Enterprise*, 337.

there in 1565 by Menéndez represented no momentary tactical maneuver. They were a vital part of the strategy adopted for the empire's defense.

The Florida colony, in the words of Professor Herbert E. Bolton, was the first of several defensive salients thrust out to counter the moves of aggressive opponents.[17] That the place was potentially dangerous had been demonstrated by the French. The English followed shortly with a challenge at Roanoke Island. Though events proved they had been a bit hasty, they later returned to the James River and in time even offered defiance on the lower Carolina coast. Thus Florida remained primarily a defensive frontier province. It attracted little Spanish settlement, and much of its terrain at the time of its final surrender to the United States was as wild and untouched by the white man as it had been at its first occupation. Here the Spaniard relied upon that combination of military and missionary outposts which for so long characterized his frontier defenses.

Upon the missionaries fell an especially heavy responsibility for extending Spanish influence northward along the coast. Without minimizing in any way the sincere zeal that often brought them to a martyr's end, it should be noted that extension of the Kingdom of God and of the Spanish Empire went hand in hand. The policy effectively expressed the two loyalties so strongly joined in the life of Menéndez, who had prepared the way within a year of his expulsion of the French. By the close of 1566 he had coasted the shores of his province, of which he was *adelantado,* and established posts from Tampa Bay on the west side to Santa Elena (Port Royal) in the north. On Santa Catalina Island below the Savannah he left a small garrison by agreement with its native chieftain, Guale, whose name was eventually applied to the entire coastal area extending from Santa Elena southward to the St. Johns River. The missionary task, fittingly, was committed to the Society of Jesus, a new order and already one of the most vigorous forces within the Catholic Counter Reformation.

The first Jesuits to undertake established mission work in Guale

[17] Herbert E. Bolton, "Defensive Spanish Expansion and the Significance of the Borderlands," in *The Trans-Mississippi West, Papers Read at a Conference Held at the University of Colorado* (Boulder, 1930), 15.

arrived in 1568. Two years later a native uprising seriously disarranged their plans. After a final bid made so far north as to have been placed by some writers on the Rappahannock River in Virginia, the Jesuits abandoned the field in 1572. They were replaced by the Franciscans, who for nearly two hundred years taught the savages and guarded Spain's outposts. They established their stations principally on the islands lying off the mainland savannahs, traveling to and fro by means of the intervening passage. With the Jesuits had departed Menéndez, who died in Spain in 1574. His former responsibilities fell partly to a nephew, Pedro Menéndez Marques. First a seaman, as was his uncle, he had been trained in Menéndez' service, and as governor of Florida, from 1577 to 1589, he became that region's dominant personality. French corsairs were a frequent source of trouble, harrying the coast, trading for sassafras, and intriguing with the natives. After Drake had sacked St. Augustine in 1586, the Santa Elena post was withdrawn, and for almost a century thereafter Santa Catalina de Guale marked the northern frontier. A native uprising that swept the coast in 1597 threatened to destroy the work accomplished by the first generation of missionaries, but the rebellion was suppressed and the missions rebuilt. By the time of Virginia's founding in 1607 the Franciscans stood on the threshold of the golden age of their mission in Florida.[18]

But the story of the Spaniard's early efforts in America is not alone the story of conquistador and missionary, nor is its pertinence to other national efforts restricted to areas of conflicting titular claims. Of special interest to students of Southern history is his

[18] Herbert E. Bolton (ed.), *Arredondo's Historical Proof of Spain's Title to Georgia* (Berkeley, 1925); Jeannette T. Connor (ed.), *Colonial Records of Spanish Florida, 1570–1580* (De Land, 1925–1930); John T. Lanning, *The Spanish Missions of Georgia* (Chapel Hill, 1935); Maynard Geiger, *The Franciscan Conquest of Florida (1573–1618)* (Washington, 1937); Maynard Geiger, *Biographical Dictionary of Franciscans in Spanish Florida and Cuba (1528–1841)* (Paterson, N. J., 1940); Michael Kenny, *The Romance of the Floridas; the Finding and the Founding* (New York, 1934), a frequently uncritical story mainly of the Jesuits; Mary Ross, "French Intrusions and Indian Uprisings in Georgia and South Carolina, 1577–1580," in *Georgia Historical Quarterly* (Savannah), VII (1923), 251–81; Mary Ross, "The French on the Savannah 1605," *ibid.*, VIII (1924), 167–94; James G. Johnson, "The Yamassee Revolt of 1597 and the Destruction of the Georgia Missions," *ibid.*, VII (1923), 44–53; and for a more recent study, Verne E. Chatelain, *The Defenses of Spanish Florida, 1565 to 1763* (Washington, 1941).

profitable development in the West Indian plantations of such commodities as sugar, ginger, tobacco, and hides—the products of a successful transplanting into the New World of Old World staples or the fruit of agricultural experiment with plants indigenous to America itself. Indeed, the history of Southern agriculture with its emphasis on tobacco, rice, indigo, and cotton has its true beginning, like the closely related story of American Negro slavery, in the Spanish colonies. Here began a chronicle of agricultural adventure that is basic to any understanding of Europe's response to the discovery of America, and that is particularly pertinent to an appreciation of the hope and faith which led to settlement of the southern portion of the United States.

It was a new land in fact as well as name that Columbus had discovered, and no European people, economic necessity aside, could have failed to be stirred by thought of its untested potentialities. Though inspired primarily by economic needs and aspirations, the initial tests drew also upon the increasingly active intellectual interests of modern Europe and the age-old love of man for what is novel and curious.

It long had been the custom for travelers, whether on some pilgrimage, a political mission, or a commercial voyage, to bring home seeds and plants for trial in their own gardens or to present as flattering tokens to their friends. The age of maritime adventure greatly extended the range of this activity and joined it more closely to considerations of national advantage and commercial profit. To reconstruct a picture of the age in all its richness of detail, it is necessary to take note of the elder Richard Hakluyt as, in 1582, he recorded for an English factor at Constantinople a list of plants and other things not native to England but at that time adding richly to its life. He urged the factor to be ever vigilant to aid in further imports of the sort in the belief that he might in this way "do more good to the poore . . . then ever any subject did in this realme by building of Almeshouses, and by giving of lands and goods to the reliefe of the poore." [19] It is no less necessary to recapture the younger Richard Hakluyt's "singuler delight" on viewing the "rare and strange curiosities" collected by Sir Walter Cope, a leading figure in the settlement of Virginia and in other commercial ven-

[19] Tayor (ed.), *Writings & Correspondence of the Two Richard Hakluyts*, I, 193–95.

tures of the day.[20] Notice must be taken even of such items as "the strange litle fish" sent from Bermuda in 1618 by the Reverend Lewis Hughes to his friend and patron the Earl of Warwick, or the box of Bermuda "pepper" forwarded to Sir Nathaniel Rich with instructions for its use as a specific "against the wyndeness in the stummack" from which Sir Nathaniel seems to have been a chronic sufferer.[21]

Not only did the discovery of America extend the range of search, but at the same time it challenged men to try a wide variety of possibilities in a new soil and a new climate. The prospect was the more inviting because of experience previously gained in Madeira, the Azores, and the Canaries. In Madeira the Portuguese had experimented with grapes and produced a wine destined to win an enduring fame by the end of the sixteenth century. Into the Azores they successfully transplanted woad, a major source of the highly favored blue dyes. The Spaniards carried sugar cane into the Canaries, where they acquired a fund of experience upon which they later drew heavily in Hispaniola.

As they crossed over to the West Indies, their ships must often have given the impression of a Noah's Ark. On board they carried cattle, horses, hogs, sheep, dogs and cats, wheat and other European grains, and the seed or plants for rice, woad, sugar cane, radishes, lettuce, melons, olives, palms, dates, pomegranates, figs, peaches, oranges, lemons, and vines of various sorts. In the pages of Gonzalo Fernández de Oviedo's *Natural hystoria de las Indias* of 1526 as translated by Richard Eden in his *Decades of the Newe Worlde or West India* (1555), Englishmen read of how "all such sedes, settes, or plantes" brought out of Spain and planted in Hispaniola became "muche better, bygger, and of greater increase" than in Europe. Beasts increased "in lyke abundaunce," were "much bygger, fatter, and also of better taste then owres in Spayne." [22] Actually, many of the experiments proved unsuccessful. With wheat, for

20 *Ibid.*, II, 408.

21 Manchester Papers (Public Record Office, London), 232, 233. This substantial and especially revealing collection of private papers pertaining to early colonization includes correspondence of the Rich family with their relatives, tenants, and friends in Bermuda.

22 Edward Arber (ed.), *The First Three English Books on America* (Birmingham, 1885), 239.

instance, there were difficulties comparable to those later experienced in the North American colonies, where as a result the Indian corn early acquired a prominent place in the American diet. On the other hand, cattle thrived and the export of hides became commercially profitable. Mulberries took root and silks—velvets, satins, taffetas—of good quality were produced. In Mexico wool was grown, and both cloth and hats were exported. Vines and olives thrived in Peru, where there were also textiles. In Hispaniola ginger prospered and the production of sugar was developed into a staple industry destined with time to spread throughout the West Indies. By 1542 the annual export of sugar had reached two and one-half million pounds.[23]

Many an old mulberry in the back yard today, or wild grape plucked in the woods, testifies to the effort of our English forefathers to duplicate these achievements of the Spaniards and the Portuguese. Those who prefer more exact evidence may follow the long record in the English colonies of experimental projects for the production of silk, sugar, wine, olive oil, indigo, and rice, to mention only the more important, projects which enlisted the active interest of such men as the two Hakluyts, Sir Edwin Sandys, Sir William Berkeley, Edward Digges, the Earl of Shaftesbury, and other worthy forerunners of Eliza Lucas. For documentary evidence that much of the faith inspiring these efforts originally was based on the achievement of Spanish and Portuguese planters, it is necessary to cite only the dedicatory epistle of Hakluyt's edition of Laudonnière's journal in 1587. The dedication is to Raleigh, and was written the very year his second colony reached Roanoke. Though disappointed over the failure of the first colony, Hakluyt was convinced that the project would yet prosper, "partly by certaine secret commodities already discovered by your servants, & partly by breeding of divers sorts of beasts in those large and ample regions, and planting of such things in that warme climat as wil best prosper there, and our realme standeth most in need of." "And this I find," he continued, "to have bin the course that both the Spaniards and Portugals tooke in the beginnings of their dis-

---

[23] Clarence H. Haring, *Trade and Navigation between Spain and the Indies in the Time of the Hapsburgs* (Cambridge, Mass., 1918), 124–28; Ulrich B. Phillips, *American Negro Slavery* (New York, 1918), 19; Bourne, *Spain in America.*

coveries & conquests." When the Spaniards first came to Hispaniola they "found neither sugar-canes nor ginger growing there, nor any kind of our cattel," but they sent cattle and "other profitable beasts . . . & transported the plants of sugar-canes, and set the rootes of ginger: the hides of which oxen, with sugar and ginger, are now the chiefe merchandise of that Island." Having cited Portugal's success with wine in Madeira and woad in the Azores, he concluded: "if our men will follow their steps, . . . I doubt not but in due time they shall reape no lesse commoditie and benefit." [24]

The very range of the Spaniard's explorations heightened his appreciation of the opportunities for agricultural experiment, a fact that lends more than passing significance to his several unsuccessful attempts to colonize the southern parts of what is now the United States. Though he was repeatedly forced to withdraw, the chances are that some seed or plant new to the area took root. Therefore, care must be exercised in relying upon the accounts of subsequent travelers for identification of indigenous flora. The native flora of the Caribbean islands appears not to have been very rich, but elsewhere, especially in Central America and southern Mexico, the Spaniard chanced upon the areas giving origin to the greatest number of the cultivated species of American plants.[25] Some of these, like maize, beans, and pumpkins, were already widely distributed over the two continents. Others, including potatoes, cacao, chili peppers, and New World cottons, received wider distribution at the hands of the Spaniard. Some, among them potatoes, maize, and tobacco, were early carried to Europe, whence their cultivation spread to other parts of the world.

Of native plants developed commercially by the European settler, tobacco was the most important.[26] The most valuable of its several species, *Nicotiana tabacum,* was widely distributed over

[24] Hakluyt, *Voyages,* VIII, 441–42. See also, Henry Hawks's informative report of 1572, after five years in Mexico, to the elder Hakluyt, in Taylor (ed.), *Writings & Correspondence of the Two Richard Hakluyts,* I, 96–114.

[25] Donald D. Brand, "The Origin and Early Distribution of New World Cultivated Plants," in *Agricultural History* (Chicago, Baltimore), XIII (1939), 109–17.

[26] The following discussion is drawn principally from the informative introductory essay in Jerome E. Brooks, *Tobacco, Its History Illustrated by the Books, Manuscripts and Engravings in the Library of George Arents, Jr.* (New York, 1937–1938). See also, Charles M. MacInnes, *The Early English Tobacco Trade* (London, 1926).

the areas brought under Spain's control. To the north as far as Canada and eastward from the Mississippi Valley, the natives relied upon a second and commercially less promising species, *Nicotiana rustica.* As is well known, tobacco held a significant place in the social and ceremonial life of many, though by no means all, of the American Indians. Over much of the two continents reliance was placed on a natural growth, but in some parts, especially around Yucatán and Tabasco, the cultivation of tobacco and a skilled technique in its curing were rather advanced. In this region, apparently, it was popularly taken in the form of a roll, the prototype of the cigar. To the north, it commonly was used in a clay pipe or another such container. Nowhere, it is worthy of note, is there much evidence that the natives assigned to tobacco the therapeutic qualities so shortly given it by Europeans. Early explorers, no doubt, regarded it chiefly as a curiosity, and as such it must have been first carried to Europe. Curiosity, however, leads naturally to an experimental mood. Those of us who have known the excruciating experiences of tobacco sickness probably hold the key to the earliest conviction that here indeed was a new and powerful drug.

Whatever the origin of the belief, it was as a therapeutic that tobacco first won wide popularity in Europe. In the late 1550's a Flemish mariner carried *N. rustica* from Florida to Lisbon. There its sovereign qualities as a cure-all had by 1560 become literally the rage, and its fame had begun to spread. Jean Nicot, French ambassador to Portugal, introduced the magic weed to Catherine de Medici with the result that his name has been associated with it since. Rapidly thereafter tobacco came to hold a favored place in the physic gardens of Europe as its popularity ran the course of the first great Indian-medicine illusion to which the European fell a victim. It was taken internally as a purgative and emetic (and who can doubt its effectiveness?), applied externally to wounds and sores, inhaled for asthmatic and rheumatic troubles, and was even regarded as of benefit in cases of failing eyesight and deafness. The survival, even in our own day, of a belief in the curative qualities of tobacco lends emphasis to the strength of these earlier convictions. Many now living have seen it applied to an aching tooth or to the sting of a wasp on a boy's arm, and can recall some

22

elderly woman smoking a pipe by her doctor's prescription, perhaps worrying a bit because she had learned to like it. The first advocates of tobacco went so far in their insistence on its virtues, however, that no small part of the discredit that soon overtook the weed may be charged to the exaggerated claims of its earliest devotees.

The use of tobacco as a therapeutic agent afforded little commercial profit to any save those of the pharmaceutical fraternity. Quantities used were relatively small and were provided largely out of European gardens. But meanwhile the social use of tobacco was steadily growing and preparing the way for a most profitable market. Settlers in America early acquired the habit, and it was probably for their own use that they first undertook its cultivation. Prior to 1535 planters imported into Hispaniola the cultivated variety of *N. tabacum,* and applying something of the techniques of the Yucatán natives, produced an extraordinarily fine leaf. Sailors and other returning adventurers were the principal agents in carrying the habit to Europe. It seems first to have taken hold in seaport towns, where the smoking sailor became a familiar sight and his initiates a growing company. He was to be observed before 1570 in England, where the first introduction of tobacco from America may have coincided with Hawkins' return from Florida in 1565. *N. rustica,* the species used most commonly for medical purposes, was cultivated in England after that year, and *N. tabacum,* far more preferable for smoking, by 1573. Drake's return from the West Indies in 1586 with "great store of Tabacco" is accepted as having fixed the habit. Raleigh's role was to popularize it, especially in the more polite circles. As in England, so had it spread elsewhere. By the early years of the seventeenth century the habit had reached all continents except Australia.

Tobacco was cultivated in almost as many places as it was smoked, but the finest leaf came from the Spanish plantations. There, in response to a growing demand, its cultivation had been expanded until by 1590 the Spaniards were producing in Trinidad, Cuba, Venezuela, and at other points large quantities of the best grade.[27] The very names of Trinidad, Caracas, and Varinas (the last two

27 See Brooks, *Tobacco,* I, 82-83.

being important points of export in Venezuela) were terms synonymous with the best tobacco to be had. This development came late enough in the century to make no evident impression on plans for Raleigh's venture at Roanoke Island. However, by 1607 tobacco had been added to the list of staples likely to be supplied by an English colony in America. Through the following decade experiments conducted both in Virginia and in Bermuda gave the colonists hope of capturing a part of Spain's rich market with tobacco as good "as ever came from the Indies." [28]

No less significant for the future of American settlement than the tobacco, sugar, and ginger of Spain's New World plantations was the beginning there of the long and tragic history of American Negro slavery. There the European settler, with characteristic lack of thought for the morrow, first found a ready answer to his ever-present need for labor in a forceful levy on the natives of Africa; there the enslaved African experienced an early identification with a type of agricultural endeavor destined to remain his principal occupation in America.

The European trade in Negro slaves predated the discovery of America by many years. Some seven hundred or eight hundred were imported annually into Portugal by 1461. In Spain by the close of the century they served in smaller numbers, and it is not impossible that the first Negro to reach America did so with Columbus. But the earliest reliable evidence is found in Ovando's instructions of 1502, which authorized the transportation to America of Christian slaves, those born in Spanish or Portuguese territories as distinct from the "bozal" Negroes out of Africa. Absorption of Spanish man power in the more adventurous undertakings of the day and the unsatisfactory character of native labor in the West Indies, however, soon created a demand for Negroes in excess of the number that could be provided from Spain. A license granted in 1518 by Charles V for the transportation of four thousand marked the yielding of imperial authority to pressures which opened the way to a direct trade in slaves between Africa and America. There-

---

[28] The official disapproval of an overemphasis on tobacco which marked the later years of the Virginia Company should not be misread to represent the attitude during the earlier phase of the project. See below, p. 123; and also Wesley F. Craven, *An Introduction to the History of Bermuda* (Williamsburg, 1938), 64, 86–87.

after, the Negro played an increasingly important part in the developing plantation economy of the West Indian area.[29]

The record indicates no inclination on the part of the original English settlers to borrow this feature of Spanish settlement. But it is interesting to note that a considerable proportion of the Negroes introduced into the English colonies of the seventeenth century bore Spanish or Portuguese names. Picked up in the West Indies or as pirates' booty from Spanish and Portuguese ships, they must have served in some measure to transmit the accumulated experience of England's predecessors in the field of transoceanic planting. And such, in fact, is a matter of record in Bermuda, where the Negro was first introduced in 1616. A letter of 1618 from Robert Rich, Bermudian planter, to his famous brother Sir Nathaniel in England recorded the possession of a Negro used for his special knowledge of "West Indy plants," and urged the purchase, even at a cost of £100, of another by the name of Francisco, recently brought into the islands as booty by a Captain John Powell. Francisco's "judgment in the caring of tobackoe" was such that Rich would "rather have him then all the other negers that bee here." [30] Not to be overlooked is the rather forceful suggestion that the Negro in his earliest identification with English settlement was valued as much for his skill as for his brawn. The fact that Latin names appear, too, in the fragmentary record of Virginia's early Negro population tempts one to give the point heavier emphasis than can be justified by documentary evidence. But the question must be left in the realm of conjecture.

In closing this discussion of influences flowing along the line of Spanish adventure into the New World to shape the earlier chapters of our history, it would be a mistake to ignore other points which unavoidably fall in the realm of conjecture and of the intangible. The Spaniard was the first pioneer of American settlement, and, like all pioneers, his actions governed in some degree those who followed him. It was he who charted the way from Europe and wrote the first dependable guides. To his charts and

---

[29] Phillips, *American Negro Slavery*, Chap. I; Blake, *European Beginnings in West Africa;* Elizabeth Donnan (ed.), *Documents Illustrative of the History of the Slave Trade to America* (Washington, 1930–1935).

[30] Manchester Papers, 220; Craven, *Introduction to the History of Bermuda*, 91–94.

narratives rivals necessarily turned for guidance in planning their own projects.[31] It was he who first provided indisputable proof of America's promise, and by his outstanding achievements associated its name with wealth and fortune. Through his missionary endeavors he set a standard of conduct toward the natives that other nationals, despite his own frequent lapses, never dared altogether ignore. Through his corruption of native words, such terms as "canoe" passed into the speech of other Europeans to describe novel features of American life. In this and other ways he rendered substantial aid to later settlers in the frequently difficult problem of adjustment to an unfamiliar environment. If nothing else, the Spaniard had made this strange new world of forests and savages a little less strange.

[31] In this connection an unusually valuable discussion is found in George B. Parks, *Richard Hakluyt and the English Voyages* (New York, 1928).

CHAPTER II

ROANOKE ISLAND

THOUGH considerations of balance and completeness require attention to Spanish and French imperialism as factors in the early history of the South, the roots of her development as a society lie deeply imbedded in the original English settlements of the Eastern seaboard. Despite the industrious efforts of modern scholars, local antiquarians, and special groups who seek the support of a tradition identifying them with the earliest chapters of American history, names and dates other than those associated with English settlement remain for the most part easily and quickly forgotten. Even in those areas where the Spaniard or Frenchman pioneered as explorer and settler, the land was later overrun by a people who spoke an English tongue, worshipped according to English rites, and settled their differences by appeal to English concepts of law and justice. The historian who would trace the main threads woven into the pattern of Southern life must, therefore, turn first to England.

The England that holds his attention is the kingdom given shape and form through the long and troubled reign of Queen Elizabeth. For it was the Elizabethan Englishman who planned and undertook the settlements to which most of us look back as on our beginnings. The Elizabethan tongue that once rang out across the James and the York may still be heard in certain out-of-the-way spots of the South. The Elizabethan devotion to Protestantism, born of a long defense of Elizabeth's church settlement and fed on the fiery materials of John Foxe's *Book of Martyrs*, still survives to shape the fundamental tenets of the great majority of Southerners. Even the institutional pattern our forefathers adapted to the

27

peculiar requirements of a new-world environment was more Elizabethan than anything else. Though sheriffs, coroners, constables, justices of the peace, juries, and representative assemblies were ancient parts of the English scene, it was as their place and function had been defined under Elizabeth that the early colonists understood them. Here, too, has the South, ever prompt to recognize individual achievement, discovered the first heroic figures of her history—Elizabeth herself and Raleigh.

A more discriminating assignment of credit might well have given first place to two students of geography, both named Richard Hakluyt. The one, commonly known as the elder Hakluyt, was a gentleman of Hereford origins, a lawyer of Middle Temple, a close student of England's economic and social problems, and a frequent consultant of merchants and other adventurers. Adviser to Frobisher, Gilbert, and Raleigh, he helped to shape the program for an English settlement of America at the point of its genesis and exerted an enduring influence on its subsequent development. The other was a younger kinsman, *the* Richard Hakluyt, clergyman, scholar, and editor, whose life's work was to mobilize available information in the interest of English maritime adventure.[1] In addition to his role as consultant and publicist in the early efforts of Gilbert and Raleigh, he served to keep alive through years of flagging interest a vision of the possibilities of America.

To explain the urge to expansion which these and other leaders directed toward the attainment of definite objectives in America, it is necessary first of all to recognize that the forces at work were dynamic. It is not enough to note merely the difficulties under which English society then labored, or the decline of older branches of England's trade as though America served but to take the place of things long familiar in European life. The far-reaching changes then affecting the social structure of Western Europe provided not only widespread dislocations producing the poverty and misery which American students have been inclined to emphasize but also many opportunities for a fuller and richer life. The dominant trend may be followed in the growing wealth and size of London, and in such evidences of a rising standard of living as the more

---

[1] See especially, Parks, *Richard Hakluyt and the English Voyages;* Introduction in Taylor (ed.), *Writings & Correspondence of the Two Richard Hakluyts,* I, 1–66.

pretentious dwellings built by the English gentry and merchants of the sixteenth century, or Hakluyt's observation that "in this age every man desireth to fill his house with all manner of goodd furniture." [2] The historical problems involved are complex; generalizations by way of explanation are best avoided unless space permits full discussion, but the conclusion is certain. No mere summary of Old World ills will suffice to explain the settlement of America. It must be viewed as one of many expressions of the abundant energies called forth by the challenging opportunities of a truly new age. The emphasis properly falls on the peculiar hopes and aspirations called forth by America itself.

It is necessary, however, to take notice of the economic problems England faced through the second and third decades of Elizabeth's reign. Space permits no more than a sketch, but that may be enough to lend due emphasis to a significant interrelation of economic and political needs during the years which witnessed the genesis of a movement for American settlement. As before, the requirements of the cloth trade claimed first attention. This was the staple, and the domestic economy depended greatly upon its prosperity.[3] In established markets English merchants encountered a variety of uncertainties arising partly from increased production of woolens by other nations and partly from international tension. Fed by the conflict between Protestantism and Catholicism, this tension brought wartime disturbances of trade, as in the Netherlands where Antwerp had long been a principal English mart, and threatened other interruptions as serious. There was an obvious need for the development of new markets.

But the problem was not so simple as that. To hold as well as expand her markets, England faced the necessity of giving attention to subsidiary problems of production. The elder Hakluyt explained their importance succinctly if somewhat repetitiously as follows: "if Forren nations turne their Wools, inferiour to ours, into truer and more excellent made cloth, and shall die the same in truer, surer, and more excellent, and more delectable colours, then shall they sell . . . their Clothes, when the English cloth of better wooll

---

[2] Taylor (ed.), *Writings & Correspondence of the Two Richard Hakluyts*, II, 281.
[3] Foster, *England's Quest of Eastern Trade*, provides the most suggestive discussion of the relation of the needs of the cloth trade to overseas adventure.

shall rest unsold." [4] The difficulty lay in the fact that while England was well supplied with greens and yellows, she depended on imports for the highly favored blue dyes and for indispensable vegetable oils. The situation was made more serious by the fact that a principal source of supply of the last-named commodities was the trade with Spain.[5]

So much has Drake overshadowed the age, that many students have tended to overlook the continuing importance of the Anglo-Spanish trade. As the foremost Protestant state, England was compelled after 1568 to look with increasing concern to the defenses of her religious and political freedom against forces rallying under the banner of Philip II. Neither Philip nor Elizabeth, however, was inclined to rush into war. The claims of Mary Queen of Scots to the English throne suggested to Philip the cheaper methods of political intrigue, while Elizabeth, to gain time for the unification of her people, took the calculated risk of forgoing from year to year the execution of her famous rival and prisoner. Not until 1586 did she invite and get a showdown by beheading Mary. These were years, then, neither of peace nor yet of war: the years of Drake's fame and of Englishmen who fought side by side with the rebellious subjects of Philip in the Netherlands, but at the same time a period of unbroken commerce between England and Spain under the provisions of ancient treaties. Only three years before the sailing of the Spanish Armada of 1587 the younger Hakluyt warned Elizabeth, though probably with some exaggeration, that by continuance of the trade Philip was in position to arrest almost half the English merchant marine.[6]

As Hakluyt's point suggests, the need for new markets and for guaranteed access to essential materials could not be divorced from urgent considerations of national security. No mere bookkeeping concept of economic interest can account for the nascent imperialism of the day. It was a time of national emergency ending in war, and, though men differed as to the specific action re-

---

[4] Taylor (ed.), *Writings & Correspondence of the Two Richard Hakluyts*, I, 185–86.
[5] *Ibid.*, 187–92; and see below p. 35. Hakluyt had earlier declared that "the price of a cloth, for a fifth, sixth, and seventh part riseth by the colour and dying." *Ibid.*, 137.
[6] For Hakluyt's discussion, see *ibid.*, II, 218–21, 267; for a modern discussion of the trade, Ephraim Lipson, *The Economic History of England* (London, 1915–1931), II, 364–66.

quired, circumstances argued strongly for a greater degree of economic self-sufficiency.

In the search for a solution to the problem, the Elizabethans were persistently challenged by the idea of opening a new route to the East.[7] Not until the turn of the century would they be strong enough to overthrow, with aid from the Dutch, Portugal's monopoly of the route by way of the Cape of Good Hope. Moreover, there were, through the earlier years, compelling reasons of state for not taking a step that would hasten the open break with Spain which Elizabeth sought to postpone, and study of winds and currents argued the existence of a more direct approach to those parts of Asia in which a man might profitably dispose of woolens. So it was that the disappointing first efforts of the Muscovy Company in the northeast were followed by high hopes of a northwest passage. Gilbert was among the early advocates of the adventure, which Frobisher undertook from 1576 to 1578 in three successive voyages.

The search for a northwest passage was to be repeatedly joined to a belief in the existence of another great and undiscovered continent lying beyond America in the South Seas.[8] Such a body of land, to which the nearest reality is found in New Zealand and Australia, could be expected to offer markets for English goods, perhaps another Peru or Mexico, areas suitable for settlement, or at least some base of use in reaching and exploiting the known wealth of the Orient. An obvious approach to its discovery was by way of the Strait of Magellan, over which the Spaniard had established no effective control, but Englishmen were encouraged to seek another approach by an assumption that the Northwest Passage might run in a southwesterly direction from its eastern entry to debouch on the Pacific side at a point perhaps no farther north than forty degrees.[9] As early as 1574 Richard Grenville, a

[7] In addition to the works of Foster, Parks, and Newton, see for a comprehensive survey, Williamson, *Age of Drake;* and as an indispensable aid to all students of the period, Eva G. R. Taylor, *Tudor Geography, 1485–1583* (London, 1930).

[8] For a discussion of the origins of the belief and its influence on maritime adventure, see James A. Williamson, "The Exploration of the Pacific," in *Cambridge History of the British Empire* (New York, 1929–), VII, Pt. I, *Australia,* 24 ff.

[9] Notice, for instance, in the records of seventeenth-century Virginia the normal presentation of westward adventure in terms of a quest of the South Seas.

west-country gentleman and adventurer who later would lead Raleigh's first colony to Virginia, projected unsuccessfully an expedition to the South Seas. Three years afterward, the original plans for Drake's most celebrated voyage called for a South Seas venture westward from the Strait of Magellan.[10] Ever a realist, Drake elected the more certain rewards of plunder along the western coasts of South America. But it should be noted that he proceeded thence, in the next stage of his circumnavigation, to the California coast and northward to a point probably in the neighborhood of modern San Francisco. Frobisher had already claimed discovery of the eastern entry to the Northwest Passage, and though Drake found in California no sign of its western outlet, he took a step toward assuring its control by England when he proclaimed annexation of the area as New Albion.

Despite repeated disappointment, the hope of an English-controlled route leading to the South Seas and to Cathay was destined again and again to shape the story of English adventure in America.[11] Contrary to popular assumption, however, that interest seems to have had little if anything to do with the origins of Sir Humphrey Gilbert's ventures. Though Gilbert was among those who in the early years of Elizabeth's reign argued the existence of a northwest passage, the latest student of his efforts finds no evidence that after 1576 he contemplated any expedition to America above fifty degrees north latitude. Apparently, Frobisher's failure cured

[10] Eva G. R. Taylor, "The Missing Draft Project of Drake's Voyage of 1577–80," in *Geographical Journal* (London), LXXV (1930), 46–47; Taylor, "More Light on Drake," in *Mariner's Mirror* (Cambridge), XVI (1930), 134–51.

[11] In the year of Francis Drake's return home, 1580, the Muscovy Company sought again to open a northeast passage. That same year the younger Hakluyt advocated seizure and fortification of the Strait of Magellan, arguing with reference to an impending union of Portugal and Spain under the rule of Philip II that "whenever the rule and government of the East & West Indies . . . shalbe in one Prince, they neither will receive English clothe nor yet care for anie vente of there commodities to us, having then so manie places of there owne to make vente and enterchange of ther commodities." Taylor (ed.), *Writings & Correspondence of the Two Richard Hakluyts*, I, 143. While Sir Walter Raleigh's agents at Roanoke pondered the chances of a way through to the South Seas, John Davis, with Raleigh's aid, carried on the quest in the north. The South Seas myth was not fully disposed of until the very eve of the American Revolution by the voyages of Captain James Cook. Belief in the existence of a northwest passage rested upon sounder assumptions. Though not successfully negotiated until the present century, it did in fact exist.

Sir Humphrey of whatever interest he may have had theretofore in attempting the passage himself. Indeed, the evidence supports a view that Gilbert's interest lay in the south rather than in those northerly regions toward which the search for a passage was currently directed. His first voyage of 1578–1579 remains shrouded in the mysteries of an incomplete record, but the most plausible solution of the problem is found in a purpose "to establish a colony . . . fairly near to the West Indies and capable of being used as a base against Spain." [12]

That the advantages of such a base help to explain the continued interest of early English colonizers, like the French Huguenots before them, in the more southern parts of North America would appear to be a reasonable assumption. Many and unmistakable are the evidences that English settlement in its genesis was based partly on a desire to challenge the power of Spain. To impose a levy on the Spaniard for meeting the expenses involved was in the circumstances an attractive idea. But any hope that may have been entertained of securing substantial assistance for purposes of settlement from the privateering interests of the day proved illusory.[13] Gilbert's interest in colonization extended back at least to 1567, when he had been identified with a proposed English settlement of northern Ireland.[14] Financial embarrassment rather than loss of interest apparently explains a delay in the revival of his American project from 1579 to 1582.[15]

Valuable evidence of the existence of a broadly based plan of settlement, probably as early as 1578, survives in certain "Notes" on colonization prepared by the elder Hakluyt and subsequently

[12] David B. Quinn (ed.), *The Voyages and Colonising Enterprises of Sir Humphrey Gilbert* (London, 1940), I, 45. This collection of extant documents pertaining to Gilbert's venture is prefaced by a scholarly Introduction of 104 pages which provides the most up-to-date and authoritative account of Sir Humphrey's place in the American story.

[13] As the record on its face clearly indicates, privateering was in no way dependent upon settlement for its success. Through years which have been appropriately marked as the age of Drake, the movement for a permanent occupation of the North American continent remained feeble for lack of adequate funds.

[14] See Quinn (ed.), *Voyages and Colonising Enterprises of Sir Humphrey Gilbert*, I, 12–19, for a summary of his activity in Ireland and suggestions as to its importance in the background of his American ventures.

[15] The dispatch in 1580 of one small vessel for purposes of reconnaissance represents the chief effort between 1579 and 1582.

printed in the spring of 1582 by the younger Hakluyt in his well-known *Divers Voyages touching the Discovery of America*. It is questionable that these notes were originally drafted for the specific guidance of Gilbert, but there is no doubt that they represent ideas which influenced the development of his project.[16] Nor can there be any doubt as to their long-term significance in the history of English colonization.

In characteristic fashion, Hakluyt deals almost exclusively with the practical problem of the moment—the choice in a preliminary voyage of a suitable site, or sites, for occupation and fortification.[17] But in his methodical recording of considerations that should guide the selection, he necessarily reveals some of the more important objectives of settlement. Though suggestions for the location of a "first seate" throw a helpful light on the later choices of Roanoke Island and Jamestown,[18] there is greater interest in his attention to broader aspects of the problem. Hakluyt well understood that the establishment of a successful colony depended upon an opportunity to provide marketable staples for exchange with England. As he explained, if "the people there to plant and to continue . . . shall live without sea trafficke, at the first they become naked by

16 The document appears in Richard Hakluyt, *Divers Voyages touching the Discovery of America and the Islands Adjacent* (London, 1582), itself a major promotional effort in the revival of Gilbert's project, as "Notes framed by a Gentleman heretofore to bee given to one that prepared for a discoverie, and went not." Its probable date has been accepted as 1578, and the customary assignment of authorship to the elder Hakluyt is undoubtedly correct. In a later printing it was described as "Notes framed by M. Richard Hakluyt of the Middle Temple Esquire, given to certain Gentlemen that went with M. Frobisher in his Northwest Discovery, for their directions," but the author obviously had in mind regions below that to which Sir Martin Frobisher's attention was directed. That the paper was intended for Gilbert's guidance seems a sounder view. For modern reprints with pertinent discussion, see Taylor (ed.), *Writings & Correspondence of the Two Richard Hakluyts*, I, 13–15, 116–22; Quinn (ed.), *Voyages and Colonising Enterprises of Sir Humphrey Gilbert*, I, 36, 181–86. See also, Parks, *Richard Hakluyt and the English Voyages*, 50–51.

17 In this connection it is well to recall the distinction made in Gilbert's charter of 1578 between "this jorney for discovery" and "the seconde jorney for conquest." Quinn (ed.), *Voyages and Colonising Enterprises of Sir Humphrey Gilbert*, I, 191.

18 For example: "To plante upon an Ilande in the mouth of some notable river, or upon the poynt of the lande entring into the river, if no such Iland be, were to great ende. For if such river were navigable or portable farre into the lande, then would arise great hope of planting in fertil soyles, and trafficke on the one or on thother side of the river, or on both, or the linking in amitie with one or other petie king, contending there for dominion."

want of linen and wollen, and very miserable by infinite wantes that will otherwise ensue, . . . and so the interprice becomes reprochfull to our nation, and a lett to many other good purposes that may be taken in hande." Accordingly, he urged "that great observation be taken what every soyle yeeldeth naturally, . . . and what it may be made to yeeld by indevour, . . . that thereuppon we may devise what meanes may be thought of to rayse trades."

In considering action that might be taken "to rayse trades," Hakluyt enjoined careful consideration of climate as well as soil. If salt water could be let into flats "where the sunne is of the heate that it is at Rochell, in the Bay of portingall, or in Spaine," with skilled direction there might be had "one noble commoditie for the fishing, and for trade of merchandize by making of Salt." If "the soyle and climate bee such as may yeelde you the Grape as good as that at Burdeus, as that in Portingale, or as that . . . in Spaine, or that in the Ilands of the Canaries," wine and raisins might be produced. "If you finde a soyle of the temperature of the South part of Spaine or Barbarie, in which you finde the Olif tree to growe," he continued, "you may bee assured of a noble marchandize for this realme, considering that our great trade of clothing doth require oyle, and weying how deere of late it is become by the vent they have of that commoditie in the West Indies." In "the berrie of Cochenile with which wee colour Stammelles, or any Roote, Berrie, Fruite, wood or earth fitte for dying," he saw the promise of "a notable thing fitt for our state of clothing." Hides would provide a "merchandize right good," and if the soil "shall yeelde Figges, Almondes, Sugar Canes, Quinces, Orenges, Lemons, Potatos, &c. there may arise some trade and trafficke by figges, almonds, sugar, marmelade, Sucket &c." "If great woods bee founde," then pitch, tar, rosin, and turpentine might be had, and timber for chests, casks, and ships. And "if we may enjoy any large Territorie of apt soyle," Hakluyt concludes, "we might so use the matter, as we should not depende upon Spaine for oyles, sacks, resinges, orenges, lemons, Spanish skinnes &c.," nor upon France "for woad, baysalt, and gascoyne wines, nor on Estlande for flaxe, pitch, tarre, mastes, &c." to the exhaustion of England's treasure and the enrichment of "doubtfull friendes." Opportunities for individual profit were thus joined to considerations of national interest. Attention was focused

35

on the land and what it might be made to yield. The emphasis pointed southward.

As already noted, the document was published for promotional purposes by the younger Hakluyt in 1582. Since by that date the six-year term placed on rights of discovery and settlement by Gilbert's patent of 1578 had but two years to run, time was of the essence in preparations undertaken for a second voyage. Consequently, as one of his associates later observed, he "refused not to entertaine every person and meanes whatsoever" to fit out the necessary ships. Having in 1580 assigned to John Dee all rights of discovery above fifty degrees north latitude, an assignment effectively disposing of any idea that he still intended to attempt the Northwest Passage, he now made extensive grants of land to prospective gentleman adventurers. His immediate purpose was twofold: to raise funds for his own voyage and, as a hedge against its failure, to encourage separate undertakings which might serve as the basis for a continuation beyond 1584 of rights under the royal charter. He thus became the first in a long line of promoters to use generous land grants as a means to underwrite the highly speculative business of American development.

In so doing he appealed to the land hunger that characterized the propertied classes of England at this time. Speculation in landed properties had been encouraged by the plundering under Henry VIII of the vast estates of the Catholic monasteries, a development which had revealed for many new families the means whereby they might acquire one of the accepted evidences of social position. Appetites had been further whetted by exploitation of the forfeited estates of Irish rebels. And now in the fertile and undeveloped lands of North America there was offered a third and, though distant, hardly less inviting prospect.

The chief of Gilbert's grantees were Sir George Peckham and Sir Thomas Gerrard. Catholics both, they planned a settlement designed to serve among other purposes as a refuge for their coreligionists. To Peckham and his associates Gilbert assigned between June, 1582, and the following February no less than eight and one-half million acres on the mainland of North America. Another grantee was Sir Philip Sidney, who was assigned three million acres. He later joined hands with Peckham, whose project early lost the peculiar character of a Catholic effort. The papers involved, together with Gilbert's plan of government, reveal a pattern of settlement suggestive of that later followed in the proprietary colonies of the seventeenth century.[19] In other words, the American venture had acquired at the very outset some of the qualities of a gigantic land speculation, and had been marked by a purpose to transfer to the New World an Old World type of land-lordism.

To translate a grant of land lying three thousand miles across the Atlantic into an established and profitable estate at this stage of the effort, however, was beyond the means of the relatively small group of gentlemen Gilbert was able to recruit. Though they might dream of distant prospects in terms of conventional rights of landholding, the immediate need was for substantial assistance from the mercantile community. Only the merchants possessed the means to bridge with any degree of promptness the distance between England and America, a fact reflected in the emphasis placed by promotional tracts through many years on the commercial advantages of settlement. Whether because of the indifference of London's merchants, who alone except perhaps for those of Bristol had the resources to underwrite so ambitious an undertaking, or for other reasons, Gilbert turned for assistance to the secondary outport of Southampton. There, in return for exclusive privileges of trade he received a subscription of something less than £1,000.[20] Sir Francis Walsingham through the younger Hakluyt undertook in the fall of 1582 to enlist the aid of Bristol. The effort met with limited success, but not before Gilbert had made an agreement with Southampton. Walsingham's stepson, Christopher Carleill, whose place in reference to Sir Humphrey's plans remains somewhat uncertain, in the spring of 1583 attempted to interest the Muscovy Company in a settlement to be established under Carleill's leadership at about forty degrees north latitude. The

[19] Dr. Quinn has gone far toward untangling the confused story of Gilbert's later associates. It is doubtful that much, if indeed anything, can be added to his discussion. On contemporary land hunger, see Charles M. Andrews, *The Colonial Period of American History* (New Haven, 1934–1938), I, 54–57.

[20] Quinn (ed.), *Voyages and Colonising Enterprises of Sir Humphrey Gilbert,* I, 81. The second voyage appears to have been financed largely by Gilbert, Sir John Gilbert, Raleigh, and other members of the family.

response was favorable, but the conditions demanded were impossible to meet so long as Gilbert's charter held.[21] There is reason to believe, as this experience suggests, that the financial assistance needed from the great merchants could have been won only by concession to them of a greater degree of control than Gilbert and his associates were prepared to make. Whatever the fact, the merchants of London displayed a preference for other ventures. Not until the years following 1606 did London lend substantial support to the movement for American settlement, and, significantly, only then did success crown the effort.

The story of Gilbert's last tragic effort is quickly told. He sailed early in June, 1583, with 5 vessels and 260 men. Inadequate provisions, apparently, prompted a last-minute decision in favor of a northern course by way of Newfoundland, where additional supplies were to be secured from the fishing fleets. The full detail of his plans cannot be given, but it is reasonable to assume that he intended, in a voyage primarily exploratory, to coast down the North American shores until a suitable site, or sites, for settlement had been selected. A small holding force left in possession would have made secure, for the time being at least, extensive rights under the charter,[22] and would have provided the foundation for another promotional effort. Having reached and laid claim to Newfoundland, he again sailed westward, but mismanagement and misfortune

[21] *Ibid.*, 76–80. Gilbert's several grants had opened the way for separate undertakings looking toward a congeries of settlements joined together for purposes of control under the authority established by the royal patent. It is possible that with the term of the charter drawing toward a close, Sir Francis Walsingham and Christopher Carleill intended to double-cross Gilbert. On the other hand, they may merely have counted on their ability with a promising project in hand to secure satisfactory terms from him. Carleill's "Briefe and Summary Discourse upon the Intended Voyage to . . . America," written in April, 1583, *ibid.*, II, 351–64, ranks among the ablest statements of the case for settlement. Directed specifically to the Muscovy merchants and reprinted in Hakluyt, *Voyages*, it exerted considerable influence on later promotional efforts. He set the cost at £4,000, indicated Bristol would subscribe £1,000, and asked of the Muscovy merchants £3,000. The company agreed, but on the condition that a royal patent, incorporating a monopoly of trade and prohibition of planting within 200 leagues of the first seat, be secured.

[22] Under the charter, rights in the land were dependent upon actual settlement and covered the area or areas "within two hundreth leages of any the said place or places where the said Sir Humfrey or his heires or assignes or any of them or any of his or their Associates or companyes shall inhabite within six yeares nexte ensuing the date hereof." *Ibid.*, I, 188–94.

had already turned him back toward home when his vessel disappeared on a September night in the North Atlantic.

He had recently remarked to one of his masters "that this voyage had wonne his heart from the South, and that he was now become a Northerne man altogether." [23] Though he spoke of sending out an expedition the following spring by the southern route, he indicated, in an extraordinary display of optimism, a purpose to lead a second voyage to the north himself. Those of his associates who undertook to continue the work he had begun were unavoidably bound to an attempt to extract from his last voyage whatever promotional advantage it afforded.[24] Thus the projects born of Gilbert's leadership ended with emphasis on the northern approach to America. But with their failure the leadership passed to Sir Walter Raleigh, who chose in a new effort the southern route.

Sir Walter is one of the more difficult figures of history to estimate; one repeatedly hesitates for fear of doing him either more or less than justice. Perhaps the very versatility of his gifts and interests explains his failure to rank among the first men of his age, as well as his attraction for biographers exceeding that of more-important contemporaries. He had been a soldier, in France and Ireland, from his youth, and a courtier of rising favor from 1581. Now he was the holder of estates, sinecures, and monopolies, the rewards of royal favor from which he generously contributed to the American venture. Half brother to Gilbert, he was among the members of the family on whom Sir Humphrey had drawn heavily for financial support. The royal charter Raleigh secured in March, 1584, conveying rights of discovery and settlement for another six years, was essentially a renewal of Gilbert's patent.[25]

[23] See Edward Hayes's narrative, the source of most of our information on the events of the voyage, *ibid.*, II, 418.

[24] Witness the title of Sir George Peckham, *A Trve Reporte of the Late Discoueries, and Possession, Taken in the Right of the Crowne of Englande, of the Newfound Landes: By that Valiaunt and Worthye Gentleman, Sir Humfrey Gilbert Knight* (London, 1583), reprinted *ibid.*, 435–82. The distinction between north and south at this time was largely a difference of routes, of the approach. Peckham's pamphlet itself talked of settlement between thirty degrees and sixty degrees north latitude.

[25] Printed in Hakluyt, *Voyages*, VIII, 289–96. There was added a denial of monopoly over the Newfoundland fisheries which Gilbert in his last voyage had apparently come to view as a source of revenue. On Raleigh, see especially David B. Quinn, *Raleigh and the British Empire* (London, 1947).

Like Gilbert, Raleigh necessarily placed discovery first. He had to bear in mind, as Carleill had stated the initial problem of settlement, that men "would be well content to goe in the voyage if they might onely be assured that there is such a Countrey, & that their money should not be wasted to nothing in the preparations." [26] Accordingly, Captains Philip Amadas and Arthur Barlow were dispatched in April on a voyage of reconnaissance to accomplish a task of preliminary exploration which Sir Humphrey had left unfinished. With the Portuguese Simon Fernandez as pilot, they dropped down to the Canaries and sailed west along the route Columbus had given to Spain. Having reached the West Indies, they drifted up with the Gulf Stream until they fell in with that chain of islands and sand bars that lock the upper Carolina coast. It was July, and within the bar both first and second impressions were good. After a short stay, devoted to exploration and trade, they reached England in mid-September with two natives and a bracelet of pearls for Sir Walter, who named his discovery Virginia.[27]

By all appearances this new-found land of Virginia was well suited for the purposes in mind. There were difficulties, as many have since learned, in the navigation of the Carolina coast. But might not these difficulties, once their mysteries had been fathomed by the English, prove of advantage for purposes of defense? Let "the first Seate be chosen on the seaside so as . . . you may have your owne Navie within Bay, river or lake," and "so as the enemie shalbe forced to lie in open rode abroade without," the elder Hakluyt had counseled in 1578. Let it be so located, he continued, perhaps "uppon an Ilande in the mouth of some notable river, or upon the poynt of the lande entring into the river," that the settlers might enjoy "the ayde of some Navigable ryver, or ample lake." [28] In a paper prepared for Raleigh's guidance in 1585, he commented favorably on the evidence brought by Barlow and Amadas that the

---

[26] *Ibid.*, 142.   [27] For Arthur Barlow's account of the expedition, see *ibid.*, 297–310.
[28] Taylor (ed.), *Writings & Correspondence of the Two Richard Hakluyts*, I, 116, 118, 121. Notice should be taken too of his advice for Arthur Pet and Charles Jackman's voyage of 1580 in quest of a northeast passage, *ibid.*, 146–58. The problem of establishing fortified posts for securing English control of the route was basically the same as that of establishing fortified outposts in America for the purpose of assuring control of its land and its trade.

English might in Virginia make themselves the "lords of navigation," [29] a consideration of great importance to the development of
any plan of settlement. The evidence, briefly summarized, was this:
Roanoke Island, sixteen miles long and somewhat less across, with
other islands, should this one not prove suitable for occupation,
helped to form a virtually inclosed sea that extended for an estimated two hundred miles from north to south and ten to fifty
miles across. Into it flowed mighty streams, offering highways into
the interior. The soil was fruitful, the waters full of fish, the climate
comparable to that of Portugal, Spain, and southern France. The
natives, weakened as potential enemies by many political subdivisions, were willing to trade. The one thing missing was a really
good harbor, but Raleigh's agents had not been there in that season
of the year which could best demonstrate how serious a disadvantage this might be. If Hakluyt's thinking, from 1578 forward, guided
the leaders, where better, except in Chesapeake Bay, could they
have found just what they sought?

Of the guiding influence of the two Hakluyts on the further development of Raleigh's project there is ample evidence. In September of 1584, the month in which Sir Walter's scouts returned
from America, the younger Hakluyt in an audience with Queen
Elizabeth presented "at the request and direction" of Raleigh a
"Discourse on the Western Planting." The document, more important than any other single paper to an understanding of the
genesis of England's colonial program, had been prepared as an
appeal for the Queen's financial support.[30] Indeed, it must ever be
read with an eye to its purpose of opening the one purse in England
deep enough to permit the work to be carried forward on a grand
scale. It was, of course, heavily weighted with arguments of a political nature. Stripped, however, of its effort to justify England's
claim to America, its attempt to demonstrate the relation of Spain's
threatening power in Europe to the resources of her New World
empire, and of such things as its shrewd suggestion of the reproach
to Protestantism implied in the contrast with the record of Cath-

[29] *Ibid.*, II, 329–30, 334.

[30] As such it was confidential and remained unpublished until late in the nineteenth century. For the best printed copy, taken from an original manuscript copy in
the New York Public Library, see *ibid.*, 211–326. See Parks, *Richard Hakluyt and
the English Voyages*, 87–98, for discussion.

olic missionary endeavor, the meat of the argument is this: no one of England's existing trades was without serious disadvantage. In Russia there was heavy expense and competition from the Dutch; in the Baltic, opposition from the Hanseatic merchants and exactions on the traffic by Denmark; in the newly developing trade with Turkey, the expense of embassies and presents to Eastern potentates, the hostility of the Italian cities, tribute to the Knights of Malta, and depredations by the pirates of Algiers and Tripoli; and elsewhere comparable disadvantages. Thus did Hakluyt call the roll of England's trades to give point to his conclusion that "it behoveth us to seeke some newe and better trade of lesse daunger and more securitie, of lesse dommage, and of more advauntage."

The answer to the problem, in Hakluyt's opinion, was clear. America, "whereunto we have juste Title . . . from Florida northwarde to 67. degrees," offered such variety of climate and soil as to "yelde unto us all the commodities of Europe, Affrica and Asia, . . . and supplye the wantes of all our decayed trades." The way there from England by the open sea was "easie and shorte," passable at all seasons of the year, and lay outside the power of any prince to impose obstructions or exactions. If apprehension existed as to Spain's power to interfere, assurance was offered by a detailed analysis of the true extent of her possessions and strength in America. Two or three forts between Florida and Cape Breton not only would make secure English possession; at the same time they would place in hazard Spain's fleets voyaging homeward from Havana and leave at England's mercy the Spanish and Portuguese fishermen off Newfoundland. Settlements planted under the protection of these forts would assure the benefits of an expanding trade and make possible a prompt and complete search, "as well by River and overlande as by sea," for the Northwest Passage. There was in this presentation little that was original with Hakluyt, except the truly national scale on which the program was projected.[31]

Unfortunately, the state's financial resources were limited, the claims upon them heavy. Elizabeth could not be persuaded to recognize the program as a charge upon the royal treasury. Her decision, reaffirmed by later rulers, is of more than passing sig-

[31] He borrowed heavily, for instance, from Carleill's paper prepared the preceding year as an inducement to the Muscovy merchants.

nificance, for it fixed a basic condition that was to govern England's colonial expansion. With the state's contribution restricted to the giving of sanction and encouragement, the size of the effort was limited by the amount of private capital that could be drawn into a highly speculative investment. Hakluyt had sketched the outlines of a national program, but Elizabeth's refusal to finance it dictated that it should be the ultimate goal rather than an immediate objective.[32]

To the elder Hakluyt fell the task of drafting a plan of action to be followed in the absence of state aid. The paper he prepared for Raleigh's guidance in 1585 is in some ways of even greater importance than his kinsman's "Discourse." Read with his "Notes" on colonization of 1578, it records the development of ideas which not only shaped the first venture to Roanoke Island but influenced the history of the Southern colonies for three quarters of a century thereafter.[33]

The elder Hakluyt, no less than the younger, was primarily concerned with England's commercial prosperity. He did not overlook the aid an American outpost might provide to further search for the Northwest Passage. He understood that the first task was one of discovery, and that no chance of advantage should be ignored, including the possibility of profitable mineral discoveries.[34] He estimated shrewdly the promise of a traffic with the Indians;

[32] The point has been too often forgotten, as shown by a tendency to use the "Discourse" as a statement of what Raleigh and his associates hoped to find or develop within the immediate environs of Roanoke Island. Hakluyt actually wrote of opportunities from Florida northward to Baffin Land in the hope that Elizabeth would advance funds for their prompt exploitation. In reference to this ambitious objective, Raleigh's venture can be viewed as no more than a step on the way.

[33] Taylor (ed.), *Writings & Correspondence of the Two Richard Hakluyts*, II, 327–38.

[34] Neither of the Hakluyts, however, laid great emphasis on gold and silver. The experience of Frobisher, whose northern venture had ended in a disastrous gold mania of 1578, apparently still exercised a sobering influence. The prevailing attitude is clearly indicated by Carleill's comment in his appeal to the Muscovy Company of 1583: "What Minerall matter may fall out to bee found, is a thing left in suspence, untill some better knowledge, because there be many men, who having long since expected some profits herein, upon the great promises that have bene made them, and being as yet in no point satisfied, doe thereupon conceive that they be but wordes purposely cast out for the inducing of men to bee the more ready and willing to furnish their money towards the charge of the first discoverie." Quinn (ed.), *Voyages and Colonising Enterprises of Sir Humphrey Gilbert*, II, 358.

43

foresaw, indeed, an increasingly profitable native market. But he had enough appreciation of the primitive state of native society to recognize the immediate limitations of an American market and to find in the civilizing influences of English settlement the principal hope of the Indian's conversion to European dress and to an economy more productive of goods acceptable in exchange for English cloth.[35] And so he came to the central argument for colonization, as distinct from mere trade, which was the necessity to develop the resources of North America beyond the limited capacity of its native inhabitants. As he himself put it, the training of natives "to plant Vines, . . . or to set Olive trees" was a "small consideration" when compared with the opportunity "to conquer a countrey or province in climate & soil of Italie, Spaine, or the Islands from whence we receive our Wines & Oiles, and to man it, to plant it, and to keepe it, and to continue the making of Wines and Oiles able to serve England." [36]

Though his scheme of settlement differed somewhat from that which later became the familiar pattern, it helps to explain much that was attempted in the early years of colonization. The project of which he wrote was designed to embrace activities extending over a much larger area than the Carolina coast. No exact bounds are given, but his discussion of possibilities to be explored covered the region from about thirty-six degrees in the south to forty-two degrees in the north, limits corresponding closely with those incorporated in the Virginia charter of 1606. The plan, apparently, was to develop at selected points along the coast a chain of fortified posts. Under the protection of these outposts men would engage in a wide variety of activity, including agricultural endeavor where the soil and climate proved suitable to the purposes in mind. This chain, it seems, would have been developed under the leadership, or presidency, of a settlement to be located on Roanoke Island or at some more favorably situated location made known by further discovery. The Roanoke venture, in other words, was regarded as

[35] Notice, too, Carleill's hope "that they will daily by little and little forsake their barbarous and savage living, and growe to such order and civilitie with us, as there may be well expected from thence no less quantitie and diversitie of merchandize then is now had out of Dutchland, Italie, France or Spaine." *Ibid.,* 357. See also, Peckham, "Trve Reporte," *ibid.,* 468.

[36] Taylor (ed.), *Writings & Correspondence of the Two Richard Hakluyts,* II, 333.

no more than the first step toward opening the coastal region above Florida to English exploitation and development.

There is no evidence that Hakluyt foresaw the vast emigration to America that was to come. Certainly he had no thought of establishing control over this extensive coast line by means of a continuous line of settlement.[37] His plan emphasized the fortification of key points and control of the intervening navigation, a proposal that tends to focus the attention of modern students on the commercial ends sought. Yet, colonization, whatever be the test applied to the term, was definitely a part of the scheme.

The elder Hakluyt's chief contribution to the development of an American program was the joining of an awakening interest in American land to definite proposals for its profitable use. He pictured for Raleigh communities producing, in time, grapes for wine and raisins; sugar to relieve England of a dependence on "infidels or our doubtful friends"; olives for their oil; anil, woad, saffron, and madder for dyes; silk, hemp, and flax for textiles and cordage; hops for brewing; and fruits—oranges, lemons, figs, pomegranates, and the common pears, apples, plums, peaches, and apricots of England—for drying and preserving.[38] It will be immediately noted that a goodly number of the commodities listed, considering the sources from which England then secured them, placed a premium on a southern soil and climate for the experiment; and

[37] In this connection it should be noted that the Hakluyts did not advocate colonization as a means for drawing off a surplus population. Indeed, the younger Hakluyt was so far from accepting the idea of overpopulation that he argued in 1584 that England was capable of supporting five times its current population. They recognized that emigration to America would currently provide a limited measure of relief from unemployment, but the real hope lay in the stimulus expected for the revival of England's trade and industry. The relatively few Englishmen who went out would open a trade with the natives, return home raw materials for processing, guarantee England's supply of materials essential to the cloth trade, develop commodities relieving her of the necessity of imports where the exchange was unfavorable, provide employment for shipping and seamen, and so on. In other words, the solution for unemployment was to give vitality to the nation's commercial and industrial system, and colonization would serve, as John Donne subsequently put it, not only as "a spleen to drain ill humours of the body, but a liver to breed good blood." Quoted by Andrews, *Colonial Period of American History*, I, 61 n. For the opinion of the Hakluyts, see Taylor (ed.), *Writings & Correspondence of the Two Richard Hakluyts*, I, 195; II, 233–39, 281–82, 317, 319.

[38] Compare his list of 1578, and notice his emphasis there on the products of Spain, Portugal, and southern France.

so closely interwoven is Hakluyt's program with the history of the Southern colonies of the seventeenth century as to persuade one that here lay a principal reason for selecting a southern site for the initial experiment.[39] If by contrast with what later proved feasible the plan seems visionary, it must be noted that Hakluyt was guided by study of many successful experiments with the transplanting of flora from one part of the Old World to another, from the old to the new, and even from America to Europe.[40] What the Portuguese had done in Madeira and the Azores and the Spaniards in the West Indies the English could do in Virginia. In so modeling his plan on Spain's achievement he did not overlook the importance of cattle and hides.

Though he betrayed no doubt of eventual success, the program was frankly experimental in character and, tried alone, would obviously require long-term and large-scale financing. With the best of fortune it would be several years before the returns from agricultural efforts could in themselves justify the dispatch of shipping from England. That this consideration had not escaped him is shown by his query: "But admit the soile were in our disposition (as yet it is not), in what time may this be brought about?" For wine he allowed a lapse of three years between the planting of the vine and its first yield; his estimate of the time required for production of olives was the same.[41] Such facts made it doubly necessary that in outlining the program he offer proof of its practicability. In the circumstances, this meant proof that it could be accomplished under conditions imposed by limited funds and the

[39] The point, however, must not be pressed too far. The simple choice, perhaps for secondary reasons, of the southern sailing route over the northern could well become a determinant factor. Another consideration, no doubt, was the necessity to fortify some position reasonably close, but not too close, to Florida in order to assure a hold on the coastline which had been marked out for English endeavor. It must be borne in mind, moreover, that there was a tendency, in the absence of exact geographical knowledge, to assume that the products of Spain, for instance, could be grown in America in latitudes comparable to those of Spain. See Carleill, "Briefe and Summary Discourse," in Quinn (ed.) *Voyages and Colonising Enterprises of Sir Humphrey Gilbert*, II, 356.

[40] For Hakluyt's interest in this, see Taylor (ed.), *Writings & Correspondence of the Two Richard Hakluyts, passim.*

[41] He noted, however, that wild vines, reported by Philip Amadas and Barlow as growing in abundance, by pruning and dressing might be brought "to profit in shorter time." *Ibid.*, II, 333.

natural insistence of investors in a speculative venture on an early return of their capital. Consequently, like Peckham and Carleill before him, Hakluyt was forced to argue that much could be accomplished with little—in effect, that the American venture could pay its own way.[42]

He accordingly presented other and more immediate prospects of profit not only as ends in themselves but as means for the accomplishment of a larger program. In setting forth the promise of a trade with the natives in skins and furs, he declared that this "present gaine at the first, raiseth great incouragement presently to the enterprise." "Hides," together with the profits of whaling and fishing, he believed would "presently defray the charge in good part or in all of the first enterprise." [43] The prospect for a variety of extractive industries gave additional promise of tiding the project over the experimental period and of guaranteeing its continued prosperity. Low-lying coastal areas stirred hopes for the production of salt as a staple that might in itself "mainteine a yeerely navigation." [44] This last point, of course, was an important one, for if shipmasters could count upon a cargo of salt for the return voyage, or for exchange in Newfoundland for a load of fish on the way home, the cost of freightage between England and Virginia would be greatly reduced. As a result, encouragement would be provided for the agricultural program prior to the time when it could itself, as in the annual tobacco fleets of later years, maintain

[42] See again Carleill's appeal of 1583 to the Muscovy merchants who, as he declared, "in disbursing their money towards the furniture of the present charge, doe demand forthwith a present returne of gaine," each of them being in the position of one "who suspecteth lest this first disbursement without returne of present gaine, should not be all his charge, but that afterwards he might yet further be urged to continue the like again, as hath happened in the discovery of the Moscovian trade." Quinn (ed.), *Voyages and Colonising Enterprises of Sir Humphrey Gilbert,* II, 51, 360. See also Peckham's "Trve Reporte" and especially the seventh chapter showing "that the Planting there, is not a matter of such charge or diffycultie, as many would make it seeme to be," and that it "may be doone without the aide of the Princes power and purse." *Ibid.,* 469.

[43] Taylor (ed.), *Writings & Correspondence of the Two Richard Hakluyts,* II, 331. To the Muscovy Company Carleill had declared: "And if for the present time there doe fall out nothing els to bee found then the bare Fishing, yet doubt I not after the first yeeres planting, but by that matter only to serve halfe a dozen of your best sort of ships." Quinn (ed.), *Voyages and Colonising Enterprises of Sir Humphrey Gilbert,* II, 356.

[44] Taylor (ed.), *Writings & Correspondence of the Two Richard Hakluyts,* II, 333.

"a yeerely navigation." Further hope of assistance was found in forests promising pitch, tar, turpentine, sassafras, nuts from which oil might be extracted, herbs for dyes or medicines, and timber for the cooper, cabinetmaker, and shipbuilder. The ground might yield minerals—iron, silver, copper, or gold. His plan called for development beyond the primary stage of certain of these extractive industries. For example, with England's woods fast approaching depletion, he felt that unemployed woodworkers might be transferred to the colony to carry on their crafts, the product to be shipped to England complete except for final assembly.[45] But the emphasis given extractive industries, so familiar in early promotional tracts, seems to reflect in no small part the need for an immediate return on investment, at least to an extent that would afford some assistance in the reduction of unavoidably heavy initial charges.

In setting the ultimate objectives of settlement, Hakluyt was nonetheless concerned for the development of a varied and balanced program. He foresaw a growing trade with America, brought about through the furtherance of related enterprises—agricultural, industrial, and commercial. Such a trade, on the one hand, would bring new wealth to England, and, on the other, would afford the colonists every possible opportunity, in a true exchange of goods, to take advantage of England's peculiar needs. He depicted for Raleigh "in time, such league & entercourse . . . betweene our Stapling seats there, . . . that incredible things, and by few as yet dreamed of, may speedily follow, tending to the impeachment of our mightie enemies, and to the common good of this noble government."

Having thus surrendered for the moment to his fondest hopes, he returned in characteristic fashion to the immediate question: "What is to be done?" In answer he advised that a second expedition be recruited and equipped to test more exactly the coastal area Amadas and Barlow had reported on the year before. Vines, sugar canes, olive plants, and other roots and seeds should be secured, some of them to be carried on this voyage, others the next. An effort should be made, presumably en route, to secure such plants

---

[45] The outstanding later example of this sort of effort is the iron project in which the London Company invested so heavily.

and seeds as might be had in the West Indies. Experts from Spain and elsewhere who understood the special techniques of cultivation and production should be enlisted. Other experts—mineralogists, herbalists, fishermen "to consider of the sea fishings," saltmakers to "advise for the trade," husbandmen to test the soil, and "Men cunning in the art of fortification, that may chuse out places strong by nature to be fortified"—should be recruited for the voyage. To this company should be added craftsmen of varied skills and, finally, "A skilfull painter" to bring back a more exact description of the country, a practice "the Spaniards used commonly in all their discoveries." [46]

Raleigh's second expedition to Virginia sailed from Plymouth on April 9, 1585, under Grenville's command.[47] With him were Thomas Cavendish, later to acquire fame for his circumnavigation of the globe; Master Ralph Lane, commissioned to remain in America as lieutenant governor; Captain Amadas, who had been designated "Admirall of the country"; and others joined together as assistants, or counselors, to Governor Lane. The record is incomplete, and particularly so regarding the special skills of just over one hundred men who remained in Virginia with Lane through the following winter.[48] Yet it is full enough to indicate in several important details the influence of Hakluyt's recommendations. The absence of women and children was in keeping with his plan for an exploratory field expedition, where they would have been so much excess baggage.[49] More positive evidence of the acceptance of his ideas is found in the inclusion of a truly "skilfull painter" in the person of John White, whose paintings were to provide a unique record of the serious purpose and promotional ingenuity with which the Roanoke venture was undertaken.[50] A mathematician and Oxford acquaintance of the younger Hakluyt, Thomas Hariot, had been retained as a member of Raleigh's household for the advice he could give on problems of navigation.

46 Taylor (ed.), *Writings & Correspondence of the Two Richard Hakluyts*, II, 334–38.
47 For an account of the voyage, see Hakluyt, *Voyages*, VIII, 310–17.
48 Listed *ibid.*, 317–18.
49 Incidental reference in his paper indicates that he would have provided for the emigration of women at a later point in the project's development.
50 See below, pp. 51–52.

As a key figure in the expedition Hariot proved an intelligent and sober student of problems outlined by the elder Hakluyt.[51] That apothecaries and a physician made the voyage is shown by Lane's letters of August and September.[52] And Hariot records the opinions of several other specialists, though some of these were obviously consulted after the return to England.

The course followed on the outward voyage carried by way of the West Indies. Calls were made at Puerto Rico and on the north side of Hispaniola, where the English bargained for "horses, mares, kine, buls, goates, swine, sheepe, bull-hides, sugar, ginger, pearle, tabacco, and such like commodities of the Iland." [53] Some of these were obviously intended for sale at home in payment of expenses incurred, but others were presumably desired for transfer to Virginia. The record shows, at any rate, that sugar cane was planted after the arrival at Roanoke.[54] This was the latter part of June, too late for a proper test.

Grenville departed for England late in August with the understanding that he would return for resupply of the colony the following spring. To the men left behind on Roanoke Island the fall and winter brought many disappointments. The lateness of their arrival had permitted only an imperfect trial of the soil. With time the Indians became less friendly; and this change in attitude, together with their improvidence as husbandmen, made the problem of maintaining food supplies much more difficult than had been expected. Wintry winds and storms revealed the risk of their exposed position on Roanoke Island. The picture, however, should not be painted in colors too dark. There was no starvation such as proved so disastrous to later settlements; indeed, only four out of the group died. But there were anxious moments as spring came

[51] Thomas Hariot, *Briefe and True Report* (London, 1588), was reprinted in Hakluyt, *Voyages*, VIII, 348–86. See also, Taylor (ed.), *Writings & Correspondence of the Two Richard Hakluyts*, II, 366–67. The younger Hakluyt had earlier been instrumental in sending on Gilbert's last voyage Stephen Parmenius, "a learned Hungarian," and another Oxford acquaintance, to record "things worthy of remembrance, happening in this discoverie." Quinn (ed.), *Voyages and Colonising Enterprises of Sir Humphrey Gilbert*, II, 379–83, 413. He was lost with Gilbert.

[52] Ralph Lane to Sir Francis Walsingham, August 12 (two letters), September 8, 1585; Lane to Sir Philip Sidney, August 12, 1585, in *Transactions and Collections of the American Antiquarian Society* (Worcester, Mass.), IV (1860), 8–18.

[53] Hakluyt, *Voyages*, VIII, 314.   [54] *Ibid.*, 358.

and went with no word of Grenville. Hope revived momentarily in June when Drake, after the sack of St. Augustine, called to offer assistance, but an unkind fate seems always to have attended the English on Roanoke Island. After a small vessel agreed upon for their service had been lost in a gale while carrying greatly needed supplies, disheartened men persuaded the governor to accept Drake's offer of a passage home. Had Lane possessed a stouter heart the colony might have been saved, for approximately two weeks after its departure Grenville finally arrived to find the place abandoned. Leaving fifteen men in possession, he promptly set out in search of such adventure as the homeward voyage might offer.[55]

And so was the focal point of the experiment transferred once more to England. Fortunately, three major sources recording the information which at this point guided Raleigh and his associates have survived. The first of these is "An Account" prepared by Lane, much of it given over to an apology for abandonment of the settlement.[56] The second is Hariot's *Briefe and True Report of the New Found Land of Virginia,* a publication that has become the most famous relic of Raleigh's first colony. Printed in a quarto edition in 1588, it is so rare, offers so fine an example of the printer's art, and holds such historical significance that collectors of Americana regard it with a reverence comparable to that reserved by others for a Shakespeare folio.[57] This influential tract received wider distribution through an edition of 1590 issued by Theodore De Bry, of Frankfort, with illustrations engraved from the paintings of John White, which brings us to the third of our major sources.

Among the treasures of the British Museum are White's original water colors depicting Indian customs and manners and a wide range of other subjects in American botany, zoology, ichthyology, herpetology, and entomology. For skill in portrayal and interest of subject matter there is nothing comparable to these paintings of American life of earlier date than the eighteenth century. A few of them were perhaps done at second hand, but the others bear the

[55] *Ibid.,* 346–48.   [56] *Ibid.,* 320–45.
[57] See especially the census of known copies contained in Randolph G. Adams' Introduction to a facsimile reproduction issued at Ann Arbor in 1931. As already noted, a reprint may be consulted in Hakluyt, *Voyages,* VIII, 348–86.

mark of original study. The evidence supports a view that the bulk of the work was done in the summer of 1585 when, in keeping with Hakluyt's suggestion, White evidently was sent for the purpose. Since his name is not listed among those who remained with Lane, it must be assumed that he returned to England with Grenville toward the end of the summer. If the customary identification of this White with the Governor John White of the second colony be accepted, it is possible that he added to his paintings in 1587.[58] Of White's work De Bry engraved for illustration of Hariot's *Virginia* two maps and twenty-one paintings, to which must be accredited in no small part the fact that De Bry's *Hariot* went through as many as seventeen printings, in a number of languages, between 1590 and 1620. He chose for engraving principally subjects pertaining to the life of the natives, and for three centuries thereafter, in various plagiarized forms and for such purposes as the marginal decoration of maps, White's figures were destined to serve as the conventional representation of the North American Indian.[59]

In the existing state of the record, Raleigh's first colony of 1585 must remain for historians the most significant of his North American ventures. The men of the second colony, who might have provided revealing accounts of that project, never returned. Their

[58] On this point, see William J. Holland, "The First Picture of an American Butterfly," in *Scientific Monthly* (Lancaster and New York), XXIX (1929), 45–49; Randolph G. Adams, "An Effort to Identify John White," in *American Historical Review* (New York), XLI (1935–1936), 87–91.

[59] See William L. Clements Library, *A Brief Account of Ralegh's Roanoke Colony of 1585, being a Guide to an Exhibition* (Ann Arbor, 1935). For a catalogue of seventy-five studies by White that have survived, see Laurence Binyon, *Catalogue of Drawings by British Artists . . . in the Department of Prints . . . in the British Museum* (London, 1907), IV, 326–37. The collection is discussed by the same author, with illustrations, in the *Thirteenth Annual Volume of the Walpole Society* (Oxford, 1925). Reproductions of sixty-three of White's paintings have recently been published in Stefan Lorant (ed.), *The New World; the First Pictures of America, Made by John White and Jacques Le Moyne and Engraved by Theodore De Bry, with Contemporary Narratives of the Huguenot Settlement in Florida, 1562–1565, and the Virginia Colony, 1585–1590* (New York, 1946). While this book has served a highly desirable purpose of bringing White's paintings to the attention of a wider public, it has been sharply criticized and especially for the imperfections of its reproductions. See Samuel E. Morison in *William and Mary College Quarterly* (Richmond, Williamsburg), 3d ser., IV (1947), 395–402; Julian P. Boyd, in *American Historical Review*, LIII (1947–1948), 111–15.

fate continues to be one of the intriguing mysteries of history. It is our misfortune that modern research has provided no solution of the problem.[60] But it is even more unfortunate that the mystery enshrouding the lost colony of 1587, together with the human appeal of certain facts in the story, has so frequently led modern writers to slight its predecessor. For in the first venture, the record provides, in outline at least, the program that called forth a will to act. Moreover, it can be demonstrated that the broad features of that program still guided the men who later at Jamestown accomplished the first permanent English settlement.

Even in the attempt to fill out the bare skeleton of known facts regarding the second colony, it is necessary to draw heavily on records of the earlier effort. The first point to note is that whatever the fate awaiting the settlers of 1587 it was not intended they should meet it on Roanoke Island. There had been general dissatisfaction with that location, its inadequate anchorage for ships, and the dangerous shallows connecting it with the mainland. Lane's account of his own exploratory efforts shows that in the attempt to locate more suitable centers of settlement and control special interest had been awakened by reports of Chesapeake Bay. Exploration of Albemarle Sound had brought, too, an interest in the reputedly vast distance to the west traversed by the strong current of the Roanoke River. He declared that his purpose had been, on Grenville's return, to seek out the great bay lying to the north, to establish there his principal fort, and to provide through a series of garrisoned posts safe communication by an estimated four-day overland march to the Chowan River, whence easy access to the heart of the mainland could be had.[61] An unusually eloquent commentary on the navigation of the Carolina coast, the plan had been shaped as well by the promise that the Roanoke River would lead to a rich copper mine and even to the South Seas. By such discoveries as these, Lane argued, adequate shipping would be guar-

60 The record remains essentially as Hakluyt published it. See his *Voyages,* VIII, 386–422; and for a later compilation, Francis L. Hawks, *History of North Carolina* (Fayetteville, N. C., 1857–1858).

61 For an interesting adaptation of this plan by the later Virginia Company, see Sir Thomas Gates's instructions of 1609, in Susan M. Kingsbury (ed.), *The Records of The Virginia Company of London* (Washington, 1906–1935), III, 17.

anteed the settlers for disposal of a variety of natural commodities which "of themselves [would] not be worth the fetching." [62] No less pertinent is Hariot's observation that "as we made our journeys further into the maine . . . we found the soile to be fatter, the trees greater . . . , the ground more firme and deeper mould," finer grass, better fruit, etc.[63]

Accordingly, the settlers of 1587 arrived in America with instructions to locate their principal seat in Chesapeake Bay.[64] They called at Roanoke Island on July 22 for the sole purpose, or so they thought, of consulting the fifteen men left there the preceding year by Grenville—men, incidentally, never again seen by their fellow countrymen. But then, for reasons charged by the settlers to the double-dealing of Simon Ferdinando,[65] Portuguese seaman who commanded the fleet of three vessels, and by him attributed to the lateness of the season, they were given no choice but to unload themselves and their goods at Roanoke Island. Even so they had no intention of remaining, and promptly agreed on a removal some fifty miles into the mainland.[66]

Intriguing questions are raised by this turn of events. What exactly was the connection between this enforced alteration of plans and the necessity that led Governor White to abandon his command for a trip to England? Just what is the bearing on the colony's subsequent disappearance of the decision to move inland? Speculation is interesting, but for the most part fruitless. Having noted that the first planters of 1607 not only reached the Chesapeake but selected a seat some fifty miles inland on the James, as though taking up where Raleigh's people had left off, it is well to continue with the story.

So it is with other questions. One wonders how the project was financed. The record indicates that earlier efforts had been undertaken at the chief or even the sole charge of Raleigh. But the impressive use of a variety of promotional devices—White's paint-

[62] Hakluyt, *Voyages*, VIII, 325, 331–33. Notice again the elder Hakluyt's concern for commercial ventures that would provide the essential aid of adequate shipping for other enterprises.

[63] *Ibid.*, 383.　　　　　　　　　　　[64] *Ibid.*, 391.

[65] This was probably the same Simon Fernandez who served as pilot in the voyage of 1584.

[66] Hakluyt, *Voyages*, VIII, 398.

ings, additional pictures done by a French painter who had been with Laudonnière in Florida,[67] the several natives brought over for show in London; Hakluyt's publication in translation of Laudonnière's narrative of Florida in 1587, and the issuance in 1588 of Hariot's *Virginia*—suggests that Raleigh's assignment to other adventurers in 1589 of certain rights, notably those of trade, represented by no means his first attempt to share the cost. It was a common practice at the time for men to join as associates in support of a distant venture with the patent and other evidences of title in the name of some prime mover, whose name by its very prominence served a useful promotional purpose.

It would be interesting to know, too, the terms of settlement under which sixty-eight men, seventeen women (two of them carrying unborn children), and nine children had been recruited for the colony. That the arrangements made looked toward a permanent settlement is unmistakably indicated by the family type of emigration. A major inducement employed is revealed by incidental mention of generous land grants ranging upward from five hundred acres per person.[68] The plan of government was apparently municipal, for Governor White and twelve assistants were incorporated by charter as the "Governour and Assistants of the Citie of Ralegh in Virginia." [69] Beyond these few facts there is not much that can be added. Of the people themselves little is known except their names.

One may speak with assurance, however, of the general plan and purpose, which remained the same as that outlined by the elder Hakluyt in 1585. Faith in that program was reaffirmed by the younger Hakluyt in his dedication to Raleigh of Laudonnière's journal in 1587, and in words revealing again the influence of what Portugal and Spain had accomplished by planting in more or less comparable climates.[70] The same faith was restated, with unusual soberness, by Hariot's *Virginia* the following year. Its author readily admitted that no adequate test had been made of sugar, silk, or wine, but argued that the thrift of native vines and silkworms suggested a likely possibility with proper organization and care. Among the more important prospective staple commodities

[67] *Ibid.*, 440.   [68] *Ibid.*, 385.   [69] *Ibid.*, 386.
[70] *Ibid.*, 441–42; and see above, p. 19.

listed as having been actually tested in some degree, either in the country or by sample in England, were "silk-grass" (of the fibers of which a piece of "Silke grogran" had been made), flax, hemp, rock alum, iron ore, pearls, sweet gums, drugs, and several dyes, some of these last admittedly as yet unproved for use in the manufacture of English cloth. He further affirmed his belief in the promise of copper and woad, and emphasized the quantity of sassafras to be had and of pine for turpentine and other marketable derivatives. Emphasis, too, was given deerskins, to be bought of the natives "thousands yerely by way of traffike for trifles."

Hariot's threefold distribution of emphasis among commodities offering the promise of a profitable trade with England, the sources from which food supplies for the colonists might be drawn, and the life and custom of the native inhabitants reveals a keen appreciation of the fundamental importance to colonization of the problems of Indian relations, food supply, and marketable staples. The pamphlet's influence is to be followed through many subsequent chapters in the history of Virginia.[71]

It seems unnecessary to recount in detail the brief and familiar story of the second colony, of White's immediate return to England, of his arrival there in the excitement of preparations for war with Spain, and of his heartbreaking failure to secure relief for a group which included Eleanor and Virginia Dare, his daughter and granddaughter. Not until 1591, and then only as a passenger with an expedition primarily interested in a West Indian venture, did White return to Roanoke Island. The imperfect search that was allowed him, the failure to determine the fate of his people, and the simple prayer that God would "helpe & comfort them" expressed in a letter of 1594 to Hakluyt place a period to the story except for rumors and speculations continuing to our day. Little is known, and it is unlikely that more will be known. Perhaps no more is needed, for additional documentary evidence could alter little the meaning of this brief hour on Roanoke Island for modern Americans. There little and otherwise unimportant men,

71 For specific citations to it in the conduct of the Virginia Company's affairs as late as 1622, see Kingsbury (ed.), *Records of The Virginia Company*, III, 547, 587, 642. The problems of food and Indian relations are more fully discussed later in Chapters III and IV of the present work.

saved from the anonymity of their kind only by the faithful Hakluyt, followed a vision of a richer and fuller life, experienced momentarily the dignity of new responsibilities, no doubt betrayed at times the pettiness of those who carry unaccustomed burdens, and just as certainly on other occasions discovered within themselves unsuspected qualities of nobility and strength. There indeed was written the prologue to American history.

The years immediately following proved unfavorable for a revival of the colonial experiment. War with Spain dragged on until 1604. Capital, shipping, and energies that might otherwise have been devoted to the founding of colonies were attracted by the profits of privateering. A colony already established might well have benefited by the English ships which frequented American waters, but as Drake's co-operation in the abandonment of Roanoke Island in 1586 indicates, such an outpost was not essential to successful privateering. Other energies, later drawn upon, were now directed toward the establishment of an Eastern trade. The focus of the effort may be followed through the history of the Levant Company of 1592, an outgrowth of the older Turkey Company, and then in the founding of the East India Company of 1600. Raleigh, whom it is difficult to acquit of the heartless abandonment of the Roanoke settlers to an unknown fate, turned his attention to the quest of Eldorado in Guiana. Hariot concentrated on studies that were to bring him a measure of distinction as a mathematician. The elder Hakluyt had retired to his estates in Hereford, where he died in 1591.

The honor of keeping alive an interest in the American venture through these years falls chiefly to the younger Hakluyt. His interest in English expansion was broad, but his special concern was with the promise of North America. While the desertion of others made impossible a renewal of the experiment, his own faith seems not to have faltered. His attitude was expressed in an exhortation to Raleigh in 1587 that he "persevere only a little longer," for the depths of Virginia's wealth were as yet unprobed.[72] He was numbered among the group to whom Raleigh assigned his rights in 1589.

[72] Taylor (ed.), *Writings & Correspondence of the Two Richard Hakluyts*, II, 367. For the following discussion of Hakluyt's activities, see the introductory essay, *ibid.*, I, 1–66; Parks, *Richard Hakluyt and the English Voyages.*

In the first edition that year of *The principall Navigations, Voiages and Discoveries of the English nation* he included accounts of the Roanoke ventures. He was instrumental in persuading De Bry to publish Hariot's *Virginia* with illustrations taken from White's paintings. In 1594 he secured from White, then in Ireland, an account of his own effort to relieve the settlers in 1587. Little has been added to the record of Raleigh's colonial enterprises as published in the third volume of his expanded *Voyages* in 1600. To him is accredited a document of 1598, evidently drafted for the purpose of peace negotiations, which undertook to provide the means to restrict Spain's pretensions in America and to establish England's title.

As the war drew toward its close and interest in North American ventures revived, Hakluyt stood ready with encouragement and informed advice. There is evidence suggesting a connection with Captain Bartholomew Gosnold's voyage of 1602. Hakluyt instigated a voyage from Bristol in 1603, and it is not improbable that he shared in other projects forming the shadowy background of the Virginia Company of 1606. Of this group he was one of the patentees named in the original charter. Despite his fifty odd years of age, he actually considered going to the colony himself. He had a prominent part in the reorganization of the project in 1609, and subscribed twenty-one pounds to the joint-stock fund. That this subscription was the least of his contributions there can be no doubt.

The failure of Raleigh's experiment at Roanoke Island was easily charged to circumstances. Results would have been happier, Hakluyt had declared in the preface to the first edition of his *Voyages,* if the task "had been as seriously followed, as it was cheerefully undertaken." That the fault was not attributed to the program outlined by the elder Hakluyt in 1585 is suggested by its publication, in abbreviated form, during the latter part of 1602.[73] No one could maintain that this program had been given a real test, and it requires no great effort to determine what must have been the younger Hakluyt's explanation for that fact. At the very first he had attempted to persuade Elizabeth to underwrite the project. He had tried again in 1587, his preface to Laudonnière's

[73] Taylor (ed.), *Writings & Correspondence of the Two Richard Hakluyts,* II, 339–43.

journal being an undisguised, though indirect, appeal for royal assistance. With the peace of 1604 releasing energies for the purpose and the promise of joint-stock methods of finance so recently proved in the establishment of the East Indian trade, might not the program now be given a proper trial? There is reason for regarding Richard Hakluyt as more than a personal link between the stories of Roanoke Island and Jamestown.

CHAPTER III

JAMESTOWN

IT IS not always possible to speak with certainty regarding the Jamestown settlement. Some of the more pertinent records of the English government have been irreparably lost by fire. Official minutes of the proceedings of the Virginia Company itself are known to exist only for the years following 1618.[1] The story of the colony prior to that time must be pieced together from sources that are not only fragmentary but are frequently given over to special pleading and personal recrimination. No other period of American history has so lent itself to the inclination of some writers to read into the record whatever interpretation appeared at the moment to serve best the national or sectional interest. It has been used to demonstrate the fallacies of communism, and more recently in attempts to establish the point that fascism has also been tried in this country and found wanting. The ease with which these obviously misleading views of the period have attained wide popularity suggests the difficulty scholars have experienced in presenting a true picture.

Unquestionably, the central theme of Virginia's early history is the pursuit of that national interest which the Hakluyts had placed at the very heart of their program for American settlement. It is proper to emphasize the newly-awakened interest of the great merchants of London and their growing influence in the company under the leadership of Sir Thomas Smith, London's greatest merchant prince. Indeed, the significance of this first chapter of our history can be fully comprehended only by giving close attention to the role of the merchants and particularly to the usages bor-

[1] For the minutes from 1619 to 1624, see Kingsbury (ed.), *Records of The Virginia Company*, I, II.

rowed for management of the enterprise from the experience of England's leading mercantile community. But in this necessary emphasis lies grave danger of overemphasis and the risk that a narrow view of the merchants' interest may distort a chronicle of epic proportions. Membership in the London Company was by no means limited to the merchants; moreover, such men as Smith, whose activity in behalf of England's trade ranged from the Spice Islands and India in the East to Virginia and Hudson Bay in the West, were more than mere tradesmen. The Virginia Company, like the East India Company, must be considered in terms of the large purpose it sought to serve. Called into existence when the state chose not to assume the lead in empire building, it can be understood only as an instrument for the achievement of national ends.

This is strongly suggested when notice is taken of the place of Virginia's founding in the larger story of European expansion in America. As with the advent of the seventeenth century, Spain's competitors advanced to secure footholds on the North American continent, the English in 1607 selected a base on the James, the French in 1608 fortified Quebec on the St. Lawrence, and in 1609 Dutch exploration of the Hudson foretold still another bid for empire in New Netherland. A new phase of the international rivalry which so largely shaped early American history had begun, and in the broad perspective of that contest the London Company may well be viewed as first to enter the lists for England.

National objectives, comparable to those advocated by the younger Hakluyt in 1584, are again suggested by the provisions of the first Virginia charter.[2] Issued on April 10, 1606, this historic document recognized two groups of adventurers: the one comprising "certain Knights, gentlemen, merchants," and other men who, with headquarters in London, planned a settlement in the southern part of Virginia; and representatives of the western outports of Plymouth, Bristol, and Exeter who proposed to establish a colony in the more northern part of Virginia. The London Company, accordingly, was authorized to "begin" its colony at any point

[2] For this and the later charters of 1609 and 1612, consult Francis N. Thorpe (comp.), *Federal and State Constitutions, Colonial Charters, and Other Organic Laws* (Washington, 1909), VII, 3783–3810.

between the thirty-fourth and forty-first degrees north latitude, roughly, that is, between Cape Fear on the Carolina coast and the position now occupied by New York City. The Plymouth Company, as the second group is usually described, was authorized to "begin their said Plantation and Seat of their first Abode and Habitation, at any Place . . . where they shall think fit and convenient" between the thirty-eighth and forty-fifth degrees, which is to say, between a point coinciding approximately with the mouth of the Potomac River and a line crossing the modern state of Maine just above Bangor.

If at first glance the charter appears to provide a confusing overlapping of claims, it should be noted that the adventurers did not receive an actual grant to either one of these extensive areas. The provision merely assured to each company a wide choice in the selection of a site for its "first seat." Furthermore, the charter stipulated that there must be at least one hundred miles between the two sites so selected, and the actual area to which title would pass was quite definitely limited. From the point chosen for a "first seat" the grant in both instances would extend fifty miles northward along the coast, the same distance to the south, one hundred miles inland, and another one hundred miles at sea. Since others "of our subjects" were prohibited to settle on the "backside" of these grants, it seems to have been the policy to leave the way open for an extension of title but at the same time to avoid the creation of extensive claims serving only to obstruct more promising ventures in other hands. It appears that the Virginia adventurers were to be given every opportunity to serve their own and the national interest, but only insofar as they were successful.

No less suggestive are the provisions for government. At its head was placed a royal council of thirteen members resident in England.[3] This Virginia Council was to act with and for the King in the exercise of the broad powers of government reserved to the crown. Its jurisdiction covered both colonies, in fact, the entire region from the thirty-fourth to the forty-fifth degree. Within each colony the rights and responsibilities of government were assigned to a council of thirteen men. They were selected and commis-

[3] In addition to the charter, see "Instructions for the Government of the Colonies," in Alexander Brown (ed.), *The Genesis of the United States* (Boston, 1890), I, 64–75.

sioned by the council in England under a provision which authorized the subsidiary council to elect by majority vote its own president (the tenure of the office being limited to one year), to remove members for sufficient reason, and by co-optation to fill vacancies arising from death or removal.

It seems to have been admitted that the adventurers were entitled to decide questions of economic policy, so long as they acted within the framework of regulations dictated by national interest. Such a practice necessarily involved an attempt to maintain some sort of distinction between government and management and required that the colony function under the dual authority of the royal council and the company of adventurers. But effective co-ordination of policy between the two governing bodies was sought by giving place on the Virginia Council to leading adventurers. Indeed, it is possible that all members of the Council were actively identified with one or the other of the settlements.[4] Thus, the Council, while serving to emphasize the paramount interest of the nation and the responsibility of the crown for the welfare of its subjects in America, also provided machinery whereby the will of the adventurers could be expressed with the full weight of royal authority.

The lack of an effectively concentrated command in Virginia proved so serious a defect in the provisions for government that it has tended to discredit the whole arrangement. With that outstanding exception, however, it is difficult to find much fault with the reasoning behind the decision. If co-ordination of policy between the Council and the company of adventurers could be effected, there was every advantage in so borrowing for the stability of the colony the weight of royal authority.

The problems of colonization were many, and by no means the least was the necessity to transplant in the wilderness of America, where only the laws of nature held sway, some vestige of established and recognized authority. A state of nature was to prove theoretically attractive to many seventeenth-century Englishmen, but those

[4] Notice that in the enlargement of the council by order of March, 1607, sixteen of the additional members, among them Sir Edwin Sandys, were nominated by the London Company and ten by the Plymouth group. The quorum was fixed at twelve, whereof six were "to be members of one of the Colonies, and six more . . . to be members of the other Colony." Brown (ed.), *Genesis of the United States*, I, 91–95.

who faced the naked reality in the New World rarely found it so. What efforts they made, often with results suggestive primarily of an unpardonable pomposity, to keep alive the forms and ceremonials that traditionally bespoke authority! How heated were the early debates which turned on an interpretation of charters and instructions from England! And as though to underscore the imperfections in these first instruments of constitutional government in America, how quick were men to confuse opposition with sedition!

The need to draw upon all possible aids is written large in the record. The Virginia Council in 1609 instructed Sir Thomas Gates to use "such fourmes and Ensignes of governement as by our letters Pattents wee are enabled to grant unto you" and "the attendance of a guarde uppon your person" in order to assure "the more regard and respect of your place, to begett reverence to your authority, and to refresh their mindes that obey the gravity of those lawes under which they were borne." [5] The function of a minister in an infant colony was hardly less political than spiritual. Take along "one or twoo preachers," Hakluyt had counseled, "that God may be honoured, the people instructed, mutinies the better avoided, and obedience the better used." [6] Significant also is the attempt made in selecting governors to draw upon the authority associated in English society with high birth. And since that was not always possible, the Virginia adventurers in 1618 tried the expedient, resorted to thereafter, of securing a knighthood for Governor George Yeardley.[7] But while these things might prove helpful, there was no substitute for a commission that enabled the head of

---

[5] Kingsbury (ed.), *Records of The Virginia Company*, III, 15.

[6] Taylor (ed.), *Writings & Correspondence of the Two Richard Hakluyts*, II, 324.

[7] For George Yeardley's knighthood and a later petition by several planters for appointment of a man of more quality, see Kingsbury (ed.), *Records of The Virginia Company*, III, 216–19, 231–32. The petitioners' argument, undoubtedly colored by factional prejudice, was that the settlers included men "whom only Reverence of the Comanders Eminence, or Nobillitye (whereunto by Nature everye man subordinate is ready to yield a willing submission without contempt, or repyning) may easily perswade under those dutyes of Obedience: which Aucthoritye conferrd upon a meane man, and of one no bettar, then selected owt of their owne Ranke, shall nevar be able to compell." Some of the peculiar problems of early colonial government have been discussed at greater length in Craven, *Introduction to the History of Bermuda*, Chap. II.

a colony to meet the threat of rebellion, as did Governor Daniel Tucker a few years later in Bermuda, with the simple warning: "I bear Kinge James his authoritie with me." [8] The adventurers of 1606 may have erred on details, but on the main point their position was well chosen.[9]

Having secured the necessary legal authorization and agreed upon a plan of government, the adventurers sent to Virginia an exploratory field expedition not unlike the one Raleigh had sent to Roanoke in 1585. Its objectives included a permanent settlement in America, but its immediate task seems to have been the establishment of an outpost there to effect preliminary investigations for the purpose of determining the exact pattern of settlement to be attempted. That the adventurers accepted the necessarily experimental nature of any initial effort in America is indicated by their apparent plan to build up the colony gradually, and presumably in accordance with opportunities more or less proved by test.[10] Such a view, at any rate, finds support in the record of events.

Approximately one hundred men and four boys, a company destined to become the "first planters in Virginia," sailed from London at the close of 1606 aboard three small vessels. In command was Captain Christopher Newport, an experienced seaman. He had served the Muscovy merchants and, prior to his death a decade later in Java, he was to win a place in the history not only

[8] [Nathaniel Butler], *Historye of the Bermudaes* (London, 1882), 73.

[9] Some of the Plymouth Company had expressed opposition to the plan of a royal council, but this perhaps represented as much as anything else opposition to its location in London. In addition to the inconvenience for western adventures, there was sharp rivalry between London and the outports. See Andrews, *Colonial Period of American History*, I, 85.

[10] "We always thought at first we would send people there little by little," Lord Chancellor Thomas Egerton is reported to have said in 1609 by way of explaining a radical change of policy at that time. Brown (ed.), *Genesis of the United States*, I, 259. The statement is supported by the following figures on early immigration into the colony: the first planters, 100-105; with the first supply, 120; and with the second supply, 70. The third supply in 1609, by contrast, sailed with 600 persons. Edward Arber and Arthur G. Bradley (eds.), *Travels and Works of Captain John Smith* (Edinburgh, 1910), I, 93-94, 107-108, 129; II, 389-90, 411-12, 445-46. This work, which includes in addition to the writings of Smith himself accounts upon which he drew in the compilation of his *Historie*, has been a chief reliance in preparing the following pages. For a recent and more detailed narrative of the colony's early years, see Matthew P. Andrews, *The Soul of a Nation* (New York, 1943).

of Virginia and of Bermuda but of England's early trade to Persia, India, and the East Indies as well. From England to the Canaries and thence to the West Indies, Newport followed a course traveled by most of the early American settlers, stopping at Nevis and other West Indian isles for refreshment of sea-weary passengers and for provisions. Proceeding then northward, he reached the entrance to Chesapeake Bay late in April, 1607.

Inside the bay, the company faced its first problem—to find a suitable site for the colony's principal fort. It had been directed that this should be located some distance up a river promising deep penetration to the west so that the colonists might be advantageously situated for purposes of westward exploration, for the development of native trade over an extensive area, and for their defense against attack by another European people.[11] Settlement inland at a point approachable only by a narrow channel or an overland march, together with plans for maintaining a lookout post nearer the coast, promised escape from the fate which had befallen the French Huguenot colony in Florida. After preliminary exploration of the lower bay, the colonists moved up the most impressive of the rivers emptying there. About thirty miles upstream, they discovered a peninsular extension offering most of the advantages sought for a "first seate." Low-lying, marshy land that covered much of the peninsula must have caused some hesitation, for they had been warned to avoid such a place. Offsetting this disadvantage, however, were reassuring views for some distance both up and down the river, anchorage close inshore for seagoing vessels, and the fact that the place, almost an island, provided very real aids to forestalling surprise attacks by the natives. Accordingly, the anchor was cast, and they gave to the place the name of King James.

It was now the middle of May.

The adventurers had directed that next the force should be divided into three approximately equal parts: one for work on fortification and other necessary construction, another to put in a crop and to provide a guard down the river, and a third group to carry out certain additional exploration. In detailing the explorations to be attempted, the instructions naturally emphasized those

[11] For the adventurers' instructions, see Brown (ed.), *Genesis of the United States*, I, 79–85.

prospects promising an especially rich reward and gave first place to discovery of a passage. As the adventurers pointed out, there was a chance that the river system of the North American continent was similar to that of Russia, where the Volga and Dvina from sources close together flowed in opposite directions to provide water transportation over most of the distance from the White to the Caspian seas. The search required would serve other useful purposes, and, should the hypothesis prove correct and the Chesapeake a fortunate choice for the test, it would be possible with the aid of an overland portage to reach the South Seas. The colony then, through its control of the portage, would be in a position to enjoy peculiar and varied advantages as an entrepôt in England's trade with Cathay and with such intervening lands as might be found.[12]

Other duties actually left little time for exploration. Though Newport had been authorized to devote two months to "discovery of the river above you, and . . . the country about you," the effort he made was virtually limited to the week extending from May 21–27. During that week he explored the river to the falls, where, at the site of present-day Richmond, he discovered a formidable barrier to further search by water. His explorations, in other words, were limited to the minimum required for the colony's security and for a preliminary report on prospects to the adventurers. The remainder of the time prior to his departure for England on June 22 was devoted to work at the fort and preparation of clapboard as cargo for the return voyage.

The adventurers had frugally directed that a search for mineral specimens be combined with the quest of a passage, and it has usually been assumed that their principal thought was of gold. Indeed, a tendency to view the Jamestown project as essentially a misguided gold hunt has frequently dominated interpretations of Virginia's early history. The record, of course, does not lack evidence supporting such a view, but there is need for greater care in use of the evidence than often has been shown. Since the original instructions from the adventurers indicate merely that, in con-

---

[12] On the continuing interest in a trade with China and in discovery of a route free of the disadvantages experienced in the passage around the Cape of Good Hope, see again Foster, *England's Quest of Eastern Trade.*

junction with other explorations, a search was to be undertaken for mineral deposits, it seems reasonable to assume that the interest was broad and general rather than specific. This interest undoubtedly included the copper listed in the charter with gold and silver and already given prominence in discussions of Virginia by Captain Ralph Lane's report of a rich copper mine inland from Roanoke Island. The prospect may also have included iron. That ore received mention in reports of the first expedition to Jamestown, and the company subsequently invested a small fortune in its Virginia ironworks.[13] Naturally, the most valuable of minerals was not to be overlooked, but there is no warrant, either in the instructions or in extant records of the colonists' activity through the first few months, for an assumption that gold had been singled out for a special effort. Not until after Newport's return to the colony with the first supply in January, 1608, was the settlement stirred by the fever of a real gold hunt. Even then the fever appears to have quickly subsided.

How far the adventurers were responsible for this outbreak is difficult to say. It is not at all certain that the two "refiners" and two goldsmiths sent with the first supply reached the colony in time to assist in the effort, but their recruitment indicates a purpose to accomplish some more exact test of the possibility of a gold find than had hitherto been made and suggests that the misdirected zeal of the settlers may well have received its initial prompting from London.[14] Though Captain John Martin, of the local council, subsequently received from the colonists the chief blame, it is significant that Newport displayed every inclination to co-operate in the undertaking. To load Martin's "gilded durt" he delayed departure for England until his stay in the colony, at considerable cost to the adventurers for demurrage, had reached a total of fourteen weeks.

In any case, there was for much of this time, as Captain John

13 For the reports, see "Capt. Newport's Discoveries, Virginia," in *Transactions and Collections of the American Antiquarian Society*, IV (1860), 40–65.

14 Arber and Bradley (eds.), *Travels and Works of Captain John Smith*, I, 108; II, 412. The supply had been sent in two ships, of which the *Phoenix* did not arrive until after Christopher Newport's departure. Assuming that the refiners arrived aboard the *Phoenix*, it might be argued that their expert opinion would have saved the colony its misspent effort.

Smith's *Historie* records, "no talke, no hope, nor worke, but dig gold, wash gold, refine gold, load gold." [15] But when the *Phoenix* arrived on April 20, just ten days after Newport's sailing, Smith succeeded in outarguing Martin on the point that cedar would provide a more profitable cargo for the return voyage.[16] And this apparently put an end to a gold hunt that is more properly viewed as a significant interlude in the history of an undertaking largely devoted to other efforts than as the dominant feature of Virginia's early years.

It is true that Newport's return to the colony the following September with the second supply brought renewed attention to the possibility of gold deposits. He came at that time with a special and broad commission to accomplish several exploratory tasks remaining unfinished. He was to determine the prospects for certain extractive industries with the aid of eight Polish and German experts in the manufacture of glass, pitch, tar, and soap ashes, who had been brought for the purpose; to send a party in search of Raleigh's lost colony; to explore the river above the falls; and while so doing to seek out, with the presumably expert assistance of a refiner, such mineral deposits as might lie along the way.[17] That the execution of this commission involved some gold hunting is hardly to be disputed, but does it not speak primarily of an attempt to balance the chance of failure in any one effort with the promise of several other projects? More than that, does not this procedure suggest the opposite of that unhealthy concentration of effort popularly associated with the term "gold hunt"? [18]

[15] *Ibid.,* I, 104; II, 407.

[16] *Ibid.,* I, 104–107; II, 407–408, 411. John Martin returned to England in the *Phoenix.*

[17] No copy of this commission has been found, but its broad outlines are clearly indicated in accounts of the "proceedings and accidents with the second supply." Arber and Bradley (eds.), *Travels and Works of Captain John Smith,* I, especially p. 121. The search for news of Raleigh's people was undertaken by Michael Sicklemore the following winter, but the other assignments were executed by Newport prior to his departure for London in November. His activities included exploration of the river for approximately forty miles beyond the falls. He also carried out a special commission for the coronation of Powhatan, discussed below.

[18] Truth to tell, the all too popular gold-hunt thesis has depended for its main support, as reference to almost any textbook will show, upon two overworked quotations. The one, quoted immediately above from Smith's *Historie,* can be applied to any period of time other than the fourteen weeks there specified only by lifting it

The English interest in settlement had been prompted by a variety of prospective opportunities to develop the trade and natural resources of the North American continent in accordance with the peculiar needs of the English market. From our vantage point it is clear that a passage did not exist within reach of Jamestown, that mineral deposits of real importance were limited to iron, and that other areas proved more suitable for the several extractive industries proposed. From the contemporary point of view, however, was it not sensible to undertake the test? The broad objectives followed had been incorporated in the well-balanced program outlined by the Hakluyts, and for 150 years yet public policy was to encourage attempts in America to reach these goals.

From the contemporary point of view, also, there was reason for placing first objectives which gave promise of an early return on investment and thereby engendered the hope of reducing overhead charges in further stages of the experiment.[19] That the adventurers intended to carry the experiment beyond the steps immediately taken is clearly indicated by the charter's provision for conferring individual titles to land. The type of agriculture and related industrial activity planned is suggested by tests made with "West-Indy plants" and by assurances returned with the earliest shipping that, given skilled direction, the colonists could produce from the soil vines, sugar, olives, hemp, prunes, currants, tobacco, cotton, saffron, woad, hops, "and such like." The pros-

---

from its context. With the second, it is also enough to return it to its context in the play "Eastward Hoe" (1605, by George Chapman, Ben Jonson, and John Marston), where it will be found in Seagull's answer to Spendthrift's question of whether there was actually in Virginia such treasure as he had heard. "I tell thee," runs the reply, "golde is more plentifull there then copper is with us. . . . Why, man, all their dripping-pans and their chamber-pots are pure gould: and all the chaines with which they chaine up their streets are massie gold; all the prisoners they take are fettered in gold"; and so on to the rubies and diamonds gathered for holiday sport. This, of course, is nothing more than the broadest comedy reaching for the belly laugh in a city where John White's paintings of the Carolina natives, Thomas Hariot's faithful description of their primitive life (with illustrations by Theodore De Bry), and even Indians themselves were not unknown. If it bespeaks anything of significance for the historian, is it not of a certain skepticism protecting the public from some of the promotional efforts of early adventurers to Virginia?

[19] In seeking to understand the Jamestown story, it is helpful to study again the proposals made by the elder Hakluyt in 1585. See above, pp. 43–49.

pect thus opened, a prospect shaped by the promise of a southern soil and climate and by the achievements of Spain and Portugal, naturally challenged the men of that day. But first the ground would have to be prepared, the country explored, fortifications raised, housing built, terms reached with the native inhabitants, and an income assured for assistance in the financing of a variety of experimental ventures. Where a man's work was to be done there was no point in being encumbered with women and children. Colonization in the full sense awaited more-exact proof of the prospects for planting.

To say that objectives set were reasonable in the light of current experience is not to deny, however, that mismanagement marred the record. With thoughts of a great discovery to the fore, the Virginia project held a strong attraction for that type of Englishman who over the years past—along the Spanish Main, in Ireland, and in the Netherlands—had readily responded to the call of adventure. Though the early settlers were largely laborers or craftsmen, the lists included a considerable number classified as gentlemen. Whatever that designation may have implied regarding their social standing at home, it undoubtedly indicates some difference in the kind of employment these men expected in the colony. In view of the work planned the relative numbers were perhaps not disproportionate, but, under the circumstances which developed, the colony appears to have been cursed with a plethora of leaders. Many of them promptly exhibited the tempestuous nature that so frequently goes with the spirit of adventure. The unhappy situation resulting became the more dangerous because of an unfortunate plan of government, under which the councilors were not only empowered to elect their president but to override his will as well.

Chief victim was Edward Maria Wingfield, scion of a distinguished family, and middle-aged veteran of wars in Ireland and the Netherlands. He was elected first president of the council, a body of six men rather than the thirteen members prescribed. By fall he had been removed from office and, following an imprisonment, he was sent home in the spring of 1608. There can be no doubt of his failure to rise to the requirements of an emergency,

71

but he occupied a difficult position and at home presented a strong defense of his actions.[20]

The charges brought against him, for the most part petty and contradictory, are especially revealing as to conditions in the colony which interfered with a prompt fulfillment of its exploratory mission. It is clear that disappointment, hunger, and sickness so charged the atmosphere with fear, suspicion, and hatred that not even the conciliatory efforts of the Reverend Robert Hunt, the first minister in the colony, could preserve the peace. Nor did Wingfield's removal bring appreciable improvement. In fact, only the resources available to the London adventurers, which permitted renewed supplies; the restriction of emigration to the colony for two years to relatively small numbers; and the energetic leadership of John Smith, who succeeded to the presidency in the fall of 1608, saved the Jamestown experiment from a failure as complete as that experienced by the Plymouth adventurers at Sagadahoc.[21]

While plans were being laid through the winter of 1608–1609 for a revised and enlarged project, Captain Smith held the fort in Virginia. He took advantage of depletion in the ranks of his fellow councilors, by death, removal, and departure from the colony, to impose the discipline of his own strong will on the colonists. Though his methods and procedures were for the most part unauthorized, significantly they were in line with policies soon to be enforced by order from London.

From the earliest days to the present, Smith has remained a controversial figure. It is true that he was egotistical and frequently lacking in generosity toward his associates. Much of the prolonged was-Smith-a-liar controversy, however, has centered around relatively minor events in his career. Whether Pocahontas actually saved his life as he later claimed is not particularly important. Let it be conceded that the captain at times exercised the prerogative of a veteran in recounting his conquests of war and love. The

[20] "A Discourse of virginia," in Arber and Bradley (eds.), *Travels and Works of Captain John Smith*, I, lxxiv–xci.

[21] For a discussion of the Maine colony (founded in August, 1607, and abandoned early the next year) that throws much light on the background of the whole Virginia venture and draws significant parallels with the Jamestown story, see Andrews, *Colonial Period of American History*, I, 78–97.

important thing is the evidence substantiating, in the main, both his *Historie* and his claim to have rendered significant services to the colony.[22] While scholars have quarreled, the instinct of the public has been sound in continuing to recognize him as the first Englishman to leave the imprint of his personality and character on a distinctively American scene.

He was responsible for the most significant explorations undertaken in the early years of the colony. In two expeditions completed during the summer of 1608 he crossed over to the Eastern Shore, followed its western shore line northward from Cape Charles ("searching every inlet and bay fit for harbours and habitations") to some of the islands that break the water above Accomac. He then explored the bay to the head of navigation, brought the Patuxent and Potomac within the knowledge of the settlers, and defined with some exactness the course of the Rappahannock. Well might his men ask who else "with such smal meanes . . . did ever discover so many faire and navigable rivers"?[23]

It is not easy for the modern visitor to see the country as did its first explorers or even to grasp some of the more significant features of the society which developed there. His very approach is in almost every detail the reverse of that of our colonial forefathers. When he stands at the tip of one of the peninsulas shaped by the rivers emptying into the Chesapeake, having arrived perhaps by way of several ferries with schedules and tolls calculated to emphasize the way in which a river may become a barrier to transportation and communication, he easily forgets how under different circumstances it may serve the opposite purpose. He looks out from land over water, whereas the first settlers more frequently looked from water over land. He naturally thinks of land surrounded by water, but they thought of water surrounded by land. He tends to interpret the problem of settlement in terms of acquir-

---

22 See especially, Arber and Bradley (eds.), *Travels and Works of Captain John Smith,* I, i–cxxvi, *passim,* where the editors perhaps overstate the case for Smith, but nevertheless make a good case. On his earlier career, see *The True Travels, Adventures, & Observations of Captaine John Smith,* with an Introduction by John G. Fletcher and a Bibliographical Note by Lawrence C. Wroth (New York, 1930). Note also expressions of confidence in him contained in Sir Thomas Gates's instructions of 1609. Kingsbury (ed.), *Records of The Virginia Company,* III, 13, 18.

23 Arber and Bradley (eds.), *Travels and Works of Captain John Smith,* I, 148.

ing control over a large area of contiguous territory; they thought of it primarily in terms of the security of navigation. His view even of the relative position of places requires correction by careful attention to the manner in which waterways both lengthen and shorten distances. One of the first requirements in studying the early history of Virginia is radically to change modern habits of map reading.

The dominant feature of the seventeenth-century map of Virginia was Chesapeake Bay, over two hundred miles in extent from south to north and at its widest approximately forty miles across. Radiating outward were navigable channels provided by rivers, creeks, and inlets which gave the bay, especially in its southern part, a position not unlike that of a traffic circle in a modern highway system. In the south the Elizabeth and Nansemond mingle their waters with those of the James, the first of the great streams penetrating westward. The James has its source in the Appalachians and is fed below the fall line by the Appomattox and the Chicka-hominy. Riding down the current from Jamestown past Point Comfort and turning northward around the end of the Virginia Peninsula that is broken by the Back and the Poquoson rivers, one comes to the York, deep and beautiful to the juncture at West Point of the Pamunkey and Mattapony. Proceeding back down again and up past Mobjack Bay and the Piankatank River, he arrives at the mouth of the Rappahannock. Beyond this and the Great Wicomico River is the majestic Potomac, enclosing with the Rappahannock the celebrated Northern Neck, land of the Fairfaxes, Lees, and Washingtons. Across on the Maryland side are the Patuxent, the Severn, and at the head of the bay the Susquehanna. Traveling down the Eastern Shore one finds no such watershed as that which empties millions of gallons daily from the north and west. Even so, here will be found the Sassafras, the Chester, the Choptank, the Nanticoke, the Wicomico, and the Pocomoke, lesser streams which with numerous inlets and creeks break the coast line into a marked irregularity and carry inland relatively long distances.

In his exploration of the Chesapeake, Smith pointed the way for his successors. For a time yet, several factors tended to draw the adventurers' attention southward. There was a general assumption that the more a land "inclined to the southe" the greater its promise.

In addition, there was the hope of locating survivors of the lost colony and the desire to test Lane's report of a rich copper mine. In 1609 the Virginia Council, by instructions suggesting the influence of Lane's earlier proposals, even advised transfer of the principal seat to a point in the neighborhood of Albemarle Sound. With this seat joined by overland marches to a port of entry at Jamestown and to another seat above the falls of the James, the chief centers of control would thus have formed the points of a triangle lying for the most part below the Virginia Peninsula.[24] But settlement actually was to follow the path of least resistance. It clung to the Chesapeake and expanded northward by successive stages along the York, the Rappahannock, and the Potomac, each of these rivers serving as did the James to carry westward a line of advance outmeasuring that followed in any other direction.

Though the adventurers advised a southward move, control of the bay to its head was secured by the second Virginia charter of 1609. This same year witnessed the beginning of a post at Point Comfort, to be more or less permanently maintained for defensive purposes thereafter. On this site today stands one of the oldest and most famous of our military establishments, Fort Monroe. Within a few years, settlement had been extended across the bay to Accomac. And though the Virginia colony was compelled in time to yield some of the lands bordering the upper bay, she held, by mastery of both capes overlooking the outlet to the Atlantic, a command of the navigation of the Chesapeake until establishment of our present Federal government. The way in which the modern state of Virginia straddles the lower Chesapeake to include two counties seeming properly to belong in Maryland calls to mind a significant chapter in the history of the colony and of the nation.

No exploratory task of the first Virginia colonists outranked in importance the necessity to define more exactly than had Hariot and other early observers the problem of Indian relations. In addition to its bearing on prospects for commercial profit, it presented to the promoters of American settlement the same ques-

24 See Gates's instructions, in Kingsbury (ed.), *Records of The Virginia Company*, III, 16–17. Another governing consideration may well have been apprehension regarding a Spanish attack, for as the instructions pointed out there were advantages in such a plan for purposes of defense.

tion of right and title that has challenged more recent imperialists. "The first objection is," declared the Reverend Robert Gray in a sermon of 1609 blessing the Virginia colony, "by what right or warrant we can enter into the land of these Savages, take away their rightfull inheritance from them, and plant ourselves in their places, being unwronged or unprovoked by them." [25] The question, of course, had to be answered, and this required attention to the moral as well as other aspects of the problem. Sir George Peckham's discussion in 1583 and that of William Strachey, secretary of the Virginia colony by an appointment of 1609, are especially full and enlightening.[26]

The answer given was not only unoriginal with the English, but has continued to serve successive movements of European overseas expansion. Frequent use in its earlier forms of Biblical references, especially from the Old Testament, should not be allowed to becloud the issues or be taken to mean that men of that day were either more or less hypocritical than their modern successors. The principal point in the case was that the English in reality did not seek to dispossess the Indian, but rather to share with him the resources of a rich country and to confer upon him the benefits of a better life. The European asked first of all for trade, a right, Peckham argued, recognized since time immemorial by the "Law of Nations." As for the modest concessions sought for purposes of planting, the land was sparsely settled, virtually boundless, and its resources undeveloped by a barbarous people. That bounteous gifts of God should be allowed to go to waste, especially when his own chosen people were in need, was a proposition supported neither by considerations of equity nor the obvious lessons of Scripture.

Moreover, the question could not be considered as merely that of leaving Virginia to the Indians. If England did not take possession, Spain or France probably would. To allow the native thus to fall under the influence of Catholicism would be to fail in an obligation to give him the true faith. And to this was naturally added a consideration of Spain's unfitness at other points to assume the

[25] Robert Gray, *A Good Speed to Virginia* (London, 1609).

[26] Peckham, *A Trve Reporte of the Late Discoueries;* William Strachey, *The Historie of Travaile into Virginia Britannia* (London, 1849).

high responsibilities of imperial tutelage. Englishmen had been much impressed by the aid the *cimarrones* gave Drake in his plundering of Peruvian treasure on the Isthmus of Panama, and in building up their case against Spain's monopolistic claims in America they made good use of available evidence supporting a charge of special tyranny and cruelty in Spanish dealings with the natives. Particularly useful were the castigations of Spain's early native policy by Bishop Bartolomé de Las Casas, whose *Brevisima Relacion de la destruycion de las Indias* of 1552 received an English translation in 1583 under the pointed title of *The Spanish Colonie*.[27] And so did an essay, surely as representative of the Spanish conscience as of Spanish cruelty, serve the purposes of an English promotional campaign. Many are the evidences, even in modern textbooks, of the success which rewarded the effort.

With the rights of trade and of settlement established, there could be no question that the colonists were entitled to provide for their own security. Fortification of English "seates" would be accompanied by friendly overtures and every due regard for native rights. Let the settlers be known, counseled the elder Hakluyt in 1585, "to be more able to scourge the people . . . than willing to offer any violence." [28] But "if after these good and fayre meanes used," argued Peckham, the natives should "barbarously" respond with violence, "I holde it no breach of equitie for the Christians to defend themselves." In addition to the established right of men "to resist violence with violence," or as Strachey later put it, "to prevent our owne throats from the cutting," there was the simple fact that withdrawal by the Christians would mean for such of the natives as had been converted a "returne to their horrible idolatrie." As usual, right and duty had been neatly combined.

It is difficult to speak in unqualified terms regarding the extent of serious missionary interest. That the English people were on the whole relatively slow to respond to the appeal of this new Macedonia appears to be indisputable. However, a warning should be issued against the modern tendency to interpret the talk of mis-

27 Subsequently reprinted by Samuel Purchas in *Hakluytus Posthumus, or Purchas His Pilgrimes* (Glasgow, 1905–1907), XVIII, 80–180. For Hakluyt's use of the charge of Spanish cruelty, see Taylor (ed.), *Writings & Correspondence of the Two Richard Hakluyts*, II, 257–65.

28 Taylor (ed.), *Writings & Correspondence of the Two Richard Hakluyts*, II, 334.

sionary undertakings in contemporary promotional tracts as nothing more than a promotional device. For there was a good deal of sincerity as well as policy in this, and it is unfair to charge leaders with hypocrisy for no better reason than their failure to provide an impressive missionary establishment at the first settlement. Not only were they operating under the disadvantage of limited funds, but it was held by so influential a student as Richard Hakluyt that planting should properly precede any serious missionary effort. Attention was to be concentrated first on the establishment of English colonies, which would serve both by precept and example as civilizing agencies. Then, having earned the native's good will and learned his languages and customs, the English might carry forward their evangelical mission with security and expedition. The lesson had been drawn partly from Spain's experience, with citation by Hakluyt to "those Spanishe ffryers that before any plantinge withoute strengthe and company landed in fflorida, where they were miserablye massacred by the Savages." [29] The gospel, in short, should be offered with the backing of sufficient force to assure for it a proper respect.

This union of conscience and realism is readily apparent in the instructions of the Virginia Council to the first settlers at Jamestown. They were enjoined to observe "all just, kind and charitable courses" in their dealings with the natives under "severe paines and punishments" to be fixed by the resident council. They were further admonished, however, not to place too much trust in the Indians as guides, to keep a cleared space around their dwellings, never to entrust their weapons to them, and when firing their pieces in the presence of the red men to take care that only the best marksmen be used. It was considered advisable to hide all sickness among the settlers, and imperative that the death of Englishmen should not be advertised. Such were the simple rules laid down for upholding the white man's prestige. The instructions also recognized the importance of native trade in plans for the colony's economic development through a warning of the danger to the market in permitting seamen to trade independently. That the current limitations of the market were understood is indicated by evidence in contemporary narratives that the colonists came well enough sup-

[29] *Ibid.*, 215.

plied with those beads and trinkets which delighted the Indian customer.[30]

The Indians with whom the colonists had to deal were not greatly different from those studied by Thomas Hariot and John White at Roanoke in 1585. Primitive, savage, and divided into numerous tribal groups, perhaps the chief distinguishing feature of their life was the loose union preserved under the "confederacy" over which presided the "emperor" Powhatan. This ancient chieftain of "subtile understanding and pollitique carriage," as Strachey described him, held a superior authority not easily defined in the terminology of European politics over most of Tidewater Virginia. Among his "subjects" were the Indians of Paspahegh, the region in the immediate vicinity of Jamestown, from whom the colonists by a payment in copper purchased the right of settlement.[31]

The early Indian relations of the colony pitted one against the other Smith and Powhatan, two worthy leaders of their people. The red chieftain proved cautious and quick to appreciate the strength of European weapons. Suspicious of assurances given, he maintained a careful watch that at times told on the settlers' nerves, exchanged tokens of friendship with them, and introduced the Englishmen to the subtle art of Indian oratory. At times he resorted to the familiar trick of assuring them that everything they hoped to find was on the upper James, where resided his enemies the Monacans. The colonists soon grasped the realities of his policy, devined the meaning of his protestation on occasions of Indian assault that even King James must have some unruly subjects, and developed strong notions as to how he should be handled.

A principal difficulty in dealing with his stratagems was the restraint imposed by the admonitions of the royal council. The hopes and ideas which guided the adventurers are interestingly sug-

---

[30] Initially, the colony was forced to trade principally for corn to meet the urgent need for food, but individuals, and especially seamen, from an early date took advantage of the opportunity for a trade in skins.

[31] *A True Declaration of the Estate of the Colonie in Virginia* (1610), reprinted in Peter Force (comp.), *Tracts and Other Papers* (Washington, 1836–1847), III, No. 1, p. 6. For other indications of an inclination on the part of the early colonists to rest their titles on purchases from the Indians, see Kingsbury (ed.), *Records of The Virginia Company*, III, 96, 99; and statement of Strachey, *Historie of Travaile into Virginia Britannia*, 19, that the English would pay for every foot of land used.

gested by an order of 1608 compelling Smith, against his better judgment, to co-operate with Newport in a ceremonial coronation of Powhatan. A copper crown had been sent for the purpose, and along with it several articles of European furniture and clothing and instructions to build the chieftain an English house. By accepting the crown Powhatan might be understood to have conceded the English title, a point of considerable legal importance to the European, while in the offer of it the English gave due recognition, or so presumably it was felt, to the Indian's right in the land. The translation of that right into exact and practical terms, permitting amicable and mutually profitable relations between the two peoples, would naturally require time, but the ultimate answer to the problem undoubtedly seemed clear.

It had been taken for granted that the Indian could be converted not only to the Christian religion but to a European economy as well. Indeed, the two objectives were regarded as in large measure interdependent, and, according to any standard acceptable to the European, there could be no question of the benefit thus to be conferred upon the Indian. On the English side, the advantage obviously would be to bring the native's understanding of his rights into harmony with English laws of landholding, and to encourage the development of economic pursuits supplementing those of the colonists. The adventurers, no doubt, had been prompted in part by the hope of developing a profitable market for English cloth, but the interest was broader than that.[32] It is pertinent to note that the coronation of Powhatan, staged in the fall of 1608, came on the eve of an impressive program of recruitment in England, which looked toward immediate colonization in the fullest sense of the word. The problem of finding a *modus vivendi* effectively joining the English and the Indians in a true community of interest was basic to the execution of any such program. The idea of con-

---

[32] See again the elder Hakluyt's draft project for Raleigh in 1585, in Taylor (ed.), *Writings & Correspondence of the Two Richard Hakluyts*, II, 327–38. On Newport's commission for the coronation of Powhatan, see Arber and Bradley (eds.), *Travels and Works of Captain John Smith*, I, 121 ff. The early hope of a market for cloth should not be lightly dismissed. Efforts to convert the Indian from his primitive habits met only a very limited success, but the woolen blanket which constitutes a major detail in our picture of the North American Indian significantly records one of the more successful ventures of the European tradesman.

verting the Indian to a European pattern of life was destined to be tried repeatedly in colonial America, and since the earliest Christian missions it had often been recognized that a useful approach was the conversion of the king.

The experiment, however, proved disappointing. Powhatan not only displayed his native shrewdness by refusing to kneel at the coronation ceremonies, but he continued thereafter his covert resistance to the English intrusion. By the following spring the adventurers were prepared to entertain some of the suggestions offered by the colonists, and in drafting instructions for Gates they agreed that the key to the immediate problem lay in destruction of Powhatan's influence. This was to be accomplished by placing all of the tribes in a position directly tributary to the English, somewhat as the Peruvian natives were understood to be under Spanish rule. Tribute would be due directly from each tribal chieftain in annual payments of corn, skins, and dye materials and through the weekly labor of a specified number of men. Thus would the power of the "emperor" be broken, the labor of his people directed to securing commodities of commercial advantage to the English, and the planters given the benefits of native labor. Instead of the earlier suggestions of an alliance with local Indians cemented by cooperation in warfare against their enemies, the adventurers now suggested that friendship be cultivated with outlying tribes for the better discipline of those close at hand.[33]

This new orientation of policy should not be interpreted as an abandonment of earlier intentions to deal justly with the natives and to lead them into a better life. Rather, as the plan to make them tributary foretells the general policy of recognizing the Indian's occupancy of the land but with the fee in the English crown, so do other provisions suggest certain ideas which were to govern missionary effort from the day of George Thorpe to that of Eleazer Wheelock. Young Indians were to be placed, by agreement with their parents, in English households for training in the English language and the Christian way of life. The tribute exacted from the natives was also intended to serve the ancillary purpose of

[33] Kingsbury (ed.), *Records of The Virginia Company*, III, 14–15, 18–21; instructions to Lord De la Warr in 1610, *ibid.*, 24–29; Strachey, *Historie of Travaile into Virginia Britannia*, 87–88, 102–103.

teaching them the values and techniques of a more advanced economy. In support of these educational measures, the adventurers directed that steps be taken to break the superstitious influence of native priests. The new emphasis found effective expression in Hakluyt's advice to the Virginia Council for dealing with the natives. "Gentle courses," so long as they served, were "without comparison the best," but it might well be necessary to rely upon some of England's old soldiers "to square and prepare them to our Preachers hands." [34]

As these adjustments of Indian policy suggest, the year 1609 brought significant changes and developments in the Virginia project. Two years of experimental effort at Jamestown had proved disappointing, but the settlement there had accomplished at least enough of its exploratory mission to provide the basis of a new hope. Disappointments, moreover, could be charged to faulty procedures and the feebleness of the initial move. "We always thought at first we would send people there little by little," Lord Chancellor Thomas Egerton was reported by the Spanish ambassador as saying, "and now we see that the proper thing is to fortify ourselves all at once." [35] Accordingly, the adventurers decided upon an enlarged and broadened program designed to assure a prompt realization of the full benefits of American settlement. To launch this more ambitious venture they relied on joint-stock methods of finance already proved in a variety of commercial undertakings and on a public appeal to the national interest.

Under the leadership of Sir Thomas Smith negotiations were begun with the King's ministers for a new charter. Meanwhile, according to custom, books were opened early in February, 1609, for subscriptions to the joint-stock fund. All those subscribing by a set date were to be listed as adventurers in the charter, which would confirm a reorganization of the project then in process. At the same time, plans were laid and carried forward for sending out a great fleet to reach Virginia in the early summer. Bargaining with shipowners and shipmasters went hand in hand with a recruiting campaign to enlist ministers, physicians, gentlemen, soldiers, and especially craftsmen of all sorts as emigrants to the colony. Sir

[34] In the Preface to *Virginia richly valued*.
[35] Brown (ed.), *Genesis of the United States*, I, 259, and 317 for supporting evidence.

Thomas' house in Philpot Lane, where such old hands as Hakluyt and Hariot sat in consultation with the leading adventurers, served as headquarters.

The appeal made was broad, and skillfully directed to patriotic and religious sentiment as well as the normal desire of men to better their lot, the reward offered including the very immortality posterity has accorded those who responded. Broadsides and pamphlets were circulated and the aid of the pulpit was enlisted. Not since the 1580's had the printing press been so active in behalf of American settlement.[36] To the lord mayor of London the adventurers addressed proposals for a mutually advantageous easing of the problems of the city's poor by assisted emigration to the colony. Through him, too, they stirred up the ancient city companies to contribute to the joint stock. The west-country adventurers of 1606 were invited to recoup their losses at Sagadahoc by throwing in their lot with London. Meanwhile gentlemen at court, and even at their country seats, found themselves caught up in a campaign that came uncomfortably close to putting the appeal on a basis of *noblesse oblige*.

To the skill which characterized the management of the campaign and to the timeliness of the appeal the best testimony is the response. Within three weeks of the opening of the books for subscription the Spanish ambassador, in alarm and amazement, wrote Philip III that "fourteen Counts and Barons. . . . have given 40.000 ducats, the Merchants give much more, and there is no poor, little man, nor woman, who is not willing to subscribe something for this enterprise." Later he added: "Much as I have written

36 [Robert Johnson], *Nova Britannia: Offering Most Excellent fruites by Planting in Virginia* (London, 1609), entered for publication on February 18, was followed in April by Hakluyt's translation of the Gentleman of Elvas' account of de Soto's explorations under the title of *Virginia richly valued by the description of the main land of Florida her next neighbor.* This characteristic contribution by the great propagandist for colonization was followed in June by *Nova Francia, or the description of that part of New France which is one Continent with Virginia,* translated by Pierre Erondelle at Hakluyt's request from Marc Lescarbot's recent *Histoire de la Nouvelle-France* "to the end that comparing the goodness of the lands of the northern parts herein mentioned with that of Virginia, which . . . must be far better by reason it stands more southerly nearer to the Sun; greater encouragement may be given to prosecute that generous and goodly action." To these had already been added two published sermons: William Simonds, *Virginia. A Sermon Preached at White-Chappel* (London, 1609); Gray, *A Good Speed to Virginia.*

to Y[our] M[ajesty] of the determination they have formed here to go to Virginia, it seems to me that I still fall short of the reality." [37] When the charter received the royal seal on May 23 it listed 56 city companies and over 650 individual subscribers. The number of persons contributing was actually much larger than these figures indicate, for the subscription of a company like that of the Fishmongers represented the total of individual contributions from its membership.[38] And to these who risked their funds must be added the 600 men, women, and children who volunteered their persons.

It is never easy to explain the success of a popular campaign of this sort. Many problems of individual and group psychology are involved. Among the factors that require consideration is the skill of promoters in placing the appeal on a high plane of national and religious interest. An effective organization brought to bear on the individual a type of compulsion not easily avoided. Slogans like "Nova Britannia" proved attractive, and the very size of the proposed venture lent new force to old arguments regarding a prospective relief of England's economic and social ills. Attention, too, must be given the adventurers' plan for achieving their objectives in the colony. For whatever the goal may be and whatever the motives inspiring the quest, men hazard their lives and their fortunes only when a way to its attainment appears reasonably clear.

The ultimate ends toward which the colonists were to direct their labor remained essentially unchanged. Once again, the search for a passage to the South Seas and for gold, silver, and copper was to be pressed. But the adventurers in presenting their immediate plans now gave heavier emphasis to the less glittering prospects for a variety of extractive industries, for native trade, and for a commercially profitable type of agriculture. Several commodities destined to be long associated with the hopes and endeavors of the Virginia colony received special attention. There was much talk of the promise of a Virginia wine. In 1610, Thomas West, Lord De la Warr, a leading adventurer and member of the Council,

[37] Brown (ed.), *Genesis of the United States*, I, 245–46, 258.

[38] *Ibid.*, 238 ff., where there will be found the most complete collection of materials relating to this promotional effort. Especially valuable are excerpts from records of the city companies which reveal something of the methods used in bringing pressure for individual contributions.

brought from France both vines and experts to tend them. By this date, too, the initial effort looking toward the production of silk had been made. The King's sponsorship of similar experiments in England undoubtedly encouraged the attempt in Virginia, where the native mulberry had already attracted attention. Iron was a third major staple sought. The industry at home had felt the effects of England's depleted wood supply, and proof of iron ore discovered in Virginia brought its promise to the fore of the company's plans by 1610, when Captain Martin received appointment as master of the ironworks.[39] It should be noted, too, that sugar held a place in the plans of 1609, and that Captain Samuel Argall sailed from England in the spring of that year for a test, among other duties, of the fishing in the Chesapeake. Additional commodities indicated as likely sources of profit filled out a list familiar to promoters of American settlement since the days of the elder Hakluyt.

The distinguishing feature of the 1609 project lay not so much in a difference of objectives as in the scale of the effort proposed. It was promised that the five hundred men and approximately one hundred women, children, and servants who sailed for Virginia on June 2 with Sir George Somers would be followed in August by one thousand more under the command of Lord De la Warr.[40] Whatever else the adventurers may have been guilty of in the spring of 1609, they were not guilty of thinking in small terms.

The point receives additional emphasis when attention is turned to the conditions of settlement offered prospective colonists. Some apparently entered into a contract with the company for wages and others migrated to Virginia as servants either by agreement with the adventurers or with individual colonists. The great majority, however, went, as contemporaries were wont to say, "on adventure," that is, under the terms of an agreement specifying for their reward proportionate shares in all returns accruing to the joint stock. The Virginia joint stock of 1609 represented more

[39] *Ibid.*, 203, 248, 317, 353, 356, 395, 408, 469, 482; Strachey, *Historie of Travaile into Virginia Britannia*, 31, 117, 132; Force (comp.), *Tracts*, III, No. 1, p. 20; Kingsbury (ed.), *Records of The Virginia Company*, III, 22.

[40] In a communication of May 29 seeking to enlist English subjects in the Netherlands, Brown (ed.), *Genesis of the United States*, I, 316–18. An earlier appeal to the Plymouth adventurers shows that originally it had been hoped that 800 men could be sent as early as March. *Ibid.*, 239.

than a mere pooling of funds; it also pooled labor in a common stock with capital, through a bookkeeping arrangement establishing a monetary equivalent for the personal adventure of the colonist. The unit of investment for the adventurer who ventured only his money was fixed at £12 10s. a share. The personal adventure of the colonist was rated as equal to one share with provision for the award of additional shares for such special considerations as social quality, official responsibility, or the possession of an acquired skill.[41] Each of these shares represented a claim equal to that of any other share in the stock against all dividends declared, whether of land or of money. And each shareholder received a guarantee of "all liberties and privileges as if they had begun the first year," which was to say, in 1606.[42] The arrangement thus provided a graduated scale

[41] Thus Sir Thomas Dale's personal adventure in 1611 received a rating of £700 or 56 shares at £12 10s. per share. *Ibid.*, 452–54.

[42] [Johnson], *Nova Britannia*, reprinted in Force (comp.), *Tracts*, I, No. 6, provides the principal source of information regarding these conditions of settlement. Issued early in the promotional campaign and under the guise of a private treatise contributed by one only recently persuaded to join the Virginia adventurers, it made possible a presentation of prospects in the most optimistic terms without unduly binding the company to specific commitments. When, fourteen years later, Captain Martin undertook to use its expressed hope that dividends would run as high as five hundred acres per share to support his own claim to an irregularly issued patent based on that figure, a court of the company, which incidentally was dominated by the factional enemies of both Martin and Alderman Johnson, ruled that "the Booke was noe Act of the Court but a private mans worke." Kingsbury (ed.), *Records of The Virginia Company*, II, 181. This ruling has naturally caused some historians to reject the document as valid evidence of the plans of 1609. The present writer, however, has no doubt that it should be accepted as a valid record of the general outlines of the plan. Not only does Gray, *Good Speed to Virginia*, bear testimony that it was so accepted in the spring of 1609; but a later pamphlet by Johnson, "Published by Authoritie of His Magesties Counsell of Virginea" in 1612, bears the significant title, *The New Life of Virginea: . . . Being the Second Part of Noua Britannia* (London, 1612), reprinted in Force (comp.), *Tracts*, I, No. 7. Moreover, the second charter's provisions governing land grants, a broadside issued by the adventurers, their appeal to the lord mayor of London, instructions for enlisting the support of English subjects in the Netherlands, a bill of adventure for Sir Thomas Dale, in Brown (ed.), *Genesis of the United States*, I, 248–49, 252–53, 316–18, 452–53, and the provisions made for the declaration of dividends in 1616 and 1618—see especially *A Briefe Declaration . . . of a Diuision to be now made, of some part of those Lands in our actuall possession, as well to all such as haue aduentured their monyes, as also to those that are Planters there*, published by the Council in 1616 and reproduced by the Massachusetts Historical Society, in Americana Series, No. 11—all support in one particular or another Johnson's statement of the plan. And to these should be added his long and intimate association with Sir Thomas Smith in the management

of compensation for the colonists, and at the same time gave recognition to a basic equality between the adventurer in England and the planter in the colony that the company turned to good advantage in its promotional efforts.

Through the joint stock of 1609 the adventurers undertook to provide the basis for a successful venture in colonization by joining the adventurer and the planter in a true community of interest. Something more than chance explains the fact that the second charter was issued in the name of The Treasurer and Company of Adventurers *and Planters* of the City of London; for no one can read the record, fragmentary as it is, without detecting indications of an attempt to give reality to the idea that the two groups did in fact form one company.[43] Necessarily, certain practical distinctions were established. The requirements of sound management dictated the location of a superior authority in London, a need met chiefly by continuance of the royal council, but equality of status existed as a general proposition from which many benefits were to flow to the planter. At the outset he had gained, in addition to equal rights in all dividends, dignity of standing, and that of course is fundamental.

The arrangement also provides a key to the much misunderstood scheme of life and labor in the early Virginia colony. For the accomplishment of its many sided program the company placed its faith in a pooling of resources which naturally tended to impose on the colony a corporate form of management. The claims of the joint stock, unlike the practice in modern joint-stock corporations, did not constitute a permanent charge on the enterprise. Stocks at this time were customarily terminable at an early date by division of the original capital as well as the earnings thereon. But, though temporary, these claims represented a first charge. Before the colonists could count themselves free to pursue their individual interest, that charge had to be paid off.

There were, moreover, strong reasons in the very conditions

of the company's affairs. For evidence of his especially active part in the financial affairs of the company through the years immediately following 1609, see Kingsbury (ed.), *Records of The Virginia Company,* III, 42–43.

[43] The clearest evidence of this is found in the establishment of the Virginia Assembly of 1619 as the counterpart of the general assembly of adventurers in London. Italics added.

governing original settlement for regarding the task as necessarily a communal undertaking. Both literally and figuratively, the land had to be cleared. Housing had to be provided, churches built, fortifications prepared, stocks of cattle and other domesticated animals built up, a variety of agricultural experiments tried, a trade with the natives effectively organized, and other exploratory missions accomplished. For work of this sort there were many advantages in a community type of effort. Assignments could be made from a common labor supply as circumstances dictated, individual aptitude suggested, or special agreement with the company directed. The people were instructed to live together in two or three principal seats, a necessary thing, if for no other reason than that of security.[44] Individual houses, gardens, and orchards were promised at an early date, so that no man's standard of living need depend wholly on the common level of effort, but the colonists were to remain basically dependent upon a common store kept replenished by their joint labors. The fruits of their several efforts, whether from planting corn, trading with the Indians, or laboring in extractive industries, would go into this store, from which the men who worked as carpenters, bricklayers, or shipwrights would draw their food as did those who applied themselves principally to its gathering. Marketable products would be sent home for sale, where the surplus over necessary reinvestment of the funds would accumulate to the credit of the joint stock. Though a monetary dividend might be declared as early and as often as the returns justified, the joint stock was to continue for seven years. At its termination in 1616, the land opened up and made secure for cultivation would also be divided. At least one hundred acres per share was promised.[45]

It is not difficult to imagine the prospect thus opened for the men and women who in the spring of 1609 prepared against the day of their departure for Virginia. That all of them had the same degree of interest in the land is hardly to be assumed, for the variety

[44] See again instructions to Gates and De la Warr, though these documents are primarily concerned with problems of political and military organization. Kingsbury (ed.), *Records of The Virginia Company,* III, 12–29.

[45] [Johnson], *Nova Britannia,* indicated that it was planned to settle by that date in seven or eight plantations, or "capital towns," to be situated on or near the James River with a distance of twenty miles separating one from another. The inhabitants of each such town would "manure and husband" the dividends lying about it.

of proposed activity which characterized the company's program unquestionably brought enlistment for varied reasons. Some had responded simply to the age-old call of adventure or to that promise of quick wealth which, in one form or another, has brought so many men to America. Others seized the opportunity to enjoy an unaccustomed prestige by identifying themselves with a highly publicized venture, or else, being footloose, they came for the lack of anything better to do.[46] Still others were craftsmen who had been offered a more profitable employment of their skills than was possible at home. And to these must be added "those ungratious sons," of whom the Council later sorrowfully spoke, "that dailie vexed their fathers hearts" until as a last resort they were "thrust upon the voyage." [47]

But as the company's promotional efforts clearly indicate, many signed in the hope of winning for themselves some part of the land, a hope necessarily depending upon assurance that the title could be given true utility. That assurance, it may be assumed, lay in an expectation that the land could be put to crops tested and proved over the intervening seven years, that some of these crops would find a local market in exchange for the returns from commercial or industrial undertakings established during the same period, and that the planter would enjoy the friendly agencies of the company in marketing his produce in England. He would draw his share of cattle from a common herd which had been shepherded together for a natural increase to offset the high cost of shipment from England. For purchase of necessary tools and equipment, he would have to his credit the monetary dividends of the joint stock, a sum that might prove very handsome indeed in the event of one or two fortunate discoveries. The company's place in this picture is also easily fixed. Still possessed of countless acres of land for additional projects of colonization, it might be expected to follow up such special opportunities for trade as had been developed, and could look forward to an expanding commercial opportunity in the regu-

---

[46] Wesley F. Craven and Walter B. Hayward (eds.), *The Journal of Richard Norwood* (New York, 1945), records in interesting and suggestive detail the life of a young man prior to his migration to the Bermuda colony in 1613. It reveals the influence in this case of a simple restlessness of spirit, the lack of an established estate at home, the challenge of distant and strange places, and the promise of a fortune.

[47] [Johnson], *New Life of Virginea*, in Force (comp.), *Tracts*, I, No. 7, p. 10.

lar supply of the colony's needs. Individual adventurers at home
might offer their dividends for sale or rent to those in the colony,
unless they elected to send out tenants for their cultivation or
perchance to settle in Virginia themselves.

A vision this, but it was the vision of men united in a common
purpose to prepare the way for an unprecedented service of individual and national interests. And who can say that with good fortune, supporting the morale of each and all, the venture might
not have proved something more than the disastrous failure misfortune brought upon it?

The geographical limits fixed by the second Virginia charter were
in keeping with the company's ambitious plans. Title now passed
to an area extending along the coast two hundred miles northward from Point Comfort, an equal distance to the south, inland
"from Sea to Sea, West and Northwest," and one hundred miles
at sea on "both Seas." The adventurers were thereby assured control of the navigation of the Chesapeake, over the region of Raleigh's ventures, and of the trade that might result from their discovery of a way to the South Seas.

Provisions for the organization and government of the project
require close attention. The original plan of government through
a royal council remained essentially unchanged. His Majesty's
Council of Virginia, as the body continued to be known even after
the issuance of the third charter in 1612, received confirmation of
its authority over the colony "according to the Tenour of our former
Letters-Patents." There were, however, certain significant adjustments. Its authority now extended over only the projects of the
London Company, and its membership came entirely from that
body. In keeping with custom, the charter listed members of the
Council as though they had been selected entirely by the King.
Actually they represented a choice of the leading promoters, as did
also the designation of Sir Thomas Smith as treasurer, an officer who
presided over both Council and company with a primary responsibility for financial matters.[48] The treasurer and the councilors might
be continued in office or changed by a majority vote of the adven-

[48] Membership on the Council was offered as an inducement to large contributions.
See Brown (ed.), *Genesis of the United States*, I, 253, where the figure is set at fifty
pounds.

turers met in an "Assembly" for the purpose. But they could qualify for office only by taking a special oath before the lord chancellor, the lord treasurer, or the lord chamberlain of the household, a provision King James subsequently used to enforce his objections to Sir Edwin Sandys as treasurer.

As befitted a body that drew its authority only in part from the company, the Council enjoyed considerable independence in exercising the powers committed to it. Though its policies could be altered by the adventurers through changes in its membership, its acts did not require ratification by the company. Working through a quorum of four that included the treasurer, or in his absence a deputy who had been chosen by him and the Council, the councilors held authority to provide for the government of the colony. They could select and commission its officers and draft for them necessary instructions, orders, ordinances, and laws. An indication of the field of action regarded as properly reserved to the adventurers is found in the stipulation that land grants should be made by the adventurers "assembled for that Purpose." Again, it may be noted that the Council held the power to admit new members to the company, but that only an assembly of adventurers possessed the right to expel a member.

Only in the colony did there occur in 1609 a radical change of government. The unhappy experiment with a joint command shared by president and council was abandoned for "one able and absolute Governor," advised by a council established for his aid. This council, however, could not override his will, and the governor's independent choice extended to the removal of any officer in the colony except for those holding certain principal offices filled by appointment of the royal council.[49] There were, indeed, few limitations upon his power, except the requirement that he abide by his instructions, which undertook to give meaning to the assurance offered the colonists by both charters that they should enjoy "all Liberties, Franchizes, and Immunities" belonging to an English subject. Lord De la Warr was selected as governor and

[49] See instructions to Gates and De la Warr, in Kingsbury (ed.), *Records of The Virginia Company*, III, 12–29; De la Warr's commission of 1610, in Brown (ed.), *Genesis of the United States*, I, 376–84. The exceptions in the latter document to the governor's right of removal were limited to Gates as lieutenant governor, Dale as marshal, Sir George Somers as admiral, and Newport as vice-admiral.

captain general, but he was unable to sail in June with Somers. Sir Thomas Gates, also of the Council, went in his place as *ad interim* governor.

One other major problem engaged the adventurers' attention in 1609. The sailing route hitherto followed to Virginia, by way of the Canaries to the West Indies and then north of Hispaniola by the Bahamas to the Gulf Stream, had many advantages. But there were certain disadvantages, chief of which was the additional risk of a clash with Spain. It was recognized that the very size of that year's project for the development of Virginia constituted a new challenge to the old enemy, a thought apparent in plans for the abandonment of Jamestown as a principal seat. Until greater strength of position had been secured, it was imperative not to invite unnecessarily an attack by Spain. The old belief that the Gulf Stream above Florida ran too strong to permit cutting across it, an assumption which had argued for continued use of Spain's route, had several times been questioned by seamen on their way to Virginia. Accordingly, the adventurers decided to try a more northern course that, while offering some of the advantages of a southern route, would avoid channels and territories in which Spain held a special interest.

That mission they committed, together with a test of the Chesapeake fisheries, to Captain Argall, who sailed ahead of the main expedition on May 5. Having followed a course from England southwestward to about the thirtieth degree of north latitude, he then ran directly westward for America. A favorable report on this new route reached the adventurers in the fall.[50] Argall's discovery by no means settled permanently a question of sailing routes destined long to remain the subject of debate, but it was currently interpreted as still another step toward establishing England's economic independence.

[50] Brown (ed.), *Genesis of the United States*, I, 343. On the Spanish threat, see Andrews, *Colonial Period of American History*, I, 141–49; Irene A. Wright, "Spanish Policy toward Virginia, 1606–1612," in *American Historical Review*, XXV (1919–1920), 448–79.

CHAPTER IV

THE LONDON COMPANY

ENGLAND had never seen anything comparable to the great fleet, with its eight hundred passengers and crewmen, that sailed for Virginia in 1609 under command of Sir George Somers, veteran sea adventurer now past sixty years of age. Six of the ships had dropped down the Thames on May 15, and from a rendezvous at Plymouth the entire fleet of nine vessels set a course for the New World on the second day of June.

No letters, diaries, or other such intimate records have survived to tell us of the personal effects carried by approximately six hundred passengers as they set out to establish for themselves a new home three thousand miles across the sea. One must rely upon his imagination to gain even a glimpse of wardrobes selected for the voyage, of pieces of jewelry carefully packed with some heirloom or other memento of the old home, of an occasional book slipped in with the favored toy of a child, or of a craftsman's tool kit laden with the trusted partners of his trade. Though the names of many of these people are known, their individual traits and quirks of character remain for the most part unknown. Nor is there record of the alterations and special arrangements made to prepare the ships as carriers of passengers in the numbers and for the distance required. It can be assumed, with support from later documents, that special arrangements on shipboard were generally restricted to an enlargement of provision for the storage and preparation of food, and that at night most of the people made shift as best they could with bed rugs and other improvised pallets.[1]

[1] See itemized expenditures by the adventurers of Berkeley Hundred for "furnishing" the *Margaret* in 1619 and the *Supply* in 1620, where several payments are listed "ffor work done about the cookroome in the ship and for cawking the bread roome

Of the supplies and equipment provided as a common store by the adventurers, however, it is possible to speak with more certainty. Though no inventories for this voyage have been found, itemized lists of expenditures made a decade later by the adventurers of Berkeley Hundred for the establishment of their plantation on the upper James lend such emphasis to the commonplace tools and staples of daily life as to leave little doubt regarding the main categories of cargo shipped with Somers.[2] The very commonness of the items included will perhaps justify their listing here, for they were the things on which life itself depended and with which man had fashioned a civilized way of life.

Only the especially heavy outlay for guns and ammunition, not to mention the completeness of the list, would mark it as an inventory of things especially collected for the support of life in America. Here were the tools brought to perfection in the service of man over the centuries: the ax, adz, hatchet, hammer, chisel, knife, file, saw, pliers, reap hook, scythe, trowel, wedge, shovel, spade, shears, auger, gimlet, vise, and hoe; here too the grindstone for their sharpening and the bellows so necessary in the use of fire to repair or temper them. Other hardware included andirons, tongs, spits, nails, bolts, latches, hinges, door locks, scales, pot racks and hooks, and the pot itself. For the house there were stocks of scissors, needles, thread, thimbles, buttons. Dishes, bowls, and spoons, many of them wooden, were listed with the kettle, ladle, bottle, candlestick, and frying pan, the last destined to win for itself a new supremacy in Southern cooking. And for the grinding of grain there were millstones. There was food to tide the people over the voyage and until their first harvest. It included cheese, fish, beef, pork, bacon, oatmeal, biscuit, bread, butter, peas, onions, raisins, prunes, and dates; for its embellishment there were salt, pepper, sugar, cinnamon, clove, nutmeg, mace, vinegar, and oil; and to wash it down there was a choice of cider, beer, sack, and aqua vitae. Help expected from gardens to be planted on arrival is shown by a variety of seeds—for parsnips, carrots, cabbages, turnips, lettuce, onions,

and other work." Kingsbury (ed.), *Records of The Virginia Company*, III, 178–89, 385–92.

[2] *Ibid.* Some confirmation is found in the record of the winter spent in Bermuda by the passengers of the *Sea Adventure* after its shipwreck there. See Craven, *Introduction to the History of Bermuda*, 15–19.

mustard, and garlic. Standard staples of supply were soap, candles, chalk, drugs, tar, pitch, and starch. Clothing and household goods were represented by stores of shoes, stockings, breeches, belts, shirts, hats, rugs, mats, bolsters, and sheets. Entries for paper, parchment, and ink emphasize for us the importance in original settlement of the written deed or other record of agreement and of the letter home.[3]

For two and one-half centuries thereafter this would remain the pattern of equipment carried by the pioneers of an advancing American settlement. Whether stored in the hold of a ship crossing the Atlantic or loaded in a covered wagon on the westward march across the continent, the cargo would include chiefly tools for construction of shelter and for tilling the soil, firearms for defensive purposes, necessary utensils and clothing, staple foods to tide the passengers over the interval before the first crop, and the seeds from which the crop would grow.[4] Little if any precious space was sacrificed to articles of furniture. Men moved with the assurance of a plentiful supply of timber at the journey's end and the skills required to fashion it according to their needs. The space belonged rather to those metal devices which were the distinguishing mark of the civilization now in transit and which were to be prized in proportion to the difficulty of their replacement on the frontier.

In contrast to the practice of later days, the equipment in 1609 belonged to a common store and men counted upon the combined skills of a company recruited for a joint undertaking rather than upon the individual dexterity necessarily developed by their descendants. Through this common effort they looked forward to enjoyment of the diverse advantages of community life by settlement in towns, not to the isolated farm home destined to become typical over most of America. And though their inventories point toward a basically agrarian economy, they give little recognition to the central position, in such an economy, of the plow. Unlike later pioneers, the original settlers found it no simple matter to take

---

[3] The only substantial collection of private papers pertaining to early colonization is the Manchester Papers. See Chapter I, n. 21.

[4] At the time the list here used was made, tobacco was the staple crop and the seed could be had in the colony. Somers undoubtedly carried a variety of seeds and plants in furtherance of the company's search for suitable staples, as also the wheat listed a decade later by the adventurers for Berkeley Hundred.

along the draft animals necessary for its use. In fact, the cost of shipping livestock across the Atlantic was so nearly prohibitive that little more could be done than to send over a few animals to breed a stock for subsequent use.[5] These differences are important to an exact estimate of the immediate story. Yet they are less fundamental than are the points of similarity which help to mark the sailing of Somers' fleet in 1609 as the true beginning of one of the great folk movements of history.

Since that movement covered an area more extensive even than the United States, the full significance of Somers' expedition can be appreciated only by noting its place in the larger story of English settlement in the New World. Indeed, the natural tendency of American students to restrict their study to those colonies later incorporated in the Federal union has resulted in a tendency to present the effort of the London adventurers in 1609 as little more than a false start. But in the broader chronicle of English settlement it becomes readily apparent that the "first planters" of 1607 had served as scouts in advance of an unbroken migration which was directed between 1609 and 1612 to Jamestown, between 1612 and 1618 principally to Bermuda, from 1618 through 1623 once again and in mounting force to Virginia, after 1623 at an even more accelerated

---

[5] A beginning had been made by earlier shipments, and Somers carried six mares and two horses at least. Prior to the starving time in the winter of 1609–1610, the colony had been supplied with hogs, goats, poultry, sheep, and cattle. Since all of these were eaten during that winter, it was necessary for the adventurers to resupply the colony by shipments of 1611. That these new shipments were regarded as primarily a breeding stock is indicated by the provision in Dale's Laws "that no man shall dare to kill, or destroy any Bull, Cow, Calfe, Mare, Horse, Colt, Goate, Swine, Cocke, Henne, Chicken, Dogge, Turkie, or any tame Cattel, or Poultry, of what Condition soever; whether his owne, or appertaining to another man, without leave from the Generall, upon paine of death in the Principall, and in the accessory, burning in the Hand, and losse of his eares, and unto the concealer of the same, foure and twenty houres whipping." Ralph Hamor in 1614 reported that the colony had two hundred head of cattle, and referring to young steers, he expressed the hope that three or four plows might be kept going the following winter. That the company had planned to use the plow is indicated by its advertisement in 1610 for plow-wrights, but even after the provision of draft animals was no longer a problem its use remained decidedly limited because of the difficulty in clearing stumps and roots from new ground. See Philip A. Bruce, *Economic History of Virginia in the Seventeenth Century* (New York, 1935), I, 215–20; Brown (ed.), *Genesis of the United States*, I, 328–29, 353; Ralph Hamor, *A True Discourse of the Present Estate of Virginia* (London, 1615); Force (comp.), *Tracts*, III, No. 2.

rate to the West Indies, and through the decade of the 1630's to New England, with a lesser stream to trace once more a reviving interest in the Chesapeake area. In this continuing though frequently redirected migration is found one of the major forces shaping the development of that Atlantic community of which so much is heard today. To Sir George Somers fell the honor of leading out the first contingent.

Having been instructed to avoid Spanish waters and territories, Somers held a course between the usual route to the Leeward Islands and that so recently taken by Argall. For seven weeks the fleet sailed without event, and the sea-wearied passengers were turning their thoughts to the prospect of an early arrival at their destination when they were overtaken by one of those hurricanes that occasionally sweep the Carolina and Virginia coasts. Through three days and four nights the storm raged, driving the ships before it. The *Sea Adventure*, which unfortunately was carrying all the leading men on whom the company depended for inauguration of its new venture—Admiral Somers, Governor Gates, William Strachey, newly appointed secretary of the colony, and Captain Christopher Newport, vice-admiral of the fleet—lost contact with its consorts. Subjected to a relentless beating, the ship became so waterlogged that its 150 passengers gave up hope. But then, miraculously, as the storm abated, the vessel was deposited between two rocks just off the Bermuda Isles through the intervention of a kind fate that could be explained only in terms of God's providential care. Though the *Sea Adventure* was doomed, the people came safely ashore, salvaged from the wreck much of their equipment, and lived in health and plenty through Bermuda's gentle winter. The isles were overrun with hogs, the waters filled with fish, and birds provided additional food reminding the people of manna from heaven. Somers, Gates, and Newport set them to work on the building of two small vessels, appropriately named on their completion the *Patience* and the *Deliverance*, in which they completed their voyage to Jamestown the following May.[6] Thus early were the fortunes of Virginia linked to those of Bermuda.

---

[6] The principal accounts by Strachey and Silvanus Jourdan may be consulted in John H. Lefroy (ed.), *Memorials of the Discovery and Early Settlement of the Bermudas or Somers Islands, 1515–1685* (London, 1877), I, 14 ff.

Meanwhile, the rest of the fleet had straggled into Jamestown with approximately four hundred of the new planters, to be received by an ill-prepared community of about eighty persons under the command of Captain Smith. From the first, unexpected difficulties were experienced, and there followed an extraordinarily unhappy sequence of events which led to the "starving time" that ran through the fearful winter of 1609–1610.

At the heart of the trouble was political confusion, tragically revealing the extent of an infant society's dependence upon an older one for its stability. The governor and all other principal officers had been aboard the *Sea Adventure* and were presumably lost. In their absence the colonists lacked adequate instructions. Not only would Smith's term as president expire in September, but such authority as he might exercise prior to that date depended on provisions of the original charter, which now had been superseded by the charter of 1609. To complicate matters further some of the captain's old enemies now had returned to the colony. Moreover, the new settlers had been hastily recruited and included, as one observer reported, "many unruly gallants packed thether by their friends to escape il destinies." [7] As the Virginia Council subsequently and sadly admitted, "no man would acknowledge a superior nor could from this headless and unbridled multitude, be anything expected but disorder and riot." [8]

It was at first agreed that Smith should serve out his term and Captain Francis West, brother of Lord De la Warr, succeed him. But Smith and West quarreled violently over the location of a seat at the falls, and all chance that the former might gain control of the situation was ended by his serious injury as the result of an accidental explosion of gunpowder. Helpless, he was deposed and sent home with word that Captain George Percy, brother to the Earl of Northumberland, was to head the colony until further instruction from the Council arrived. Events were to prove, however, that this act of self-government provided no satisfactory substitute for a properly constituted authority. Discipline and co-ordinated effort were required to provide housing and food for the coming winter.

[7] Arber and Bradley (eds.), *Travels and Works of Captain John Smith*, I, 162.
[8] Brown (ed.), *Genesis of the United States*, I, 347.

Instead, men worked at cross-purposes or, sickened and disheartened, worked not at all.

Why such large numbers of Virginia's early settlers should have starved to death is a question that has repeatedly bothered historians. The answer is that their deaths came only partly from starvation. Close attention had been given the problem of food by early adventurers. Hariot's pamphlet, long the most influential in the field, not only presents a descriptive list of edibles native to the country but more than once mentions pictures presumably drawn by White for the better guidance of the planters. Out of this and other studies had come a solution that appeared, from the English side of the water, reasonable and dependable. If the settlers were provided with seeds or plants for English vegetables and fruits, with carefully compiled information regarding native sources of food, with equipment for fishing, dogs for hunting, and supplies to tide them over the months preliminary to their first harvest, they should then be able to subsist by their own efforts. Through care for the conservation of poultry and livestock sent for breeding, they could look forward to an early self-sufficiency in all matters of diet.

The trouble began with the adventurers' disposition, because of the ever-present necessity of cutting down overhead, to figure closely and to overemphasize immediate prospects for independent subsistence. Had all gone according to plan, all perhaps would have been well. But at the outset, the administrative burden involved in setting forth a large fleet often imposed a delay, as in 1609, in the departure from England. The planters consequently arrived too late in the season to contribute much to that year's crop. Having spent seven, nine, or even more weeks in crossing the Atlantic on an overcrowded ship (usually of less than three hundred tons in size), and with water stale and food in some instances rancid through the later stages of the voyage, they landed in a weakened physical state inviting epidemic disease, and not infrequently with the epidemic already in full rage. First impressions were undoubtedly disillusioning, and the marshes of Jamestown in no way helpful. Such provision as had been made for reception of new arrivals was inadequate and primitive. Exposure and overcrowding aggravated their condition and spread contagion. Many experienced a succession of attacks such as was visited on Lord De la Warr, who tells us that shortly after his arrival in 1610 he was "welcomed by a hot and violent Ague," and then in turn "surprised" by the flux and "assaulted" by the cramp. Finally, he fell a victim to scurvy.[9]

For weeks some were unable to work. The early and disheartening necessity of rationing provisions to get through the winter contributed to a continuance of this incapacity. About them was game, but these men, unlike succeeding generations of settlers, were not born to wood lore. As Captain John Smith explained, "Though there be fish in the Sea, foules in the ayre, and Beasts in the woods, their bounds are so large, they so wilde, and we so weake, and ignorant, we cannot much trouble them." [10] Help from the natives was limited, even when they were friendly, for they were notoriously improvident. In the end a disastrous shortage might result, especially if discipline crumbled, and those who survived this final assault on their weakened bodies and spirits would long remember it as "a starving time."

Such was the fate that overtook the settlers of 1609, and dashed to the ground the high hopes that had brought them to Virginia. By May, when Somers, Gates, and Newport finally arrived from Bermuda, of nearly five hundred only a few over sixty remained alive. Their cattle, hogs, poultry, and even their horses had been eaten, and one man was reported to have eaten his wife. The Indians had become openly hostile, *"as fast killing without as the famine and pestilence within."* [11] Houses had been torn down for firewood, the church was in ruins, the palisades lay on the ground, and Lord De la Warr was long overdue. Having brought from Bermuda only supplies sufficient to last out the voyage, the commanders found no choice but to abandon the colony. As June opened, preparations were being made for an attempt to return home by Newfoundland.

The disturbing delay in Lord De la Warr's arrival is easily explained. The joint-stock subscription of 1609 had been the product of what is known today as a high-pressure campaign, and many subscribers had hardly put their names to the list before doubt and regret beset them. They were slow in paying up, and some paid only

[9] *Ibid.*, 479.   [10] *Ibid.*, 202.   [11] *Ibid.*, 405.

in part or not at all. Reports reaching London in the fall of the apparent loss of Somers, Gates, and Newport and of the resulting confusion in the colony, made the problem of equipping another expedition even more difficult. In the winter a special appeal to delinquents was printed and circulated by the Council.[12] It put the best face possible on the situation, but ended with a simple appeal to conscience. Men had promised, and on this assurance other men had staked their lives; to abandon them in their misfortune was to bear the guilt of their death. Even so, it was spring before De la Warr got away.

His arrival early in June, with three ships and 150 men, proved so timely as once again to suggest the intervention of Providence.[13] The planters, actually on their way down the river, were turned back, and the colony for the moment at least was saved. De la Warr's expedition, however, had not been recruited and equipped to meet the requirements of a situation as desperate as that existing by the summer of 1610. Prompt action was required to forestall the threat of still another winter of starvation. Accordingly, on June 19, Somers and Argall sailed for Bermuda to secure a supply of salted pork; and, in July, Gates departed with Newport for England to advise the adventurers of the colony's condition.

Unhappily, the cycle of misfortune was not yet complete. Somers and Argall, meeting contrary winds, were forced to alter their course to the north. Argall then lost contact with the admiral, and though effecting important geographic discoveries that included Delaware Bay, he returned to Jamestown with little of immediate value to the settlers.[14] Somers in time reached Bermuda, but in the fall he died there. His men, apparently more interested in prospects for the settlement of those fortunate isles than in helping their compatriots on the mainland, returned to England. In Virginia Lord De la Warr restored a much needed discipline and

[12] *A True and Sincere declaration of the purpose and ends of the Plantation begun in Virginia* (London, 1610).

[13] His instructions are in Kingsbury (ed.), *Records of The Virginia Company*, III, 24–29.

[14] Strachey, *Historie of Travaile into Virginia Britannia*, 42–43; Brown (ed.), *Genesis of the United States*, I, 428–39, the latter a detailed journal of the voyage, which added much to the Englishman's knowledge of the coast southward from Cape Cod to Cape Charles.

strengthened the colony's position on the lower James by construction of Forts Henry and Charles, which were designed in part for the reception of new arrivals. He found in Captain Argall an able successor to Smith as Indian trader. But he himself fell a victim to a succession of diseases that swept through the settlement, and leaving a community reduced to two hundred souls in charge again of Captain Percy, he sailed with Argall in March, 1611, for the West Indies. Contrary winds led him to alter the course for the Azores instead of the West Indies, and from the Azores he went on to England. His landing there in June brought consternation to members of the Virginia Council and to other gentlemen who had recently subscribed additional funds for the colony's support.[15]

On Gates's return home the preceding September, the leading adventurers had sat in earnest consultation over the question of abandonment or continuance of the Virginia colony. Gates's assurance of the promise of returns in timber, sweetwoods, silk, iron, silk grass, sturgeon, wine, furs, sugar, almonds, rice, aniseed, and other valuable commodities weighted the decision in favor of continuance—a brave decision indeed. It committed the adventurers to an attempt to provide further supplies of essential materials and workmen at an estimated cost of no less than £30,000.

All former adventurers were called upon to subscribe at least £37 10s. to be paid in at the rate of £12 10s. a year, the first payment falling due at the time of subscription. New subscribers were invited at the same rates. With leaders of the enterprise setting a worthy example—Smith, Sandys, and Sir Walter Cope subscribed double the amount and Johnson, £60—a carefully planned campaign directed appeals for aid to the bishops, noblemen, and gentry, to the lord mayor and the London companies, and to all the principal towns of England. The appeal was made to patriotism and to individual and community pride. A variety of devices was used for bringing pressure to bear—devices that are familiar today to those who raise funds for community chests, the Red Cross, and other such worthy causes.[16] *A True Declaration of the estate of the*

---

[15] Notice his promptly published explanation, in Brown (ed.), *Genesis of the United States*, I, 478–83.

[16] The key to this story of finance is found in several documents discovered and published in Kingsbury (ed.), *Records of The Virginia Company*, III, 34–48, pertain-

Colonie in Virginia, With a confutation of such scandalous reports as have tended to the disgrace of so worthy an enterprise was published by the Council in November for reasons well enough set forth in the title.[17] To this was added, if not at the instigation of the Council at least in co-operation with its purposes, Richard Rich's *Newes from Virginia, the lost Flocke Triumphant,* which proclaimed in not too good verse the rescue of Somers, Gates, and Newport and the colonists' continuing purpose "to plant a Nation, where none before hath stood." Silvanus Jourdan, in the first edition of his *Discovery of the Barmudas, . . . Set forth for the love of my Country; and . . . the good of the Plantation in Virginia,* contributed another appeal. Both Jourdan and Rich drew attention to the one story in a long chronicle of misfortune that might stir the heart to hope; for in the saga of the *Sea Adventure,* as the Council affirmed in its own *True Declaration,* "was no Ariadnes thread, but the direct line of Gods providence."

In this new effort to raise funds the adventurers naturally met a good deal of resistance. The Mercers of London replied in December that they had already done as well as any other of the city companies and would contribute no more. Yet by the spring of 1611, £18,000 had been subscribed. A third of this sum presumably was available for immediate needs, and the promise of double that amount within two years provided a credit upon which the Council could draw. It thus proved possible to send out two expeditions for the immediate relief of Virginia. The first, made up of three ships carrying three hundred men, sailed in March under command of Sir Thomas Dale. Like Gates, Dale was an old soldier on leave from his regiment in the Netherlands, and had been commissioned knight marshal of the colony. About the time of his arrival in the Chesapeake on May 12 to take over the duties of deputy governor, Sir Thomas Gates as lieutenant governor made ready to sail with six ships, an additional three hundred persons, one hundred cattle, approximately two hundred swine, and with conies, pigeons, and

---

ing to suits subsequently entered against defaulting subscribers. These papers supplement documents published in Brown (ed.), *Genesis of the United States,* I, 442, 445, 461–70. The sum sought apparently had been limited originally to £10,000. See Andrews, *Colonial Period of American History,* I, 106 n.

[17] Force (comp.), *Tracts,* III, No. 1.

poultry to boot. Having on the way out met with Governor De la Warr, he reached Virginia early in August, 1611.

The cargoes carried by these two fleets and the Council's special efforts to enlist husbandmen and certain skilled craftsmen suggest the existence of a new emphasis on planting as distinct from discovery. Heretofore, the two objectives had been pursued jointly, with circumstances naturally and to some extent necessarily giving priority to the work of discovery. The dazzling prospect of an early trade with the South Seas or for discovery of a rich mine had provided the adventurers with one of their better selling points, but failure to achieve either of these goals constituted one of the sources of the disillusionment from which the venture now suffered. It seems to have been assumed, therefore, that a safer course would be to concentrate, at least until a sure footing had been secured, on the agricultural, industrial, and commercial possibilities existing in the immediate vicinity of the first settlement. Not long after his arrival in Virginia, Dale wrote Lord Salisbury that with two thousand men released from the jails of England he could clear the Virginia Peninsula of Powhatan's people or bring them into permanent subjection, make secure beyond all chance of attack the entrance to the river, fortify a strong position at the head of navigation, and thus "affoard many excellent Seates for many a thowsand Householder." [18] The newness of this was largely a matter of emphasis, but here is something more readily comprehensible to modern Americans than are the terms in which the elder Hakluyt had spoken. It would be possible to draw our kind of map of that kind of colony, and even to give the area of settlement a special and unbroken shading.

Dale did not get the two thousand men, but he moved promptly with those at hand to strengthen the settlement in many other ways. Following Gates's return in August he devoted his energies to the building, according to the Council's now two-year-old instructions, of a seat on the upper James. The town, named Henrico in honor of the popular Prince Henry, was located ten or twelve miles below the falls, but unfortunately was not to fulfill its original purpose as the colony's chief city. Dale's name is more prominently associated,

[18] Brown (ed.), *Genesis of the United States,* I, 501–508. See also, his letter of May 25 to the Council, *ibid.,* 489–94.

therefore, with the establishment in the colony of a strict discipline.

The need for this, indeed the extreme dangers to which the community was exposed in its absence, had been disastrously revealed several times, and Dale himself was only partly responsible for the steps taken to provide an adequate remedy. In 1609 the governor had been authorized to issue such orders for control of the people as were deemed advisable, subject of course to the ultimate approval of the Virginia Council, and to resort to martial law in cases of mutiny and rebellion. He was further instructed "in all matters of Civill Iustice" to "proceed rather as a Chauncelor then as a Iudge, rather uppon the naturall right and equity then uppon the nicenes and letter of the lawe." [19] Especially notable in this delineation of a legal system for the colony was the distinction made between civil and military jurisdiction, the prescription of a somewhat summary procedure for the colony's courts, and the conferring of a large degree of legislative independence upon resident officers. In accordance with these instructions, Gates on his first arrival in Virginia in the spring of 1610 had proclaimed certain laws and orders. Having been approved shortly afterward by Lord De la Warr, they were "exemplified and enlarged" by Dale on June 22, 1611. Dale's own contribution seems to have been chiefly in the field of martial rather than civil law. The whole of the laws were reduced to the form of a code by Secretary Strachey, and after his return to England it was published in 1612 by the Virginia Council under the title of *Lawes Divine, Morall and Martiall*. The publication was intended, no doubt, to provide assurance for the people at home that one of the more obvious weaknesses of the colony had been corrected.[20] To speak of this code as "Dale's Laws," it will be evident, is not altogether accurate.

Inaccurate, too, is the popular view that Virginians were by the provisions of that code made subject entirely to martial law. The fact is that they came under the discipline of martial law only insofar as and for such time as they were engaged in military duties.

[19] Kingsbury (ed.), *Records of The Virginia Company*, III, 15, 27–28.

[20] Force (comp.), *Tracts*, III, No. 2. For a penetrating study of this code, see Walter F. Prince, "The First Criminal Code of Virginia," in American Historical Association, *Annual Report*, 1899, I (Washington, 1900), 311–63.

These duties, it is true, took much more of the colonists' time than was required of their compatriots in England or is demanded of Americans today, for an infant colony was as much a military outpost as anything else. Its political head served also as commander in chief, and its men took their regular turn at guard duty, held themselves ready for a call at any moment to man the defenses, and tended to find their first distinctively American marks of political and social rank in some military title. Inevitably, effective discipline depended at many points in the daily routine of life upon the established conventions of military law. Nor was it always easy to draw a distinction between military and civil jurisdictions. Where the community's very life so obviously depended upon its military effectiveness any opposition to constituted authority unavoidably took on some of the qualities of mutiny. More than one early governor found himself forced to resort to methods as a commander which he would readily admit ill became a magistrate.[21]

All the more significant, therefore, is the fact that such a distinction was here attempted. It may seem to the modern reader not only somewhat obscured but primarily of an academic nature, for the laws relating to civil offenses appear hardly less severe than those pertaining to military offenses. But though the entire code was marked by its severity, even according to seventeenth-century standards, some of the laws which have been repeatedly cited in evidence of this harshness, such as the penalties for embezzlement of public stores or the stealing of boats, speak not so loudly of severity as they do of the importance of the stores and of the boat. A community dependent upon a line of supply three thousand miles long and upon boats as the chief means of local transportation naturally viewed theft from the stores, or of a boat, with something of the same intolerance that characterized the attitude of a later generation of frontiersmen toward the horse thief.

Perhaps the most important point of all is the one most frequently overlooked. The colonists had been provided with laws, even though severe, and their government was a government of law. To "live as free English men," if a definition sponsored by the Virginia Council that same year of 1612 may be accepted, was to

---

[21] See especially, Governor Nathaniel Butler's eloquent comment on this in his *Historye of the Bermudaes*, 261.

live "under the government of just and equall lawes, and not as slaves after the will and lust of any superiour."[22]

From this code and other documents it is possible to reconstruct in some detail the daily life of the colony.[23] Its people lived apart in individual houses with allotment of private grounds and gardens. A minimum of rations and additional supplies were drawn regularly from the public store, but the industrious might supplement these issues by their own efforts. Labor on public projects, as a general rule, required only a part of a man's time. Common gardens, as they were called, were laid out and planted to corn, hemp, flax, and the like. All those not assigned to other duties were required upon the roll of the drum at 6 A. M. to repair to these fields. There they worked under an overseer until 10, when once again the drum sounded and the church bell tolled a call to morning worship. Rations were issued following the service, and not until 2 P. M. did the drums call men back to the field, and then only for a two-hour turn that ended with the 4 o'clock summons to evening prayer. Strict observance of the Sabbath was enjoined, with ministers required to preach each Sunday morning and to catechize in the afternoon. But even with compulsory attendance at religious services thirteen times a week, ample time remained for cultivation in one's garden of the parsnips, carrots, turnips, pompions, melons, cucumbers, parsley, and chicory, which among English vegetables prospered, and the corn, potatoes, and beans that were native to America. Many must have early adopted the later Southern custom of a nap after the midday meal and worked their gardens following evening prayers. The routine, of course, was varied according to season and necessity.

The approximately seven hundred English inhabitants, of whom hardly more than thirty were women, lived in communities providing some of the advantages of town life. A small group stood guard at Point Comfort and near-by Kecoughtan, where there were found the best silk grass and two thousand to three thousand acres clear for planting. Jamestown, declared to have had in 1611

---

[22] [Johnson], *New Life of Virginea*, in Force (comp.), *Tracts*, I, No. 7, p. 17.

[23] See *ibid.;* other official communications or publications previously listed; Strachey, *Historie of Travaile into Virginia Brittania;* and documents published in Wright (ed.), *Spanish Documents Concerning English Voyages to the Caribbean.*

one hundred wooden houses, boasted, in addition to a wharf off which rode the great ships from London, shelters for horses and cattle, streets used at times for bowling, a market place, a storehouse, and a church that annually was in need of extensive repairs.[24] In the fall of that year approximately three hundred of the inhabitants moved with Dale to Henrico, where houses were built with the first story of brick. Both towns were palisaded and further secured by blockhouses against attack. To wander far from the protection of these defenses except in force was extremely hazardous. Hunting for the deer, wild turkeys, bears, raccoons, or opossums which frequented the forest, even fishing save in the nearest waters, was therefore not a quest that could safely be pursued individually. Meat more than any other staple of diet was an item to be had of the public store, which secured much of its stock by trade with the Indians. The emperor Powhatan still proved hostile, but some of the natives had been forced by Dale to take their turn at labor for the English. Others came of their own volition for trade, and Strachey subsequently recalled the "well featured, but wanton" young Pocahontas, naked, turning cartwheels in the market place at Jamestown.

The most profitable branch of the Indian trade was that opened by Argall with the natives of the Potomac. There, with the aid of the one or two small vessels usually kept on hand for the service of the colony, copper trinkets, white beads, hoes, knives, bells, scissors, and hatchets were traded for deerskins and the fur of the wildcat, fox, beaver, otter, and raccoon, not to mention the meat and corn secured for food. These skins and furs constituted a principal return to the adventurers, helping to meet bills for supplies and freightage. Homeward-bound ships were loaded principally, however, with timber, the now rare and ever popular black walnut finding an early and ready market among the cabinetmakers of England. Another staple was sassafras, the old stand-by of the French *filibustiers* who failed to pick up a more profitable cargo. Repeated references are made to the planting of hemp and flax, and some perhaps was shipped, in addition to soap ashes and silk grass, the last-

---

[24] An interesting attempt to reconstruct the picture of early Jamestown is available in Henry C. Forman, *Jamestown and St. Mary's, Buried Cities of Romance* (Baltimore, 1938).

named providing a fiber for cordage. The adventurers on one occasion actually sold some sixteen or seventeen tons of Virginia iron to the East India Company, no doubt through the good offices of Sir Thomas Smith, but the ironworks somehow failed to prosper.

Experiments, yet unsuccessful, had been made by 1612 in the planting of tobacco, not the native *apooke,* as Powhatan's people knew it, of small plant, yellow flower, and "biting" taste, but a merchantable variety imported from Trinidad. Dr. Lawrence Bohune, the physician, in addition to searching for profitable herbs, gained distinction by manufacturing as much as twenty gallons of wine at a time from the native grape. This wine, however, proved suitable only for the good doctor and his friends. The imported French vines in which so much hope had been placed proved a disappointment, as did oranges, pineapples, and silkworms.[25] After five years the colony still lacked a really satisfactory staple that could be produced and marketed in sufficient quantity to meet its need.

That fact made all the more perplexing the problems with which the leaders at home struggled in 1612. They felt, and not without reason, that, with time and greater resources than were then at the command of Gates and Dale, Virginia would still prove its worth. But though faith among the few was strong, among the others it was weak. Many subscribers, influenced by Lord De la Warr's unexpected return the preceding summer, had flatly refused payment of their second and third installments on the subscription of 1611. There existed, moreover, little if any prospect that another subscription could be secured to make up the resulting deficiency, unless it be in connection with some new project that would be free of the chain of misfortune and disappointment now principally associated in the public mind with Virginia. As the Council itself admitted, there was "no common speech nor publicke name of any thing this day, (except it be the name of God) which is more vildly depraved, traduced and derided . . . then the name of Virginea."[26]

Accordingly, the leading adventurers undertook to infuse new

[25] See especially, Strachey, *Historie of Travaile into Virginia Britannia,* 31, 38, 113, 116, 117, 120, 121, 129, 132; Wright (ed.), *Spanish Documents Concerning English Voyages to the Caribbean,* 478.

[26] From the dedication of *New Life of Virginea* (1612).

life into their American venture by capitalizing on a growing interest in the Bermudas. The "direct line of God's providence" had first directed attention to the possibility of settlement there through the miraculous rescue in 1609 of the shipwrecked passengers of the *Sea Adventure*. Somers and Newport during their ten-month stay in the islands had made a somewhat detailed survey for the information of the adventurers, and Sir George's men on their return to England early in 1611 had brought further encouragement for a project of settlement. In addition to special attractions of soil and climate, the islands offered the English an unusual strength of position in the pursuit of their objectives in America, objectives which now tended to emphasize an exclusively American venture in contrast to the original idea of joining settlement with an immediate hope of reaching the South Seas. The Bermudas were surrounded by a coral reef through which ships of size could pass only at two easily fortified points. Also, the islands' central location in the western Atlantic promised a unique strategic advantage with reference to possession of the mainland and of the West Indies and Newfoundland as well. Once the place had been fortified, the English could not be dislodged easily nor denied a share in the exploitation of America.[27]

It thus became possible to present the occupation of Bermuda as a new project, relatively free of the dead weight of former misfortune, and at the same time as a move calculated to strengthen the English position in Virginia. The adventurers even decided that the islands would be officially designated Virginiola, but happily that selection gave way to Somers Islands in honor of Sir George. For the immediate assistance of the Virginia colony, special advantages would be sought in pressing lawsuits for unpaid subscriptions, together with license to operate a public lottery as the best available means for raising new funds. And as an inducement both to the payment of old subscriptions and the making of new ones it was agreed that the government of the enterprise should be reorganized to give the rank and file of the adventurers a larger voice in its control.

[27] The founding of the Bermuda colony and its close relation to the story of Virginia for twelve years thereafter has been discussed fully in Craven, *Introduction to the History of Bermuda*.

As a step necessary to accomplish these purposes, Sir Thomas Smith and his associates secured a second and final revision of the Virginia charter. Passing the seal on March 12, the third charter extended the adventurers' title from one hundred miles to three hundred leagues at sea in order to include the Bermudas, which lie something under six hundred miles off Cape Henry. A subsidiary joint-stock association, called by one contemporary an "under company," had been formed of the more substantial and active Virginia adventurers, and early in July Captain Richard Moore landed with fifty to sixty men to begin the permanent occupation of what is now England's oldest colony in the New World. The charter having given special assurance that royal justices would favor suits for unpaid subscriptions, the suits were promptly instituted before the Court of Chancery.[28] Meanwhile, the new authorization for the operation of a lottery resulted in the opening of its headquarters in a newly erected house in St. Paul's Churchyard.[29] Near by stood the establishment of William Welby, who printed so many of the adventurers' promotional tracts as practically to justify his designation as official publisher to the company. Among the more important issues published by him is Robert Johnson's tract of that year entitled *New Life of Virginea; declaring the former successe and present estate of that plantation, being the second part of Nova Britannia*—an exhortation to renewed hope and faith.

The charter's provision for the reorganization of the government requires special attention, for it represents a development of great importance to the history of English settlement in America. Powers of government heretofore largely exercised by the Virginia Council were now transferred to the more democratic control of a "Court and Assembly" of the adventurers. This assembly already held, under the charter of 1609, a very real voice in determining the Council's membership and the main features of economic policy. But to its former functions the third charter added the privilege of admitting new adventurers, a direct control in the selection of all officers for both the company and the colony, and the fundamental right to draft "such Laws and Ordinances, for the Good

---

[28] Kingsbury (ed.), *Records of The Virginia Company,* III, 34–48; John Smyth of Nibley Papers (New York Public Library), 1.
[29] Kingsbury (ed.), *Records of The Virginia Company,* III, 54.

and Welfare of the . . . Plantation, as . . . shall be thought requisite and meet." In the course of the following years, the assembly came to meet regularly once a week as "an ordinary court," with requirement of a quorum of twenty adventurers who must include the treasurer or his deputy, and four other members of the Council. It also met four times a year in a great quarter court, for which weightier questions were reserved.[30]

The Council continued to enjoy the advantage and prestige associated with its official designation as His Majesty's Council. Its members still took a special oath. As before, it served as the principal channel of communication with royal officers and for direction of the company's officials in Virginia. In 1612 it even received additional powers to deal with seamen and prospective colonists guilty of breach of contract, with planters returning home without license, who were numbered among the more serious detractors of the enterprise, and with malefactors sent from the colony for punishment. Yet, more clearly than before, the Council now acted as a standing committee of the adventurers. In its direct responsibility to them it occupied a position paralleling that of similar councils, committees, or courts of assistants in other commercial companies. From this time until the colony passed under royal rule in 1624 the central fact in the government of Virginia was the controlling influence of the agencies and conventions of an English commercial company.

Historically and primarily the English commercial company was a governing body, composed of the merchants engaged in a certain branch of trade and existing for its effective regulation. Modern students have been disposed to classify the companies of this earlier day according to two types: in one, the joint-stock type, members pooled their resources in a common fund for investment under direction of the company's officers; in the other, the so-called regulated company, members traded individually on their own capital, subject to general rules laid down in the common interest.

[30] The company's organization, like that of any other institution, showed of course growth and progressive refinement. For an understanding of its structure and operation, the key documents are the charters of 1609 and 1612, the charter of the Somers Islands Company of 1615, in Lefroy (ed.), *Memorials of the . . . Bermudas*, I, 83–98; and the "Orders and Constitutions" of 1620, in Kingsbury (ed.), *Records of The Virginia Company*, III, 340–65.

The distinction is important, for as Englishmen turned at this period to ventures more distant and hazardous, they were increasingly disposed to rely on joint-stock methods of finance, and the commercial company underwent a transformation of great significance in the history of corporate enterprise. But joint-stock methods were as yet far from being those of the modern corporation. As already noted, stocks were terminable; and frequently, as in the East India Company and by 1612 in the Virginia Company, there was more than one joint stock. The contemporary joint-stock company is more readily understood if regarded as essentially a regulated company supervising one or more joint-stock ventures rather than, as in its older form, individually owned projects.[31] It could be all the more easily adapted, therefore, to the peculiar requirements for a depository of authority over such ventures as the settlement of Virginia or of Bermuda.

Its forms and procedures had already left their mark on the evolving framework of government in the Virginia colony. The first head of the colony had been known as the president, a term used more or less interchangeably with "governor" for designation of the chief officer of an English commercial company and not infrequently applied to leading factors, or agents, representing the company abroad. The title did not survive in America as it did in the presidencies of British India, no doubt because of its unhappy association with a discredited experiment at Jamestown. In selecting a new title in 1609, the adventurers chose the alternate of "governor," which together with the traditional courtesy designation of "His Excellency" was destined to remain a permanent feature of American colonial and state government. To advise the new governor there was established a council representative of the leading men of the colony. This was a reasonable step to take, and the term "council," which could have been borrowed from any one of several places, was as good a designation as any. Notice should be taken, however, of the close parallel to the organization existing among the adventurers at home. There the head, as frequently called gov-

---

[31] For a comprehensive study, see William R. Scott, *The Constitution and Finance of English, Scottish and Irish Joint-Stock Companies to 1720* (Cambridge, 1910–1912); for a more recent discussion with helpful bibliographical notes, see Andrews, *Colonial Period of American History*, I, 28 ff.; and for the peculiar problems of colonial government under a company, Craven, *Introduction to the History of Bermuda*, 29–48.

ernor as by his official title of treasurer, worked with a council selected from the more substantial investors. After 1612 only the establishment of a general assembly of the planters in Virginia was required to round out a framework of government reproducing in all essentials the structure of that existing for the adventurers in England.

The newly reorganized London Company made a serious effort to draw upon the aids provided in the third charter for the benefit of the Virginia colony. It was announced that Governor De la Warr, whose commission had been for life, would soon return to Jamestown together with Argall, who since 1609 had been the colony's chief reliance for trade and exploration. The Reverend William Simonds, who had preached a sermon in behalf of the 1609 venture, now came forward with the lengthiest publication yet to appear on the subject of the colony, Captain John Smith's *Map of Virginia. With a Description of the Country* and the supplementary *Proceedings of the English Colonie in Virginia* compiled from accounts by several of the older settlers.[32] And though De la Warr failed to fulfill the company's promise of a return to his post, Argall once more took up duties in Virginia which in 1613 led him to attack French intruders in present-day Maine and Nova Scotia.[33] This action testified to the broad geographical terms in which the English adventurers continued to view their American rights, but all hope of infusing new life into the Virginia project disappeared as the result of a continuing financial stringency.

Though it is impossible to say what was the outcome of suits for unpaid subscriptions, circumstances indicate disappointment. Disappointing, too, was the return from lotteries, the total amounting perhaps to less than £3,000.[34] An additional £2,000 was secured

[32] Arber and Bradley (eds.), *Travels and Works of Captain John Smith*, I, 41–174, a contribution perhaps not altogether welcome to the company's officers, for there were suggestions that mismanagement explained recent disappointments. But the main point, that the country was good, was helpful, and Smith's descriptions of Indian life were calculated to further the missionary appeal on which heavy reliance was now placed.

[33] Andrews, *Colonial Period of American History*, I, 147–49.

[34] Kingsbury (ed.), *Records of The Virginia Company*, III, 49–56. For evidence that £3,000 to £4,000 may have been collected by Chancery rulings, see Thomas Birch, *Court and Times of James I* (London, 1849), I, 263. Such funds as were thus received were in all probability applied to the company's debts.

in November of 1612 by an outright sale of the company's title in
the Bermudas to the association of adventurers formed for their
settlement, a step toward the complete legal separation of the two
projects finally accomplished by incorporation under royal charter
in 1615 of the Somers Islands Company.[35] A new appeal, in the
Reverend Alexander Whitaker's *Good Newes from Virginia*, came
in 1613. The Reverend William Crashaw, for several years a friend
of the undertaking, in a prefatory note presented the sacrificial
labors of Virginia's two ministers, Richard Buck and Whitaker,
graduates respectively of Oxford and Cambridge, as proof "that
this worke is of God, and will therefore stand, though man should
unfaithfully forsake it." Whitaker himself sounded what was primarily a missionary plea. The same note was struck, to an accom-
paniment of gold, in a great masque which served as part of the
celebrations attending the popular marriage of Princess Elizabeth
to the Protestant Frederick, Elector of the Palatinate. But Englishmen were as yet slow to hear the Macedonian call, and gold was now
an old and hackneyed theme, useful chiefly for purposes of amuse-
ment.

More faithfully reflecting the adventurers' real hopes at this time
was a shipment of silkworms, which, like so many of the company's
efforts, proved unproductive. Only in John Rolfe's experiments
with tobacco did there appear to be the promise of a profitable
staple, and these proceeded slowly. Virginia tobacco was imported
at London in 1614, but three years later it still proved unable to
compete with other tobacco in the English market and was re-
shipped by the East India fleets to points where men had learned
only to smoke and not to discriminate.[36] As Rolfe's tobacco reached
London his own thoughts were turned in another direction. In
the continuing struggle with Powhatan the English had kidnapped
his favorite daughter, the comely Pocahontas, who only recently
had arrived at the age for wearing clothes the year around. Rolfe
fell in love, tossed and worried through a sufficient number of sleep-
less nights to persuade himself that the affections awakened by

[35] The steps are outlined in the charter, in Lefroy (ed.), *Memorials of the . . .
Bermudas*, I, 83–98.

[36] "Lord Sackville's Papers respecting Virginia, 1613–1631," in *American Historical
Review*, XXVII (1921–1922), 493–538, 738–65, provides the best index to tobacco
importations. See also, Kingsbury (ed.), *Records of The Virginia Company*, III, 78.

this young savage were honorable, for the glory of God, and for the good of the plantation. His own conscience quieted, Dale's agreement won, and Powhatan yielding to persuasion, the marriage was celebrated, and with it came, at long last, peace with the Indians.

That peace coincided with termination of the three-year contracts for service in the colony by Gates and Dale. The former immediately returned home, bearing word that the "plantation will fall to the ground, if it be not presently supplied." [37] Ralph Hamor, successor to Strachey as secretary, also returned to provide the chief account of these events in his *True Discourse of the Present Estate of Virginia,* which was printed with supplementary letters from Dale, Rolfe, and Whitaker in 1615. But Dale found "a generall desire in the best sort to returne for England: letter upon letter, request upon request from their friends to returne, so as I knew not upon whom to conferre the care of this busines in my absence," and accordingly he remained at his post. His decision should go far to offset charges, of questionable historical value, brought against him by those who fell afoul his undoubtedly strict but apparently necessary discipline. As Whitaker pointed out in Dale's defense, it is difficult for the malefactor to "abide the face of the Judge."

Leaders in London seem once more to have stirred themselves to send aid. At any rate, Hamor's *Discourse* was published, and another try was made with the lottery.[38] Yet when in 1616 the seven-year term placed on the joint stock came to an end, the colony had been reduced to a mere 350 persons, the company had only the land to offer by way of a dividend, and possessed not even sufficient funds to meet the administrative costs of such a division. Adventurers, therefore, were informed by printed notice of a plan to provide now only a preliminary or "first" dividend of fifty acres per share, the division to be made of those lands lying along the James "in our actuall possession." [39] Subscribers received promise that as the area of effective occupation was enlarged there would be additional dividends, bringing the total for each share to perhaps

---

[37] Birch, *Court and Times of James I,* I, 311.

[38] Brown (ed.), *Genesis of the United States,* II, 760–66.

[39] *A Briefe Declaration of the present state of things in Virginia, and of a Division to be now made, of some part of those Lands in our actuall possession,* reprinted in Brown (ed.), *Genesis of the United States,* II, 775–79.

two hundred acres, but for the present it would be impossible to secure even the first fifty acres without paying down another £12 10s. to meet the cost of sending out a new governor and a commission of survey. As an inducement to payment of this levy, the company promised an additional fifty acres for the added £12 10s., the grant to be made immediately and in an area less remote from the principal seats of the colony than would be the future lot of those who refused the payment. Planters in the colony would receive in accordance with the original agreement fifty acres for their personal adventure, apparently without payment of a levy. As further evidence of the sad estate to which the project had sunk, an offer of fifty acres was made to any nonadventurer who would promptly pay in £12 10s.

And takers, for a time, were few. Not even Dale's return home in 1616 with Pocahontas and nine or ten other Indians and the concerted effort to play up her status as a royal convert could overcome the fact that thousands of pounds, hundreds of lives, the devoted efforts at home of Smith, Johnson, and Sandys and abroad of Smith, Newport, Argall, Gates, and Dale had seemingly been expended for nought.

Meanwhile, the Bermuda colony, as Spanish ambassador Count Gondomar had recently informed his royal master, enjoyed "a very different and creditable reputation." [40] This contrast must be explained in terms other than those of a difference in leadership, for Sir Thomas Smith served as governor of both companies and Alderman Robert Johnson as deputy governor. Moreover, the active membership of the Virginia and Bermuda companies was so nearly the same that the two courts, through the years that followed, repeatedly sat virtually as one body, and more than one historian has experienced difficulty in disentangling their records. Indeed, it is necessary only to notice the names by which Bermuda's parishes are known—Sandys, Southampton, Warwick, Paget, Pembroke, Devonshire, Smith, Hamilton—to appreciate that the founders of that colony were for the most part the same men who have been honored for their leadership in the settlement of Virginia. But while the older colony wasted well-nigh away, the younger had attracted a total of over six hundred settlers by 1615, and in its con-

[40] Brown (ed.), *Genesis of the United States*, II, 740.

tinued growth would hold a marked superiority in numbers for three years thereafter. Obviously, the difficulties of the Virginia Company reflected not so much a loss of faith in the promise of America itself as they did disillusionment regarding a specific project.

No less obvious is the pertinence of the adventurers' experience in Bermuda to an understanding of the ideas which shaped the later course of English settlement. To summarize this experience is not only to record lessons drawn from a succession of misfortunes with the older colony prior to 1612 but to explain some of the more important policies subsequently adopted by the Virginia Company.

A principal difficulty in the Virginia Company had been collection of the second and third installments of the adventurer's subscription. In launching their new project, therefore, the leaders attempted to secure his continued support by establishing for him an immediate title in the land.[41] Under the plan adopted, the investment of each individual adventurer would be directed largely to the development of his own acres. The plan, in other words, marks a declining enthusiasm for a scheme which made everything depend on one joint stock. It was recognized, of course, that some pooling of capital and labor would be necessary in order to effect the occupation and fortification of the islands. Accordingly, subscriptions to a joint stock were secured under a ruling which fixed the subscriber's right to a grant of land in proportion to his payment into the common fund. Also, it was agreed that all colonists would labor together under the governor's direction until forts had been built, a church raised, and other such public work completed. Thereafter a public estate, to be cultivated by tenants supplied and equipped through use of joint-stock funds, would be set aside for the support of government and to meet other common charges. But most of the settlers arrived in the colony at the expense of

[41] "When the Virginia business was at its height," wrote John Chamberlain to Sir Dudley Carleton in 1613, "in that heat many gentlemen and others were drawn by persuasion and importunity to underwrite their names for adventurers. But when it came to the payment, specially the second and third time, their hands were not so ready to go to their purses as they were to the paper, and in the end flatly refused." Quoted by Andrews, *Colonial Period of American History*, I, 128. For a detailed discussion of the Bermuda plan, see Craven, *Introduction to the History of Bermuda*, 26 ff.

individual adventurers for ultimate assignment as tenants on privately-held land dividends. A provision for tenancy at half shares perpetuated a policy recognizing the equal claims of adventurer and planter, and at the same time undertook to bind each of them by the promise of an immediate reward in proportion to his individual contribution to the effort. One cannot but be reminded of Dale's attempt in 1614 to enlarge the field of individual endeavor and reward in Virginia by allotment of small farms to the planters there.

The preliminary work actually required more time than had been expected. Though the Bermuda colonists escaped most of the bitter experiences suffered by their fellow countrymen in Virginia, everything did not go according to plan. Not until the spring of 1617 had there been completed a necessary survey dividing the bulk of the land into eight tribes (now parishes) and subdividing these into shares of twenty-five acres each.[42] Already, however, significant experiments with a proprietary type of colonization were under way. Sir Nathaniel Rich, lawyer and parliamentary leader, together with his cousin, the famous second Earl of Warwick, both of whom were also members of the Virginia Company, within a few months after the survey had consolidated their shares by purchase and exchange into an estate of some five hundred acres. On this estate their tenants planted grapevines, tobacco, cotton, sugar cane, indigo, plantains, figs, pomegranates, cassava, and additional "West Indy plants" not specified. To indicate the seriousness of purpose with which the venture had been undertaken, it may be noted that the Riches shipped out at their own cost two expert vinedressers secured from abroad, both of whom unfortunately died in passage.

Other adventurers, and the company itself on the "publique land," engaged in similar agricultural ventures which emphasized principally a hope for production of silk, wine, sugar, tobacco, and fruits for drying. Except in the case of tobacco, these efforts were destined to fail, but they bring attention again to the continuing influence on the early course of English settlement of objectives

---

[42] For new evidence on the Bermuda survey indicating that two surveys were run, a preliminary one by 1615 for guidance of the adventurers in determining the division and a second to lay out the bounds so determined, see Craven and Hayward (eds.), *Journal of Richard Norwood*, especially Introduction, pp. xxiii ff.

outlined by the elder Hakluyt for Raleigh. And they point to a basic reason for an active interest in the proprietorship of American land that would soon bring new strength to Virginia.

Of special interest in connection with subsequent developments in Virginia, too, is the Bermuda public estate. The adventurers' plan had emphasized an individual proprietorship of the soil, but in no society can individual enterprise be independent of certain community services. Men must have government and it must be paid for. Provision must be made for the common defense, and to the seventeenth-century mind support of the church was no less fundamental.[43] The most familiar answer to this problem of providing for the public service is to collect from members of the community a levy in the form of tax, fee, or voluntary contribution, and to such a practice our colonial forefathers were forced eventually to turn. But first they tried one of the more remarkable schemes in the long history of politico-economic experiment in America. The public estate, financed by the original joint-stock fund, in area approximately equal to one of the tribes and cultivated by half-share tenants of the company, would provide an income for the support of government and the church, for the maintenance of defenses, and for other common charges. The proprietors would thus be left to develop their own estates free of taxation. Though the plan failed to accomplish its full purpose, this failure was not yet apparent at the time of the reorganization of the Virginia project which gave to the year 1618 unusual significance in the history of American colonization.

As that year opened, a new interest stirred the older company. The sources of this interest were varied, but at its heart will be found a reviving hope for individual advantage through ownership of the land. Though the Virginia Company's failure had recently seemed well-nigh complete, on second glance it appeared that the company must be credited with one solid achievement.

[43] Since not all of the adventurers were able to provide, as were the Riches, an overseer for superintendence of their tenants, it had even been necessary for the Bermuda proprietors to make plans for sharing such administrative costs through the services of a bailiff established as the chief officer of each tribe. For the functions of this officer and points of similarity with the heads of the Virginia hundred or "particular plantation" after 1618, see Craven, *Introduction to the History of Bermuda*, 76–77.

Some of the land had been won from the wilderness and was now placed at the disposal of all who had the courage to take it.

Old planters like Martin, Hamor, and Argall, together with certain of the adventurers who saw an advantage in associating themselves with these experienced leaders by a pooling of shares, had been among the first to respond. In the months that followed the public announcement in 1616 of plans for a land dividend, the company offered a grant in proportion to the number of shares thus pooled and an additional allowance of fifty acres for every person transported at the charge of the grantees, an offer containing features basic to Virginia's subsequent land policy. Even then the general response continued to be disappointing. So much so that such patents as were issued were carelessly drawn or else the officers of the company were persuaded, in the hope of saving the colony, to agree to almost any terms upon which men were willing to go. At any rate, most of the early patents were later repudiated, with charges in one or two instances of collusion for dishonest purposes. Some of them, especially in the case of a claim by Captain Martin to five hundred acres per share, remained a subject of bitter controversy to the company's last days. The explanation would appear to be that under existing circumstances men were permitted virtually to write their own tickets.[44]

It was the middle of May, 1617, before Captain Argall arrived in Virginia as the new deputy governor to take over from Captain George Yeardley, another old planter to whom the colony had been entrusted upon Dale's departure the preceding year. Equipped largely at his own expense and that of his associates, Argall, like so many of Virginia's governors thereafter, divided his attention between the responsibilities of command and efforts to improve his own fortune. Later there would be charges of maladministration.

But for the present this willingness of old hands such as Argall and Martin to risk their lives and fortunes in a new venture to Virginia encouraged others to follow. The practice of pooling dividends to secure a common grant of land, with its promise of

[44] Chief reliance must be placed on the record of the company's later action. See Kingsbury (ed.), *Records of The Virginia Company*, III, 98–109, and 58–98 for incomplete records relating to the period from 1616 to 1618. The several topics are discussed in Wesley F. Craven, *Dissolution of the Virginia Company* (New York, 1932).

savings in administrative and other costs, seems also to have helped persuade some of the smaller investors to participate. Most men were still inclined to seek the advantages of group action in approaching the hazards of American settlement and to take for granted the necessity of settling together in units that would permit enjoyment of the diverse benefits of community life. The English village with its surrounding farm lands, not the isolated farmhouse of later America, continued to set the standard followed by those who sought some practical arrangement for turning to good account their land dividends in Virginia. The several private plantations which had their beginning or were projected at this time varied considerably in size. Some were small enough for their ownership and management to be described in terms of a partnership which united in a common effort only a few adventurers and perhaps one or more experienced planters. Others were held jointly by societies of adventurers which became large enough to require an organization not unlike that of the mother company.

Such a society was that for Smith's Hundred, later renamed Southampton Hundred, which was organized in 1617 with Sir Thomas Smith, Sir Edwin Sandys, the Earl of Southampton, and other leading adventurers among its members. Having a joint stock of its own and functioning through a treasurer and committees designated by a "general Assemblye" of the associated adventurers, the organization held a position with reference to the Virginia Company very similar to that of the subsidiary joint-stock society formed in 1612 for the settlement of Bermuda. In the more or less common plan of action followed by these societies there will be found, too, many of the basic features of the joint-stock plan of 1609. Since the societies represented voluntary associations, agreements reached by the several groups undoubtedly varied. Incomplete evidence indicates, however, that it was the practice to pool capital, labor, and the land only for a stipulated period of time, with the understanding that once the initial planting had been accomplished there would be a division for the purpose of establishing individual titles to specific acreages. In other words, the joint stock seems to have been a temporary feature of the plan. Closer parallels will be found in the voluntary associations later formed for settlement of some of the New England towns than in any subsequent development of Virginia's own history.[45]

Though the proprietary experiment undertaken in Bermuda absorbed energies and funds which might otherwise have been directed toward Virginia, there can be little doubt that part of the enthusiasm it engendered was transferred to new projects of settlement in the older colony. In Bermuda, shares were fixed at twenty-five acres each and the total area of the islands was less than that of Manhattan Island. In Virginia, where men could talk of 100-, 200-, or even 500-acre shares, there was room for more ambitious ventures.[46] Moreover, Virginia's expanding production of tobacco, even though much of it was still of such poor quality as to require reshipment from England, could hardly be ignored by men who had pinned their faith so largely on a program of agricultural experimentation in Bermuda. Of the favored place of tobacco in that program the adventurers had given proof in 1616 by sending an expert to Bermuda to instruct the colonists in the techniques of planting, curing, and packing the weed.[47]

It would be difficult to exaggerate the importance of tobacco

[45] The Smyth of Nibley Papers, which relate to the affairs of Berkeley Hundred established on the upper James in 1619, provide the only collection approaching completeness for study of one of these plantations. The more important of the papers have been published in Kingsbury (ed.), *Records of The Virginia Company,* III. For the fragmentary records of Smith's and Southampton Hundred, see *ibid.,* Index. It should be remembered, too, that the Pilgrims' settlement at Plymouth Rock had its origins under patent from the Virginia Company in one of these associations, and all students of this period in Virginia's history should read the late Professor Andrews' discussion of the Plymouth colony in his *Colonial Period of American History,* I, 249–99. The present writer, however, would take exception to his conclusion on p. 265 that the association of both adventurers and planters in one company represented a novel development, for this conclusion rests upon a misinterpretation of the joint-stock plan of 1609 and particularly his rejection (p. 106) of [Johnson], *Nova Britannia,* of that year as valid evidence of the plan. See above, p. 86 n. For Andrews' discussion of the Virginia plantation, see his *Colonial Period of American History,* I, 128 ff.

[46] Southampton Hundred, for instance, would eventually embrace, at least on paper, 80,000–100,000 acres, and in 1621 Sir Edwin Sandys pushed a proposal for establishment by the Bermuda adventurers of a 45,000-acre plantation on the mainland under patent from the Virginia Company. See Craven, *Introduction to the History of Bermuda,* 13–14, 155.

[47] See Lefroy (ed.), *Memorials of the . . . Bermudas,* I, 116.

in the history of Virginia after 1616. Indeed, the significance of the fact that the colony at last had found a marketable staple—one, moreover, promising a return on investment within a year of settlement—is so obvious that historians have been inclined to assume that this development alone offers explanation enough for the adventurers' reviving interest. But there is reason to believe that the development had for contemporaries an even broader significance than later students have assigned to it. Since tobacco all along had been merely one in a long list of prospective staples, the success achieved with it naturally tended to strengthen the promise of other experimental efforts. Such, at any rate, would seem to be the evidence offered by the adventurers' attempt over the next few years to put to a test practically the entire experimental program initially outlined by the elder Hakluyt.

If the reviving faith in that program found earlier expression in Bermuda than in the older colony, it was partly because of the need for an adequate explanation of previous failures in Virginia. It took time to overcome this difficulty, but a beginning was made in 1617, when the adventurers became agitated by charges of mismanagement against the company's leadership. Men who had recently regarded Virginia as worthy only of scorn now found her worth quarreling about. Demands were made for a closer look at the books, and under the leadership of Sandys, whose own interest in the colony apparently had been unflagging, an audit was undertaken. The accounts probably needed auditing. Some of the adventurers had invested as early as 1606, others in 1609, others only in 1611, and still others for the first time in 1616. Some had paid only in part or not at all, and some claimed their shares in lieu of prizes from the lottery. Debts had accumulated and officers had frequently advanced funds from their own pockets. In a corporation whose history had been marked by such varied transactions and by so many turns of fortune, the books might well show a certain confusion. To provide for an equitable distribution of Virginia's land undoubtedly required that they be put straight. As the audit proceeded, however, the need for proof of Virginia's promise apparently overcame all other considerations. Suggestions of dishonesty were added to those of carelessness. Feelings were aroused, and men found it increasingly difficult to co-operate. Thus did the company enter upon a period of sharp controversy that would end in its own destruction.

Other subjects of dispute soon appeared. Irregularities in early land patents were naturally called into question and, in an atmosphere of growing suspicion, were increasingly regarded with misgivings. The planters themselves contributed another cause for debate. As colonists had become free of their obligations to the company, the first of them perhaps at the close of a seven-year term ending in 1614 and others two years later, the magazine ships bringing supplies from England increasingly engaged in direct trade with individual planters. The business naturally went to merchants within the company, with Alderman Johnson, partly because of his position as deputy, in charge. The tobacco received in payment was still of poor quality, while magazine prices included freightage and allowance for other costs. It required little time for the Virginia planter to enter those charges of exorbitance on the part of the merchants that were to serve as his favorite grievance for a century and a half. His accusations won credence among adventurers who, for other reasons, were becoming suspicious of the leadership of those merchants who from the first had held the company's principal offices. In the end a real injustice was done to Smith and Johnson, than whom none had been more loyal. But a useful purpose was served, for men thereby were helped in reaching a conviction that with proper management Virginia's promise might yet be fulfilled.

These were but beginnings in 1617, and the picture here presented is, for that year, easily overdrawn. It should be regarded as no more than the portrayal of a trend, the full effect of which would not be felt until the spring of 1619. At that time Sandys, supported by a group of the lesser adventurers whose suspicions had hardened into conviction, replaced Sir Thomas Smith as treasurer. John Ferrar took Johnson's post as deputy. The group had gradually formed into a factional party, taking advantage of the democratic rule of voting by head rather than by share that held in the company's courts, and had enjoyed the leadership of one of England's most skilled parliamentarians. Even at the time of its triumph, however, it was still a minority faction, and was successful only through the momentary aid of the Earl of Warwick and Sir

Nathaniel Rich, who had quarrels of their own with Smith. Their support was given only in the Virginia court, and Smith continued in control of the Bermuda Company for two more years. Sandys soon consolidated his position with the aid of new adherents and thus assumed leadership in the last great effort of the Virginia Company.

The way had been prepared for him in 1618 through a far-reaching reorganization of the business and a reform of the company's procedures. There can be little doubt that even then the initiative belonged largely to Sandys and that the support for measures adopted came chiefly from the party forming behind his leadership. Yet Smith still controlled the company, and without his help little or nothing could have been accomplished.[48] He must have known moments of bitter reflection as he looked back over years of struggle to keep the project alive and witnessed at last a reviving faith that depended so much upon criticism of his management. But loyal as ever to the best interests of the colony, he accepted help from whatever source it came and co-operated in putting through a series of reforms that wrote a fitting climax to a long term of service.

The underlying purpose of the adventurers' legislative efforts in 1618 was well stated in a promotional tract issued two years later. "The care . . . that hath been taken by directions, Instructions, Charters, and Commissions to reduce the people and affaires in *Virginia* into a regular course," declared the company, "hath bin such and so great that the Colony beginneth now to have the face and fashion of an orderly State, and such as is likely to grow and prosper." Growth and prosperity were the end, and orderliness in the management of the colony's affairs the means proposed for its attainment. In keeping therewith, the court undertook first to set its own house in order. It codified its rules and by-laws in the well-known "Orders and Constitutions," which, though not formally adopted until June of 1619, represented for the most part legislation of the preceding year.[49] By November, 1618, the adventurers

---

[48] In addition to Craven, *Dissolution of the Virginia Company* and *Introduction to the History of Bermuda*, see Andrews, *Colonial Period of American History*, I.

[49] *A Declaration of the State of the Colony and Affaires in Virginia* (London, 1620), reprinted in Kingsbury (ed.), *Records of The Virginia Company*, III, 307–65. For the "Orders and Constitutions," see *ibid.*, 340–65; for proof that the document repre-

had also approved for transmittal to the colony by George Yeardley, its newly appointed governor, papers which established a uniform land policy, provided for the first representative assembly in America, and decreed a major reform in the laws theretofore governing the colonists.

Of these papers, the most important, as is evidenced by the fact that the colonists promptly described it as "the greate Charter," gave a detailed statement of land policies and of plans for the encouragement of those undertaking individually or by associated action the development of their dividends.[50] To all adventurers, including delinquents who would now pay up their subscriptions, the company promised a grant of one hundred acres as a first dividend for each share of £12 10s. value and another one hundred acres as a second dividend after the first had been "sufficiently peopled." Both dividends were to pass free of quitrent. Also rent free would be identical grants authorized for such of the "ancient planters" (a designation indicating arrival in the colony prior to Dale's departure in 1616) as had settled at their own expense. Those who had emigrated at the company's charge were to be given the same acreages, following expiration of a seven-year term of service, but were required to pay two shillings quitrent per hundred acres. The company thus cleared itself of commitments to the older planters by action suggestive of certain adjustments which over the intervening years had been made in the original scheme of settlement.

For those who had emigrated since 1616 or who would emigrate within the seven-year period extending from Midsummer Day of

---

sented legislation chiefly of 1618, see *ibid.*, 99. A similar constitution for the Bermuda Company was adopted in 1622 after the Sandys faction had gained control of that court. See Lefroy (ed.), *Memorials of the . . . Bermudas*, I, 182–228.

[50] Kingsbury (ed.), *Records of The Virginia Company*, III, 98–109. Historians have persisted in creating something of a mystery regarding the contents of the great charter. Assuming that a document so described must have been concerned primarily with legal and political rights, and failing to find any paper corresponding to this preconceived notion, they have concluded that it has been lost and have even attempted to reconstruct it from other evidences of the political and legal reforms decreed by the adventurers in 1618. Actually, the document usually cited as "Instructions to Governor Yeardly" and dated November 18, 1618, is established beyond question as "the greate Charter" by the proceedings of the first Virginia Assembly. See *ibid.*, 98–109, 153–77.

1618 the rules were quite different. Those who went at the company's expense would serve a seven-year term as half-share tenants of the company. Upon the expiration of that term presumably they would be free to dispose of their labor to their best advantage, but there was no provision for a grant of land to them. Men who migrated at their own cost would claim their land under the famous headright provision of the charter. This provided, in one of the more significant applications of the principle of using the land to underwrite immigration, for a grant of fifty acres, on both a first and second dividend, for every person transported to the colony prior to Midsummer Day, 1625.[51] Since the land belonged to the person who paid the cost of transportation, anyone going at his own charge would be assured of a land grant in proportion to the number of persons he took with him, but the immediate purpose undoubtedly was to provide an additional inducement for all grantees to undertake a prompt and full development of their dividends. Outlasting the seven-year term here placed upon it, the headright would serve thereafter as the basis of Virginia's land policy and, through its encouragement of those who first brought in indentured servants and then Negro slaves, would help to meet the colony's expanding need for labor.

Further encouragement of individual investment was offered in the charter's provisions for revival of the company's own projects. If for no other reason than that of an accumulated debt standing in 1618 at £8,000 to £9,000, the company had little choice but to continue as an active colonizing agent.[52] For seven years there would be no more than a small revenue from quitrents. Any attempt to retire the debt by levying on the adventurers could only discourage the type of individual investment upon which hopes now principally depended. Moreover, the Bermuda plan of a public estate jointly operated through the agencies of the company for the support of common charges would strengthen the promise that the adventurers might enjoy the full return from their current investment and this perhaps would help to persuade enough delinquents in the payment of their overdue subscriptions to provide the funds for its inauguration. The charter, accordingly, conveyed

[51] Except in the case of grants to adventurers and old planters settling at their own cost, all such grants were subject to a quitrent of one shilling for each fifty acres.
[52] Kingsbury (ed.), *Records of The Virginia Company*, I, 350.

the assurance of the company's continued activity, especially in the development of a public estate intended "to Ease all the Inhabitants of Virginia forever of all taxes and public burthens as much as may be."

The general pattern of settlement, into which this public estate would be fitted, found its focal points in four towns or boroughs. Scattered settlement was not only considered dangerous, in view of the yet uncertain relations existing with the Indians, but would involve sacrifice of many of the advantages of town life, especially in the promotion of trade and craftsmanship. It was well understood that the prosperity of a colony could not be divorced from commerce, that it depended upon such things as favorable freightage to European markets, and that this, in turn, depended on a concentration of local marketing arrangements to facilitate the speedy loading of ships. A healthy economy required, too, a degree of self-sufficiency in the provision of essential services calling for an acquired skill. Only by a concentration of settlement could there be effected those economies of time, distance, and production which permit such services to be rendered at a reasonable charge.

The four boroughs to be established were designated as James City, Charles City, Henrico, and Kecoughtan, the last subsequently renamed Elizabeth City. Though their names have been perpetuated by four of Virginia's oldest counties, a fact which conveniently fixes for us the relative location of the earlier boroughs, it must be understood that this legislation of 1618 provided for nothing comparable to an introduction of the county system of administration. Contrary to an assumption sometimes made, it did not attempt to divide the colony into four major and adjoining administrative units holding a superiority over all other units of local administration. Rather, the charter merely established four principal points of concentration for the general body of settlers, in which the pattern of life and government would be that of the English municipality instead of the county, and to which other units, like Southampton Hundred, would be co-ordinate and not subordinate.

At each of these points three thousand acres were to be set apart as the company's land for cultivation by its tenants on a half-share basis. Of the company's moiety, one half was appropriated to the support of the colony's superior officers, the governor excepted. For the governor's support an additional three thousand acres were to be laid out in the neighborhood of Jamestown and designated as the governor's land. The company would provide tenants for the land, and a half share of their produce would provide the governor's income.[53] Planters now entitled to a dividend for their personal adventure would also find their shares in lands adjoining these four towns. The communities would include, too, such craftsmen as could be induced to stick by their trades through an offer of a house and four acres at an annual rent of fourpence. For the maintenance of local administration, as distinct from the government of the colony, 1,500 acres were ordered set apart at each of the four cities as the "Burroughs Land." The services of all public officers would be thus provided free of either tax or fee.

The one exception came in the case of ministers, who, if the early practice of the Bermuda Company may be accepted as a guide, had heretofore served on contract with the company for a stipulated salary.[54] For each borough it was now ordered that one hundred acres of glebe be set aside, and that the minister's income from this source be supplemented by a sufficient contribution from his parishioners to provide a total income of £200 a year. Governmental services might be made free, but the adventurers evidently regarded it as unsound policy to make religion so.

Private plantations in process of establishment, or to be established, by the several groups of associated adventurers would fall outside the area of any of the four major boroughs. In effect, they would serve as additional boroughs and co-ordinate units of local administration. The problem of determining their status in the colony had called for especially close attention in 1618. It was obvious that for the sake of the common interest they must be incorporated in some over-all plan of government which would assure the preservation of an essential unity and uniformity of practice, and it was no less obvious that men would not invest their capital in such undertakings unless they could retain control of

[53] The company thereafter increasingly tended to follow the policy of making a special allotment of land and tenants for the support of individual offices.

[54] See Craven, *Introduction to the History of Bermuda*, 125. It should be noticed that provision had been made much earlier for glebe land in Bermuda Hundred.

them. The solution found is best understood by reading the charter together with one of the patents issued under the policies fixed by it.[55]

The associated adventurers received assurance of a necessary degree of independence in the management of the business end of the venture. This assurance was in the form of a guarantee that they would control the economic development of the estate, that they would enjoy the right to select officers for oversight of their tenants, and that they would be free of imposts levied for the benefit of the company. In addition, a considerable degree of political independence was conceded to them; for the society of adventurers might issue for the government of their people such orders and ordinances as were in conformity with the laws of England and the general regulations of the company, and the plantation itself would constitute a self-contained unit of local administration subordinate only to the government of the colony. The public estate offered the additional assurance that contributions for general expenses would be at the worst slight. Furthermore, such contributions were restricted, by a provision pointing to a significant reason for the establishment of a representative assembly, to those given "by the grant and consent of the generall Colony." Finally, and as though to emphasize the co-ordinate status of these plantations, each of them received an added grant for glebe and 1,500 acres for its borough land. On the other hand, however, the inhabitants of each of these boroughs were required to live in accordance with the laws of the colony, to answer for their acts before its superior courts, and to hold themselves ready for a call to military service.

This elaborate plan of settlement was followed only in part, and certain of its details had no more than momentary significance. Yet, only by understanding it can one comprehend the colony's problems in that highly important transitional stage of its history following the collapse of the London Company or view intelligently

[55] See the indenture between the company and Sir William Throckmorton, Sir George Yeardley, Richard Berkeley, and John Smyth of February 3, 1618/19, authorizing them "to erect and build a Towne" in Virginia and to "settle and plant dyuers inhabitants there for the advancement of the generall plantačon of that country." Kingsbury (ed.), *Records of The Virginia Company*, III, 130–34.

some of the enduring features of the Virginia scene. For a century and a half the lower house of the Virginia Assembly would be known as the House of Burgesses, though its members came almost entirely from the most rural of communities. And long after Jamestown, which alone of the four boroughs ever developed any real likeness to a town, had surrendered all other pretensions to being anything more than an unfortunate choice of the first planters, it clung to that ancient privilege of corporate existence—a parliamentary seat. The public land, the governor's land, and the borough lands all disappear in the twilight of Virginia's incomplete records, but a policy of relying on the glebe for a part of the minister's support survived, though it was to be but imperfectly followed. Destined also for survival as a familiar American practice was the basic idea of appropriating land for public purposes.

And, as though to foretell the especially significant place of this practice in the development of American education, "the greate Charter" directed that ten thousand acres be set apart at Henrico for endowment of a "University and College." The college, in its beginning at any rate, was to be an Indian college. Missionary opportunities in Virginia had received increasing emphasis in the company's promotional efforts after 1612. More recently the well-managed visit to England in 1616 of Pocahontas and her entourage had been used effectively to stir up popular interest. The King and the church subsequently co-operated with the adventurers in soliciting a national contribution "for the building and planting of a college," as the great charter put it, "for the training up of the Children of those Infidels in true Religion moral virtue and Civility and for other godly uses." Whether these "other godly uses" included a plan for the training of English as well as Indian youths is debatable. Such a plan later became a part of the company's program, but there can be no doubt that the primary aim in 1618 was to found an Indian mission. Actual establishment of the college was indefinitely postponed by a decision to handle the funds raised by the so-called bishops' appeal as an endowment for investment in a 10,000-acre plantation to be known as the "College Land." No other decision of 1618 spoke more strongly of the confidence with which the adventurers made their plans for the colony's economic development.

132

Identification with this Christian and humanitarian effort must be counted as part of the appeal that persuaded men to emigrate to Virginia in large numbers through the years immediately following. Of greater importance, however, was the assurance offered by legislation of 1618 that they might live under a government guaranteeing the full rights of Englishmen. Though the original justification for establishing a rigid discipline had been strong, its maintenance and especially its association in the popular view with martial law had become major factors in bringing the name of Virginia into ill repute. So the adventurers undertook to establish, as the charter put it, "a laudable form of Government by Majestracy and just laws for the happy guiding and governing of the people there inhabiting like as we have already done for the well ordering of our Courts here." The charter itself, except in its provisions for the support of this magistracy, was only incidentally concerned with the problems of government. Instructions issued for the accomplishment of legal reforms were evidently incorporated in another paper which unfortunately has not survived. But their intent happily is recorded for us in a statement of a later promotional tract that "The rigour of Martiall Law, wherewith before they were gouerned, is reduced within the limits prescribed by his Maiestie: and the laudable forme of Iustice and gouernment used in this Realme, established, and followed as neere as may be." [56]

The meaning of this is clear enough. It is no more accurate to say that martial law had been abolished than it is to suggest that theretofore Virginians had known no other. The effort, rather, was to draw a clearer distinction between civil and military authority and to limit the latter insofar as it proved possible in the interest of the colonists' liberties. Major reforms came, no doubt, through an attempt to substitute, where practical, courts formally assembled at regular term times and generally bound by rules of the common law for the more or less summary procedure theretofore characterizing the judicial action of officers. That, at any rate, is what occurred in Bermuda, where Governor Nathaniel Butler arrived in 1619 with instructions to effect reforms duplicating many of those adopted the preceding year for Virginia. It was the evident purpose, too, of a requirement, apparently dating from 1618, that

[56] *Ibid.*, 310.

the governor and his council sit at Jamestown as a general court in quarterly sessions.[57]

That Dale's Laws were suspended, at least in part, seems apparent from the fact that the first Virginia assembly enacted more moderate legislation as a substitute for some of its severe provisions. Furthermore, in 1620 the adventurers undertook, at the colonists' request, to provide in its place a code of "the Lawes of *England* proper for the use of that Plantation, with addition of such other, as the nature of the place, the novitie of the Colony, and other important circumstances should necessarily require." [58] Among the four committees to which the task was assigned, it should be noted, was one "For Millitary Discipline." It is not certain that the new code was ever completed, but clearly the guarantee contained in the royal charter of a right to live under the laws of England had acquired an added meaning of great importance to our institutional development. The commander and the magistrate were still one, but the commander had been enjoined not to forget that he was primarily a magistrate. Civil authority, as any American knows, properly takes precedence over the military.

No less significant for our later life was the act establishing a representative assembly for the colonists.[59] Among the several reasons for this step, the changing structure of the colony itself holds a place of primary importance. The introduction of new proprietary ventures now brought a diversity of interest and a dispersal

[57] The parallel experience of Bermuda is worthy of study, and Butler's own *Historye of the Bermudaes* is a valuable document. The need for this reform was not so great as in Virginia, but it was occasioned by similar complaints of "arbitrary rule," a term directing attention again to procedure, by Governor Daniel Tucker, formerly of Virginia, who was accused of following Dale's Laws in the younger colony. See Craven, *Introduction to the History of Bermuda,* 139–44. Butler's action reinforces the suggestion, contained in the document itself, Kingsbury (ed.), *Records of The Virginia Company,* III, 472–80, that the Virginia Company's instructions of 1621 for the holding of quarterly sessions by the governor and council merely duplicated an earlier order that had perhaps not been too faithfully observed.

[58] Kingsbury (ed.), *Records of The Virginia Company,* III, 311; I, 394–96.

[59] *Ibid.,* III, 482–84. This is not the original, but a duplicate sent out in 1621 along with copies of other orders of 1618. It should be read with John Pory's account of the proceedings of the first Assembly, *ibid.,* 153–77; Governor Butler's account of the Bermuda Assembly meeting in 1620, in *Historye of the Bermudaes,* 190–203, 308–13; and the statutes enacted by that body, in Lefroy (ed.), *Memorials of the . . . Bermudas,* I, 165–79.

of settlement unknown in the primitive and relatively compact community of earlier years. A resulting threat to the unity of the colony had caused the adventurers grave concern. That Englishmen, seeking a rule of action adequately balancing the requirements of local particularism and the necessities of an essential union, should have adopted the principle of representative government need cause no more surprise among modern students than it apparently did in contemporary observers. Moreover, the fact that these private plantations represented the investment of important groups of adventurers provided a strong argument for having their interests directly represented in the government of the colony. Some of the adventurers were planning to go to Virginia themselves for the purpose of taking personal command of their ventures. Others saw perhaps a better prospect of enlisting men of ability by giving some more complete expression to an already established principle of equality between adventurer and planter.

It was no accident that the body was described as "the generall Assemblie," a term commonly used to designate meetings of the adventurers in London. Nor was it accidental that its first important function, as it met in the church at Jamestown the following summer, was to consider the charter and other such documents previously passed upon by the general assembly of the company, with a view to suggesting amendments to them. The adventurers, it is true, were not bound to act on suggestions from the Jamestown assembly. Practical considerations of business management forbade as yet any too literal an application of the principle of equality. The governor, in a body where the council and burgesses sat together in one house, held a right of veto, and legislation enacted was of force only insofar as the company approved. But it was promised, and in the very document creating the assembly, that once the colony and its government had been securely established, "No orders of our Court afterwarde shall binde [the] colony unles they bee ratified in like manner in ther generall Assembly." In that promise one finds the final assurance of an equality of status conceded by the adventurers nine years before, and of a degree of self-government as great as the colonists could have asked for.

Other considerations may be quickly noted. The adventurers

described the assembly as one of two "Supreame Counsells." The first was a council of state made up of the governor and others appointed to it by the company; the second comprised this council and two burgesses "Chosen by the inhabitants" of every town, hundred, or other "particular plantation." It thus would be so constituted as to provide through its annual meetings a regular channel for the presentation of grievances. Among the more fundamental of human rights is the right of petition, the right to a hearing, and from its first session the assembly devoted much of its time to receiving and acting upon petitions. Only with the passage of years were its judicial functions overshadowed by the growing importance of its legislative powers. As a legislature, the body in its origin testified to the adventurers' understanding, to quote from the instruction for summoning the first Bermuda Assembly in 1620, that "every man will more willingly obey lawes to which he hath yielded his consent." It testified also, if the action of the first assembly to temper the severity of the colony's laws may be taken at face value, to a keen understanding of the connection between the right of representation and the protection of other fundamental rights.

No doubt the developing contest in England between King and Parliament played its part. A heightened sense of political and legal rights characterized the Englishman of this day and was reflected in the demands of those who considered emigration to America. It is unnecessary, however, to seek any more direct connection between the adventurers' action and political developments in England. The basic task of the London Company in 1618 was to persuade men to settle in Virginia. To accomplish that purpose it proved necessary to overcome the ill repute into which, by a succession of misfortunes, the colony had fallen. The company had long since established a policy of offering economic conditions of settlement that were not only in themselves liberal but conceded to the planters a status which naturally carried implications of legal and political advantage. The reforms of 1618 may be considered, therefore, a logical culmination of policies adopted by the adventurers much earlier. Through the years that followed, America would exert an increasingly strong attraction on the men of Europe, but the difficulties to be overcome remained such as to force upon those who sought to promote its settlement the granting of liberal terms.

In April, 1618, the population of Virginia stood at only four hundred persons, but by the close of the year it had grown to approximately a thousand. This increase represented no more than the vanguard of an unusually significant folk movement known to students as the Great Migration [60]—a movement that would carry into Virginia during the five-year period remaining of the active life of the company some 4,500 persons. After the company's bankruptcy and dissolution had cast a new shadow over Virginia's promise, the migration would flow in other directions. It would seize for English enterprise St. Kitts, Barbados, and additional West Indian isles, complete the occupation of Northern Ireland by Protestant English and Scots, effect the settlement of New England, and make secure England's control of the Chesapeake by the settlement of Maryland.

It is with a view to this continuing migration that one must interpret the reforms undertaken at its very outset by the Virginia adventurers. Designed specifically for the encouragement of emigration to a new and distant land, the reforms are of more than momentary or local significance, for they fixed a pattern of fundamental guarantees which Englishmen thereafter, and wherever they went, were disposed to regard as proper and necessary.

[60] The writer follows here the English usage rather than the American practice of restricting the term to the especially heavy migration into New England through the years following 1630. This Puritan migration, however significant in itself, was only a part of a much larger and more broadly significant movement. See especially, Arthur P. Newton, "The Great Migration, 1618–1648," in *Cambridge History of the British Empire*, I, 136–82.

CHAPTER V

VIRGINIA

TO SIR EDWIN SANDYS by election in the spring of 1619 fell the leadership of the Virginia Company in its last great effort. Son of an archbishop of York, leader in the parliamentary cause, and for many years a prominent adventurer of both the Virginia and Bermuda companies, he now proved himself to be one of the more skillful promoters in the long history of English colonization. He had an eye for order and organization, and a persuasive gift in the presentation of plans that remains after three hundred years the most impressive feature of the recorded proceedings of the company. His task was that primarily of an executive, for the major policies identified with his administration had been adopted by the adventurers in 1618. Indeed, Sir George Yeardley had sailed for the colony in November of that year with detailed instructions for the inauguration of the new policies, and at the time of Sir Edwin's election Yeardley had already taken steps to put into effect the desired political and legal reforms. The main outlines of a new economic program had also been decided upon in 1618, but there remained for Sandys the heavy responsibility of proving its practical worth.

The record offers ample proof of his very real accomplishment in shouldering this responsibility. In the three years following Sandys' election, emigration to the colony reached a figure of 3,570, thus bringing the total for the four-year period opening with 1618 to over 4,000; and more were yet to follow.[1] As an earnest

---

1 Kingsbury (ed.), *Records of The Virginia Company*, III, 546. Cf. *ibid.*, I, 351–52; III, 115–16, 239–40, 639. The last years of the company's activity may be followed in detail in Andrews, *Colonial Period of American History*, I, 118–205; Craven, *Dissolution of the Virginia Company*; Craven, *Introduction to the History of Bermuda*, 123–73.

of the company's intention to carry through with its own projects, 871 of the 1,261 persons who went out between the spring of 1619 and the summer of 1620 migrated at the company's charge or by the use of funds entrusted to its care.[2] To finance this effort Sir Edwin depended chiefly on the Virginia lottery, which he and John Ferrar, who had succeeded Alderman Johnson as deputy, promoted with such vigor that it apparently became in short time a national nuisance. At any rate, the privilege was recalled in 1621 at the request of Parliament; but not before Sandys had launched the company's program with such an impressive show of strength as to persuade many adventurers that they might safely loosen their own purse strings in support of their several proprietary projects. After 1620 the bulk of emigration to the colony represented an investment by individual or associated groups of adventurers rather than of the company itself, and by 1622 the total number of patents for private plantations had risen to fifty.[3] Included in this number was one to John Pierce under the authority of which the Pilgrim Fathers set sail for Virginia to land instead on Plymouth Rock.

These patents conferred upon the grantees rights of trade as well as an allotment of land. That the original plan of the Pilgrims to take out a small vessel for trading with the natives was not unique in its indication of a purpose to promote trade is shown by the "trucking stuff"—beads, hatchets, copper, shoes, and knives—forwarded to Virginia in 1619 by the adventurers for Berkeley Hundred.[4] Further assistance was expected from the planting of tobacco, a crop now sufficiently well established to offer assurance of some return on the investment within a year. Important as was this prospective help in persuading the adventurers to take the risk, however, tobacco by this time could provide no more than a very insecure foundation on which to base long-range plans. In 1619 the company's seven-year exemption, conceded by the royal charter, from customs duties on its goods entering England had terminated. The government promptly imposed duties expressive not merely of the financial needs of the royal treasury but also of the King's

[2] In this latter category, the fund for the Indian college was chief.

[3] Kingsbury (ed.), *Records of The Virginia Company*, III, 546. See also, *ibid.*, 118, 241, 643; IV, 210–11.

[4] *Ibid.*, III, 178–89, 196, 201.

well-known dislike of tobacco. That His Majesty was not alone in this disapproval would be pointedly revealed two years later when Parliament threatened to prohibit all importation of tobacco into England. Appeals from the Virginia and Bermuda adventurers saved the day, but the signs were clear for all to read. From 1619, negotiation of favorable terms for the import of colonial tobacco became an increasingly difficult problem.[5] Of necessity, therefore, the chief hope lay in experiments looking to the development of a wide variety of new staples.

All parties in some measure shared the effort. The records of Berkeley Hundred reveal that steps were taken there for the production of tar, pitch, hops, woad, wine, and silk, and that the plans of the adventurers included attempts to produce rice, flax, iron, silk grass, and vegetable oils.[6] But since experiment with some of these commodities required a heavy investment of time and money, there naturally fell upon the company a special obligation to take the lead and show the way. Its public estate was the logical choice for a proving ground where the major experiments could be conducted under direction of experts employed at the common charge and to which the planters could look, as to an experimental farm, for seeds, plants, and technical guidance.[7] Hence the special importance of Sir Edwin's promptness in sending out tenants for the public lands, for thereby he provided an added assurance of early success with at least some of the products to be tested.

The economic program to which Sandys devoted his closest attention, and for which he deserves chiefly to be remembered in American history, followed closely the ideas of the elder Hakluyt. Most of its objectives at one time or another had been pursued by the London adventurers in either Virginia or Bermuda, but the balance and completeness of the current effort marked it as an

[5] See especially, "Lord Sackville's Papers respecting Virginia, 1613–1631," loc. cit., 493–538, 738–65; George L. Beer, Origins of the British Colonial System, 1578–1660 (New York, 1908).

[6] Kingsbury (ed.), Records of The Virginia Company, III, 109, 178–89, 197–98, 208, 261. In addition to over forty varieties of garden seeds, the Berkeley adventurers sent out (presumably for trial) aniseed, mustard, and wheat.

[7] For an interesting parallel in instructions of 1669 from the Carolina proprietors for establishment of an experimental farm to test cotton, indigo, ginger, sugar, grapevines, and olives, see Chapter IX. Such experimental work was also a function of the public estate in Bermuda.

extraordinarily courageous endeavor to accomplish at one stroke, so to speak, well-nigh the entire Hakluyt program of settlement. A second attempt to establish an iron industry near the falls of the James received first place in Sir Edwin's plans. A total of 150 persons were sent out for the purpose within a year of his election, and the full expenditure on this project ultimately reached the sum of £5,000, a truly impressive figure for that day.[8]

In a search for the greatest possible variety of staples, attention was given to the development of other extractive industries. These were to include the production of pitch, tar, potash, and soap ashes under the guidance of Polish experts already in the colony; of gums, dyes, and such like, for which purpose apothecaries were now provided; of timber, for the cutting of which "Dutchmen" from Hamburg and sawmill equipment were sent out; and of salt, for which experts, including a Frenchman from Rochelle, were recruited. Like Hakluyt, Sandys saw an opportunity through the production of salt to gain great advantages for the colony by supply of the northern fisheries. Of special interest, too, is a project of 1621 for establishment in Virginia, with the aid of Italian experts, of a glass furnace for the manufacture principally of beads, chief stock in trade with the Indians. Further evidence that trade was still regarded as a necessary adjunct to agriculture and industry in the development of a well-balanced program appears in the dispatch from England in 1621 and 1622 of twenty-five shipwrights.

The list of agricultural commodities tried foretells the whole story of Southern agricultural experiment. Cotton was imported from both the West and East Indies. Indigo thrived, according to reports of 1622, but the colonists lacked a necessary skill to extract its profitable dye. Reports were secured from French experts on the production of olives and rice. Sugar canes, cassava roots, oranges, lemons, pineapples, and potatoes were imported from Bermuda, though there is no evidence that any of these were tested with the serious purpose that had marked earlier attempts at their cultivation in the younger colony. But nothing save good fortune was wanting in the determined effort to produce wine and silk. John

---

[8] The details of the company's program may be followed in the well-indexed volumes of Kingsbury (ed.), *Records of The Virginia Company*. In addition to secondary works already cited, see Bruce, *Economic History of Virginia*.

Bonoeil, French master of the King's experiments with silk production at Oatland, was a close consultant of the company and author of *Observations to be followed . . . to keepe Silk-wormes . . . as also, for the best manner of planting Mulberry trees to feed them.* The work, first printed in 1620, was reissued in 1622 for distribution to all the heads of families in Virginia with additional information on the production of wine and a word of encouragement and warning from the King and the Virginia Council. Bonoeil lent assistance, too, in securing men experienced in the production of both wine and silk, among them eight men from Languedoc. Silkworms were provided out of the King's own store, and additional supplies of them were secured in Valencia, France, and Italy. Vine cuttings were brought from several foreign lands, and by 1621 as many as ten thousand had been set upon the College Land alone. Though these experiments failed, some of the experts—Polish, German, French, and Italian—lived on to form a part of Virginia's basic stock.

No one of the new Virginia projects stirred wider interest than that for a college. From the bishops' appeal had come a fund of approximately £1,500, to which there was added £300 by a bequest in the will of the elder Nicholas Ferrar, the sum to be used when at least ten Indians were in residence at the college. Other gifts included a handsome communion set; St. Augustine's *City of God;* the works of "Master Perkins," popular among the Puritans; the bequest of a library valued at one hundred marks by the Reverend Thomas Bargrave; and other books and maps not catalogued. Total receipts for the college were listed in the spring of 1620 at over £2,000, a sum that may have included an anonymous gift of £550 in gold for the training of Indian youths "in the Knowledge of God and true Religion" and "in fit trades whereby honestly to live." The latter fund was separately invested, but had an obvious relation to the work of the college. For the College Land the company sent out one hundred tenants during the first year of Sandys' leadership, their command being entrusted to Captain Jabez Whitaker. These were followed by fifty more, the moiety of whose earnings was intended to provide for the training of thirty Indian youths in "true Religion and civility." Sir Edwin also moved promptly to strengthen the provision for the spiritual welfare of the colony by directing that fifty of the tenants supplied by the company should be assigned to cultivation of the glebe.[9]

Plans did not work out satisfactorily the first year, and in 1620 Captain George Thorpe, a leading member of Berkeley Hundred, was placed in charge as deputy of the College Land. Ten additional tenants were assigned to the support of this new office. Thorpe himself is one of those shadowy figures that move across the early pages of American history about whom we would like to know much more than has been discovered. As deputy, he was responsible primarily for making good the invested endowment of the college. But what is known of him indicates that he did more, that he stands first, in point of time, among those spokesmen of humanitarian and religious interests who in the colonies sought to make the record of relations between the English settlers and their Indian neighbors something other than what it became. A worthy forerunner of Father White, John Eliot, and Eleazer Wheelock, he found time to court the friendship of the natives, and especially of Powhatan's successor Opechancanough. For the latter he built an English house with a door and lock that so delighted the simple savage he was reported to have stood by the hour locking and unlocking his door.[10] Upon the colonists, suspicious and contemptuous of the Indians, he urged fair dealing and co-operation in the training of their children, so much, indeed, that he was frequently charged with responsibility for the Indian massacre of 1622, in which, ironically, he was among the first to fall. A man of remarkable energies, he seems also to have been the first to establish the possibility of producing a satisfactory alcoholic beverage from the Indian corn.

The company's plans for mission work in the colony were rounded out by the provision made in 1621 for establishment of the so-called East India School. That project had its beginning when the Reverend Patrick Copeland, chaplain of the *Royal James* on a voyage homeward from India, persuaded seamen and passengers contribute to a fund for some charitable work in Virginia. A little over seventy pounds was collected and subsequently

---

[9] Kingsbury (ed.), *Records of The Virginia Company*, I, 220, 352, 354–55; III, 115–16, 217, 226–27, 240–41, 575–76.

[10] *Ibid.*, III, 552. See also, ["Voyage of Anthony Chester"], in *William and Mary College Quarterly*, IX (1900–1901), 203–14; Smyth of Nibley Papers, 43.

turned over to the Virginia Company, which in the fall of 1621 decided that it should be used to establish a "publique free schoole" in the colony. Among the reasons advanced for this decision was the prospect that it would save the planters from the necessity of sending their children to England for schooling. The stipulation that the school "should have dependance upon the Colledge in Virginia which should be made capable to receave Schollers from the Shoole into such Scollershipps and fellowshipps as the said Colledge shalbe endowed withall for the advancement of schollers as they arise by degres and deserts in learninge" leaves no doubt that, by this date at least, the college was intended to be something more than a mere Indian school.[11] Anonymous gifts of twenty-five and thirty pounds were added to the original fund, and passengers on board two other vessels of the East India Company subsequently contributed an additional sixty-six pounds. Once again, the sum was invested in Virginia land by sending out tenants for its development. The adventurers ordered one thousand acres set aside in Charles City for the purpose, and in 1622 sent out seven persons to work the land for support of the schoolmaster and usher who were to follow.

While continued misfortunes of the sort that had beset all English efforts in Virginia prevented the actual establishment of either college or school, the adventurers' plans nevertheless merit serious attention. Not only does the action taken suggest that earlier professions of humanitarian aims should be treated with more respect than at times they have been accorded, but it lends emphasis again, especially in the decision to provide educational opportunities for children of the colonists, to the extraordinarily ambitious objectives English colonizers had set for themselves in America. To look only at what they were able to accomplish is to lose sight of the full vision they followed. And there is a useful lesson in the company's approach to the problem of establishing a college, for it was representative of views that governed the action of leaders, from the elder Hakluyt to Sir Edwin Sandys, in their approach to the larger problem of settlement. Hardheaded men of affairs as well as dream-

---

[11] Kingsbury (ed.), *Records of The Virginia Company*, I, 538–41; III, 537–40, 576, 640, 642; Edward D. Neill, *Memoir of Patrick Copeland, Rector Elect of the First Projected College in the United States* (New York, 1871).

ers of great dreams, they had a way of putting first things first. So fundamental to the achievement of their objectives in America was the establishment of the colony's material prosperity on the secure foundation of a profitable list of staple commodities that they tended in their planning to make all else depend upon a variety of economic experiments offering the hope, as the elder Hakluyt had said, of "incredible things, and by few as yet dreamed of." Brickmakers were sent in preparation for the construction of college buildings, a schoolmaster was engaged, and provision was made for supply of the necessary books. But with the failure of the company's program of economic development all was lost, save the idea that schools and missionary endeavor, like certain legal guarantees and advanced concepts of self-government, had a proper place in the life of an American community.

It is not difficult to explain the tragic failure of Sir Edwin's program for the colony's development. The program itself, which called for heavy investments in a number of highly speculative ventures, was too ambitious and altogether out of proportion to the financial resources available for its continued support. The principal source of the company's income had been the Virginia lottery. After the government's recall of that privilege Sandys and Deputy John Ferrar found no really adequate substitute, although they showed ingenuity in the promotion of special stocks for particular projects and in their resort to other devices. Nor does the record indicate that any substantial part of the proceeds from the lottery, or of such a fund as that for the college, had been held in reserve. Like other leaders of early English settlement, Sir Edwin's responsibility was largely that of a promoter, and he used the funds at hand accordingly.[12] With the hope of encouraging individual investment in the colony by the adventurers, he gambled boldly with the company's funds and allowed himself to be tempted into overhasty action. Close figuring on requirements of supply, on prospects for an early return from investment, and on such details as the number of passengers that could safely be carried in ships

[12] The decision to invest the college fund in the development of a plantation undoubtedly reflected in part the limited funds available from other sources for underwriting the company's several projects. It should be noted that the College Land seems to have been a main center for the experiment with the production of wine.

sailing for Virginia left him entirely too dependent on good fortune. He thus invited the penalties of overcrowded shipping, of inadequate preparation in the colony, and of a consequent disarrangement of carefully laid plans. Misunderstanding and mutual discontent between leaders at home and in the colony developed within the first two years of Sandys' administration of the company's affairs.[13] Yeardley, accordingly, was displaced at the end of his three-year term in 1621 by Sir Francis Wyatt, whose instructions directed that he immediately put into effect plans and policies theretofore imperfectly followed.[14] Special concern over lack of progress in efforts to develop new and more profitable staples led to the appointment of George Sandys, brother to Sir Edwin, as treasurer of the colony with responsibility chiefly for the furtherance of all such projects.

Wyatt and Sandys were hardly settled in their new posts when the colony fell victim to the great Indian massacre of March, 1622. The Indians had become alarmed at the growing numbers of the English; the planters had been thrown off their guard after several years of peace and much talk of a great missionary effort. Taking advantage of the dispersed settlement which characterized the colony's development after 1618, the natives fell upon the unsuspecting colonists with savage brutality and killed no less than 347 persons. Even more serious was the consequent disorganization of the colony's life. It was necessary to withdraw from many points to positions of greater safety. Facilities became overcrowded. Stores and equipment had been lost. At the very beginning of the planting season, men had to drop their tools in order to stand guard or to join in punitive expeditions against the foe. Stark tragedy, such as had not been faced since 1610, was the prospect for the coming winter unless the company came promptly to the colony's aid. But this the company, its treasury long since empty, was unable adequately to do. It did what it could, but no less an authority than George Sandys estimated that an additional five hundred

[13] Because of the King's insistence, Sir Edwin was not re-elected in 1620, when the Earl of Southampton succeeded him as treasurer, but Sandys remained the guiding spirit of the company.

[14] Kingsbury (ed.), *Records of The Virginia Company*, III, 468–91. It is to this action that we are indebted for a record of some of the most important policies adopted in 1618.

146

persons died in the year following the massacre. A census taken early in 1624 showed a total population for the colony of only 1,275 persons.[15] Approximately four thousand people had emigrated to Virginia since 1618, at the close of which year the colonists had numbered perhaps a thousand. Meanwhile, some of these had returned home to England in disappointment and disgust. Even when making an allowance for them, however, it is difficult to avoid the conclusion that the colony had suffered a mounting death rate, in the end not far short of three out of four for the five-year period extending from the spring of 1619 to the spring of 1624.

That fact in itself more than justified the investigation of the company's affairs undertaken by the English government in 1623. Since the beginning of the preceding year the company's difficulties had multiplied, at home hardly less than in the colony. News of the massacre had forced upon leaders a further postponement of hopes for profitable staples other than tobacco, and gave new urgency to a financial problem in which the central and inescapable fact was that tobacco alone offered any immediate prospect of a return on investment. Continuation of efforts both public and private, even of those projects designed to supplant it as the colony's staple, clearly depended upon an advantageous market for this weed that so readily took root in soil where more desirable commodities perversely withered and died. More urgent than ever before was the necessity of negotiating favorable terms for its importation into England. Consequently, during the summer following the massacre leaders at home had concentrated primarily on problems of the market. In behalf of the Virginia and Bermuda companies (Sandys' partisans had captured control of the younger company in 1621) they negotiated a contract with the government for a farm of the royal customs collected on tobacco imports. That is to say, they agreed to meet the King's demand for a revenue from this source in return for a monopolistic control of all tobacco brought into England. Such a contract, of course, touched directly the interest of most adventurers in American plantations, including many of the

---

[15] *Ibid.*, IV, 65, 71, 74; W. Noël Sainsbury (ed.), *Calendar of State Papers, Colonial Series, 1574–1660* (London, 1860), 43, 57. See also, Sir Francis Wyatt's testimony that not all of the company's troubles could be attributed directly to the massacre, in *William and Mary College Quarterly*, 2d ser., VI (1926), 114–21.

heavier investors in Bermuda who, like the Earl of Warwick and Sir Nathaniel Rich, were already ranged in opposition to Sir Edwin's management of that enterprise. Objections were entered and pressed amidst a growing feeling fed by old hatreds that in some instances extended back to the quarrels of 1617.

By the spring of 1623 the factional quarrels of the Virginia and Bermuda adventurers had become a public scandal. At that point news of the colony's fate following the massacre reached England. Quick to seize the advantage offered, Sandys' opponents petitioned for a full investigation by the Privy Council. The fact that the King's council included men in no way reluctant to injure Sir Edwin does not alter the no less well-established fact that the investigation was needed.

The affairs of both companies, by proceedings that are best compared to a receivership, were placed in the hands of a special commission headed by Sir William Jones. Public hearings brought out unmistakable evidence that the Virginia Company was hopelessly divided, that its colonists were facing a desperate situation, and that it, moreover, was bankrupt. Perhaps as much as £100,000 had been expended in its successive joint-stock ventures; unless the many obligations of the company were to stand as a charge on the colony for years to come, thereby retarding its development, they would have to be written off the books. There was no effective way of doing this except by complete dissolution of the company, an action accomplished by order of the court of King's Bench in 1624.[16] The dissolution occasioned bitter debate at the time and has been since then the subject of scholarly controversy, but, after all is said, it must be judged as essentially an attempt to save the colony from further penalties of the company's past mistakes and misfortunes. While the decision was pending, the colonists experienced some apprehension over the possible loss of political privileges enjoyed under the company's liberal policy. For a few years thereafter they probably would have welcomed any plan for the revival of the company that promised substantial relief of the colony's many urgent needs. When the immediate crisis passed, however, experience already had shown that the agencies of royal rule were much

---

[16] The record of this action and of the events leading up to it may be followed in Kingsbury (ed.), *Records of The Virginia Company,* II, IV.

less vigilant than had been the company. And so, counting upon time to provide a full guarantee of the political privileges of the colony, the planters thereafter vigorously opposed all suggestions that a proprietary authority be re-established over them.

Almost two decades after the fall of the company fear of its revival remained a potent factor in the colony's political life. That this should have been true is in itself indication enough of the English government's failure to reach a prompt and definitive settlement of the problem presented it by the collapse of the London Company. But the subject merits more than passing attention, for it lies at the very heart of Virginia's history in one of the colony's most significant transitional periods.

Despite the inexperience of a government which heretofore had assumed for the most part a negative role in the work of settlement,[17] the King's ministers in 1624 moved with reasonable promptness to a clear statement of fundamental policy. Immediate authority over the colony and instructions to provide for a permanent settlement of its affairs were given in July of that year to a special commission headed by Lord President Henry Mandeville.[18] Before a final disposition of the problem had been made, however, the powers of the Mandeville Commission were terminated by the death of James I, and in the spring of 1625 the whole question of Virginia was redebated before the privy councilors. It was then that the Sandys faction, in a plea for re-establishment of the company's charter, submitted its well-known "Discourse of the Old Company," [19] but the experience of the two preceding years argued too strongly against such an action. Instead, the privy councilors concluded, in a decision regarded as of such general significance as to warrant its announcement in the form of a royal proclamation, that powers of government in the colony properly depended upon the crown and should "not be committed to any Company or Corporation, to whom it may be proper to trust matters of Trade and Commerce, but cannot bee fit or safe to communicate the ordering of State Affairs be they of never so Meane Consequence." [20]

---

[17] Notice the tendency, as in the appointment of a special committee of Chichester, Carew, and Grandison in 1623 to advise on the government of Virginia, to rely on experience gained in the administration of Ireland. *Cal. St. Pap., Col., 1574–1660*, p. 50.

[18] Kingsbury (ed.), *Records of The Virginia Company*, IV, 490–97.

[19] *Ibid.*, 519–51.   [20] Thomas Rymer, *Foedera* (London, 1726–1735), XVIII, 72.

To that principle the King's ministers would hold, at least insofar as Virginia was concerned. But broad and sweeping as were the implications of the statement, it actually covered no more than half the problem. Among the heavier charges of colonization, as any old adventurer could tell, were those for the support of government. Immediate and repeated requests from the colony for financial assistance in the re-establishment of its peace and security emphasized the obvious need of a new capital investment.[21] Nothing in the proclamation, however, indicates that the English government in King Charles's day was any more willing than it had been in Queen Elizabeth's to contribute from its own funds; nor do other records offer any such evidence. It would appear, then, that there was no recourse but to fall back on the plan of 1606, with a royal council holding ultimate authority over the colony and a reorganized company of adventurers enjoying rights with reference to Virginia's land and trade that would serve to encourage new investments of capital. Such a plan, at any rate, became the favored solution of the problem, and under the circumstances it was perhaps the best that could be offered. But there were difficulties which had received pointed emphasis in the recent argument of Sandys' partisans before the Privy Council that the question of government properly depended on the question of who was to bear the cost, and a nice problem it was. Since men were unlikely to invest heavily when they were uncertain as to the policies affecting the security of the investment, how was the necessary assurance to be provided without at the same time destroying the reality of royal control?

While the King's ministers hesitated in the face of that question, their mismanagement in other fields led the country into a disastrous war. Political difficulties mounted, and through years marked by increasing controversy between King and Parliament questions of colonial government became relatively unimportant. Already the Bermuda Company had been permitted to re-establish its control of the Somers Islands. The situation in the younger company had differed from that in the older: its factional divisions represented differences rooted principally in the quarrels of the Vir-

21 Kingsbury (ed.), *Records of The Virginia Company*, IV, 568–69, 571–74; *Cal. St. Pap., Col., 1574–1660*, pp. 76, 88; *Virginia Magazine of History and Biography* (Richmond), II (1894–1895), 50–55, 369–72.

ginia courts, its people had escaped the disasters visited upon the
Jamestown planters, and once more the Bermuda colony had a
population exceeding that of Virginia. It is true that ambitious
schemes for the production of silk, sugar, and wine had met with
complete failure, but the colonization of Bermuda had been under-
written largely by privately invested capital; individual adventurers rather than the company had absorbed the major part of the
loss sustained. Since 1620 the adventurers had put their land chiefly
to tobacco. The company's debt was relatively small, and in providing for the retirement of that indebtedness it had not been difficult for the more substantial investors to reassert their control of
the court.

No action was taken against the Bermuda charter itself, and any
apprehension that may have been occasioned by the royal proclamation regarding the government of Virginia seems to have been set
at rest by the passage of time. For sixty years yet the Somers Islands
Company would continue to serve as the governing authority over
Bermuda.[22] Moreover, a proprietary patent was issued in 1627 to
James Hay, Earl of Carlisle, for the infant West Indian plantations. In 1629 the Massachusetts Bay Company received a royal charter that was in no essential different from the one formerly enjoyed by the Virginia Company. The next year a similar charter
was granted the Providence Island Company. Perhaps only the
bitter factionalism which divided the Virginia adventurers prevented an early reincorporation of the London Company with
all its former powers. But whatever the case, the war closed with
Virginia's problem having received as yet no formal disposition.

A new commission for settlement of the question was appointed
in 1631. It had nothing more to offer, however, than recommendations for the re-establishment in England of a royal council and of
a newly chartered Virginia Company with rights and responsibilities falling principally in the field of the colony's economic development.[23] Opposition to revival of the company, which included
representations from the Virginia Assembly, proved strong enough

[22] For Bermuda's place in the controversies of 1623 and 1624, see Craven, *Introduction to the History of Bermuda;* Andrews, *Colonial Period of American History,*
I, Chaps. VII–IX.

[23] *Virginia Magazine,* VIII (1900–1901), 29, 36–39.

to prevent adoption of the plan, but the victory was definitely of a negative character.[24] The issue remained alive for another decade, during which the attitude of the colonists toward proposals for the company's revival hardened into bitter opposition. That opposition expressed, among other things, a growing concern for property rights established since 1624 which might be called into question by restoration of the company's proprietary title. The colonists, accordingly, countered by requesting a royal charter of their own. Such a charter would serve not only as an effective bar to revival of the company, but for protection against such further encroachments as had been witnessed in the grant of Carolina to Robert Heath in 1629 and of Maryland to Lord Baltimore in 1632.[25]

The demand for re-establishment of the Virginia Company came largely from those adventurers who through the last storm-ridden years of the company had followed the factional leadership of Sir Edwin Sandys, and it was none other than Sir Edwin's brother, George Sandys, who next brought the issue to the fore. He had been commissioned by the Virginia Assembly of 1639 to make certain representations in its behalf at London. Whether because of misunderstanding or for some other reason—the Assembly later charged deliberate misrepresentation—he was instrumental in bringing before the House of Commons a petition for the company's revival so couched as to indicate that the colonists desired it. Sir William Berkeley, who had been designated governor in 1641, arrived in Virginia the following year as bearer of a new assurance from the crown that the company would not be revived and as the first of a long line of royal governors to claim a special reward for services rendered the colony prior to departure from England. A grateful Assembly that spring presented him an orchard and two houses, and spread on the record in the form of a statute a strongly worded statement of its objections to the company's restoration. Disowning the action of George Sandys, the Assembly proclaimed that any settler who thereafter supported such a move would be re-

[24] See especially, William W. Hening, *The Statutes at Large; Being a Collection of all the Laws of Virginia, from the First Session of the Legislature, in the Year 1619* (Richmond, 1810–1823), I, 231.

[25] See below, pp. 188–90.

garded as an enemy of the colony and become liable to confiscation of his entire estate.[26]

As these developments indicate, some of the more fundamental questions raised by the dissolution of the Virginia Company remained a subject of debate eighteen years afterward. Through the intervening period proposals to establish a superior council in London were usually joined to plans for a revival of the company, with the result that rejection of the latter proposal brought postponement of action on the other. Since anything more than a tentative decision on governmental problems in Virginia seemed inadvisable until the superior authority to be established in England had been determined, the colony was left dependent upon year to year decisions regarding the management of its affairs. And in the end, it was decided simply to let stand what had been established by custom and usage.

In attempting to trace the development under these circumstances of a pattern of royal government, principal emphasis is due the continuity of practice which joined in a single story the periods falling before and after 1624. The King had taken over at a time of grave emergency in the colony. Its already serious condition had been further aggravated by the unsettling influences attending the dissolution of the company. Indeed, the Virginia Assembly, meeting in the spring of 1624, had been sufficiently concerned for the internal peace of the community to enact a statute providing that "no person within this Colonie uppon the rumor of supposed change and alteratione presume to be disobedient to the presente Government, nor servants to theire privatt officers masters or overseers, at their uttermost perills." [27] Authorities in England were hardly less alert to the dangers of an "interregnum." Consequently, the Mandeville Commission in its first action was guided chiefly by a desire to remove promptly disturbing uncertainties as to the basis and extent of public authority in the colony. This it sought to accomplish by forwarding a royal commission to Governor Wyatt and a council of eleven men, of whom five were of the former council, authorizing them to act together "as fully

---

[26] Hening, *Statutes*, I, 230–36, 267; Force (comp.), *Tracts*, II, No. 6.

[27] Kingsbury (ed.), *Records of The Virginia Company*, IV, 584.

and ampley as anie Governor and Councell resident there at anie tyme within the space of five yeares now last past." [28]

Upon Wyatt's retirement Sir George Yeardley received in 1626 a similar commission, explaining that the King, "being forced by many other urgent occasions in respect of his late access to the crown," would continue the existing government until he "should find some more convenient means upon mature advice to give more ample directions for the same." [29] Sir John Harvey, the next governor sent out from England, was authorized in 1628 to execute his office as fully as any governor there resident within the preceding three years.[30] And so it went. A comparison of Yeardley's instructions in 1626 with those issued to Sir Francis Wyatt in 1639 and to Sir William Berkeley in 1641 reveals that not only were royal instructions to the governor based in the first instance on instructions previously issued by the company to its own governors, but that these royal instructions became over a sixteen-year period in no small part stereotyped.[31]

Little change occurred in the composition, organization, or position of the governor's council, except for a certain extension of its power traceable to a failure of the King's ministers to maintain the same alert oversight of its actions as had the company. The rule of the company's later days binding the governor by a majority vote of the council, with a casting vote in case of a tie, was continued.[32] As before, the council held the authority to fill temporarily vacancies in the governor's chair arising from death or other cause by election, a right exercised no less than three times within a decade of the company's fall. Governor and council continued to act as the chief administrative agency of the colony, to sit in quarterly sessions as a superior court, and to join with the burgesses in forming a general assembly.

The transition, however, was not without its difficulties. Governor Harvey became involved in a long controversy with the council. Though precipitated largely by Harvey's poor judgment

[28] *Ibid.*, 501–504.

[29] Quoted in Andrews, *Colonial Period of American History,* I, 196.

[30] *Cal. St. Pap., Col., 1574–1660,* p. 88.

[31] *Virginia Magazine,* II (1894–1895), 393–96; XI (1903–1904), 54–57; II, 281–88.

[32] Kingsbury (ed.), *Records of The Virginia Company,* III, 480, 483; *Virginia Magazine,* II (1894–1895), 282.

and ill temper, the dispute had an additional cause. The joining of governor and council in one commission with provision for majority rule presented, in the absence of the company's former and close superintendence, a very real question as to the extent of the governor's independent powers. Harvey insisted on his prerogative as lieutenant of the King, while the councilors, in actions indicative of their role as representatives of colonial sentiment, were no less insistent on the letter of the commission. With the aid of an irregular assembly, Harvey was sent home in 1635. Authorities in England responded chiefly by sending him back the next year, an action which served as an effective reminder that he was indeed, whatever else might be said, the King's lieutenant.[33]

The event, however, resulted in no radical alteration of the governor's position. Harvey's conduct, both before and after his return, was of the sort to emphasize the wisdom in the company's decision to use the council as a restraint on arbitrary action by the governor; and happier choices, of Wyatt in 1639 and of Berkeley in 1641, proved the practicability of a common commission. The council came to accept the fact that it had no existence apart from the governor. Theoretically, its members were appointed by the crown, but actually and from an early date the governor's choice ruled. On the other hand, the governor was bound by a majority vote on all important decisions, shared with the council control over patronage, and did not even possess an independent power to remove his advisers.[34] A gradually forming community of economic and political interest between the governor and his councilors completed the transition to a smoothly functioning agency of colonial government.

Further difficulties arose in providing for the support of the colony's officers and for other public charges. The plan of 1618 had

---

[33] The details of the story may be followed in Thomas J. Wertenbaker, *Virginia under the Stuarts* (Princeton, 1914), 60–84.

[34] Although the standard authority, Philip A. Bruce, *Institutional History of Virginia in the Seventeenth Century* (New York, 1910), has the common fault of its time in an analytical and topical treatment of the subject that is better suited to the interest of the political scientist than of the historian, it is nevertheless a study to which repeated reference must be made. The early records of the council, unfortunately incomplete, may be consulted in Henry R. McIlwaine (ed.), *Minutes of the Council and General Court of Colonial Virginia, 1622–1632, 1670–1676* (Richmond, 1924).

been to relieve the settlers of this burden through the returns from a public estate. But that hopeful project had failed to serve its purpose even under the company, despite a surprisingly large number of tenants sent out for the public lands after 1619 and an adjustment of the scheme to provide a more effective oversight of their labors through allotment of a specified acreage and number of tenants to each of the major offices.

Public tenants died as easily as did other colonists, and a system of half-share tenancy offered little encouragement, especially in the absence of extraordinarily valuable staples, for either party to the sharing.[35] Officers, in fact, frequently elected to hire out their tenants, who thus formed the first considerable body of wage laborers available to the planters. Some of these tenants still had time to serve under their contracts after the dissolution of the company, as did also at least thirty-seven general tenants of the company who in the fall of 1626 were distributed among the leading officers of the colony with eighteen of them assigned to the governor.[36] The crown, however, proved no more willing than had the company in its later days been able to provide replacements. Just exactly what thereafter became of the land allotted for a public estate cannot be said. Fragmentary evidence indicates that in some instances at least it remained attached for a time to the office to which it had been assigned and was possibly turned to some advantage by successive incumbents, while in other instances it was leased on terms providing a small revenue for public charges.[37] Whatever the full story of its surviving remnants, the public estate itself quickly became of such slight importance in the life of Virginia that few of her historians have even bothered to understand its place in the earlier plan of settlement.

[35] See George Sandys on the subject, in Kingsbury (ed.), *Records of The Virginia Company,* IV, 74; and III, 472, on rearrangements of the scheme between 1618 and 1621.

[36] *Virginia Magazine,* XXVII (1919), 148–49; McIlwaine (ed.), *Minutes of the Council,* 154; Edward D. Neill, *Virginia Carolorum* (Albany, 1886), 14 n., 17 n.

[37] See abstracts of land patents, in *Virginia Magazine,* II (1894–1895), 68, 77–80, 310–11; *William and Mary College Quarterly,* IX (1900–1901), 86; and for a 99-year lease of 675 acres of the governor's land given Phillip Ludwell in the eighteenth century by Governor Dinwiddie at 37 barrels of corn annually, *Virginia Magazine,* V (1897–1898), 245–48. See also, *Cal. St. Pap., Col., 1574–1660,* p. 263; Bruce, *Economic History of Virginia,* I, 412–13; Bruce, *Institutional History of Virginia,* II, 341.

Where the charge would fall already had been made clear. Complaints, as early as 1621, of exorbitant fees exacted from the settlers indicated the imperfect execution of the company's plan for a public estate and foretold its total collapse. Failure of the plan would fasten upon the colonists, in addition to an elaborate system of fees, the necessity of paying taxes as did other men.[38] When, through the years after 1624, the colonists took up almost the full burden of the public charge, they relied chiefly for relief on other forms of compensation for public service than financial. Witness the effort, both conscious and unconscious, to make the badge of office a mark of honor and standing in the community. This, of course, was by no means new, for the custom reflected a need felt by all societies, and one felt, as already noted, with a special keenness midst the primitive conditions of an infant community. But the consistency with which members of the council after 1624 received the courtesy designation of esquire seems so unmistakable an example of the borrowing of a mark of social distinction in the old country for reward of public service in the new as to merit special notice.[39] It is not strange that the traditions of the later South should have emphasized the public responsibility that went with social position, for from the earliest days the assumption of that responsibility constituted a first claim to social distinction.

Nor is it strange that the resulting political control should have been open to abuse. In addition to the plain facts of human nature, there was a background of custom having its origin in the peculiar needs and limitations of early colonial days. For a while after 1624 it is doubtful that members of the council received any compensation other than the opportunity afforded them, as men selected from the more substantial planters, to protect a common interest. And if some of them used the advantage of their position to extend in one way or another their stake in the community, it should be remembered that a land grant was the oldest form of reward in Virginia, and that it was natural to use land, the colony's major

---

[38] Kingsbury (ed.), *Records of The Virginia Company*, III, 478, 490.

[39] This seems to have been an invariable custom from the first royal commission in 1624. For evidence of the need of some additional inducement, see a letter of 1623 by George Sandys, in Kingsbury (ed.), *Records of The Virginia Company*, IV, 110–11.

asset, to subsidize public services.[40] It appears that for a time during the following years the governor and his councilors held a monopoly of Indian trade in the Chesapeake. Later, it was provided by royal instruction and act of assembly in 1639 that each councilor should enjoy for himself and ten servants exemption from all public levies.[41] In years to come, when the rewards of the office were greater, the practice was regarded as an abuse, but at the time of adoption it is best viewed perhaps as a policy well suited to the primitive economy of the community.

The charges falling upon the governor were naturally far heavier than those of any other office. Not until 1641 did the colony possess a Statehouse, and nine years earlier Harvey complained that so much of the public business was transacted at his residence in Jamestown, "where is no other hospitalitie for all commers," that he might "be as well called the hoste as gouvernor of Virginia." [42] The problem, indeed, was especially acute under Harvey, for little could have remained of the former provision for the governor's support except the land and perhaps a few head of cattle. In response to his repeated complaints, and in addition to an allowance for transportation to his post and the proceeds of all fines, he was allowed by the crown, possibly as early as 1634, £1,000 a year as salary, the allotment apparently to come out of the customs on Virginia tobacco.[43] This placed the cost on the colonists, but by a form of indirect taxation assuring to the chief executive a desirable independence.

He enjoyed, however, no such independence with reference to the ordinary revenues of his government. The crown obviously had been reluctant to part even with the funds necessary for the governor's support, and for relief of the colony's other financial needs proved willing to entertain only the suggestion that new capital might be enlisted through reincorporation of the company. When

40 For examples suggesting this use, see *Cal. St. Pap., Col., 1574–1660*, p. 185; *Virginia Magazine*, II (1894–1895), 421; III (1895–1896), 280–81.

41 McIlwaine (ed.), *Minutes of the Council*, 479; *Virginia Magazine*, XI (1903–1904), 55; Hening, *Statutes*, I, 228; *William and Mary College Quarterly*, 2d ser., IV (1924), 157. The last indicates enjoyment of certain exemptions theretofore.

42 *Virginia Magazine*, VIII (1900–1901), 150.

43 *Ibid.*, VII (1899–1900), 370, 371, 372–73, 378; *Cal. St. Pap., Col., 1574–1660*, pp. 221, 273–74, 276.

that project failed to materialize, the colonists were left to bear their own common charges, and to make the best of a situation in which the principal opportunity was to turn an economic disadvantage into a political advantage. The inclination of the colonists had been unmistakably indicated as early as 1624, when the assembly faced a problem of public charges that had been reopened by failure of the public estate and aggravated by the calamities befalling the colony after the massacre. That problem presented no mere question of taxes, but involved the governor's right to call men to labor on public projects, to summon them or their tenants for guard duty, and to control fees for official services rendered. The planters, in view of assurances given them in 1618, were in an unusually strong position, and among several enactments asserting their right to distribute a now inescapable common burden, the most significant declared that "the Governor shall not laye any taxes or impositiones uppon the Colony, theire landes or comodities otherwise then by the awthoritie of the generall Assemblie, to be levied and imployed as the saide Assembly shall appoint." [44] The act lends added significance to the colonists' petition this same year that they might retain the liberty of their general assembly, "than which nothing can more conduce to our satisfaction or the public utilitie." [45]

In the end, the right of taxation, along with the older privileges of petition and legislation, would be conceded to the Virginia Assembly. But for a time there was some uncertainty as to whether the Assembly would be permitted to survive the company, a fact re-emphasizing the importance of the English commercial corporation to the origins of representative government in America. The primary explanation is probably to be found in nothing more than the general uncertainty that currently overhung the whole question of Virginia's government. The long-popular view that the existence of the Assembly had been a major factor in bringing the company into disrepute with the government has been ex-

[44] Kingsbury (ed.), *Records of The Virginia Company*, IV, 581. The parallel story of the Bermuda Assembly, where an earlier failure of plans for the public estate had brought this question to the fore, should be noted. See Craven, *Introduction to the History of Bermuda*, 133–47.

[45] Henry R. McIlwaine (ed.), *Journals of the House of Burgesses of Virginia, 1619–1658/59* (Richmond, 1915), 27.

ploded. There were those among the King's ministers, it is true, who doubted the wisdom of committing colonial administration to a popular body. Such a body had been the general court of the Virginia Company, where party divisions and tumultous, almost riotous, sessions had persuaded many observers to reject "democraticall" rule by many voices. The alternative to which they were disposed to turn is shown in plans for vesting control in a relatively small council of responsible men. There may well have been some doubt in the minds of the privy councilors as to how suitable to this plan of control in England would be a scheme in the colony marked by a rather wide distribution of powers. In any case, it was natural that a decision on the question should be postponed until the superior authority in England had been more exactly determined.

The Assembly found no place in the royal commission to Wyatt in 1624. Though it met in an irregular "convention" in 1625 to formulate petitions to the crown, including another for its own revival, Yeardley, who carried the petitions to England, returned the year after with only a vague assurance of "all such reasonable privileges as they have formerly enjoyed." [46] Not until 1629 was the body to reassemble with anything like the powers held under the company, and for ten years thereafter its position was marked by uncertainty.

The initial steps toward its revival were more closely related to economic than to strictly political considerations. The principal change in the economic life of the colony through the early royal period came in the disappearance, for the most part, of absentee ownership. The colonists' servitude to tobacco remained unbroken, and problems of marketing were but slightly altered. The task of establishing credit in the English market proved, with increased production and falling prices, as difficult as had the earlier dual necessity of establishing that credit and at the same time repaying the English adventurers. The government's attitude toward, and its relationship to, the problem also remained essentially unchanged. Indeed, the earnest efforts of the company through its last years to provide substitutes for tobacco reflected in no small

[46] The best discussion of the Assembly's history in relation to the fall of the company is in Andrews, *Colonial Period of American History*, I, 180–205.

160

part the government's insistence that its continued sanction of colonial projects depended upon a true service of the national interest. The King's officers now, as had so recently the company's agents, urged upon the planters the need for a variety of approved staples. Confronted by the depressing failure of the company's effort and the perplexing problem of how to finance another, they also showed a certain disposition to emphasize anew the possible rewards of exploration for the Northwest Passage.[47] As before, royal imposts on tobacco imports were based on the twofold consideration of the King's financial needs and a disinclination to encourage its production.

The difference was in those with whom the government now had to deal. Heretofore, contracts for importation of Virginia's tobacco had been arranged between the King's fiscal officers, or farmers holding a monopoly under royal grant, and the London adventurers acting through their designated officers. Now, not only was the company gone, but the individual adventurers had for the most part lost an active interest in their Virginia dividends. The story may be briefly summarized in the fate befalling Berkeley Hundred, a plantation undertaken in 1619 by John Smyth of Nibley, Sir William Throckmorton, Richard Berkeley, and George Thorpe. At a cost of no less than £2,000 the adventurers had sent out over ninety persons in 1619 and 1620, of which number almost two thirds are listed in the papers of Smyth as dead at an early date. Eleven, including Thorpe himself, were killed in the massacre, and by the summer of 1622 only nineteen of their servants remained alive and in the colony.[48] Some of these continued as residents of Virginia, but their term of service, normally three to seven years, soon expired, and of this once hopeful project there soon remained only the land and a few head of cattle. The adventurers in 1632 considered plans for a modest revival of their project by

[47] The company itself, contemplating the failure of its expensive projects, had also been disposed to turn to the old idea of aid through some major discovery. Kingsbury (ed.), *Records of The Virginia Company*, III, 541, 547–48, 572–75, 642; IV, 109, 166, 237. See also, Neill, *Virginia Carolorum*, 52, 104.

[48] Kingsbury (ed.), *Records of The Virginia Company*, III, 196, 197–99, 213, 230, 260, 292, 385, 392, 396–97, 404, 405, 426, 567, 619, 674; IV, 79. The Smyth of Nibley Papers provide an unusually valuable record of this type of project. Miss Kingsbury has published those falling within the company's period.

sending out a half-dozen men on agreement with two of their former servants, but by 1636 they had sold out to a group of London merchants.[49]

Southampton Hundred had gone the same way. Its associates asserted in 1635 that for an investment of over £6,000 they had "nothing left but a stock of cattle." [50] Martin's Hundred, located some seven miles from Jamestown and below modern Williamsburg, had been virtually wiped out by the massacre, seventy-eight persons being killed there on that ill-fated March day. The project survived principally as a title in mortmain obstructing the colony's natural development. In the interest of the community the title was in time set aside, and the associates were left with only individual claims to allotments of land in proportion to their original investment in the company's joint stock.[51] Records of the land office suggest that such claims, if not entirely forgotten, were largely disposed of on easy terms to persons planning to settle in Virginia.[52] Residents of England, and especially merchants engaged in the Virginia tobacco trade, acquired and even developed plantations in the colony through the years that followed. But such absentee owners became the exception rather than the rule. From 1624 the real Virginia adventurer was the planter in Virginia.

His was the land, his the tobacco, and it was with him that the King's ministers now had to deal in matters pertaining to the importation of Virginia tobacco. Development of the government's policy may be followed in detail in George L. Beer's able analysis.[53] Here perhaps it will be sufficient to note that a distinguishing feature of that policy was an attempt to enlist the co-operation of the planter with plans which admitted his immediate dependence on tobacco but looked toward his ultimate emancipation from that dependence. When seeking co-operation of this sort, the company had resorted to a representative assembly, and so, now, did the King. In William W. Hening's *Statutes* are recorded an unbroken succession of laws seeking, in accordance first with the company's instructions and then with recommendations

[49] Smyth of Nibley Papers, 40, 41, 42; *Virginia Magazine*, VI (1898–1899), 185.
[50] *Virginia Magazine*, VIII (1900–1901), 401–402.   [51] See below, pp. 173–74.
[52] For example, *Virginia Magazine*, III (1895–1896), 177; IV (1896–1897), 315; VI (1898–1899), 189, 194.
[53] Beer, *Origins of the British Colonial System*, 134 ff.

from the King, to limit the production of tobacco and to promote the planting of mulberries, vines, hemp, flax, and other useful commodities. No one can read through these laws without recognizing that representative government in America owes much in its origins to an attempt to win men's support of a common economic program by means of mutual consent. The first assembly to meet under authority from the King convened early in 1628 to consider proposed arrangements for the importation of tobacco and recommendations for the promotion of other staples. The assembly apparently confined its activities to that one function, and represented in no full sense a revival of the older privilege.

Another step toward its revival, however, is marked by an assembly which met in October, 1629. For several years theretofore the colonists had sought royal assistance in solving certain urgent problems of defense. And now, in lieu of that aid, they were authorized to meet in assembly for action on a proposal, advanced some five years before, to clear the natives out of the lower Peninsula and to construct a defensive pale running across from Jamestown to the York.[54] The subject under consideration was again limited, but it touched upon several matters of broad significance: defense, native policy, title to the land, and the imposition of a common burden. Still another step was taken upon Governor Harvey's arrival the next spring with instructions authorizing a "grand assembly" to "set downe an establishment of the Government, and ordaine lawes & orders for the good thereof, and those to send hither to receive allowance, and such as shall be soe allowed to be returned thither . . . and put in execucon, the same to be temporary & changeable at his majesty's pleasure." [55] Whether that instruction was regarded as anything more than authorization to call one special assembly for the purpose of canvassing colonial sentiment on the unsettled problem of the colony's government is open to question. Certainly the careful phrasing suggests that there was no intention of prejudicing the freedom of action of His Majesty's advisers when opportunity should arise for a final decision.

But important precedents for consultation on special occasions

---

[54] For the origins of this project, see *Virginia Magazine*, II (1894–1895), 51–52; Kingsbury (ed.), *Records of The Virginia Company*, IV, 103.

[55] *Virginia Magazine*, VII (1899–1900), 371.

had been established, and the colonists had a strong will to self-government. There was hardly a man who came to America, from the early days of the company on, who was not soon persuaded that he knew more of the actual conditions here faced than all the men in England. "I often wish little Mr. *Farrar here*," wrote Governor Wyatt to his father in 1623, *"that to his zeale he would add knowledge of this Contrey."* [26] The sentiment would be many times repeated in both public and private letters from the colony.

Now that the King had for five years done little to meet the problems laid before him, beyond advising the colonists on ways in which they might help themselves, they proceeded to take the fullest possible advantage of the situation. A governor for whom no adequate provision had yet been made could be counted upon for a liberal reading of his instructions. Assemblies met annually from 1630, with a possible exception in 1636. Those of 1634 and 1637 were specifically authorized for consultation on the ever-present problem of tobacco. The others, presumably, sat by royal sufferance. In fact, the King's ministers, though several times canvassing such possibilities as the condition of the royal treasury would permit, were unable to find any acceptable solution of Virginia's problem except to leave the solution to the colonists themselves. Finally, after years in which no laws of the Assembly had been disallowed, and when a special effort to enlist the colonists' aid in reducing the tobacco crop had been agreed upon, Governor Wyatt sailed for his post in 1639 with instructions that the Assembly should be called annually. [57] As the late Professor Charles M. Andrews has well concluded, much of the credit for this final confirmation of usage should be assigned to the Virginians themselves.

To them must be assigned, too, the major share of the credit for meeting realistically through their Assembly the problems of a

[56] Kingsbury (ed.), *Records of The Virginia Company*, IV, 237. "Many things are Principles with us here that are disputed there as Problemes, and often decided against our opinions," he declared in an interesting letter of the following year which frankly admitted the justification for some of the more damaging charges then being made against the company. *William and Mary College Quarterly*, 2d ser., VI (1926), 114–21.

[57] For the statutes of 1639/40 dealing at length with the tobacco problem, see *William and Mary College Quarterly*, 2d ser., IV (1924), 17–35; for authorization of the 1634 Assembly, *Virginia Magazine*, VIII (1900–1901), 159–60.

growing community. Governor and council still sat in one body with the burgesses, thus preserving many of the forms identified in origin with the alert supervision of the company. But the alertness had not been transferred to the agencies of the crown. The royal governor enjoyed no such strength of position as had his predecessors, and the councilors, as is indicated by the Harvey affair of 1635, were primarily spokesmen for a colonial point of view. And insofar as they were coming to be joined by interest and privilege to the governor, the effect was somewhat offset by the burgesses' efforts to strengthen their bargaining power through the first tentative steps toward the creation of a bicameral assembly.[58]

Taking up where they had left off in 1624, the burgesses asserted, and in the same language, the Assembly's right to apportion the public burden.[59] That burden now fell upon the colonists chiefly in the form of a public levy, a head tax which both in form and name represented a direct borrowing from the English commercial company. The first levy had been imposed by the burgesses of 1619 for compensation of their speaker, clerk, and sergeant-at-arms. The second, probably, was the "contribution" agreed to by the Assembly of 1621 for construction of a guesthouse for the reception of newcomers to the colony. Other levies were imposed in 1624. The burgesses continued the practice of imposing the levy on all male inhabitants above sixteen. These were the tithables, as they came to be known, and this the origin of the poll tax, a form of taxation that in some sections of the South still survives. The Assembly's control of finances was detailed and almost complete. Claims against the colony were submitted for its consideration and were allowed by specific appropriation, the rate of the levy being finally determined by dividing the sum total of the claims allowed by the total number of tithables.[60] The burgesses themselves, prior

[58] The exact date at which the Assembly became bicameral is not known, but there is evidence of separate action by the burgesses as early as 1632, and unmistakably of the existence of two separate houses by 1663, considerably in advance of the long-accepted date of 1680. See Introduction in McIlwaine (ed.), *Journals of the House of Burgesses of Virginia, 1619–1658/59; ibid., 1659/60–1693* (Richmond, 1914).

[59] Cf. Hening, *Statutes*, I, 171–72, 196, with the acts of 1624.

[60] For example, see Hening, *Statutes*, I, 142, 171; *William and Mary College Quarterly*, 2d ser., IV (1924), 159–62. Appropriations authorizing future expenditures with a specific levy for the purpose were also made. *Ibid.*, 145–46.

to the appointment of sheriffs, served as agents for certifying the list of tithables and then for both collection and payment of the levies.[61] The right to impose a local rate rested upon authorization from the Assembly, which assumed also the power to fix and regulate the fees of all officers.[62] It even successfully asserted a right to lay impositions upon all vessels entering the colony. Having at the colony's charge constructed a fort at Point Comfort, the Assembly in 1632 met the problem of providing necessary ammunition by levying a contribution of powder and shot upon every vessel engaged in the Virginia trade. English merchants protested, but this first customs measure was upheld by authorities in London, was successively re-enacted, and effectively enforced in the colony's courts.[63]

No less effective was the Assembly's voice in solving the problem of local administration. That problem proved to be basically one of adjustment to an economic and social pattern increasingly marked by a wide dispersal of settlement. Under the pressure of this trend in settlement the municipal scheme of local government established in 1618 gave way to practices borrowed from the English county, but the story of local administration in Virginia traces directly from that year. For then it was that the colony came to be marked by a diversity of interests compelling attention to several questions of local government. Chief among these was the problem presented by the adventurers' plans for development of their own "particular" plantations, and though these units were destined soon to disappear, the action fixing their relationship to the provincial administration was to leave its mark on the governmental structure of the colony through many years. According to the company's decree, the several plantations would fall under the general authority of the colony's superior government, but would be recognized as local administrative units possessed of extensive powers of self-government. The proprietors were authorized to designate a man for the government of their tenants and to invest him with

61 Hening, *Statutes*, I, 143. For other administrative duties assumed by the burgesses, see *ibid.*, 175.

62 *Ibid.*, 160, 176–77, 201, 220, 265–67.

63 *Ibid.*, 176, 192, 218, 247; *William and Mary College Quarterly*, 2d ser., IV (1924), 159; *Virginia Magazine*, XI (1903–1904), 46–47, 280.

requisite economic and political powers.[64] The governor of the colony, in turn, would concede to him the status of chief officer, or "commander," of the place occupied by his people. In other words, he was to be recognized by the central government as a local magistrate and militia officer, and accordingly held to account.

If we may judge by Berkeley Hundred, his responsibilities were shared with certain assistants designated for his counsel by the proprietors, and he was bound in all important decisions to accept the majority voice of that council.[65] Thus in addition to a local magistrate whose position is suggestive of that subsequently occupied by the justice of the peace, there seems to have existed, in one instance at least, a body very similar to the later county court.

The progenitor of the county court has long been recognized in the so-called monthly court. Just how early that institution appeared is not clear. The great charter of 1618 refers incidentally to a government of "Majestracy and just Laws," and the Assembly of 1619 appears to have taken for granted the residence in each community of some sort of "magistrate." The term as there used, however, is probably to be understood in its generic sense, that is, as having reference to a varied assortment of local officials who performed according to circumstance such public duties as were required. In some places, resident members of the governor's council acted, as occasion demanded, to meet the community's need with an authority that required no other warrant than that provided by their high office, and in a manner foretelling their active association through many years with the work of the later county court. In other communities the local "commander," such as the officer in charge of the ironworkers at Falling Creek, probably served in a capacity not unlike that of the commander of Berkeley Hundred. The long continued association of the term "commander" with the chief magistrate of the county emphasizes for us the combination of functions that characterized offices of local government in early Virginia.

Through these first years expediency, rather than some formal and uniform arrangement, was probably the guiding rule, at any

[64] See the commission to Captain John Woodlief for Berkeley Hundred, in Kingsbury (ed.), *Records of The Virginia Company*, III, 199–201.

[65] *Ibid.*, 209. Woodlief was given a board of five assistants.

rate until 1622, when according to Captain John Smith courts were appointed "in convenient places" to save the trouble of carrying all causes to Jamestown.[66] It is possible that Smith refers here to the earliest establishment of the monthly court, but the first clear evidence of its existence falls in 1624. An act of that year's Assembly provided that courts should be held once a month "in the Corporations of Charles City & Elizabeth City" for the settlement of civil suits not exceeding one hundred pounds of tobacco and for the punishment of petty offenses. The court was to be comprised of the commander and such others as were commissioned for the purpose by the governor and council. The commander must be of the quorum, and decisions were to be reached by majority vote of the court.[67]

Two courts were thus established within easy reach of the inhabitants of the upper and lower parts of the colony, whose remoteness from the seat of government at Jamestown placed them at a disadvantage. That further steps to carry the government to the people were soon taken is indicated by a special authorization in 1625 to the commander at Accomac, on the Eastern Shore, for administering such oaths as might lead to a "compremise" adjudication of petty causes and so save the trouble of sending witnesses to Jamestown.[68] The earliest extant commissions for the monthly courts, those of 1626, suggest that the commissioners were expected to meet as occasion required in more than one part of their precinct, and the commissions of 1629 showed additional consideration for the convenience of all parties by fixing the quorum of the court at three.[69] Not only was the monthly court itinerant, but an early provision for a formal commission to some "sufficient man" in every plantation, precinct, hundred, or "neck" to act as commander with the powers of a conservator of the peace broadened still more the base of local self-government. Submission to the quarter court in 1627, and again in 1629, of the records of a "monthly" court at Warrosquyoake, on the south side of the James, a section later known as Isle of Wight, suggests that these con-

---

[66] Arber and Bradley (eds.), *Travels and Works of Captain John Smith*, II, 571.
[67] Kingsbury (ed.), *Records of The Virginia Company*, IV, 582, 584.
[68] McIlwaine (ed.), *Minutes of the Council*, 50.
[69] *Ibid.*, 106, 484; Hening, *Statutes*, I, 132–33.

servators of the peace promptly followed the precedent provided by the petty session of one or more local magistrates so familiar to students of the English justice of the peace.[70] There remained as late as 1629 only two monthly courts of the rank provided by the law of 1624. But the tendency, under the pressure of an expanding population that was to reach five thousand by the spring of 1635, was obviously toward the creation of many small precincts and the grouping of these into such larger units as the convenience of the community required.

By 1632 provision had been made for five monthly courts of equal rank: one for the "Upper Parts," and for the people who lived below Jamestown, one each for Warwick River, Warrosquyoake, Elizabeth City, and Accomac.[71] As had been the case with the two older courts, a member of the governor's council headed each of the five commissions and was designated one of the quorum. Through preceding years the commissioners had more than once been instructed to model their proceedings after those of the justices of the peace in the English quarter sessions, and there now remained only a short step to formal adoption of the county scheme of local government.

That step was taken in 1634, when the Assembly divided the colony into eight counties.[72] For each of these a monthly court was established by commission from the governor and council. While the court's power to act in criminal causes continued to be limited to cases not involving life or limb, its civil jurisdiction was now extended from five-pound to ten-pound suits. In form, the commission was much the same as that issued for the English county. The commissioners, who individually acted as local magistrates

[70] McIlwaine (ed.), *Minutes of the Council,* 105, 484, 192–93, 200; Hening, *Statutes,* I, 130–32, 145. Governor John Pott in 1629 renewed commissions to commanders in no less than sixteen precincts. The Warrosquyoake proceedings were presented by John Upton and Thomas Jordan, described as commissioners of that place. Neither appears in the commissions of 1626 and 1629 for the Elizabeth City court, but both are of the commission for a separate Warrosquyoake court in March, 1632.

[71] Hening, *Statutes,* I, 168–70, where is found the form of the commission and of the oath, together with the five to seven commissioners named for each precinct. For the census of 1635, see Neill, *Virginia Carolorum,* 114–15.

[72] Reading from west to east, they were Henrico, Charles City, James City, Warwick River, Charles River (York), Warrosquyoake, Elizabeth City, and Accomac. Hening, *Statutes,* I, 223.

for their neighborhoods, collectively formed a board of county commissioners who assumed in addition to their judicial duties many administrative responsibilities. Members of the county court, as the board came increasingly to be known, were selected for qualifications that tended also to commend them to their neighbors in the choice of burgesses; even before 1634 there was a marked duplication in membership with the Assembly.[73] A necessary co-ordination of local and central agencies of government received further assistance through the requirement that a member of the council should "have notice to attend and assist in each court of the shire." [74] For the provost marshal, who had served as the chief police officer wherever there was need for one, and whose title suggests again the military structure of government in early Virginia, the Assembly in 1634 substituted the sheriff. It also created the office of lieutenant, which in England carried responsibility for the county militia.

The sheriff was destined to become a key figure in the American county, but the lieutenant's office, at least during the seventeenth century, had little existence outside the statute. Command of the militia continued to be so all important that the selection tended naturally to fall upon the most capable and responsible member of the community, and those very qualifications were likely to dictate the choice of the same man as chief magistrate of the county court, or even as the representative for his section of the colony on the governor's council. To designate such a man as lieutenant of the county was merely to add another title, in a community where a captain had long since outranked a lieutenant. Consequently, the older title of commander, carrying with it a twofold obligation to "command and govern" the people, survived for a time in a practical arrangement of local administration that imposed upon the county court responsibilities with reference to military affairs which foretold the distinct but overlapping commissions sub-

[73] Comparison of the 1632 list of commissioners with the names of the burgesses for 1629, 1630, and 1632 presents an interesting result. Of the total of thirty-one commissioners, seven were of the council, and of the remaining twenty-four no less than twenty-two served at one or more of these assemblies.

[74] One is reminded of the practice in early Massachusetts, where to such assistants or magistrates, the equivalent there to the councilors in Virginia, as resided in the community were added by commission several responsible men to form a local court.

sequently issued for the militia and for the court.[75] In seeking an effective co-ordination of effort, the commander in chief of the colony naturally found in his councilors convenient instruments, and often conferred on them the honor and responsibility of a superior command.

The story is of general as well as special interest, for it touches upon the question of the extent to which our institutions were borrowed from England. To that question there is no simple answer. More than once our forefathers proclaimed the borrowing of some English institutional usage, and the origins of the county in Virginia provides one of the more familiar examples. Yet little is heard of the lieutenant beyond the statutory provision for the office; the Virginia sheriff bore a definite similarity to the English sheriff but he was at the same time quite different; and the county court possessed both a broader and a narrower field of action than did the quarter sessions of the English county.[76] In truth, our institutions, like those of other peoples, were shaped by a long succession of separate decisions made by men who were seeking a practicable solution to an immediate problem rather than consciously shaping an institution. That problem was in most instances the product of a situation peculiar to America, and many times peculiar to some one section of America. Insofar as any one rule of action was followed, the rule was to do what appeared to be reasonable under the circumstances. That Englishmen would find a reasonable course of action differing in some particulars from that tried by Frenchmen is to be expected, but that Englishmen would always adopt identical courses is well enough disproved by the distinctive institutional patterns marking their settlements in Virginia and New England. Though there were, of course, important similarities in form, terminology, and procedure, the chief thing that bound

[75] The earliest surviving county records, those for Accomac (dating from 1632) and for York (from 1634), though incomplete, bear interesting testimony to the nature of the transition from earlier to later practices. See especially, Northampton County Records, No. 1, Orders, Wills, Deeds, etc., 1632–1640 (photographic copy, Virginia State Library, Richmond), 31–32. Accomac became Northampton County in 1643.

[76] A useful study in comparative government is Cyrus H. Karraker, *The Seventeenth-Century Sheriff; A Comparative Study of the Sheriff in England and the Chesapeake Colonies, 1607–1689* (Philadelphia, 1930).

Massachusetts and Virginia to a common institutional heritage was a thing of the spirit, a feeling for what was appropriate in a community of Englishmen. Overshadowing all differences is the fact that these early Americans laid hold of the cardinal principle of English local administration—a somewhat unusual combination of central authority and local representation. In Virginia as in the homeland, the Englishman depended, in that area of government most intimately identified with his interests, upon officials who bore the King's commission but were at the same time neighbors of the men they judged.

Through the years that followed, the expanding frontier of Virginia's settlement is conveniently marked for us by the creation of new counties.[77] On each frontier the earliest expression of the will to self-government was a demand for the creation of a local court that would bring the government within easy reach of the people and entrust it to representative members of the community. At times, no doubt, the demand reflected in part a desire for separate representation in the Assembly, but that was for a while of secondary importance. It is true that the county was becoming the basic electoral unit, but a right of any one community within the county to send at its own cost a separate burgess survived through several years to remind historians of the earlier and very practical rule that representation in the Assembly should be given all those communities which properly should be represented. Significantly, the privilege seems to have been used principally to demand a greater measure of local autonomy in the fields of civil and ecclesiastical administration.[78]

Of special importance to an understanding of the colony's expansion after 1624 is the Indian problem. The planters, far too many of whom recently had looked upon their dead, now had dropped all thought of missionary effort to grapple realistically with a situation that threatened their very existence. They proclaimed a settled policy of relentless warfare upon the natives, and year after year implemented it by organized destruction of towns

[77] On the origin of the several counties, of their names, and for their boundaries and pertinent changes, the standard reference is Morgan P. Robinson, "Virginia Counties," in *Bulletin of the Virginia State Library* (Richmond), IX (1916).

[78] Hening, *Statutes,* I, 250, 277, 299–300, 421, 520–521, 545; *Virginia Magazine,* XVII (1909), 127.

and crops and by other actions calculated to harass the Indians and keep them on the defensive. By proclamation and legislative enactment the date of the great massacre was annually celebrated to remind the people of the continuing necessity for the utmost vigilance. The council in 1629 even decided to abandon a peace agreement recently made with their enemies, on the ground that a necessary vigilance could be assured only through a policy of "perpetual enmity" with the Indians.[79]

The chief threat came from Opechancanough, whose warriors held the region up and across the York River. The planters managed to retain their hold on the upper James, where the counties of Henrico, Charles City, and James City extended across the river, a fact reminding us that in those days a waterway joined rather than divided the peoples on its opposite banks. But the location east of Jamestown of the other five original counties, as was to be the case with the next two counties added (Nansemond and Lower Norfolk), indicates that the westward advance characterizing Virginia's early settlement had given way in the face of Indian resistance. The advantages of deep-water communications in the marketing of tobacco perhaps were of even greater importance in leading the planters along the waters emptying immediately into the lower Chesapeake and across it to extend the area of their settlement on its Eastern Shore. But a glance at the Indian trade after 1622 suggests that the native problem constituted a contributory factor of no slight significance. That trade, unavoidably affected by the policy of perpetual enmity with immediate neighbors, was chiefly pressed along a line conveniently marked for us by William Claiborne's Kent Island post in the upper Chesapeake.[80]

The withdrawal, however, had been largely a tactical move. Almost from the day of the massacre, men had debated the possibility of clearing the Indians from the lower Peninsula, and in 1629 steps

[79] McIlwaine (ed.), *Minutes of the Council*, 184–85; Hening, *Statutes*, I, 153, 177, 202. To include all pertinent citations is impossible. Suffice it to say that even a cursory examination of the records emphasizes the fact that few historians have managed to convey a feeling for the full extent to which the Indian problem absorbed the energies and thought of the colonists.

[80] The purchase of cloth, "bayes and cotton," for exchange with the Indians reached such a point that the Assembly of 1633 took steps to prohibit the diversion of stores needed by the planters. Hening, *Statutes*, I, 219.

were taken to put the policy into effect. Several of the more prominent planters, by an arrangement foretelling a major feature of Virginia's land policy, agreed to provide a specified number of men for occupation of a point on the York River above modern Yorktown known as Cheskiack in return for a grant of fifty acres of land for each man provided. The logical development of this move was an attempt to assure a strongly held line of settlement across the Peninsula from Cheskiack to Jamestown. Accordingly, the Assembly of 1632 offered a grant of fifty acres and a term of tax exemption to any freeman who would settle at a point approximately halfway across the Peninsula, to which was given the name of Middle Plantation, a site later occupied by the city of Williamsburg. An act of 1633 imposed a labor levy of one man in every forty residing below the line to aid in the construction of necessary buildings and fortifications. By the next year a pale some six miles in extent and joining two creeks, the one flowing into the York and the other into the James, had further strengthened the defenses raised against Indian incursions.[81] Three hundred thousand acres, roughly, had been cleared of the Indian title. A claim had been entered to the York, next river to the north. And warning had been given, as the English faced back up the river, of a relentless advance destined with time to extend across a continent.

By no means the least significant feature of this action was a decision to set aside the proprietors' title to Martin's Hundred, for it touched upon one of the more serious uncertainties that affected the colony's growth. Following the recall of the company's charter, upon which depended all land titles in Virginia, the planters sought a royal charter confirming them in their own estates, and some further action that at the same time would void such of the adventurers' titles as were unoccupied and stood in the way.[82] The question thus raised was intimately joined to that of the revival of the company, and so remained unsettled in any final sense while the larger question of the company's restoration continued under debate. Meanwhile, the colonists received general assurances of

[81] *Ibid.*, 139–40, 199, 208; *Virginia Magazine,* VIII (1900–1901), 157–58.

[82] On this request and the response, see *Cal. St. Pap., Col., 1574–1660,* pp. 76, 79, 94; *Virginia Magazine,* II (1894–1895), 50–55; VII (1899–1900), 369–72; *William and Mary College Quarterly,* 2d ser., VI (1926), 119–20.

their rights and estates, and the crown gave at least tacit approval to certain projects, chief among them the occupation of Cheskiack and Middle Plantation, that tended to superimpose on the original map of the colony a new mosaic of property rights. There was probably little cause for worry about the titles issued at Cheskiack and Middle Plantation, but the general situation was far from satisfactory.

Governors after 1624 continued to issue land patents under the terms of the great charter of 1618. Bills of adventure and headright claims were accordingly honored, but that charter had fixed a term on the rights offered that closed on Midsummer Day of 1625. Headright claims based on immigration prior to that date were legal enough, but claims honored for immigrants subsequently entering the colony could have rested at any time prior to 1634 on nothing but custom, and not a very old custom at that. Moreover, the colonists had been disposed to take the fullest possible advantage of the company's earlier ruling that occupation of the land was necessary to perfect a title, as also of the fact that in many places there was no one at hand to challenge a counterclaim. It is no less pertinent that such surveys as had been made were both imperfect and incomplete.

This was the problem that explains in no small part the planters' hardening opposition to revival of the company, and their apprehension over the disregard in the Heath and Baltimore grants to Carolina and Maryland of the boundaries fixed by the second Virginia charter. Issuance of the Maryland charter was followed promptly by renewal of the colonists' plea for some royal confirmation of their own estates and rights. Employing Captain William Bulton as a special agent in 1634 to press their petition, the Virginians sought especially to secure an authorization extending the powers of the governor and council under the great charter beyond the term there fixed. By order of the Privy Council in July, 1634, the requested grant was made, to be afterward confirmed by a new clause in the governor's instructions specifying a right of fifty acres for every person entering after midsummer, 1625.[83] The privilege was subject to recall, and, strictly speaking, the crown had done

[83] *Virginia Magazine*, XVII (1909), 8–9; VIII (1900–1901), 155–56, 158; *Cal. St. Pap., Col., 1574–1660*, pp. 184–85; McIlwaine (ed.), *Minutes of the Council*, 481.

no more than give assurance of the integrity of such titles as were issued while the edict held, but the trend of royal policy had taken a turn favorable to the colonists.

From this point forward, in fact, the King's ministers displayed an increasing disposition to let stand those arrangements of the colony's life that had been shaped by events and by the will of the planters. In 1637 they took a significant step toward confirmation of the great charter by appointment of a treasurer for the colony with the duty of collecting the quitrents originally specified in that document. Wyatt's instructions of 1639 ruled in favor of the colonists on questions involving unoccupied or abandoned lands patented to the adventurers and subsequently taken up by the planters. Final agreement came through re-enactment of the essential provisions of the great charter, including its schedule of quitrents, by the Assembly of 1639.[84] The chance remained, of course, that the planters might yet be subjected to the overlordship of a company or of some English nobleman. But for the time being, at any rate, Virginia's land system, like her political structure, had been stabilized in accordance with policies and principles first outlined in 1618.

The title by which the planter now held his land made him in effect a freehold tenant of the King. He could have asked for no more absolute a grant. The patent was awarded on four main conditions: in return for a contribution to the colony's founding, for meritorious services to the community, as inducement for settlement on an exposed frontier, and in return for evidence of having paid the cost of importing a laborer into the colony.

Already the last of these outranked all others in importance, for it was this headright system that enabled the community to underwrite the immigration upon which Virginia's fortunes were rebuilt. Following 1624, British capitalists turned their attention elsewhere; those whose faith survived were the hardened and "seasoned" planters in the colony, men already touched by that love

According to *ibid.*, 480, petitions for large grants had been theretofore referred to the King's commissioners for Virginia for confirmation.

[84] McIlwaine (ed.), *Minutes of the Council*, 243; *Virginia Magazine*, IX (1901–1902), 43; XI (1903–1904), 54–57; *William and Mary College Quarterly*, 2d ser., IV (1924), 153–55. Attention should be given supplementary action by the Assembly in 1642 and 1643.

of the land which would distinguish their descendants through generations to come. Subsistence farming and the cultivation of tobacco, a proved "money" crop, opened before them a prospect by no means so dazzling as that which first brought them to America, but one nonetheless offering the rewards of an independent freeholder. To win the full measure of those rewards a primary need was cheap labor. A few Negroes had been provided as early as 1619, but the real answer to the planter's problem came in the increasing number of little and unimportant Englishmen who sought for themselves a new lot in a new world. Some of them possessed enough to pay their way across, claim their headrights, and start at once as freeholders; but most of them, perhaps as many as 75 per cent, took advantage of an opportunity to work out the cost of their passage through a term of service to some planter.[85] Many, no doubt, came with some misunderstanding of the headright system; but whether or not they knew that the fifty acres belonged to the master rather than the servant, there can be little question that they came in the faith that labor and patience would win for them the status of a freehold tenant of the King. One thousand persons were reported as recent arrivals in 1628; 2,000 as having entered in the year closing with the spring of 1635; and 1,600 for the year that followed. By 1640 the population had reached an estimated 8,000.[86]

To provide for the religious life of a population growing at that rate, and marked in its every move by an increasing dispersal of settlement, proved one of the more difficult problems of the colony's early years. Virginia had been settled at a time when the religious differences of the seventeenth century had not as yet brought into question the allegiance of the vast majority of Englishmen to the Church of England. There were, of course, small groups of Separatists; but Puritanism, the real forerunner of English nonconformity, still represented an attempt to accomplish reforms within the Established Church itself. Only the Separatists, who included the Pilgrim Fathers, had felt sufficient repression to

85 *Virginia Magazine*, VIII (1900–1901), 441; IX (1901–1902), 37; Thomas J. Wertenbaker, *Planters of Colonial Virginia* (Princeton, 1922), 80–82.

86 *Virginia Magazine*, I (1893–1894), 4; VII (1899–1900), 259; VIII (1900–1901), 302; IX (1901–1902), 36–37; *William and Mary College Quarterly*, 2d ser., IV (1924), 31.

make persecution a major factor in the decision to emigrate. The settlement of the Pilgrim Fathers in New England rather than in Virginia saved the latter colony from the disturbances normally arising from religious controversy. When religion later became a major factor in the Great Migration, Massachusetts naturally proved more attractive than Virginia to those who left England in protest of the apparent triumph of Archbishop William Laud's party over the Puritans. The rituals and doctrines of the Church of England, therefore, were accepted as a matter of course in early Virginia.[87]

This does not mean, however, that religion was taken for granted or slighted. Not only was the age an age of faith, but there existed by no means as many marked differences between the several religious factions as has often popularly been assumed. A glance at the statutes, from Dale's code on, suggests that sabbatarianism, for example, was hardly less strong in Virginia than it was in Massachusetts. Indeed, it seems not altogether improbable that the principal difference lay in the fact that town life in New England permitted a more effective enforcement than was possible in Virginia. Surviving evidence indicates that the few books it proved possible for the colonist to bring over to the Chesapeake were largely of a devotional character. A significant and oft-recurring entry in the inventories of seventeenth-century estates is "one old bible and the practice of piety." [88]

Nor is it to be assumed that the church established in Virginia was an exact copy of its parent at home. For the Anglican Church, though a product of the Protestant Reformation, was an ancient institution, and its elaborate organization more than an infant colony could support. There was never to be a bishop of the Virginia church, nor were the colonists to know in their new home those ecclesiastical courts that existed in England for the enforce-

[87] The story might have been different had more of the Puritan clergy, like Lewis Hughes in Bermuda and perhaps Alexander Whitaker in Virginia, responded to the opportunity in the colonies. See the latter's appeal, in Brown (ed.), *Genesis of the United States*, I, 499.

[88] Colonists sent out for the settlement of Berkeley Hundred in 1619 were provided with two "church bibles," two "common prayer books," three "books of the practice of piety," and three "books of the playne man's path way." Kingsbury (ed.), *Records of The Virginia Company*, III, 178.

ment of orthodoxy and the exercise of a jurisdiction covering such things as marriages, wills, and probates. For reasons of practical necessity the ordinary courts of the colony at an early date assumed or were granted superintendence over all such matters. The result was a highly significant extension of lay control, a trend which became no less noticeable in the relative insecurity which marked the minister's position.

The clergy of the English establishment enjoyed a very helpful independence of the vestry, elected governing body of the parish. The power of appointment lay outside the vestry. Once inducted by the bishop, the minister enjoyed an independent right to the income of his living. There were, also, limited grounds upon which a motion for his removal would be entertained. Appointment by the company or by associated groups of adventurers of the early ministers in Virginia, the order of 1618 for the provision of glebe land, and the accompanying requirement that parishioners contribute to assure each minister a fixed income were obviously intended to confer upon the clergy in the colony something of their customary independence. The plan, however, suffered from the collapse that overtook all other features of the company's program. Had the crown been willing and able to assume the responsibility in 1624, or had there been some such missionary organization as the later Society for the Propagation of the Gospel, the situation might have been saved. But the crown had other and more important interests, and the energies of the church were increasingly absorbed in a contest with Puritanism that would develop into a long and bitter struggle by nonconformity to establish itself in England. Meanwhile, the Virginia church went its own way.

Support of the church even more than the support of government was left to the colonists. In response to a special appeal for ministers in 1629, the King did nothing more than agree that any who would pay his own passage and could find accommodation in the colony might go.[89] To this the governor's instructions later added the requirement that two hundred acres of glebe be provided in each parish. Authorities in the colony gave testimony of their purpose to follow the English church "as neere as may be." A series of statutes required conformity with its canons, defined

[89] *Virginia Magazine*, VII (1899–1900), 369–72.

the duties of the minister and other officers of the parish, imposed a fixed tax on every tithable for the minister's support, and specified a schedule of fees for his particular services. Supplementary efforts, however, such as the award of land grants for meritorious services to individual ministers or the assessment by law in 1632 of the twentieth calf, kid, and pig for the benefit of the clergy, speak eloquently of the inadequacy of that provision. The glebe was of uncertain value unless supplied with servants, and the tithe, with the market moving generally downward, remained fixed at ten pounds of tobacco and a bushel of corn per poll.[90] Thus, in effect, the earlier principle of a fixed income for each minister came to have little meaning.

It is not surprising that there was a shortage of ministers, or that the filling of a pulpit might depend upon the willingness of the parish to offer some compensation in addition to that fixed by law.[91] The resulting agreement between the vestry and the minister left with the former virtual power to force the latter's resignation by withdrawal of the extra compensation. This control of the purse proved with time to be of greater importance even than the law of 1643, conferring on the vestry the right to choose the minister subject to induction by the governor.[92] Under the circumstances existing, the better-qualified men were rarely attracted to Virginia. The poor quality of those available naturally caused the vestry to hesitate to give them even such security of tenure as presentment and induction in Virginia could provide. In time it became a common custom for vestries not to make a formal presentment, but rather to enter into annual agreements that were accurately, though coarsely, described as "hiring" the minister.[93]

[90] See especially, Neill, *Virginia Carolorum,* 69 n.; McIlwaine (ed.), *Minutes of the Council,* 22, 174, 471; Hening, *Statutes,* I, 159–60, 183–85, 207, 220–21, 240–43, 289–91; *William and Mary College Quarterly,* 2d ser., IV (1924), 34–35, 155–56; *Virginia Magazine,* III (1895–1896), 280–81.

[91] For early examples, see *Virginia Magazine,* I (1893–1894), 327; XLI (1933), 53; *Lower Norfolk County Antiquary* (Baltimore), II (1897–1899), 63; also an act of 1646, in Hening, *Statutes,* I, 328.

[92] Hening, *Statutes,* I, 241–42. The vestry was to elect its minister with the allowance of such of the county commissioners as resided in the parish. Though induction was by the governor, only an Assembly could remove a clergyman.

[93] See Henry Hartwell, James Blair, and Edward Chilton, *The Present State of Virginia, and the College,* edited by Hunter D. Farish (Williamsburg, 1940), 66, *passim.*

Conditions in Virginia proved equally unfavorable for an exact reproduction of that close-knit unit of community life, and of ecclesiastical and lay administration, that was the English parish. The colonial parish inevitably was large. It often coincided in extent and in its boundaries with the county, and its population was subject to many shifts and changes. As would be expected, the vestry showed a marked duplication in membership with the county court, which exercised a general superintendence over parish activities, and the two bodies were not always careful to keep themselves apart. Chief among officers of the vestry were the churchwardens, men charged with the collection of parish levies and the making of presentments for trial on complaints of drunkenness, swearing, sabbathbreaking, recusancy, fornication, adultery, bastardy, and other such offenses. Indictments necessarily were brought before the civil courts, and principally those of the counties. In the recording of vital statistics on marriages, christenings, and burials, parish officers acted essentially as agents of the county court, if indeed they acted at all.[94] There were many things to remind men of the parish at home, but the differences were no less marked.

The minister frequently became something of a "circuit rider," holding services here one Sunday, there another. Lay readers often substituted for him. Difficulties arose over the building of churches which unavoidably had to be placed at a point remote from some parts of the parish, and "chapels of ease" for the convenience of especially remote communities became rather common. The family burying ground, speaking in its somber way both of the problems of dispersed settlement and of man's love for his own land, made an early appearance despite repeated efforts to provide more appropriately for burial of the dead. Like the home wedding, it

Helpful studies of recent date are Elizabeth H. Davidson, *The Establishment of the English Church in Continental American Colonies* (Durham, 1936), and George MacLaren Brydon, *Virginia's Mother Church and the Political Conditions Under Which It Grew* (Richmond, 1947).

[94] Kingsbury (ed.), *Records of The Virginia Company,* III, 172; Hening, *Statutes,* I, 126, 145, 155–56, 160–61, 227, 240–41; *Virginia Magazine,* IX (1901–1902), 52. The county records bear interesting testimony. For the early period, see Northampton County, Orders, No. 1, etc., 16, 20, 54, 63, 73, 85; *Lower Norfolk County Antiquary,* I (1895–1896), 140–43; II (1897–1899), 13; *Virginia Magazine,* V (1897–1898), 35; XXXIX (1931), 15; XL (1940), 134.

would become a mark of Southern life. Despite these and other necessary accommodations to altered circumstances, however, these early Virginians held true to a great spiritual tradition. *The Book of Common Prayer* and the King James Version of the Bible remained unchanged.

Thus was the old and the new compounded to round out the most significant transition in Virginia's institutional life at any time prior to 1776. The story holds a double significance. No other colony offers the same opportunity for study of the continuous development of that experiment in American settlement which had its origins in the minds and hearts of the Elizabethans. No other colony, save Massachusetts, was to exert a comparable influence on the further stages of that experiment; for, like the great Puritan commonwealth to the north, Virginia was destined to serve as a mother colony and state. Her way of life would be carried near and far by emigrant sons who in their new homes adapted it to their immediate requirements. And so when we of the South return today to the site of old Jamestown, there to stand in the tower of the brick church begun in 1639, or to walk over the foundations of the first Statehouse, acquired in 1641, buildings that helped to overcome what John Pory had earlier described as the "solitary uncouthnes of this place," [95] it is to think of some of the first men and influences to give shape to a Southern way of life.

[95] Kingsbury (ed.), *Records of The Virginia Company,* III, 222.

CHAPTER VI

MARYLAND

THROUGH the years following 1624 Virginia was in many ways a backwater, outside the main currents of England's maritime expansion. The old name still possessed enough of its former magic to attract several thousand settlers, but Virginia's population of 8,000 in 1640 was slight when compared with the approximately 20,000 persons who had through the preceding decade found their way into the New England colonies. An even larger group had followed the old quest of fortune in southern climes to the West Indies, where St. Christopher, Barbados, Barbuda, Nevis, Monserratt, and perhaps other islands had been occupied by English adventurers. St. Kitts, with a population in the neighborhood of 14,000, supported England's most populous colony. Massachusetts Bay, with over 12,000, ranked second. Barbados held a population approximately the same as that of Virginia, and Nevis boasted half as many people. By 1640 perhaps 40,000 persons, in an emigration dating from the reign of James and drawn partly from England but chiefly from the Lowlands of Scotland, had moved out to occupy the northern counties of Ulster.[1] The tide of emigration would turn again, and once more Virginia would become England's largest colony. But for the moment her priority was simply one of age.

The waters, however, were frequently stirred by eddies from the

[1] For some of the more important studies in these related fields of English expansion, see Vincent T. Harlow, *A History of Barbados, 1625–1685* (Oxford, 1926); Arthur P. Newton, *The Colonising Activities of the English Puritans* (New Haven, 1914); Newton, *European Nations in the West Indies*; James A. Williamson, *English Colonies in Guiana and on the Amazon, 1604–1668* (Oxford, 1923); George P. Insh, *Scottish Colonial Schemes, 1620–1686* (Glasgow, 1922); Theodore W. Moody, *The Londonderry Plantation, 1609–41*; *The City of London and the Plantation in Ulster* (Belfast, 1939).

main currents. New England, expanding at a rate beyond her capacity to produce food, drew upon Virginia for some of the staples of life, and before many years the Yankee trader would become a familiar figure in the Southern colonies.[2] Though a part of the surplus population that early beset Bermuda contributed to the re-establishment of the fortunes of its sister colony, the newer colonies exerted on the older the usual attraction of novelty and booming prospects. So strong was this attraction, in fact, that legislation regulating the right of emigration from Virginia was required.[3] Especially important were the problems raised by the grant of Maryland to Lord Baltimore.

Sir George Calvert, in 1625 first Lord Baltimore of the Irish peerage, had been a subscriber of the Virginia Company, a member of the New England Council, and the promoter of a settlement in Newfoundland prior to his development of plans for a colony on the upper Chesapeake. The settlement undertaken there, which drew its name from the French Catholic queen of Charles I, grew directly out of Baltimore's earlier activities and stands as the first of the great proprietary colonies on the mainland. It was to be followed in turn by the Carolinas, New York, New Jersey, and Pennsylvania. As the list itself suggests, a proprietary form of management dominated the later phases of English settlement no less than the usages borrowed from the London merchants had the earlier stages.

The hope of acquiring a title to American land had been from the first a consistent, and possibly the chief, inspiration of the New World venture. From the first, too, some of the more important leaders had identified the promise of America with the most ambitious schemes of landed proprietorship. But those leaders had recognized that the land itself would be of little value until joined by established channels of trade to some European market, or unless some market for the primary produce of agricultural endeavor could be established in America. Moreover, they lacked the means to bridge the distance between England and the New World.

---

[2] *Virginia Magazine,* VIII (1900–1901), 155, 157–58; *William and Mary College Quarterly,* 2d ser., IV (1924), 148.

[3] *Virginia Magazine,* VIII (1900–1901), 302; Hening, *Statutes,* I, 200. The chief fear seems to have been of unpaid debts left behind.

Accordingly, they had sought to enlist the co-operation of commercial groups possessed of resources more nearly equal to the task, and when that aid was finally won it tended for a time to dominate the effort. Joint-stock methods of finance, and a decision to rely generally on a co-operative approach to the problems of initial settlement, left little or no immediate opportunity for extensive individual proprietorships.

By the 1620's, however, conditions were changing. Co-operative projects now tended to give way to individual effort, and, where they were still relied upon, the temporary nature of the expedient together with a more immediate recognition of individual claims received greater emphasis. Meanwhile, the Englishman's knowledge of America, and of its opportunities, had been greatly expanded. Uncertainties and peculiar hazards remained, but they had been measurably reduced. At the same time, discontent—economic, political, and religious—provided a growing number of persons ready to emigrate. They were for the most part little men who offered principally their labor, but many of them were able and willing to pay their own way and to invest some additional capital besides. As a result, fortunately placed members of the landed classes responded to an apparent opportunity to transfer the Old World's long-established forms of proprietorship to America. If political influence could be counted upon to secure from the King an extensive grant, the traditional rights and responsibilities attached to lordship of the land might be used to effect a familiar and not altogether unsatisfactory arrangement of community life. The income from quitrents and other normal jurisdictional prerogatives could be expected to provide the proprietor with a necessary compensation for the responsibilities of leadership he assumed.

The response to the new opportunity is readily apparent. It may be followed in the ambitious schemes advanced by Sir Ferdinando Gorges through the New England Council, a body at first wholly representative of the landed classes and in its origin associated with elaborate plans for feudal proprietary rights. These plans came to little, but they underscore for us the sense men had of a new and expanded opportunity. More easily read is the record entered on the map of a coast which initially, from Florida to Canada, had been only Virginia. As now Nova Scotia, Maine, New Hampshire, Maryland, and Carolina were added, each name gave notice of another impressive proprietary grant.

Of the early proprietary undertakings, Calvert's estate in Newfoundland ranks among the more significant. It was purchased in 1620 from Sir William Vaughan, who had received it from a London and Bristol company of adventurers which for several years after 1610 had sought to promote English settlement in the island with a view to control of the fishing. The grant lay in the extreme southeastern portion of the island.[4] Since the land was held nominally by grant of the company and the company was in decline, Calvert felt the need of a more secure title and a more ample definition of his authority. Fortunately, he was in a position to do something about it, being a man of influence that carried high in the English government. A graduate of Oxford in 1597, he had become secretary to Sir Robert Cecil. He served in Parliament from 1609 to 1624. Having been raised from a post as clerk of the Privy Council to that of a principal secretary of state in 1619, he secured a royal patent in 1623 enlarging his grant and erecting it into the province of Avalon, a name borrowed from the traditional birthplace of Christianity in England.

His desire, of course, was the desire of any adventurer or group of adventurers: as secure a title and as unqualified a power for direction of the investment as could be had. The solution of that problem in the case of a group of adventurers joined in a corporation like the Virginia Company had been a grant expressed in terms of a corporate monopoly. A comparable grant to an individual, however, presented a somewhat different legal problem. Lawyers, then as now, were bound in some measure to the use of conventional forms of conveyance, and it is doubtful that they could have found any other form for conveying to an individual so extensive a grant of land and authority than that of a feudal charter. Feudalism, it is true, was declining as a force in English life, and its survivals were rapidly becoming archaic; but among the last things to reflect a gradual change of the sort involved are the forms and usages of the law. And so the Avalon patent was drawn in the form of a feudal charter.

These limitations of the law by no means ran counter to Calvert's

[4] *Cambridge History of the British Empire*, VI: *Canada and Newfoundland*, 125–28.

own wishes. A member of the landed class, he was accustomed to think in terms of its conventional rights. In seeking the most effective expression of the authority desired, he turned not to some new and uncertain device, but rather to the precedent provided by the most extensive separate jurisdiction existing within the framework of medieval England. Such, at any rate, would appear to have been the origin of the celebrated Bishop of Durham clause, destined to appear later in both the Maryland and Carolina charters and included in the Avalon patent apparently at Calvert's own instance. Avalon thus became in effect a county palatine with an authority vested in the lord proprietor equal to that held by the Bishop of Durham "at any time" theretofore. The medieval palatine lordships were of diverse origins, and in their development there were other differences shaped by circumstances. No one description will serve. In general, however, they represented the greatest degree of independent authority consistent with an acknowledged allegiance to the King. It may be well to note also that in England these palatine jurisdictions, of which the bishopric of Durham was chief, offered a solution to the problem of maintaining the peace in distant frontier regions. Where border problems were troublesome, or distance caused the King's authority to shade into relative insignificance, the solution was to leave some one lord in control with power that was in itself sufficient to meet the need. It was often said of the bishopric of Durham, "what the king has without, the bishop has within," and whatever the accuracy of that description, it unquestionably stated correctly enough what Calvert desired in Newfoundland. The high point of the bishop's authority had been reached in the fourteenth and fifteenth centuries. Improved agencies of the modern state had brought thereafter a marked decline in his independent jurisdiction. But what was outworn in England might well serve the purpose on the new and even more distant frontier of America.[5]

Baltimore's interest in Avalon carried him to Newfoundland in 1627 and again in 1628, where, as might be expected, his thoughts

[5] Decidedly the best discussion of the background of Maryland's history, and especially of those ideas and influences shaping the feudal features of the proprietary scheme, is found in Andrews, *Colonial Period of American History*, II, 195 ff. On the palatinate, see Gaillard T. Lapsley, *The County Palatine of Durham; A Study in Constitutional History* (New York, 1900).

were turned to the advantages of a more southern climate. In 1629 he went with his wife and family to Virginia, expressing in a letter to the King a desire to settle in that colony or somewhere to the south of it. But his welcome at Jamestown brought him little encouragement. He had become a convert to Catholicism, not long perhaps before his surrender of the office of secretary of state on the accession of Charles I. Refusing the oath of supremacy tendered by the colony's officials, he returned to England with hopes now centered on the region immediately below the Virginia Peninsula.[6] The experience, no doubt, strengthened an additional purpose that had entered into his plans for settlement, a desire to provide a refuge for fellow Catholics who might wish, like the Pilgrim Fathers at Plymouth, to emigrate without surrender of their allegiance as Englishmen. The idea of such a colony extended as far back as 1583, and under the leadership of the Catholic Sir Thomas Arundel, sometimes credited with Calvert's conversion, it had played a part in one of the several projects immediately preceding the Virginia grant of 1606.

The location of the Maryland grant of June 30, 1632, on the upper reaches of the Chesapeake rather than to the south of Virginia as had first been requested, suggests the probable influence of a developing rivalry between England and Holland. The English state played an essentially negative role in the colonial and commercial expansion of the time. Nevertheless, the inspiration of the movement had been from the days of Elizabeth in no small part national, and periods of intensified effort had frequently coincided with critical developments in the nation's foreign relations. Since Raleigh's day Catholic Spain had provided a continuing challenge to English adventure. Indeed, so close had been the last great effort of the Virginia Company to the hope that England would again assume the leadership of the Protestant cause in Europe that some even saw the hand of Spain in the downfall of the company. A second Spanish war actually accompanied the occupation of the British West Indies, and was still running its unhappy course when in 1629 Sir Robert Heath received his grant to Carolina, a region forming a natural buffer between Virginia and Florida. But that same year brought an end to hostilities for all practical purposes

[6] *Archives of Maryland* (Baltimore), III (1885), 15–17.

in preparation for a formal peace reached in 1631, when the Dutch, as if to remind the English that other rivals existed, undertook to extend their activities in North America from a base on the Hudson into the Delaware.

The new rivalry with Holland was economic and imperial, and lacked the reinforcement of ideological differences. Indeed, men on both sides were reluctant to consider the possibility of a serious clash of interests. There had been talk on occasion of collaboration between these two Protestant states, in economic pursuits abroad as well as in the politics of Europe. Yet, interest persistently overruled sentiment. The celebrated Amboyna massacre of 1623 had signaled the virtual exclusion of the English from the Dutch East Indies, as that rich archipelago was destined to be known, with the result that England perforce directed her energies to the Asiatic subcontinent that would serve for three hundred years as the base of her East Indian empire.[7] Contemporaneously, the occupation of New Netherland had driven a wedge between the English settlements to the east and south of the Hudson River. The Delaware venture of 1631 proved abortive, but it carried a threat to England's interest in the Chesapeake area comparable in significance with the current challenge of Dutch traders on Long Island Sound and along the Connecticut River to the new settlements in New England. It was as a trader that the Dutchman was most to be feared, and by the 1630's he was frequently found bargaining for Virginia's tobacco.[8] The threat was yet insufficient to strain the relations between the two countries, but was enough to lend new importance to the upper Chesapeake and to Delaware Bay.[9] Of aid in suggesting the point to the King's officers, no doubt, were protests from some of the old Virginia adventurers, who saw after 1631 a new prospect for the revival of their patent, against a plan to settle Baltimore in southern Virginia.

They could hardly have been much more displeased with the original proposal, however, than with the grant actually made. For the ten million to twelve million acres patented to Cecilius, second

[7] See again, Foster, *England's Quest of Eastern Trade,* for an admirable discussion of this phase of the subject.

[8] *Cal. St. Pap., Col., 1574–1660,* pp. 250–51; *Virginia Magazine,* VIII (1900–1901), 149–50, 302; IX (1901–1902), 176–78.

[9] *Virginia Magazine,* VIII (1900–1901), 153–54.

Lord Baltimore (the first had died while the charter was passing through the seals), included a considerable part of the grant made to the Virginia Company in 1609.[10] The northern boundary ran westward from Delaware Bay along the fortieth parallel (a line some distance above the present extension of Maryland and including all of Delaware) to the "first fountain" of the Potomac River. On the south, the line followed the southern bank of that river (a fact of no small historical significance) to its mouth; from there it ran across the bay to Watkins Point and thence to the Atlantic. At one time in the negotiations, the southern extremity had been placed at Cape Charles, but on objection from the Virginia adventurers the line had been moved northward to exclude the Virginia settlements on the Eastern Shore. Thus the older colony was left in possession of both capes commanding the outlet to the sea. This and other features of the grant foretold problems in sharing the navigation of the Chesapeake and the Potomac that would occasion more than one conference between responsible officials of the two communities, including the Annapolis Convention of 1786.

In addition to the land, the grant contained, as did other American charters, extensive rights of jurisdiction. The difference lay in the fact that powers of government were in this instance conferred upon one man rather than a group of men, and thus in a sense constituted a grant somewhat more "absolute." Modeled closely after the Avalon patent, the Maryland charter entrusted to Lord Baltimore prerogatives that had been denied any one subject in England for approximately a century; in short, it made of him a palatine lord. Even the statute of *Quia Emptores* was suspended to permit a subinfeudation of lands granted by the lord proprietor. The illiberality of such an arrangement, so obviously ill-suited to the actual conditions of American settlement, stands among the first and most pertinent facts in Maryland's history. The point for the moment, however, may easily be overemphasized.

[10] Misleading statements at times have been made through failure to understand that it is the charter of 1609 that counted, and that the grant there made had no standing in law after 1624. Strictly speaking, nothing was taken from Virginia, but the Maryland grant did fall in a region that both the old adventurers and the colonists hoped to have confirmed, each group to itself. The adventurers and planters were at one only in their dislike of the Maryland grant.

There was a contractual relationship between lord and tenant offering guarantees to the latter and traditionally implicit in the feudal scheme Lord Baltimore sought to introduce. Also, once again men facing the hazards of a frontier venture may well have found a reassuring promise of effective authority and order in what to us appears objectionably restrictive, and soon indeed would so appear to them.

Since apparently there had never been an intention to establish a colony exclusively Catholic in faith, it became necessary to offset through a well-executed promotional program the normal suspicion that would be entertained by Protestants of a Catholic leadership. Printed tracts, as in earlier ventures a leading feature of the effort, are suggestive, especially in the exactitude with which such things as costs for labor and equipment are specified, of the advantage gained by the later colonists from the experience of those who had gone before them. The extent to which the information offered was compiled on the basis of known conditions in Virginia, and the suggestion made that four to five pounds laid out in England for clothing, wine, and assorted groceries would find in Virginia a ready exchange for a cow or several breeding sows reminds us once more of how much the task of the early settler there had been to prepare the way.[11] To his credit stands in no small part the fact that later colonists, including those in Maryland, escaped the intense suffering which repeatedly had been his lot.

The chief inducement offered prospective settlers was the promise of a grant of land in proportion to the investment made. For the "first adventurers," every man going at his own cost, or sending a deputy in command, with able men between the ages of sixteen and fifty, would receive two thousand acres for every five such men. The land would lie in one place and be erected into a manor "with all such royalties and priviledges, as are usually belonging to Mannors in England," the right to hold courts leet and baron included. Those following within two years after the first settlement would receive, with similar rights of jurisdiction, two thousand acres for every ten men. When migrating in less force, a man

---

[11] See especially, *A Relation of Maryland* (London, 1635), reprinted in Clayton C. Hall (ed.), *Narratives of Early Maryland* (New York, 1910), 70–112. The document includes the Maryland charter as an Appendix.

could claim one hundred acres each for himself, wife, and every servant, and fifty acres for every child under sixteen. Though in detail and form there were significant differences, Lord Baltimore had followed the basic features of the Virginia land system: use of the land to underwrite the settlement of the colony and use of the headright as a unit of apportionment. As in Virginia, special consideration was accorded those bearing the brunt of the first effort. By 1642 it required the transportation of twenty persons to secure a manorial grant of two thousand acres, and the headright for those carrying a lesser number had been reduced to fifty acres, which was the headright in Virginia. The quitrent, too, was fixed at the Virginia rate of two shillings per hundred acres.[12]

Two vessels, the *Ark* and the *Dove,* left England for Maryland late in the fall of 1633 after much trouble and a delay caused in part by the obstructive tactics of the old Virginia adventurers. Having followed the southern route by way of Barbados and St. Kitts, the mixed group of probably less than three hundred prospective settlers sailed into Chesapeake Bay toward the close of February. In command was Leonard Calvert, brother to the lord proprietor and destined to serve as governor of Maryland until his death in 1647. Joined with him in a commission for the government of the colony were Jerome Hawley, who was to be appointed treasurer of Virginia in 1637, and Thomas Cornwallis, one of the outstanding leaders in early Maryland. Perhaps the most interesting member of the party was Father Andrew White, a Jesuit priest who with his colleague, John Altham, came in the hope of founding a mission that would redound to the credit both of their church and of their country. White deserves to be remembered also for his charming chronicle of the first settlement.[13] Two lay brothers and sixteen

---

[12] For the successive conditions of settlement, see *Archives of Maryland,* III (1885), 47–48, 99–100, 221–28, 231–37; Hall (ed.), *Narratives of Early Maryland,* 91–92. The two-shilling rate was adopted in 1635.

[13] See his "Briefe Relation of the Voyage unto Maryland," in Hall (ed.), *Narratives of Early Maryland,* 27–45. Among secondary accounts of Maryland's early history, Andrews, *Colonial Period of American History,* II, 274 ff., is the most enlightening. Other useful references are John L. Bozman, *The History of Maryland, from its First Settlement, in 1633, to the Restoration, in 1660* (Baltimore, 1837); John T. Scharf, *History of Maryland, from the Earliest Period to the Present Day* (Baltimore, 1879); William H. Browne, *Maryland; The History of a Palatinate* (Boston, 1884); Clayton C. Hall, *The Lords Baltimore and the Maryland Palatinate* (Baltimore, 1902); and the

gentlemen-adventurers completed the list of leading figures, the majority of whom were Catholic. The remainder of the settlers, chiefly Protestant in faith, were for the most part servants, laborers, and craftsmen, with a few yeomen included. It appears that, from the first, Protestants outnumbered Catholics in the Maryland colony.

The explanation is simple. Few of Baltimore's coreligionists found in their hearts sufficient response to his appeal to hazard the risks of emigration. On the other hand, his promise of religious toleration carried sufficient conviction to persuade many men of Protestant faith to take the additional risk of settlement under Catholic leadership. That promise received confirmation in instructions to Leonard Calvert which enjoined him to "suffer no scandall nor offence to be given to any of the Protestants," and required as an additional safeguard that the Catholics maintain silence "upon all occasions of discourse concerning matters of Religion." [14] Surely, the latter injunction must be numbered among the most difficult to observe of all the instructions issued by English authorities for the guidance of American colonists. It is no mere figure of speech to say that Maryland was founded on the principle that men were entitled to worship according to the dictates of their own consciences, and as Charles, third Lord Baltimore, later declared, it is doubtful that the project could have been carried through without the concession thus made to Protestant participants.[15]

From Governor Harvey in Virginia, Lord Baltimore's people received, according to the King's specific instructions to Harvey,[16] material and other assistance. After a brief visit in Virginia, the *Ark* and *Dove* early in March entered the mouth of the Potomac, its majestic sweep so impressing White that the Thames seemed "but a little finger to it." Landing on St. Clement's (now Blakiston) Island, the colonists took possession in the name of the lord proprietor. Exploration and consultation with native chieftains con-

chronological narrative of Bernard C. Steiner, *Beginnings of Maryland, 1631–1639* (Baltimore, 1903); *Maryland during the English Civil Wars* (Baltimore, 1906–1907); and *Maryland under the Commonwealth; A Chronicle of the Years 1649–1658* (Baltimore, 1911).

[14] Hall (ed.), *Narratives of Early Maryland*, 11–23.
[15] *Archives of Maryland*, V (1887), 267–68.   [16] *Ibid.*, III (1885), 22–23.

sumed several weeks, during which the nimble-witted and veteran Indian trader Henry Fleet served as guide and interpreter, before the site of St. Mary's was chosen and purchased of the local Yaocomico Indians. Approximately seventy miles from Jamestown as the crow flies but somewhat farther away by water, the site lay a short distance up the Potomac and to the right on what came to be known as St. Mary's River. As all who have visited St. Mary's know, the choice fell in one of the more attractive places selected by our forebears for a first seat. Above and overlooking a good anchorage, lying well for the farmer's tools, and supplied with good water, it became in the spring of 1634 a place of bustling activity as men hurried to build a temporary palisade and to get in the first seed, meanwhile sleeping and offering their worship in the rude dwellings left by the departing natives.

Today St. Mary's, like Jamestown, lies off the main road. It is a place not only rich in historical associations but one that affords the student of history an opportunity to stand in reverie with only a few reminders of the modern age to block the free play of his imagination. The memorials and the markers erected by later generations are few. The visitor easily reconstructs his own image of the place as it appeared to the first settlers, and while taking advantage of an inviting view of the surrounding country, he tends to contemplate the significance of the names they gave to the places about them. Perhaps it is just as well that this should be the case, for place names are often a more helpful guide than could be any other historical mark.[17]

Consider, for example, the names of our rivers. The river on which colonists came in, and upon which they subsequently depended for communication with the outside world, naturally acquired for them an overshadowing importance. Its designation usually fell among the earliest formal acts of a newly arrived colony, and the European name given it—whether the James, the Cooper, the Ashley, or some other—was likely to survive wherever the settlement proved permanent. But streams lying beyond the area of initial settlement, including tributaries of rivers which themselves bore European names, have tended to carry an identification that

[17] Students of American history will find George R. Stewart, *Names on the Land* (New York, 1945), a most rewarding book.

bespeaks their original association in the minds of the settlers with the native Indians who lived along their banks. Such was the case with the Appomattox, the Chickahominy, the Rappahannock, the Potomac, the Susquehanna, and the Connecticut. Here and there the colonists attempted to substitute another name, as when the founders of Maryland undertook to redesignate the Potomac as St. Gregory's River, but prior usage fortunately tended to prevail. When naming their towns, plantations, manors, or perhaps it is better said, their New World homes, the colonists frequently gave expression to nostalgia for the old home and to a variety of other moods and sentiments with which they viewed their new situation. The word "hope" appended to the family name was ever popular, as in Archer's Hope. A man in Virginia simply and eloquently described his place as World's End, and another in Maryland with misplaced optimism chose for a name the Ending of Controversie. As the colonial communities grew and political subdivisions became necessary, the names more commonly used appropriately bespoke allegiance to an established political tradition by honoring some public figure at home, not infrequently a patron of the settlement, or called to mind the ancient shires of England. Each community, too, bears the markings of its own peculiar origins. In Maryland, St. Mary's, St. Clement's, St. Inigoe's, to mention but a few, speak as forcefully of the Catholic faith and purpose of its first leaders as elsewhere the name Providence records the spiritual resources of a Puritan settlement.

Among the more important of Maryland's problems was that of establishing a proper relationship between its people and their neighbors in Virginia. Of help were a community of tradition and outlook as Englishmen, a sense of sharing in the laudable work of expanding His Majesty's dominions, and mutually advantageous opportunities for the exchange of goods. In the larger community of the Chesapeake, the influx of Marylanders represented an investment of new capital, a fact as important then as it was in later years to the primitive economy of any frontier community. The older colony provided a source of supply promising a more speedy establishment of the younger settlement, while in Maryland the Virginians found a new market for their staple produce. Over against these considerations there existed certain jealousies and apprehensions that had caused Lord Baltimore to forbid his officers to bring the *Ark* and *Dove* within command of the guns at Point Comfort. The warning had been ignored to the very real advantage of his people, but another likely source of friction is amusingly noted in Father White's reference to the unsatisfactory nature of his first discussions of religion with the native chieftains because of a necessary dependence on Protestant interpreters from Virginia. Moreover, there was a clash of economic interests affecting influential Virginians.

The trade of the Chesapeake, it will be recalled, had been assigned to members of the governor's council in Virginia as a partial compensation for their services. How effective was the restriction thus established, or for how long a term it held, is difficult to say, but it is unlikely that there were many persons outside the council who possessed the capital to press the trade seriously. Indeed, it is not known how many even of the council bothered to exercise the prerogative, though it is significant that Governor Harvey's befriending of the Marylanders was an obvious source of the increasing friction between him and the council that led to his expulsion in 1635. The prolonged and bitter controversy over the bay trade centered largely around one man, William Claiborne, who had come to Virginia in 1621 as surveyor general.

Like other promoters, Lord Baltimore had looked to the beaver and the deerskins which featured the trade with the Chesapeake Bay Indians as a source of income. He had entered into an agreement for exploitation of the trade with adventurers in the first expedition, and counting the licensing of traders a normal prerogative of the proprietorship, looked forward to a continuing revenue from that source.[18] On the other hand, Claiborne as a member of the Virginia council had been engaged in exploratory and trading ventures in the upper Chesapeake, and had established a post there on Kent Island. In 1630, the year after Baltimore's visit to Virginia, Claiborne had gone to England in the double hope, apparently, of obstructing Baltimore's grant and of securing capital for a more ambitious undertaking of his own. He returned to Virginia in 1631, having won the backing of a small group of London merchants, among whom William Cloberry was chief. With the

---

[18] *Archives of Maryland,* I (1883), 42–44.

funds so provided he began the work that was over the next few years to transform his Kent Island trading post into a full-fledged settlement of colonists following agricultural as well as trading pursuits. It was, in effect, a new though small colony, founded with the benefit of a base in Virginia, but representing essentially the investment of London merchants. As Professor Andrews has observed, it was "in no sense a Virginia undertaking." [19] Only in a secondary way was the quarrel that centered about it a clash of interests between Virginia and Maryland.

It proved, nonetheless, an irritating factor in the relations of the two colonies. Claiborne and his associates had only a trading license, while the title to Kent Island under the subsequent Maryland charter unquestionably belonged to Lord Baltimore. The latter's approach to Claiborne was conciliatory, but unyielding in the demand that his title be recognized. Claiborne's rejection of these advances was partly inspired by strong anti-Catholic convictions. In the ensuing contest he naturally found much sympathy in Virginia, where dislike of Catholicism was joined to the apprehensions of men whose rights and titles lacked the security afforded by a royal charter. But Virginia could advance no legal claim to Kent Island, and there must have been some who hesitated to back Claiborne too far lest they lend comfort and support to the old Virginia adventurers who, in their current effort to revive the company's charter, attacked the validity of Baltimore's grant. Thus the quarrel continued primarily between Claiborne and Baltimore, both of whom pursued it with uncompromising stubbornness.

The spring of 1635 brought an exchange of blows over Claiborne's insistence on a right of trade without the proprietor's license. This contest proved for the moment indecisive, but decisive enough in its results was the implied repudiation of Claiborne by his partners. In 1636 they sent over George Evelyn with full power of attorney and instructions for Claiborne's return to England to explain his accounts and actions. During the next year and in Claiborne's absence, Evelyn, as perhaps his employers had intended, agreed upon the island's submission to Governor Calvert, a sub-

---

[19] Andrews, *Colonial Period of American History*, II, 302–307, is the clearest discussion of the complex issues involved.

mission made good, per agreement, by military force. Henceforth Kent Island was in fact as well as law a part of Maryland. But it remained, hardly the less, a center of recurring trouble; and Claiborne, the subject of an altogether unfair bill of attainder passed by the Maryland Assembly of 1638, continued alert to the opportunities provided by whatever disturbance might arise. For the moment faced with defeat, he was yet to have his innings.

Colorful and pertinent as is the story of the Claiborne affair, its overemphasis should be guarded against, for there is danger of slighting a more significant fact. Virginia's official position with reference to the quarrel was for the most part correct, and in accord with the King's injunction "to hold that good correspondence" and to provide "such lawfull assistance, as may conduce to both your safeties and the advancement of the plantation of those Countries." [20] Through the years during which Claiborne remained a troublemaker for Maryland, and they cover virtually a quarter of a century, the two Chesapeake colonies were working out the procedures for that exchange of amenities that is appropriate to fellow members of a larger political community. Not to be overlooked were such things as Virginia's protective statutes to guard against the invasion of Catholics.[21] But co-operation was early sought and given in the apprehension of fugitive servants. Agreements were made regarding rights of trade, and those doing business across the line found standing in courts where faith and credit were accorded documents executed in the other colony.[22] As Article IV of our Federal Constitution amply attests, these were developments of enduring importance.

A community of institutional development provided further encouragement for this exchange of intercolonial amenities. The commission by which Leonard Calvert ruled spoke, it is true, both of absolute ideas of government and of elaborate plans for arrangement of the colony's life that were unfamiliar in Virginia. By it

[20] *Archives of Maryland,* III (1885), 22–23; and see *ibid.,* 79–80; *Virginia Magazine,* VIII (1900–1901), 151–52; IX (1901–1902), 36–37.

[21] *Virginia Magazine,* IX (1901–1902), 56; Hening, *Statutes,* I, 268–69.

[22] On the subject of servants, see Raphael Semmes, *Crime and Punishment in Early Maryland* (Baltimore, 1938), 110–11, and his specific references, especially to records of the provincial court, p. 287. For a trade agreement of 1642, see Hening, *Statutes,* I, 276. On the general topic the county court records form a pertinent source.

Calvert had been constituted lieutenant general, admiral, chief captain and commander, chancellor, chief justice, and chief magistrate. He held power to appoint necessary officers; to hear and judge pleas civil and criminal; to issue edicts, ordinances, and proclamations so long as the penalties attached did not extend to a deprival of life and goods. He was also empowered to hear appeals with a reservation of capital offenses for final action by the proprietor; to grant pardons except for treason; to issue land patents; and to superintend generally and specifically the commercial life of the colony. In the exercise of his many-sided functions he enjoyed the aid of a council. By the commission of 1637, the earliest extant, that council was comprised of three men: Jerome Hawley, John Lewger, and Thomas Cornwallis. Lewger was also designated secretary, with duties comparable to those of the secretary in Virginia, and collector of proprietary rents and revenues.[23] The governor's authority was at all points paramount, and technically free of restrictions then operating in Virginia. The elaborate recitation of powers conferred suggests an influence proceeding directly from the lord proprietor conducive to a more exact observance in early Maryland than in Virginia, and possibly most of the colonies, of the technical distinctions and procedures of English law.[24] The governor's commission prepared the way, too, for distinctive institutional developments, as in the appointment of a separate chancellor in 1661.

Circumstances in the first days of a colony, however, tended to reduce the most elaborate formulas to the simplest terms. An interesting example is afforded by a discussion that took place in the Maryland Assembly of 1638. A body of laws submitted by the proprietor for approval by the Assembly had been rejected. The question then became that of what laws the colony should be governed by until further word came from the proprietor. It was proposed that the Assembly frame laws of its own. The governor denied the right. Cornwallis suggested the laws of England might serve. Calvert agreed that they would do for civil causes and

---

[23] *Archives of Maryland*, III (1885), 49–55.

[24] See especially Judge Carroll T. Bond's introduction to the "Proceedings of the Court of Chancery of Maryland, 1669–1679," in *Archives of Maryland*, LI (1934), xxii–xxxi.

criminal actions not extending to life or limb, but that for the more serious offenses he was restricted to the laws of the province. And to this it was "answered, that such enormous offences could hardly be committed without mutinie & then it might be punished by martiall law." [25] One is reminded of the difficulty in distinguishing between martial and civil authority during the early days of Virginia, but of greater immediate importance is the suggestion that Calvert's elaborate commission simply conferred upon him all necessary powers.

The point of departure for developing agencies of provincial administration was in Maryland not greatly different from what it had been in Virginia. Through the years that followed, governor and council in each colony sat in consultation on questions of policy, acted as the highest provincial court, undertook to assume the leadership of the general assembly, and exercised such administrative functions as the occasion required. [26] Outranking in importance all technical differences are these essential similarities.

The field of local administration presents even clearer evidence of the way in which circumstances tended to take charge. Baltimore's plan of government depended heavily upon his feudal scheme of settlement. He intended that the manor should exist in something more than name only, and erected no less than sixty manors by patent in addition to those set aside for himself and members of his family. [27] Fragmentary records, extending over the period from 1659 to 1672, have survived to reveal something of the proceedings of one manorial court. [28] But that is all, and other records of the province show remarkably little evidence that manorial courts functioned. The fact appears to be that only a very

[25] *Ibid.*, I (1883), 9.

[26] The proceedings of the council are in *Archives of Maryland*, III (1885); V (1887); VIII (1890); XV (1896); XVII (1898). where the judicial proceedings have been printed separately. The standard authority on the institutional story is Newton D. Mereness, *Maryland as a Proprietary Province* (New York, 1901), which like Bruce on Virginia is arranged topically.

[27] Andrews, *Colonial Period of American History*, II, 294. See also, Donnell M. Owings, "Private Manors: An Edited List," in *Maryland Historical Magazine* (Baltimore), XXXIII (1938), 307–34; Annie L. Sioussat, *Old Manors in the Colony of Maryland* (Baltimore, 1911–1913).

[28] That for St. Clement's Manor, granted Thomas Gerard in 1639, in *Archives of Maryland*, LIII (1936), 627–37.

few manor lords ever bothered with the exercise of their jurisdictional prerogatives, and most of those few soon gave it up as pointless and unprofitable. As the editors of one of the more recent volumes of the Maryland *Archives* have pertinently remarked: "To look upon seventeenth-century Maryland as a land in which some seventy or more large landowners lived in ample manor houses and held feudal sway over numerous freehold and leasehold tenants, is a romantic picture which is not justified either by the Provincial records or by the economic conditions of the time." [29]

The ground, in fact, was for the most part quickly cleared to give full play to circumstances very similar to those which had guided the institutional growth of Virginia. Through the first stages of the colony's development men found practically no occasion to distinguish between provincial and local administration. A small and compact community centering around St. Mary's required little more in the way of a government than could be provided easily by the governor and his councilors. As the expansion of settlement brought some necessity for special provision in outlying areas, the governor and council continued through several years to serve well enough for the home settlement at St. Mary's. So it had been in Virginia, where the county court in Elizabeth City, for example, was considerably older than that now sitting for James City.

The earliest unit of local administration to appear in Maryland, apart from the manor, was the hundred. Where settlement advanced into some area lying far enough out to present a special problem, the region would be constituted a hundred, and one of its more responsible inhabitants appointed high constable with the authority belonging to that office in England. [30] Maryland stood almost alone among the seventeenth-century colonies in giving some reality in America to the English hundred. For a while it served, in a confusing and shifting pattern of local administration, as an important electoral, judicial, and administrative unit, but its importance declined, almost from the time of its appearance. At an

---

[29] *Ibid.*, lxiii.

[30] *Ibid.*, III (1885), 59–60, 70–71, 91, the last conferring conjunctively the powers of a coroner. There are also references to St. Mary's Hundred as early as 1637 and 1638. *Ibid.*, IV (1887), 4 ff.

early date commissions issued to local magistrates placed in each of the several communities a "Conservator of the Peace" with powers defined as those of any two English justices of the peace.[31] That action in itself did not dispose of the need for the hundred, but, as events soon proved, the step marked a move toward reliance upon the same county-court machinery of local government that had been established in Virginia. With the development of the county, both the hundred and its constable assumed increasingly a junior status. The one survived primarily as a constablewick, while the other became a minor police officer of the sort making his appearance about this time in Virginia, where he served for a local precinct under the county court. In both colonies the term of office became a year. Its duties being somewhat onerous, the job was avoided, and rotated among those eligible whenever possible.

Lord Baltimore's plan interposed no serious obstacle to the introduction of such agencies of the English county as might be deemed useful. The bishopric of Durham had also been a county, and early references are made in Maryland to St. Mary's County. Close examination reveals, however, that this was in effect merely another designation for the province, as appears by the fact that Kent Island, some distance away from St. Mary's on the Eastern Shore of the bay, was considered a hundred of St. Mary's. The Assembly of 1639 had under consideration a bill for the establishment of a county court, but the measure appears to have proposed little more than another refinement of the multiple functions of the governor and his councilors.[32] Such items of record are perhaps significant primarily as a clue to those influences which led to the introduction, as a matter of course, of the familiar English officers of local administration. Though the records of the American colonies are often incomplete, it is nonetheless significant that sheriffs, coroners, and constables frequently make their first appearance by incidental reference.

In tracing the origins of the county in Maryland, it is necessary to turn again to Kent Island. When that island finally came under the proprietor's authority, its distance from St. Mary's and the disgruntled attitude of many of its people presented a special

---

[31] *Ibid.*, III (1885), 60–61, 89–90.
[32] *Ibid.*, I (1883), 47–49, 55–57; IV (1887), 9, 161, 162.

problem of government. There was need for someone both to "command and govern" the people, and, where so many of the people came from Virginia, it was only natural that the precedent provided by the commander of the county in Virginia should have been followed. In December, 1637, Evelyn, in keeping perhaps with the terms of his recent submission, received a commission as commander of the isle of Kent. He had power to choose six or more able men for his consultation and assistance, to hold courts for civil causes not exceeding ten pounds sterling and for criminal actions not extending to life or member, and to appoint such other officers as might be necessary for the execution of justice and the preservation of the peace with allowance of fees identical with those "usually belonging to the same or the like offices in Virginia." Commissions issued subsequently were of a similar import.[33] Between 1640 and 1642 Kent Island, which had had its own sheriff as early as 1638, was given the status of a county; as more than once had been the case in Virginia, the county court in Kent predated the county itself. How early such a court existed for St. Mary's is uncertain, but its presence by August of 1644 is established by the issuance at that time of the now familiar commission to a commander and two other commissioners.[34] By the end of the decade, the institution had acquired a position in the government of the Maryland colony comparable in all important particulars to that of the county court in Virginia. Thereafter, the administration of each new county established was promptly entrusted to a chief magistrate and board of commissioners. As in the older colony, the title of "commander" lingered on through several years.

The parallels between the county court in Maryland and in Virginia extend beyond those arising merely from a similarity of origins. Functions were equally broad, and successive stages of

[33] *Ibid.*, III (1885), 59, 62–63, 80–81, 88–89, 105, 124–25, 127. It would be interesting in this connection to know just what administrative arrangements for the island existed under Claiborne. The limits fixed in 1637 for the court's jurisdiction were identical with those holding at the time in Virginia.

[34] *Ibid.*, 150–51. The most recent and the best discussion of the early history of the county court in Maryland is available in the introductory essays by the editors of Volumes LIII (1936) and LIV (1937) of the *Archives of Maryland*, where records of seventeenth-century county courts are published. Bruce, *Institutional History of Virginia*, I, 484 ff., remains the principal account of the court in Virginia.

development were alike. Members enjoyed individually the authority and the prestige of a local magistrate, a source of pride through a man's life that would often in the Old South find record on his tombstone. For the county as a whole there were usually from six to eight magistrates, one or more of whom carried a special responsibility indicated by the requirement that they be of the quorum when the court sat. The chief magistrate, or chief justice as he was at times called, held a casting vote at a table where decisions were reached by majority rule. Through the early years a courthouse was a luxury beyond the means of an infant community, and the court tended to carry its services to the people. It often met successively at the residences of the several commissioners, who had been chosen partly with a view to providing a resident magistrate in each section of the county. At other times some tavern that was a natural focal point of the county's life served as a regular meeting place, and perhaps also to encourage the idea that court day was a good day to find congenial company at the bar. The governor and members of his council exercised a well-established right to sit with the commissioners of any county as opportunity or the occasion might suggest. Commissions issued for newly created counties usually included one or more men who had served in an older court, who often in fact had acted as magistrates for that end of an older county which now was erected into a new jurisdiction for the convenience of an expanding community. Thus, in a way that would be typical of the political development of the American frontier, men built anew on the foundations of experience in the older areas of settlement. To sum it up, circumstances were giving shape through these years to a community of institutional usage between the two Chesapeake settlements as markedly English in spirit, as unmistakably American in character, and as distinctly regional in form, as that which in Massachusetts, Connecticut, Rhode Island, and New Haven centered about the New England town.[35]

Among the more important influences working toward this end was Lord Baltimore's enforced absence from the province. Like his father, his interest in colonization was immediate and personal.

[35] For a discussion of the further development of the county court and its jurisdiction in the Southern colonies, see below, pp. 269–89, 293–94, 302–309.

There can be little doubt that had he been able to follow his own inclination he would have been, for most of the time at any rate, a resident proprietor. Instead, successive attacks upon his charter and other considerations kept him in England for a time that was indefinitely prolonged by the outbreak there of civil disturbances which placed at special hazard the interests of a Catholic nobleman and friend of the King. In fact, he was never to visit Maryland. The differences between resident and absentee landlordism are many and significant. The one is personal, prompt in action, and possessed of a certain elasticity permitting concessions in special circumstances without surrender of essential prerogatives. The other is marked by delay and misunderstanding, both of them calculated to strengthen the determination of either party to a conflict and thus to draw out differences to a point at which men are divided on principle.

The story of the Maryland Assembly offers a case in point. Baltimore's charter conferred on him "free, full, and absolute power" to make laws "with the advice assent and approbation of the Freemen of the . . . Province," who as occasion dictated were to be assembled by the proprietor and his heirs "in such sort and form, as to him or them shall seem best." For the earliest Assembly, that of 1635, there is no extant record. The first of which anything is known in detail met in 1638.[36] Some of those present had responded to individual writs, as did members of the English House of Lords; the others to general writs calling for the attendance of all freemen, either in person or by deputy and proxy. They met as one body under the presidency of the governor, who as lieutenant of the proprietor and in his behalf insisted upon full control over adjournment, dissolution, and the initiation of legislation. Had the proprietor been resident in the colony he undoubtedly would have presided, and there is no difficulty in picturing the scene, somewhat medieval in flavor, as surrounded by his chosen and intimate advisers, together with the freemen or their deputies, the lord proprietor proceeded to promulgate laws for his province with the "assent" of its people. "Be it enacted by the Lord Proprietarie of this Province of and with the advice and approbation of the

---

[36] The proceedings and acts of assembly may be followed in *Archives of Maryland*, I (1883); II (1884); VII (1889); XIII (1894).

freemen of the same," reads the common form in which was cast Maryland's early statutes. The right to legislate was a right of the proprietor, but out of his grace and in keeping with the charter he sought the "advice and approbation" of the people in its exercise —something quite different from a right in the people to make their own laws.

For that right a contest was immediately opened. Laws sent over by the proprietor, or framed in accordance with his instructions, frequently met with something less than the approbation of the freemen. Some laws they were disposed to reject outright, others to amend in important particulars, and still other bills they wished to introduce in their own behalf. On the second and third points the issue was joined in a struggle destined to continue through many years. The proprietor proved unyielding on the principle at stake, but, hard pressed from many quarters, he occasionally made practical concessions that tended to move the legislative power in Maryland toward a position long familiar to the inhabitants of Virginia.[37] In that colony orders and instructions from the company or from officers of the crown, as the case may have been, had frequently received legislative sanction by an action of the burgesses that was in effect a counterpart of the rule denying validity to an act of the Assembly without approval of the company or the crown. A comparison of instructions to the early royal governors of Virginia with the record provided in Hening's *Statutes* shows that many of the royal instructions were mere paraphrasing of laws previously enacted on the initiative of the Assembly, just as more than one statute merely paraphrased specific instructions from the King.[38] A reciprocal arrangement this, and one which divided the legislative power both as to place and authority. The arrangement continued in some measure to be honored throughout the colonial period, and is interestingly suggestive of Joseph Galloway's subsequent proposals for an accommodation of the differences between the Continental Congress and Parliament.

Through the early days of Maryland the thoughts of Englishmen

[37] For example, see *ibid.*, I (1883), 238–43, 262–72, 322–23; and notice the later attempt of the Carolina proprietors to secure ratification by the Assembly of the Fundamental Constitutions of 1669.

[38] Berkeley's instructions of 1642, in *Virginia Magazine,* II (1894–1895), 281–88, are especially useful in this connection.

were frequently drawn to a consideration of the rights of Parliament, and of the place parliamentary authority and usage held in the English tradition. The issues raised at home were easily transferred to America, and especially to Maryland, where a proprietary authority regularly expressed in such terms of royal right as "We have therefore of our Meer grace," "in the fifteenth year of our dominion," or "our city of St. Mary's," invited an obvious comparison. The Assembly was quick to model its actions after Parliament, to demand the usual parliamentary privileges, and more significant perhaps, to observe those conventions governing a joint deliberation and decision that, ingrained in the habits of a people, have formed so large a part of the genius for self-government in the New World as in the old. Whatever crudities may have marked their speech, dress, or place of assembly, men took the floor in an attitude of respect for a great tradition. They referred to their colleagues in such acceptable terms as "the gentleman who spoke last," and when on this point or otherwise forgetting the rules of the house or of common courtesy, they found themselves open to indictment for a breach of the dignity of the house.[39]

The parallel with Parliament's development is further suggested by two other particulars. Judicial functions, similar to those exercised in Virginia, remind us of the role historically identified with the "high court of parliament." More pertinent to topics of later interest were the influences working toward a bicameral form of organization. Those persons summoned by special writ tended naturally toward an identification with the larger propertied interests, and thus with the interests of the proprietary circle and the expanding membership of the governor's council. As time passed and the colony grew, any attempt to give each freeman a voice directly or by proxy proved expensive and awkward. It had been from the first a privilege of the freemen in a community to send a deputy, and there was a natural tendency to identify his representative role with such units as the hundred or county. The somewhat mixed membership holding for a time reflected not merely the original rules of representation, but as well the same practical considerations that in Virginia awarded representation, as is possible in a small community, to any group having a good reason to

[39] See *Archives of Maryland,* I (1883), 91–92, 215–16; Hening, *Statutes,* I, 507–508.

be represented.[40] The demand for a separate house was made as early as 1642, but the separation did not come until 1650,[41] a date not far from that at which the Virginia Assembly was similarly divided.

The period of this transition was marked, both in Maryland and in Virginia, by a growing mastery of parliamentary techniques and skills. One of the more profitable exercises for the modern student is to read through Hening's *Statutes,* and to notice there the increasing skill with which bills were drafted. Less and less frequently did it prove necessary to go back and restate the intent of the Assembly because of imperfect draftsmanship in an earlier effort.[42] A more impressive display of technical and legal knowledge generally characterizing the laws of Maryland reflects the influence of the proprietor, as no doubt does a marked improvement in Virginia evidence the aid of Governors Wyatt and Berkeley. Not only did the proprietor and his attorneys supervise more closely the laws passed in Maryland than did crown officials, but the statutes sent over by him, even when drastically modified or rejected, offered a worthy model. Too often perhaps have Americans been inclined to emphasize the restrictive, or negative, side of an English authority over the colonies at the expense of the constructive tutelage provided.

Similarities in institutional development suggest the existence of an underlying unity in the basic fabric of neighboring societies, and so it was with Virginia and Maryland. Joined closely by waterway communication, separated only by lines principally of political and legal significance, the Chesapeake colonies formed essentially one community, its life drawn chiefly from the soil and its people tending to ever wider dispersal as they took advantage of waterways carrying on all sides to new and better land. Tobacco was the main crop; the "tobacco house," serving a variety of purposes, the most important of the outbuildings on a man's place; and the tobacco stick, stout and ever ready to hand, a common instrument of chastisement as cases involving abuse of servants frequently testify.

[40] *Archives of Maryland,* I (1883), 74–75, 81–82, 259.   [41] *Ibid.,* 130, 272–73.

[42] For an example in Maryland, see *ibid.,* 298–99. Another point of significance is the drawing of a clear distinction between orders and statutes by the 1640's in Virginia. McIlwaine (ed.), *Journals of the House of Burgesses of Virginia, 1619–1658/59,* p. xxxix.

Indeed, the importance of the American weed is written so unmistakably across the record that its significance is easily exaggerated. Much has been said of a one-crop economy, and certainly laws requiring the planting of at least two acres of corn per head indicate that some members of the community were disposed, as have been many farmers of the South since, to devote too much of their time to the staple crop.[43] Nevertheless, tobacco is more accurately described as the money crop, the crop with which men paid their taxes and their minister and with luck met their debts. Energies were largely absorbed by the varied duties of subsistence farming; meat and bread were no more to be thought of as imports than elsewhere, or at any time, on an American frontier.

The characteristic economic unit was the small farm. References to manors and plantations should not mislead us, for one was no more representative of the established position and wealth associated with the term in England than is the other of any group comparable to the relatively small class that later monopolized the name "planter." In the usage of these early days, "planter" was synonymous with "colonist," any colonist who was free, and his plantation was simply his farm.

There were differences, of course, in the size of the farm. Some of the early grants were quite impressive in their extent, and there is evidence that some men whose beginnings in the New World had been modest were accumulating larger holdings by the middle of the century. But that such estates were promptly put under cultivation as large units, except in rare instances, remains unlikely and unproved. It must be remembered that land was more easily acquired than was the labor and capital equipment for its development, and that a title to 1,500 or 2,000 acres does not of itself prove that a plantation of that extent was actually in operation. It is pertinent to inquire how much of the grant had been cleared for cultivation and to remember that the difficulty of clearing new ground was so great that it provided succeeding generations of Americans with one of their more forceful figures of speech denoting hard work. Pertinent, too, is the question of the acreage ac-

---

[43] *Archives of Maryland*, I (1883), 79, 96; Hening, *Statutes*, I, 152, 166, 246, 419, 481, these last indicating that such laws extended considerably beyond the earliest period of settlement.

quired and held for purely speculative reasons. The abuses which marked the headright system, and the advantage taken of them for speculative purposes, are well known.[44] Equally well known is the practice, growing with a wasteful agricultural system, of acquiring land in excess of one's immediate needs to be held in reserve for later use.

Of interest in this connection is the evidence in the county records that much of the land brought under cultivation was leased, some of it for rent and some on shares, the leases collectively presenting a wide variation both as to the acreage involved and the terms of tenancy. Stipulations frequently entered into between landlord and tenant indicate that the lease proved one of the more useful devices for getting the land cleared and placing upon it improvements calculated to add to its value. Usage of the device suggests that large holdings tended to be scattered rather than concentrated, and is indicative of a measure of absentee ownership, especially in the case of land owned by English merchants. Tenancy seems to have been a principal opportunity awaiting the servant at the end of his term of service. Finally, the evidence reinforces the view that large holdings, insofar as they were brought under cultivation, tended to be worked in small units, where the tenant farmer, often enjoying advantageous terms, was the central figure.[45]

As for those members of the community who worked their own land, Professor Thomas J. Wertenbaker's careful analysis of land patents, inventories, wills, and rent rolls for Virginia, outside the Northern Neck, has established beyond challenge the fact that even at the close of the century the small farm and a yeoman class of farmers remained the dominant feature of the picture.[46] A more

[44] The abuses were such that Lord Baltimore abandoned the headright system in 1683, substituting sales. *Archives of Maryland,* V (1887), 390–91, 394–95.

[45] For examples in Virginia, see York County Records (Office of Clerk of Court, Yorktown), No. 1, Deeds, Orders, Wills, 1633–1657, pp. 104–108; No. 3, Deeds, Orders, Wills, 1657–1662, p. 163; in Maryland, *Archives of Maryland,* LIII (1936), 127, 365; LIV (1937), 12, 79, 133, 201, 244, 425. The evidence is perhaps less conclusive for Maryland than for Virginia. The present writer has had only an opportunity to sample the county records, and a closer study is required. An indication of the possible results of such study, supporting the conclusions advanced above, may be found in Susie M. Ames, *Studies of the Virginia Eastern Shore in the Seventeenth Century* (Richmond, 1940), 37–42. Leases often included servants, cattle, and even hogs.

[46] Wertenbaker, *Planters of Colonial Virginia, passim.*

recent study for Virginia's Eastern Shore brings out an interesting trend from original grants that were for the most part small to larger units by the middle of the century. This trend reached its high point in the third quarter of the century, and thereafter was reversed, as through the fourth quarter larger units were broken up by wills and sales.[47] A study for Maryland, based upon land conveyances from person to person, indicates a similar tendency toward smaller holdings throughout the period extending from the Restoration to the close of the century.[48] The earlier trend probably reflects chiefly the liberal land policies which characterized the initial period of settlement. As for the later period, democratic customs of inheritance and an expanding population evidently brought about, under unfavorable conditions of the tobacco market, the subdivision of many of the larger holdings.

Naturally, there were exceptions to the general tendency, exceptions prophetic of later developments, but clearly the roses and old lace interpretation of Southern life, whatever reality may attach to it in subsequent periods, has no place in the seventeenth century. There was an occasional wig at church on Sunday, though without the powder of the eighteenth century, and the simple lines of the church often bore testimony to a discriminating taste in its conception, as did at times the homes of those who worshiped.[49] But through the week, life was hard and men smelled of tobacco, cattle, and sweat.

Over the span of three centuries, life on a small Southern farm has not greatly changed in its essential qualities. During the crop season first thought naturally went to the money crop, but land was put as well to European wheat and Indian corn.[50] The special favor allotted a surprising number of fruit orchards is amply attested by the extent to which alcoholic beverages ran to ciders and other fruit derivatives, and by frequent choice of this part of a man's ground

[47] Ames, *Studies of the Virginia Eastern Shore*, 16 ff.

[48] Vertrees J. Wyckoff, "The Sizes of Plantations in Seventeenth-Century Maryland," in *Maryland Historical Magazine*, XXXII (1937), 331–39.

[49] For a recent and authoritative discussion of seventeenth-century architecture, see Thomas J. Wertenbaker, *The Old South; The Founding of American Civilization* (New York, 1942), 73–88.

[50] The standard authority is Lewis C. Gray, *History of Agriculture in the Southern United States to 1860* (Washington, 1933).

for a burial plot. Horses or other draft animals were for a while exceedingly scarce, but cattle, hogs, goats, and sheep were common. Indeed, wealth was counted in no small part, as hundreds of wills and inventories show, in terms of cattle. Their pet names of Prettie, Bess, Bossie, Spot, Brownie, Whiteface, Lady, and others familiar on the farm since, so repeatedly appear in the record as to suggest that they often received more care, and were kept closer to the house, than has been generally assumed. The cowbell, its note jarring in other surroundings but musically blending with the varied evidences of life on a farm, soon rang out its helpful peal. The bark of a dog, the crow of a rooster, the cluck of a fretting mother hen, or the cry of children at their play, were among the sounds that carried over the water a familiar notice of the farmer's clearing in the woods.

The hog, a hardy animal, rooted for himself until hog-killing time in the fall put an end to his brief tenure of life. Pork was the staple meat. Chicken, game, and fish provided variety of diet. Where settlement was scattered, mills for the grinding of grain were relatively few and substitute arrangements often primitive. Dishes such as succotash, roasting ears, and hominy, utilizing the whole grain, acquired the popularity they enjoyed among the natives. From the natives, also, came the corn pone and the ash-baked potato.

All agricultural communities face a fundamental problem in the question of whether to fence in the crop or to fence in the live-stock. Since the latter solution calls for a heavy investment of time and labor to provide feed or to fence an area large enough to permit the stock to feed itself, it is not surprising that under conditions existing in early Virginia and Maryland the colonists elected, as men of a later generation put it, to "fence in the crop and turn out the stock." Laws required that every man must provide a fence "sufficient" for the protection of his crop, or else sacrifice all claims for damage done. As the legislature from time to time undertook to define more exactly the term sufficient, there gradually evolved the fence destined to be described in common parlance as "pig-tight, horse-high, and bull-strong." [51]

[51] Hening, *Statutes*, I, 176, 199, 244, 332, 458; *Archives of Maryland*, I (1883), 96, for

Whatever inclination may have existed at first to follow tradi-tional methods of fencing, there was an early trend toward a com-mon use of the rail fence that would lend to the American farm one of its distinctive marks for generations to come.[52] The Tidewater area boasted relatively few stones; the planting of a hedge would have been in the circumstances pretentious and wasteful of time; but close at hand to every field stood a plentiful supply of timber, and though sawmills were few and far between, every farmer had an ax and soon knew how to use it. It did not take long to discover that the three-sided rail, split with the grain, provided the most fence to the felled tree, or that in building the fence a zigzag arrangement of the rails, with stakes driven at each interlacing or "corner," avoided the labor of digging postholes and saved a scarce and ever-prized supply of nails. Mention might also be made of the additional ad-vantage of a fence which readily could be torn down and reassem-bled. Like the clearing of new ground and the cutting of firewood, rail splitting was an off-season job—a task destined to be credited in the tradition, for encouragement of the young, with the building of character no less than of muscle.

The decision having been made to turn out the stock, it became necessary to provide for it identifying marks of ownership. Of the several possibilities, the simplest and the one adopted was to cut with a knife some mark or combination of marks on the animal's ear, a relatively insensible member of the body and of practically no utility to any other than the beast itself. Earmarks—nicks, slits, croppings, underbits, overbits, and holes—placed on either or both of the ears offered for the convenience of the community an amaz-ing number of combinations. Each man had his own mark, which usually was made a matter of record with the clerk of the county court, where charges of hog stealing became so common that it

the earliest law in Maryland. "Hogsties" were not unknown, and a law of Virginia in 1640 even required the shutting up of all hogs by night and attendance of a keeper by day. Hening, *Statutes*, I, 228; Forman, *Jamestown and St. Mary's*, 315. Maryland in 1674 enacted penalties for the malicious practice of fence burning. *Archives of Maryland*, II (1884), 398–99.

[52] Bruce, *Economic History of Virginia*, I, 316, places the introduction of the rail as early as 1621 and cites an order of the General Court five years later requiring that men "rail, pale, or fence" their tilled land where cattle ranges were situated.

proved advisable at hog-killing time to save the ears as evidence of title even to meat on the table.[53] The accusation carried a special offense, suggesting as it did both petty thievery and the taking of a particularly unfair advantage of a neighbor. Men were quick to fight it in and outside court.

The daily duties of farm life, then as later, were many and varied, so varied in fact as to exercise a possibly decisive influence on the type of labor employed by the seventeenth-century colonists. There were as yet few Negroes: from the 22 who had been listed at the time of the company's fall as residents of Virginia, the number had probably increased to about 150 in 1640 and to 300 in 1649. According to Governor Berkeley, there were in 1670 only 2,000 Negroes out of Virginia's total population of 40,000 persons.[54] The explanation for this slow growth undoubtedly lies partly in a problem of supply; England's leadership in the African slave trade came later, and for a while yet English colonists could increase greatly the number of their Negro laborers only by depending upon a foreign source of supply. But the Dutch, who now led in the African trade and were active during the middle period of the century in the Chesapeake trade, could have provided them; more than that, they probably did provide most of those brought in at that time. Moreover, the problem of supply seems not to have been insurmountable in the neighboring British West Indian isles, where imported Negro labor and the cultivation of sugar cane by 1660 had set under way a major economic and social revolution. It would appear that consideration must be given the question of demand as well as of supply in attempting to explain the slow growth of Negro slavery in the mainland colonies. An influential factor may well have been the simple fact that the Negroes

[53] Hening, *Statutes*, I, 244, 350–51, 454; *Archives of Maryland*, I (1883), 251, 295. The author is indebted to his late father, who was "raised" on a North Carolina farm at a time when the fencing laws remained substantially the same as those adopted by the seventeenth-century colonists, for the following definitions: the crop—a smooth cut from the end of the ear; the slit—a split in the end of the ear; the underbit—a nick cut in the under part of the ear; the overbit—a nick in the upper part of the ear. On the chance that the records of North Carolina's Randolph County may be deficient in this particular, it is hereby recorded that the mark of B. Y. Craven, whose stock during much of the nineteenth century ranged in the neighborhood of Coleridge, was a crop and underbit in the right ear and an underbit on the left.

[54] Wertenbaker, *Planters of Colonial Virginia*, 124–25.

then available were not so well suited to the needs of the small farmer as were the white servants, the most loutish of whom brought to their task more of the skill and responsibility required than could any Negro fresh from Africa.[55] What the small farmer needed was a man for whom he could set a task, and then go about another himself; his helper must be a man having some familiarity with the techniques of a European agricultural society, or else too much of the master's time would be required for the duties of instructor and overseer. It is significant that the European servant remained the principal dependence in the colonies for so long as the small farm was the dominant type.

To deal with the peculiar problems of a servant class, set apart legally and otherwise from the rest of the community, was an early and frequently recurring task of legislature and court in the Southern colonies. An increasing group of servants who lacked under law the responsibility that goes with freedom and the ownership of property, and who not infrequently included in their number some of the baser elements of English society, found in their hard lot and the remote isolation of life in America a strong temptation to escape. To control this group it was necessary to enact a series of statutes which added up to a detailed code requiring only some modification and further elaboration to meet the need later felt for a slave code. In an attempt to cope with the most difficult and serious of early problems, that of the fugitive, the law inflicted upon the runaway servant heavy corporal punishment together with a prescribed addition of time to his term of service. It also enjoined all public officials and private citizens to render their utmost assistance in effecting his apprehension and punishment.[56] Under conditions which made it difficult for the law alone to overcome a natural temptation to entertain any stranger, for his company if not for his much needed labor, the right of a master to the co-operation of his fellow citizens in the return of a fugitive servant

---

[55] Negroes brought from other European communities fall, of course, in a different classification, but the number of them available was decidedly limited.

[56] Some of the more significant pieces of early legislation are in Hening, *Statutes*, I, 253–55, 401, 439–40, 483, 517–18; *Archives of Maryland*, I (1883), 107–108, 124, 249. An act of 1639, *ibid.*, I, 73, listed harboring another's servant among the "enormious offences." For early enactments against trade with servants, see Hening, *Statutes*, I, 274–75, 445.

became one of the oldest and most deeply ingrained convictions of the Southerner.

No less old and certainly no less significant was the assumption by the state of a responsibility for the servant's welfare. Men in these first days of settlement commonly used the term "family" not merely to include the blood relations of its head but his servants as well, and it was understood that a man enjoyed a well-established, if not too well-defined, right of discipline over his wife, his children, and his servants.[57] This was something old, and peculiar neither to America nor to the South. The exercise of that right was coupled with a sense of responsibility colored by other conventions of the day. If, under the influence of modern humanitarian sentiment, some of us find ourselves inclined to horror at evidences of earlier severity, it is well to recall that the lashes dealt a servant were often only slightly in excess of those a man would lay on the rump of his own son with no thought but that he had done his Christian duty. And as in the thrashing of his son, the point at which public authority might properly interfere with the discipline of his servant presented a delicate question. It is not so remarkable, therefore, that government failed to save the servant from all abuses the system invited as that the courts did actually intervene in his behalf.

The complaint of a servant against his master at times was found to be without justification, as was often undoubtedly true, and on other occasions the master was reprimanded even, in rare instances, to the extent of suffering action which freed the servant.[58] The "custom of the country" governing a servant's right on expira-

[57] The law not only recognized the right but specifically held him to account for the discipline of his servants, as in laws for Sabbath observance and religious instruction. Hening, *Statutes,* I, 261, 311, 434; *Archives of Maryland,* I (1883), 53.

[58] More common perhaps was the action of a Lancaster County court in 1675 binding the master in ten thousand pounds of tobacco not to abuse his servants or to give them "correction" except in the presence of a neighbor or his overseer. *William and Mary College Quarterly,* VI (1897–1898), 117. The right of complaint was a statutory privilege. Hening, *Statutes,* I, 440. The indexes in *Archives of Maryland,* LIII (1936); LIV (1937), provide a convenient guide to pertinent source material. Useful discussions of the servant problem based on court records are Semmes, *Crime and Punishment in Early Maryland,* 80 ff.; Ames, *Studies of the Virginia Eastern Shore,* 72 ff.; Bruce, *Economic History of Virginia,* II, 10 ff. See also, Force (comp.), *Tracts,* III, No. 14, p. 16. A recent and authoritative general study is Richard B. Morris, *Government and Labor in Early America* (New York, 1946).

tion of his term to a minimum of clothing, tools, and other equipment repeatedly was upheld in the courts. Still more impressive is the protection afforded the large number of servants arriving in the colony without indentures, that is, without contracts fixing the terms and conditions of their servitude. Servants had quickly become an article of commerce and a principal export to the colonies, their recruiting imperfectly supervised by authorities at home and often falling under the control of unscrupulous shipmasters.[59] The legislature fixed the term of service according to age, and as a safeguard, required masters to appear within a stipulated time before the county court for entry on record of such indenture as might exist and of the servant's age as adjudged by the court.[60] The fact that such a record might be of advantage to the planter as well as the servant is suggestive of the way in which self-interest often supports the public conscience.

The Negro's status under the laws and customs of these early days is a debatable question on which the records do not always speak clearly. As the late Professor Ulrich B. Phillips and others have shown, slavery first developed as a custom of the country, considerably in advance of its sanction as an institution by law.[61] There were no special laws covering the Negro's standing in Virginia prior to the era of the Restoration, and the slave code, both in Virginia and Maryland, belongs primarily to the eighteenth rather than the seventeenth century. It is a mistake, however, to make too much of this delay in the enactment of a full-fledged slave code, for where the number of Negroes was small, most of the peculiar problems of slave discipline were adequately covered by the increasingly elaborate servant code. The principal risk, as with the white servant, was of escape, and significantly the first statute in Virginia dealing directly with a problem peculiar to the Negro's status, a law of 1661, related to runaway "negroes who are incapable of making satisfaction by addition of time." [62] That phrasing, of course, does not necessarily include all Negroes, and the very

---

[59] See Abbot E. Smith, *Colonists in Bondage; White Servitude and Convict Labor in America, 1607–1776* (Chapel Hill, 1947), a recent and definitive study.

[60] Hening, *Statutes*, I, 257, 411, 441–42, 471; *Archives of Maryland*, I (1883), 80; and LIII (1936); LIV (1937), *passim*, for the court record. One consideration, of course, was the time at which the servant would become a "tithable." Hening, *Statutes*, I, 361.

[61] Phillips, *American Negro Slavery*, 75–77.   [62] Hening, *Statutes*, II, 26.

evident reliance for a time on the servant code naturally raises a question of their right to its benefits. There were cases of Negroes freed at the end of a fixed term, but there is danger in generalizing too much from the relatively few cases recorded.[63]

In attempts to arrive at some general conclusion regarding the Negro's position, one bit of evidence usually overlooked is a statute passed by the Bermuda Assembly in 1623 for restraining "the insolences of the Negroes." [64] The first of its kind in the English-speaking world, it denied the Negro's right to free movement, to participation in trade, and to bear arms, three deprivals which were basic in the later slave codes. That this legislation, enacted by a sister colony closely joined at the time to Virginia, reflected the attitudes held at least by some of the colonists on the mainland, not to mention those Bermudians who over the next few years migrated to the older settlement, appears to be a safe assumption. More direct evidence is found in the fact that the highest court in Virginia promptly drew the color line, a point pertinent to the modern assumption that prejudice against the Negro is largely a product of slavery.[65] Not without significance is the separate classification regularly given in a census, in tax and similar lists, and in inventories of estates to "negroes" or "negro servants." [66] Notice should be taken of a specific exception of Negroes in a Virginia statute of 1640 requiring all other men to be armed, and

[63] The view that servitude preceded slavery traces principally to James C. Ballagh, *A History of Slavery in Virginia* (Baltimore, 1902); John H. Russell, *The Free Negro in Virginia, 1619–1865* (Baltimore, 1913). A pertinent criticism of their conclusions, based on study of the county records, is presented by Ames, *Studies of the Virginia Eastern Shore*, 100–106. Helen T. Catterall (ed.), *Judicial Cases concerning American Slavery and the Negro* (5 vols., Washington, 1926–1937) is a standard reference. See especially, I, 53–81.

[64] Lefroy (ed.), *Memorials of the . . . Bermudas*, I, 308–309.

[65] "Hugh Davis to be soundly whipped, before an assembly of Negroes and others for abusing himself to the dishonor of God and shame of Christians, by defiling his body in lying with a negro." Hening, *Statutes*, I, 146. Ten years later, in 1640, a similar offense seems to have been treated only as fornication. *Virginia Magazine,* XI (1903–1904), 281.

[66] For example, Neill, *Virginia Carolorum*, 16 n., 22; Accomac Records, No. 1, p. 52; *Virginia Magazine*, V (1897–1898), 40; XL (1932), 144; *William and Mary College Quarterly*, II (1893–1894), 269; XX (1911–1912), 138; XXII (1913–1914), 235–48. No special significance can be attached to the common usage of Negro instead of slave, for the usage was common long after the institution of slavery was well established.

of the stipulation in an act of 1643 that Negro women from the age of sixteen must be included in the list of tithables, a requirement not applying to white female servants.[67] It should be noted too that by the 1640's Negro servants brought prices higher than those generally paid for white servants, and that important exceptions in the case of "slaves" appear in the earliest Maryland statutes.[68] Finally, consideration must be given to the probable influence of the fact that Negro slavery was an established institution in the law and custom of other European peoples. When all is said, it is difficult to avoid the conclusion that, while the individual lot of the Negro might vary according to the attitude of the master in whose hands it was his lot to fall, the trend from the first was toward a sharp distinction between him and the white servant.

In Maryland no less than in Virginia, it was the land policy which fathered white servitude and Negro slavery. The proprietor's elaborately feudal scheme of settlement, even with its awards of title and position, counted for little beside the simple fact that the original grant had been drawn in proportion to the investment made, and that it was most easily expanded by the acquisition of additional headrights. For the planter to negotiate with men in England for settlement on his land as freehold or leasehold tenants was both inconvenient and expensive, but shipmasters offered for sale each year in the colony, in return for the colony's produce, stout fellows who might be quickly trained to the duties of a useful "hand." The law and the court, responding to the planter's need, made secure his claim to a term of service commensurate with the price paid the shipmaster, and made easy for him the establishment of a headright claim against the land office.[69] The goal of the Maryland planter, like that of his neighbor in Virginia, was to acquire enough servants to develop the land under his own immediate supervision, and in the acquiring to extend his holdings. The proprietor's original intent would be reflected for many years in the technicalities of the law, but thus the New World planta-

[67] Hening, *Statutes,* I, 226, 242; *William and Mary College Quarterly,* 2d ser., IV (1924), 147.

[68] Bruce, *Economic History of Virginia,* I, 51–52, 89–90; *Archives of Maryland,* I (1883), 41, 80.

[69] A first step in establishing the headright claim was action by the local county court certifying the right.

tion, rather than the Old World manor, early took option on the future.

Through the preceding pages frequent reference has been made to the wide dispersal of settlement which increasingly had come to characterize the Chesapeake colonies, a feature of their life which commonly has been attributed to the influence of tobacco. There can be no doubt that the imperative demands of the American weed exercised an especially important influence, but the frequently popular view that tobacco led immediately to the large plantation and thus to dispersed settlement overlooks unimpeachable evidence that the small farm rather than the large plantation was the typical unit of cultivation. The influence of tobacco would appear to have been, rather, that it required good land, drew heavily upon the soil, and therefore encouraged men, whose resources were limited, to spread out in search of fields that would produce the finest leaf in return for a minimum investment of capital and labor. The chief limit imposed on a tendency so natural as this, of course, was the distance a man might go without sacrificing ready access to the market, but in this instance that factor counted for little. The Chesapeake, with its multitude of inlets and tributary rivers and creeks, provided the most marvelous system of inland waterways on the Atlantic coast; indeed, one of the most remarkable in all the world. An elaborate pattern of natural highways carried in well-nigh every direction to new and more fertile fields, all in practical terms nearly equidistant from the market, for the market was in Europe, and at hundreds of different points in and off the Chesapeake might ride the proudest ships engaged in the New World trade. No one place offered greater security from foreign attack than another, since entrance from the sea ran only between Capes Henry and Charles and under the guns of Point Comfort. The natives of the region, moreover, were small in number, were divided politically, and from the middle of the century they proved amenable to policies dictated by the English. Other and secondary factors, such as the extent of speculative holdings and the generally wasteful methods of cultivation, lent their support to the trend. But the very wealth of natural riches lay at the foundation both of the speculation and of the waste.

The unusual improvidence that so early characterized Southern

AN INDIAN TOWN. From Theodore De Bry, *Admirando Narratio Fida Tamen* . . . (Frankfort, 1590). De Bry's engraving from a painting by John White shows (A) the house serving as a tomb for chieftains, (B) place of prayer, (C) ceremonial dance, (D) feast, (E) tobacco, (F) watchman in field, (G) corn, (H) squash, (I) pumpkins, (K) ceremonial fire, (L) water.

ST. AUGUSTINE. This view, issued in 1588 and from the Phelps Stokes Collection of American Historical Prints in the New York Public Library, represents Francis Drake's attack of 1586. The English fleet is in the foreground; the hexagonal figure is the fort; the town is shown in upper left corner.

AN INDIAN MEAL. Engraved from John White's painting by Theodore De Bry for *Admirando Narratio Fida Tamen* . . . (Frankfort, 1590).

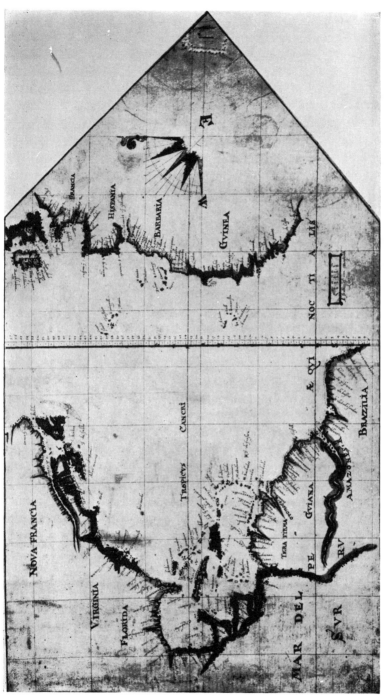

THE VIRGINIA COMPANY CHART. This map, with green coloring to mark the limits fixed by the Virginia charter of 1606, was probably drawn for the Virginia adventurers as indicated by I. N. Phelps Stokes and Daniel C. Haskell in the catalogue of *American Historical Prints, Early Views of American Cities, Etc. from the Phelps Stokes and Other Collections* (New York Public Library, 1933), 2. The designation of Capes Henry and Charles and of Jamestown, together with the imperfect delineation of the coast line between Cape Charles and Cape Cod, suggests a date falling between the settlement of Jamestown and some time in 1609.

THE · PORTRAICTUER · OF · CAPTAYNE · IOHN · SMITH · ADMIRALL · OF · NEW · ENGLAND ·

Æt⸗ 37
A° 1616

These are the Lines that shew thy Face; but those
That shew thy Grace and Glory, brighter bee:
Thy Faire-Discoueries and Fowle-Overthrowes
Of Salvages, much Civilliz'd by thee
Best shew thy Spirit; and to it Glory Wyn;
So, thou art Brasse without, but Golde within.

THE PORTRAICTUER OF CAPTAYNE IOHN SMITH. From the map in Smith's
A Description of New England (London, 1616).

CAPTAYNE WOODLEEFS BILL. SEPTEMBER 1619. From the Smyth of Nibley Papers, New York Public Library. This bill of charges submitted by Captain John Woodleefe in September, 1619, emphasizes the importance of such items of supply as nails, hooks, hinges, locks, bolts, and tools.

VIRGINIA. From John Smith, *The Generall Historie* of *Virginia, New-England, and the Summer Isles* (London, 1624).

A LYST OF THE MEN NOWE SENT FOR PLANTACON UNDER CAPTAYNE WOODLEEFE GOVERNOR. From the Smyth of Nibley Papers, New York Public Library. This list of men sent in 1619 to Berkeley Hundred in Virginia tells its own story. Note especially the later entries on the left in another hand which show one man returned to England in 1620, one "slayne," one drowned, and all but two others dead.

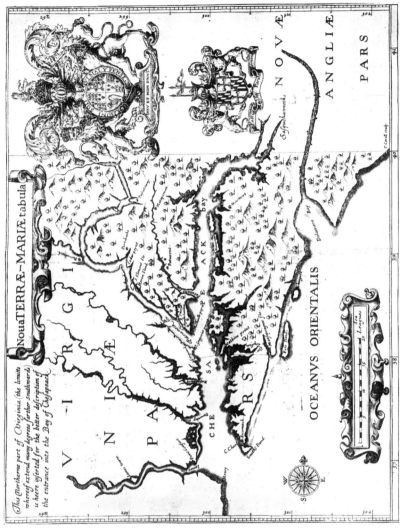

TERRAE-MARIAE. From *A Relation of Maryland* (London, 1635). The dotted lines indicate the boundaries under the Maryland charter.

49

A note for the adventurers memory, of such things as hee may (if he please) carry with him, either for his owne better accommodation (on ship-board, or for some time after his arrivall in Maryland) or for trade; according to his abilitie.

Provision for Ship-board.

Fine Wheate-flower, close and well packed, to make puddings, &c. Claret-wine burnt. Canary Sacke. Conserues. Marmalades, Suckets, and Spices. Sallet Oyle. Prunes to stew. Live Poultry. Rice, Butter, Holland-cheese, or old Cheshire, gammons of Bacon, Porke, dried Neates-tongues; Beefe packed up in Vineger, some Weather-sheepe, meats baked in earthen pots, Leggs of Mutton minced, and stewed, and close packed up in tried Sewet, or Butter, in earthen pots: Iuyce of Limons, &c.

Provision for trade in *Virginia,* or *Maryland.*

If hee be minded to furnish himselfe with
Cattell

G 3

50

Cattell in *Virginia,* his best way is to carry a superfluitie of wollen, or linnen cloth, calicoes, sayes, harts, shooes, stockings, and all sorts of clothing; of Wine, Sugar, Prunes, Rasins, Currance, Honey, Spice, and Grocery ware, with which hee may procure himselfe cattell there, according to the stocke he dealeth withall. About 4. or 5. Pound laid out here in commodities; will there buy a Cow, and betweene 20. and 30. shillings, a breeding Sow. The like Commodities will furnish him either there, or in *Maryland,* with Hogges, Poultry, and Corne. Hee may doe well also to carry a superfluity of Knives, Combes, and Braceles, to trade with the women Natives; and some Hatchets, Howes, and Axes, to trade with the men for Venison, Fish, Turkies, Corne, Fawnes to store a Parke, &c.

Provision for his House.

Iron, and Locks, and Hinges, and bolts, &c. Mustard-feede, Glasse and Leade for his windowes, Mault for beere, a Hogshead of Beefe or Porke: Two or three Firkins of Butter, a hundred or two of old Cheeses; a gallon of honey, Soape and Candles, Iron wedges, Pookes for Rennet to make cheese, a good *Mastiffe,* &c.

Provision

A NOTE FOR THE ADVENTURERS MEMORY. From *A Relation of Maryland* (London, 1635).

A COURT HOLDEN FOR THE COUNTY OF YORKE. From the York County Records, No. 2, Wills and Deeds, 1645–1649, included here through the courtesy of the Virginia State Library. See Appendix, p. 416, for transcription.

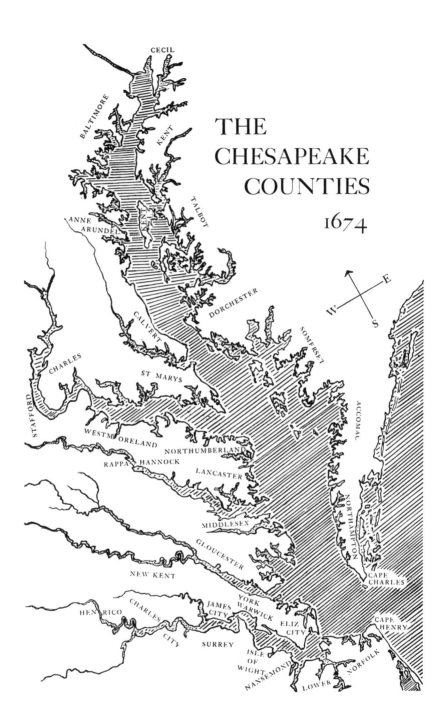

THE
CHESAPEAKE
COUNTIES
1674

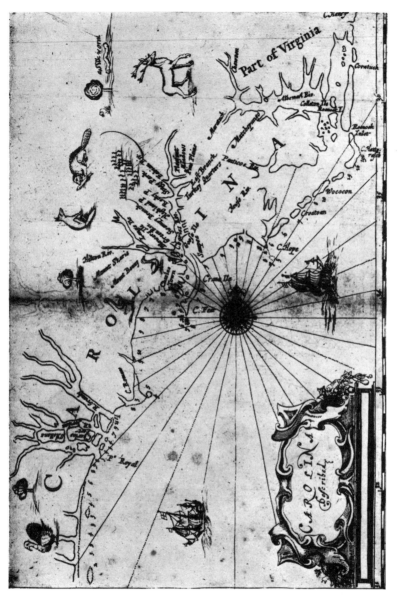

CAROLINA. From *A Brief Description of the Province of Carolina on the Coasts of Florida* (London, 1666).

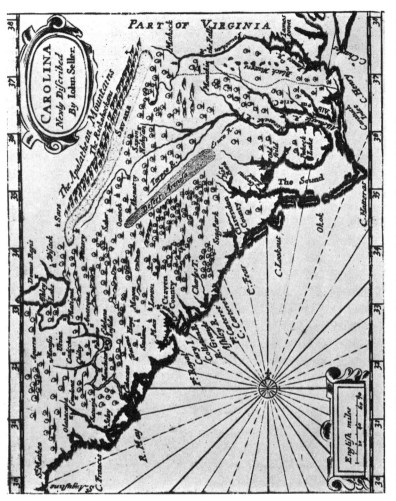

CAROLINA NEWLY DISCRIBED. Map inserted in New York Public Library copy of *An Account of the Province of Carolina in America* (London, 1682). It is obviously of earlier date.

THE KING WILLIAM COURTHOUSE. Built prior to 1675; it served originally New Kent County, Virginia. Reproduced through the courtesy of the Virginia Conservation Commission.

AN

ACCOUNT

OF THE

Province

OF

CAROLINA

IN

AMERICA.

TOGETHER WITH

An Abſtract of the PATENT,
and ſeveral other Neceſſary and Uſeful Particulars, to ſuch as have thoughts of Tran-
ſporting themſelves thither.

Publiſhed foʒ their Infoʒmation.

Samuel Wilson

LONDON:
Printed by *G. Larkin* for *Francis Smith*, at the Elephant
and Caſtle in *Cornhil*. 1682.

AN ACCOUNT OF THE PROVINCE OF CAROLINA IN AMERICA. Title page
from the New York Public Library copy. As the penciled notation indicates, Samuel
Wilson was the author.

agriculture requires, however, closer attention. It is well enough to attribute its wastefulness to environmental factors, and chiefly to the natural wealth of the area. But this can provide no more than an escape from the problem that is presented by the simple fact that other men have settled in fertile regions to treat the gifts of God with more respect. In any society a first factor is the human one, and who can doubt that there would have been important differences had the original settlers been German peasants, such as later settled in Pennsylvania, or, God save the mark, had the Puritans of Massachusetts with their remarkable unity of purpose and its attendant inspiration found the Chesapeake open and inviting their settlement? [70]

But how shall we judge of this human factor? Was there some special quality characterizing those who on leaving England set their course toward the Chesapeake? Obviously, they were a representative group of Englishmen bearing no marked differences from their fellows except on occasional points of religious or political faith. Shall we, then, place the blame on the fact that so large a proportion of the population migrated as servants, learning here the ways of sloth in another's service and finding in their hard-won freedom insufficient incentive to change their ways? The point is worth consideration, but overlooks unmistakable evidence of the response of humble immigrants to the highest opportunities of the New World.[71] No thesis involving an assumption of inferiority as the distinctive mark of any one group of men can find substantial support here or elsewhere in American history. The answer, instead, must be sought in the operation of those social forces which normally, with the aid of natural environment, shape the life of a community.

When the Chesapeake settlements are examined from that point of view, the most noticeable feature of their life is the absence of a

[70] For an interesting discussion of this phase of the problem, see Richard H. Shryock, "British versus German Traditions in Colonial Agriculture," in *Mississippi Valley Historical Review* (Cedar Rapids), XXVI (1939–1940), 39–54. The influence of cultural backgrounds on agricultural methods has of recent years received attention from the Department of Agriculture. See, for example, Walter M. Kollmorgen, *The German-Swiss in Franklin County, Tennessee, A Study of the Significance of Cultural Considerations in Farming Enterprises* (Washington, 1940).

[71] See, for example, Wertenbaker, *Planters of Colonial Virginia*, 73–78.

common purpose and goal except such as was dictated principally by the requirements of individual interests. Here, in short, was the first typically American frontier community, its development planless in any larger sense and its end the service of individual wants. It had not always been so. There had been a comprehensive plan and purpose in the days of the Virginia Company, but the influence of the company had been removed in an hour of defeat and disillusionment. With it disappeared the high hopes of an ambitious program for a diversified economy, together with other influences that had joined men in the sense of a common and great undertaking. No substitute for the company's leadership was provided, and men thrown back on their own resources had proceeded to build a society that gave as free play to individualism as any America was to know. In Maryland, the proprietor's plan not only proved antiquated and unsuited, but he had been denied the opportunity to supervise closely its inauguration. Meanwhile, his people took their cue from Virginia, and were united principally in resistance to the intent of the proprietary plan. The particular type of individualism bred of these circumstances, and nurtured in the disorderly advance of successive frontiers of settlement, holds in American life a twofold significance. It provided a very fertile field indeed for the growth of a political tradition emphasizing individual liberty, but that same liberty in the economic sphere of man's activity has entailed far too much of thoughtless waste. Already, by the middle of the seventeenth century, the need for "fresh" land had entered into the forces shaping an expanding area of settlement.[72] Already, too, the old field and the old-field pine served to give men a peculiar sense of age in a society that was really new.

New as it was, the members of that society as they approached the mid-century could take satisfaction from many evidences about them of achievement and progress. Few of the Chesapeake planters were articulate, and historians have been forced to depend on fragments of such writing as they did to piece together a story of the disillusionment which had followed their initial expectations and then finally had been overcome by a new hope and faith. It may be

[72] For example, Hening, *Statutes*, I, 353, where the demand for a new area of settlement is justified by "the mean produce of their labours upon barren and over-wrought grounds."

permissible in closing, therefore, to borrow from an account written two hundred years later by an Englishman out of experiences in Australasia comparable to those of the first settlers in Virginia and Maryland. Of the settler, "after his outlay has been made, and before he receives his returns," wrote this Englishman of a later day, "what a long, careful, dissatisfied face is his. How he grumbles. How he repines. How thin he gets. Now is the time for quarrels, and outcries, and remonstrances. Now, all who advised and assisted him to emigrate are fearfully cursed. . . . To conclude, he writes to England furiously, denouncing the settlement, declaring its originators are swindlers and imposters, and protesting he is utterly undone, without a single penny, heartbroken, beggared. . . . But along with all this there is a change going on; he begins to learn the secret of making his way in a new country; . . . his cattle and sheep multiply; many little things turn out advantageously, as if to repay him for former losses. His house is now finished; he makes cheese and butter; . . . he becomes strong and merry; . . . whistles as he walks. . . . Presently he launches out in praise of the country, and wonders what his relatives are about, 'why they don't come out' . . . and 'though many of your readers (he writes to the editor of his own old county newspaper in England), affect to disbelieve in the prospects of this colony, they cannot refuse to accept the testimony of one whose own case is a proof of the *bona fide* soundness of the inducements held out to settlers on the great Swamptown Plain, in New Dalmatia.' " [73]

With only a few changes, this might have been written by one of the older Chesapeake planters at some time in the 1640's.

[73] Thomas Cholmondeley, *Ultima Thule; or, Thoughts Suggested by a Residence in New Zealand* (London, 1854), 44–47, quoted in Johannes S. Marais, *Colonisation of New Zealand* (London, 1927), 144–45. Cf. John Hammond, *Leah and Rachel* (1656), in Force (comp.), *Tracts*, III, No. 14.

CHAPTER VII

CIVIL WAR

W HEN the body is disturbed the members needs bee affected, therefore wee here can expect no Setled times, till England is in peace." [1] Thus wrote William Byrd I of the situation in Virginia immediately after the English Revolution of 1689. His observation is no less applicable to the earlier days of the Civil War and the interregnum rule of Oliver Cromwell. Maryland was less than six years old and Sir Francis Wyatt hardly settled in his second term as governor of Virginia when the Long Parliament, most famous of England's Parliaments, assembled to put a period to eleven years of personal rule by Charles I. Sir Edwin Sandys, Sir Edward Coke, Sir John Eliot, and the redoubtable John Hampden, names of immortal fame in the struggle for the rights of Parliament and the Common Law, were now followed in the leadership of the cause by the shrewd and indefatigable John Pym. Through two years King Charles, unhappily embroiled with the covenanters of his Scottish kingdom, pursued an uneven contest with "King Pym." The issues at stake were so fundamental that compromise proved impossible, and by 1642 men were facing the unhappy necessity of choosing sides in what promised to be a final showdown through the arbitrament of arms. In August the King raised his standard at Newport and the Civil War was on. [2]

As so frequently is the case with civil wars, men were torn by conflicting loyalties, and the division was not clear-cut. Those ranged

---

[1] *Virginia Magazine*, XXVI (1918), 130.

[2] George M. Trevelyan, *England under the Stuarts* (London, 1904; 12th ed., 1925), remains the most entertaining and suggestive short account of England's history during the seventeenth century.

on the side of Parliament advanced no scheme of government without a King, and even proclaimed, on their own terms, their loyalty to His Majesty. Those who followed the royal standard sought neither the destruction of Parliament nor of the Common Law. Behind the King stood most of those who approved William Laud's High Church policies, and so many of the Puritans sided with Parliament that their name proved a useful designation for the party led by Pym. But there were Anglicans, such as the Earl of Warwick, in the ranks of the Puritan party, and men of puritanical ideas, such as Edward Hyde, later Earl of Clarendon, among the Royalists. The division cut across family, class, and geographical region. A confusing picture even for him who watched it day by day, it was doubly confounding to the colonist who followed it at great distance and with only an occasional glimpse.

To the planters in America, nonetheless, it was remote only in terms of time and distance. No more serious mistake can be made than to assume that their recorded attitudes reflect only conventional sentiment and loyalty expressed by men comfortably removed from the center of the disturbance. As Englishmen and members of an English community, they held both sentiments and convictions that were deeply involved. Moreover, the upheaval tearing at the metropolis of their world touched directly their most vital interests. As with men at home, the position taken by the colonists reflected a normal mixture of sentiment and interest.

In Virginia the planters were well-nigh unanimous in their allegiance to the Anglican establishment of which the King by the laws of Elizabeth was the accepted head. Through ingrained habit, loyalty to all those things appropriately claiming an Englishman's devotion was expressed in the forms of allegiance to His Majesty the King. Leadership in the colony was entrusted, just at the outbreak of war, to the young and popular Sir William Berkeley, a Royalist. His very popularity, however, was for the moment based primarily upon the fact of his recent arrival as bearer of new assurances from the crown on the ever-recurring threat of a revival of the Virginia Company. It had been through the colleagues of Pym that George Sandys had so recently co-operated with the old Virginia adventurers in an attempt to re-establish their charter through parliamentary action. No one reading the Assembly's sharply worded remonstrance that year can doubt the apprehension and indignation that effort called forth in Virginia.[3] In short, Virginians on the very eve of war had occasion to see in the action of Parliament a challenge to the security of their most cherished rights, and to find in assurances from the King their chief guarantee.

The renewed threat of the company's revival not only helped to shape the initial decision, but served thereafter to hold their allegiance unchanged. For the danger remained very real in the minds of the colonists, and would be reflected in their actions even as late as the surrender of the Virginia colony to Cromwell in 1652.[4] That their continuing fears had some foundation is strongly suggested by the fact that these were the very years during which the story of the company's dissolution in 1624 became so encrusted with interpretations drawn from the issues of the 1640's as to mislead more than one later historian on the true history of its bankruptcy and collapse. Alexander Brown's well-known thesis, attributing the company's fall to the King's interference for political reasons, depended largely on a pamphlet written about 1644 (but not published until 1651) by Arthur Wodenoth, former Virginia adventurer, a relative of the Ferrars, and by his own description, "a true friend" of "the Parliament-interest."[5] Just how serious a risk of the company's revival existed after 1642 is difficult to say, but there can be no question as to the reality of the fear besetting the colonists.

Significant, too, is the connection between that concern and other apprehensions which governed attitudes in the colony toward the trouble at home. Since 1624 the institutional structure of the community had taken shape on the foundation of royal authority. This meant in Virginia no mere tribute to the legal theory that all lawful authority stemmed from the crown, for it was true in hard fact as well as in theory. The colonists had no charter, visible evi-

---

[3] Hening, *Statutes*, I, 230–36. See above, pp. 152–53.   [4] See below, p. 256.

[5] *A Short Collection of the Most Remarkable Passages from the originall to the dissolution of the Virginia Company* (London, 1651); Alexander Brown, *First Republic of America* (Boston, 1898); and for a discussion of Brown's dependence on Arthur Wodenoth, see Craven, *Dissolution of the Virginia Company*, 16–19. It had been argued in opposition to a revival of the charter in 1631 that the courts of the company had been used for consultation by opponents of King James. *Virginia Magazine*, VIII (1900–1901), 39–43.

dence of rights conceded and bulwark for their defense in the courts. Instead, public authority, which is to say all law, order, and security for life and property, rested on custom and usage sanctioned merely by the more mutable forms of royal consent. Virginia, first of the royal colonies, was thus uniquely tied, even in the most minute detail of its administration, to the royal right of government. To call that right into question was to invite the penalties of civil war and anarchy.

Let us look again at the celebrated statute of 1649 passed by the Virginia Assembly on the occasion of Cromwell's execution of Charles I. Its oft-quoted denunciation of the "unparalel'd treasons" of the regicides, and of all doctrines calculated to lend the color of legality to this the highest treason, undoubtedly expressed the sentiment of most Virginians, as did, too, the proclamation of "the undoubted & inherent right of his Majesty" King Charles II "to the collony of Virginia, and all other his majesties dominions." The immediate and practical purpose behind the act, however, finds expression in the fear that "arguments easily and naturally deduced from the aforesaid cursed and destructive principles" might be used to "press and perswade the power of the commission to be void & null, and all magistracy and office thereon depending to have lost their vigor and efficacy." Now, that is no mere expression of outraged Royalist sentiment, but the voice of men who feared for their lives and their property. They consequently further declared "That what person soever, by false reports and malicious rumors shall spread abroad, among the people, any thing tending to change of government, or to the lessening of the power and authority of the Governor or government either in civill or ecclesiasticall causes (which this Assembly hath and doth declare to be full and plenarie to all intents and purposes) such persons . . . shall suffer such punishment even to severity as shall be thought fitt." [6] Not until the arrival three years later of a parliamentary commission, backed by some show of force, did the majority of Virginians see either the necessity of, or any safety in, a transfer of their allegiance.

The problem faced, though especially acute in this particular instance, was by no means new; nor were its dangers entirely to pass until England knew again a settled peace. The Assembly of 1624,

---

[6] Hening, *Statutes*, I, 359–61.

apprehensive over uncertainties attending the fall of the company, had strictly prohibited all disobedience to existing authority in the colony "upon rumur of supposed change and alteration." Proposals for the company's revival after 1631 again flooded the colony with disturbing reports, with the result that a statute identical in all essentials with that of 1624 was enacted at each of two sittings of the Assembly in 1632. Three years after passage of the act of 1649, the colonists came to terms with Cromwell's government, thus safely negotiating a difficult transition. However, in the spring of 1658, the year of the Protector's death and the succession of "Tumbledown Dick," the Assembly was forced again to provide special penalties for the circulation of "false or dangerous news" tending to disturbance of the colony's peace. Once more, in 1660, just prior to the restoration of Charles II to his father's throne, "the late frequent distractions in England" provided the occasion for an act declaring that "all persons whatsoever that shall . . . say or act any thing in derogation of the present government hereby established shall be proceeded against as enemies of the peace of this collonie." [7] And there is the point of them all—to preserve the peace of Virginia.

The same end dictated on the outbreak of the Civil War a greater care to assure conformity within the church. A tightening of the law was undertaken by the Assembly of 1643.[8] Designed to ward off the dangers of religious controversy, the action probably had been prompted in part by arrival in the colony the preceding year of three Puritan divines from Boston. They had come in response to an invitation from Richard Bennett and others of Nansemond County, men of a puritanical persuasion, if not profession. Of the three, only William Thompson stuck by his post in the face of disapproval by the colony's authorities, but among the converts of the next few years was Thomas Harrison, clergyman of the establishment and minister in Lower Norfolk County prior to his expulsion from the colony in 1648. The number of conversions came nowhere near the harvest foreseen by friends and correspondents in New

---

[7] Kingsbury (ed.), *Records of The Virginia Company,* IV, 584; Hening, *Statutes,* I, 128, 174, 198, 434–35, 531, 532. Baltimore advised in 1651 the enacting of a law "for the punishment of all such as shall publish false news to the disturbance of the minds of the People and the publick peace." *Archives of Maryland,* I (1883), 334–35.

[8] Hening, *Statutes,* I, 241–43.

England. They were enough, however, to raise up, especially in Nansemond and Lower Norfolk counties, a sizable "schismaticall party, of whose intentions," declared the Assembly of 1648, "our native country of England hath had and yet hath too sad experience." [9] Where the overwhelming majority of the people remained loyal to the Anglican faith, it was not necessary to resort to the severer forms of persecution, but the pressure brought to bear proved sufficient to persuade a goodly company of the Puritans finally to seek refuge in Maryland. There should be no difficulty, whatever our modern views may be, in understanding and even sympathizing with the policy thus pursued in Virginia. For religious differences provided some of the most disruptive political issues of the day.

Nor should there be any trouble in comprehending the persecution of the Quakers that was soon to follow. Representatives of that group first became troublesome in the years of the interregnum when the Virginians, despite the fact that they had come to terms with the established government in England, still lived with the fears normally bred of political uncertainty at home. The Quaker of that day was not always the quiet and peaceable citizen known to later generations. He at times defied public authority, consistently scorned such symbols of deference to that authority as uncovering in the court, and in other ways appeared to lack the respect considered appropriate, even necessary, toward ministers and public officers. As the records repeatedly testify, county judges sitting at some improvised table in a private home or public tavern had to be especially persistent on such points, and civil war in England had emphasized this urgent necessity of the frontier. There were other objections. The Quaker refused an oath in a community possessed of fewer means for holding men to account than exist today, and where its consequent importance was such that thought was even given to limiting its use for fear of cheapening it by overuse. His meetings, necessarily secretive, aroused suspicion, especially when servants were thus brought under his influence. Respect

[9] *Ibid.*, 355. For a discussion of the Puritan group, see Bruce, *Institutional History of Virginia,* I, 252–61; and for an act of 1647 relieving parishioners of the obligation to pay tithes when the minister did not follow the common prayer book, Hening, *Statutes,* I, 341–42.

for public and private authority—that of the husband over his wife, of the father over his children, or of the master over his servants as well as that of the sworn officer or of the ordained minister—were closely joined in the contemporary mind. Hardly less than in New England did some of the Quaker doctrines suggest blasphemy and a cheapening of Holy Writ, itself at the very foundation of law and order.

Virginia's statute of 1660 speaks clearly enough. An "unreasonable and turbulent sort of people," it reads, "teaching and publishing, lies, miracles, false visions, prophecies and doctrines, which have influence upon the communities of men both ecclesiasticall and civil endeavouring and attempting thereby to destroy religion, lawes, communities and all bonds of civil societie, leaving it arbitrarie to everie vaine and vitious person whether men shall be safe, laws established, offenders punished, and Governours rule, hereby disturbing the publique peace and just interest." [10] The act all too frequently has been discussed as simply an evidence of bigotry and of an inclination to ape the intolerant policies of Restoration England. But that is to ignore the fact that Virginia acted in advance of the celebrated Clarendon Code at home and to overlook the evidence provided in at least one county that legislative action had come in response to the demands of lower units of government which for some time had experienced difficulty in coping with the problem.[11] And whatever note of hysteria may be detected in the action taken, no thoughtful student can question that under existing circumstances the Quakers did present to the community a real problem. There is need perhaps among students today for more tolerance of the intolerance of yesterday.

Had the Virginians been in any way inclined to try a broad policy of toleration, Maryland's experience would surely have warned them off. There, too, the issues of the war came directly home to

[10] Hening, *Statutes*, I, 532–33.

[11] York County Records, No. 3, 1657–1662, pp. 63b, 66, where the county court formally called the attention of provincial authorities to a problem considered especially serious in that county. See also, *ibid.*, 125–27, 130b, 131; *Virginia Magazine*, V (1897–1898), 41, an excerpt recording the action of the Northampton court early in 1657 by which Henry Vaux was sent up to the governor on a charge of entertaining William Robinson, a Quaker; and Bruce, *Institutional History of Virginia*, I, 225 ff. One of the distinguished studies in early American history is Rufus M. Jones, *The Quakers in the American Colonies* (London, 1911).

all parties. A royal charter gave Lord Baltimore an advantage that had been denied the planters of Virginia, but the proprietor was Catholic, a personal friend of the King, and he had much to fear from the Puritan leadership of Parliament. Those members of the colony who were consciously joined to the proprietary interest easily saw an important connection between that interest and the fate of the Royalist cause. Others, already resisting the proprietary prerogative in Maryland, might by the same token look for an escape from its restrictions through a victory by Parliament. There was risk that the Protestants, uneasy partners with Catholics in a daring experiment, might react dangerously to the anti-Catholic sentiment which, though largely based on mistaken assumptions, was a significant factor in the opposition to Charles and Laud. The only certainty in the situation was that there would be trouble, and to make the outlook doubly dark, it could be anticipated that William Claiborne would fish wherever the waters became troubled. Whatever influences in Virginia may have worked to make of that old enemy of the proprietor a Royalist, the Maryland situation held forth a promise persuading him to the side of Parliament.

The years of the Long Parliament were for Baltimore a time of disappointment and recurring difficulty in the defense of his chartered rights. Numbered among the disappointments was a failure of the Indian mission. For a time it had stirred the patriotic and religious zeal of the English Jesuits, heretofore denied the stimulation of a mission field of their own. Father White and his colleagues, seeking out Indian villages by the riverways, preaching and healing through the day and camping on the river's bank of an evening, present a charming picture that stands with that of Thorpe in Virginia and of Eliot in New England to prove that English colonization was not wholly divorced from a Christian and humanitarian concern for the welfare of the natives.[12] But here, as elsewhere, the harvest was Indian wars rather than converts.

An increasing number of brushes with local tribes is followed

[12] The standard authorities are John G. Shea, *History of the Catholic Missions among the Indian Tribes of the United States, 1529–1854* (New York, 1899); John G. Shea, *A History of the Catholic Church within the Limits of the United States* (New York, 1886–1892); and see especially extracts from annual letters of the English Provincials of the Society of Jesus, in Hall (ed.), *Narratives of Early Maryland*, 115–44.

in the records by the outbreak of a protracted struggle with the powerful Susquehannocks. Unrest in Maryland contributed, no doubt, to a growing apprehension among the Indians of Virginia, where time had brought some relaxation in the colonists' vigilance and where the now ancient Opechancanough awaited the hour of vengeance. It came in 1644, bringing to the planters the unspeakable horrors of another massacre and a second holiday for annual commemoration of the escape of the more fortunate members of the community. Governor Berkeley won new favor by the vigor of his efforts to suppress the uprising.[13] New Englanders saw a judgment visited upon a Godless people for their recent rejection of proffered spiritual aid, and at least one Virginian, Thomas Harrison, appears to have reasoned likewise in the moment of his conversion to Puritanism.[14] The people of Maryland read a warning lesson, perfected in their own use the techniques of security learned by the hard experience of their neighbors, and more than once proposed co-operation in meeting a common danger. The fires of evangelical zeal flickered out as signal fires ran from hilltop to hilltop or three guns echoed through the forest to warn the whites.

Contributing to the declining promise of the Indian mission had been a quarrel between Baltimore and the Jesuits. Though he had encouraged the work, Baltimore was jealous of his proprietary prerogative and had no intention of permitting the development of a spiritual dominion independent of his own authority. Not only would such a rival dominion reduce the prestige and profit of the proprietorship, but the proselyting zeal of the Jesuit fathers, thus reinforced, might well become a threat to his established policy of religious toleration. He brought the issue to a head in 1641 by forbidding the Jesuits to acquire land from the Indians and by declaring in force the ancient statute of mortmain against gifts of land to such societies and corporations. The ruling was bitterly contested, appealed to the English provincial, incidentally a direct descendant of Sir Thomas More, and then referred to Rome, where Baltimore emerged victor.[15] It is still impossible to acquire land

[13] Wertenbaker, *Virginia under the Stuarts*, 88–91.

[14] Bruce, *Institutional History of Virginia*, I, 255.

[15] Andrews, *Colonial Period of American History*, II, 312–13, and the citations there given.

in Maryland for religious purposes except by act of the legislature, in which members of the clergy are denied a seat. Virginia faced no such problem as that raised by the Jesuits in Maryland, but during the interregnum, perhaps after some contemplation by Virginians of the handiwork of religious zealots in England, ministers were excluded from the Assembly on the ground that such a privilege entailed unhappy consequences for the community.[16] In both colonies strong influences were at work for the supremacy of lay authority.

Hard on the quarrel with the Jesuits followed trouble between the Catholics and the Protestants. Prior to 1642 Protestant and Catholic had even worshiped in the same chapel at St. Mary's. But that year the Protestants appealed to the Assembly, asserting that the door had been locked against them and their books taken away by Thomas Gerard, a Catholic. Though the Assembly promptly ordered their readmittance and imposed a fine on Gerard to be used for the support of the first minister that should arrive in the province, the incident signaled the failure of Lord Baltimore's unique experiment.[17] Events at home had placed an abnormal strain on efforts to control the most normal of impulses. Such good will as had existed among the planters gave way to suspicion and bitterness, threatening a complete overthrow of the proprietor's policy and an end to the colony's peace.

Into this unhappy breach stepped William Claiborne, not long back from England as another "true friend" of Parliament, and Captain Richard Ingle, Protestant master of the *Reformation,* a London tobacco ship trading to the Chesapeake. Leonard Calvert had gone to England for consultation with his brother when in 1644 Governor Giles Brent indiscreetly arrested Ingle for treasonable remarks anent the King. The upshot was a vigorous championship of Protestantism and all forms of opposition to prerogative right that served Ingle during the following year as a convenient cover for brigandage. Leonard had returned in the fall of 1644, unfortunately the bearer of a commission from the King for arrest of ships whose owners adhered to Parliament's cause. He and Berke-

---

16 Hening, *Statutes,* I, 378.

17 *Archives of Maryland,* I (1883), 119. On the chapel itself, see Forman, *Jamestown and St. Mary's,* 203.

ley apparently decided to forget the commission. Not so Ingle, who used the report of it to advantage, and Calvert was forced to take refuge in Virginia. Father White and his colleague, Philip Fisher, were carried prisoners to England, where the former remained an inmate of Newgate until 1648. Claiborne seized Kent Island, and for a two-year period incomplete records show principally that the colony was uproariously unsettled.[18] With Berkeley's help Calvert regained control shortly before his death in 1647.

His success did not remove, however, the continuing threat to Baltimore's charter at home, where Ingle, Claiborne, and others were active against the proprietor. His opponents enjoyed many advantages, but Baltimore showed tact and good judgment in the defense of his chartered rights. In the success which rewarded his efforts, he possibly was indebted to friends such as the Earl of Warwick, who served after 1643 as head of a parliamentary committee on plantations. Of greater importance, however, were the proprietor's attempt to hold a neutral course through the troubles dividing his countrymen, his failure to press openly and objectionably the Catholic mission, the appointment in 1648 of the Protestant William Stone as governor to succeed the Catholic Thomas Greene who had been selected by Leonard Calvert on his deathbed, and a shrewd move in providing an asylum for the persecuted Puritans of Virginia. Richard Bennett and an estimated four hundred to six hundred coreligionists accepted an invitation from Stone in 1648 to move to Maryland. Settled on the Severn, with thoughts turning now and again to the Severn in old Gloucestershire, they named their community Providence.[19]

It was at this point that Lord Baltimore sent over his justly famous "Act concerning Religion." No doubt he desired among other things to provide some additional protection for the now considerably outnumbered Catholic minority. The act was offered with an eye to evidences of a nascent sentiment in England favoring liberty of conscience, a new phrase then gaining some currency. Protecting the "conscience in matters of religion" for all who

[18] For an account of the period, see again, Steiner, *Maryland during the English Civil Wars*. On the controversial question of Richard Ingle, the writer is in agreement with Andrews, *Colonial Period of American History*, II, 308–309.

[19] As events soon proved, this Puritan settlement was destined rather to perpetuate the memory of a leading Catholic lady in England, Anne Arundel.

accepted the divinity of Christ, the act provided an effective rejoinder to the repeated charge of Baltimore's enemies that Maryland was a hotbed of popish schemes. Also, it served as a well-timed
invitation to other Protestants to settle in the province, and finally,
but by no means least, it expressed once more the policy to which
for years he had consistently held.[20]

Considering its fame, some who bother to read the law as enacted by the Assembly of 1649 will be disappointed.[21] For there
is little of the sweeping and compelling force that marks Thomas
Jefferson's later indictment of the union of church and state in
Virginia's "Act for Religious Liberty," and among Baltimore's
contemporaries, Roger Williams supported the cause with arguments more eloquent and more advanced than any contained in the
Maryland statute. Nonetheless, Baltimore's act stands as one of
the more important milestones in the history of America's way of
life. Sober and sound in its reasoning, the product of good sense
rather than of an extraordinary intelligence, it called for no surrender of basic convictions, and urged only that men of different
faiths live in peace, concede to one another the free right of worship, and eschew in their daily intercourse the use of terms which
served merely to breed ill will. Specifically, the colonists were to
avoid the use "in a reproachful manner" of such designations as
"heritick, Scismatick, Idolator, puritan, Independant, Prespiterian
popish prest, Jesuite, Jesuited papist, Lutheran, Calvenist, Ana-
baptist, Brownist, Antinomian, Barrowist, Roundhead, Sepatist, or
any other" the like. No such radical doctrine as the separation of
church and state was included.

By these very limitations Lord Baltimore cut to the heart of the
problem that was to be so peculiarly America's. That problem has
been to live together in peace, and only slowly and by an uneven
course did men come to a general acceptance of the separation of
church and state as a necessary means to that end. And if any be
disposed to think the road was easy, or to view too seriously occa-

[20] See Bradley T. Johnson, *The Foundation of Maryland and the Origin of the Act
concerning Religion of April 21, 1649* (Baltimore, 1883); Andrews, *Colonial Period
of American History*, II, 310–12; and for general background, Wilbur K. Jordan,
*The Development of Religious Toleration in England from the Convention of the
Long Parliament to the Restoration, 1640–1660* (London, 1938).

[21] *Archives of Maryland*, I (1883), 244–47.

sional departures today from the way advised by good sense, Maryland's experience stands as a useful lesson. In no other place was the peace more frequently broken, or was there more common resort to the very terms of reproach indexed by the act. The prolonged controversy, inside and out of scholarly circles, as to where most of the credit and most of the blame belongs is pointless except for the purpose of continuing an ancient fight, the fallen heroes of which still hover in their ghostly fashion about a monument that stands at the entrance to the site of old St. Mary's to proclaim that hoary field of battle the birthplace of religious tolerance in America. It undoubtedly is one of the places of its origin, and one of the more important, though hardly in the sense ordinarily implied. The point is that men came after a long and bitter struggle, despite continuing dislikes and misunderstandings, to accept the commonsense rule advised by Baltimore at the outset. We are reminded that religious tolerance in America stems not so much from sentimental devotion to a high ideal as from the triumph of good judgment. And because the victory was hard won, perhaps we shall all value it the more.

Questions of religious and political allegiance were but two aspects of a problem embracing serious economic considerations as well. The trade of the colonists, except for an occasional Dutch ship, had remained largely in the hands of London merchants. Each year perhaps as many as thirty vessels sailed from England for the Chesapeake, their arrival there being timed to suit the convenience of a community which harvested its tobacco crop in the late summer and had it ready for the market by early fall. On this side of the water, as the coloring of fall touched the forest and a new crispness in the air joined the aroma of freshly cured tobacco, the planters made haste against a day that would mark the event of the year. The first ships of the annual tobacco fleet brought in addition to much-needed supplies equally welcome news and gossip from home. The word carried quickly over the colony, and while men hurried to complete their preparations, women took stock of larders that might entice some shipmaster ashore for dinner and an evening's conversation. The hope of the shipmaster, as he went about a round of duties extending from the delivery of token gifts from friends and relatives in England to appearances in court for collection of overdue accounts, was that he might reach London again by March, a hope more than once destined to disappointment.

A wide dispersal of settlement occasioned serious waste of time and effort in transactions with individual planters. The difficulty could not be entirely overcome even by the growing practice which concentrated much of the trade in the hands of leading planters acting as factors and attorneys for the English merchants. Nonetheless, it is important to notice the effort made and its increasing effect upon the economy of the community, for the first fortunes of the region seem to have been built upon a combination of planting and commercial activity. Perhaps the wealthiest man in Virginia during the 1640's was Samuel Mathews, whose plantation was advantageously situated in the lower part of the Peninsula. There he produced beef, pork, wheat, and dairy products for the supply of outgoing ships.[22] If, in return for that supply, he did not take merchandise to exchange with his less fortunate or less provident neighbors for their tobacco, he missed an opportunity many later planters turned to advantage. The store would become a featured item in inventories of the larger estates. In its stock of soap, nails, pots, knives, pans, tools, ammunition, as well as stockings, shoes, and other items of clothing, one finds a ready list of the common articles imported from England.[23] In the final analysis, of course, all trade rested upon an exchange for tobacco; with tobacco, plus occasional part loads of furs, skins, clapboard, pipe staves, and walnut or cedar timber, payments were made in London.

It follows that the fortunes of the colony rose and fell with the tobacco market, and that the problems of that market were among the first concerns of the planter. For their solution he looked to political action. That it was a responsibility of government to pro-

22 Force (comp.), *Tracts*, II, No. 8, p. 15. A useful account of trade is that of the Dutchman, David P. De Vries, in *Collections of the New York Historical Society* (New York), 2d ser., III (1857), especially pp. 77–78, 124. County records offer helpful clues, as the York County Records, No. 2, Wills and Deeds, 1645–1649, pp. 56, 64, 93, 96, 140, 215.

23 York County Records, No. 3, Deeds, Orders, Wills, 1657–1662, pp. 108–109, provides an example in the estate of Colonel Thomas Ludlow (1661). The word "store" is not to be read necessarily in its modern sense, for it was basically a storehouse for the planter's own supplies. Its stocking, however, with an eye to some commercial advantage in meeting the needs of the surrounding community was a natural development.

tect the community against the particular hazards of its economic position was, in contemporary thought, an accepted postulate reinforced for the colonist by the sense of common economic interest arising from the basic conditions of colonial life. Government, accordingly, did not stop with fixing the Winchester measures of England as standard, or upon the passage of strict laws against engrossing and forestalling. It engaged in price-fixing efforts extending from the issuance of compulsory price lists for the tavernkeeper, or stipulation of a fair compensation for the physician who effected a cure, to varied schemes for boosting the price levels of the colony's staple.[24] Expanding production in the Chesapeake and West Indian plantations had glutted the market, while large quantities of an inferior grade of leaf gave Virginia tobacco a poor name. The colonies suffered, too, from competitive production in England, where, as late as the middle of the century, a contest between plantation interests and English tobacco farming proved an occasional source of stormy trouble. In England a prohibition of the growth of tobacco in favor of the American plantations had featured public policy since the time of King James, and in America crop control, designed both to reduce the quantity and to improve the quality of the market product, had long been the favored remedy. Orders issued at the company's direction for burning all bad weed had been followed by a succession of laws passed on the initiative either of the King or of the colonists themselves to limit the number of plants per head that might be cultivated, and even the number of leaves per plant that might be cured. Tobacco "viewers" and other officers were sworn to an obviously difficult task of enforcement.[25]

Earlier efforts having availed little, an especially radical proposal from the English merchants was accepted by the Virginia Assembly in 1640. All of the bad and half of the good of that year's crop was to be destroyed, and a production limit of 170 pounds per

[24] For example, see Hening, *Statutes*, I, 229, 287, 300, 316, 319, 347-48, 446, 450. A useful study is Edgar A. J. Johnson, *American Economic Thought in the Seventeenth Century* (London, 1932).

[25] Hening, *Statutes*, I, 141-42, 162-65, 188-90, 203-207, 209-13. Maryland followed within six years of her settlement by appointment of tobacco viewers. *Archives of Maryland*, I (1883), 97-99.

poll was fixed for each of the two ensuing years.[26] But such an effort depended upon co-operation of other colonies for real success, and problems of enforcement were extraordinarily difficult. Moreover, the plan rested upon an agreement between the Virginia planters and the London merchants, and under conditions produced by civil war at home it could provide no permanent answer to the colony's problem.

The effects of the war on trade naturally were disturbing. It brought upon the commercial communities of England a depression and stagnancy felt in time by all those in any way dependent upon them. Contributing to that result were not merely political uncertainty and conflict at home but additional risks of interference on the seas and in colonial ports, risks reflected in insurance and freight rates. The Virginia colonists, though Royalist in their political sentiments, on the whole promptly recognized that economic interest dictated a practical policy of neutrality that would not embarrass established relations with London, where the merchants generally adhered to Parliament in an alliance strengthened by the Earl of Warwick's prompt seizure of most of the royal navy. And for a time the policy thus established met with a gratifying measure of success. The Assembly in 1643 took the precaution of easing the conditions for Dutch traders, but a Dutchman visiting the colony that year found the usual number of English vessels and only four from Holland. An occasional caller at Jamestown over the preceding decade, he noted no radical change in trade relations with England. He returned home aboard one of eleven ships sailing together for London, and reported, as he had done after earlier visits, that prospects for Dutch trade in Virginia were slight.[27]

However, war, especially civil war, has a way of taking charge. In the spring of 1644 two London ships were forced to return home without cargo because of an attack on a Bristol ship in the lower James. The penalty was probably imposed chiefly for a violation of the colony's neutrality in matters of trade. Yet, the report of it

[26] *William and Mary College Quarterly*, 2d ser., IV (1924), 17–35, 146–47; *Virginia Magazine*, XIII (1905–1906), 381–82.

[27] Hening, *Statutes*, I, 258; De Vries, in *Collections of the New York Historical Society*, 2d ser., III (1857), 122–29. For a general discussion of the problem, see Beer, *Origins of the British Colonial System*, 352–59.

in London, together with the King's commission to Calvert and Berkeley for seizure of parliamentary shipping and with prejudiced accounts of Ingle's experiences in Maryland, seemingly had the effect of dissuading some London merchants from their usual ventures to the Chesapeake. Early in 1645 the Virginia Assembly hastened to assure the Londoners that the colony's policy remained, as it had been from the first, one of free trade with all English subjects, and that all rumors of an intended stoppage were entirely false.[28] Nevertheless, the London trade thereafter declined. Of the thirty-one ships trading in Virginia at the close of 1648, ten were from London, two were from Bristol, twelve were from the Netherlands, and seven were from New England.[29]

There were advantages in this diversification of trade for the colonists. Bristol merchants, who continued to be active in the Chesapeake, apparently assumed more of the risks in the trade than did their London competitors, who moved increasingly toward a scheme of trade based on consignments to London houses under agreements whereby the planter assumed most of the risks.[30] The Dutch, more efficient in the management of their business and possessed of better marketing facilities through their widespread commercial activities, offered prices better than the depressed levels obtaining in previous years. Indeed, the Virginia planter was long to recall, and often with great bitterness, the price his tobacco had fetched through this period of free trade with the Dutch. It does not follow necessarily, however, that the new trades provided an altogether satisfactory substitute for the older. Price, after all, is but one criterion in a trade.

The basic problem of a colony is one of supply. For its well-being it must have those goods from abroad which make possible an advancing standard of living, and at the same time it must enjoy a continuing investment of capital and labor in order to expand the range of economic opportunity. Without those aids its needs are inadequately met, whatever price in other terms its

[28] Hening, *Statutes*, I, 296.

[29] Force (comp.), *Tracts*, II, No. 8, p. 14. For evidence of Dutch trade in Maryland, see *Archives of Maryland*, I (1883), 252-53.

[30] Both De Vries and the county records indicate that the planter early fell behind in transactions with London. The merchants undoubtedly took full advantage of this indebtedness in fixing the general rules of the trade.

produce may bring.[31] And it was here that the new trades fell short. The Bristol trade seems never to have been large enough to promise a satisfactory substitute for a trade of supply from London. In fact, it is questionable that any other port in England could successfully compete with London in the supply of goods suited to the English taste, a point which may help to explain the subsequent "enslavement" of the planters to the London merchants. New Englanders, having little produce aside from fish that could command a market in Europe, were in the Chesapeake as in the West Indies looking for returns of value on a London market, or else for the goods of London. They were more likely to take essential goods out of Virginia than to increase its supply, and to offer such commodities as molasses or rum in exchange than items of more enduring value to the colonists. A footnote on the New England trade is suggested by a Virginia statute of 1659. It affirms that "the necessities of this country are relieved chiefly by the importation of English goods," and that the relief had been greatly obstructed by those bringing in unnecessary commodities to exchange for tobacco which was in turn sold for substantial goods such as clothing to be carried out of the colony leaving the "country destitute of her owne supplies." [32] The act forbade thereafter the export of any English goods except by him who first brought them in.

The Dutch, of course, were better equipped than the New Englanders for supply of the colony's needs. On occasion representing English merchants resident in Holland, they offered an exchange chiefly for "linen and coarse cloths, beer, brandy, and other dis-

[31] The fundamental importance of supply is emphasized by a long series of statutes directed against forestalling and engrossing. The latter offense was described in a statute of 1643 as the buying of shoes, stockings, woolens, linens, liquors, candles, soap, sugar, spices, fruit, ironware, nails, ammunition, arms, "or any necessarie commoditie whatsoever" and selling them at a "dearer rate." Hening, *Statutes*, I, 245. A statute of 1633, *ibid.*, 216–17, had prohibited any ship from having any more freight of the colony's goods than was equivalent to the goods imported by the vessel. And notice especially Maryland's proclamation of 1643 forbidding the loading of other ships until the English ships had secured a full cargo on the ground that the colony's essential supply depended upon shipping from England. *Archives of Maryland*, III (1885), 144.

[32] Hening, *Statutes*, I, 519; II, 127–28. Adversely affecting the New England trade was a ten-shilling duty of 1658 on exports not bound for England, a duty which significantly for the encouragement of New England traders was withdrawn in 1665 on goods shipped by them. *Ibid.*, I, 469; II, 218.

stilled spirits." [33] That the Virginians in the circumstances should have welcomed the trade is natural, and that they desired its continuance is readily apparent in their long-continued effort to maintain a right of "free" trade. Such a right would have afforded an opportunity to sell their tobacco in a more competitive market and to dispose of a surplus production which had served only to depress prices on the English market. But there is little reason to believe that the Dutch trade ever promised to relieve the colonists of a basic dependence on England. Aside from important political considerations which called into play the normal loyalties of the planters as Englishmen, there were several economic arguments against placing too great a reliance on the new trade. Dutch cargoes ran perhaps a bit too heavily to spirituous goods, and there is some question of the Hollanders' ability at other points to meet fully the demands of a market governed by English tastes.[34] More important was the very limited investment of capital and labor the Dutch were prepared to make. Traders rather than colonizers, they offered no adequate substitute for the several hundred immigrants who had for years constituted the principal annual import from England. They brought a welcome supply of Negro labor, but the numbers were relatively few and there is reason to believe that white servants from Britain, even if they were Irishmen fleeing the wrath of Cromwell, were preferred.[35] No more than a handful of the Dutch themselves actually settled in the colony.

The fundamental importance of the problem of supply finds emphasis in a renewed attempt to provide for the colony a greater degree of local self-sufficiency that would reduce the need for imports. Acts for the encouragement of specific trades were supplemented by those which sought provision of general conditions

[33] Bruce, *Economic History of Virginia*, II, 310, whose discussion of the Dutch trade contains much valuable information.

[34] The problem of liquor imports was perennial and was closely joined to that of the basic supply of the colony. The danger, of course, was that the colonists would pay out so much for spirits that little or nothing would be left for the purchase of essential goods. Efforts to restrict the trade included a statutory provision that debts for wine and strong drink should not be recoverable in the courts, a regulation repealed in 1645 and re-enacted as a "perpetual" law two years later. See Hening, *Statutes*, I, 295, 350; and II, 128, for an act of 1662 seeking to restrict the rum trade particularly.

[35] *Ibid.*, I, 411, 471, 538-39, 540.

favorable to craftsmanship and experimental endeavor.[36] Of such a purpose were laws seeking to systematize the marketing arrangements of the colony in the hope of securing at least some of the advantages of town life.[37] To encourage Virginians to earn a part of the freightage on their own goods, ships owned by Virginian traders were exempted from the "castle" duties imposed on all other shipping.[38] Another effort, prophetic of some of the more significant chapters of American history, sought to attract and hold in the colony hard money. It was an accepted and well-grounded opinion of the time that coin provided distinct advantages over a commodity exchange as a stimulant to trade and craftsmanship. Also, a constant drainage of specie in payment of an unfavorable balance with Europe had been associated in the colonist's mind with a depression of prices that acted as a general deterrent on enterprise. Accordingly, in 1645 plans to mint a local coin were accompanied by legislation decreeing that Spanish pieces of eight should circulate at an exchange value of six shillings, an inflated rate subsequently reduced to the still-inflated figure of five shillings. The measure was counted upon to hold the coin in Virginia.[39] Prompted by circumstances which effectively reduced the prospect of interference by the home government and passed with an eye to opportunities for attracting foreign coin through the channels of Dutch trade, the legislation expressed a policy that for the remainder of the seventeenth century was frequently resorted to by the colonies in their quest for a well-rounded economy.

Of similar intent was the concern reflected in contemporary legislation for a more equitable distribution of the tax burden than had been provided by the now traditional poll tax. In meeting the extraordinary expenses occasioned by the massacre of 1644, the Assembly supplemented its customary levy by special imposts on property other than servants. The experiment was abandoned in

[36] *Ibid.*, 307, 314, 330, 336, 351–52, 488–89, 524.

[37] *Ibid.*, 362, 397, 417–18; Charles City County Records, Orders, Wills, Deeds, 1655–1665 (Virginia State Library, Richmond), 2, 16, 19.

[38] Hening, *Statutes*, I, 402, 480; York County Records, No. 2, pp. 202, 377, for an early example of a planter possessing share rights in a ship. Such joint ownership or, at least, joint participation in ventures beyond the bay were not uncommon. See Bruce, *Economic History of Virginia*, I, 448–49.

[39] Hening, *Statutes*, I, 308–309, 397, 410–11, 493.

1648 on the ground that it had never been anything more than an emergency measure, but through the following years sentiment came to favor a reliance principally upon customs revenues. An act of 1658 imposed a duty of two shillings per hogshead on the export trade of the colony. The line of reasoning that led to its adoption is clearly indicated in the act. The poll tax, though roughly apportioning the levy according to ability to pay and having an obvious administrative advantage, imposed the burden directly on the colony's labor supply. To place it rather on the common product of the colonists' labors, measured by exports, appeared not only to be more equitable but also likely to stimulate individual endeavor. By withholding the incidence of taxation through an experimental period, the measure was designed to provide an indirect subsidy for all experimental efforts. Payable in coin, bills of exchange, or commodities at a 30 per cent advance over the European price, the duty was also expected to prove a further aid in solving the colony's monetary problems.[40] It was destined, of course, to supplement rather than displace the poll tax.

In this quest of a greater degree of self-sufficiency, little was done that was actually new. A cardinal feature of the original program of the Virginia Company had been just such an effort. Many of the policies now adopted were no more than revivals of those by which the company had sought the recruitment of craftsmen of all sorts for the colony and the assurance of conditions favorable to their continued activity in the hope of holding to a desirable minimum unavoidably expensive imports from England. And now as then, the attempt represented but one part of a broader program designed to assure for the colonists the most secure position possible in the service of a European market. As Virginia's founders had well understood, the basic problem was to assure a mutually advantageous trade, and for this purpose it would be necessary to provide, in addition to a certain degree of colonial self-sufficiency, staple products sufficiently varied and attractive to command the continued services of European capital and labor. The collapse of the company in 1624 had left the colonists disillusioned with all its ambitious projects. In the face of that feeling attempts to escape the disadvantages of an unvaried economy had

40 *Ibid.*, 305–306, 337–38, 341, 351, 356; and for the two-shilling duty, pp. 491–92, 498.

proved as feeble as they were fitful, but necessity now forced a different attitude. Whether trading with the Dutch or with the English, with London or with Bristol, it was clear to thoughtful leaders in the colony that some escape must be found from an unhealthy reliance upon tobacco. And so once more there was serious talk of silk, sugar, wine, and other such rich commodities; talk in terms familiar to all who have read Hariot, Hakluyt, and the minutes of the Virginia Company; talk that in its return to the original objectives of Virginia's settlement overlooked not even Hariot's silk grass or Captain Lane's passage to the South Seas by way of the Roanoke River.

A leading figure in the revival of these old hopes was Sir William Berkeley. More than a royal governor of the colony, he was in many ways its leading planter. His estate at Greenspring boasted the first great house of Virginia and an orchard of 1,500 trees to which men pointed, along with his efforts to cultivate rice, in proof of the promise of further agricultural experimentation. The interests that were to guide him through many years as governor and planter in Virginia and as a proprietor of the Carolinas were already taking shape. A London tract of 1649 announced his intention to lead an expedition southwestward in search of a passage to the South Seas by which Virginia might "gain the rich trade of the *East India*." [41] The pamphlet also enlarged on the prospects for production of sugar, indigo, ginger, cotton, and the like, and sought in other ways to revive the high hopes that had once been so closely associated with the very name of Virginia. To remove the imputations still remaining from the disastrous failure of the Virginia Company in just such an effort as was now proposed, a leaf was lifted from those who had for so long sought a revival of the company's charter. Readers were assured that there had been no fault in the company's plan and no lack of promise in Virginia itself. Rather, the failure should be attributed to Spanish intrigue at the court of James I, an argument which reminds us of the imminence of Cromwell's attempt to seize the Spanish West Indies.

Reviving hopes in Virginia, as the publication of this pamphlet in London suggests, grew partly out of opportunities seemingly presented by the trend of events in England. The Civil War had by

[41] Force (comp.), *Tracts*, II, No. 8, pp. 8–9.

1646 run its course to a military victory for Parliament that proved extraordinarily difficult to translate into a satisfactory political settlement. King Charles, who became first a prisoner of Parliament and then of the more radical army of Cromwell, gambled all on the divisions separating his opponents and in January of 1649 paid with his head. Cromwell had paved the way for this denouement by purging Parliament of a "Presbyterian" group more moderate in its opinions than were the religious Independents of the army. Only a "Rump" of the Long Parliament remained, and the substance of power lay with the army. For a time the revulsion of public sentiment at the execution of the King, the resentment of the "Presbyterians," the rallying of the Scottish Highlanders to the cause of Charles II, and a desperate rebellion of the Irish held forth some promise of a Royalist restoration, but Cromwell proved to be the master. As the troubled decade of the 1640's reached its close, the controversies which for so long had divided Englishmen were apparently drawing toward some sort of conclusion. A final settlement, as events proved, awaited the passage of another decade, but a significant turning point was reached with the re-establishment by the army of one effective authority over the British Isles. An unpalatable fact for many, it had to be reckoned with by all Englishmen at home and abroad.

Among those especially affected were the Royalists, many of them in exile or facing exile, their estates sequestered or threatened with sequestration. It was natural that some of them should turn their thoughts to America. It was natural, too, that an exiled king possessed of little with which to reward his followers should offer such an aid as the grant in 1649 of the Northern Neck of Virginia to Lord John Culpeper, Lord Ralph Horton, Lord Henry Jermyn, Sir John Berkeley, Sir William Morton, Sir Dudley Wyatt, and Thomas Culpeper. And it is not surprising that Sir William Berkeley, whose brother was numbered among the grantees and whose own plans had undoubtedly been laid in the hope of a Royalist triumph, should seek in the circumstances producing the patent whatever advantage might be found for Virginia. For a time his position in the colony, backed by the Assembly's strong condemnation of the regicides, appears to have held out some real promise of a Royalist refuge on the Chesapeake that would have brought to

246

the aid of the Virginia colony men of substantial quality and ability if nothing else.[42] Such hopes as may have been associated with that prospect, however, were soon dissipated; the Royalists lacked both the means and the will to serve a major colonial enterprise. While some of them now acquired an active interest in colonial questions that would continue into the Restoration era with important results, and some actually migrated to the colonies, principally it seems to the West Indies, most of them clung rather to the hope of a re-establishment of their fortunes in England. When forced into exile, they usually took up a temporary residence on the Continent. Such evidences of their interest in America as the grant to the Northern Neck had never, in fact, promised much beyond the sort of overlordship of the land that the colonists had feared and fought since the days of the first Lord Baltimore.

Over the ensuing years, Virginia could boast of gentlemen who in every way met the test of a Cavalier, but, though their influence on social standards was possibly greater than their number, there were only a few of them. Among English immigrants of middle-class or more humble origins who reached the colony after 1649, many no doubt counted themselves as having been on the side of the King, but for the most part they came to a community that already had made its peace with Cromwell and for reasons having little to do with politics. Virginia's now timeworn Cavalier tradition has little basis in historical fact.[43]

Though some of the colonists may have been slow to realize it, the promise of effective aid from the Royalists had disappeared with the collapse of their political fortunes in England. The most

[42] See especially, *A Voyage to Virginia by Colonel Norwood, ibid.,* III, No. 10.

[43] See especially, Thomas J. Wertenbaker, *Patrician and Plebeian in Virginia, or the Origin and Development of the Social Classes of the Old Dominion* (Charlottesville, 1910); and notice that the cavalier tradition finds no place in Robert Beverley, *History and Present State of Virginia* (London, 1705). A reprint of this work (Chapel Hill, 1947), has been edited by Louis B. Wright for the Institute of Early American History and Culture, Williamsburg, Virginia. The relatively heavy migration into Virginia and Maryland during the 1650's was related to the politics of the period chiefly through the consequent disturbance of English economy. Thus William Hallam wrote to Daniel Llewellin in September, 1656, of the unsettled condition of England: "I would wish I could heare in what condicon you live in, for I fear if these times hold long amongst us, we must all faine to come to Virginia." *William and Mary College Quarterly,* VIII (1899–1900), 238–39.

urgent of the colony's economic needs was a re-establishment of normal relations with the mother country. So much has modern thought been shaped by the advantages of a later independence that we easily overlook the essential difference in seventeenth-century conditions, and at times have assumed that in this earlier day the colony could have pursued an independent course. Virginia had in 1650 a population of approximately 15,000 souls as against half a million in 1776; it needed capital, the continuance of a readily assimilated flow of immigration, and the assurance of an established market for the purchase of supplies suited to its requirements and tastes. Whatever temptation the Dutch trade may have offered, the inducement was certainly insufficient to warrant such a severance of economic and social ties with the homeland as would be involved in a refusal to come to terms with the government that now held jurisdiction over all the British Isles. To most Virginians, no doubt, an ideal arrangement would have been one in which the colonists enjoyed the good will of the home government and were left free in their trade. But even this arrangement obviously would require as its very first condition an accommodation of differences with Cromwell's regime.

Of assistance in persuading the colonists to an acceptance of that necessity were developments at home which mark the genesis of a new imperial mood. The prospect of even a limited degree of political stability had turned men's thoughts toward a restoration of England's trade, which had suffered a serious decline during the years of civil war. There were many indications, including an evident purpose to re-establish normal trade relations between England and her colonies, of a growing concern over the threat to English interests arising from Dutch competition in all quarters of the globe.[44] The risk that the rivalry between the two states might lead to war gave new weight to those considerations of national self-sufficiency which since Elizabeth's day had helped to promote an interest in colonization and other projects of maritime expansion. Indeed, there is evidence that more than one contemporary turned back to the pages of Hakluyt, with results serving to mark

[44] See especially, Andrews, *Colonial Period of American History*, IV; Lawrence A. Harper, *The English Navigation Laws; A Seventeenth-Century Experiment in Social Engineering* (New York, 1939); Beer, *Origins of the British Colonial System*.

the developments of the day as in some measure a conscious revival of the economic nationalism of the Elizabethan promoters.[45] Indications that the state itself might now more nearly assume the positive role desired by these early leaders were to be found in the beginnings of modern English naval power under Robert Blake and in the Navigation Acts of 1650 and 1651, with their warnings both to the colonists and to the Dutch. As negotiations were undertaken for an amicable settlement of differences with Holland, negotiations that would end in failure, the colonists faced a prospect of having to choose between membership in either a British or a Dutch empire. And should the choice come to that, who could doubt where the decision would fall?

England's reviving imperialism, moreover, promised a renewed interest in Virginia and its neighboring regions. That this should be true is not in itself surprising, but there is a certain irony in the fact that it was particularly true of those features of the new mood which were definitely traceable to the influence of Puritanism. The Puritans were in many ways Elizabethan, and their long-continued opposition to the Stuarts had fed upon a tradition of England's greatness in the age of Elizabeth. That tradition still argued, despite the greater menace of Dutch competition, for hostility to the "arrogant" Spaniard, as yet twenty years away from formal concession even of the English title to Virginia. Hostile attitudes toward Spain had been encouraged by the activity of prominent Puritans in piracy along the Spanish Main, and through the English settlement of isles lying within the Spanish sphere. Especially important was the memory of the English settlement on Providence Island, off the Mosquito Coast, a settlement founded in 1629 under the leadership of such outstanding Puritans as Sir Nathaniel Rich, the Earl of Warwick, and John Pym. With time it became chiefly a pirates' base and was finally destroyed by the outraged Spaniards in 1641.[46] In the desire to even that score men found encouragement in the growing profits from sugar planting in the British West Indian plantations, and in the ease with which a free-booting Captain William Jackson, in the service of Warwick, had

[45] This is especially noticeable in contemporary pamphlets on the possibilities in Virginia and Carolina. For a list, see below, n. 50.
[46] Newton, *Colonising Activities of the English Puritans.*

249

seized and held momentarily the Spanish colony of Jamaica in 1643.[47]

During the civil-war years energies that might otherwise have been directed toward an extension of English interest in the West Indies were largely absorbed by the controversies at home. Older and established plantations in the Lesser Antilles continued and throve, but infant communities founded by Bermuda settlers under Warwick's patronage on Trinidad and Tobago disappeared. In 1642 the fate which had befallen Providence Island also overtook the Ruatan settlement, established in the Bay of Honduras under a patent of 1638 from the Providence Island Company to none other than William Claiborne, recently withdrawn from his defeat on Kent Island in the Chesapeake.[48] The settlement established in 1646 at Eleuthera in the Bahamas by a band of Puritan emigrants from Bermuda remained a small and relatively unimportant venture, even after receiving additional immigrants in 1649 as the result of the triumph in Bermuda of a Royalist faction. It was important enough, however, to receive that year the notice of Parliament in England, where still echoed Pym's ringing condemnation of King Charles's failure to act on a great opportunity for West Indian conquest in the interest both of England and of Protestantism.[49] Pym was now gone, but in his place stood Cromwell, who deplored the prospect of war with Protestant Holland and earnestly sought over a three-year period to negotiate some settlement of differences. Failing in that, he withdrew at the earliest opportunity from the first (1652–1654) of three wars with the Dutch in the hope of freeing England's resources for his own grandiose "Western Design" for the conquest of the Spanish West Indies.

That the West Indian project was thus delayed, and its ultimate reward no more than the conquest of Jamaica in 1655, in no way alters the significance of the story in the background of our own. For the objectives identified with this "Western Design" were

47 Vincent T. Harlow (ed.), *The Voyages of Captain William Jackson (1642–1645)*, in *Camden Miscellany* (London), XIII, No. 4 (1923).

48 Newton, *Colonising Activities of the English Puritans*, 267, 315. Evidently Claiborne did not go to Ruatan. Andrews, *Colonial Period of American History*, II, 309 n.

49 Leo F. Stock (ed.), *Proceedings and Debates of the British Parliaments Respecting North America* (Washington, 1924–), I, 98, 210, 211.

obviously conducive to a new interest in Virginia, and in the Carolina region to the south of it. The West Indies rather than the mainland held the focus of attention, but the Spanish outpost in Florida argued the strategical significance of the southeastern coast of North America in any plan for control of the West Indies. Moreover, any such expansion of the southern area of English settlement as was now proposed naturally lent a certain pertinence to the record of English effort in Virginia, oldest of the southern colonies.

If the examination of that record helped to clear away doubts regarding the promise of a West Indian venture, it served no less to suggest that another trial be made in Virginia. In addition, it called to mind projects, like the quest of a southerly passage to the Orient, which had once claimed the attention of Englishmen and still invited investigation. Such, at any rate, is the evidence offered by several contemporary pamphlets marking the first significant public discussion in a quarter of a century of the Virginia colony and neighboring Carolina.[50] Both a stimulant and a response to the new expansionist mood, these pamphlets dwelt chiefly on the hope that silk might be developed as a major staple. The colonists received detailed advice on sericulture, and those who offered the advice quite evidently had listened sympathetically to suggestions that Virginia provided at one and the same time a logical base of operations for a southward thrust and living proof of the promise which lay in that direction.

There was, of course, more talk than action. No major English investment resulted, and even the grant to the Carolina proprietors remained a decade in the future. Not only did the Dutch war interpose and the rewards of West Indian conquest prove disappointing,

---

[50] *Virginia impartially examined, and left to publick view. . . . Under which title, is comprehended the degrees from 34 to 39, wherein lyes the rich and healthfull countries of Roanock, the now plantations of Virginia and Maryland. . . . By William Bullock, gent.* (London, 1649); *A Perfect Description of Virginia . . .* (London, 1649), in Force (comp.), *Tracts,* II, No. 8; *Virginia: More especially the South part thereof. Richly and truly valued: viz. The fertile Carolana, and no lesse excellent Isle of Roanoak. . . . The second Edition, with Addition of the Discovery of Silkworms, with their benefit . . . . By E. W. Gent* (London, 1650), *ibid.,* III, No. 11; *The Reformed Virginian Silk-Worm, Or, a Rare and New Discovery of A speedy way . . . found out by a young Lady in England . . . in May, Anno 1652. For the feeding of Silk-worms in the Woods, on the Mulberry-Tree-leaves in Virginia . . .* (London, 1655), *ibid.,* No. 13.

but political uncertainty in the homeland continued and became an increasingly disturbing factor as the years of the interregnum passed. The record speaks frequently of a new imperial purpose, but for the time being there was more of promise than of achievement.

On the other side, the Virginia farmer, true to a character shaped by hard experience, in most instances undoubtedly remained as skeptical as his means were limited. Nevertheless, several acts of the Assembly passed during and after the Civil War for the encouragement of southwestward exploration display a keen sense of the direction interests at home would take.[51] It is in this same light, too, that the actual beginnings of settlement in the Albemarle Sound region, several years in advance of the Carolina charter of 1663, are properly viewed. There is no occasion to argue that the genesis of William Byrd's Lubberland presents a coherently organized chapter of major significance in England's quest of southern empire. Essentially, it represents merely one segment of an expanding Virginia frontier, the opening of a hinterland that even today finds its natural metropolis in Norfolk, and a movement of population that was by no means so impressive as the northward thrust of settlement from the James across the York and up the Rappahannock. As between the northern and southern extensions of that frontier, however, there was one important difference. Those who now moved toward Albemarle sacrificed the many advantages of an unexposed, all-water connection with arteries of transportation providing the only established line of communication with Europe. The map of the day shows clearly that such advantages were not surrendered without cause. And in seeking an explanation in this instance, it is perhaps well to recall how frequently on the American frontier the trends of migration were to reveal a sensitive response to every indication of the gathering tides of empire.

Actual experiments with silk production appear to have been largely the work of one man, Edward Digges, son of Sir Dudley Digges, former parliamentary leader and member of the Virginia Company. A leading figure in Virginia through the interregnum, he brought over for the direction of his projects two Armenian

[51] Hening, *Statutes*, I, 262, 376–77, 380–81, 422, 548; *Virginia Magazine*, IX (1901–1902), 55.

experts, at least one of whom was active in that work for several years. The community, though leaving the task chiefly to Digges, was by no means wholly indifferent. In addition to legislative policies designed to encourage just that kind of experiment, the Assembly revived an old law of the company requiring the planting of a specified number of mulberries on every dividend, offered bounties for the production of silk, wine, flax, wheat, hops, or any staple other than tobacco, and in 1656 even appropriated four thousand pounds of tobacco for the support of one of the Armenians.[52] That appropriation stands alone, however, and serves principally to emphasize the need for capital to tide such enterprises over an unavoidably expensive experimental period.

The continued effort to produce silk, extending well into the Restoration era, with a marked revival under the later patronage of Berkeley that actually won a degree of experimental success, testifies to the fact that Digges's efforts were no mere product of a passing fancy.[53] The measures adopted were intelligent, but, altogether aside from natural factors that apparently made a commercial success problematical, there was an imperative requirement for capital resources beyond the limited means of a poor and primitive community. The promise of a future bounty could in no way meet the actual and immediate need for funds. And so it was that when in the early stages of a hopeful experiment an offer of a political settlement with Cromwell came, there were additional economic arguments for its acceptance.

It perhaps would be too much to say that the surrender to the Commonwealth was dictated primarily by economic factors, but there can be no doubt that the weight of such considerations favored the action. The surrender followed parliamentary legislation threatening a complete boycott of the colony's trade with England and affirming a determined purpose to exclude the Dutch.[54] The proposal of terms came, moreover, when England

[52] Force (comp.), *Tracts*, III, No. 13, pp. 27–28, 35; Hening, *Statutes*, I, 420, 425, 469–70, 481, 487, 520, 521; York County Records, No. 3, p. 2a.

[53] For a useful condensation of the story, see Gray, *History of Agriculture in the Southern United States*, I, 184–85.

[54] The Navigation Act of 1650 was designed to force the submission of rebellious colonies to the new government. The act of 1651 laid down the principles of an imperial trade policy designed especially to exclude the Dutch. That Virginia clung

and Holland were already at war, and under circumstances promising favorable conditions of surrender.

A commission of Captain Robert Dennis, Captain Thomas Stagge, Captain Edmond Curtis, Richard Bennett, and William Claiborne was constituted in the latter part of 1651 for the reduction of the Virginia colony. Both Dennis and Stagge were lost with their ship on the passage out, and thus, upon the arrival of Curtis' frigate in the spring of 1652, negotiations were in the hands of three commissioners, among whom Bennett and Claiborne assumed the lead.[55] There seems little reason to doubt that Claiborne was primarily concerned with an opportunity in Maryland, and that Virginia stood to benefit by that as well as by his long-standing identification with the colony. He had already given ample testimony of an inclination to take every advantage of the political situation at home in his protracted and bitter contest with Lord Baltimore, and had maintained political connections in England which set him apart from most of the Virginia planters. Bennett's position is not so easily explained. A leader of the Virginia Puritans who had only recently taken advantage of Baltimore's offer of a haven in Maryland, his subsequent contribution to the disturbances of that community raises questions that can perhaps be answered only in the light of the intense feelings called forth by the issues of the day. His religious identification gave him much in common with the Independents at home, and probably produced an attachment to political principles which appeared to be at stake in America no less than in England. Also, he was apparently not averse to an opportunity to re-establish in some measure his position in Virginia, nor to visit discomfort upon Berkeley.

Sir William's well-known display of an intention to resist presents an interesting puzzle. In the presence of a by no means over-

---

to the hope of continuing her policy of economic neutrality is shown by the Assembly's response to the act of 1650. Challenging the claims of Parliament in accordance with an eloquent address by Berkeley, the burgesses in 1651 declared their resolve "to Continue our Allegeance to our most Gratious King, yet as long as his gratious favour permits us, we will peaceably (as formerly) trade with the Londoners, and all other Nations in amity with our Soveraigne." *Virginia Magazine*, I (1893–1894), 75–81; and for a full recounting, see Wertenbaker, *Virginia under the Stuarts*, 96–98.

[55] For background, see Beer, *Origins of the British Colonial System*, 362 ff.; for useful data pertaining to the mission, Stock (ed.), *Proceedings and Debates*, I, 226, 227, 229–32; *Virginia Magazine*, XI (1903–1904), 38–41.

whelming force, he both talked and acted bravely, but quickly surrendered to the counsels of wisdom and took an active part in the negotiations that followed. The governor of Virginia held, of course, no arbitrary power, and he may have been overpersuaded by his advisers, but there is more than a suggestion that from beginning to end he played the role of a politically experienced man whose chief anxiety in circumstances beyond his control was to keep the record straight for future reference.[56] That his actions contributed to securing the most favorable terms appears highly probable.

The terms of submission were recorded in two documents, both of them dated March 12, 1651/52.[57] By articles of agreement between the commissioners, as the first party, and the governor and council as the second, the governor and his councilors were exempted from any oath or engagement to the Commonwealth for one year, during which they were assured of a privilege to depart the colony with full guarantee of property rights. During that year they were also permitted individually and among themselves to pray for and speak well of the King. The paper promised that no person would be penalized for a former service to the King either "here or in England," and stipulated that a general act of indemnity should be promptly issued as a part of the settlement.[58] A second paper, drawn between the commissioners and a grand assembly of governor, council, and burgesses, embodied the general terms of a submission that was to be acknowledged as a "voluntary act" carrying with it a guarantee of "such freedomes and priviledges as belong to the free borne people of England." All former commissions and instructions upon which the government had stood were now nullified. A general indemnity for all persons permitted any not desiring to take an engagement to the Commonwealth to depart without molestation or interference with the disposal of their property within a term of one year. The document confirmed the Assembly's position in the government, all existing land titles, and established land policies, which included provisions for the headright and an exemption for

[56] Among the terms of surrender was Berkeley's right to send a full explanation to Charles II. Hening, *Statutes*, I, 366.

[57] *Ibid.*, 363–67. For the commissioners' account of the proceedings, see *Virginia Magazine*, XI (1903–1904), 32–35.

[58] For the act, also dated March 12, 1651/52, see Hening, *Statutes*, I, 367–68.

seven years of title from quitrent exactions. The right of worship according to *The Book of Common Prayer,* and of the clergy to their accustomed dues, were also allowed for a year, provided "those things which relate to kingshipp or that government" should not be "used publiquely."

Several provisions are of special interest. The fourth article declared that Virginia would have and enjoy the ancient boundaries granted by the royal charter, and assured aid in securing a parliamentary grant to that effect. One is reminded at once of Claiborne's interests in Maryland, for there could have been no more likely move to enlist for their support the sympathies of the Virginia planters. That they desired at this time the annexation of Maryland is doubtful, but there were unsettled boundary differences between the provinces on the Eastern Shore. The King's recent grant of the Northern Neck to a group of gentlemen had undoubtedly raised anew the colonists' apprehension of encroachment upon Virginia's natural area of expansion that had for so long made a charter of its own one of the community's cherished hopes.[59] This hope had been more than once associated with the planters' attempts to prevent a revival of the claims of the Virginia Company. That they were even now not entirely free of their old fear of such a revival is suggested by article twelve, which declared that "no man's cattell shall be questioned as the companies unless such as have been entrusted with them or have disposed of them without order." It appears likely that in accepting the settlement there was some thought for the assurance of Parliament's good will in resisting any move to resurrect the company.[60] The seventh article, stipulating that Virginia should enjoy "free trade as the people of England do enjoy to all places and with all nations according to the lawes of that commonwealth," is of interest because of the

[59] The colonists were already moving into the Northern Neck where they extended their settlement during the interregnum, and they strongly opposed revival of the 1649 claim after the Restoration.

[60] The publication in 1651 of Wodenoth's pamphlet (see above, n. 5) was possibly the chief occasion for apprehension at this time. In England the question of a charter for the Virginia colony was joined principally with the troublesome issues of Maryland. Stock (ed.), *Proceedings and Debates,* I, 231–32; Hall (ed.), *Narratives of Early Maryland,* 170, 209 ff.

subsequent attempt to use it to support a right of trade with the Dutch. There seems to have been very little justification for that view in the article itself, which was framed by men well aware of the Navigation Acts. The eighteenth article declared: "That Virginia shall be free from all taxes, customes and impositions whatsoever, and none to be imposed on them without consent of the Grand Assembly, And soe that neither Forts nor castles bee erected or garrisons maintained without their consent." It provided a guarantee of self-government no less welcome than was the additional assurance that the colony would bear no part of the cost of its reduction. Whatever else about the surrender may be debatable, there can be no question that the terms were good.

Whether it had been the intention in England for the commissioners to interfere in Maryland is not clear. No such power was specified in the instructions, which, nowhere mentioning Maryland by name, offered cover for the action only under the equivocal order "upon your arrival in Virginia . . . to reduce all the Plantations within the Bay of Chesepiak to their due obedience to the Parliament and the Commonwealth of England." [61] It was claimed during the following year that Maryland's name had been stricken from the original instructions on representations from Lord Baltimore.[62] The claim receives some support from his very evident inclination in preceding years to curry the favor of the victorious parliamentary forces, as when he admitted Virginia's Puritans into Maryland and appointed the Protestant William Stone governor. Indeed, early in 1650 Charles II had been moved to set aside the proprietor's authority through a commission to Sir William Davenant to act as governor of the province.[63] It is true that the indiscreet zeal of Thomas Greene, a Catholic and former governor who served during the absence in 1651 of Stone on a visit to Virginia, in proclaiming the accession of Charles II had threatened Baltimore with the displeasure of both Parliament and King.[64] Nevertheless, there appears to be some basis for an assumption that

[61] For the instructions, see Hall (ed.), *Narratives of Early Maryland*, 206–208; *Archives of Maryland*, III (1885), 264.

[62] See especially, *The Lord Baltemore's Case* (London, 1653), in Hall (ed.), *Narratives of Early Maryland*, 167–80.

[63] For his commission, see *ibid.*, 179–80.   [64] *Ibid.*, 164.

Claiborne and Bennett, neither of whom had been in England at the drafting of the instructions, were unintentionally left, through the untimely death of the senior members of the commission, to take full advantage of an equivocal phrasing.

In any case, while Bennett remained in Jamestown to supervise the establishment of an interim government, Claiborne hastened to St. Mary's, where on March 29, 1652, he effected the "reduction" of Maryland. Governor Stone and his council were ousted, and another council appointed for the government of the province received instructions to tender to all inhabitants an engagement to the Commonwealth. That Claiborne had been overhasty is made clear by an early reinstatement of Stone and a part of his council under the terms of a compromise which provided that writs would run in the name of the Commonwealth but permitted officials to regard their oaths to the proprietor as binding until further instructions came from England.[65] The authority of the Commonwealth had been asserted and men were required to give their engagement to it, but at the same time the proprietor's right still stood and officials were bound by oath in an obedience to his commands. Such a situation was obviously fraught with a danger to the peace of the colony that could only be removed by prompt and decisive action by the home government.

Unfortunately, the required action was not to be had. The issue of Baltimore's charter came before the council of state and Parliament promptly enough. With Samuel Mathews in London to press Virginia's claim under the terms of her recent surrender to a grant incorporating the bounds of the old royal charter, bounds which overlapped those conveyed by Maryland's charter, the question was in August referred for study to the navy committee. In December the committee drafted a report not unfavorable to the

---

[65] *Archives of Maryland*, III (1885), 271–72, 275; LIV (1937), 4–5, 7–8. On this subject and subsequent developments the best brief discussion is in Andrews, *Colonial Period of American History*, II, 315–20. Contemporary accounts, for the most part decidedly partisan, are *The Lord Baltemore's Case*, in Hall (ed.), *Narratives of Early Maryland*, 167–80; *Virginia and Maryland, or the Lord Baltamore's Printed Case Uncased and Answered* (London, 1655), *ibid.*, 187–230; *Babylon's Fall* (1655), *ibid.*, 235–46; *A Just and Cleere Refutation of a False and Scandalous Pamphlet Entituled Babylons Fall* (London, 1655), *ibid.*, 254–75; *Leah and Rachel* (London, 1656), *ibid.*, 281–308; "Heamans' Brief Narration" (1655), in *Maryland Historical Magazine*, IV (1909), 140–53; "Hammond vs. Heamans," *ibid.*, 236–51.

hopes of Claiborne and the Virginia planters.[66] But the problem was returned to Parliament without specific recommendation, and the ensuing year proved one of successive crises in Cromwell's attempt to reach a satisfactory political settlement in England itself. The Rump Parliament, last remnant of the old constitutional system, was dissolved in April. The ill-fated experiment of Barebone's Parliament followed; and then came the inauguration of the Protectorate under the Instrument of Government in December. The end was not yet in sight and, moreover, the country was at war. As a result, Lord Baltimore emerged with a negative victory which unhappily he sought to turn to a positive advantage in Maryland. On the eve of 1654, Governor Stone received instruction that the charter remained in force and that accordingly the arrangement with Claiborne should be ignored. The council should be reconstituted and the inhabitants required to take a new oath of fidelity to the proprietor, in whose name all writs would now run, under penalty of the loss of their land. In consequence, Maryland again knew at firsthand the meaning of civil war.

Leading the opposition were the Puritans of Providence, a group which only recently had been the special beneficiary of proprietary policies. Having a keen sense of the very real advantage for Baltimore in their move from Virginia, and being stubborn in the way of that day, these men had surrendered none of their inherited distaste for the Catholic Church and its communicants in general. Grounded in the political tradition of Virginia, where the King had never bothered to assert pretensions comparable to those of the lord palatine of Maryland, they had enjoyed in their new home the benefits of a remote situation which left them largely to their own self-government and thus strengthened inclinations running counter to the proprietary pattern of government. Many of them undoubtedly had responded with enthusiasm to the establishment of a Puritan commonwealth at home, and it was only natural that some should have regarded nullification of the proprietary charter as a desirable step toward the achievement of one Chesapeake commonwealth uniting the provinces of Maryland and Virginia. Though the Puritans are hardly to be charged with a primary

66 Hall (ed.), *Narratives of Early Maryland*, 209–11; Stock (ed.), *Proceedings and Debates*, I, 231–32.

responsibility for the attack on Baltimore's charter, the move appears nonetheless to have aroused anticipations which fed upon deep-rooted convictions.

Of more immediate significance was the simple fact that the proprietor's requirement of a special oath raised in the circumstances a challenging question of conflicting allegiance. To yield that submission under orders bearing the unmistakable sanction of the Commonwealth was one thing; to do it under circumstances suggestive even of the repudiation of a higher allegiance to that government was quite another thing. "We see [not] by what lawful power such an Oath, with such extream penalties can by his Lordship be exacted of us who are free Subjects of the Common-wealth of England, and have taken the Engagement to them," declared a petition from the commissioners and inhabitants of Anne Arundel County addressed to Bennett and Claiborne as "Commissioners of the Commonwealth of England." [67] In reply came instructions to hold "your due Obedience to the Commonwealth of England" because "we, nor you, have not as yet received, or seen sufficient order, or directions from the Parliament and State of England, contrary to the form to which you were Reduced and Established by the Parliaments said Commissioners." [68] On the other hand, Governor Stone, who could be stubborn in the performance of duty and had in 1652 insisted upon honoring his oath to the proprietor, felt called upon to carry out an order, as he explained, "not any wayes contradictory, so far as I understand, to any Command from the Supream Authority in England." [69] Neither party in Maryland could be wholly blamed for a situation that by the summer of 1654 threatened bloodshed.

Claiborne and Bennett, up from Virginia, in July ousted Stone, appointed in his place the Puritan William Fuller, and called for the fall an Assembly to be elected only by Protestants. The Assembly, meeting in October, repudiated the proprietor's authority in its entirety, repealed his statute of religious tolerance, and by one of the most ungenerous acts of colonial times deprived Catholics of the protection of law. [70] The contest, let it be understood, was by no means the product of a clear-cut division between Protestants

[67] Hall (ed.), *Narratives of Early Maryland*, 218.   [68] *Ibid.*, 221.   [69] *Ibid.*, 225.
[70] *Archives of Maryland*, III (1885), 311–13; LIV (1937), 23–25; I (1883), 339–56.

and Catholics. Stone was himself Protestant, as had been half the council appointed with him in 1648. Subsequent to the meeting of the Assembly a renewed attempt to assert the authority of the proprietary government won in general the support of the lower counties, while the Puritans of Providence were joined by the residents of that old center of unrest, Kent Island. In an effort to force the submission of this upper region, Stone was defeated in a battle on the Severn in March, 1655. He was himself wounded and imprisoned; four of his followers who survived the fight were executed; and for three years thereafter the Puritans kept possession of the province. Once more Maryland paid the price of political uncertainty at home and the lack of unity among its own people.

CHAPTER VIII

INTERREGNUM AND
RESTORATION

NO SUCH political upheaval as occurred in Maryland marked the years of the interregnum in Virginia. It has been popular to present the events of the period as a contest reflecting in miniature the conflicts of the homeland, and so to balance the victory of a parliamentary faction in 1652 with a Royalist triumph in 1660, but upon close examination the facts appear in a somewhat different light.

The terms of Virginia's surrender to Parliament having been determined, a newly elected Assembly met with the commissioners in April, 1652, for settlement of the colony's government. In the absence apparently of specific instructions from Westminster, an agreement was reached on April 30 for the establishment of a temporary government that would function "untill the further pleasures of the states be knowne." By the terms of that agreement Bennett became governor; Claiborne became secretary of state with rank next to the governor in the council; and thirteen additional councilors were designated. These officers were required to act in accordance with instructions from the authorities at home, the laws of England, and the established acts of the Assembly, but of far greater significance was the stipulation that the authority now exercised by governor, secretary, and council depended upon a grant from the Assembly.[1] That this last meant in effect a grant from the burgesses is indicated by their action to admit the governor and the councilors to membership in the Assembly on the condition that they take the oath of a burgess.[2]

The control of the government thus established proved to be much more than a temporary expedient. Though during the ensuing years moves were made in England for some formal disposition

[1] Hening, *Statutes*, I, 371–72.   [2] *Ibid.*, 373.

of the problem of Virginia's government, nothing came of any of them and the colony was left to govern itself. As a result, the agreement of 1652 continued to serve as the basis of the colony's government through an eight-year term marked by the unyielding determination of the burgesses to retain in their own hands the substance of power. Bennett continued as governor until the spring of 1655, when Edward Digges succeeded to the office. He in turn was followed by Samuel Mathews.[3] Councilors served at the pleasure of the burgesses, at least until 1659. All lesser offices also were made subject to the election of the burgesses by act of May, 1652. In actual practice it proved convenient to allow the governor to issue commissions for the county magistrates, but the Assembly took care to indicate the source from which the authority came and to stipulate that appointments be made on the nomination of the several county courts.[4] The consequent reduction of the governor's influence on local administration is hardly less significant than the radical change in his position as the chief officer of the province.

Three constitutional crises served to clarify further the relationship of the governor to the Assembly. In the summer of 1653, Governor Bennett took exception to the burgesses' choice of a speaker, an exception apparently so well grounded that the quarrel seems to have ended in agreement on withdrawal of the speaker-elect, but not without protest from the burgesses concerning the governor's right to interfere.[5] A more serious difficulty arose in 1658 when the governor and council undertook to dissolve the Assembly. The burgesses, who had been forehanded in strengthening their position as "representatives of the people" by extending the franchise two years earlier to all freemen,[6] refused to accept dissolution and flatly rejected a compromise proposal that would have allowed the house to continue in session with the question of dissolution referred to England. Taking the position that no power of dissolution existed outside "the House of Burgesses," they made the point stick by declaring vacant the offices of governor and secretary and all places on the council, and then by returning Mathews, Clai-

[3] *Ibid.*, 408. Samuel Mathews is referred to in December, 1656, as governor-elect in an order requesting Edward Digges to continue in office for so long as he remained in the colony, with Mathews taking the next place in the council. The latter was elected, or re-elected, in March, 1658. *Ibid.*, 426, 431–32.

[4] *Ibid.*, 372, 376, 480.   [5] *Ibid.*, 377–78, 385.   [6] *Ibid.*, 403.

borne, and all but two of the council to their places on conditions written by the house.[7] Despite that victory, the issue of dissolution was raised again the next year. The occasion, apparently, was the receipt of a letter from the council of state in England announcing the death of Cromwell and promising more exact instructions on the government of Virginia in the near future. Governor Mathews, himself one of the more substantial planters of the colony, expressed a willingness to co-operate with the burgesses in securing new recognition for the colony's privileges. Nevertheless, the governor issued an order of dissolution; he may have had specific instructions from London or he may have sought to take advantage of the traditional rule that the death of a monarch terminated all commissions. It cannot be said that the order was obeyed, but a strengthening of the governor's hand by the turn of events in England is strongly suggested by proposals from the burgesses for a compromise which specified a two-year term of office for the governor, the selection of his successors from the membership of the council, and the establishment of life tenure for all councilors.[8]

The threat of interference by the government of Richard Cromwell soon disappeared. But the collapse of the Protectorate only replaced one problem with another. Governor Mathews died at the close of 1659, and an Assembly meeting in March, 1660, cited the absence of any "absolute and generall confessed power" in England to justify assuming unto itself "the supreame power of the government of this country" until "such a comand and commission come out of England as shall be by the Assembly adjudged lawfull." [9] Sir William Berkeley, who had remained a resident of Virginia throughout the preceding eight years, now accepted the governorship at the Assembly's hands. True to his convictions and to a sense of coming events at home, he refused the office when first offered on condition that he submit to whatever government might be established in London. It had then been agreed that he would serve under the authority of the Assembly until the government of England had been settled, whereupon he was to surrender his commission.[10] There was nothing in that arrangement, of course, entitling Virginia, as popular tradition has

[7] *Ibid.,* 499–504.   [8] *Ibid.,* 509–12, 514, 515, 516–17, 537.   [9] *Ibid.,* 530.
[10] *Ibid.,* 530–31, 544, 545; Wertenbaker, *Virginia under the Stuarts,* 109–13.

often argued, to the distinction of having been the first to restore the monarchy. It did, however, place the colony in a fortunate position with reference to the restoration of Charles II, which followed on May 29.

As with many Englishmen, news of the Restoration brought to Virginians a welcome promise of release from disturbing uncertainties, and at the same time some apprehension lest the King be not gracious enough to overlook parts of the record. On September 20, nearly four months after the return of Charles II to London, Berkeley issued an order requiring forthwith a proclamation in every county of the King's rule, continuing all officers in their places, and stipulating that writs should henceforth run in the King's name. In October the burgesses assembled to address His Majesty for a pardon.[11] It remained only to dispatch Sir William on an embassy to England, and for a professedly penitent Assembly to bring the total of Virginia's official holidays to four in commemoration of its survival of two massacres, the execution of a King, and the restoration of another.[12]

Any disposition to interpret the history of Virginia between 1652 and 1660 in terms of a conflict between Royalist and parliamentary parties must depend upon the superficialities of the record rather than its underlying substance. In effect, after 1652, the colony became a self-governing commonwealth, with the assertion of a local parliamentary authority the most significant feature of her political development. To see in that a triumph of local partisans of the "parliamentary" party in England, however, is to ignore a pertinent fact. The power of the Assembly was asserted principally against the very men who must be accounted, if anyone is, the leading spokesmen in Virginia of the parliamentary cause at home. Berkeley, an undoubted Royalist, was ousted from office for the time being, and the influence thereupon won by Bennett and Claiborne bore an obvious relation to their political affiliations in the mother

---

[11] York County Records, No. 3, Deeds, Orders, Wills, 1657–1662, pp. 93, 96; Hening, *Statutes*, II, 10, 11. The proclamation ceremonies in York County cost 3,604 pounds of tobacco for items including a barrel of powder, 211 gallons of cider, the rent of several "great guns," and the fees of a minister and several trumpeters. Berkeley's own commission appears to have been dated July 30, 1660. *Virginia Magazine*, XII (1904–1905), 288.

[12] Hening, *Statutes*, II, 17, 24, 25.

country. It was natural that some men should have joined Berkeley in refusing office except under the crown, and equally natural for other men who accepted the logic of events to respond in some instances to the Commonwealth sentiment of the day. But neither in 1652 nor 1660 was the transition marked by anything approaching a revolutionary overturn of those in power.

The records are incomplete, and they become more difficult because of a continuing practice of passing around, among the leading members of the county, the burdensome duty of attending the sessions of the Assembly at Jamestown. Nevertheless, a full enough check can be made to reveal in the membership of the successive Assemblies a significant continuity of political control during the era extending from the 1640's through the Restoration of 1660.[13] No-

[13] *Ibid.*, I, 282–83 (October, 1644), 288–89 (February, 1644/45), 298–99 (November, 1645), 322–23 (October, 1646), 339–40 (November, 1647), 358–59 (October, 1649), 369–71 (April, 1652), 373–74 (November, 1652), 379 (July, 1653), 386–87 (November, 1654), 429–31 (March, 1657/58), 506–507 (March, 1658/59), 526–30 (March, 1659/60), provide lists of the burgesses returned for the years indicated. Of the thirty-five burgesses listed for April, 1652, a total of nineteen and possibly twenty had served in one or more of the Assemblies meeting from 1644 to 1649. Of these thirty-five only six had sat with the Assembly of 1649, but that is not in itself remarkable, for a check of the lists preceding 1649 shows that of the twenty-four burgesses for that year, of whom a total of ten, possibly eleven, had served in one of the earlier sessions, six had attended in 1644, three in February, 1644/45, eight in 1645, four in 1646, and only one in 1647, and that of the twenty-nine burgesses in 1647 only five had served in the Assembly of 1646. A check forward from 1652 reveals that of the thirty-two burgesses meeting in November of that year only thirteen had been present the preceding April, that of the thirty-four listed for 1653 only fifteen had attended one of the sessions in 1652, and that of thirty-seven burgesses in 1654 the number of those who had attended in 1652 had dropped to thirteen, of which number only six had participated in the deliberations of 1653. That a practice of passing the job around continued is indicated by the fact that the Assembly of March, 1657/58, included no more than three of those who served as burgesses in 1654. Of the burgesses sitting in the spring of 1660 there were four who had been burgesses in 1649 and only three who in that capacity had participated in the surrender to Oliver Cromwell, but four additional burgesses of the spring of 1652 now sat with Berkeley as members of the governor's council. The lists for seven sessions of the Assembly in the period 1652–1660 show an average of thirty-seven burgesses and a total of at least forty-one men who had served in one or more of the Assemblies from 1644 to 1649. And of the forty-four burgesses who in the spring of 1660 returned Sir William to office at least twenty-four had sat in one or more of the sessions from 1652 to 1659—three of them in November, 1652, three in 1653, five in 1654, eight in 1657/58, and fourteen in 1658/59. Of the thirty burgesses present at a slimly attended session of 1663, a total of thirteen had served at some time from 1653 to 1660; additions or substitutions in 1666 added five more with a previous service falling in that period. McIlwaine

ticeable, too, is a similar continuity in the membership of the council,[14] and when one turns to that increasingly important seat of political power, the county court, the evidence, in one county at least, supports the same conclusion.[15]

(ed.), *Journals of the House of Burgesses of Virginia, 1659/60–1693*, viii. It is pertinent to consideration of the figures given above to note that the average membership of thirty-seven through the years 1652–1660 represents an increase of eight over the average for the period 1644–1649. That increase is explained chiefly by the addition of burgesses from newly created counties, which usually sent men who had not previously sat in the Assembly.

[14] Hening (see citations in preceding note) lists the members of the governor's council attending the Assemblies of 1644, 1644/45, 1646, and 1647. Of the men there listed, seven—William Claiborne, John West, Argall Yeardley, Thomas Pettus, Humphrey Higgison, George Ludlow, and William Bernard—stand with Samuel Mathews, another old councilor, at the head of the council of sixteen men elected with Governor Digges in 1655. Hening, *Statutes*, I, 408. Of the remaining eight, at least four had served as burgesses during the 1640's. In the list of councilors sitting with Berkeley in the spring of 1660, only Claiborne, Bernard, and Pettus, to whom there was now joined Richard Bennett, remained of the group active in the 1640's, but of the other ten members seven had served as councilors during the 1650's, eight as burgesses, three as speaker, and at least three had a record of service in the Assembly extending well back into the 1640's. *Ibid.*, 526.

[15] A list of the justices for York County compiled by the author from the record of attendance in proceedings of the court is presumably complete from 1633 to 1648 and from 1652 forward. Its examination reveals a marked tendency toward an increase in the size of the county commission, a tendency which seems to have been general and without check prior to the act of 1661 fixing the limit for each county at eight commissioners on the ground that excessive numbers had brought the office into contempt and had encouraged factionalism. *Ibid.*, II, 21. To the six commissioners active in 1633 there had been added during the ensuing seven years seven new members of the court; in the period 1641–1648 a total of eleven new names appears; but from 1652 to 1660 the new commissioners number no less than thirty. The average attendance of just under seven for this last period compares with the average of just over five for the 1640's, and a third of the new justices are noticeable chiefly for their relative inactivity on the bench. One suspects that the convenience of local communities in having a resident magistrate was a chief, if not the chief, factor operating to increase the number of commissioners. Whatever the case, the major change in the composition and leadership of the functioning court came in and after 1655 rather than in 1652. Under date of May 8, 1652, a commission of thirteen justices for the York court placed at its head Nicholas Martian, an original member of the bench and for several years prior to 1649 its ranking member. York County Records, No. 1, Deeds, Orders, Wills, 1633–1657, 1691–1694, p. 93. Next came John Chew, a member of the court since 1634. Christopher Calthorpe, in third place, apparently had not been on the bench prior to 1649, but he had at least twice represented the county as a burgess. Francis Morgan had been an active member of the court since 1645; Augustine Warner, a member since 1648; and Henry Lee went on the bench that same year. William Taylor, another active member during the

Continuity of leadership is also suggested in the record of individual men. For example, John West, brother to Lord De la Warr and himself a former governor of the colony, over many years had served as a leading figure on the council and in 1652 continued next in rank after Bennett and Claiborne. Colonel Edward Hill had been speaker in 1644 and 1645. He held the same office in 1654 and 1659, and sat as a member of the council in 1655 and from 1660 to his death three years later. Considerably in advance of the Restoration, he had become strongly entrenched as the leading spirit of the Charles City court, where a son of the same name, inheriting his father's position, would become the object of some of the most bitter attacks delivered by Nathaniel Bacon's rebels in 1676.[16] Fran-

---

1640's, was now on the governor's council; and Hugh Gwin sat in the Assembly of 1652 as representative for the recently created Gloucester County, across the river. The remaining seven commissioners for York in 1652 were either new or had come on the bench since 1648. Of their number only William Barber and John Hansford would be distinguished over the ensuing years by active participation in the work of the court.

By the end of the decade, however, a well-nigh complete change had been accomplished. Judged by the records of attendance, the leading members of the court then were, in order: William Barber, Daniel Park (commissioned 1655), William Hay (1656), Edmund Peters (1656), George Read (1655 and a member of the governor's council after 1658), Jerome Hane (1655), John Hansford (1652), Joseph Croshaw (1655), Ralph Langley (1655), Thomas Ludlow (1657), Robert Baldry (1658), Christopher Calthorpe (1652), James Goodwin (1656), Christopher Harris (1658), and Henry Gooch (1658). Whatever justification may exist for viewing the changes after 1652 as the product of political differences of opinion (and there are considerations of age, death, and removal from the county on which no check is here attempted), there can be no question that those who had gained control during the 1650's remained in command after 1660. On January 24, 1660/61, Colonel George Read, Esq., by appointment of Governor Berkeley administered the oaths of supremacy and allegiance to Barber, Langley, Park, Peters, Hay, and Gooch, all of whom took at the same time the oath of office as commissioners of the peace. Croshaw seems to have been sworn separately, as was Baldry, who on May 23 took the oath in accordance with an order which also directed the removal of Calthorpe, who had moved out of the county "to the Southward," and Goodwin, who had "gone for England." See York County Records, No. 3, Deeds, Orders, Wills, 1657–1662, pp. 102b, 117b, 119b. The statute of March, 1661, in fixing a limit of eight men had specified that the first eight men in each commission should serve thereafter except where some "known defect" or "to neare relation" to another commissioner argued otherwise. See also, n. 16.

[16] No less than five of the active members of the Charles City court after 1655 had represented the county in one or more of the Assemblies from 1644 to 1649. All of the justices sitting on the bench between the fall of 1660 and June, 1661—Thomas Drew, Anthony Wyatt, Thomas Stegge, John Epes, Robert Wynne, Edward Hill,

cis Moryson, who as a Royalist had emigrated to Virginia after the surrender to Cromwell, affords another suggestive example. He served as speaker in 1656, on the council in 1660, as lieutenant governor during Berkeley's absence from 1661 to 1662, as agent of the colony on a mission to England in 1675, and shortly thereafter as a royal commissioner for the post-Bacon settlement in Virginia. Even Bennett, who had held high office in the colony prior to 1648, apparently used the occasion of the colony's surrender in 1652 principally to re-establish his own fortunes in Virginia, where he died on the eve of Bacon's Rebellion in peace and affluence and as an officer of the crown.[17]

The point receives additional emphasis from a study of the more significant developments of the period in the colony's government. Because of their prominence in the grievances expressed by the colonists at the time of Bacon's Rebellion, many features of the contemporary political scene have been made familiar to all students. There has been a tendency, however, to exaggerate the influence of Berkeley and of the Restoration, and that tendency has obscured to some extent the highly important fact that the system against which the protest arose was a thing of long and steady growth. Only in the later stages of its development, and then more often incidentally than fundamentally, had it been shaped by influences proceeding directly from the Restoration.

For two decades before 1660 the most impressive feature of the political scene had been the expanding jurisdiction and power of the county court. The fundamental explanation for this extraordinarily significant development must be sought in an especially rapid extension of the area of settlement. Though an increasing population was but one of several factors involved in this expansion, it is well to note that the population grew from approximately 8,000 in 1640 to 15,000 in 1649 and to an estimated 40,000 by 1666.[18] There had been only ten counties in 1643, but that total was exactly doubled through the years extending from 1648 to 1673 by

John Holmwood, Stephen Hamelin, and Francis Epes—had served in that capacity during the 1650's. See Charles City, Orders, Wills, Deeds, etc., 1655–1665, in the Virginia State Library.

[17] For his will, proved in the Nansemond court on April 12, 1675, see *New England Historical and Genealogical Register* (Boston), XLVIII (1894), 114–15.

[18] Wertenbaker, *Virginia under the Stuarts*, 114.

the addition of Northumberland, Gloucester, Lancaster, Surry, Westmoreland, New Kent, Rappahannock, Accomac, Stafford, and Middlesex.[19] All of these except Middlesex had been formed by 1664, a fact which lends emphasis to an unusually significant movement of population during the years of the Civil War and the interregnum in England. In general, each new county may be considered the result of an extension of settlement beyond the reach of a county court sitting at points convenient to the older areas of settlement.[20] The difficulties experienced by the people may be followed in a series of acts and orders (some of them preliminary to the creation of a new county) which authorized some convenient division of the commission in its actual work, or required the court to sit at regular intervals in different sections of the county.[21]

Similarly, each step in this outward movement of population increased the distance between the people and the seat of provincial government at Jamestown. No longer could the governor and council serve as a court of easy access for hearing the more important original pleas and such appeals as the occasion might direct. Statutes subjecting the quarter court to new and more exact rules regarding the time and extent of its terms and the order of its proceedings, sought to effect a necessary adjustment to the requirements of a larger community.[22] An inevitable result, however, was the removal of the body still further from the people in another sense by giving it more of the formality of a high court. The Assembly repeatedly showed concern over the cost to the community of needless appeals; and, while taking appropriate steps for their discouragement, the burgesses did not neglect to keep an unfriendly eye on the price lists of Jamestown tavernkeepers. To save the people unnecessary expense and at the same time to keep some of the traditional guarantees of the English law, it became necessary to make certain compromises, as in the well-known rule re-

[19] Robinson, "Virginia Counties," in *Bulletin of the Virginia State Library*, IX, 90–93. Accomac and Northampton were temporarily reunited from 1670 to 1673. Susie M. Ames, "The Reunion of Two Virginia Counties," in *Journal of Southern History*, VIII (1942), 536–48.

[20] For example, see Hening, *Statutes*, I, 427.

[21] *Ibid.*, 335–36, 376, 409, 424, 426, 497, 550.

[22] For example, *ibid.*, 270, 461; II, 58–64.

garding use of the jury at Jamestown. The seventeenth-century juror still retained much of his original function as a bearer of fact, both as to the circumstances of the case and the character of its contestants. No small part of the benefit of jury trial, therefore, depended upon an ancient rule that jurors should be men "of the vicinity." But to bring a full jury from the Eastern Shore or the Northern Neck to Jamestown was too expensive, hence the rule stipulating that no more than six men "of the vicinity" would be required.[23] As for the testimony of witnesses, it was reduced wherever possible to sworn affidavits taken by local magistrates.[24]

That practice was but one of many moves, all of them made in answer to the compelling force of circumstances, to increase the duties and expand the jurisdiction of the county commissioners. The jurisdiction of the county court had been fixed in 1634 under a law that made its judgment final in all actions up to ten pounds sterling. Since that sum was regarded in the next decade as the equivalent of 1,600 pounds of tobacco, a large part of what a man could produce in a year by his own labor, it is not surprising that the figure remained unchanged for as long as possible.[25] Even before 1634, however, it had apparently been the practice to enlarge the competence of the more distant courts, and in 1641 the court of Accomac, on the Eastern Shore, held final determination of causes up to twenty pounds. The exceptional situation of Accomac tended thereafter to become more nearly the rule than the exception, and, with a growing population imposing a heavier burden on the quarter court, the general limit for the county court was raised by act of 1658 to sixteen pounds. This and the earlier limit, it should be understood, did not preclude the entertainment of actions for larger sums. The difference lay in the right of appeal. As early as 1645 the county court had been specifically authorized to hear causes involving any sum whatsoever.[26]

The bare detail of the statutory provisions, moreover, tells only a part of the story. It had been from the first a regular practice for

[23] *Ibid.*, II, 63–64.   [24] *Ibid.*, 23–24, 67–69. Criminal causes were excepted.
[25] *Ibid.*, I, 272, 345, 398.
[26] *Ibid.*, 303, 345, 477; II, 65–66; Bruce, *Institutional History of Virginia*, I, 540–42. The limit for Accomac was raised in 1659 to £30. Hening, *Statutes*, I, 520.

members of the governor's council to add the weight of their office and experience to the deliberations of the county commissioners. When the number of counties had been small and the duties of the council itself not too heavy, the practice had proved useful and not too difficult to follow. But the custom tended now to fall increasingly into abeyance with the result that the county commissioners, altogether aside from additional duties imposed by statute, bore a heavier responsibility.[27]

Of the statutes imposing new burdens none was more important than an act of 1645 charging the county commission with the manifold duties of a probate court. Prior to that year the probating of wills belonged to the quarter court, but there had been increasing complaints of administrative costs occasioned by attendance at Jamestown and of abuses by executors which obviously called for a closer watch than could be maintained at a distance. The commissioners had already been charged by an act of 1643 with a special superintendence over the estates of orphans. Guardians and overseers were required to make an annual accounting to the local court, where it became customary to hold each year, usually in the fall, an orphan's court for the purpose.[28] The duties involved were not limited merely to the allowance of costs and the entry on record of each new calf or other interest on the principle, but included as well a general surveillance of the child's education and training. The statutes were emphatic in requiring that an orphan be assured in these matters the benefit of the estate and station to which he was born. The laws also provided that the magistrates take advantage of an opportunity in the case of the less fortunate children to increase the technical skills of the community.[29] The execution of articles of apprenticeship or inquiries into a child's knowledge of reading, writing, arithmetic, and the catechism might thus be added to the more normal routine of issuing letters of

[27] Members of the council still sat in on occasion, and especially in their own county.

[28] Hening, *Statutes*, I, 260, 302, 400, 416, 443, 480; II, 27, 90–95. For an early orphans' court, see York County Records, No. 2, Wills and Deeds, 1645–1649, pp. 399–403.

[29] For a special project for the technical training of poor children ordered by the Assembly in 1646, see Hening, *Statutes*, I, 336–37. And for a most useful general discussion, see Marcus W. Jernegan, *Laboring and Dependent Classes in Colonial America, 1607–1783* (Chicago, 1931), 141–88.

administration, fixing bonds, accepting accounts (with a careful eye to charges for the funeral), and granting finally a quietus.

Court records reveal that the commissioners had carried important responsibilities in these matters, at times by reference from Jamestown, considerably in advance of the statutes bestowing the power upon them.[30] The acts are properly viewed as not so much creating a new jurisdiction as rather recognizing the necessity for one already developing through the sheer force of circumstance. It is probably in the same light that acts of 1645 and 1658, conferring respectively the powers of an equity court and of an admiralty court, must be considered.[31]

An enlightening illustration of the varied sources of the court's expanding power and influence is found in its authority with reference to the institution of marriage. It was almost inevitable that in seventeenth-century Virginia the state should assume a heavier responsibility for the regulation of marriages than was the case in England, and that much of the work occasioned should fall to the county court. A shortage of ministers and the size of parishes made the traditional requirement that marriage bans be thrice published before the ceremony an insufficient warning to interested parties. An understandable laxity on the part of ministers in following rules better suited to the requirements of small and well-knit communities than to the conditions of frontier life added to the difficulty. The problem became especially acute when a man wished to marry another's female servant, for unless care was taken the conflict between the property rights of a master and the normal prerogatives of a husband might lead to complex questions of law, not to mention a nasty situation. To make more certain of the consent of parents, guardians, and masters, the marriage license had been introduced by 1642 under statutory provisions requiring use either of the license or the bans, and with a differential in the minister's fee calculated to encourage a proper use of the latter. The governor, who in the absence of a bishop had perforce assumed important episcopal functions, issued the license. But as time passed, his remoteness became an increasing disadvantage to most parties, and by acts of 1661 and 1662 the license was to be issued by the

[30] *Virginia Magazine*, XL (1932), 240; XLI (1933), 121.
[31] Hening, *Statutes*, I, 303, 466–67.

head of the county commission upon certificate from the clerk of the court.[32] A provision in the statute outlawing all marriages of subsequent date not performed by a clergyman, with illegitimacy of the issue as penalty, suggests that even the civil ceremony had not been unknown.

The county court had long since been made responsible for the recording of marriages and the keeping of other vital records. Though the county and the parish were legally distinct, they so frequently coincided both in extent and in their official personnel that the county commissioners acquired many obligations traditionally belonging to officers of the parish. Moreover, the court answered to higher authority for the settlement of parish or interparish disputes, the enforcement of laws governing the church, the vestry's choice of a minister, the location and construction of church buildings, action on the churchwardens' regular presentment of those offending against the moral code, and for the relief and care of indigent persons.[33] The board was not always faithful in the performance of its duties. At times it ignored the minister's departure from *The Book of Common Prayer,* and its records of births, marriages, and deaths were often kept with an indifference calculated to encourage reliance on some such family record as an entry on the flyleaf of a Bible. On the other hand, where the community's welfare was immediately involved and action was required to "save the parish harmless," one finds not only an alert sense of responsibility but a noticeable willingness to try such innovations of practice and law as the circumstances might require.

Charged with a primary responsibility for orphans, the court was easily led to an active part in the negotiation and enforcement of prenuptial contracts that were usually designed for the protection

[32] *Ibid.,* 243, 252, 332, 433, 438; II, 28, 50, 54, 114.

[33] *Ibid.,* I, 240–42, 399, 425, 469, 542. For examples from the county records, see Charles City, Orders, Wills, Deeds, 1655–1665, pp. 3, 7, 13, 41, 67, 186; York County Records, No. 1, 203; *Lower Norfolk County Antiquary,* I (1895–1896), 139–42; II (1897–1899), 12, 63; III (1901), 29, 31–32; *Virginia Magazine,* V (1897–1898), 288–89; XII (1904–1905), 289–91; XLI (1933), 324, 342, 343; *William and Mary College Quarterly,* XX (1911–1912), 137, 138–39; XXII (1913–1914), 39–43. A revealing case in York County in 1662 shows the court not concerned with a case of fornication when it was revealed that the offense was committed in another county, and when the woman's master promised that the child would not be a burden to the county. York County Records, No. 3, p. 175.

of children by a prior marriage. Postnuptial contracts for this or other purposes, including separation agreements, also received early recognition.[34] The practice marks a significant break with the principles of English law and reveals the developing importance of the county court in molding the basic assumptions of an American law and an American society. Agreements of this sort were among the more influential customs lending to marriage the essential qualities of a civil contract, with implications of a new equality between the contracting parties of great importance to the legal status of women.[35]

The county court was no mere court in the modern sense of the word. Its duties embraced the entire field of local government, and its administrative responsibilities constituted a heavy claim upon its time. The county commissioners, to use a designation more indicative of the full scope of their functions, were obligated to provide standard weights and measures against which those used by local merchants, tavernkeepers, and millers were to be checked and certified.[36] The Assembly showed a tendency especially to place taverns under the watchful eye of the court. Licensed by the governor on the county's recommendation in 1644, the keeper of the tavern received his license from the court itself by 1655.[37] The commissioners were instructed to enforce a variety of price regulations set by the Assembly, and at times acquired, as with tavern rates, the power to determine themselves the extent of a lawful charge. Virtually every economic regulation for the control of tobacco or the promotion of new staples imposed some special duty of enforcement upon the county magistrates.[38] As settlement expanded and moved inland from the rivers there came new responsibilities

[34] See York County Records, No. 1, pp. 96, 168–69; No. 2, p. 166; No. 3, p. 93; Charles City, Orders, Wills, Deeds, 1655–1665, p. 55.

[35] On this and other equally interesting subjects in early American legal history, see Richard B. Morris, *Studies in the History of American Law, with Special Reference to the Seventeenth and Eighteenth Centuries* (New York, 1930).

[36] Hening, *Statutes*, I, 268, 391, 473; II, 89–90.

[37] *Ibid.*, I, 287, 411, 521; II, 19, 112.

[38] For example, by an act of 1655 they were required to locate and regulate one or two markets in each county. *Ibid.*, I, 417; *Virginia Magazine*, V (1897–1898), 40–41. After 1660 they were charged to provide at the county's cost a tanhouse and to secure for its use a tanner, currier, and shoemaker. Hening, *Statutes*, II, 123; York County Records, No. 3, p. 145; Charles City, Orders, Wills, Deeds, 1655–1665, p. 253.

for the maintenance of ferry service and of highways, "church-ways," and bridges.[39] Since the life of the colony through this mid-period of the century was in a remarkably fluid state, it became necessary both to strengthen and decentralize the controls over the right of removal from the county or the province. The license to depart for England or a neighboring province still issued from Jamestown, but only on certificate from the county that adequate notice of intention had been given and security taken for the pay-ment of debts. For transfer of residence into another county, the clerk of court was empowered to issue the license under similiar rules, but with an additional requirement that four neighbors view the stock to be moved and certify that its earmarks were correct.[40] The English farmer's intrusion into the forest soon upset the bal-ance of nature, and by the 1640's the settlers struggled against a plague of wolves. The county court held the key position in the administration of the bounty system that was for so long to remain the favored American weapon against natural foes of this sort.

New crises in Indian relations inevitably accompanied the resistless expansion of white settlement and kept to the fore prob-lems of security, especially through the years following 1644. From the earliest days, the civil and military leadership of the county had been joined in the office of commander, a title which con-tinued through the 1640's to be a hardly less accurate description of the position held by the head of the county commission than it had been a decade earlier. He was commander in fact as well as name: subordinate officers of the militia served by his appointment with the governor's approval; and, through his authority in civil affairs, problems of overlapping or conflicting jurisdiction were effectively eliminated. The title of "commander" disappeared after the middle of the century, when separate militia commissions were issued for each county to a board of officers whose head usually car-ried the rank of colonel, but the basic administrative principle of

---

[39] The commissioners were responsible for the location of roads as early as 1632, and for their maintenance, in which task the people were often called out at appointed times for road work according to a usage that was long to characterize arrangements in rural America for road repair or, on a voluntary basis, the cleaning up of a grave-yard. The law in the 1650's required appointment of surveyors of highways. Hening, *Statutes*, I, 199, 436; II, 103; *Virginia Magazine*, VIII (1900–1901), 175–76; Charles City, Orders, Wills, Deeds, 1655–1665, p. 145.

[40] Hening, *Statutes*, I, 243, 436, 465; II, 88, 130.

the earlier system continued in effect. The county and militia commissions were distinct, but, as with the parish, there was a marked overlapping in personnel and responsibility.[41] The chief magistrate and the colonel were more often than not the same man, and everywhere a majority of the commissioners of militia held place in the county court. The county remained a convenient unit of apportionment in all military levies. Upon its official family fell the obligation to apportion the levy among its men of military age, to provide required supplies by a further levy upon all inhabitants, or if the call came in crop season to make an assessment of labor for care of the soldier's crop. Whatever authority the commissioners of militia may have lacked the county commissioners had, and to seek a clear line of demarcation between the two jurisdictions would be to bother about questions that rarely bothered the commissioners. In times of a serious and common emergency the joint task was carried out under general rules and assignments emanating from Jamestown. On other occasions there appears to have been some inclination to regard local trouble with the Indians as a distinctly local problem, and to leave a county to work its way out of its own difficulties at its own cost.[42] Needless to say, such a policy tended to strengthen the county's demand for local self-government on points more advantageous to itself.

It was as a court of record that the county court rendered some of its most important services. Its entry of the age of a newly arrived servant constituted a major assurance of his legal rights, as did also a subsequent certificate of his freedom. The transcribed will of a dying and grateful master stood as proof that an aging Negro was his own man.[43] Through the crabbed and now faded script of a seventeenth-century clerk the historian is introduced to the intimate details of contemporary life as recorded in contracts, let-

[41] See especially, a list of civil and military officers for 1680, in *Virginia Magazine*, I (1893–1894), 225-26, 246-52. For illustrative material from county records, see Charles City, Orders, Wills, Deeds, 1655–1665, pp. 20, 44, 61, 102, 279, 283, 284–86; York County Records, No. 2, pp. 65, 121, 152; No. 3, p. 95; *William and Mary College Quarterly*, VII (1898–1899), 179–81; VIII (1899–1900), 24–25; XI (1902–1903), 81–86; XX (1911–1912), 140–41; *Virginia Magazine*, VIII (1900–1901), 189–91; XII (1904–1905), 195, 196, 197–98.

[42] Even in 1644 there was a disposition to levy the costs principally against the counties most affected. Hening, *Statutes*, I, 285; and see also, pp. 389–90.

[43] York County Records, No. 3, p. 16.

ters of attorney, confessions of debt, deeds, articles of apprenticeship, and even personal correspondence conveying at times, in
addition to instructions for the disposal of property, the further
news that, at home in England, Uncle John or Aunt Mary and more
frequently trade, was dead. In clearing accounts, so many persons
found the safest record in a judgment of court that, for the ease of
all parties, proceedings were reduced to the bare minimum required
to establish the record.[44] An item in the records of Charles City
County suggests the full range of the board's services as a court of
record. A foresighted parent appeared before the court one day to
submit evidence that an unusual disfiguration of his son's ear had
been occasioned by a fall and to secure a certificate to that effect,
with full entry on record, lest by "the mistakes or malice of future
times" the blemish be converted into a "mark of Infamy." [45]

Of all the records kept, none compared in importance with those
which testified to a title in land. Wealth was not counted in terms
of money, nor even of tobacco, but of the land a man held, the
improvements he had put upon it, and the stock that ranged over
its acres. The county court now held a key position in the issuance
of original titles. Grants were commonly made on headright claims
certified by the county to the secretary's office in Jamestown, where
upon the submission of a certificate with a plot of survey the patent
was issued, on condition that the land be occupied within three
years.[46] Many men obviously patented more land than they could
develop, and the principal reliance for enforcement of the rule
requiring occupancy within three years was the right of others to
repatent "abandoned" land. No adequate definition of occupancy
existed, however, and prior to the Restoration the rule was enforced under policies so liberal as to leave untouched the original
grantee's claim to another patent of the same extent in some other
location.[47] Among the beneficiaries of, and contributors to, a
loosely administered land policy were the surveyors. Holding office

[44] Hening, *Statutes*, I, 304, 447, 449, 455; II, 87, 110; York County Records, No. 2,
pp. 110, 147.

[45] Charles City, Orders, Wills, Deeds, 1655–1665, p. 37.

[46] See Thomas Ludwell's description of the colony's government (1666), in *Virginia
Magazine*, V (1897–1898), 54–59. The three-year limit, like other features of the
policy, was first fixed by the Virginia Company.

[47] Hening, *Statutes*, I, 468; II, 95.

since the days of the company from the surveyor general, a royal appointee after 1624, their professional and ethical shortcomings proved so serious that their appointment and supervision were placed during the interregnum under the direct control of the county court.[48] With the Restoration the older type of commission returned, and the colony again depended for its protection upon the enactment of statutory regulations governing the duties of the office.[49]

So many persons after occupying their land found the title challenged by a later survey that the Assembly sought in characteristic fashion to cut through the legal complications by insisting that the claimant must either compensate the occupant for all improvements made or accept a fair price for his title. It was further enacted that no challenge to a title could be made after five years of peaceful occupation.[50] Trees, marked or unmarked, served to fix boundary limits, and when to the "insufficiency" of the surveyor was added the owner's carelessness in keeping fresh his bounds, many "contentious disputes" followed. Experience rarely recommended a call for the surveyor's aid, for as the Assembly of 1662 explained, "the least variation of a compasse alters the scituation of a whole neighbourhood." Accordingly, the law required that the county commissioners have the vestry divide each parish into a convenient number of precincts, and that in each precinct all the inhabitants should once in four years walk the bounds of every man's land for the "preservation of ffriendshipp among neighbors." [51] A preventive measure designed to serve worthy ends both of the law and of the church, its special possibilities were not ignored by a people inclined to improve every opportunity for a social occasion.

From the many difficulties experienced in the operation of a loosely administered land system there arose, in addition to disputes at law and partly because of them, a growing inclination to rely upon the court's record for evidence of title. The original record of the patent in the secretary's office made unnecessary its entry on the local books except as an extra precaution or for some other special cause, but when conveyances were made there was an obvious advantage in their recordation with the court. Indeed,

[48] *Ibid.*, I, 404.   [49] *Ibid.*, 335, 452, 518; II, 99.
[50] *Ibid.*, I, 260, 331, 443, 451; II, 96–98.   [51] *Ibid.*, II, 101–102.

during Wyatt's second term the Assembly had required, as a safe-guard against fraudulent mortgages, the acknowledgment and registry of conveyances in either the quarter or the county court.[52] An exception was made, however, for bona fide bills of sale accompanied by an actual delivery of possession, and it was not so much the law as it was the force of circumstances that caused men to rely increasingly upon a court record for proof of title. Given the lack of safe depositories in the average home, the shifting character of the population, the frequent subdivision of original grants for purposes of sale, the extraordinary confusion of claims which developed, and the genesis of an official registry in the intial record of patents issued, nothing could have been more natural than to depend upon such successive entries in the official record as have come to characterize the American system of registry.[53] The convenience of the people in this, as in other matters, dictated some decentralization of governmental aid, and by the middle of the century no small part of the duties of the clerk of court was that of a registrar of deeds.

The clerk's office had grown apace with the expanding activity of the court. His commission came from the governor; his remuneration principally from fees fixed by act of Assembly. So many of these fees were for services formerly rendered almost exclusively by the secretary's office that it is not surprising that the clerk was required to make some "composition" with the secretary. Nor is it surprising that this member of the council held an important voice in the appointment of the county clerk. During the interregnum the courts asserted for all practical purposes the power to select their own clerks; and though with the Restoration the older usage returned, there is little doubt that the will of the court remained an important factor in the choice.[54] The office became so remunerative that, later in the century, one gentleman of Stafford County accepted a commission in the quorum of the court only

[52] *William and Mary College Quarterly*, 2d ser., IV (1924), 149; Hening, *Statutes,* I, 248, 417; II, 98.

[53] In this connection, see Morris, *Studies in the History of American Law,* 69–73; and for a parallel development in Maryland, see below, p. 305.

[54] Hening, *Statutes,* I, 305, 448, 464; II, 145; *Virginia Magazine,* XLIV (1936), 191–92; Bruce, *Institutional History of Virginia,* I, 588–91.

on the condition that he retain his clerkship.[55] The duties of the place called for relatively high educational qualifications, but there were marked differences among clerks in this and other particulars. Some kept the records with great faithfulness and neatness while others were careless and untidy. Some of them restricted their entries of proceedings to the barest legal details and some, given the excuse of a spicy suit for slander or charge of immorality, were likely to become downright gossipy. To study the old records is quickly to acquire a feeling of acquaintance with the old clerks. And if the study be pursued in a modern clerk's office, little time is required to sense the important fact that the clerk of court so familiar today had made his appearance by the middle of the seventeenth century.

Hardly less familiar is the seventeenth-century sheriff. Ranking police and financial officer of the county, he bore a commission from the governor that clothed his office with the full majesty of the law but did not disguise unmistakable evidence that his tenure of office depended chiefly upon a local political influence. His responsibility for the service of warrants, subpoenas, and other such documents, or for the apprehension and custody of the King's prisoners, became all the more heavy because of the dispersed settlement which characterized his rural precinct. Indeed, it was necessary to restrain him from a growing custom of making his arrests and serving his summons at the church door on a Sunday, or on general muster days, a usage properly viewed as likely to encourage men who had done those things which they ought not to have done to leave undone those things they ought to do.[56] The compensation for the burdens of his position, however, was by no means inconsiderable.

The settlement of accounts, public and private, was an annual business of the fall season. In a community lacking the convenience of money and depending principally upon a crop that matured but once a year, men were "carried on the books," whether by the

---

[55] *Virginia Magazine*, I (1893–1894), 4. In addition to regular fees for warrants, recordings, etc., he received a percentage for inventories and appraisals made by order of court or by agreement with the parties involved. Hening, *Statutes*, I, 295.

[56] Hening, *Statutes*, I, 457.

minister or the tavernkeeper, the secretary of state or the clerk of court, the local merchant or the surveyor, and even on occasion by the ferryman, until the crop had been cured. Then all accounts fell due, unless it had been otherwise specified, and with the ships from England timing their arrival by the same season of the year, it was in most cases a question of collecting at that time or waiting another year.[57] Many modern Southerners, among them the country preacher, will require no further elaboration of the point. With public as with private business there were accounts payable as well as receivable, and the bulkiness and perishable quality of the commodity that passed in payment dictated a common-sense rule of paying out insofar as it was possible at every point of receipt with the tobacco there received. Convenient places of payment were fixed, and the actual transactions became largely a matter of bookkeeping, with the tobacco passing from farm to ship's hold by whatever route entailed the least possible handling of the standard hogshead of 350 pounds. Indeed, a hogshead of tobacco, or even a portion of it, might be accepted by the sheriff in payment of taxes, then assigned by him to another planter in return for services rendered the county or the province, and by him in turn paid over to a local merchant without the tobacco having been so much as once moved from the tobacco house of its original producer until, properly marked or sealed, it was collected for direct shipment to England. Under such conditions there were, of course, strong reasons for concentrating the responsibility for collecting and paying public accounts in the hands of some one officer, and no choice was more natural than the sheriff.

Though the sheriff was charged primarily with the collection of the public levy, it was found convenient to rely upon his services for collection at the same time of the minister's dues, the King's quitrents, the county's levy for its own expenses, and fees due the governor, secretary, or clerk of court. The established allowance for collections was 10 per cent, and to this was added the regular fees allowed the sheriff for executing the several duties of the county's

[57] Public levies were due in November, and payment of private debts, unless demanded between October 10 and the last of January, could not be forced until another fall. *Ibid.*, 319, 334, 489; II, 104.

chief police officer.[58] The job paid well, but perhaps in no other way could a position of great difficulty and heavy responsibility have been made sufficiently attractive.

The opportunities for abuse of the sheriff's office were so many that the county court acquired an early and growing responsibility for its conduct. By an act of 1643 the commissioners were charged to place the sheriff in adequate bond or else to bear themselves the full penalty of his defections, and by a statute of 1648 the county itself became responsible for all arrears due the provincial treasury.[59] The problem of assuring the provision of honest and complete tax lists proved especially difficult. Whether the levy was rated only by the poll of tithable persons or whether it fell, as from 1645 to 1648, upon dividends of land and the head of cattle, horses, sheep, and goats, concealment was often easy, and its apprehension required, over and beyond official honesty, an expenditure of time and energy frequently out of proportion to the return. Neither the taxpayer nor the sheriff could be fully trusted to provide an adequate list, so its provision became an annual obligation of the county court. The law in its final form required that the county be divided into precincts, in each of which a commissioner appointed by the court should be responsible for compilation of the list. Upon public notice from the commissioner every head of a family was to submit his list by June 10, under a penalty of treble the amount due. The commissioner made his return to the court in August, and the full list was to be certified by the county to the clerk of the Assembly during the September term of the general court.[60] The commissioners designated for the purpose were, in most cases, themselves members of the bench, a fact indicative of their sense of the extent to which the ultimate responsibility had been imposed upon the court. Consideration must be given also to the court's own immediate interest in the collection of taxes, for in addition to serving as an agent of the provincial government in the assessment of the public levy the county commissioners held the power to appropriate

[58] *Ibid.*, I, 288, 318, 465; Karraker, *Seventeenth-Century Sheriff*, 130 ff.
[59] Hening, *Statutes*, I, 259, 284, 354; II, 87.
[60] *Ibid.*, I, 306, 329, 341, 361, 388, 454; II, 19, 83–84. For the Surry list of 1668, see *William and Mary College Quarterly*, VIII (1899–1900), 161–64.

and levy for the necessary expenses of the county. Appropriations made by the Assembly for provincial purposes were apportioned among the counties, where each court added the total of the county's charges, divided the sum by the number of tithables, and so fixed the annual tax due.[61]

The colonists experimented with the use of collectors other than the sheriff and his deputies, but the experiment was soon abandoned. In 1647 special collectors were appointed in each county under a plan that was well enough liked to be tried again the following year, the right of appointment lying with the county court.[62] Thereafter it apparently remained a right and duty of the court to designate such collectors of the public and county levies as it saw fit. The appointments, however, tended to go to members of the bench, who were thereby entitled to the established 10 per cent allowance, and from about 1654 it became increasingly the practice of the court to assign the collector's office once more to the sheriff. Two considerations appear to have been involved. There was a certain efficiency in having the responsibility centered in one financial officer, and appointment to the sheriff's office had now been brought more effectively under the control of the local court. An act of 1654 requiring that the sheriff be selected from a list of three men submitted by the county court was followed by the celebrated act of 1661 which required that he be taken from the bench itself. Fixing the size of the court at eight, the act stipulated that the sheriff's office, its tenure already limited to one year, should pass in turn to each of the county commissioners.[63]

In these acts there was little actually new. The county courts had long enjoyed the right of nomination for the office; governors had usually made appointments from lists submitted by the courts; and nominations had increasingly been made from the membership of the court itself. Not even the assurance of a share in the financial

[61] York County Records, No. 2, pp. 298–99; No. 3, pp. 2, 37, 96, 134; No. 4, Deeds, Orders, Wills, 1665–1672, p. 39, which show allowances both for the sheriff and the justices in compensation for preparing the lists.

[62] Hening, *Statutes*, I, 342, 356.

[63] *Ibid.*, 392; II, 21; Bruce, *Institutional History of Virginia*, II, 570 ff. There is evidence that the courts appointed sheriffs under the act of May, 1652, giving them control over local officers. *William and Mary College Quarterly*, XX (1911–1912), 132–33. See again, Karraker, *Seventeenth-Century Sheriff*, 72–75.

rewards of the collector's office was new. Nevertheless, those acts properly have been regarded as among the more significant indications of the growing power of the county court. But perhaps too much attention has been paid the financial advantages thus gained by the magistrates, and too little has been given to the extent of the court's responsibility for the sheriff's office. As a supplementary act of 1662 explained, the commissioners of the county court were by law made answerable for the levies collected by the sheriff, and in that fact they found a warrant for taking the job.[64]

Whatever may be the credit due the argument, it must be admitted that there was a measure of simple justice in allowing the county magistrate the rewards of the sheriff's job one year in eight. For in addition to the heavy responsibilities shared with other members of the commission, there were many duties that fell to him as a local magistrate. Complaints of every sort—of a master's treatment of his servants, of an excessive toll taken by the miller, of an overcharge at the tavern, of a ferryman's failure to keep appointed hours, or of a neighbor's slanderous tongue—were carried to "the nearest magistrate." To him men repaired for a certificate of freedom to "hire out," or of the extra time due from a runaway servant. Others brought wolves' heads in evidence of a claim to the bounty or hogs' ears in proof of title to meat. By the court's assignment he superintended the appraisal of a local estate or inquired into the care of a local orphan. He administered oaths, took affidavits of testimony, conducted preliminary hearings, acted as coroner, and bound over to court or ordered the release of parties as the occasion required. His own power to render a judgment was raised from the 20s. or 200 pounds of tobacco fixed by act of 1642 to 350 pounds by an act of 1658, and if he was sitting with another magistrate the jurisdiction was extended to 1,000 pounds.[65] His duties included the swearing in of appraisers of goods taken in execution by the sheriff, and he intervened in such other common disputes with the sheriff as those involving the quality of the tobacco offered in payment of taxes.

[64] Hening, *Statutes*, II, 78.

[65] *Ibid.*, I, 272, 335, 435; II, 70, 72. The last two acts cited, respectively, conferred the authority of any justice of the peace in England and apparently restored the older twenty-shilling limit.

Important and varied were his responsibilities for keeping the local peace. A hog in a garden patch carried the threat of a lawsuit for damage or slander, and often for both; but the law required that the garden be adequately fenced, and the magistrate's intervention to determine the fault in the fence might well save a troublesome suit. Many differences were settled by his arbitration outside court, and under conditions revealing the significant fact that he was not dependent upon the power of his commission alone. Indeed, if the county magistrate had been selected in accordance with the best requirements of a now-established custom, he was a man whose word carried in the community an authority of its own, the kind of man to whom his neighbors naturally turned for arbitration of their differences. Though the royal commission was always at hand in case of need, an easy informality commonly characterized his work, so much so that the Assembly of 1662 felt compelled to speak out against the abuse of "private" courts.[66] In short, think of him as the local squire, a rapidly disappearing figure today, but one still remembered by many of us as he sat in a front pew at church on Sunday or "held court" on Monday, in the summer where the shade was best and in the winter where the fire was near.

The seventeenth-century justice of the peace, first a farmer and then a judge, was even more of a layman than were his successors in office. To cope with the juridical problems of an increasingly complex society, he relied principally upon his own experience and that of his colleagues. The conventions which governed his choice, and which dictated that he should remain at his post for so long as his conduct and service were reasonably satisfactory, constituted the chief safeguard against a general lack of formal training for the job. The rule of the quorum placing a special responsibility upon the more seasoned and capable members of the bench proved of further help, as did the magistrate's personal knowledge of the men and problems with which he dealt. Deficiencies in his knowledge of the law were often compensated by an understanding of his neighbors.

Though necessity now forced upon the full court a certain formality in its proceedings, and the holding of its sessions at regular terms adjusted to those of neighboring counties and of the quarter

[66] *Ibid.*, II, 73.

court, it remained distinctly a layman's court. There was respect for the essential principle and spirit of the law, but impatience with the lawyer and his kind of argument. Expressing discontent with "excessive charges and greate delaies . . . by reason of small mistakes in writts and formes of pleading," the Assembly of 1658 ordered all courts to "proceed and give judgement according as the right of the cause and the matter in lawe shall appeare unto them, without regard of any imperfection, default or want of forme in any writt, returne plaint or process or any other cause whatsoever." [67] In the adjudication of disputes the court often acted as a board of arbitration; and though juries were occasionally used, there appears to have been on both sides of the table a general preference for the speedier and less costly summary proceeding. In the matter of punishment, too, the judges displayed a preference for that which was simple and administratively inexpensive, usually a whipping or a fine. Like the Kentucky judge of a later date, not knowing enough law to do the wrong thing and so trying simply to do the right, the county magistrate of this day was more frequently than not an honorable and faithful public servant, able within his limits, and one who found a justifiable pride in his position.[68]

Nevertheless, his neighbors had their doubts about the squire. The feeling finds occasional expression in such contemptuous statements as that of William Hatton, who was arraigned in 1662 for describing the justices of York County as "Coopers, Hogg trough Makers, Peddlars, Coblers, Tailors, weavers," and generally "not fitting to sit where they doe sit." [69] Despite the heavy expense involved in proceedings at Jamestown and the precedent provided by the quarter sessions of the English county, the county court was

[67] *Ibid.*, I, 486. Beginning in 1642 the court days, staggered for the convenience of those having business in more than one court, were fixed by act of Assembly. *Ibid.*, 272, 462; II, 69–70. As for the lawyer himself, the attitude of the Assembly alternated between attempts to regulate his practice and fees and decisions to throw him out entirely as one more often concerned with his own "inordinate lucre" than the good of his clients. *Ibid.*, I, 275, 302, 313, 349, 419, 482, 495, 522; II, 105.

[68] As with most such bodies, some men carried more than their share and others made it necessary to impose penalties for absence. *Ibid.*, I, 350, 454. On criminal procedure, see Arthur P. Scott, *Criminal Law in Colonial Virginia* (Chicago, 1930); and on the general subject of procedural simplification, Morris, *Studies in the History of American Law*, 46–62.

[69] York County Records, No. 3, p. 175.

denied jurisdiction over any crime involving life or limb. During the interregnum the rule momentarily had been abandoned, but in a prompt move to repeal the act which had given that jurisdiction to the court, the Assembly of 1656 significantly declared: "Wee conceive it no ease nor benefit to the people to have their lives taken away with too much ease, And though we confesse the same to be done in England, yet wee know the disparity between them and us to be so great that wee cannot with safety follow the example." [70] Accordingly, an exclusive jurisdiction over felonies was returned to the quarter court, which after 1662 became, in official terminology, the general court.

Necessity rather than choice had led to the extraordinary expansion of the county court's responsibility over the twenty years preceding the Restoration. Still struggling with the problem in 1662, the Assembly tried the expedient of sending the governor and councilors on circuit as itinerant justices. The governor and one councilor, or in the event of the governor's absence two members of the council, were annually, in August, to visit the several county courts and to sit with them in the exercise of an intermediate jurisdiction. A special provision forbade any councilor to travel the circuit of his own river. The new court was empowered to hear appeals and such original actions as had been referred to it. But, alas, these visitations proved more of a burden than a trip to Jamestown, and the experiment was promptly abandoned on the ground that it entailed too great a charge to the country. [71] And so was the county court left in full charge of its expanded responsibilities by a people who seemingly had no choice but to hope that the magistrates would act on the burgesses' instruction of 1666 to purchase for the use of each commission a few standard books on the law. [72] To say that the colony had found now a satisfactory solution to its problem is to ignore the plain facts of the record.

[70] Hening, *Statutes*, I, 397–98.

[71] *Ibid.*, II, 64–66, 179. The cost to York County was nine thousand pounds of tobacco. York County Records, No. 3, p. 168; Bruce, *Institutional History of Virginia*, I, 498.

[72] Hening, *Statutes*, II, 246, which recommended particularly the *Statutes at Large*, Michael Dalton's *Justice of the Peace* and *Office of Sheriff*, and Henry Swinburne's *Book of Wills and Testaments*. The York court ordered the first of these in 1661. York County Records, No. 3, pp. 125, 134.

There can be no question that a lingering doubt as to the competence of the county court contributed thereafter to a growing discontent over its extraordinary powers.

Hand in hand with the consolidation of the county magistracy's control of local affairs had gone a highly significant extension of its influence in provincial politics. There was, of course, nothing more natural than that the magistrates should have insisted upon a larger share in the determination of provincial policy. Not only were they now charged with a primary responsibility for its execution, but no other group within the colony could speak with the same degree of that authority which comes from experience and a knowledge of local problems. The Assembly provided the obvious channel for expression of their will, and no violence to established convention or proper political practice was required to convert the House of Burgesses into a body speaking chiefly for the county magistrates.[73] It is true that the electoral machinery of the colony operated under the supervision of the county court; that the sheriff, through whom the governor issued writs of election and by whom returns were certified, served as chief electoral officer; and that there were complaints of laxity and even of occasional misconduct of elections.[74] But to overemphasize the extent of unwarranted interference is to overestimate the need for it. Under normal circumstances the natural choice for burgess was one of the magistrates or some man closely allied to them in station and interest. They possessed the requisite experience, were the natural leaders of the community, and, moreover, they were in every sense representative of it.

To the work of the Assembly they brought the skill of a widening experience in the conduct of public affairs. Well practiced in the ways of self-government, they turned to good advantage the Assembly's control of the purse, its well-established legislative right, and the peculiar political uncertainties of the Civil War years which forced upon those in authority a courting of popular unity. Even before the interregnum, the distribution of political power

[73] Of the burgesses listed by Hening (see above, n. 13) for York County during the period 1644–1660, only five men were not at the time members of the local court, and one of them was subsequently added to the commission.

[74] Hening, *Statutes*, I, 227, 300, 333–34, 403, 411–12, 475, 532; II, 82; *Virginia Magazine*, XXXIX (1931), 240; Karraker, *Seventeenth-Century Sheriff*, 117–21.

in Virginia already suggested the outlines of a pyramid having its base in the county courts and reaching a vertex through the relative positions assumed by Assembly, council, and governor. To speak in terms of the governor's arbitrary power then or at any time thereafter is to lose sight of the hard facts of a political situation in which he had little choice but to fit himself in as best he could at the top. He could lead, but not arbitrarily direct.

Both the opportunities and the restraints affecting his leadership are interestingly suggested by an action of the Assembly in 1648. The crisis of Virginia's second Indian massacre having been safely negotiated, the people, in a manner prophetic of their descendants' attitude toward executive power under the Federal Constitution, voiced some doubt of the legality of certain emergency powers assumed by Governor Berkeley while suppressing the uprising. Whereupon the Assembly formally declared that his actions had been adequately covered by his royal commission as commander in chief, that they accordingly constituted no infringement of the "liberties and the lawes of the collonie," and that it should be understood that in the life of a community there came emergencies "not admitting delay of time nor those slow motions of great counsells." [75]

Though willing enough to concede to the governor necessary war powers in one kind of emergency, the burgesses soon demonstrated an inclination to take full advantage of any political emergency. In 1652 the Assembly took complete charge, with results that were to have a lasting effect upon its own structure. A growing effectiveness in its organization was shown thereafter through an increasing use of committees and in the development of a separate House of Burgesses. The General Assembly originally had incorporated governor, council, and burgesses in one body, but it was the presence of specially chosen representatives of the planters which explained its peculiar authority. From that fact there naturally developed among the burgesses a sense of distinct existence and a consciousness of common power. These feelings undoubtedly drew nourishment from the trend of the parliamentary struggle in England and were further strengthened by a unique combination of circumstances giving into the hands of the burgesses the appoint-

[75] Hening, *Statutes*, I, 355.

ment both of the governor and of his councilors during the years of
the interregnum. At times of dispute over the choice of speaker and
the right of dissolution, incidental references in the record to the
House of Burgesses mark a tendency for the elected members to
assume the position of a separate house of assembly. The dominant
influence of the burgesses extended well beyond 1660, and by 1663
the bicameral form of legislature had become an established part
of Virginia's constitution.[76]

Welcoming the restoration of royal authority for its stabilizing
effect, the burgesses in 1660 showed a first concern for appropriate
representations in London regarding amnesty and other matters
incidental to the re-establishment of normal relations with the
mother country. Of particular importance to them were the policies
to be followed by the new government in London with reference
to colonial trade and to such opportunities as might exist for
enlisting the aid of a reviving interest there in overseas projects.
Berkeley, who for several years yet would prove an able advocate
of interests he shared with other Virginia planters, was the obvious
choice as agent to press their cause. Preparatory to his departure,
the Assembly directed special attention to the needs of the church.
Nonconformity had made little progress among Virginians, and
the burgesses were prompt to point out the great need for a well-
trained and orthodox ministry in the upbuilding of the restored
establishment. They dwelt especially upon the advantages of a
college for this purpose in Virginia and upon the opportunity
such a project would afford the re-established church at home to
undertake a worth-while mission.[77] Sir William left for England in

[76] See especially, McIlwaine (ed.), *Journals of the House of Burgesses of Virginia,
1619–1658/59;* his introductory discussion in *Journals of the House of Burgesses,
1659/60–1693;* Hening, *Statutes,* I, 373, 497, 500–504, 511–12.

[77] The Assembly in March ordered land purchased for a free school and a college
of the liberal arts and sciences; took subscriptions of its own members for support
of the project; instructed the county magistrates in like manner to take the lead
in their own meetings and to issue similar instructions for action by the vestries; and
petitioned the King for his letters patent to solicit "the charity of well disposed
people in England" and for his intercession with the universities at home for the
supply meanwhile of qualified ministers. Hening, *Statutes,* II, 25, 29, 30–31, 37. In a
general effort to increase the inducements for the immigration of orthodox ministers,
the burgesses the next year attempted to restore the old principle of a fixed income
at the figure of eighty pounds over and above the perquisites and the return of the
glebe, which again was ordered laid out in every parish. *Ibid.,* 45. For the financing

the spring of 1661. His early identification with the Carolina proprietorship suggests that there were personal as well as public interests requiring his attendance there. He did not return to Virginia, it is important to note, until late in 1662.

In his absence the burgesses turned to the task of writing a political settlement, a task accomplished through one of those periodical revisals of the laws that so generally characterized colonial legislative methods. Though considerable progress had been made toward mastery of the legislator's art, it remained necessary periodically to go through the whole body of statutes to provide a clear and comprehensive statement of the law. That work had been undertaken and completed as recently as 1658, however, and the occasion for the revisal adopted in 1662 must have been largely political.[78] The return of the royal commission to its traditional place in the constitution required surrender of the more extraordinary of the burgesses' recently exercised powers and an adjustment within other agencies of government to a legal presence of the utmost significance.

No more than a cursory reading of the revisal of 1662 is necessary to appreciate that the primary concern of its draftsmen was the local rather than the provincial government. The attention of modern students has naturally been directed so largely to the role of the representative assembly in time of crisis that it is easy to forget that in colonial America the demand for self-government often emphasized a local rather than a provincial right. Indeed, the right of representation in a general assembly was at times valued chiefly as a means of forcing some more adequate provision for local administration. Instances are not wanting to suggest that satisfactory arrangements in that field could even relegate to a position of relative unimportance the right to a seat in the Assembly.

of Berkeley's mission the sum of 200,000 pounds of tobacco was appropriated by an act suggesting that among the reasons for his trip was the old fear of a revival of the company. *Ibid.*, 17.

[78] The revisal of 1662, the most important of the seventeenth century and representing the main body of the law until the very close of the period to which this study is devoted, is found in Hening, *Statutes*, 41–148. It appears to have been the work largely of Francis Moryson and Henry Randolph, and was printed by order of the Assembly. *Ibid.*, 34; Bruce, *Institutional History of Virginia*, II, 509. The next revisal came in 1705. That of 1658 will be found in Hening, *Statutes*, I, 432–95; and that of 1643, the most important theretofore, *ibid.*, 239 *et seq.*

As early as 1648, Northampton County, which for geographical reasons enjoyed an unusual degree of local autonomy through the special competence bestowed upon its county court, had elected to forgo the privilege and save the expense of sending burgesses to Jamestown. That was going a bit too far, especially when the county subsequently refused to pay its share of the public levy on the ground that it was unrepresented in the Assembly imposing the tax, and the people of the Eastern Shore were forced to reassume their normal relation to the provincial government.[79] It is only an incident in the long history of self-government in Virginia, but it lights the way for the modern student.

Under the Restoration settlement, the county courts were left in possession of their greatly expanded jurisdiction, and for all practical purposes they kept control of their membership and other key offices of the county. It is true that the court lost the right to appoint surveyors; that its clerk again sought office through the traditional channels; and that the justices of the peace, as the county commissioners were now officially designated, became once more subject to the governor's right of commission. The surveyors excepted, however, these were changes chiefly of legal significance, for the governor's authority in such matters was limited by the most practical of political considerations. The right of the justices to be consulted upon a vacancy in their midst is accurately enough measured by the extent of their heavy responsibilities. Experience had demonstrated that there was no alternative to an arrangement imposing upon them collectively the heaviest burden of government, as is shown by the prompt abandonment of the experiment with itinerant justices. It thus proved difficult to ignore the desire of the county magistrates in making appointments, and, unless the circumstances were unusual, it was not wise. Further reinforcement of their position came in the statutory award to them of the sheriff's office and of a virtual control of the parish. Laws for the re-establishment of the church made of the vestry a self-perpetuating body and thus in effect guaranteed the county magistracy full control over all phases of local administration.[80] Almost

---

[79] *Virginia Magazine*, V (1897–1898), 35; Ames, *Studies of the Virginia Eastern Shore*, 8.

[80] Hening, *Statutes*, II, 44–45, provided "that twelve of the most able men of each

superfluously, the county court also received in 1662 a new statutory right to enact such bylaws as were deemed necessary, an authority destined to survive until 1683 as a significant token of local autonomy.[81]

It will readily be seen that the distinguishing feature of Virginia's colonial constitution, which received now a more or less permanent form, was a wide distribution of authority. It mattered little that the burgesses had surrendered direct control over the offices of governor and councilor. Not only did the right to govern again in the name of the King more than compensate for the loss, but the burgesses had won a new position of influence in the Assembly, an influence they used to establish firmly comprehensive rights of local self-government. In the process one detects a growing tendency to concentrate political control in the hands of a relatively small group of the leading planters. The very nature of the county-court scheme of administration—imposing a special obligation upon the more responsible members of the community and depending for its effectiveness upon the accumulated experience of the county board—dictated that this should be so. With the Restoration, Virginia was well on the way toward acquiring a governing class, not one imported from England or anywhere else, but a class produced by its own administrative needs with the aid of economic opportunities which were themselves frequently related to the possession of political influence. Before the system of government thus established had acquired the advantage of age, the colony passed through the most famous of colonial rebellions,

---

parish be by the major part of the said parish chosen to be vestrymen out of which number the minister and vestry to make choice of two churchwardens yearly, as alsoe in the case of the death of any vestry man, or his departure out of the parish, that the said minister and vestry make choice of another to supply his roome." That the statute thus specifically authorized the usage by which the vestry became a close corporation has been overlooked at times.

[81] *Ibid.*, 171–72, an act which conferred the same authority on the vestry. This right of local self-government seems to have been granted particularly with a view to problems of servant discipline, and for that purpose had been given to Gloucester County in 1661. *Ibid.*, 35, 195. But again action growing out of the peculiar situation of the Eastern Shore had foretold a policy of general application, Northampton County having received in 1656 a limited right to enact by-laws. *Ibid.*, I, 396, 476. Middlesex County later used the authority for a conservation measure against "fishgigging," apparently an all too popular night sport. *Virginia Magazine*, VIII (1900–1901), 186.

but the system possessed the strength to survive even Bacon's Rebellion.

Sir William Berkeley's return to the colony in 1662 left untouched in any marked way the political settlement written in his absence. Historians have been inclined to draw a parallel between his second term as governor and the reign of King Charles at home, thus suggesting that he imposed a largely undesired rule upon the colonists. However, it seems better to regard him simply as a leading Virginia planter with ideas and aims not greatly different from those of other planters with whom he shared direction of the colony's affairs. His voice was often raised through the years that followed in eloquent condemnation of the new parliamentary trade acts, and other causes he championed, such as the suppression of Quakerism, are readily explained without reference to outside prompting. That he served now in any special sense as spokesman for interests outside Virginia appears to be as unlikely as the oft-heard suggestion that the peculiar irascibility he displayed at the time of Bacon's Rebellion marked his conduct throughout his second governorship.

If for a number of years paralleling the term of King Charles's celebrated Cavalier Parliament there was no new Assembly elected in Virginia, and the one chosen shortly after the Restoration met infrequently, it need cause no astonishment.[82] For a generation theretofore the colony's relations with England and problems of adjustment within its own expanding frontiers had lent a special importance to the work of the Assembly and hence to the right of representation in it. But now that the right was no longer in question and an administrative adjustment emphasizing local self-government had been achieved, it was natural that indifference

[82] A tendency to follow the practice of adjourning from session to session rather than accepting dissolution, which called for a new election, developed during the interregnum, as also did a growing awareness of the cost of the Assembly as an actual or potential grievance of the people. It was proposed as early as 1658 that because of the cost, counties be limited to two burgesses each, and that became the law in 1661. Hening, *Statutes*, I, 498; II, 20. At the same time another act fixed the allowance for expenses at 150 pounds of tobacco per day to limit excessive charges and as a safeguard against bargain-rate candidates, while still another measure authorized the governor and council to meet in the fall for "raising and apportioning" the public levy, which was a function of the Assembly, on the ground that the cost of its own sitting often exceeded all other taxes imposed on the people. *Ibid.*, II, 23, 24, 31–32.

toward the Assembly should have appeared. The men who customarily made and enforced the law were, in the main, satisfied with it as it stood. Such additional legislation as was passed left untouched, save for incidentals, the system given shape in 1662. A statute of 1670,[83] tightening the franchise requirements, marks the first unmistakable indication of a challenge to established leadership that might measurably have altered the Assembly's complexion. The subsequent development of this challenge to the point of open rebellion, and the intrusion thereafter of a more strong-willed imperial policy, were to bring a returning vitality to the Assembly. For the moment, however, it was passing through an interlude joining more significant phases of its development.

In contrast with the experience of Virginia, the Restoration in Maryland brought difficult problems of adjustment. Unhappily, the political unrest which characterized the years of the interregnum in the more northerly of the two colonies extended to the very day of the Restoration. The Puritan control of the province, established in 1655, had been promptly challenged by Lord Baltimore in England, where during the next year Bennett and Mathews pressed anew Virginia's case against the Maryland charter. Interruptions occasioned by the urgency of more important affairs of state delayed action by the English government, and in the end the interest of Virginia seems to have been directed chiefly toward the achievement of some compromise that would bring peace to her neighbor rather than the furtherance of her own ambitions. It is difficult to say whether that attitude of the older colony should be attributed to the influence of officials of the home government, to a distaste for the Puritan regime in Maryland that tended to move Virginians to the side of the proprietor, to the apparent fact that the implications of Baltimore's grant had been more important from the outset than any specific objections to the grant itself, or to some combination of these and other influences. Whatever the case, Mathews and Digges, especially the latter, played an active part in the negotiation of an agreement of November, 1657, which recognized Baltimore's right to his province on the understanding that a general amnesty would ensue and that the property rights of all men would be protected. More than a year before that date

83 *Ibid.*, II, 280.

Josias Fendall had been designated proprietary governor, and in March of 1658 Fuller formally surrendered the government to him.[84] Once more Lord Baltimore had defended his patent successfully.

He was to face yet another attack, however, and this time from his own Governor Fendall. Baltimore's ideas on the extent of his authority were so absolute and inelastic that many persons who had opposed the extreme action of the Puritans shared with them in substantial measure an inclination to oppose the proprietary prerogatives. Among such persons, apparently, was Fendall. He had fought on the side of the proprietor in 1655, and as a reward had become successor to Stone, but Baltimore had misjudged the man, as was clearly demonstrated by the events of 1660.

An Assembly convening in March of that year was marked by a demand of the lower house that it be recognized as the "highest court of Judicature" and "without dependence on any other Power in the Province." To that demand Fendall not only acceded, agreeing that, if they sat at all, the governor and council should sit with the burgesses and that the burgesses under their own speaker should have full control of dissolution, but he contributed to the debate a remarkable interpretation of the charter with reference to the location of the legislative power. Though he felt that the proprietor or his deputy ought to be present and to hold "a Casting voice," he declared a belief that "the intent of the King in his lordship's Pattent was that the ffreemen by writt assembled either by themselues or their deputies should make and Enact lawes, and those lawes soe made were to be published in his lordship's name, and then to be in full force. Provided they be agreeable to reason, and in noe case repugnant to the Lawes of England." [85] Short of an outright repudiation of the proprietor's title, it would have been difficult to frame a more radical doctrine in contemporary Maryland.

It is possible that Fendall had grievously misjudged the trend of events at home and now, in an ill-timed venture, sought for himself the role of Cromwell in a Maryland commonwealth. But circumstances suggest another interpretation. Unhappily, the records of

---

[84] *Archives of Maryland*, III (1885), 332–34; I (1883), 369–71; and see again, Andrews, *Colonial Period of American History*, II, 320 ff.

[85] *Archives of Maryland*, I (1883), 388–91.

his subsequent rule were by later order destroyed, and much must depend on conjecture. Enough has survived to reveal that in time he completely repudiated the proprietary authority, but the fragment shows too that he sought to rule in the name of the King.[86] It seems likely that his original intent was to take advantage of an apparent opportunity created by the political situation in England to place the colony in a position to bargain for a more satisfactory settlement of its government than had been provided by the agreement of 1657, a document which had restored the full rights of the proprietor under a now defunct Protectorate. Throughout the colonies in 1660 men were no less alert to the opportunities provided by a new turn in the political fortunes of England than they were to the special hazards of the day.[87] The Maryland settlement of 1657–1658 had set something of a precedent for negotiation in these matters, and though at that time the proprietor's rights had gone unimpaired, men clearly guilty of rebellion also had gone unpunished. An official record is easily misleading but evidently the initiative lay with the burgesses rather than with Fendall. Prominent among them were leading Puritans, including Fuller, but any calculation of the majority required to force the issue in the Assembly must lead to the conclusion that the move was supported by a much more representative group than had been joined together in the earlier Puritan venture.[88] Finally, it should be noted that the rights asserted by the Assembly were not greatly different from

[86] *Ibid.*, LIII (1936), xvi–xvii, 93–94, where in the Charles County Records will be found a writ of September for an arrest "at his Majestyes suite." There are no provincial records for the period from March 7 to November 11, and of the county records only those of Charles County survive.

[87] Notice in addition to Sir William Berkeley's mission to London the extraordinary success of agents for Connecticut and Rhode Island in winning from the newly established government royal charters which so far met the provincial desire for self-government that they were destined to serve the needs of those two communities well into the nineteenth century.

[88] Of the twenty-six burgesses attending the session, eight had participated in the Assembly of 1654, and two others had attended an Assembly of September, 1657. The speaker of 1660, Captain Richard Ewen of Anne Arundel, had sat in both of William Fuller's Assemblies. The Council in 1660 was divided, with Philip Calvert, Baker Brooke, and John Price standing by the patent, while Nathaniel Utye and Thomas Gerard, a member of the upper house by special writ, went on record with the governor. *Archives of Maryland*, I (1883), 339, 359, 382, 383–84, 389–90. Both Catholics and Protestants seem to have participated in the "rebellion." *Ibid.*, LIII (1936), lxvii.

those successfully maintained this same year by the House of Burgesses in Virginia.

There was a fundamental difference, however, in the situation of Maryland and that of Virginia, and if Fendall did not try the part of Cromwell he might as well have done so. The difference lay in the existence of a royal charter which in the very nature of things made difficult any appeal in defiance of it without a resort to those revolutionary doctrines of government Englishmen were now hopefully putting behind them. In Virginia, circumstances gave the Assembly's action every appearance of a laudable step preparatory to the restoration of duly constituted authority, but in Maryland the whole move inevitably smacked of a Commonwealth venture.

The situation could have been saved only if Charles II had shown a disposition to dwell upon Baltimore's marked willingness to follow the main chance and do business with Cromwell. But such proved not to be the case. In July royal letters instructed the authorities in Virginia and all shipmasters trading to Maryland to lend aid in the restoration of Lord Baltimore's lawful authority. The proprietor's brother Philip, already in the colony, and as secretary a dissenter from the action of the preceding March, was appointed governor. On November 19 he proclaimed the succession of Charles II, with an appropriate expression of regret that conditions through the preceding eleven years had not permitted an earlier proclamation of His Majesty's unquestioned right. Later in the month he proclaimed an amnesty with few exceptions.[89] Even Fendall eventually won a pardon, though with a permanent disbarment from office. Thus did the Restoration bring a final victory for Baltimore.

At the same time, however, it set the stage for a continuing contest between the proprietor and his people that would be pressed on both sides as a war of attrition until it reached yet another climax in the year of England's Glorious Revolution. The royal confirmation of the proprietor's patent in 1660 not only freed him from the fear of renewed attacks by old enemies such as Claiborne, but offered an opportunity to support his own prerogative by an appeal to that royal right of government which Englishmen of the Restoration era were so generally inclined to admit. When in 1669 the

[89] *Ibid.*, LIII (1936), 102–104.

burgesses complained of the erection of offices with fees contrary to acts of the Assembly, they received a reply that such action represented no more than was allowed by his lordship's patent "and whatsoever he lawfully doth by power of his Pattent must not be Styled a Grievance unless You mean to quarrel with the King who granted it." [90] Whatever modification of the doctrines of absolutism may have been forced upon the government in England by the events preliminary to its restoration, Lord Baltimore had no intention of conceding any of the broad and absolute powers stipulated in his charter. That attitude stemmed from no stubborn loyalty to an abstract political theory. His primary interest in Maryland was economic rather than political,[91] but concern for the returns from an overlordship of the land argued that the reins should be tightly held.

The proprietor remained in England after 1660, but the administration of the colony again took on the quality of a family rule appropriately suited to the feudal concepts which had shaped its origins. To his son and heir, Charles Calvert, who in 1675 succeeded to the proprietorship as the third lord Baltimore, the proprietor in 1661 entrusted the responsibilities of governor. Philip Calvert at that time took the office of chancellor, a post he filled until his death in 1682.[92] Through the control of appointments and of the land office, practical steps were taken to bind the more substantial planters to the proprietary interest. From that group were drawn the members of the council, whose perquisites proved hardly less advantageous to them than those enjoyed by councilors in Virginia. Other men of substance, called by special writ, joined with the councilors to form an upper house of assembly. With ties of marriage binding together these and members of the proprietary family, Maryland in time came nearer than any other colony to reproducing the English peerage and House of Lords.[93] It again was made clear that the right to legislate belonged to the proprietor by and

---

[90] *Ibid.*, II (1884), 176.

[91] See Andrews, *Colonial Period of American History*, II, 339 n.

[92] See *Archives of Maryland*, LI (1934), *Proceedings of the Court of Chancery, 1660–1679*, and especially the editor's introduction.

[93] Andrews, *Colonial Period of American History*, II, 376–78, and the foregoing pages which provide decidedly the most helpful discussion of Maryland's history from the Restoration to the Revolution.

with the consent of the freemen assembled at his call. The full power to summon, prorogue, and dissolve the Assembly was reasserted by a proprietor who, in theory at least, still refused to concede others a right to initiate legislation.

Though capable of developing strong political convictions, the American has always been a practical man whose primary interests lie outside the field of politics. In 1660 to the people of Maryland the most important political desire undoubtedly was to achieve some settlement that would bring a lasting peace to the colony with an appropriate adjustment of provincial life to duly constituted authority in England. The shortest road to that end lay in an acknowledgment of the proprietor's charter, and it is not surprising that for over eight years the colony enjoyed a term, relatively speaking, of good will and co-operation. The decent sentiments which characterized the Calvert family were helpful to the maintenance of that spirit. The Calverts were stubborn and their thinking inelastic on points involving their prerogatives, but kindliness and graciousness usually marked their insistence on the proprietary right. When in 1661 the lower house sought a statutory right of freedom of speech for the Assembly, the burgesses were informed by the governor in person "that there was noe necessity of making such an Acte," for "they should have as much liberty as any Burgesses had or haue in the Parliament of England or Magna Charta did afforde them in England." [94] A disarming method this, one which conceded the fact while preserving the principle that the privilege proceeded from his lordship's grace.

Such an action, however, did not provide the guarantee of an indisputable right. And so, instead of relaxing in the assurance of firmly established rights, the Maryland colonists of necessity remained ever on the alert. They read the charter with a lawyer's eye to the extraction of its fullest advantage, appealed wherever possible to the statutes of England and the precedents of Parliament, and came to their Assemblies in a frame of mind which promised to make great issues of small matters. The submission of seven articles of grievance by the burgesses of 1669, articles which involved the two houses in a protracted quarrel, put a period to the years of relative good will. One easily imagines the feeling with which the

[94] *Archives of Maryland,* I (1883), 398.

burgesses listened while the governor informed them that they were "not to Conceive that their privileges run parallel to the Commons in the Parliament of England, for that they have no power to meet but by Virtue of my Lords Charter," and that their position was "but like the common Council of the City of London." [95] The maddening thing was the lack of a substantial base upon which to rest what were regarded as legitimate demands— the ease with which under the prevailing theory of government the burgesses could be maneuvered into the position of men challenging the very basis of public authority. And this was particularly galling because so many members of the Maryland Assembly had been charged as county magistrates with a heavy responsibility for the maintenance of that authority in their own communities.

Through the interregnum and the decade following its close the county court in Maryland had advanced to a position in the government of the colony hardly less important than that held by the county commission of Virginia. And once again, the development reflected parallel conditions and problems in the two provinces. Maryland's population had grown apace with that of her sister colony. From Virginia, Puritans had been followed by Quakers seeking the benefit of a tolerant policy re-established on the return of proprietary authority, while others came, as had Governor Stone before them, in response to the appeal of new frontiers. Servants from England and Ireland constituted the bulk of an annual immigration, though after 1649 there was a scattering of Dutch, Swedish, and French settlers, drawn mainly from the Delaware region. By 1660 the natural increase of the original stock had become, as it had somewhat earlier in Virginia, a factor of major importance. There is need for a study of Maryland's population in the seventeenth century, but probable estimates give 11,000 for 1660; 16,000 for 1670; and approximately 25,000 for 1689.[96]

[95] Ibid., II (1884), 168–69, 173–84. The major grievances were delay in the confirmation of laws, the governor's dissent from renewal of statutes previously confirmed, the right to impose a levy without "the Consent of the Freemen," and the question of control of fees.

[96] Ibid., LIII (1936), lviii. The Assembly in 1671 gave a total of 5,641 tithables, which by law included all native-born males above sixteen, imported male servants above ten, and all slaves. Ibid., II (1884), 341; John C. B. Nicklin, "Immigration between Virginia and Maryland in the Seventeenth Century," in William and Mary College Quarterly, 2d ser., XVIII (1938), 440–46.

The same general factors producing a wide dispersal of settlement in Virginia operated with similar effect in Maryland.[97] Indeed, at an even earlier stage of the colony's development the peculiar situation of Kent Island in the upper bay had brought into the picture a problem of distance from the provincial seat. The Puritan Anne Arundel County of 1650, on the opposite side of the Chesapeake, was no less remotely situated. Calvert County in 1654 and Charles County in 1658 met the needs of an expanding settlement west of the Chesapeake, and Baltimore County in 1660 marked a northward extension toward the head of the bay. On the Eastern Shore, Kent County after 1658 extended its jurisdiction onto the mainland. Talbot was added in 1662, and, the area adjoining the Virginia plantations in the south having been opened to grant as early as 1660, Somerset County was organized by 1666. Dorchester was established in 1668, and six years later Cecil County was added in the northeast. Thus by 1674 ten of the sixteen counties into which colonial Maryland ultimately would be divided had been established, eight of them since 1650.[98]

A corresponding expansion of the court's jurisdiction had accompanied this extension of settlement. The ten-pound limit originally set for civil cases had by the interregnum been approximately doubled, and at three thousand pounds of tobacco remained fixed until late in the century. A concurrent jurisdiction belonged to the provincial court, but after 1661 it refused to entertain original actions for less than 1,500 pounds of tobacco. Even before that date it had not been uncommon for the provincial court to refer cases to the county court for fuller information or even final deter-

[97] For a suggestion of the influence of speculative holdings, see an act of 1663 for the aid of Baltimore County. *Archives of Maryland,* I (1883), 499.

[98] See again, *ibid.,* the very helpful introductions to Volumes LIII (1936), and LIV (1937), which provide the latest and best discussion of county administration in early Maryland. The two volumes incorporate proceedings of the county courts for Charles County, 1658–1666; Kent, 1648–1676; Talbot, 1662–1674; Somerset, 1665–1668. An important reference for the formation and subsequent boundary changes of the counties is Edward B. Mathews, *The Counties of Maryland, Their Origin, Boundaries, and Election Districts* (Baltimore, 1907), in *Maryland Geological Survey* . . . , Special Publication, Vol. VI, Pt. V. Useful surveys of extant county records by Louis D. Scisco are available in the *Maryland Historical Magazine,* XXI–XXIV (1926–1929). The distribution of tithables in 1671 was as follows: Calvert, 1,028; St. Mary's, 868; Talbot, 785; Anne Arundel, 784; Charles, 726; Baltimore, 534; Somerset, 386; Dorchester, 263; and Kent, 257. *Archives of Maryland,* II (1884), 341.

mination. As in Virginia, criminal jurisdiction did not extend to life or limb.[99] Though the authority for so doing is uncertain, the Maryland county court had become almost as concerned with testamentary affairs as was the Virginia court. Whether actually proving wills and granting administrations, or establishing a record for use in subsequent action by the governor, secretary, and chancellor who successively were designated probate judge, or merely acting for the convenience and security of all parties concerned through the maintenance of a local record and supervision, the court filled its books with the documentary evidences of probate and administration and kept a watchful eye on executors and administrators.[100] An important consideration in this development was the fact that after 1654 the court had been charged with a special responsibility for the protection of orphans.[101] The varied duties of an orphan's court, of course, carried with them much of the reality as well as the appearance of a probate court.

The recording of wills, inventories, and other documents pertaining to testamentary affairs was but one of many similar services provided the community. Bills of credit and of sale, receipts, deeds of gift, leases, letters of attorney, indentures of service, and other forms of contract were regularly entered by the clerk of court. Though many of these appear in the proceedings as a part of the evidence submitted for the judgment of the court, more impressive are those entered for the sake of a record, occasionally with some such explanatory note as "the oldnes of the paper and naughtines of the inke," or perhaps the loss of an original.[102] In requiring the

[99] *Archives of Maryland*, LIII (1936), xiv, 129; LIV (1937), 261, 354, 634; XLI (1934), 414; for cases referred to county courts, *ibid.*, LIII (1936), 18–19, 23, 624; LIV (1937), 26, 243; and for a reference from the Assembly, *ibid.*, I (1883), 403.

[100] See especially, *ibid.*, LIII (1936), xxxvii, 267, 268, 407, 502–503; LIV (1937), 13, 39, 100, 123, 196, 209, 219, 276–83. Though the evidence suggests that during the interregnum, at least, the county court actually on occasion granted probates and administrations, the general picture indicates that, while legally the authority was placed higher up, much of the actual work was done by the county court for the same reasons which had in Virginia brought an assignment to it of full powers. The secretary seemingly held office as judge of probate from 1642 to 1673, when the chancellor was so designated.

[101] *Ibid.*, I (1883), 353, 374–75, 493–95; II (1884), 325–30; and for examples from proceedings, LIII (1936), 410, 504–505; LIV (1937), 92–99, 308, 341, 386.

[102] *Ibid.*, LIII (1936), 76, 153. For illustrations from Charles County of the great variety, see *ibid.*, 55, 68, 74, 127, 131, 169, 180, 221, 466–77, 543.

registry of livestock or cattle marks Maryland was ahead of Virginia, while the magistrates in both colonies showed alertness to their responsibility for judging and entering the age of newly arrived servants.[103] The absence of an established church, or for that matter of any adequate provision for religious life over large areas and periods of time, brought upon the court in Maryland an even heavier responsibility for the performance of duties traditionally belonging to parish officers. After 1654 the clerk was required to keep a registry of all marriages, births, and burials, a duty performed with varying degrees of regard for the law.[104] An act of 1640, as amended in 1658 and 1662, required publication of marriage bans in either church, chapel, or county court, and in a community where at least one man sought recognition for a common-law marriage on the ground that there was no Protestant minister to perform the ceremony, the civil ceremony received early recognition.[105] Again, the records bear eloquent testimony to the fact that men lived primarily by the land. A proposed act of 1639 undertook to provide for the recording of land conveyances, and a statute of 1663 made this obligatory in either the provincial or county court. The latter act, however, received in 1669 the proprietor's dissent and not until the 1670's did the requirement become established by law.[106] Long before this, however, the needs of the community had been such that the statute finally enacted hardly did more than confirm an established practice. Indeed, the county records of Maryland for this period appear to contain more evidences of land conveyance than do the records in Virginia.

The court's administrative duties increased the range of its responsibilities to include the whole field of local government. Whatever administrative arrangements may have been preferred by Lord

---

[103] *Ibid.*, I (1883), 251; LIII (1936), xxxvii, 563–64. Wives frequently entered a separate cattle mark of their own. The first law requiring registry of all indentures and entry of the age of those not indentured was that of 1654. *Ibid.*, I (1883), 352. The resultant records emphasize the youthfulness of servants brought over, and are a major source for any study of the institution.

[104] *Ibid.*, I (1883), 345, 373; LIV (1937), 38, 129–30, 186–88, 267.

[105] *Ibid.*, I (1883), 97, 374, 442; II (1884), 148, prescribing a form of ceremony; LIII (1936), 599. Special license from the governor might be substituted.

[106] *Ibid.*, I (1883), 61–62, 488; II (1884), 305, 389; LIII (1936), xxxv.

Baltimore, circumstances and the trend of legislation through the Restoration era were to confirm for the county court a position in the administrative structure of the province comparable to that of its counterpart in Virginia. Thus, an act of 1671 conferring upon the commissioners a power to levy for county expenses merely endorsed an already well-established practice.[107] The court served in some measure, too, as a channel through which the people received announcement of the public levy. But the sheriff rather than the commissioners was charged with the preparation of tax lists, and the court appears not to have had quite the same degree of responsibility as in Virginia for the performance of the sheriff's financial duties.[108] Otherwise there is little difference to note. The licensing and supervising of taverns, provision for the operation of ferries, the maintenance of roads and of bridges, the relief of the poor, designation of custodians for standard weights and measures, the payment of bounties for wolves' heads, approval of passes for departure from the province, the appointment of constables, enforcement of regulations for the discipline of servants, the award of bounties for the production of new staples, occasional certification of headright claims, execution of contracts for the provision of courthouse facilities, superintendence, with the sheriff, of elections, authorization of charges for the county's burgesses, and action on local problems of defense were among the varied duties claiming the board's attention.[109] The office of commander, which had emphasized an early combination of military, political, and judicial leadership in the county, disappeared after 1658. Thereafter, the presiding justice in the commission was commonly known as the judge, a title that served to mark a new distinction between civil and military commands. Perhaps it was only the less serious nature of the Indian problem in Maryland that explains the relatively few references in the records to military affairs, for problems of supply and those involving care of the absent soldier's crop or of the

[107] *Ibid.*, II (1884), 273; LIII (1936), 55, 273, 522, 618–20; LIV (1937), 104, 122, 173, 231, 273, 305, 317, 363, 376, 428.

[108] See again, Karraker, *Seventeenth-Century Sheriff*, 139.

[109] *Archives of Maryland*, I (1883), 375, 410, 413, 534; II (1884), 134, 149, 219, 225, 279, 300, 301, 321, 325; LIII (1936), xiv, lvi, 7, 560, 601; LIV (1937), 28, 51, 104, 233, 272–73, 299, 320, 322, 324, 328, 344, 482, 652.

wounded veteran received attention as the occasion required.[110] As a local magistrate, the individual commissioner acted much as did the justice of the peace in Virginia.

The successive political upheavals of the interregnum had brought more-frequent changes in the personnel of the county commissions than occurred through this period in Virginia. A significant result is seen in the difficulty occasionally experienced in finding a sufficient number of men possessing the requisite character and ability. Some appointments, to say the least, were unfortunate.[111] With the Restoration, however, it was possible to follow the general principle of entrusting local government to the more substantial and responsible planters, a group containing some former opponents of the proprietary interest. Thereafter, the magistrates enjoyed a marked security of tenure and a considerable degree of independent control over their own communities. This development was attributable to the court's expanding responsibilities, to a consequently growing appreciation of the value of experience, and to the political necessity compelling the proprietary authority to court an alliance with the more influential men of the province. The sheriff's office, which in addition to its fees offered the reward of 10 per cent of the proprietary, provincial, and county revenues collected, was in Maryland too the principal plum of local patronage. Having enjoyed an early right of nomination and even of appointment on occasion during the interregnum, the court after 1661 nominated three persons from whom the governor was by statute required to make a selection; and so did the commissioners control and with marked regularity occupy the office. The limitation of tenure to one year was frequently ignored, and prior to 1666 the job was at times combined with the increasingly lucrative post of clerk. The clerk was usually appointed by the governor, though in the middle of the century appointments were occasionally made by the court, and later the right was attached to the secretary's office.[112] The trend was toward the creation

110 *Ibid.* LIII (1936), xlvi, 522–25, 617, 618, 620; LIV (1937), 415, 419, 421.

111 The introductions to *ibid.*, LIII (1936); LIV (1937), provide helpful discussions of the personnel of the courts.

112 *Ibid.*, I (1883), 308, 412, 450; II (1884), 132, 137, 222; LIII (1936), xxxviii; Karraker, *Seventeenth-Century Sheriff,* 87–91.

of a relatively small and compact governing clique whose members shared the offices of magistrate, sheriff, and clerk.

And as had been the case in Virginia, that same group tended to exercise a strong influence in the lower house of assembly, which through later years would be marked by a close identification of its membership with the county magistracy.[113] One of the principal problems of the proprietor was to enlist the support of that increasingly powerful group. That the necessity was appreciated is apparent in concessions made to the demand for control of local affairs and by selections for higher political preferment. Indeed, the proprietor's own ideas regarding social and political leadership reinforced other factors working to give the province a governing class similar in character and position to the group now dominant in Virginia. In both colonies, undoubtedly, benefits flowed from the custom of entrusting public affairs to men long experienced in their handling; in both, the system invited serious abuses. But marked as were the similarities, there was one all important difference: Maryland lacked the political stability that had been gained in Virginia.

The county magistrates of the Chesapeake colonies enjoyed a strength of position attributable largely to the administrative needs of their communities. With the position went advanced ideas of self-government, pride of place, and an independent spirit, all of which naturally clashed with archaic ideas of government. In Virginia the burgesses had worked out a comfortable accommodation with the agencies of royal authority which left undisturbed in any serious way a well-established political control, but in Maryland, where internal disturbance and time had not permitted the magistrates to consolidate their position or to gain the strength of men long accustomed to govern, the proprietor after 1660 challenged the right of any but himself to rule. The outburst of 1669 marked the beginning of a long struggle, and when to the fundamental divergence of opinion reflected in that struggle one adds the poten-

[113] Mereness, *Maryland as a Proprietary Province*, 214–16, 237. As in Virginia, the changing membership of the Assembly, together with incomplete records, make an exact check impossible, but compare the names of individuals active in the county courts for Charles, Kent, Talbot, and Somerset, in *Archives of Maryland*, LIII (1936); LIV (1937), especially the editorial introductions, with records of attendance in the proceedings of the Assembly, *ibid.*, I (1883); II (1884); VII (1889).

tial trouble over abusive usages among the magistrates themselves, it becomes readily apparent that Maryland was doubly vulnerable to political unrest. Add in the divisions bred of a continuing religious strife, and the situation becomes thrice confounded.

CHAPTER IX

CAROLINA

UNTIL past the middle of the century the Chesapeake colonies had formed a small if scattered community that was remotely situated with reference to all other European settlements in America. Except for the periodical necessity of adjusting trade and political relations with the mother country, the planters had been left to their own devices, and their attention had been absorbed principally by problems arising within the framework of their own nascent society. The ever vital question of the tobacco trade aside, the basic records of their life reveal a concern chiefly for the adjustment of land policies and of the machinery of government to the peculiar requirements of expanding frontiers. But just when more or less permanent, if not wholly satisfactory, adjustments were near achievement, new problems born of expansion thrust their way into the foreground.

A Virginia statute of 1659 emphasizes this new turn of affairs. It had long been established policy to prohibit a trade in firearms with the natives. The restriction, however, was now repealed on the ground that neighboring English and foreign plantations engaged in the trade; thus the law placed Virginians at a disadvantage without in any way adding to their security.[1] The action touched upon only one facet of a many-sided problem of Indian relations that would move relentlessly, with the aid of pressures arising both from within and without the English settlements, toward a third disastrous explosion. At approximately the same time that Virginia repealed the restriction on a trade in firearms, the Maryland colony, whose expansion northward was drawing a ring of English farms

[1] Hening, *Statutes*, I, 525. An act of 1665, citing the conquest of New Netherland in explanation, restored the prohibition. *Ibid.*, II, 215.

310

around the upper Chesapeake and bringing within reach the Delaware outposts of the Swedes and their Dutch conquerors of 1655, exchanged diplomatic missions with the New Netherland authorities in a dispute over conflicting claims to the west bank of the Delaware. It was one of the earliest in a long list of boundary disputes which have given color and technical difficulty to the story of American settlement, and to the list Virginia and Maryland promptly added a difference over the exact location of their common boundary on the Eastern Shore.[2] On the south, Virginians already had carried into the upper edge of Carolina, there to lay the foundations for still another English colony, a pattern of settlement developed along the Chesapeake. Additional projects for the occupation by English colonists of areas lying closer to Spanish Florida and a renewal of the Anglo-Dutch war by the English conquest of New Netherland in 1664 heralded the arrival of a new era of imperial effort and strife.

Nowhere were the evidences of the response to the opportunities of this new hour more apparent than in London, once more the metropolis of a united nation. Midst one of the most famous contests for place and position in England's history, an atmosphere of materialism and self-seeking hung over Whitehall, and the actions of the English government often bespoke an underlying lack of direction. Yet the outlines of a coherent and comprehensive imperial policy now began to emerge. Special councils of trade and plantations served to bring spokesmen of the government, leading merchants, and men such as Berkeley into consultation on problems of common interest. Guided partly by the information thus assembled, Parliament through the well-known Acts of Trade of 1660, 1661, and 1663 confirmed the essential principles of Cromwell's Navigation Acts by restricting the trade of the colonies to English ships, by reserving for sole export to England or her possessions certain enumerated commodities, and by making England a staple in the trade between foreign countries and the colonies.[3]

[2] Mereness, *Maryland as a Proprietary Province*, 30; Louis N. Whealton, *The Maryland and Virginia Boundary Controversy (1668–1894)* (New York, 1904); *Archives of Maryland*, LIV (1937), xxviii–xxix.

[3] On the question of colonial policy, see Andrews, *Colonial Period of American History*, IV; Harper, *English Navigation Laws;* George L. Beer, *The Old Colonial System, 1660–1754* (New York, 1912).

Tobacco, oldest staple of colonial production and the main support of the Chesapeake colonies, stood high on the list of enumerated commodities. The established policy of allowing a rebate of payments due the King's customs on that part of the tobacco re-exported for sale abroad continued to be followed. But the costs of thus maintaining an English staple in the trade with other countries were considerable, and the policy denied to the planter an obvious advantage in marketing surplus produce directly through agencies provided by Dutch merchants. That the intent of the statute was partly to cripple Holland as a competitor is beyond question, but there is also reason to believe that other fundamental considerations were involved. The very rivalry with Holland gave new emphasis to the desirability of a self-contained empire, and it apparently was felt that to discourage the over-production of tobacco would encourage the development of other staples—a point of imperial policy with reference to Virginia almost as old as the colony itself. The Privy Council sought an agreement among the merchants, shipmasters, and Berkeley, as a representative of the planters, for a "restraint" of tobacco. Agreement proved impossible, but Berkeley returned to Virginia under orders, dated September, 1662, to take up the question in the Assembly and to appoint commissioners for negotiation of a joint agreement with Maryland. The instructions at the same time directed attention to other steps required for a healthy readjustment of the colony's economy. With citation to the worthy example of "their neighbours of New England," the Virginians were ordered to build a town on each river and to afford every possible encouragement to the production of silk, flax, hemp, pitch, potash, and other promising staples. A special project for the establishment of an ironworks was considered so important that the government promised, upon the submission of satisfactory evidence of its practicability, to make available royal funds for underwriting the effort in whatever amount proved necessary to supplement private subscription.[4]

Though by no means in full accord with the government on all details of its policy, Governor Berkeley had long been active in efforts to diversify the colony's economy and apparently set forth

[4] *Virginia Magazine,* III (1895–1896), 15–20.

with a will to carry out as much of his instructions as he could. Upon his return to Virginia, he promptly summoned the Assembly, which enacted an elaborate measure for the immediate building of a town of brick construction at Jamestown through the imposition of a general levy and of a specific obligation upon each county to provide one house for the town. It was announced that the same procedure would be followed in each of the succeeding years for the construction of similar towns on the York, Rappahannock, and Potomac and then for the building of a town on the Eastern Shore. Little need existed for the enactment of new legislation to encourage the production of additional staples. Inspired to some extent perhaps by a desire to show a proper interest in those things reportedly of interest to Englishmen at home, the burgesses had already revived and revised older statutes for encouraging such trades as shipbuilding and the production of flax, silk, salt, leather, and wool. Except for lowering at points the quantity of production required for the award of a bounty, the statutes reveal little change in the policies tried over the preceding years. The Assembly already had reindorsed, too, the long-favored policy of crop control, but it was unprepared to go the length proposed by the English government, and the efforts made to secure an effective agreement with Maryland failed.[5]

Though the act for towns is probably to be credited with some of the improvements made thereafter at Jamestown, it accomplished no change in the pattern of Virginia's life. As Anthony Langston reported, an easy land policy had fixed a custom whereby "every man builds in the midst of his own Land, and . . . provides beforehand to take up so much at the first Patent, that his great Grandchild may be sure not to want Land," while the convenience of riverway transportation had led the people "up and down by these famous Rivers" to the establishment of "stragling" seats from which they could be drawn only at the price of what would be

[5] Hening, *Statutes*, II, 12, 26, 32, 38, 85, 119–24, 128, 136, 172–75, 178, 179. Francis Moryson went to London in 1664 as agent for the colony in this matter, and after hearings before the Privy Council and meetings with Lord Baltimore "and others concerned in the Colony of Virginia," the Privy Council accepted a counterproposal exempting from customs for a five-year term all hemp, pitch, and tar produced in Maryland and Virginia. William L. Saunders (ed.), *Colonial Records of North Carolina* (Raleigh, 1886–1890), I, 74–75; *Virginia Magazine*, XVIII (1910), 423.

regarded as "the greatest oppression in the world." [6] His estimate of £2,700 as the cost of an ironworks emphasizes again the basic requirement of a new investment of capital and skilled labor in all efforts to diversify the colony's economy.

Once more it was the hope of silk that came nearest to enlisting the required interest. Perhaps the rapidly growing silk manufacture of London, which reportedly employed 14,000 persons in 1664 and was declared to provide employment for some 40,000 families by the 1680's, explains the special strength of this old favorite among projects of colonial experimentation.[7] Perhaps, too, the encouragement for all types of experimental effort provided by the recently organized Royal Society played a significant part. Certainly, Virginia's attempt to produce silk, and the colony's botanical and mineral resources in general, together with the flying squirrel, the opossum's sack for its young, the chinquapin, the stature of the natives, and the color of their children at birth were among the subjects, both academic and practical, claiming the attention of that unique community of scientific interests which centered about the society.[8] Through the decade following its formal organization in 1660, and the grant of a royal charter in 1662, there were more men than at any time since Sir Edwin Sandys' day who engaged their time and capital in the effort to produce silk in Virginia. Berkeley proved a persevering leader in the enterprise, and by 1670 Edward Digges returned to an active participation in projects which first had enlisted his interest fifteen years earlier. The average planter undoubtedly looked on with a confirmed skepticism, and he protested against the nuisance of laws requiring that he plant mulberries. Others, however, found some encouragement in an occasional experimental success which seems not to have been without effect upon the post-Restoration migration to Virginia.[9]

Of newcomers who participated, none could have been more

[6] *William and Mary College Quarterly*, 2d ser., I (1921), 100–106.

[7] James E. Gillespie, *The Influence of Oversea Expansion on England to 1700* (New York, 1920), 135.

[8] See especially a "Letter from Mr. Povey concerning the Naturall Products of Virginia in Behalf of the Royall Society" of March 4, 1660, in *William and Mary College Quarterly*, 2d ser., I (1921), 66–69.

[9] *Virginia Magazine*, XVIII (1910), 295, 409–10; XIX (1911), 261, 348–49, 357–59; XX (1912), 17, 126–27, 240–41, 358; XXI (1913), 34; Hening, *Statutes*, II, 191, 199,

interesting than the Reverend Alexander Moray, Scotsman and relative of Sir Robert Moray, one of the founders of the Royal Society. In 1665, Moray wrote from Virginia to his kinsman that he was putting in one thousand fruit trees, and in the following spring wrote that he had planted ten thousand mulberries, from which effort he hoped for silk within three years. His experiments also included trials of barley and rice, and he planned a test of the coffee bean and of such other commodities "from the Straits" as Sir Robert through the "merchants in your society" might be able to provide.[10]

Among the more articulate and sensitive of Virginia's early settlers, Moray wrote one passage that is worth quoting if for no other reason than its uniqueness. Surviving correspondence of contemporary planters is concerned almost entirely with the hard and practical things of their life, but in a letter of June, 1665, Moray declared poetically: "Could a publick good, consist with a hermetik condicon, I should prefere [it] before all others, but the nixt to it which is the settling in a wilderness of milk and honey: non can know the sweetness of it: but he that tasts it: one ocular inspection, one aromatik smel of our woods: one hearing of the consert of our birds in those woods would affect more then a 1000 reported stories let the authors be never so readible." Of no less interest is his comment on the difficulties confronting Scottish settlers. "I should think myself very happy in living in this Country," he declared, "but that the emulations, and differences betwixt us and the English, not only give discouragement but that when wee have occasion, we meet many disappointments in justice." Though recalling the common saying that Scotsmen were like the Jews in that they thrived on "being crost" and noting the example of "many of our Country men, living better than ever ther forfathers, and that from so mean a beginning as being sold slavs here, after hamiltons engagement and Worster fight," some of them already "great masters of many servants themselfs," he saw in Carolina rather than Virginia the brightest prospects for his countrymen. Indeed, he and

201, 241–42, 272. In 1666 a present of three hundred pounds of silk was sent to the King, and in 1671 Berkeley promised sixty or seventy pounds made that year in his own house. At the same time, however, he urged the need of skilled men.

[10] *William and Mary College Quarterly*, 2d ser., II (1922), 157–61.

other Scottish associates had already "made discoveries" for a projected settlement there, it "being the hopefullest place in the world," and he planned to return home after a couple of years to recommend this course of action to his fellow Scotsmen.[11]

It is readily apparent that the settlement of Carolina, as Moray's plans suggest, owed much to the current attempt to diversify the colonies' economy and thus to find through colonization an answer to the problem of national self-suffiency. Not only had the region been joined repeatedly to the most hopeful discussions of Virginia's promise, but several of the proprietors named in the charter of 1663 were actively identified with public policies designed to encourage the necessary experimentation. The charter itself invited settlers to occupy the grant on terms promising exemption from customs duties on all wines, silks, raisins, currants, capers, wax, oil, olives, and almonds imported into England for a term of seven years, that term to be dated from the satisfactory completion of experimental tests. Upper Carolina, sharing the fortunes and misfortunes of its older neighbor, remained outside the area of principal endeavor. But the men who founded South Carolina, finding little encouragement for production of either the tobacco of the Chesapeake settlements or the sugar of the West Indies from which so many of them came, experimented with a long list of likely staples that included silk, olives, wine, hemp, flax, wheat, barley, indigo, cotton, and rice. With rice they won a success that ranks among the more significant achievements in a long chronicle of agricultural experimentation.[12] Perhaps no greater mistake can be made in the study of the Southern colonies than to underestimate the influence of forces which in the contemporary view joined the soil and climate of the southeastern portion of North America to special opportuni-

---

[11] *Ibid.*

[12] A seven-year exemption from customs on the staples listed, "to commence and be accompted, from and after the first importation of four tons of any of the said goods, in any one bottom," was granted in the charter and frequently cited in the proprietors' promotional efforts. Saunders (ed.), *Colonial Records of North Carolina,* I, 27, 45, 47, 48; Alexander S. Salley, Jr. (ed.), *Narratives of Early Carolina, 1650–1708* (New York, 1911), 61, 71. On the range of agricultural experimentation, see especially, Thomas Ashe, *Carolina; or a Description of the Present State of that Country* (London, 1682), in Salley (ed.), *Narratives of Early Carolina,* 138–59; and on the important topic of rice culture, see below, p. 356. Notice, too, the proprietors' early interest in wine. Saunders (ed.), *Colonial Records of North Carolina,* I, 51, 101.

ties for profitable planting suggested by the very range of England's peculiar needs and of her expanding imperialism. Though elsewhere men may have undertaken initial settlement in quest of the contentment to be had from a modest but independent subsistence, and though most Southerners have certainly been forced from the first to be contented with just that, the genesis of their settlements usually encouraged the most ambitious projects of planting.

In an unusual degree the Carolina proprietors sought to capitalize on an opportunity that was not a product of their own efforts. It is not intended to slight the important role of promoter which they assumed. Far too much of the modern discussion of the administrative arrangements upon which American settlement depended has been tainted with the suggestion that the promoter's role was essentially parasitical. In the work of settlement, someone must assume the responsibilities of leadership, if for no other reason than to assure a desirable unity of command and clarity of title resting upon some accepted legal power, and though there were probably better ways of providing this necessary assistance, the proprietors under the authority of their royal charter made a definite contribution to the orderly occupation of Carolina. At the same time, it must be recognized that the area's possibilities had been the subject of public discussion for several years past, and that much of the preliminary promotional work had already been accomplished by others when the proprietors' charter was issued in 1663.

Moreover, settlement in the newly created province had actually begun several years before. It is impossible to speak definitely of the first permanent settlement of Carolina. However, it is known that Francis Yeardley, acting with his brother Argall, a leading planter of the Eastern Shore, had expended by his own account some £300 in the furtherance of explorations there and the purchase of lands from the Indians in 1653 and 1654. The investment was substantial enough to lend credence to his plans announced, in a letter of 1654 to John Ferrar, for experimentation with silk, olives, and wine in a land not only rich but, as he reported, free of Virginia's "nipping frosts." [13] That active interest in the region had

13 Salley (ed.), *Narratives of Early Carolina*, 25–29. John Ferrar and a daughter, Virginia, were active in efforts to encourage experiments with silk and other staples.

not been restricted to the Yeardleys is indicated by Hening's record of an authorization of December, 1656, to Colonel Thomas Dew and his associates for the exploration of navigable rivers between Cape Hatteras and Cape Fear. Statutes of the Virginia Assembly in 1655 and 1658 authorizing attachments for the creditors' security against persons about to move to distant and remote plantations either "northerly or southerly" convey the distinct suggestion that actual settlement was under way.[14] It was the proprietors' understanding in 1663 that two communities of settlers existed, the one "on the north east parte of the river Chowan" and the other "on the Larboard side entring of the same river." In September they instructed Sir William Berkeley to designate two governors for the region if he saw fit. His issuance that same month of grants, in the regular form of the Virginia land patent and in return for headright claims against the secretary's office at Jamestown, for acreages surveyed on the "River of Carolina" and on streams severally identified as "Pasquotank," "Raspitanck, "pyquomans," "paspatanck," and "Curatuck" suggest that here had been no slackening of interest among Virginia's planters.[15]

Nor was Virginia the only likely source of an immigration of seasoned and experienced colonists. In New England no less than on the Chesapeake the early settlers held close to deep water and the advantages of oceanway contacts with the outside world, leaving a deeper penetration of the interior for later generations. In terms of the contemporary pattern of settlement, the New England colonies offered a surplus of population for the occupation of other

---

See especially, *Reformed Virginian Silk-Worm* (1655), in Force (comp.), *Tracts*, III, No. 13.

[14] Hening, *Statutes*, I, 409, 422, 471. Worthy of note also is an order of July, 1653, authorizing a grant of 11,000 acres to Roger Green, clerk, and other inhabitants of Nansemond River for a settlement of one hundred persons to be made on the Moratuck or Roanoke River "and the land lying upon the south side of Choan river and the branches thereof." *Ibid.*, 380. Henderson Walker's statement in 1703 that "we have been settled near this fifty years in this place," Saunders (ed.), *Colonial Records of North Carolina*, I, 571, is helpful, but offers no exact clue to the actual date of settlement. The writer sees no reason for believing that it came at any time prior to 1654.

[15] Saunders (ed.), *Colonial Records of North Carolina*, I, 49, 53, 54, and 59–67 for Berkeley's patents of September 25, 1663. The suggestion that two governors might be appointed is explained on the ground of religious differences separating those on opposite sides of the river.

regions. Their people, in a rapidly developing contest for mastery of the strategic footholds along the Eastern seaboard, had already brought strong pressure on the Dutch of New Netherland, and following hard upon the removal of that barrier in 1664, the Puritans moved across from Connecticut and Long Island to make a major contribution to the settlement of New Jersey. Enterprising seamen from Boston and other New England ports had been for several years frequent visitors in the Chesapeake, and they now provided ready channels of information and ready means of transportation for those desiring to participate in new projects of southern expansion.

Indeed, at the time of the granting of the Carolina charter, a New England outpost, reportedly well stocked with cattle, had recently been established near the mouth of the Cape Fear River, toward the other extreme from Albemarle of the bounds of modern North Carolina. Unfortunately, an incomplete record tells little of its history. Whether it was an independent project of the sort so familiar in the history of Puritan colonization, or whether comprised of advance agents for groups at the time negotiating with the proprietors regarding a prospective settlement, cannot be said. Whatever the case, the undertaking was soon abandoned in disappointment and apparently with strong feelings anent the region itself. William Hilton, prospector for Barbadian planters contemplating a move to Carolina, on his return in 1664 from an exploration of the Cape Fear region, directed his efforts principally to disproving "a Writing left in a Post at the Point of Cape Fair River, by those New-England-men that left Cattel with the Indians there, the Contents whereof tended not only to the disparagement of the Land about the said River, but also to the great discouragement of all those that should hereafter come into those parts to settle." [16]

Hilton's explorations were especially significant, for his reports

[16] Salley (ed.), *Narratives of Early Carolina*, 53; Saunders (ed.), *Colonial Records of North Carolina*, I, 71. A letter of August 6, 1663, from London associates of a group of New England adventurers indicates that an independent project of settlement, with headquarters in New England, had been launched prior to the granting of the Carolina charter, that land had been purchased of the Indians, that a royal patent had been sought in confirmation of the title so acquired, and that the party whose presence is noted by William Hilton were advance agents for this group. *Ibid.*, 36–39. There

of this and a prior voyage encouraged a growing interest among West Indian and Bermudian planters in a settlement of the Carolina mainland. The British West Indian plantations of the Lesser Antilles had drawn a larger number than had any other single region of those who during the period of the Great Migration left England for America. To their exports of tobacco, cotton, indigo, and ginger had been added after 1640 increasing quantities of sugar, and by the time of the Restoration, sugar planting, combined with a rapid development of Negro slavery, had wrought an economic and social revolution of far-reaching effect. The small planter, who heretofore had dominated the scene, now found himself at an increasing disadvantage in competition with the larger units of cultivation associated with the growth of sugar and of slavery. White servants completing the term of their indentures, and finding neither land nor suitable employment available, swelled the totals of a surplus population. Emigration from the original settlements long since had effected an occupation of additional and neighboring isles and had been drawn upon after 1650 for the English planting of Surinam in Guiana and for settlement of the newly conquered island of Jamaica after 1655. In Barbados, by the time of South Carolina's founding, conditions were especially favorable for the launching of new projects of colonization.[17]

Perhaps New England's seamen, again, should be credited with an assist. They plied a regular trade with the West Indian plantations, which they often joined to their commerce in the Chesapeake, and they had been prompt in establishing a trade with Albemarle Sound. It would have been natural for them to offer aid in the exchange of ideas, the co-ordination of plans, and the provision of passage and freightage to the mainland. The Bermudas had early faced the problems of a surplus population and had contributed to the settlement of Virginia, the West Indies, and Jamaica.

---

appears to be no real evidence supporting the tradition that a New England settlement existed on the Cape Fear as early as 1660, or indeed that anything in the nature of a real settlement was actually made even later. See also, *ibid.*, 46–47.

[17] On the British West Indies in this period, see Harlow, *History of Barbados;* James A. Williamson, *The Caribee Islands under the Proprietary Patents* (London, 1926); Williamson, *English Colonies in Guiana and on the Amazon;* Charles S. S. Higham, *The Development of the Leeward Islands under the Restoration, 1660–1688* (Cambridge, 1921); Andrews, *Colonial Period of American History,* II, 240–73.

The islands lay only a few hundred miles off Cape Hatteras, and a project for the settlement of Carolina had been associated with their history as early as 1620.[18]

Significantly, proposals for the new proprietorship seem to have originated with men whose acquaintance with the opportunity traced to their own experience in America. Perhaps the prime mover in the undertaking was Sir John Colleton, a Royalist soldier who after the King's execution had become a planter in Barbados. Returning to London at the time of the Restoration, he left his son Peter in charge of the family's interests in the colony, received from the King the cheap reward of a knighthood, and cast about for such advantages as the moment might offer. He was thoroughly familiar with the difficulties of the Barbadian planters, among whom his son and a kinsman, Sir Thomas Modyford, would assume leadership in the subsequent development of plans for a settlement in Carolina by agreement with the proprietors. To London in 1661 came also Sir William Berkeley, whose sponsorship of exploratory efforts extending southwestward toward Carolina went back to his first term as governor of Virginia. He had been named in advance of his arrival to membership on a special Council for Foreign Plantations which included Colleton and Sir Anthony Ashley Cooper, better known to students of history by his later title of first Earl of Shaftesbury. Cooper had owned a modest property in Barbados from 1646 to 1655, and had invested in slave-trading ventures to Guinea. Being formerly of the Presbyterian party, he had widened his experience in the conduct of public affairs by an occasional service to Cromwell. Though understandably now regarded with suspicion in several quarters, he was able and enterprising, had the recommendation of General George Monck, newly created Duke of Albemarle, and stood on the threshold of one of the most significant political careers of England's history.[19]

18 For an account of Bermuda's history prior to 1684, see Henry Wilkinson, *Adventurers of Bermuda* (London, 1933); and for a project to enlist the Bermuda adventurers in a settlement on the mainland under the Virginia Company, see Craven, *Introduction to the History of Bermuda*, 13 n., 155. Hall (ed.), *Narratives of Early Maryland*, 364, indicates that Barbados received an annual supply of provisions from Maryland.

19 See especially, Louise F. Brown, *The First Earl of Shaftesbury* (New York, 1933) 151 ff.; Andrews, *Colonial Period of American History*, III, Chap. V.

There were ample opportunities for an exchange of ideas among these men and for the framing of joint plans of action. It is doubtful that, without assistance, they could have swung the weight required to secure a royal charter, however, and the full list of eight proprietors who received the Carolina grant in 1663 contains in itself eloquent testimony to the skillful political maneuvering that had prepared the way. Lord John Berkeley, brother to Sir William, privy councilor, active in naval affairs of great interest to members of the royal family, and soon to become by grant from the Duke of York a proprietor of New Jersey, was an obvious choice as an agent for the enlistment of more influential men. Albemarle, Cromwell's old soldier who had recently turned king-maker and who was a relative of Colleton and known to be greedy, represented an equally obvious choice. Sir George Carteret, vice-chamberlain of the household, treasurer of the navy, and a man known chiefly for his defense of the Jerseys during the Civil War, would share with Berkeley the proprietorship of New Jersey. William, Earl of Craven, was an old soldier of the King, had money and an adventurous spirit, and was marked for later favors. Edward Hyde, Earl of Clarendon, carried the weight of the King's first minister. Nothing could be further from the truth than the frequently repeated suggestion that King Charles, in a light and offhand manner, conferred on these men the grant of Carolina as a special mark of his royal favor. The fact is that he probably opposed the grant but found this skillfully assembled group too many for him.

It is worthy of note that the proprietors both now and later were closely identified with the framing and administration of imperial policy. Their names appear repeatedly among the ranking members of the Council of Trade of November, 1660, of the Council for Foreign Plantations created the following December, and of the Joint Council for Trade and Plantations, forerunner of the celebrated Lords of Trade.[20] As already noted, some of the

[20] The Councils of Trade and for Foreign Plantations (1660) each included Lord Berkeley, Carteret, Colleton, Clarendon, and Cooper; the joint council of 1668, York, Rupert, Albemarle, Craven, Berkeley, Ashley, and Carteret; and of the council of 1672 Ashley, now Shaftesbury, was president while York, Rupert, and Carteret belonged ex officio. See especially, Charles M. Andrews, *British Committees, Commissions, and Councils of Trade and Plantations, 1622–1675* (Baltimore, 1908).

proprietors were also active in naval administration. This was an interest closely related to colonial questions in an era of imperial conquest and one which offered a point of contact with the Duke of York and his cousin, Prince Rupert, whose enthusiasms extended into several fields of maritime expansion. There were strong influences, representative notably of the merchants, opposing the creation of further chartered colonies. But England's method of expansion still emphasized a reliance on private initiative, and gentlemen of high rank and place were still alert to opportunities for pressing their own advantage while serving the larger ends of national interest. As a result, a relatively small group of highly placed men in the government and at court assumed the leadership of England's post-Restoration expansion, and had York and Rupert been added to the Carolina proprietors, the membership of that board would have provided a well-nigh complete list.

The Duke of York, Lord High Admiral and heir to the throne, had been a leader in the organization of the Company of Royal Adventurers to Africa in 1660. Its business included the provision of slave labor for American plantations, and among its members were Lord John Berkeley, Carteret, and Colleton. Having secured a charter for New Netherland in 1664, the Duke promptly deeded New Jersey to Berkeley and Carteret. The Bahama grant of 1670 went to six of the Carolina proprietors—Shaftesbury, Albemarle, Craven, Lord John Berkeley, Carteret, and Peter Colleton, heir to his now deceased father. The Hudson's Bay Company that same year presents Rupert, Albemarle, Craven, Shaftesbury, Carteret, and Colleton associated together again, this time in a quest of the Northwest Passage. Even William Penn, son of Admiral Sir William Penn of Jamaica fame, friend of York, active in Berkeley's share of New Jersey following its sale in 1674, and the founder of Pennsylvania, had the credentials for membership in the group.

By the terms of a charter dated March 24, 1663, the Carolina proprietors acquired title to a vast acreage lying between the thirty-sixth and thirty-first degrees of latitude and running westward to the "south seas." [21] For all practical and immediate purposes they

[21] Saunders (ed.), *Colonial Records of North Carolina*, I, 20–33. By the second charter of 1665, *ibid.*, 102–14, the bounds were extended northward half a degree and southward to a point well below the present Georgia-Florida line.

received possession of that very considerable portion of the Eastern seaboard which extended from Virginia to modern Florida, with a title held of the King in free and common socage for no more than twenty marks annually. The charter set forth their authority over the area in the full and absolute terms of the now familiar Bishop of Durham clause. Like Baltimore, they held the power to legislate "with the advice, assent, and approbation of the freemen . . . or of the greater part of them, or of their delegates or deputies" in assembly. Aside from that provision of the charter and the customary stipulation that "laws be consonant to reason, and as near as may be conveniently, agreeable to the laws and customs" of England, few practical limits affected the proprietors' right to manage the affairs of the province as they chose. Exceptions allowable to the oaths and forms of service required under the religious establishment of Restoration England undoubtedly were included at the instance of the proprietors with a view to attracting nonconformist settlers. Such a policy of religious freedom was commonly adopted by promoters of that day, and, when placed alongside the traditional assurance for the colonists of denizenship and the full privileges of English subjects, the policy marks a step forward in the use of a colonial charter for the guarantee of fundamental rights. The political and religious liberalism which has become so characteristically American has deep roots in the economics of colonial promotion.

The proprietors' immediate plan of operation was simple and somewhat elastic. They intended chiefly to operate a land office and contemplated no expensive venture of colonization from England. Not only had the assumption of an earlier generation that emigration promoted the national interest undergone revision, but the cost of emigration from England was great and the men thus to be had were inexperienced in the work of settlement. In America, on the other hand, seasoned colonizers were available, experienced men who were prepared both to pay and to make their own way. The neighborhood of older settlements could be counted upon, as in the earlier occupation of Maryland, to facilitate the provision of stock and other basic supplies.[22] A saving clause for titles already acquired had been introduced into the charter, and the

[22] See, for example, *ibid.*, 38; Salley (ed.), *Narratives of Early Carolina*, 72, 84, 122–24.

grantees' first concern, after legal obstructions raised by claimants under Sir Robert Heath's patent of 1629 had been cleared, was to forward instructions to Sir William Berkeley for the organization of Albemarle.

Hardly if any less prompt was the proprietors' action to encourage correspondents in New England, Bermuda, and Barbados to undertake still other settlements. In "A Declaration and Proposals to All That Will Plant in Carolina," the board outlined the conditions that would be offered.[23] In advance of actual settlement, the participants in any project should submit a list of thirteen men from whom a governor and council of six would be commissioned for a term of three years. At the expiration of this term, their places were to be filled on nomination by the freeholders of the community. Laws were to be made by an assembly with the consent of the governor and council, subject to the proprietors' allowance. Freedom of religion would be granted to the extent desired by the community and allowed by the charter. The land would be divided according to the following headrights: every undertaker would receive for himself one hundred acres, fifty additional acres for every manservant capable of bearing arms and so equipped, and thirty acres for every woman servant brought into the colony within the first five years. As a further subsidy to immigration, servants were to receive, according to their sex, ten and six acres at the expiration of their terms. The colony was to support its own local administration, and the proprietors for their pains and in recognition of their rights were due a halfpenny per acre rent. In addition, twenty thousand acres would be reserved for them in every settlement undertaken.

Documents forwarded to Berkeley bring the proprietors' ideas into an even clearer light. He was authorized to appoint for the settlers of upper Carolina a governor and council of six men with power to designate subordinate officers and to legislate with the advice of an assembly. Exceptions were made in the case of the secretary and the surveyor, officers whose duties embraced a primary responsibility for the issuance and recordance of land patents and whose appointment was reserved for the proprietors in an action significantly indicative of where their chief interest lay. A

23 Saunders (ed.), *Colonial Records of North Carolina*, I, 43–46, 46–47.

copy of the "Declaration and Proposals" was forwarded for Berkeley's advice but with the hope that a "more fassil people" could be brought to accept terms more favorable to the proprietors. He was instructed to persuade the older settlers to accept such allotments as were to be generally allowed and to provide for a more compact form of settlement. If necessary, the people might be given three to five years before imposition of the halfpenny rent. A proprietary reservation of twenty thousand acres should be laid out in parcels, some of it near a likely location for a town. Another part, according to an instruction suggestive of the sort of direct investment possibly contemplated by the proprietors, should be selected with an eye to the planting of vineyards, which reportedly brought annually sixty pounds an acre in the Canaries. Adequate fees were to be fixed for the surveyor and secretary, and if no other way could be found for the governor's support, a monopoly of the fur trade might serve for the time being. The kind of common expense the proprietors themselves were willing to bear is shown by Berkeley's authorization to fit out a modest expedition for exploration of the waters below Albemarle Sound.[24]

In October, 1664, a commission from the proprietors named William Drummond governor and commander in chief of Albemarle County, as the original settlement had been officially designated, and after a three-year term he was succeeded by Samuel Stephens.[25] At some time prior to June, 1665, a general assembly sat for Albemarle. According to instructions for Governor Stephens in 1667, twelve deputies chosen by the freemen to act with the governor and council for purposes of legislation would constitute an assembly until the establishment of parishes or other appropriate precincts made it possible to choose two deputies from each such unit.[26] The same provision is found in the "Concessions and Agreement" of January, 1665, a lengthy document drafted in consultation with Barbadian and New England adventurers joined together for settlement on the Cape Fear and at Port Royal, but a paper also containing both general and specific conditions of settlement applying to Albemarle.[27] To the Assembly in each of the settlements undertaken the proprietors conceded those powers which had

[24] *Ibid.*, 48–55.   [25] *Ibid.*, xiii, 93, 162.   [26] *Ibid.*, 101, 167.
[27] *Ibid.*, 79–92. For the circumstances attending its drafting, see below, p. 330.

become customary in the American colonies, and the people received a specific guarantee against all taxes not imposed by their own consent. Statutes, however, would remain in force for only a year and a half unless ratified by the proprietors and could not affect such proprietary policies as the assurance of religious freedom. Nor could they alter the basic terms governing land grants.

These terms had been fixed by Drummond's instructions and the "Concessions" of 1665 at eighty acres per head for every freeman settled prior to January, 1666. The same amount would be allotted for his wife and every able-bodied manservant brought in before that date, and forty acres each for such "weaker" servants as women, children, and slaves above fourteen years of age. Thereafter the acreage allowed would follow a sliding scale downward, according to the year of arrival, until there would be due those entering in 1667 no more than forty and twenty acres severally.[28] That total, of course, fell considerably below the standard fifty-acre headright of Virginia, and a halfpenny rent came to a higher figure than did Virginia's quitrent. Immigration from above the line naturally slackened in the face of terms less favorable than were offered in the parent colony, and an attempt to assure compact settlement by limiting the bounds of the county to 1,600 square miles discouraged the kind of investor who, for all the wastefulness of his speculative ventures, had elsewhere proved a useful promoter. "Rich men (which Albemarle stands in much need of) may perhaps take up great Tracts," wrote Surveyor Thomas Woodward in a revealing letter of 1665, "but then they will endeavour to procure Tenants to helpe towards the payment of their Rent, and will at their owne charge build howseing (which poore men cannot compasse) to invite them." [29]

As Woodward and other men in America well knew, there was no escape from Albemarle's dependence on Virginia. Navigational obstructions along a sand-locked coast hindered the establishment of normal commercial relations with Europe, and thus tended to cut off Albemarle's settlers from that regular and easy supply of labor and other essential commodities which had been the basis for so much of the growth of the Chesapeake colonies. Failure in these circumstances to subsidize immigration to the same extent as above Cape Henry could only reinforce that natural barrier. Thus the earliest major grievance of Carolina's planters found expression in a demand for conditions of settlement at least equal to those of Virginia.

In Stephens' instructions of 1667 the proprietors so far relented as to fix the headrights respectively at sixty and fifty acres, where they remained. The idea, presumably, was that the larger headright, together with an assurance of fifty acres for time-expired servants, might offset the higher rent and certain other conditions imposed in the Carolina grants.[30] The Assembly, however, felt differently and promptly petitioned for the right to hold their lands "upon the same terms and conditions that the Inhabitants of Virginia hold theirs." The petition was granted in May, 1668, but the concession was destined to be short-lived indeed.[31] Within a year the proprietors took an occasion, bred of successive disappointments in other parts of their grant, to revise through the "Fundamental Constitutions of Carolina" their whole scheme of settlement. In doing so, though the larger headrights were retained, the proprietors restored the original rent. Later they even increased it. Thus, from the first the Albemarle community had paid the penalty of policies poorly adjusted to the peculiar requirements of its situation. Its development would continue to be slow and painful.

The explanation lies partly in the fact that the more southerly

[30] *Ibid.*, 169–70, 172–75. Baltimore had also seen an advantage in offering a headright claim to the servant as well as to the master, but Virginia's experience indicates that what really counted was the subsidy provided the master. Rents were not due until 1670. Other conditions imposed required the maintenance of one manservant or two other servants for every hundred acres over a term of thirteen years, that each manservant be armed with a gun, ten pounds of powder, and twenty pounds of bullets, and that the grant be occupied within three years.

[31] *Ibid.*, 175–76. By instructions of 1670, *ibid.*, 182–83, the sixty-acre headright was due all free persons above sixteen and for every able-bodied manservant, and the rent was given as a halfpenny. The Fundamental Constitutions had fixed the rent at one penny from and after 1689, *ibid.*, 204, as did instructions of 1679 which continued the above-given headright claims for all those entering up to Christmas, 1684. Provision was also made in these instructions allowing those who had received patents from Berkeley prior to Christmas, 1663, to hold their land under the Virginia rents, and safeguarding the rights of those who had subsequently patented land at the prevailing halfpenny rent; but there was no exception made for such lands as may have been patented under the concession of 1668. The phrasing of the document is apparently unmistakable, but it is possible that it was not intended to affect rents. See *ibid.*, 236–39, 253–54.

regions of the grant attracted a much greater interest. As the north-ward extension of Carolina's bounds under a second charter of 1665 indicates, the proprietors were not indifferent to that section of their province which drew its life largely from Virginia. However, they considered both New England and Barbados to be more promising fields of recruitment, and the more liberal features of their promotional policies had been shaped by that assumption. It would be too much to suggest that the proprietors merely followed the lead given by prospective settlers, but it is pertinent to note that Barbadian and New England adventurers had shown interest principally in areas lying south of Albemarle Sound.

The hope of assistance from New England proved to be for the most part an illusion. Negotiations entered into between the newly established proprietary board and a group of New England and London adventurers previously organized with plans for a settlement on the Cape Fear River came to nought; and though as late as January, 1665, the proprietors considered the Puritan colonies the most likely source of emigration to the southernmost parts of Carolina, all other efforts were similarly abortive.[32] Some of the Barbadian adventurers active in Carolina had New England associates, but in these agreements the West Indian influence was clearly the dominant one.

Under the leadership of Modyford and Peter Colleton a group of Barbadian associates had sent William Hilton at their own charge on two important voyages of discovery along the Carolina coast. His report of the second of these, a voyage extending from August to December in 1663, provided a useful promotional tract on its publication in London the following year.[33] It served especially to discount the disparaging reports regarding the Cape Fear made by earlier agents from New England and to focus attention on the even more southerly site of Port Royal. Though negotiations with the original group of Barbadian adventurers hit a snag in proposals for a corporate form of self-government which the proprietors were unwilling to concede, and some of the undertakers apparently with-

---

[32] *Ibid.*, 36–39, 94.

[33] William Hilton, *A Relation of a Discovery lately made on the Coast of Florida* (London, 1664), in Salley (ed.), *Narratives of Early Carolina*, 37–61. No account of his first voyage survives, and its exact date cannot be given.

drew, others persevered. On May 29, 1664, they undertook, as had the New Englanders before them, to settle the Cape Fear, then called the Charles River. With a principal seat some twenty or thirty miles upstream at Charles Town, the community reportedly had grown by 1666 to include a total of no less than eight hundred colonists.[34]

Peter Colleton continued to serve as spokesman for his fellow planters in negotiations with the proprietors, but leadership in the actual work of settlement passed into the hands of John Yeamans, another Barbadian planter. Acknowledgment by the proprietors in a letter of January, 1665, of his "forwardness to setle neare Cape Faire before you had an assurance of any conditions from us" [35] suggests that he had taken the initiative in establishing Charles Town. Whatever may be the fact in that instance, there can be no doubt regarding his responsibility for an ambitious project of settlement in the Port Royal region, which also had its origins in 1664.

Yeamans' son William reached London in the fall of that year, bearing proposals both for the new undertaking and for the organization of the Cape Fear colony. As a result, Yeamans and his associates of Barbados, New England, the Leeward Islands, Bermuda, and England received the promise of 500 acres for every 1,000 pounds of sugar subscribed for the financing of the venture, and in addition a 150-acre headright was assigned to all those who would accompany him to Port Royal in the first fleet. As a part of the proposed contract, the proprietors appended the previously mentioned "Concessions and Agreement" of January, 1665,[36] a document outlining in detail provisions agreed upon for the government of three widely separated settlements. Each of the settlements—the two already established in Albemarle and on the Cape Fear and the one to be established at Port Royal—was constituted a county and given a separate administration along provincial lines with its own governor, council, and representative assembly. But

---

[34] Saunders (ed.), *Colonial Records of North Carolina*, I, 39–42, 46–48, 55–59; Robert Horne (?), *A Brief Description of the Province of Carolina* (London, 1666), in Salley (ed.), *Narratives of Early Carolina*, 66–73.

[35] Saunders (ed.), *Colonial Records of North Carolina*, I, 98; but see *ibid.*, 144–45.
[36] See above, p. 326.

for the time being Yeamans, for whom the proprietors had secured a baronetcy, was commissioned governor of the county of Clarendon, as the Cape Fear colony had been designated, and of all the proprietary grant lying south of it on the understanding that the Port Royal settlement, once established, would be erected into the county of Craven.[37] As this arrangement indicates, the attempt to settle Craven would be based on Clarendon, and for that purpose Sir John Yeamans had been given such authority as he might need.

The accompanying business arrangements bring the economics of proprietary promotion into a very revealing light. In addition to the 500 acres for each 1,000 pounds of sugar invested and the 150-acre headright for those going with the first expedition to Port Royal, Yeamans himself received the promise of 6,000 acres and his associate Captain William Merricke, 1,500. Settlers who followed during 1665 were promised 120 acres for themselves and for each able-bodied manservant, and 60 acres for every "weaker" servant above fourteen years of age. For those arriving in the year 1666 the allotments fell respectively to 90 and 45 acres, and if the venture was postponed until 1667 it would be undertaken in expectation of only 60 and 30 acres. For the people settled in Clarendon, headrights began at 100 and 50 acres and came down by 1667 to 50 and 25 acres. The proprietors further agreed to provide 12 pieces of large ordinance, 100 firelocks, and 100 matchlocks with ammunition for the fort at Port Royal.[38] As in Albemarle, the inhabitants of Clarendon and Craven were expected to support their own government, and rents at a halfpenny per acre would fall due on March 25, 1670. In short, the settlers assumed all of the risks except for a single contribution for purposes of defense by the proprietors, who hoped to underwrite the work of settlement by promising liberal land grants and thus to convert an undeveloped estate into a rent-producing property. It was as simple as that, or so it seemed.

Yeamans sailed from Barbados for the Cape Fear with a vessel of 150 tons, a small frigate, and a sloop, in October, 1665. The larg-

---

[37] Saunders (ed.), *Colonial Records of North Carolina*, I, 75–78, 78–92, 93–98.

[38] *Ibid.*, 77–78, 86–89, 94. In addition to rents, the proprietors were entitled to land reserves equal to approximately an eleventh part of all land surveyed, and there is a possibility that the proprietors may have borne some part of the cost of subsequent exploration. *Ibid.*, 121. The twelve guns were secured as a gift from the King. *Collections of the South Carolina Historical Society* (Charleston), V (1897), 49–50.

est of his vessels went down in a storm at the very entrance to the river; and, though he and his people reached shore safely, the larger part of their supplies had been lost. Yeamans' luck continued bad, for he found the Charles Town settlers in a state of great need and unrest. To meet the unexpected emergency, he sent the sloop to Virginia for provisions and, giving up his own plans for a voyage to Port Royal, returned to Barbados with the frigate. "Yett that the designe of the Southern Settlement might not wholly fall," he left a commission with Robert Sandford, formerly of Surinam and Barbados and now secretary for Clarendon County, to undertake a southward voyage of discovery either in the sloop upon its return from Virginia or in a ship to be sent back by Sir John from Barbados. But these plans fell victim to a new series of misfortunes. The sloop, on its way back from Virginia, was driven ashore in a storm, its crew fortunately finding their way to Albemarle. The ship from Barbados was delayed by stormy seas and the loss of its captain, who went insane and jumped overboard. Not until June, 1666, did Sandford with a company of twenty men get away from Clarendon. He returned to Charles Town on July 12, with reports confirming Hilton's favorable impression of the Port Royal region.[39]

The projected settlement there, however, was not to be made. Discouraging as had been Sir John's attempt to settle a second colony, the situation in the Cape Fear colony itself provided even greater cause for concern. Settled in advance of the "Concessions and Agreement," its people were discontented with conditions of settlement which favored the Port Royal project at the expense, they felt, of Clarendon. An Assembly, meeting prior to Governor Yeamans' return to Barbados in January, also protested a plan of survey and allotment which not only ignored titles already located but the lay of the land itself. Much of the surrounding country was swampy and sandy, a fact that had encouraged the people to scatter their settlement along a stretch of the river extending some sixty miles. The colonists declared that provisions calling for proprietary reserves would result in an even more dangerous dispersal. Moreover, other policies announced by the proprietors

[39] Saunders (ed.), *Colonial Records of North Carolina*, I, 118–39; Salley (ed.), *Narratives of Early Carolina*, 77–108.

would enforce payment of the same rent for large acreages of swamp and sand as was imposed on fertile land and would require the maintenance of servants under penalty of forfeiture on lots wholly unequal to meeting the charge.[40] A state of warfare with the local natives of such intensity that Sandford found the news of it far down the coast added to the causes for discontent. Complaints finding their way to Barbados discouraged further support from that quarter. And Yeamans himself, whose sense of responsibility is certainly open to question, became involved in the frequently turbulent politics of the island to the apparent neglect of his interests on the mainland.

The proprietors became sufficiently alarmed to seek a reinforcement of the colony by raising the headrights to one hundred acres and fifty acres and by joining this increase to the promise for settlement before June 24, 1667, of rents no more than half those due in Virginia. But this was not enough, and it came too late. By the fall of 1667 the Cape Fear settlement had been abandoned, its people dispersing some to Albemarle, some to Virginia, some to New England, and others back to Barbados.[41] Of once hopeful projects in southern Carolina nothing survived except an evil report of the Cape Fear, a good report of Port Royal, and land claims against the proprietors destined through later years to bring many Barbadians to South Carolina.

It was time for the proprietors to take stock. An accounting of proprietary expenditures from June, 1663, to April, 1666, shows a total of £600 8s. 3d. charged against a fund of £600 which had been provided by levies amounting to £75 each. No doubt these figures represent very nearly, if not entirely, the sum total of the proprietors' investment. Significantly, the major charges in round figures were £106 for the first patent, £71 for the second, £40 for a great seal, and £284 for the arms and ammunition contributed to the Port Royal venture.[42] Surveyor John Vassall's complaint during the next year that a supply costing no more than £200 would have saved the Cape Fear settlement emphasized the obvious lesson

[40] Saunders (ed.), *Colonial Records of North Carolina*, I, 144–49.

[41] *Ibid.*, 153–55, 157–61; *Virginia Magazine*, XXI (1913), 122.

[42] *Collections of the South Carolina Historical Society*, V (1897), 56–57. This volume is made up largely of "The Shaftesbury Papers and Other Records Relating to Carolina and the First Settlement on Ashley River Prior to the Year 1676."

of a niggardly policy.[43] Unless the proprietors were prepared to assume more of the responsibilities properly belonging to their position, the successful colonization of Carolina was hardly to be expected. In the poor and discontented state of Albemarle, the only surviving settlement, little could be found pointing to another conclusion.

Fortunately, Cooper, now Lord Ashley and in 1672 to be elevated to the earldom of Shaftesbury, provided in this emergency a new and vigorous leadership. The Earl of Clarendon had been forced out of the country as a political exile; Colleton was dead; Sir William Berkeley remained inactive and his brother John indifferent; Albemarle, Carteret, and Craven were old. But Ashley, who was only forty-seven in 1668, found time and energy through the years of his greatest political activity to make one of the most significant contributions to the English settlement of America. In this work he received some aid from John Locke, his physician and consultant on a variety of problems. The turning point came with the spring of 1669, when on April 26 the proprietors reached an agreement that each of them should contribute £500 sterling to a fund for the purchase of shipping, arms, ammunition, tools, and provisions for a settlement to be located at Port Royal. The agreement also provided that in each of the ensuing four years the proprietors severally would pay in an additional sum not to exceed £200. Though only five members of the board were prompt in honoring the obligation, a total of £3,200 16s. 6d. was laid out for the equipment of an expedition that sailed from The Downs late in August.[44]

The distinguishing feature of this new venture was the proprietors' assumption of a direct responsibility for its promotion. Yet, there appears to be little reason for regarding the develop-

---

[43] Saunders (ed.), *Colonial Records of North Carolina*, I, 160.

[44] For the agreement, see *Collections of the South Carolina Historical Society*, V (1897), 91–93. In case of default the other proprietors could acquire title to the defaulting share by payment of such contributions as had been previously made plus 10 per cent interest. The funds were to be deposited with a London goldsmith, and a husband was to be employed for effecting necessary arrangements. An accounting of expenditures on the expedition, *ibid.*, 151–52, shows that Albemarle, Craven, Colleton, Carteret, and Ashley had paid in their shares, and that the first three of these had evidently contributed an additional £145. It was later stated that Sir William Berkeley had never contributed a penny toward the settlement of the province. Saunders (ed.), *Colonial Records of North Carolina*, I, 337–38.

ment as evidence of a radical change in basic policies. Not many more than a hundred prospective colonists sailed from London, and even had plans for procuring additional servants in Ireland been fully successful, the total number would hardly justify an assumption that it was now intended to colonize Carolina chiefly from the British Isles.[45] Nothing in the several instructions given the proprietors' agents indicates such an intention, and the known financial plans for the ensuing four years left little if any room for expensive ventures of that sort. On the other hand, efforts to enlist the aid of seasoned planters from the older colonies continued, as did the practice of relying on these communities as convenient bases of supply. Moreover, land policies shaped by the requirements of earlier projects underwent little essential change. Indeed, the proprietors seem simply to have drawn from experience the rather obvious conclusion that it was incumbent upon them to provide and maintain through the hazardous stages of first settlement the leadership necessary for a clear proof of Carolina's promise. That, at any rate, was what they attempted through plans drafted in 1669.

Three ships purchased at a cost of over £600 were refitted with the evident intent of keeping them in the regular service of the province. Appropriately renamed the *Carolina, Port Royal,* and *Albemarle* and made ready for sailing by August, they carried to America, in addition to passengers, a stock of provisions, seeds, clothing, arms, ammunition, tools, ware, tackle, and trading truck representing an investment of better than £1,500. An additional £270 in goods were forwarded direct to Virginia under a plan to establish a credit in the older colony against which the proprietors' agents at Port Royal could draw for the provision of livestock and other staples.[46] Captain Henry Brayne, who had accompanied Sand-

---

[45] *Collections of the South Carolina Historical Society,* V (1897), 134–36, which gives the total number of passengers aboard the *Carolina* before sailing as ninety-two. The list seems not to have been wholly complete but was undoubtedly nearly so, and, since the other vessels were much smaller, the list must come close to including all the English colonists. Captain Henry Brayne speaks of plans to take on a "great number" of passengers in Ireland, but the hope of getting additional servants there met with serious disappointment. Others joined in Barbados, and a letter of March, 1671, gives the colony's population at about 200. *Ibid.,* 137, 152–55, 156–57, 302.

[46] For an unusually valuable itemized account of expenditures for the expedition, see *ibid.,* 143–52. The *Carolina* had been purchased at a cost of £430, not counting the sums expended for its repair and equipment. Five hundred and forty pounds were

ford to Port Royal in 1666, sailed now as master of the *Carolina* with orders to call first at Barbados. His instructions for the period following the landing at Port Royal necessarily were elastic, but the general nature of his intended employment is clear. Guided by circumstances, he was to go to Virginia for cattle and other cargo to be picked up as directed by William Burgh of the James River; or back to Barbados, taking on timber and such additional freightage as could be had, to load passengers and cargo for a return voyage to Port Royal; or if the proprietors' Barbadian correspondents thought it best, he was to load products of the island for Virginia and return to England by way of the Chesapeake. It is impossible to offer a full chronicle of the *Carolina*'s later services. Let it be noted, though, that a letter of September, 1670, brought word from the colony of the ship's recent return from Virginia with an eight months' supply of provisions, and stated that it had since gone to Barbados for additional colonists. There, on November 4, Captain Brayne proclaimed a purpose to sail for Carolina in thirty days and advertised that subscribers to earlier ventures might now claim land dividends to their definite advantage. He offered both passage and supply to such persons as were unable to meet their own charges, in return for an obligation to repay the proprietors within two years in tobacco, cotton, or ginger.[47]

Instructions to Joseph West, who was in command of the fleet prior to its arrival at Barbados, provide equally interesting testimony to the sort of aid the proprietors now undertook to provide. A commission as governor and commander in chief was forwarded in blank by him to Sir John Yeamans, who was to assume the post himself or to assign it to some other fit person. Having thus surrendered the command, West's first duty became that of securing from Thomas Colleton a supply of cottonseed, indigo seed, ginger roots, sugar cane, vines, and olive sets, a supply that was to be supplemented in case the ships called also at Bermuda. On arrival at Port Royal he was to select a site, with an eye to the variety of its

---

sent in provisions, £212 in clothing, £397 in arms and ammunition, £188 in tools and ironware, and £50 in trading goods.

[47] *Ibid.*, 129–30, 163, 178–81, 210–13. Brayne seems to have taken the opportunity while in Virginia to increase his own stock, and to secure the services of an experienced overseer. *Ibid.*, 214–17.

soil, for an experimental farm. Thirty servants to be procured on the proprietors' account in Ireland on the way out were assigned to him. With them he was to clear the ground, erect necessary housing, and make experimental plantings in March, April, May, and June on several varieties of soil, not neglecting to try both low and high ground. Except for the time and ground devoted to food crops, his efforts were to be for the moment wholly experimental and according to instructions which read: "you are never to thinke of makeing any Comodity your buisiness further than for experience sake & to have your stock of it for planting encrease till you have sufficiently provided for ye belly by planting store of provisions which must in all contrivances be looked upon by you as ye foundation of your Plantacon." The farm was to be laid out in accordance with the proprietors' headright claims for thirty servants, and having served its experimental purposes it would be divided.[48] One is reminded of a similar function of the public estate in the early days of Virginia and of Bermuda.

Hardly less interesting are separate instructions carried by West as storekeeper for the proprietors.[49] Immediately upon arrival at Port Royal, he was to erect a storehouse within the fort for the supplies sent from England. His responsibility included charge of the trading truck shipped for purchase of provisions from the Indians as the occasion required. Also, he was to pay out to the settlers both supplies and provisions on order from the governor and council in return for a written obligation to pay back to the proprietors at 10 per cent interest for the duration of the account. Payment was to be received in ginger, silk, cotton, olive oil, indigo, and other such marketable commodities at the English rather than the American price. The difference is important, for as Shaftesbury later explained "we ayme nott at the profit of merchants but the incouragement of landlords." [50] Thus, he embodied in a single sentence the sum total of the proprietors' purpose in 1669. It is true that they demanded 10 per cent on advances made to the settlers, required of Brayne a regular accounting of freightage earned, and

---

[48] *Ibid.*, 123-27. He was to secure twenty to twenty-five servants in Kinsale and six young sows and a boar in Barbados. The cattle from Virginia were also to be entrusted to his care.

[49] *Ibid.*, 127-29.   [50] Quoted in Brown, *First Earl of Shaftesbury*, 171.

proved thereafter nowise indifferent to opportunities for commercial exploitation. But the real return on the investment now made was expected in that later day when the lords proprietors of Carolina might relax in the enjoyment of well-earned rents.

The proprietors continued to rely on the headright as the chief of their promotional devices, a fact that has been somewhat obscured by the historian's concern with the elaborate provisions of the Fundamental Constitutions of Carolina. That famous document, dated in March of 1669 and apparently drafted by Shaftesbury with some help from Locke, contains no mention of headrights. Nevertheless, its intricacies are perhaps best approached by way of the headrights and plan of survey specified in other instructions forwarded by West.[51] Headrights began at 150 acres for all free persons above sixteen and for all menservants, and 100 acres for women servants and boys under sixteen, who entered the colony prior to March 25, 1670. The acreage due thereafter was graduated downward until it stood at 70 and 60 acres, respectively, for those settling between March, 1671, and March, 1672.[52] Instructions for the surveyor reveal plans for an orderly, even symmetrical, plan of settlement. The land was to be laid out in squares of 12,000 acres each, forty such squares to constitute a county. Eight squares in each county would be reserved as seigniories for the eight proprietors, and another eight squares, making in all two fifths of the total, were to be held as baronies for a hereditary nobility to be established. The remaining twenty-four squares, officially designated as colonies and to be divided for administrative purposes into four equal precincts, would be occupied by persons holding headright claims against the proprietors. The land would be granted in free and common socage at a penny per acre rent, its payment due annually after 1689. As settlement advanced, each new county was to be laid out according to the same pattern. Thus would a constant

[51] The Constitutions may be conveniently consulted in Saunders (ed.), *Colonial Records of North Carolina*, I, 187–205; for the instructions, see *Collections of the South Carolina Historical Society*, V (1897), 119–23.

[52] Servants at the expiration of their time would receive one hundred acres. Those persons settled between March, 1670, and March, 1671, were entitled to claims in the amounts of one hundred and of seventy acres severally, with seventy acres constituting the later right of the time-expired servant. The headrights for Negroes were now the same as for white servants. See *Collections of the South Carolina Historical Society*, V (1897), 164.

balance be maintained, with three fifths of the land held by free-holders and two fifths by the proprietors and the colony's own hereditary nobility.

The ideas which had shaped this pattern of settlement found clear expression in the preamble of the Fundamental Constitutions. The stated purpose of that historic document was to establish "the interest of the Lords Proprietors with equality," to provide a government "agreeable to the Monarchy under which we live," and to avoid the dangers of "a numerous democracy"—objectives that immediately suggest the probable influence of the currently popular political philosophy of James Harrington. "A nobility of gentry overbalancing a popular Government is the utter bane and destruction of it," wrote Harrington, "as a nobility or gentry in a popular Government not overbalancing it, is the very life and soul of it." [53] Such was the ideal inspiring the attempt to guarantee in Carolina an economic and political balance between the aristocracy and the democracy.

The charter having authorized the establishment of titles of nobility, that right was now exercised for the first time in the creation of two hereditary ranks. In each county four of the baronies, which is to say 48,000 acres, would be held by a landgrave, the title being borrowed possibly from the usages of northern England. The remaining four squares reserved for the nobility would be shared equally by two caciques, whose liabilities included a title taken from the Spanish designation for an Indian chieftain—a title sometimes spelled "Cassock," for the benefit of those who wonder how the English pronounced it. Manors and manor lords might also be patented with a grant of not less than 3,000 acres and, since the manor must lie wholly within one "colony," not more than 12,000. These patents would confer customary and hereditary rights of manorial jurisdiction, but other prerogatives of the manor lord were by comparison with the landgrave or cacique much less extensive.

Outranking all other noblemen, of course, were the lords proprietors, the eldest of whom became the lord palatine of Carolina. Carrying still further an analogy with the ancient palatinate jurisdiction of the Bishops of Durham, the Constitutions made of the

[53] Quoted in Andrews, *Colonial Period of American History,* III, 213 n.

eight proprietors a palatine court, the highest governmental authority to which the settlers were directly subject. The document had been drafted on the assumption that the proprietors might with time take up residence in the province, and in such an event the oldest resident proprietor automatically became governor. When not in residence, the proprietors' interests, including the development of their seigniories, were to be in the hands of appointed deputies. The governor had to be at least a landgrave. The Assembly, comprised of the governor, proprietors or their deputies, the landgraves, the caciques, and a freeholder from each precinct, would sit as one body. Possession of a fifty-acre freehold was necessary to the exercise of the franchise, and title to five hundred acres for election to the Assembly. A requirement that the whole of this five hundred acres lie within the precinct from which the assemblyman was elected marked another step in confirming the already well-established American custom that parliamentary delegates should have residence in the constituencies they represented. Statutes were made subject to the allowance of the palatine court, and an elaborate scheme for a grand council, borrowed again from Harrington, imposed a check on the Assembly's right of initiation. At this time, as in later years, America frequently invited a test of some of the more advanced theories of the day. And more often than not they proved, as did the grand council of Carolina, to be among the most unworkable schemes proposed.

It would be a serious mistake, however, to assume that the Fundamental Constitutions contained nothing more than impractical theories and archaic survivals of the feudal age. Like other plans of settlement drafted by English promoters of colonization, it subsequently proved unacceptable to the colonists and indeed unsuited to the conditions of their life. But given the objectives of the proprietors, it is possible to reconcile the general features of the plan with the apparently unassailable fact that they reflect chiefly the ideas of one of the most practical and hardheaded political leaders of seventeenth-century England. The elaborate political and social structure outlined by the proprietors, however absolute may have been the terminology of the document itself, clearly was intended to serve as an ultimate rather than an immediate objective. According to instructions, it was to be followed for the time being only insofar as found applicable to existing circumstances.[54] The effort to transplant into America the feudal usages of England's rural society may seem foolish in the light of previous and subsequent experience. Yet, it should be recognized that the proprietors naturally saw a worthy model in a familiar social and political order which offered substantial testimony to the advantages in that age of some sort of balance between an aristocracy and the more popular forces of "democracy." Let it be noted, too, that the effort did not prove a complete failure; though landgraves and caciques in Carolina showed an early disposition to drop the title in recognition of its inappropriateness, many of the conventions of a landed aristocracy took root. And if it be said that the aristocracy of later Carolina was distinctively American, its place won by enterprise and merit with the aid of favorable land policies, it must also be admitted that the aristocracy envisioned in the proprietors' plan was essentially the same. Stripped of feudal verbiage, their plan to award large acreages with contingent responsibilities and prerogatives to selected individuals becomes a very practical promotional device. It was one way, and one very familiar in American history, of using the land to subsidize the development of a new country by encouraging men of means or enterprise or of both to invest their time and funds as subsidiary promoters. In this connection it may be well to recall Thomas Woodward's earlier insistence on the urgent need for "rich men" in Albemarle.[55]

The Constitutions, moreover, contain much evidence of a practical knowledge of America and its special problems. Serious as was the talk of using leetmen for the occupation of seigniories, baronies, and manors, the document imposed no barrier to the introduction of Negro slave labor. On the contrary, it was invited. Not only did the headright system offer inducements for the importation of slaves, but articles 107 and 110 defined the master's

---

[54] *Collections of the South Carolina Historical Society,* V (1897), 119. See also, instructions to the governor and council of Albemarle, in Saunders (ed.), *Colonial Records of North Carolina,* I, 181–83. The stated purpose "to come as nigh it as we cann in the present state of affairs," however, was to prove a troublesome stipulation. Uncertainties as to the exact extent of its application inevitably followed. For an able and significant defense of this much derided document, see Brown, *First Earl of Shaftesbury,* 155–61.

[55] See above, p. 327.

authority in absolute terms and removed all doubt as to a possible effect on the Negro's status of his conversion to the Christian religion, a troublesome question in some of the colonies even a generation later. Another provision repeated an earlier requirement for the registration of all land conveyances. The aid thus expected in keeping tab on proprietary rents is not to be overlooked, but neither is the fact of a growing American usage. A prohibition of professional lawyers not only restated an ideal repeatedly associated with man's dreams of a utopian society, but a purpose already recorded in more than one vigorously worded American statute. The proprietors were alert to the importance of towns and to the advantages of New England's form of settlement over that of the Chesapeake colonies.[56] A full and explicit reaffirmation of the established policy of religious freedom—a policy embracing the Jew and offering concessions to the special sensibilities of the Quaker, providing no religious establishment but demanding of the people identification with some organized faith, forbidding the use of reproachful or abusive language regarding another's religion and seeking to encourage an orderly worship of Almighty God— speaks not only of sound principle but of an intelligent assessment of a business opportunity. It is perhaps necessary only to add that aliens might be naturalized through the simple act of swearing an oath of allegiance to the King and of good faith to the proprietors.

The further plans of the proprietors in 1669 offer ample testimony of a continuing purpose to rely chiefly upon experienced men in the actual work of settlement. Whether because of some feeling of a prior commitment to Yeamans or because of a conviction that the planters of Barbados would enlist more readily under the leadership of one of their own number, Sir John was requested

[56] Brown, *First Earl of Shaftesbury*, 163. The first task of the Port Royal expedition, according to instructions of July 27, was the location of a fort and town. If located on an island, the whole of the island was to be laid out as "colonies," and if on the mainland, the next six adjoining squares were to be "colonies" so that no seigniories and baronies could interfere with compact settlement of the community about the town. The Constitutions provided for port towns, guaranteed them special privileges of the market, stipulated that the first such town on every river should be located in a "colony," and promised incorporation with government by a mayor, aldermen, and common council. It was the hope that in each "colony" the people would draw together in a town.

either to assume the governor's post himself or to fill in the name of some fit person of his selection.[57] The ships under West's command reached Barbados in October, and from there early in November he wrote Ashley of the hope of providing a total complement of two hundred settlers for Carolina by recruitment among the local planters.[58]

That fall in the Caribbean proved to be one of storms and generally unfavorable weather. A gale which wrecked the *Albemarle* at Barbados delayed the departure for Port Royal, and when the expedition got under way again, the *Albemarle* having been replaced by a Barbadian shallop, additional misfortunes overtook it. Separated from the rest of the fleet, the *Port Royal* in January suffered shipwreck in the Bahamas. The *Carolina* and the Barbadian shallop found their way to Bermuda, where some refitting was required and where, it would seem almost incidentally, the colonists picked up a governor. Yeamans had sailed with them from Barbados, but in Bermuda he seems to have grown impatient with the delay. Desirous of making a prompt return home, he filled in the governor's commission with the name of William Sayle. By Yeamans' own admission, Sayle was "a man of no great sufficiency yet the ablest I could meet with." [59] An old Puritan now approaching the age of eighty, Sayle had known the years of his greatest activity in the mid-century. He had been identified during the English Civil War with the Puritan settlement at Eleuthera in the Bahamas, islands to which the Carolina proprietors in 1670 acquired title, and he had served as governor of Bermuda prior to his resignation

[57] *Collections of the South Carolina Historical Society,* V (1897), 117–19. Dated July 26, 1669, the commission covered the region west and south of Cape Carteret (Romain).

[58] *Ibid.,* 156–57.

[59] Quoted by Edward McCrady, *The History of South Carolina under the Proprietary Government, 1670–1719* (New York, 1897), 124, a work which continues to serve as a principal reliance of all students of early Carolina history. For a more recent and comprehensive survey, see David D. Wallace, *The History of South Carolina* (New York, 1934). It is hardly necessary to add that all students find themselves heavily and repeatedly indebted to Alexander S. Salley, Jr., of the Historical Commission of South Carolina, and especially for his efforts to provide publication for the more basic records of the province and the state. In connection with the immediate subject, see Salley (ed.), *Narratives of Early Carolina,* 111–24.

in 1662.[60] After little more than a year of service as a pioneer governor in Carolina, he died there in the spring of 1671.

Governor Sayle and his new charges had left Bermuda in February of the preceding year. The weather continued unfavorable but the *Carolina* reached the Port Royal region toward the close of March. Driven south of its course, the Barbadian shallop did not come in until the latter part of May and even then there were missing a few of its passengers who had fallen into the hands of the Spaniards on St. Catherine's Island, northernmost of the Spanish outposts based on Florida. Meanwhile, a decision had been made to abandon the Port Royal area for another site of settlement. Perhaps it was some recollection of Ribaut's early and unsuccessful challenge to Spanish monopoly in that very area which served to remind the colonists that the place lay "in the very chops of the Spaniards." [61] Perhaps of greater influence were the urgent entreaties and invitations of the friendly Kiawahs, who sought an ally against the warlike Westos on the Savannah River, to occupy a part of their own country lying north of Port Royal. It may be well not to overlook the all too familiar inclination of experienced colonists to substitute their own judgment for instructions from England. Whatever the case, Governor Sayle and his advisers, after some preliminary exploration, agreed upon a site which they called Albemarle Point, located some twenty-five miles inland on the western bank of the Kiawah or Ashley River.

In recording the early history of the settlement undertaken there, even in the briefest way, one is repeatedly tempted to pick up some of the more colorful threads woven into the pattern of Carolina's later history, for they were all there from the first. The unintended visit of the Barbadian shallop to Santa Catalina de Guale, the resultant imprisonment of several of the Carolinians at St. Augustine, and the dispatch from that now venerable fortification in late summer of an abortive expedition by sea for expulsion of the new intruders foretold the unfolding of yet another chronicle

[60] On William Sayle, see Wilkinson, *Adventurers of Bermuda, passim;* and on the circumstances attending the acquisition of the Bahamas, Brown, *First Earl of Shaftesbury,* 166.

[61] Andrews, *Colonial Period of American History,* III, 201.

of imperial rivalry, one that in time would take a place of first significance in the greatest struggle of all for the possession of North America. Reports brought by friendly natives of the hostile movement of "Spanish" Indians in the south, together with the first accounts of advantageous trades with local tribesmen for deerskins, at once recall the story of a rich and colorful trade destined to become a principal bone of contention between England and France. Similarly, the first election in South Carolina—an election held at Port Royal in accordance with instructions for the freemen to choose five of their number to sit as councilors with those men who had been designated for the purpose by the proprietors, an election promptly challenged on legal grounds and consequently rerun but with no change in results—tempts the historian to launch into an immediate discussion of a complex political history that would find its focus in resistance to proprietary control until the expulsion of that authority had been achieved through the revolution of 1719. But to yield to these temptations would be to run ahead of the story and thus to neglect subjects of greater importance at this initial stage of the colony's development.

If it is permissible to paraphrase a later American reported to have said that the business of America is business, it may be worth observing that the business of the first generation of colonists in any part of America was colonization. To that observation South Carolina provides no exception. When its early history is properly viewed, the cardinal fact becomes neither the inadequacies of the Fundamental Constitutions nor the way in which the stage was set for an eighteenth-century conflict with France, but rather the successful administration of a shrewdly conceived land policy. Feudal terminology and feudal concepts of social and political organization notwithstanding, the hard reality underlying the proprietors' land policy was the now tried and proved headright system. This it was that brought men in increasing numbers from Barbados, Bermuda, England, New York, Ireland, and France, each to pick for himself a part of the land and by the simple procedures established to secure a title to it, to clear the land, and then to plant it. In this effort lies the central theme of Carolina's history through its first years.

For a while progress necessarily was slow. At Albemarle Point the colonists undertook to fortify a position of natural strength and to build a town which, in honor of the King, they named Charles Town. The alarms raised by the Spanish expedition of late summer held the people close to their defenses, "more like souldiers in a garrison than planters," [62] and interfered with the accomplishment of initial objectives which West described for Sir George Carteret in the following spring as "being . . . in the first place to provide for the Belly and to make some Experiment of what the land will best produce." [63] For provisions during the first winter the colony depended chiefly upon an eight months' supply of Indian corn, peas, and meal brought in by the *Carolina* from Virginia near the end of the summer. With this food came also a stock of cattle and hogs, but at a price which led Thomas Colleton to advise Sir Peter that New York offered a more advantageous source of supply.[64] Relieved thus of the fear of want, the colonists bent their energies to clearing and building. As early as September, 1670, Stephen Bull reported to Ashley that a semicircle about the town had been marked out for grants of ten acres per head "for present planting." [65] Such grants were obviously intended chiefly for subsistence farming, but already men were testing a variety of seeds and plants brought for the purpose—oranges, lemons, limes, pomegranates, figs, plantains, wheat, potatoes, tobacco, cotton, flax, and others. It had been planned to try ginger, but the roots intended for that test had been lost with the ill-fated *Port Royal*.[66] The Barbadians, whose experience lent special weight to their opinions, were reported as regarding the soil and climate especially promising for the production of sugar, wine, silk, tobacco, and cotton.[67]

The return of the *Carolina* from Barbados in February with sixty-four new settlers brought substantial proof of a growing interest in the new project among the Barbadian planters. During the same month another forty-two came in on a vessel provided for

[62] *Collections of the South Carolina Historical Society,* V (1897), 184.   [63] *Ibid.*, 269.

[64] *Ibid.*, 174, 179, 241–42. Colleton advised that the *Carolina* carry sugar, molasses, and rum from Barbados to New York, cattle from New York to the Ashley, and from there a cargo of lumber back to Barbados. Thus would the lumber make payment for the cattle.

[65] *Ibid.*, 193.   [66] *Ibid.*, 174, 175, 188, 193, 269, 270.   [67] *Ibid.*, 175, 266–68.

the voyage largely through the efforts of Thomas Colleton.[68] A report in the following March indicated a total population of about two hundred persons, of whom some forty to fifty were freeholders.[69] The people still lived in a relatively compact community immediately surrounding Albemarle Point, and were still subject to the limitations of life in a garrison. But West reported to Sir George Carteret that in addition to having cleared about thirty acres, which he intended to use immediately for food crops and experimental planting, he had "taken up" three hundred acres of land near the town on the joint account of Carteret, Ashley, and Colleton.[70] Through a letter of William Owen's, we gain a glimpse of the hopes with which others looked about for favorably situated land that year. "If I had 10000 £ per. annum in England," he wrote, "yet would I have an Interest here and if Ginger continues a price no doubt not of more then an ordinarie Liveing." [71]

Unfortunately, the year proved a dry one in Carolina, and comments on experimental plantings began to be marked by certain reservations. There was discouragement over the prospects for sugar cane and cotton, but hopes survived for indigo, ginger, wine, silk, oil, hemp, flax, and tobacco "as good as ever smoked." [72] The records suggest that from an early date men displayed an understandable inclination to seek out and mark for their own particular use favorably situated lands lying beyond the immediate environs of the town. An indication of the main lines of exploration followed in this quest, as well as the advent of another stage in the colony's development, is found in the council's appointment of a special commission in October, 1671, charged with "convenient speed" to view all those places on the Ashley and Wando (Cooper) rivers which might be "most convenient to situate Towns upon soe

[68] McCrady, *South Carolina under the Proprietary Government,* 143; Wallace, *History of South Carolina,* I, 79.

[69] *Collections of the South Carolina Historical Society,* V (1897), 302.

[70] *Ibid.,* 269. This letter indicates that only these three of the proprietors originally participated in the financing of Joseph West's special mission of planting, but a letter of Ashley's written in April informed West that the plantation thereafter should be considered as on the account of all the proprietors. *Ibid.,* 317.

[71] *Ibid.,* 305.

[72] *Ibid.,* 333–34, 376–83. A ship sent by the proprietors in the spring of 1671 carried instructions for the procurement of mulberries and silkworms from Virginia. *Ibid.,* 321.

the same may be wholy reserved for these and the like uses." [73] The council gave anticipated further additions to the population as the chief reason for the action taken. New arrivals from England and New York during that summer and fall contributed to the colony's growth. On January 20, 1671/72, an official report to Ashley declared "that 337 men and women 62 children or persons under 16 years of age is the full number of persons who have arrived *in*, and *since* the first fleet out of England to this day, whereof 43 men 2 women 3 children are dead, and 16 absent so as there now remains 263 men able to bear arms 69 women, 59 children or persons under 16 years of age." [74]

For the accommodation of new settlers the council had taken steps during the preceding September to locate below Charles Town a second town in the neighborhood of Stono Creek, and in December a thirty-acre plot "in a Creeke Southward from Stonoe Creeke" was ordered laid out and given the name of James Town. [75] Oyster Point at the juncture of the Ashley and the Cooper, where the later city of Charleston would rise, had been selected as still another townsite as early as February, 1672. [76] Additional evidence of an attempt to follow the proprietary instructions emphasizing the desirability of settlement in towns is found in the council's decision of the following April to lay out three colonies of 12,000 acres each, one for Charles Town, another for James Town, and a third at Oyster Point. [77] The actual warrant to the surveyor for laying out this third colony has survived. The warrant was dated April 30 and directed him to survey 12,000 acres of the land beginning at Oyster Point and lying between the Ashley and

---

[73] Alexander S. Salley, Jr. (ed.), *Journal of the Grand Council of South Carolina, August 25, 1671–June 24, 1680* (Columbia, 1907), 10. This action was followed in January, 1672, by appointment of another commission to view the Wando and its several creeks for the purpose of marking "such place or places as they shall thinke most convenient for the situacon of a Towne or Townes," and by a strict prohibition "that noe Person or Persons upon any pretence whatsoever doe hereafter run out or marke any lands in Wandoe River" until the report had been returned. *Ibid.*, 24.

[74] Quoted in McCrady, *South Carolina under the Proprietary Government*, 144.

[75] Salley (ed.), *Journal of the Grand Council of South Carolina*, 5–6, 19–21.

[76] *Ibid.*, 29. A warrant for survey of the townsite was issued on July 27 following. Alexander S. Salley, Jr. (ed.), *Warrants for Lands in South Carolina, 1672–1679* (Columbia, 1910), 22.

[77] Salley (ed.), *Journal of the Grand Council of South Carolina*, 31.

the Wando "in a square as much as Navigable Rivers will per-
mitt." [78] Surviving, too, are subsequently issued warrants for the
survey of individual grants which show some care to protect such
townsites as had been set aside and a concern for deduction from
the total acreage to be surveyed of such town lots as may have
been received by the grantee. According to the usual phrasing, the
land would be situated for the grantee "in such place as you [i.e.,
the surveyor] shall be directed by him or his Attorney soe as the
same be not within the compass of any lands heretofore layd out
or marked to be layd out for any other person or Towne." [79] But
somehow the modern student tends to linger over the evidence thus
provided of a reasonably free choice of site enjoyed by the grantee,
for that kind of freedom runs counter to the procedures of planned
settlement.[80]

For evidence of the increasing prevalence of a free choice, which
with a growing disregard of the proprietors' orderly plan of settlement followed the natural highways provided by the Ashley and
Cooper rivers, one has only to look further into the land warrants.[81]
At first glance this fundamental source appears monotonously un-
interesting for all save the genealogist, but when conscience prompts
a second examination, the men and women whose names are
recorded there begin once again to take on life as one follows them
in their quest of favorably situated land. The governing consideration in their minds, as it had been with men pursuing a similar
quest in Virginia and Maryland, was ready access to those waterways upon which the community chiefly depended for transportation. Each warrant stipulated for the surveyor's instruction that if

[78] Salley (ed.), *Warrants for Lands in South Carolina, 1672–1679,* p. 3.

[79] For example, *ibid.,* 8.

[80] Notice, for instance, the purpose in settling James Town first to lay out uniform
plots of a half acre each and then to have the people draw lots for them. Salley (ed.),
Journal of the Grand Council of South Carolina, 21.

[81] See, in addition to the volume previously cited, Alexander S. Salley, Jr. (ed.), *Warrants for Lands in South Carolina, 1680–1692* (Columbia, 1911); and notice the statement of the council in May, 1672, that "divers persons have taken up severall quantities of land in this Province which said lands have not yett been surveyed or bounded
as they ought to be thereby impedeing the propagacon of a regular settlement," with
the accompanying order that all should secure a survey within three months on
penalty of having all unsurveyed land thrown open to any who would secure a proper
warrant. Salley (ed.), *Journal of the Grand Council of South Carolina,* 32.

the grantee's choice of land lay "upon any navigable River or any River capable of being made navigable you are to allow only the fifth part of the depth thereof by the water side." Indeed, it might almost be said that the first settlers divided among themselves not so much the land as they did the land's water frontage.

Of the proprietors' elaborate scheme of settlement one gains an occasional glimpse, as in the warrant for laying out a seigniory of 12,000 acres for Shaftesbury in 1675 and another for Sir Peter Colleton in 1678.[82] Here and there a landgrave or cacique makes his appearance.[83] Expansive grants made in the spirit of the Fundamental Constitutions, for the most part prior to 1700, would carry over into the eighteenth century land titles held chiefly for speculative purposes which contributed to one of the most sordid chapters in the history of American land speculation.[84] But one gains an impression from the warrants that at least through the first decade of settlement grants were made largely in return for services rendered, albeit in accordance with a purposely liberal land policy.[85]

The main burden of the story told by the warrants is of grants received in payment of headright claims under the several conditions laid down by the proprietors. Thus to Henry Wood on June 29, 1672, goes 200 acres of land "for himselfe and Alice his wife arriveing in the first ffleet"; on May 21 to Henry Jones, "arriveing a servant in the first ffleet," 100 acres; to Thomas Clutterbrooke of Barbados on June 23 a grant of 670 acres "for his disbursements on the discovery of this province by Capt. Hilton" and for two servants, Robert and Mary Thomas, who had arrived in February, 1671. Joseph Dalton in July received 1,150 acres for George Prideaux, Thomas Young, William Chambers, John Dawson, William

82 Salley (ed.), *Warrants for Lands in South Carolina, 1672–1679*, pp. 103, 155.

83 *Ibid.*, 150, 170, 203; Salley (ed.), *Warrants for Lands in South Carolina, 1680–1692*, pp. 3, 34, 105, 106, 116, 144, 157, 196.

84 Wertenbaker, *Old South*, 339 ff.

85 Even in the very considerable grants made to members of the Colleton family, the claims of that family on the province were substantial. An early development of policy was the granting of land in advance of the establishment of headright claims but on the understanding that the required number of persons subsequently would be transported. Notice, too, the warrant for two thousand acres issued on January 3, 1677/78, in accordance with instructions from Shaftesbury to the benefit of Dr. Henry Woodward, Indian agent and explorer.

Rhodes, William Burges, and Jane Lawson, all of them brought in as servants with the first fleet; for the same number of servants arriving in February and June of 1671, Major Thomas Gray received on August 24, 1672, the lesser figure of 700 acres. A warrant in November of that year issued in behalf of the executors of the late Governor William Sayle allowed 1,300 acres for the governor himself, Captain Nathaniel Sayle, Mrs. Mary Gand, Charles Rilley, George Roberts, "John Senr. a Negroe Elizabeth a Negro and John Junr. a Negroe arriveing in September 1670." Record of the early arrival in the colony of other Negroes is provided in the warrant of September 5, 1674, issued in the right of Simon Berringer for 3,000 acres "for himselfe and soe many Servants and Negroes arriveing in the yeare 1671 & 1672." Notice should also be taken of a warrant of the same date which allowed Lady Margaret Yeamans, widow to the late deceased Sir John, a grant of 1,070 acres. Of this grant 880 acres were "for her self and eight of her own proper Negroes namely Hannah, Jone, Jupiter, Rentee, Gilbert, Resom, Jossee & Simon, and one man servant John: Hopkins arriveing in August 1672, and ffebruary 1674." The remaining 190 acres were granted on the understanding that she would transport "soe many persons more to settle the same as shall be sufficient for that Appropriation." [86]

That the proprietors enjoyed some success in their effort to enlist the aid of persons capable of making substantial investments of capital and labor in the development of the province is amply attested by these and other warrants.[87] But not to be overlooked in considering the contributions made to Carolina's growth are such grants as that of 180 acres on October 14, 1682, to William Driver "for himselfe, wife, & two Children arriveing in October 1682," or the laying out in October, 1680, of a town lot in Charles Town for John Cottingham, "one of the free persons of this province" who in April, 1681, received a grant "of one hundred acres of land not yett layd out or marked to be layd out for any other

[86] Salley (ed.), *Warrants for Lands in South Carolina, 1672–1679*, in order, 17, 14, 15, 24, 28, 52–53, 84, 82, 112; and for those cited later in this paragraph, *ibid.*, 114; and Salley (ed.), *Warrants for Lands in South Carolina, 1680–1692*, pp. 70, 14, 40.

[87] Ashley had expressed this attitude in a statement of 1671 that he was "not very fond of more Company unlesse they be substantiall men." Brown, *First Earl of Shaftesbury*, 164.

Person or use." Nor can we slight the "seaventy acres of land" brought, among other attractions no doubt, to Evan Jones by his marriage with "Jone his wife," who, according to a warrant of June 17, 1676, had reached Carolina "a servant in March 1672."

In the end there remained of the original plan for a town type of settlement only Charles Town and its unique position in the life of the province. The custom among the great planters of the eighteenth century of keeping a town house in Charles Town in addition to the fine dwellings on their outlying plantations carried over into the years of the colony's maturity a faint trace of the founders' intention that a man's property in Carolina should be divided between a town lot and the acreage he cultivated outside the town. It is not too much perhaps to suggest that the earlier plan helped to shape the peculiar features of South Carolina's social and political life resulting from that custom. But in the very movement of population which after 1680 so quickly built up Charles Town one finds chiefly an adjustment, with the abandonment of other townsites, to a basic geographical consideration. The settlers, in their quest of favorably situated land, had followed the waterways of the Ashley and the Cooper. The confluence of those two rivers at Oyster Point in a good harbor readily accessible from the sea lanes leading in from England, the Antilles, Bermuda, Virginia, New York, and New England made that site the logical choice for the colony's first city.

The site itself had been chosen for a town as early as 1672. Warrants for town lots there date from the spring of 1677, and by June, 1680, the name "Charles Town" had been transferred across the Ashley to take the place of "Oyster Point." For a short time yet men felt an occasional need to specify "New Charles towne," but the old town already had become "Kaiawah sometimes called Charles towne," and soon was "Kaiawah formerlie called Charles towne" or simply Kiawah.[88]

In laying out the new city, the colonists held not only to the proprietors' choice of a name, which incidentally would not become Charleston until 1783, but also to the symmetrical pattern

---

[88] Salley (ed.), *Warrants for Lands in South Carolina, 1680–1692*, pp. 19, 20, 38; Salley (ed.), *Journal of the Grand Council of South Carolina*, 84.

decreed by the proprietors for the survey of a town.[89] The cities of western Europe, growing with little or no planning out of the conditions of medieval life, were marked by their narrow, winding, and often almost twisted streets. The same tendency toward disorderly growth was noticeable in the older American settlements at Boston and New York. But whether because of the influence of London's great fire of 1666, which turned the thoughts of some men to the advantages of a more orderly arrangement, or because the vast expanse of undivided land in America naturally encouraged reliance on the straight line of the surveyor and an expansive mood in the act of division, or because men already felt moved to express that love of form and order which so characterized the eighteenth-century European, or because of some combination of these and other influences, the later colonial towns bore the distinctive mark of the American city with streets that are straight and broad and which usually turn at a right angle, as in Charleston, Philadelphia, Williamsburg, and Savannah. And of these, the oldest is Charleston.[90]

The town itself, indeed the whole province, was as yet a small thing. A contemporary estimate gives the population at the opening of the colony's second decade as 1,000 to 1,200 souls,[91] and though the years immediately following seem to have been years of substantial growth, southern Carolina would acquire the weight of numbers only with the eighteenth century. Consequently, one finds no special· cause for comment on the institutional structure of the colony during the period falling within the limits of this volume.

[89] For Ashley's even more ambitious ideas, see Brown, *First Earl of Shaftesbury*, 164.

[90] Of Charles Town, Ashe wrote in a promotional pamphlet in 1682: "It's very commodiously scituated from many other Navigable Rivers that lie near it on which the Planters are seated; by the Advantage of Creeks, which have a Communication from one great River to another, at the Tide or Ebb the Planters may bring their Commodities to the Town as to the Common Market and Magazine both for Trading and Shipping. The town is regularly laid out into large and capacious Streets, which to Buildings is a great Ornament and Beauty. In it they have reserved convenient places for Building of a Church, Town-House and other Publick Structures, an Artillery Ground for the Exercise of their Militia, and Wharfs for the Convenience of their Trade and Shipping." Salley (ed.), *Narratives of Early Carolina*, 157–58.

[91] *Ibid.*, 158.

Through the first years in all colonies men had little occasion to draw a distinction between provincial and local areas of government. Control at first was centralized, and only gradually did the need appear for some parceling out of the right to govern among lesser and geographically distributed agencies. Thus it had been in Virginia and in Maryland, and now in Carolina government had its beginning in the control exercised by a governor and a council which, for all practical purposes, was distinguished only by the presence in the council of specially elected representatives of the freemen. An even fuller recognition of the principle of representation had been provided in the Fundamental Constitutions, and though the clumsy question of the rate at which its elaborate scheme should be effected apparently postponed the calling of an assembly beyond the time considered desirable by some of the planters, a local parliament met as early as July, 1670. There soon developed a contest for the right to initiate legislation by the more representative element of the Assembly, a controversy given certain special turns by James Harrington's notions regarding the function of a Grand Council. Other complications in the early political scene arose from the presence of men who had been designated proprietary deputies, landgraves, and caciques. But their numbers were few and the designations seem to have served principally to mask the normal struggle for place and influence on public policy and occasionally to give an advantage in that struggle. Of greater importance, or so it would seem in a general survey of the sort attempted in this volume, is the fact that the governor in Carolina did not enjoy absolute powers, that like the governor of Virginia he tended as one of the larger landholders to be identified with the interest of the community itself, and that he found his office dependent upon some working alliance with the leading planters.[92]

Adjustments of the machinery of government to a growing dispersal of settlement came as early as 1673. They consisted of provision to eliminate expensive jury proceedings through agreement

[92] In addition to the detailed discussion of the early years in McCrady, *South Carolina under the Proprietary Government,* reference may be made to Herbert L. Osgood, *The American Colonies in the Seventeenth Century* (New York, 1904–1907), II, 211 ff.

of the parties to civil actions before the council, and "for ye speedy & more easy administracon of justice" through authorization to any two members of the council, one being a proprietary deputy, to call to their aid two or more freeholders to hear "small misdemeanors." [93] But the legal establishment in 1682 of three counties—Berkeley to include Charles Town, Colleton lying south of it, and Craven to the north—was not followed by development of the usual machinery of county administration. This failure is chiefly significant for the promise it gave of a continued concentration of governmental agencies in Charles Town that would long restrict the normal development of local self-government both in and outside that city.

Of the more recent immigrants into the colony, forty-five Huguenots reaching Charles Town in 1680 on His Majesty's ship *Richmond* are especially interesting. Not only were they forerunners of other French Protestants destined to contribute significantly to the life and the tradition of the province, but they came with a special commission to introduce the production of silk and wine.[94] The silkworms, unhappily, hatched aboard ship and died before they reached Carolina, and wine would remain among the perennial hopes of the English colonizers of America. Though abortive, the project serves again to remind us of a continuing interest in agricultural experimentation that was heavily relied upon in current efforts to promote emigration to the colony.[95] Of the many commodities already tried in the colonists' search for staple crops, the easiest success apparently had come with tobacco, but "the great Quantities which Virginia, and other of His Majesties Plantations make, rendring it a Drug over all Europe" lent little encouragement to its production.[96] Discouragement with cotton, in later years to shape so much of Carolina's history, had come early. Optimism regarding indigo, another great staple later perfected, per-

[93] Salley (ed.), *Journal of the Grand Council of South Carolina*, 58, 67.

[94] Salley (ed.), *Narratives of Early Carolina*, 143. These French immigrants, however, were apparently not the first Huguenots to reach the province. See McCrady, *South Carolina under the Proprietary Government*, 180–81.

[95] See Ashe, *Carolina*, in Salley (ed.), *Narratives of Early Carolina*, 138–59; Samuel Wilson, *An Account of the Province of Carolina, in America* (London, 1682), *ibid.*, 138–59, 164–76.

[96] Ashe, *Carolina*, in Salley (ed.), *Narratives of Early Carolina*, 147.

sisted for a time, but, whether because of difficulty in extracting its profitable dye or for other reasons, the planters gave up attempts to grow the plant.[97] Rice rather than cotton or indigo would be the first great staple of South Carolina's plantations.

As with most such developments it is impossible to tie the origins of rice planting to any specific date. But that its rich and colorful history traces directly from the experimental interests of the colony's first years seems beyond question. As early as January, 1672, the proprietors had shipped to Carolina a barrel of rice, for which Joseph West gave his receipt the following April. Five years later they wrote to the colony of an effort to secure "in Severall places of ye world . . . plants & seeds proper for your Country and . . . Persons that are Skill'd in planteinge & produceinge vines, Mulberry trees Rice oyles & wines and such other Comodities that enrich those other Countryes that enjoy not soe good a climate as you." [98] Agricultural experimentation is a slow process involving in addition to a test of the soil, tests of the season best suited to the planting, of the variety of seed best adapted to the conditions of soil and climate, of the techniques of preparation for the market, and finally of the market itself. And whatever may have been the exact time at which men were justified in regarding rice as a proved crop, experimental effort for its further improvement, as in the search for a finer grain by importation of new varieties, undoubtedly continued for many years thereafter. Alexander S. Salley of the Historical Commission of South Carolina is inclined to believe that rice was produced successfully in the colony as early as 1684 and that rice of superior quality from Madagascar was tried before 1690. Another eminent authority, while not discounting the weight of Mr. Salley's evidence, feels that the "development of the industry" began about 1695.[99] The present writer is content to suggest that the achievement came in accordance with an original plan for the encouragement of all such effort and with a vision worthy even of the elder Richard Hakluyt.

Meanwhile, the planters had confronted the necessity of finding

[97] See discussion of agricultural experimentation in Gray, *History of Agriculture in the Southern United States*, I, 52–55.

[98] Alexander S. Salley, Jr., *The Introduction of Rice Culture into South Carolina*, Historical Commission of South Carolina *Bulletin*, No. 6 (Columbia, 1919), 3–4.

[99] *Ibid.*, 13; Gray, *History of Agriculture in the Southern United States*, I, 277–79.

immediate means of subsistence and of making payments called for especially in Barbados and England. Like others before them, they experienced trouble in attempts to grow European grains. Finding in the Indian corn a natural staple of amazing hardiness and reproductivity, they made a not too difficult adjustment of taste and undoubtedly at an early date some of their number preferred cornbread to any other, as well they might. The hogs brought down from Virginia found the rooting good, and who can question that the gravy soon ran red in Carolina, or that vegetables on the table were not left dependent for flavor on their own juices? Among the vegetables were the potato brought from Barbados and the English pea, ready to eat in late April. Game, the ubiquitous American turkey included, and fish gave variety to the diet, as did also in season wild strawberries, blackberries, grapes, and peaches, not to mention the hickory nut and the black walnut; but the Carolinian was already noted, like his contemporary in Virginia, as a man who had little time for gardens.[100]

That in addition to pork he frequently ate beef is suggested by the fact that his cattle at an early date provided a chief staple of export. Samuel Wilson declared in 1682 that some of the planters "have already seven or eight hundred head," and commenting on the custom of allowing stock a free range and the absence of need to provide fodder for "the little Winter they have," he declared "an Ox is raised at almost as little expence in Carolina, as a Hen is in England." He forecast that these natural advantages would soon permit a flourishing trade in supply of meat for the northern provinces, where men were compelled to "spend a great part of their Summers Labour in providing three or four Months Fother for the Cattle in the Winter." On this point he proved to be wrong, but Carolina did and would continue to share with the more

[100] Ashe, *Carolina*, in Salley (ed.), *Narratives of Early Carolina*, 145, declared: "Gardens as yet they have not much improved or minded, their Designs having otherwise more profitably engaged them in settling and cultivating their Plantations with good Provisions and numerous Stocks of Cattle." Beverley in his delightful *History and Present State of Virginia*, 292, 314–16, suggests that among his fellow planters a "Kitchin-Garden" for its vegetables received some attention, but commenting upon the plentiful supply of fruit provided by natural growth and the almost universal neglect of grafting or any other effort to improve the supply, he concludes: "A Garden is no where sooner made than there, either for Fruits, or Flowers. . . . And yet they han't many Gardens in the Country, fit to bear that name."

northern plantations in the provision of food, especially of salt pork and beef, for the West Indies. Thus the first planters made payment in Barbados, or secured title there to sugar and molasses for payment to London. Wilson wrote as a promoter of the Carolina settlement, but he compressed much of its history into a few words when he described "many Planters that are single, and have never a Servant, that have two or three hundred Hogs, of which they make great profit; Barbados, Jamaica, and New-England, affording a constant good price for their Pork; by which means they get wherewithal to build them more convenient Houses, and to purchase Servants, and Negro-slaves." [101]

Also, payments abroad increasingly were made with peltries acquired through an expanding Indian trade and, unhappily, with Indian slaves, but we will return to that subject later. For the moment, there appears to be some advantage in closing this discussion of the settlement of Carolina by noting other details of advice given by Wilson to prospective settlers in 1682. In behalf of the proprietors he advertised that passage from England to Charles Town might be had at five pounds for a man or woman. For the benefit of those who wished to settle free of quitrents, the land could be bought at fifty pounds for a thousand acres. Men were advised to take with them "An Ax, a Bill, and a Broad Hoe, and grabbing Hoe, for every man, and a cross cut Saw to every four men, a Whip-saw, a set of Wedges and Fraus and Betle-Rings to every family, and some Reaping Hooks and Sythes, as likewise Nails of all sorts, Hooks, Hinges, Bolts and Locks for their Houses." For "the Provision he hath need of," a man should take the "Merchandizes which sell best in Carolina"—"Linnen and Woollen, and all other Stufs to make clothes of, with Thread, Sowing Silk, Buttons, Ribbons, Hats, Stockings, Shoes, etc."

For further advice one of the proprietors or their secretary might be consulted at eleven o'clock every Tuesday at the Carolina coffeehouse in Birching Lane near by the Royal Exchange.[102] There, presumably, a man might secure with his coffee some elaboration

[101] Wilson, *Account of the Province of Carolina,* in Salley (ed.), *Narratives of Early Carolina,* 171–72. On the livestock industry, see Gray, *History of Agriculture in the Southern United States,* I, 55–57.

[102] Wilson, *Account of the Province of Carolina,* in Salley (ed.), *Narratives of Early Carolina,* 175–76.

of the promise that in Carolina the "Ayr gives a strong Appetite and quick Digestion, nor is it without suitable effects, men finding themselves apparently more lightsome, more prone, and more able to all Youthful Exercises, than in England, the Women are very Fruitful, and the Children have fresh Sanguine Complexions." [103]

[103] *Ibid.*, 169.

BACON'S REBELLION

WITH the establishment of Carolina the initial settlement of the Southern colonies, Georgia excepted, had
been completed, and as the southward extension of
English imperialism clashed with Spain's outer defenses in Florida
to bring into the story new diversities of interest and geography,
life in the older provinces took on a new complexity. Indeed, in
considering the general significance of the last years falling within
the scope of this volume the historian is frequently tempted to
resort to some favored oversimplification. He must follow developments within communities where few if any men could remember
the hardships of the first years; at the same time he must trace anew
the experience of men in other communities who were engaged in
the work of original settlement. It is necessary to take notice of
new problems in the white man's relations with the Indian, problems arising from the expanding area of European activity, and
this must be done without neglect of the fate overtaking those tribes
who first smoked a pipe of peace with the English settler. It becomes no less necessary to trace, at least in outline, the growth of
a new imperial policy and its effect on problems of control as old
and as new as settlement itself; nor can there be overlooked in
this connection one of the most important chapters in England's
political history. It is significant that the curtain rises on Bacon's
Rebellion, a popular uprising in Virginia which many have seen
as a forerunner of the American Revolution, and that it falls on a
revolution in England to which the leaders of our own Revolution
repeatedly harked back.

In such a context one finds a certain appropriateness in the
necessity for observing at the outset that no simple answer can be

found for the complex problem of Bacon's Rebellion. The irascibility of an old man who had outlived his usefulness, the temperament of a young man whose career suggests more of spirit than of balance, an accumulation of economic and political grievances, and a tragic inability to cope with the fundamental problem of Indian relations—all have their place in the narrative. Authorities differ as to the weight to be assigned these several factors, but on one point agreement can be had: the trouble started in a dispute over Indian policy. Thus the discussion immediately comes to a focus on one of the major failures of early American history, a failure emphasized no less forcefully by the outbreak of King Philip's War in New England than by the almost simultaneous pillage and massacre which in Virginia precipitated Bacon's Rebellion.

In these twin tragedies nothing is more tragic than the fact that they followed the most sincere and persistent efforts yet made by the English colonists to deal humanely and fairly with the Indian. The New England story, featuring the ideas of Roger Williams, the work of the Mayhews on Martha's Vineyard, the missionary zeal of John Eliot, his Indian Bible, and the Indian college at Harvard, is well known. Familiar, too, is the support given these efforts from England by the Society for the Propagation of the Gospel in New England. Brafferton Hall at the College of William and Mary stands as a constant reminder of the interest in the work of the Society shown by Robert Boyle, who served as its president after the Restoration, and of the connection between his activities and ambitious undertakings of the eighteenth century.[1] Less familiar is another story, recorded principally in the statutes and court records of Virginia, which requires now a fuller narration.

Parallels of time and policy suggest that Virginia's effort may have drawn some inspiration from the trend of sentiment reflected in the more comprehensive program in New England. The story appears, however, to represent essentially nothing more than another phase of the colony's current attempt to adjust satisfactorily

---

[1] Under the provisions of Robert Boyle's will, income from Brafferton Manor in Yorkshire became available for the support of Indian missions. In the eighteenth century the College of William and Mary was successful, as Harvard also had been, in drawing upon these funds for support of its Indian school.

its own internal problems. It presents the struggle of an American community to find within its own limits and capacities the answer to one of the more difficult problems of frontier life, and it foretells with remarkable completeness the ultimate failure overtaking all such effort.

The narrative must be picked up in 1644, when the second great massacre in Virginia's history forced re-examination of the Indian problem. As a result, the leaders of the colony decided upon the construction of blockhouses or forts at key points for the maintenance of a watch along the frontiers of settlement and as outposts for forays into Indian territory as occasion might require. Forts Royal, Charles, and Henry, located respectively at Pamunkey on the Mattapony, at the falls of the James, and at the falls of the Appomattox, were built under the provisions of statutes enacted in 1645 and 1646. When peace came in the latter part of 1646, the command and custody of the forts, together with liberal grants of adjoining land, were awarded to certain men on condition that each should maintain over a three-year period a garrison of ten men.[2] Only the name of Fort Henry, on the site of modern Petersburg, survived as a place name for any length of time. Its use as a point of departure in 1650 for an exploratory expedition toward Carolina, which included Captain Abraham Wood, the fort's original commander, suggests that its importance thereafter lay principally in the development of Virginia's Indian trade.[3] Whatever the case, it was to this policy, identified with one of the notable accomplishments of Sir William Berkeley's early administration of the colony, that the elderly governor later returned with results that are written large in the history of Bacon's Rebellion.

A second and more important policy had its origins in the peace treaty of 1646. By its terms Necotowance, successor to the implacable Opechancanough, acknowledged the overlordship of the English King, bound himself to pay tribute of "twenty beaver skins att the goeing away of Geese yearely," and ceded all claims to the area

---

[2] Hening, *Statutes*, I, 293–94, 315, 326–27. Except for a lesser fort on the Chickahominy, six hundred acres of land were granted in each case. The land was deeded in perpetuity in line with an established policy of using land grants for the compensation of public service.

[3] See *The Discovery of New Brittaine, Began August 27 . . . 1650* (London, 1651), in Salley (ed.), *Narratives of Early Carolina*, 5–19.

between the York and the James from the falls downward. Except for official messengers garbed in striped coats obtained at Forts Royal and Henry, no Indian was to enter that area on pain of death. In return, the natives received exclusive right to the land and hunting north of the York, except for a stipulation that the lower reaches of that river, where in fact English grants within the later county of Gloucester had already been made, might be opened subsequently to settlement. As an aid to enforcement of the agreement, the presence of any colonist in the region thus assigned to the Indian became, in the absence of a license from the governor, a felony.[4]

The peace itself marked a major development of policy, for the colonists through the years which followed the first massacre had rejected any such formal settlement of their differences with the natives.[5] It is noteworthy, too, that the promise of aid to Necotowance against his enemies finally resolved an old question of alliance against or with the nearest tribesmen in favor of the latter principle. Outranking all other features of the treaty, however, was its recognition of the Indian's need for a guarantee of his right in the land. There was nothing new in the attempt to exclude him from the principal area of English settlement, but the purpose to set aside a reservation in which he would be free of the white man's varied intrusions represents a turn of policy of first significance.

Unhappily, the colony's leadership thereafter faltered. The peace of 1646 had been made on the eve of one of the most important periods of expansion in Virginia's history. For two years Berkeley suspended the right of occupation across the York, even where the treaty would have allowed it and where earlier grants had been made. In further testimony of good faith the planters seem also to have been kept out of the Rappahannock, but they passed on in such numbers to the Potomac that Northumberland County was established for their convenience in 1648. Beyond lay Maryland, and Lord Baltimore offered favorable terms of settlement. Perhaps Berkeley had no escape when in October, 1648, the burgesses unan-

---

[4] Hening, *Statutes*, I, 323-26, 328-29. Ten striped coats, possibly intended for a similar use, were among the Indian truck forwarded by the Carolina proprietors in 1669.

[5] See above, pp. 172-74.

imously complained to him of "the great and clamorous necessities of divers of the inhabitants occasioned and brought upon them through the mean produce of their labours upon barren and over-wrought grounds and the apparent decay of their cattle and hoggs for want of sufficient range." Insisting upon considerations of security, he won their agreement to another year's postponement, but gave his consent to an opening of the York and the Rappahannock on and after September 1, 1649.[6] It was no longer a felony to be caught across the York without license; indeed, surveys might be made in advance of the opening day set. When that day came, the movement across the line must have begun with an expedition destined to become familiar on such occasions in the relentless advance of the American farmer, for by 1651 the farms of Gloucester and by 1652 those of Lancaster were placed under new county commissions. With the passage of another year, Westmoreland County, on the Potomac above Northumberland, was added to the list.

An overhauling of the militia system, which occurred at approximately the same time, is suggestive of the consequences felt. By the fall of 1654 the men of Lancaster, Northumberland, and Westmoreland had been called out to cope with the "injuries" and "insolencies" of the Rappahannocks, and once more the threat of open war hung over the colony.[7] With the English now planted on all four of the major rivers, the Indians were being pushed back from the water on which they depended for important staples of diet.[8] Where the planter cleared the land the Indian's game disappeared. Or the native in pursuit of wild hogs, a by-product of white settlement upon which the Indian frequently fed, ran afoul of the Englishman's laws of trespass and theft. The treaty's exclusion of the Indian on pain of death from a proscribed area of settlement had strengthened an all too common custom of using a gun in answer to trespass, and when death resulted, the law required no more than the planter's unsupported oath in proof of the trespass. The Assembly in 1656, declaring its "sad apprehension of the small account . . . of late made of shedding Indians' blood, though never so innocent," sought remedy by prohibiting the killing of any Indian under English protection except when caught in an

---

[6] Hening, *Statutes*, I, 353–54.   [7] *Ibid.*, 389–90.   [8] *Ibid.*, 415; II, 140.

act that done by an Englishman would be adjudged a felony, and that to be proved by two witnesses. To reduce "these mischiefs" the Indian now was required to secure from a designated person at the head of each river a ticket of entry in evidence of such legitimate errands as fishing, fowling, or the gathering of berries. As a further safeguard, no native could be "entertained" thereafter by the planter, whatever the purpose, without the consent of the local county court.[9]

The heart of the problem, as this legislation so clearly reveals, lay in the difficulty experienced by both peoples, with their contrasting social and economic systems, in attempting to live in close neighborhood with one another. That basic fact had received recognition in the effort of 1646 to draw a line between the two communities by reserving a sufficient tract for exclusive use by the Indians, but the planters forced a prompt repudiation of the agreement. There was apparently no way to stem the tide of an advancing English settlement, and so no alternative to the assumption that intermingling of the two peoples must continue. Such an assumption left only the hope that an equitable division of the land, if joined with some conversion of the Indian economy, might provide an answer.

The county commissioners of Gloucester and Lancaster were ordered by the Assembly in 1653 to apportion the land among the two peoples within their jurisdiction according to the general provisions of a statute enacted the preceding year. That statute apparently is not extant. The direction of policy, however, is well-enough indicated by provisions in the revisal of 1658 establishing as a first claim in all new areas of settlement an allowance of fifty acres for every bowman. This land was to be surveyed and patented in a common allotment for each native town.[10] The new policy, in other words, conceded a rough equality of right in the land by adopting the established headright claim of the English colonist as the measure for its apportionment. At the same time, it undertook to reduce the Indian's claim to compact units and well-defined limits.

Attributing the succession of Indian troubles to "our extreame

9 *Ibid.*, I, 410, 415.
10 *Ibid.*, 382, 456–57; *Virginia Magazine*, VIII (1900–1901), 173–74.

pressures on them and theire wanting of something to hazard & loose beside their lives," the Assembly through a statute of March, 1656, sought further remedy. In the first place, the natives were encouraged to bring in wolves' heads, a thing in itself desirable, by the promise of a cow to be awarded for every eight such heads brought in. Presumably, the cow was intended to serve both as a civilizing agency and as a means to enforce upon the native a degree of legal responsibility theretofore wanting. A second provision sought to give new assurances regarding one of the oldest features of the colony's Indian policy. The practice of taking Indian children into English households for the professed purpose of converting them to Christianity and to a European pattern of life had its origins in a sincere belief that it would prove a useful step toward solution of the native problem. But the children had been classified officially as hostages and the usage provided an obvious cover for their enslavement. Accordingly, it was now promised that they would not be used "as slaves," and the county courts were charged with a new responsibility for upholding the promise. That the law was not without effect is suggested not only by the continuing relative unimportance of Indian labor in the economy of the colony, but by the pains taken at the time of Bacon's Rebellion in 1676 to stipulate that all captives might be enslaved for life.[11]

A third part of the act provided that all land allotted the Indians in accordance with acts and orders of the Assembly should be thereafter unalienable except with the consent of the Assembly, lest the natives be "allwaies in fear of what they hold not being able to distinguish between our desires to buy or enforcement to have." The tendency to substitute for a presumptive right the more exact forms of an English title to specified acreages obviously had opened the way for one of the more serious invasions of the native's interest. The act of 1656 was supplemented in the revisal of 1658 by an assurance to the Indians of all "seats of land" they then held. The law included a strict prohibition of English plant-

[11] Hening, *Statutes*, I, 393–96, 455–56, 481–82; II, 346; Almon W. Lauber, *Indian Slavery in Colonial Times within the Present Limits of the United States* (New York, 1913), 108, 117; Ames, *Studies of the Virginia Eastern Shore*, 73–74. Indian slavery in colonial America developed largely as a by-product of Indian wars. It showed some tendency to develop in Virginia during the 1640's, but thereafter public policy sought to keep the use of Indian labor within the limits of indentured service.

ing in all places claimed or desired by the Indians except with the specific allowance of the governor and council, and restricted land sales to such as were actually made in the presence of the quarter court.[12]

There existed as yet, however, no safeguard against the dishonest interpreter, "rendering them willing to surrender when indeed they intended to have received a confirmation of their owne rights." Nor was there any defense against the unscrupulous trader who advanced goods on credit beyond the native's ability to repay and then sought an attachment against his person and goods. When in the spring of 1660 the arrest of the King of the Weyanokes by his creditors brought home to the colony a grave risk of retaliatory warfare, the Assembly provided that such credit should be entirely at the creditor's risk with no right of recovery in court.[13] And during the next year the burgesses took still another step when they withdrew all fur-trading privileges except for those persons receiving a license from the governor, who was requested to grant the license only to men of "known integrity." [14] It has become the custom to deal cynically with this right of license, but, whatever opportunities it may have provided for monopolistic developments in the Indian trade, it must be considered in its origin as a measure well and honestly conceived. The "inordinate covetousness" of "ill-minded" traders to which the Assembly referred is no more to be challenged than is the serious danger to which their activities exposed the colony.

The Indian question, with special committees examining both individual and general problems, engaged much of the Assembly's attention during the sessions of 1660 and 1661. Out of these and other deliberations there came in the revisal of 1662 a comprehensive statute "Concerning Indians." [15] Noting that "the mutuall discontents, complaints, jealousies and ffeares of English and In-

---

[12] Hening, *Statutes*, I, 467–68.　　[13] *Ibid.*, 541, 547.　　[14] *Ibid.*, II, 20.

[15] *Ibid.*, 138–43; and see also, 13–16, 34, 35, 36, 39, 124, 149, 150–56, 161–62. Of interest in this connection is the instruction from the Carolina proprietors in 1669 prohibiting settlement by the colonists within two and one-half miles of any Indian town unless on the opposite side of a river. The purpose "in time to drawe ye Indians into our Government" found further expression in an order that 12,000 acres should be left about "every Cassiques house or Towne." *Collections of the South Carolina Historical Society*, V (1897), 119–23.

dians proceed chiefly from the violent intrusions of diverse English made into their lands forcing the Indians by way of revenge to kill the cattle and hogs of the English," and that it was "as easy to affright them to a publique as well as a private acknowledgment" of willingness to sell, the act prohibited any alienation of land "now justly claymed or actually possest by any Indian or Indians." Their persons and their goods were placed, moreover, under the protection of the same laws that governed the rights of Englishmen. Where settlement had been extended legally to within three miles of an Indian town, the English must provide fences for the Indian cornfields, and persons who had encroached upon Indian lands were to be removed upon complaint and their housing and other improvements destroyed. It is evident that little hope remained for a conversion of the Indian economy.

The native's right to gather oysters, berries, and fruits outside the bounds of his town was recognized under license from any two justices of the peace. The law established new penalties for un-licensed trade, and reserved all disputes between traders and Indians for settlement by the governor or his special appointees. No native chieftain could be imprisoned save by special warrant from the governor and two members of the council, lest "the making of peace and warre" be "wrested out of those hands it is by his majesty's commission intrusted into." Special commissioners, the first of commissioners thereafter to be annually appointed, were to proclaim the peace in each Indian town, to view and determine all bounds, and to see that fences required by the act were constructed. The "Great Man" of each town became answerable for pilfering or other damage done by his people, who for identification would wear specified badges whenever outside their own limits. Colonists could "entertain" the Indians as servants or for other purposes, but only by special license from the governor. No Indian could be enslaved, nor could he be required to serve for a longer term than that fixed by statute for the English servant of like age.[16]

The law now was well-nigh complete, though by no means per-

16 For evidence from the county records, see in addition to Ames, *Studies of the Virginia Eastern Shore*, 73–74, *William and Mary College Quarterly*, IV (1895–1896), 177–79; VI (1897–1898), 118; VIII (1899–1900), 23; *Virginia Magazine*, VIII (1900–1901), 173–74; V (1897–1898), 33, 35, 39; IV (1896–1897), 408–409.

fect. Prohibition of land sales still left the way open for leases through which men accomplished further inroads on the Indian reserve.[17] Yet, the failure experienced in this mid-century attempt to solve a difficult problem came not so much in the effort to provide some equitable distribution of the land and to safeguard the Indian title so established as in the hope that a European title to a fair share of the land might save the natives from the disintegrating influence of English settlement. Indeed, the Indian title at more than one point would outlast the Indian himself. Tribes which first had contested the issue with Captain John Smith and his successors had been broken. Now nominally allied with the English, they had become in fact dependents, and, having lost their independence, they surrendered their vitality also.[18] No less marked was the failure to meet even temporarily the special problems of an expanding frontier of settlement and to find some formula that would prove its worth at each new stage of the colony's growth by preventing a sickening repetition of earlier massacres and wars. Instead, recurring difficulty along the margins of settlement led directly into the uprisings immediately preceding Bacon's Rebellion.[19]

Against this record of failure in attempts to deal with the special problems presented by neighboring Indians stands a promising achievement in the development of trade with outlying tribes. Since the days of Samuel Argall and of William Claiborne's early activity in the upper Chesapeake the most profitable branches of the Indian trade had been developed in regions located considerably outside the area of English settlement. Lord Baltimore's triumph over Claiborne at Kent Island had marked a victory primarily for the interests of settlement, and as the migration of the English settler northward along the waterways of the Chesapeake staked out its surrounding lands for farming, the trader moved westward along the major rivers to the head of navigation, or, as if to em-

17 McIlwaine (ed.), *Minutes of the Council and General Court*, 370–71, 384.

18 For a contemporary list of the tributary tribes, see Hening, *Statutes*, II, 274–76; and compare with Beverley's list of 1705 in *History and Present State of Virginia*, 232–33, where he describes the Indians of Virginia as "almost wasted." His description of Indian life is, of course, a classic. See also, Bruce, *Economic History of Virginia*, I, 497–99.

19 Hening, *Statutes*, II, 185, 193–94, 205, 209, 218–20, 237–38, 289.

phasize a fundamental conflict of interest, he turned toward the south in a direction that led away from the main movement of settlement. For his encouragement in this last and especially significant development there existed certain hopes as old as the English interest in North America—the possibility of some major discovery leading to the South Seas or the proof of some other promise lingering with the tradition of Raleigh's initial venture.

The new awakening in mid-century to the importance of Carolina contributed additional incentives. When Abraham Wood, foremost of the early Indian traders in Virginia, set out in 1650 on a discovery that carried him southwestward some sixty-five miles to the point at which the Dan and the Staunton join to form the Roanoke River, he was accompanied by Edward Bland, who returned to press for rights of settlement.[20] But three quarters of a century later William Byrd II could describe the same general area as a fresh discovery of Eden. The land itself, as Byrd's later description suggests, was attractive enough, but no waterway led back to an established market for the relatively bulky produce of the farm. It is true that the horse as a beast of burden was becoming now increasingly common in Virginia, so much so that the Assembly in 1668 repealed a restriction on the exportation of horses and even in the next year prohibited their importation,[21] but the ownership of a horse was still regarded in 1670 as the mark of a rich man.[22] On the frontiers of settlement horses offered assistance chiefly as pack animals. Consequently, the trader, whose commodity carried a relatively high value in proportion to its weight, rather than the farmer first found the horse an aid to distant penetrations of the interior.

The record provides only an incomplete view of Abraham Wood. It is clear, however, that from his post at Fort Henry he carried on an expanding trade with the Indians, that his vision of its

[20] See especially, Clarence W. Alvord and Lee Bidgood, *The First Explorations of the Trans-Allegheny Region by the Virginians, 1650–1674* (Cleveland, 1912), 47–51; and 105–30 for reprint of *The Discovery of New Brittaine*, the original account published in London in 1651. See also above, pp. 251–52, 362.

[21] Hening, *Statutes*, II, 267, 271.

[22] *Ibid.*, 279, a law which required owners to restrain their horses from trespass between July 20 and the last of October, "it being much fitter that rich men who have the benefitt of such horses should provide for their restraint, then the poore enjoyned to the impossibility of [very] high ffences."

possibilities extended far beyond the bounds of the Virginia colony, and that as an Indian trader, planter, and land speculator he became a man of wealth and great influence in the colony.[23] It can only be surmised that he conducted the trade from Fort Henry along lines later described by William Byrd II as the common custom. "Gentlemen send for Goods proper for such a Trade from England," wrote Byrd, "and then either Venture them out at their own Risk to the Indian Towns, or credit some Traders with them of Substance and Reputation, to be paid in Skins at a certain Price agreed betwixt them." [24] Byrd's own father, William Byrd I, had settled by the early 1670's at the falls of the James, where as planter, merchant, and Indian trader he founded one of the principal fortunes of colonial Virginia.[25] From surviving fragments of the elder Byrd's correspondence of the 1680's, one gains a closer view of the trade.[26] He seems both to have sent out his own traders, two of whom were killed at a point four hundred miles from the falls in 1686, and to have dealt with independent traders, for he complained of losses suffered because of inadequate information on the market. From the well-known house of Perry and Lane in London and from others, he imported, in addition to goods for disposal to local planters, the common stock of the Indian trade—textiles (with more than one plea for a good dark blue), guns and ammunition (with suggestions to those who supplied him that the Indian would not take just any gun), hoes (not too small), kettles (free of holes),

<hr />

23 Alvord and Bidgood, *First Explorations of the Trans-Allegheny Region by the Virginians*, which rescued Abraham Wood from an undeserved oblivion. He apparently had come to Virginia as a servant in the later days of the London Company, and perhaps served his apprenticeship under Samuel Mathews, one of the first planters to demonstrate the possibilities for a profitable combination of planting with commercial activity. The six hundred acres which went with his command of Fort Henry in 1646 were only a fraction of the total acreage patented in his name. He served as a burgess from Charles City as early as 1644, was elevated to the council in 1658, and in the Virginia militia rose from a captain to become one of the three major generals who after the Restoration received command of the militia with rank next to Berkeley.

24 John S. Bassett (ed.), *The Writings of 'Colonel William Byrd, of Westover in Virginia, Esqr'* (New York, 1901), 235.

25 *Ibid.*, especially Bassett's account of the family in the Introduction.

26 Published in *Virginia Magazine*, XXIV (1916), especially 228, 230, 234, 351, 352, 354; XXV (1917), 49–50, 50–52, 132, 133, 252–53. Other of Byrd's letters may be consulted in the *Virginia Historical Register* (Richmond), I (1848); II (1849).

small white beads, plain belts apparently made up for the trade, hatchets, etc. Whether the rum imported from Barbados was intended for his English or for his Indian customers, or for both, cannot be said. In return he shipped to England tobacco, furs, and skins, all packed in hogsheads.

Like Wood, Byrd was no mere trader, for in furtherance of the Virginia trade he contributed importantly to westward exploration. Record exists of at least one venture by him with a "great company" as far west as the Valley of Virginia in 1671.[27] But to Wood belongs the greater credit. There is reason to believe that for a time he may have traded chiefly with the Occaneechees, who, on their island just below the confluence of the Dan and the Staunton, figured so prominently as middlemen in the trade with more distantly situated tribes as to give their name to the path followed by the later Virginia traders into Carolina.[28] But it is clear that by the 1670's Wood's interests, if not his traders, ranged far beyond Occaneechee Island. In September, 1671, he sent out from Fort Henry, Captain Thomas Batts and Robert Fallam, who moving westward accomplished the first recorded passage of the Appalachian barrier to the New River, one of the tributaries of the Ohio. Again, in the spring of 1673 he sent James Needham and Gabriel Arthur, the latter probably one of Wood's servants, on a southwestward discovery across the modern state of North Carolina and the Blue Ridge Mountains to the land of the Cherokee.[29] Thus, before Bacon's Rebellion, Virginia's Indian traders had found the way to Kentucky and Tennessee. Their influence extended in fact as far south as the Savannah, for the settlers at Charles Town found on that river in the Westos a tribe which terrorized its neighbors with guns secured through the Virginia trade.[30]

As in matters of trade, so in questions of internal security the Indian problem had become one involving considerations extend-

[27] Alvord and Bidgood, *First Explorations of the Trans-Allegheny Region by the Virginians*, 77, 192.

[28] Notice also the difficulty traders passing Occaneechee experienced because of resentment over loss of the advantage of the middleman.

[29] Alvord and Bidgood, *First Explorations of the Trans-Allegheny Region by the Virginians*, 70–89, 181–226, and especially 210–26 for an account by Wood himself which significantly was found in the papers of the Earl of Shaftesbury.

[30] Verner W. Crane, *The Southern Frontier, 1670–1732* (Durham, 1929), 12, 16.

ing across provincial lines and beyond the control of any one province. Behind the difficulties which precipitated Bacon's Rebellion lay not only the tensions produced by Virginia's own expansion, but the external pressures born of the growth of other European settlements and of the effect of this growth upon the contentions dividing the North American tribes themselves. Among the older of these rivalries was that between the Seneca, of the Iroquois group, and the Susquehannocks. Famed for their strength, build, and warlike character, the Susquehannocks had proved since the middle of the century a useful ally of the Maryland colony in guarding the northern approaches to that settlement against the more northerly situated Seneca. By 1674, however, Maryland's plantations had been extended to the upper reaches of the bay, grants even had been made along the lower Susquehanna River, and during that year the colony in effect abandoned its former allies to make a separate peace with the Seneca. Before the superior strength of that tribe the Susquehannocks fell back on the Patuxent and thence to the north bank of the Potomac near Piscataway Creek, where their presence presented to the colonists an embarrassing and dangerous problem.[31]

Reluctant to act on a proposal of the Maryland Assembly that they move up beyond the falls of the Potomac, the Susquehannocks became a disturbing influence among the Indians of the Potomac area, including the Doegs, with whom Virginia's frontiersmen had carried on a long-standing feud. One inevitable result of the situation was a shortage of food, which encouraged raids upon neighboring plantations and thus brought a train of incidents and misunderstandings leading finally to a major explosion. A planter mortally wounded on a Sunday morning in Stafford County, Virginia, lived long enough to gasp an accusation against the Doegs. His aroused neighbors, on crossing the river into Maryland, displayed an all too familiar carelessness in distinguishing one Indian from another with the result that Susquehannocks as well as Doegs were killed. The response of the outraged Susquehannocks caused Maryland to bury her own complaint against the intrusion of the

---

[31] Thomas J. Wertenbaker, *Torchbearer of the Revolution; The Story of Bacon's Rebellion and Its Leader* (Princeton, 1940), 74–84, provides an excellent account of the origins of the Indian troubles.

Virginians in a common effort to force her former allies up the river. The attempt, resisted by the natives, was mismanaged from the first, and in the end the Susquehannocks escaped a decisive defeat at the hands of the Virginia and Maryland militia. Breaking up into roving bands of embittered savages, the Indians crossed the Potomac and vengefully fell upon the exposed plantations of the upper Virginia counties. Early in 1676 they killed some thirty-six persons along the Rappahannock and two other men apparently as far south as the James.[32]

As the planters in the exposed area drew together to improvise some defense, or in panic abandoned their plantations for the security of more settled areas, the governor responded encouragingly by ordering a punitive expedition, to be led by Sir Henry Chicheley, Royalist soldier of the English Civil War. But an offer of peace from the chieftain of the Susquehannocks seems to have caught Sir William off his guard. Perhaps it was the governor's advanced age; perhaps he was guided too much by a sense of the just grievances of the offending Indians; perhaps he underestimated the danger or was overly concerned for the unsettling influence of his planned action on the Indian trade; perhaps, having led such an expedition himself, he knew it probably would lead to a general war; and in this connection, perhaps he was influenced by reports of the appalling cost of such a war to the people of New England—whatever the cause, he countermanded the orders to Sir Henry and was successful, though not without some dissent, in persuading an Assembly, meeting early in March, to adopt a defensive rather than an offensive policy.[33] Forts were to be erected and manned in Stafford, and on the Rappahannock, Mattapony, Pamunkey, James, and Appomat-

[32] Such are the figures given by Berkeley in a letter of April 1, 1676, to Thomas Ludwell, which significantly suggests that at that time the governor took these figures to represent the total casualties. *Virginia Magazine,* XX (1912), 246–49. See also, *ibid.,* III (1895–1896), 35–36.

[33] In addition to the letter to Ludwell, Berkeley wrote on April 1 to Secretary Williamson in London. The two letters suggest that the Governor was greatly impressed by news of the losses suffered by the New England colonies, including their anticipated losses in the "beaver trade," that he was inclined to see a connection between King Philip's War and the Indian trouble in Maryland and Virginia, and that he was further inclined to attribute the trouble generally to the fact that the English settlers had dispossessed the American Indian of more land than they were able to hold against him. See *ibid.,* XX (1912), 243–49.

tox; two additional forts on the south side of the James would complete a ring about the colony. Five hundred men would be enlisted for garrisons. Indian allies were promised appropriate rewards for assistance. Finally, and once again, a trade in firearms was strictly prohibited.[34]

It soon became evident that the governor had misjudged both the Indian situation and the temper of his own people. The Susquehannocks seem to have gotten beyond all control, even by their own leaders. With aid from other discontented tribesmen they renewed their depredations along the frontier, and Sir William found himself committed to a policy which required time and a heavy expenditure of funds for its fulfillment. He might have been pardoned for the original error of judgment had he displayed any inclination to revise an unpopular policy. Instead, he showed a stubborn disinclination to yield to popular pressure and thus called into question the whole structure of a government which many colonists were coming to regard as altogether too unresponsive to the will of the people. By late spring, when the Indian terror swept as far south as the James, the issues dividing the governor and his people had already passed beyond a simple question of Indian policy.

The colonists had many grievances.[35] For several years past, taxes had been heavy. After a Dutch fleet had successfully invaded the Chesapeake toward the close of the second Anglo-Dutch war to destroy or capture a score of English ships, the Assembly decided to construct forts in each of the rivers and charged the several county courts with responsibility for their construction through concerted action. Yet, when the third Dutch war came in 1672 these forts, by the Assembly's admission, were in a serious state of disrepair. And despite additional costs incurred for their rehabilitation, the enemy

[34] Hening, *Statutes,* II, 326–39, legislation which also prohibited the export of any provisions prior to the last of July. The act prohibiting trade in firearms authorized county courts to designate not more than five "sober persons" for trade in other commodities with allied Indians but "utterly barred" any of "the late traders," their factors, or servants.

[35] See especially, grievances submitted after the rebellion to the royal commissioners, in *Virginia Magazine,* II (1894–1895), 166–69, 169–70, 170–73, 289–92, 380–92; III (1895–1896), 35–42, 132–47; Wertenbaker, *Virginia under the Stuarts,* 115–45, a discussion of "The Causes of Bacon's Rebellion."

again staged a successful attack on English shipping in the Chesapeake.[36] A defensive policy depending chiefly upon the construction of forts had for the Virginians of the day unpleasant associations. They remembered too the special taxes imposed on each county for the improvement of Jamestown, an expenditure for which little if any advantage had been gained. More recently, the public levy had been made heavier to meet the expenses of commissioners sent to England to oppose the proprietary grant of all Virginia, insofar as its soil and regalities were concerned, to the Earl of Arlington and to Thomas, Lord Culpeper, heir to one of the original grantees of the 1649 patent to the Northern Neck.[37] These additional burdens had fallen, moreover, on a people already carrying the heavy weight of an unfavorable tobacco market. Sir William could hardly be blamed for the low price of tobacco; indeed, he had protested repeatedly and vigorously against restrictions of the Trade Acts which the colonists seem to have regarded as the principal cause for a depressed market. Nor could he be blamed for the epidemic which in the winter of 1672–1673 took half the colony's cattle, any more than for the great and destructive storm which in 1667 had swept through the province. But acts of Providence and the government at Whitehall aside, there was little for which the governor could not be blamed.

The very nature of the colony's government, depending as it did upon a self-perpetuating control by key men in each county whose authority was formally derived from a commission issued by the governor, made of him the natural target of all complaints.[38] County levies, hardly if any less than provincial levies, also had been heavy of recent years. There had been suspicion, as so frequently thereafter would be the case when Americans took the

---

[36] In addition to Wertenbaker's account, see Hening, *Statutes*, II, 255–59, 291–92, 293–95.

[37] Andrews, *Colonial Period of American History*, II, 234–35, is helpful at this point.

[38] Notice the charge by the residents of Charles City "that Sir Wm. Berkeley haveing by these wayes and meanes, and by takeing uppon him contrary to law the granting collectors places, sherifs, and other offices of profitt to whome he best pleased, he soe gained uppon and obliged all or the greatest number of the men of parts and estates in the whole country (out of which it was necessary our representatives and Burgesses should be elected) hath thereby soe fortifyed his power, over us, as of himselfe without respect to our laws, to doe what soever he best pleased." *Virginia Magazine*, III (1895–1896), 135.

time to look at their county government, of misappropriation of funds and of special favors to members of the bench. In the county, where men had their chief opportunity to observe the functioning of their government, they had taken particular notice of the lack of popular control over taxation, of "the custome of County Courts att the laying of the levy to withdraw into a private Roome by which meanes the poore people not knowing for what they paid their levy did allways admire how their taxes could be so high." [39] They had noted, too, with growing discontent the monopoly enjoyed by members of the court over the lucrative post of sheriff and the way in which the same group controlled the militia and the parish vestry.

Nor did the people miss the connection between this local control and the special privileges enjoyed by the ruling hierarchy of the province. They seem to have paid less attention than have modern students to the fact that no general election had been held for several years. [40] They complained more perhaps of too frequent Assemblies, of their exorbitant costs, and of the way in which the prosperous members of the community took advantage of the indebtedness of their fellows to perpetuate their hold on the government. "The poverty of the Country is such," declared Bacon, "that all the power and sway is got into the hands of the rich, who by extortious advantages, having the common people in their debt, have always curbed and oppressed them in all manner of wayes." He saw little hope of redress when the appeal must be made "to the very persons our complaints do accuse." [41] Members of the governor's council had enjoyed for many years an exemption by law for ten heads in the levy of the poll tax. At the time of its institution, the rule had made sense. [42] Now, however, it was impossible to overlook the fact that these very men, who enjoyed special advantages in the allotment of collectorships, in securing patents for purposes of land speculation, or in the distribution of licenses for the Indian trade, were better able to pay high taxes than were their poverty-stricken fellows. Midst a growing demand for some

[39] *Ibid.*, II (1894–1895), 172.

[40] But notice that the royal commissioners later recommended "a New Assembly to be elected and chosen every two yeares." *Ibid.*, XIV (1906–1907), 275.

[41] Quoted in Wertenbaker, *Virginia under the Stuarts*, 135.   [42] See above, p. 158.

accounting of the return from the two-shilling duty which had been intended to distribute the load more fairly, and which the colonists pointed out they and not the English merchants paid, sentiment developed for a scheme of taxation more nearly adjusted to ability to pay.[43] As the residents of Isle of Wight County put it after the rebellion: "Wee desire you our Burgesses to give none of our estates away as formerly ye have done, but if ye must give such great summes dispose of your own." [44]

Popular protest of abuses in provincial administration received substantial support from many of the county magistrates.[45] Their position in the developing contest reflected again the dual nature of the authority they exercised as commissioned agents of the crown and as representatives of their respective communities. They repeatedly had demonstrated a strong sense of the right of local self-government, and if on the one hand they had shown a human inclination to interpret that right in terms of a somewhat exclusive reliance on their own wisdom and experience, on the other they were now alert to the need for restricting unwarranted interference by the governor. In 1660 they had welcomed the restoration of the royal commission and no doubt had shown since then some inclination to extract undue advantage from it, but they had expected that the governor would not take improper advantage of a necessary restoration of certain powers traditionally belonging to his office in the appointment of sheriffs, clerks, and other local officers. Unfortunately, Sir William too was human, and of recent years evidently had been inclined to interpret his authority in terms more nearly absolute than its historical foundations would justify. Thus the administration of public affairs, at all echelons, had drifted since 1662 toward an arbitrary type of control.

The grievances of the people more than once reflected their discontent over the fact that political and economic advantage in their society belonged so frequently to the same men. Circumstances tended to pit debtor against creditor, but the issues raised were political, not economic. It is profitable to draw a parallel with

[43] On origins of the two-shilling duty, see above, p. 244.

[44] *Virginia Magazine*, II (1894–1895), 387.

[45] This fact becomes clear from legislation passed by the famous Assembly of June, 1676, discussed below, pp. 383–84. The grievances cited in n. 35 above offer further supporting evidence.

later divisions in American political life, but in so doing it should be noted that this group of rebels made no proposals for the issuance of paper currency, for the formation of a land bank, or for the free coinage of silver. The issue was that of political privilege, privilege based to some extent on economic advantage and joined in the popular mind with strong suspicion of corruption, especially the corruption of public policy. Perhaps no one thing stirred more bitterness than the stake highly placed officers of government had in the Indian trade. Berkeley himself, if not a participant in the trade, had certainly encouraged the enterprises of such men as Abraham Wood, a member of the council. The governor therefore stood vulnerable to the charge that he and his advisers in their ineffective action for quelling the Indian uprising showed greater concern for the protection of their trade than for the lives of the planters. Bacon put the grievance quite simply when he cried: "these traders at the head of the rivers buy and sell our blood." [46]

Nathaniel Bacon had been a resident of Virginia for less than two years when he assumed leadership of the popular protest. He himself was identified with the ruling oligarchy, and few men in Virginia had a clearer claim to the distinction of gentle birth. This "spoiled child of a wealthy English squire," as Professor Wertenbaker has recently described him, had grown up in a Suffolk manor house, and had been schooled at Cambridge. He had made the grand tour of the Continent, which traditionally was relied upon to put the polish on a gentleman's education, and had studied law as a resident of Gray's Inn, where earlier his distinguished kinsman, Lord Francis Bacon, had studied. [47] Until very recently, indeed, his destiny had been that of an English country squire. But the record in 1670 takes a surprising turn when Bacon's marriage to the daughter of a neighboring Suffolk squire, a marriage that would seem to have met all conventional requirements, promptly led to the disinheritance of the bride by an outraged father. Soon thereafter the groom found himself involved, innocently or otherwise, in an unsavory deal to defraud another of his inheritance, and not

---

[46] Alvord and Bidgood, *First Explorations of the Trans–Allegheny Region by the Virginians,* 76.

[47] The writer is chiefly indebted to Wertenbaker, *Torchbearer of the Revolution,* for biographical information on Bacon.

long after that, Bacon's father concluded that Virginia rather than England was the place for his heir. The record is incomplete and conjecture may be misleading, but Bacon himself presents one of the most intriguing questions of the rebellion.

Having been provided with a stake of some £1,800, Bacon arrived in Virginia in 1674, being then twenty-seven years old. He came as the relative of another Nathaniel Bacon, who had migrated to the colony at an earlier day, had married a wealthy widow, and, aided by the education that was his lot as the son of an English clergyman, had risen to a seat on the governor's council. The younger Bacon thus enjoyed expert advice and influential assistance in settling near William Byrd on the upper James in Henrico County. The advantage to be gained in contemporary Virginia through a powerful relative is further indicated by Bacon's prompt elevation to a seat on the governor's council. As he settled down, every indication must have suggested that while he had lost the privileged position of a squire in England, he soon would gain its equivalent in Virginia. But in the spring of 1676 the Indians killed his overseer.

The people up the river had had enough, and as they gathered in Charles City County to consider action for the security of their lives, they talked, too, of security for their liberties. In Bacon they found a natural leader—young, impetuous, eloquent, and one, moreover, who enjoyed the prestige of a seat on the governor's council.[48] The immediate action proposed was a punitive expedition against the Indians. For this the governor's authority was asked, but the request went from men who had agreed to defy his will if necessary. Bacon moved first into New Kent County in search of additional volunteers and perhaps for some action against the Pamunkeys, regarded by the upcountry planters as traitorous allies of the Susquehannocks and by Berkeley as faithful and valued allies of the English. The Pamunkeys withdrew in the face of this new threat, and Berkeley proclaimed Bacon's action rebellious.[49]

[48] In the part played by William Byrd and other men of substance in persuading Bacon to take the lead, as in later complaints of the people that they had been misled, one finds a strong suggestion that this last consideration carried considerable weight both in the choice of Bacon and in the response he won. See Wertenbaker, *Virginia under the Stuarts*, 155.

[49] *Ibid.*, 155–94; and Wertenbaker, *Torchbearer of the Revolution*, 93 ff., provide

He offered pardon to all concerned if they would lay down their arms. But that was a hard condition to meet in the circumstances, and Bacon instead led his force into the forest where, according to report, some of the Susquehannocks had encamped near Occaneechee. In the hope of forestalling Bacon, the governor early in May hastily assembled three hundred horsemen whose ride up the river must have served to emphasize some of the grievances of the people, for the ownership of horses had now introduced into Virginia that ancient and important distinction between men who ride to war and those who walk to it. Frustrated in his purpose to apprehend Bacon, the governor soon found himself in a difficult position. He again proclaimed Bacon a rebel, this time removing him from his seat on the council. The governor even went out of his way to warn Mrs. Bacon that he intended to hang her husband. But to a people whose attitude toward the Indians was all too frequently summed up in the simple statement that "it matters not whether they be Friends or Foes Soe they be Indians," [50] Bacon had done no more than Berkeley himself should long since have done.

An evident rallying of support for Bacon forced the governor to make his own bid for popular support. Consequently, he returned to Greenspring, where, taking note of the grievances of the people, he issued writs for a newly elected Assembly, with authorization for all freemen to exercise the franchise.[51] Whether his strategy was to hold out the promise of relief of grievances in the hope of leaving Bacon isolated in his conviction for rebellion, or some other, the fates proved unkind. For Bacon soon emerged from the forest to bring the word that he had killed Indians. Having found a band of Susquehannocks on the Roanoke, he had destroyed it with the aid of the Occaneechees. Then in a subsequent quarrel with the Occaneechees he had destroyed all but a remnant of them.

---

detailed and highly readable accounts of the subsequent development of the rebellion. These should be read in conjunction with the original narratives of the rebellion, in Charles M. Andrews (ed.), *Narratives of the Insurrections, 1675–1690* (New York, 1915), 11–141, which includes "A True Narrative of the Late Rebellion in Virginia, by the Royal Commissioners, 1677," pp. 105–41.

[50] Andrews (ed.), *Narratives of the Insurrections,* 123.

[51] Wertenbaker, *Torchbearer of the Revolution,* 106. A statute of 1670 had restricted the franchise to "ffreeholders and housekeepers who only are answerable to the publique for the levies." Hening, *Statutes,* II, 280.

As a result, Bacon the Indian fighter was elected in late May by the people of Henrico to Berkeley's forthcoming Assembly, an Assembly destined to be associated chiefly with the name of Bacon, not Berkeley.

The newly elected burgess came down the river attended by a guard of some forty men. Off Jamestown on June 7 he sent in an inquiry as to whether he would be permitted to take his seat and received from Berkeley an unqualified answer delivered by gunfire. Bacon moved out of range, but the next day he was captured by the *Adam and Eve,* under its master, Captain Thomas Gardiner. "Now I behold the greatest Rebell that ever was in Virginia," the old governor is reported to have cried on receiving his prisoner. However, after expressing the hope that Bacon still was a gentleman, he released him on his own parole.[52]

This gesture can be interpreted as an initial move toward some such reconciliation with Bacon as would assist the governor in riding out the storm of popular protest, of which by now he must have been thoroughly aware. Circumstances and Bacon's own later protests strongly suggest that the younger man's primary concern was to secure some authorization for prosecuting the war which would of itself remove the taint of rebellion from his former actions. If this be true, it is clear that there were grounds of agreement between the two men because of the governor's need to eliminate the personal quarrel with this newly risen hero of the people in order better to deal with the general discontent. It is not surprising, therefore, to find Bacon two days later making his formal submission to the governor and council in keeping with all traditional requirements by a show of humility, a confession of guilt, and a plea for pardon. Thereupon the governor, remarking on the joy in heaven at the return of one sinner, granted the pardon and restored the sinner to his seat on the council. The action can be viewed as a clever strategem for keeping Bacon out of the House of Burgesses and for remedying a personal grievance the people seemed inclined to make their own. It must be admitted that Bacon at the time was a prisoner, but he had behind him the rebellious mood of the country and men both near and far who were ready to fight. Surely he must have received in advance of his submission

[52] See especially, Andrews (ed.), *Narratives of the Insurrections,* 114-15.

certain assurances over and beyond that of his restoration to the council, and it is difficult to avoid the conclusion that they included a promise of the commission for command of a war against the Indians, commonly understood to have been part of the bargain.

Bacon thus had no opportunity to take his seat as a burgess, and the question of his direct influence on the legislation passed by the Assembly then in session is intriguing. Laws enacted by this Assembly have been known since 1676 as Bacon's Laws, but they include action of which he could hardly have approved.[53] One measure, which struck broadly at abuses of government, demanded that no person not a native of Virginia or a minister be admitted to public office until he had resided in the colony for three years immediately preceding his elevation. This law stated further that no person guilty of any "notorious crime" should be allowed to hold office.[54] Extensive research might turn up other targets, but the act bears the mark of one aimed at Bacon and none other. That supposition lends added interest to other provisions which forbade the appointment of the same man as sheriff for two years in succession; which outlawed a growing practice of plurality in office-holding; which struck at inefficiency in the secretary's office at Jamestown; which set new penalties for exaction of exorbitant fees by sheriffs, escheators, collectors, clerks, and other officers; which required justices of the peace to act ex officio as coroners; and which declared it to be "an inherent and unquestionable right belonging to the . . . county courts to nominate, appoint place and displace their clerks as they see cause." Also passed were acts that repealed the statute of 1670 restricting the franchise to freeholders; gave to the freemen a right to elect every three years freeholders or substantial householders to the number of twelve as vestrymen of the parish; and directed "that some of the discreetest and ableest of the inhabitants of each county" be elected to sit with the county court in laying the annual levy. Still other acts forbade members of the governor's council to sit with the county court; reserved to the court appointment of all collectors of public and county levies; dispensed with need for the governor's signature on probates and administrations by authorizing any two local magistrates of the quorum to sign in his stead; and placed council members on a

[53] For the laws, see Hening, *Statutes*, II, 341–65.   [54] *Ibid.*, 353–55.

common basis with other residents of the colony in the payment of the poll tax.[55]

Among the attempts to deal directly with the current disturbances was a call for enforcement by all civil and military officers of the laws of England against "unlawfull tumults, routs and riotts." This act specifically authorized the governor to use military force for their suppression. At the same time, the burgesses ousted Edward Hill and John Stith from their places on the Charles City court and disqualified them for the holding of any office thereafter, on the ground that they had been "the greatest instruments and occasion of raiseing, promoteing and stirring up the late differences and misunderstandings that have happened between the honourable governor and his majesties good and loyall subjects" of Charles City and Henrico.[56] In still another effort to cope with current unrest, the Assembly provided amnesty for "all treasons, misprision of treasons, murders, fellonies, offences, crimes, contempts and misdemeanors, councelled, commanded, acted or done" between March 1 and June 25, except for violations of the laws governing trade with the Indians.[57]

Given a record like that, what is one to say? Clearly the ruling magistrates of the several counties had not all been unhorsed by Bacon's footmen. Clearly, too, they shared in some measure the popular complaints against the governor, and while yielding to the demand for a more popular control over county court and vestry, they substantially strengthened their own position with reference to the provincial authority. It could be argued that Berkeley's influence is reflected in some of the acts, but he can hardly be credited with others. As for Bacon's influence, it is pertinent to note that for most of the time the Assembly sat (from June 5 to June 25) he was not even in Jamestown. If during his stormy visit to the town toward the close of the Assembly's session he forced or persuaded the burgesses to adopt some of the more popular measures, he did not bother to secure repeal of the less popular. A likely conclusion seems to be that Bacon's Laws in the

[55] *Ibid.*, 359–60, an act which substituted for the former exemption an allowance of one hundred pounds yearly out of the returns from the two-shilling duty over and above allowances already made.

[56] *Ibid.*, 364–65.   [57] *Ibid.*, 363–64.

main reflect the work chiefly of a House of Burgesses broadly representative of the varied emotions evoked by recent events, and that agreement was reached most easily on the question of a general amnesty and on the necessity for action against the Indians.

There may have been disagreement over some provisions of the act for raising a force of one thousand men for prosecution of the war, and particularly to that part which designated Bacon as general and commander in chief. It is to be hoped that at least a few spoke out against the provision permitting the enslavement of all captive Indians. Surely there were some who saw the danger in an act authorizing repossession of abandoned land previously assigned to Indians and its sale to meet expenses of the war. But agreement must have come easily on the decision to have done with Sir William's plan of fortification and to outlaw *all* trade with the Indians.[58]

It would appear that Governor Berkeley and Speaker Thomas Godwin gave their formal approval to the legislation, whether perforce or otherwise. An Assembly meeting in the following February, after the death of Bacon and the collapse of his cause, declared all of these acts (for good measure) null, void, and repealed.[59] Some of the people in submitting their grievances to royal commissioners who arrived early in 1677 asked that "many good laws" enacted "before the rebell Bacon came" be confirmed. The commissioners, however, had an answer that was logical enough: the Assembly possessed the power to re-enact all such laws as were deemed desirable.[60]

It is not surprising that the work of the burgesses in June, 1676, should thus have been branded with the mark of rebellion. Bacon, following his reconciliation with Berkeley on June 10, remained in Jamestown, apparently expecting to receive the governor's commission. After a few days of fruitless waiting and after having received warning of a plot on his life, he left town with the governor's permission, on the excuse of a sick wife. One must rely entirely on conjecture for an answer to the puzzling problem of Berkeley's conduct. Politically wise enough to recognize the need for concession to popular sentiment, was he nevertheless deter-

[58] *Ibid.*, 341–50, 350–51, 351. [59] *Ibid.*, 365.
[60] *Virginia Magazine,* II (1894–1895), 167.

mined at all costs to win the personal contest between himself and Bacon and thus reluctant to yield to him the honor he had promised? Had there been some misunderstanding between the two men as to what had been promised? Was the governor awaiting action by the Assembly? Did he place too much confidence in the evidence there of distaste both for rebellion and for Bacon? It was a time of great excitement and tension; no doubt, of many ill-founded rumors. Was Bacon, always, it would seem, impetuous, precipitate in his decision to return home? Or was Berkeley now simply the "old fool" Charles II is reported later to have called him?

Whatever the fact, the governor blundered in permitting Bacon to return to the upper parts of the country without a clear statement of intentions regarding the Indian war. No sooner had Bacon reached home than the impatient people, "exclaiming still more and more against the Indians," came in "to ask how affairs Stood" and "if he had yet a comission." Finding that he did not, they "cry'd out aloud that they would either have a comission for Bacon that they might serve under his conduct or else they would pull downe the Towne or doe worse. . . , and if Bacon would goe but with them they would gett him a commission." And so, in the words of the royal commissioners, "the Raging Tumult came downe to Towne." [61] The scene enacted at Jamestown has become familiar by many tellings—the irate old governor rushing out to accuse Bacon as a rebel and a traitor; his offer, sword in hand, to settle the difference between them man to man; Bacon's refusal "to hurt a haire of your honor's head" and his "God damne my Blood, I came for a commission, and a commission I will have before I goe"; the burgesses looking on from the upper windows until on order from Bacon his soldiers took aim; and then the cry "For God's sake hold your handes and forebear a little, and you shall have what you please." [62] On the next day, commission in hand, he marched away with his men to settle at last the score with the Indians.

With a royal commission and the backing of a statute of the Assembly, Bacon found ready co-operation from a people long since impatient to finish the job. But just as he was ready to move against the "Heathen," as he often called the foe, word came that Sir William once more had proclaimed him a rebel and was en-

[61] Andrews (ed.), *Narratives of the Insurrections*, 116.   [62] *Ibid.*, 116–17.

gaged in an effort to raise forces against him. And at this point Bacon made his mistake, by deciding to turn back and settle first the score with Berkeley. It is pertinent to note the report rendered later by the royal commissioners, which on this development reads: "Now in vaine the Governor attempts raising a force against Bacon, and although the Industry and endeavors hee used to effect it was great, yet at this Juncture it was impossible, for Bacon at this tyme was so much the hopes and Darling of the people that the Governor's interest prov'd but weake, and his Friends so very few that he grew sick of the Essay." [63] Indeed, when Berkeley heard that Bacon was marching against him he had no choice but to flee for refuge to the Eastern Shore. Bacon might have ignored the reports of Berkeley's activity and pressed on against the Indians with confidence that if success attended his efforts not even Berkeley could touch him. The decision not to fight with a formidable enemy at his back is understandable from a military point of view, but it was obviously based upon an inadequate estimate of the governor's current strength. Moreover, it committed Bacon irrevocably to rebellion.

Few men have placed themselves so much in the wrong as had Berkeley, and Bacon soon found himself undisputed master of all Virginia, except for the Eastern Shore. But Sir William had the King's commission and other advantages in presenting his case to London. Bacon had the backing of popular support, but that he saw grave danger of its loss is evident from his attempt now to bind the people to him by special oath. The Indian war waited while the leading men were called into conference at Middle Plantation, where, after much debate, as the royal commissioners later reported it, "many by threats, Force and Feare were feigne to subscribe" to an oath that they would oppose such forces as might be sent from England "till such tyme I [i.e., Bacon] have acquainted the King with the state of this country, and have had an answer"; that they recognized the governor's action to have been illegal, Bacon's legal; and that they accepted the latter's commission as "lawfull and legally obtained." [64] Through the county courts an attempt was

[63] *Ibid.*, 121.

[64] *Ibid.*, 122. In addition, the oath required secrecy regarding Bacon's plans and the divulging of "what you shall heare at any time spoken against mee." As for the

made to secure administration of the same oath to the people, of whom, according to the commissioners, "none (or very few) for feare or Force durst or did refuse." [65] Bacon coupled this effort with an abortive attempt to seize the governor for the announced purpose of sending him to England for trial and with a call for a newly elected Assembly to meet early in September.[66] Then, once again, he prepared to deal with the Indians, who by this time must almost have felt neglected.

Though Bacon's purposes have been debated by scholars, there appears to be no valid reason for not accepting the commissioners' account as a substantially accurate statement of his objective— that is, to hold the people of Virginia united until a fair hearing could be had of the King. Bacon had the bull by the horns. A combination of Berkeley's irascibility and his own impetuosity had set Bacon on a course from which there was no turning back and left him no hope except that of winning out in a final hearing. That he had an independent spirit and that his followers frequently displayed the spirit of independence so characteristic both of Englishmen and Americans can hardly be disputed, but the parallel sometimes drawn with the American Revolution seems to be without real justification. Virginia had a population at this time of not many more than forty thousand; in a contest with the might of England there could be but one outcome. And if through foreign aid one saw a chance of success, what advantage would be gained? There were unpopular features of British policy, but where in this age of mercantilist empires could this community of Englishmen have gained a better bargain?

Let it be admitted for the sake of argument, however, that Bacon was ahead of his day in sensing the need for American independence. The important point is that once committed to open and unmistakable rebellion against the King's appointed agent he was unable to hold the people in line.[67] Indeed, one of the most im-

---

use of threats and force, it should be remembered that the commissioners took their information from witnesses anxious to clear themselves of the taint of treason. It is probable, however, that Bacon did appeal to the fears of men already deeply involved.

[65] *Ibid.*   [66] *Ibid.;* Wertenbaker, *Virginia under the Stuarts,* 173 ff.

[67] Wertenbaker, *Torchbearer of the Revolution,* 135–37, quotes at length from a reported conversation in September between Bacon and one John Goode which

pressive facts of the whole rebellion, which at times takes on a character close to that of a comic opera, is the fact that Sir William, for all his faults and the grievous complaints of the people, was able to reassert his authority without assistance from England. In September, Bacon turned from a somewhat indecisive campaign against the Pamunkeys, not to meet an assembly of his followers, but to march against a Jamestown reoccupied by the governor, who had moved back by water from Accomac.[68] In its capture Bacon's soldiers fought with better spirit than did its defenders, but his subsequent decision to burn the town speaks more of desperation than of confidence in his strength. Already too many men sought the safety of a neutral position, and after Bacon's death from exposure and exhaustion late in October his cause collapsed. Though some fought on with the desperate courage of men irrevocably committed, the key men were run down and hanged by late January, when the King's commissioners arrived to confront instead of the rebel Bacon a governor who once more was so much possessed of his old assurance as to offer gratuitous insult to the man commissioned to take his place. Soon shipped off to England to answer for his faults, the old man made his exit from a stage where, it should not be forgotten, he had for most of the time played a distinguished part.

And what of Bacon and his place in American history, a place surely as large for the length of time he spent in the country as that of any other man? To deny that he stood for all of the things for which Jefferson stood a hundred years later is not to deny that he fought for some of the things for which Jefferson would fight. Hotheaded and impetuous, a man who appears to have been carried at times further than he intended by his emotions, Bacon apparently was moved primarily by resentment against the governor's ineffective policy for defense of the exposed frontiers. Indeed, it might

---

shows Bacon's mind at that time ranging over all the possibilities, even of help from other colonies and of independence. It is an extraordinarily interesting document, but to this writer it suggests the desperate graspings of a man who already sensed that his cause was lost, and is of interest primarily for Goode's clear statement of the arguments for Virginia's dependence. Notice, too, his warning that "your followers do not think themselves engaged against the King's authority, but merely against the Indians."

[68] Wertenbaker's discussion, *ibid.*, 142 ff., of the naval aspects of the rebellion is especially helpful.

be argued that an interpretation of his rebellion couched in the old-fashioned terms of a sectional contest makes as much sense as the more recent tendency to interpret it in terms of a class conflict. But, as so frequently would be the case thereafter, a protest rooted in sectional interest broadened into a general attack on special privilege and on abusive use of political power. Thus its leader has been accorded a rightful place among those who have shaped the long tradition of political liberalism in America. Perhaps the dispute regarding his place with reference to the American Revolution can be resolved by recalling again the twofold character of that revolution. It was more than a contest for independence from England; it sought also readjustment and reform within the several provinces in the interest of a more popularly controlled government, and for this last objective Bacon made an early fight. More immediately, the effect of his efforts undoubtedly is to be followed in the warning given to those who held office in Virginia. If he did not succeed in destroying the special privilege of a governing class, he succeeded in underscoring for a group to which he himself belonged the responsibility which properly goes with privilege. His very name, celebrated in verse and song down through the years, was destined to correct abuses in a system of government from which the nation, through Washington, Jefferson, Madison, and others, would draw great advantage.

By no means the least significant feature of Bacon's Rebellion was the prompt reaction of the home government to news, first received in September, of the disturbances in the colony. Having decided at once on the removal of Berkeley, the government on receipt of additional information prepared to send an expedition which all told would comprise eleven vessels (three being men-of-war) and over 1,100 soldiers under the command of Colonel Herbert Jeffreys. He received a commission to replace Berkeley and was joined in a special commission of investigation with Captain Sir John Berry, who commanded the fleet, and Francis Moryson, who had been in England as agent for the colony in its protest against the Arlington and Culpeper grant. The first ship reached Virginia on January 29, 1677, and all were in by mid-February.[69]

[69] Andrews (ed.), *Narratives of the Insurrections*, 101–104; Wertenbaker, *Virginia under the Stuarts*, 195 ff.

The presence in Virginia of so many vessels and soldiers of the King spoke more impressively of a new imperial policy than did the almost coincidental launching of Edward Randolph's campaign for the reduction of New England to a due submission to His Majesty's will. Thoughtful men must have recognized that these soldiers represented a purpose destined to have enduring influence on the life of the colony. Perhaps some of them saw a connection with the recently established Lords of Trade, a committee of the Privy Council, which over the ensuing two decades would accomplish much toward the shaping and reshaping of an empire.

For the moment, however, the problem of restoring peace to a war-torn province engaged the chief attention of all. If Berkeley, whose resourcefulness together with the timidity of Jeffreys enabled him to hang on for a few weeks,[70] interpreted that problem in terms primarily of running down and executing his remaining enemies, the commissioners directed their attention in accordance with the royal instructions to receiving the grievances of the people and seeking to restore peace with the Indians. A newly elected Assembly, meeting at Greenspring on February 20, passed an act of general indemnity, though with exceptions reflecting far too much of Berkeley's vindictiveness,[71] and re-enacted some but by no means all the legislation adopted at the extraordinary session of the preceding June.[72] Accusations and recriminations continued to divide the people,[73] but by July it was considered safe to send most of the soldiers back to England.

Colonel Jeffreys remained in the colony as lieutenant governor until his death in November, 1678. Since 1675 Thomas, Lord Cul-

[70] Wertenbaker, *Virginia under the Stuarts*, 199–211.

[71] Hening, *Statutes*, II, 366–73. See also, *ibid.*, 373–80, 428–30.

[72] See especially, *ibid.*, 389–92, 396, 398–99, 404. The right of the county court to appoint collectors was reaffirmed; pluralism in the holding of the offices of justice and clerk of court was prohibited; the right of councilors to sit with the county court was conceded but on condition that they assume full responsibility and liability with other members of the court; the requirement of a three-year term of residence before appointment to office was renewed. Also renewed were the acts permitting two justices of the quorum to sign probates, and removing the exemption of councilors (except for their own persons) from levies. One act authorized the election of six freeholders and householders to sit with the parish vestry in levying parish dues. Another cut the allowance for the expense of the burgesses. Title to captured Indians received confirmation.

[73] See an act of October, 1677, *ibid.*, 409.

peper, one of the Virginia proprietors, had held commission as successor to Berkeley, but not until the spring of 1680 was he persuaded to leave the pleasures of London for the governor's post in Virginia. Meantime, Sir Henry Chicheley, an elderly and now a somewhat infirm member of the council, served as acting governor. Sir Henry's interim rule marks conveniently enough the reestablishment of conventional controls in the life of the colony.

Meanwhile, relations with the Indians also had been restored to an accustomed basis. The royal commissioners had argued with the burgesses in February, 1677, that the settlers should be content with the land they had, "being more than they either will or can cultivate to profitt," [74] and neighboring tribes, of which the Pamunkey was chief, escaped the confiscation of their lands which had been threatened in the heat of Bacon's Rebellion. The Susquehannocks and other outlying tribes having quieted down, in October the Assembly began to relax the restrictions on Indian trade.[75] When in 1678 the colony faced new alarms it entrusted plans for defense to none other than Abraham Wood,[76] who would render his last-recorded public service in Indian negotiations of 1679–1680.[77]

The Assembly undertook to supplement Wood's negotiations by adopting a modification of Berkeley's plan of frontier forts. At the head of each of the four great rivers housing and stores were to be provided for a permanent garrison, recruited by imposing a responsibility for the provision of one completely armed man with horse on every forty tithables.[78] Each garrison would enjoy the services of four Indian scouts, and it is apparent from the phrasing of the act that these garrisons were expected to maintain "ranging" patrols for the warning both of the Indians and of the English. In fact, the experiment is significant chiefly as a step toward reliance on a less expensive system of rangers that was destined to

[74] McIlwaine (ed.), *Journals of the House of Burgesses of Virginia, 1659/60–1693,* pp. 91–92.

[75] Hening, *Statutes,* II, 410–12. For evidence of the enslavement of Indians after 1676, see Ames, *Virginia Eastern Shore in the Seventeenth Century,* 74.

[76] Bruce, *Institutional History of Virginia,* II, 91.

[77] Alvord and Bidgood, *First Explorations of the Trans-Allegheny Region by the Virginians,* 43.

[78] Hening, *Statutes,* II, 433–40.

hold a large place in the history and tradition of the American frontier. By legislation first passed in 1682 provision was made for the compensation of rangers to be recruited from the frontier counties.[79] They would have no obligation to stand guard at any one place, but, armed and mounted at their own expense, they were expected to maintain regular patrols for intelligence of Indian movements.

No longer guided by fanciful notions of living in permanent peace with the Indians, not even concerned, in Hakluyt's phrase, to square and prepare them for the preacher's hand, and too poor to maintain a standing defense, the English planter now sought chiefly to assure for himself some warning of the native's intended retaliation.

[79] See discussion in Bruce, *Institutional History of Virginia,* II, 115 ff.

CHAPTER XI

YEARS OF CHANGE AND DISCONTENT

THE detailed history of the several provinces during the later years of the seventeenth century fortunately has no place in a work of this scope. Viewed separately, each province underwent developments of major significance in its own history and experienced varying degrees of unrest among its people pointing to problems of adjustment which generally characterized the period. Followed in detail, however, these stories tend to lead one away from those things that are of general interest into a confusing chronicle of petty politics and protest. Accordingly, the concluding pages of this volume are restricted to a broad discussion of developments which lend meaning to the period as a whole.

Some of the more important forces at work have been suggested in the preceding chapter. It is more than mere chance that explains a common inclination to regard Bacon's Rebellion as marking both the end and the beginning of an era in American history. Not only did other communities share in considerable measure the popular discontent which overflowed in that historic protest, but the spirit of rebellion thus awakened undoubtedly contributed to the unrest which subsequently found expression in neighboring provinces. There, hardly less than in Virginia, men struggled with problems occasioned by the low price of tobacco, found reason to associate the hardships of their life with abuse of political power, and sought remedy through political action. But in Maryland and Carolina one fundamental difference existed: the right to govern did not stem directly from a royal commission. Rather, it depended upon an intermediate authority established by earlier proprietary charters. Popular protest, therefore, found a natural focus in opposition to the proprietary right to rule, and in the end men of rebellious spirit in America found powerful allies in agencies of the crown which for their own reasons sought to restrict proprietary authority in the colonies. Some few men may have entertained early notions of independence from England, but a much more common objective among Americans for many years to come would be that of winning the right to be governed by the King.

In setting that objective, colonists in the proprietary settlements received encouragement from the growing activity of a committee of the Privy Council commonly known as the Lords of Trade. Established in 1675 as successor to a series of special committees and councils which since Cromwell's day had sought with imperfect success to implement the commercial policies laid down in the Navigation Acts and Trade Acts, the Lords of Trade were engaged in the development of an administrative policy that has been well described by the late Professor Andrews as one of "centralization." [1] Its purpose was to overcome the administrative disunity of an empire which had developed with little central direction, and to establish in the interest of a more effective enforcement of the Trade Acts a necessary control of colonial administration by agencies of the crown. In a running contest with Massachusetts, most flagrant of the offenders against the King's laws, the Lords of Trade converted New Hampshire into a royal colony by 1679. Though they failed in the subsequent attempt to obstruct the grant of Pennsylvania as a proprietorship to William Penn, they succeeded in denying to him some of the extensive powers held by Lord Baltimore in Maryland. In 1684 they won in the courts an annulment of the charters of Massachusetts and of the Bermuda Company. And after New York had passed automatically to the crown with the Duke of York's accession to the throne as James II in 1685, the Lords of Trade undertook their most ambitious experiment in the establishment of the Dominion of New England—a short-lived attempt to consolidate all of the New England colonies and New York under a single royal government. During the brief interval that remained before the English Revolution of 1688, New England continued to receive chief attention.[2] But while undertaking to

---

[1] See especially, Charles M. Andrews, *The Colonial Background of the American Revolution* (New Haven, 1924), 27.

[2] Viola F. Barnes, *The Dominion of New England, A Study in British Colonial Policy* (New Haven, 1923), tells the story in detail.

reduce the Northern provinces to an appropriate submission to royal authority, the Lords of Trade had not neglected to attempt a suitable revision of the pattern of royal government as it had developed in Virginia.

Culpeper's instructions of 1680 specified that thereafter the Assembly should be called into session only after the consent of the King's ministers in London had been obtained. It was further directed that the governor and council in seeking this consent should forward drafts of necessary legislation for approval by the King's ministers before its submission to the burgesses "for their consent," a provision which carried an unmistakable threat that the House of Burgesses would be deprived of its long-established right to the initiative in the legislative process. On these points, happily, the governor disregarded his instructions, and was upheld because of considerations of distance and time. That the authorities in England intended, however, to assume the initiative in securing enactment of desired legislation was forcefully emphasized by three statutes Lord Culpeper presented, per instruction, for passage by the Virginia Assembly.[3]

The practice, it should be noted, was not entirely new. Since the days of Yeardley and Wyatt the governor's instructions repeatedly had served to shape legislation in the colony,[4] but the long tenure of Sir William Berkeley had been in an unusual degree a period of self-government and the burgesses rightly saw in the formal drafts submitted to them a new cause for concern. They could find little ground for opposing an act of general indemnity intended to end the quarrels left from Bacon's Rebellion, and felt little if any inclination to object to the provisions of a proposed act of naturalization. But the burgesses stood their ground on the question of a bill for levy of the two-shilling duty. The duty itself, of course, was one long since placed in the statutes on the initiative of the burgesses themselves. The trouble came from a provision granting the proceeds "to the king's most excellent Majesty his heires and Successors for ever to and for the better support of the Government." [5] This clause raised a fundamental issue of control of the purse, but the burgesses fought at a disadvantage.

---

[3] Wertenbaker, *Virginia under the Stuarts*, 226–27.   [4] See above, p. 206.
[5] Wertenbaker, *Virginia under the Stuarts*, 227, 229–31.

Large arrears in unpaid quitrents hung over the colony, and a threat that payment in full might be demanded put through the measure.

The details, however, have relatively little importance for the purposes of this study. The point is that the Virginia Assembly had been alerted to the necessity for defending its traditional rights in the government of the colony, and that men theretofore divided by the memory of Bacon's Rebellion tended to draw together in defense of the colony's rights. Lord Culpeper proved to be a feeble instrument of the new policy, but in Lord Howard of Effingham, who took the oath as replacement for Culpeper in October of 1683, the Lords of Trade found a much more dependable man. Over the next few years the Assembly was denied the right to act as the highest court of appeals in the colony through a decision which enlarged the power of the governor and council as the final resort in Virginia; saw the clerk of the burgesses removed and the authority to designate a clerk for the house vested thereafter in the crown; had some of its members dismissed for petition in behalf of the Assembly to the King; struggled again over the old question of fees unregulated by legislative action; disputed the royal prerogative on questions of disallowance and prorogation; and for its pains was labeled "obstinate and peevish" by the governor.[6] New issues brought forward new leaders: men like Robert Beverley, ousted clerk of Assembly, and Philip Ludwell, ousted member of the council, both of them having been stalwart supporters of Berkeley at the time of Bacon's Rebellion.

In these and other efforts made by the English government during the 1680's one finds the origins of a permanent policy, destined to be pressed with persistent vigor by the Board of Trade, which in 1696 took over the functions of the Lords of Trade. But as yet the policy was imperfect and incomplete in its application, even its enforcement was marked at times by a note of incongruity. Lord Culpeper, for instance, in his own person represented the very proprietary interest against which the new policy so largely was to be directed. The Culpeper-Arlington patent of 1673 carried no rights of government, but Lord Culpeper's designation in succession to Berkeley as early as 1675 is more than suggestive of official

6 *Ibid.*, 241-55.

attitudes which had enabled Sir George Calvert in 1632 to secure in addition to his proprietorship of the soil of Maryland full powers of government. During the very years of Culpeper's active gubernatorial service in Virginia, he acquired by purchase the rights of all other claimants, including, in addition to Arlington, claimants under the patent of 1649. After the governor's recall in 1683, he sold to the crown all rights except those in the Northern Neck, but that more restricted proprietorship would survive as the Fairfax estate of eighteenth-century fame.[7]

Other features of imperial policy during the later years of the seventeenth century were destined to have a more profound effect on the life of eighteenth-century Virginia. The colony's place in the empire depended upon its production of tobacco, and thus the most important actions of the government in London were those which pertained to the marketing of that weed. From the point of view of the planter, the critical problem continued to be that of a low price for his annual crop, but in seeking remedy through the long-favored device of crop control he now met an additional obstacle in the attitude of the King's ministers. Not only did they refuse to accept the threatened losses in royal revenue, but their attitude seems to have been shaped in part by a desire to assist the English merchant in capturing European markets of great potential value.[8]

If the policy carried the promise of ultimate benefit for the planter, that promise was more than offset by the hardships currently resulting. When hope of some effective action by the Virginia Assembly had been frustrated in the spring of 1682 by its prorogation on other grounds, the anger of the people found expression in the famous tobacco riots of that year. The troubles began in Gloucester, but the idea soon caught on in other counties as men banded together to destroy the tobacco as it grew in the field. After the militia made raids too hazardous by day, some carried on the destruction under cover of darkness. Authorities in England saw the specter of rebellion; many arrests were made and two leaders were later hanged. But the riots seemed to have been spontaneous outbursts of angered farmers who had no other purpose than to

[7] Andrews, *Colonial Period of American History*, II, 234–37.
[8] Wertenbaker, *Planters of Colonial Virginia*, 117; *Virginia under the Stuarts*, 238.

emphasize their protest at the failure to provide remedy for unbearable conditions of the market. By the end of summer quiet had been restored.[9]

Complaints continued to be heard against the requirement that all tobacco should be shipped to England. That policy in its application, however, guaranteed substantial advantages for the colonial product in the English markets and permitted reshipment abroad of the surplus, with favorable allowances on the customs due the King. In the end, the very bulk of the colonies' production drove down the price to such an extent that the English merchants captured for their tobacco an expanding market on the Continent and elsewhere. And as the very cheapness of tobacco helped to spread its use, foretelling its place as the poor man's luxury around the world, even the planter began to feel the benefit. Indeed, the very next year after the riots in Virginia a favorable turn of the market gave promise of better days.[10]

Unquestionably there was much to be said for a policy which recognized that the future of tobacco lay in the encouragement of its popular consumption rather than in the maintenance of prices restricting its sale as a luxury. The transitional stage, however, frequently imposed heavy penalties on the planters and left permanent marks on the colony's economic and social structure. In the struggle to combat the disadvantages of a falling market, many planters found an additional stimulus to mercantile and other activity long to be identified with plantation life. Ventures in shipping, despite favoring legislation for locally owned vessels, proved none too successful. Similarly abortive were renewed attempts to encourage the growth of towns in the hope, among other things, of effecting economies in the wasteful system by which tobacco was collected for shipment to England. But those planters who dealt as local merchants in the distribution of imported goods, who extended to their neighbors credit through the year and took their crop in payment at the end of the year, reportedly lived better than any others.[11] If the practice served to emphasize a sense of

---

[9] Wertenbaker, *Virginia under the Stuarts*, 231–38.

[10] See especially, Wertenbaker, *Planters of Colonial Virginia*, 115 ff.; Gray, *History of Agriculture in Southern United States*, I, 252–53, 265–68.

[11] Henry Hartwell, James Blair, and Edward Chilton, *The Present State of Virginia*,

indebtedness and disadvantage among the poor, it provided relief for the not so poor. The hold of this latter group on the government had been only momentarily shaken by the rebellion, and the rewards of office—whether from fee, salary, or special favors in the granting of land—strengthened a natural inclination of the more favorably situated planters to seek office.

Though much of the land secured through a loosely administered policy was held for speculative purposes, which imposed additional penalties on the poor man who sought to improve his lot, some of the planters were exploring the possibility that an answer to the problem of a low-priced staple might be found in production on a scale that would offer compensation for a low rate of profit. Conditions of the market placed new premiums on the use of fresh land, and the larger planters at times cultivated widely scattered acreages, using overseers for superintendence of outlying quarters.[12] If anything, agriculture around the Chesapeake became now even more wasteful of natural resources than previously. Indian troubles and a probably more important consideration of the bar to navigation provided by the fall line on the several rivers tended to restrict momentarily the area of settlement. As freed servants and other less fortunate members of the community put to cultivation lands of marginal fertility or location, they helped to preserve a statistical basis for demonstrating that Virginia was still the land of the small farmer, as indeed it remained. But there were indications that it might not always so remain.[13]

Among these indications was the growing use of Negro labor. The colony continued to depend chiefly upon an annual importation of approximately 1,500 white servants from England, a supply that would not be seriously diminished until after 1689,[14] but the estimated number of Negroes in the colony had jumped from three

---

and the College, ed. by Hunter D. Farish (Williamsburg, 1940), 10–11. This account, written in 1697, attributed the failure of attempts to stimulate the growth of towns to the fact that the burgesses of each county wanted the town in their own county or else a town for each county. See also, Bruce, Economic History of Virginia, II, 380–85.

12 Bruce, Economic History of Virginia, I, 429; II, 17–18.

13 See again, Wertenbaker, Planters of Colonial Virginia.

14 In addition to ibid., 41, see Smith, Colonists in Bondage; White Servitude and Convict Labor in America, 1607–1776, Appendix.

hundred at mid-century to two thousand by 1671 and to three thousand by 1681.[15]

In seeking an explanation for this significant development, one is inclined, first, to emphasize the ever present shortage of labor in a new country, even in times of adversity. It seems to be a likely conclusion that the colonist initially found in the Negro not so much a different type of laborer to be substituted for some other available laborer as rather an additional workman who helped to narrow the gap between the demand and the supply. But with the passage of time there is increasing evidence that it was the larger planter who found the Negro most useful, a fact which argues that there existed in connection with the development of larger units of cultivation a definite advantage in the use of Negroes. That advantage probably lay in the relative economy of Negro labor where no special considerations, as on the small farm, gave preference to the European laborer. For while the initial cost was greater, the purchaser might expect to enjoy the Negro's services for a lifetime and even to build up over the years a stock of labor which reproduced itself.[16] Since most of the Negroes reaching the Chesapeake at this time seem to have come from the West Indies through the agencies of New England traders, one finds little occasion for considering here the growing slave trade of the Royal African Company or the interest of the English government in its encouragement.[17]

Let it be emphasized again that the Chesapeake colonies still remained a community of European settlers. But in the growing number of Negroes, and the continued necessity for economy in the production of a commodity which depended so much for a market on its cheapness, one traces the forewarning of a tragic commitment to human slavery.[18]

[15] Evarts B. Greene and Virginia D. Harrington, *American Population before the Federal Census of 1790* (New York, 1932), 136–37.

[16] Gray, *History of Agriculture in the Southern United States,* I, 361–71; Wertenbaker, *Planters of Colonial Virginia,* 126 ff.

[17] Gray, *History of Agriculture in the Southern United States,* I, 353.

[18] Apparently the earliest figures available for Maryland are those of 1707, which show then a total of 4,657 slaves as against 3,000 white servants. Greene and Harrington, *American Population before the Federal Census of 1790,* p. 124. Jeffrey R. Brackett,

Already the statutes reflected developing customs that tended to draw a sharp distinction between the white and the black. The statute of 1661, passed in recognition of the fact that runaway Negroes bound to life servitude could not make satisfaction by serving additional time,[19] had been followed by a law of 1662 which settled the question of whether children "got by any Englishman upon a negro woman should be slave or free" by declaring they should take the status of the mother.[20] The provision of double penalties for "any christian" guilty of fornication "with a negro man or woman" contained in the same act expressed a purpose, as had earlier action of the courts, to maintain the racial integrity of the whites. As the phrasing of the law indicates, the Virginia Assembly followed a long-established tradition in basing the distinction between slave and free on the difference between the heathen and the Christian. That ancient rule still guided the burgesses as in 1670 they faced the question of whether an Indian enslaved by other Indians and then sold to an Englishman could be held for life. The Indian was also a heathen, as Bacon would frequently remind the people, but there were special considerations operating for protection of the native American. And so the burgesses settled the question by ruling "that all servants not being christians imported into this colony by shipping shalbe slaves for their lives; but what shall come by land shall serve, if boyes or girles, untill thirty yeares of age, if men or women twelve yeares and no longer."[21] At the same time, the Assembly forbade any "manumitted, or otherwise free" Indian or Negro, even "though baptised," to hold a Christian in bondage, though they might buy "any of their owne nation."[22]

There appears to be little occasion for debate as to the intent of this legislation. The law is a technical thing, and there are subtleties in the law of slavery which this generation of Virginians had had as yet little occasion to appreciate. Many more statutes would be required to settle all questions, and the so-called slave code of Virginia is properly identified with a later period of time.

The Negro in Maryland; A Study of the Institution of Slavery (Baltimore, 1889), like Ballagh on Virginia, is concerned with the legal aspects of slavery rather than the economic.

[19] See above, p. 217.   [20] Hening, *Statutes*, II, 170.
[21] *Ibid.*, 283.   [22] *Ibid.*, 280–81.

But disregarding the sort of technicality that might enable a man to make his point in court, can we question that the English settler already proposed to treat the growing number of Negroes. coming into the colony as slaves, that his approach to the problem was founded upon a belief in his own superiority, and that he rejected any idea that the new stock might be incorporated into his society without regard for the integrity of his own stock? By a statute of 1682 which removed conversion to Christianity as the basis for a claim to freedom,[23] the colonist also took a significant step toward shifting the fundamental basis of his distinction between free and slave from a difference in religion to a difference of race.

In seeking to preserve the racial integrity of the English community, men gave some thought to the future, but in their attempt to find through use of the Negro a ready answer to their problems of labor, they paid little heed to the consequences of what they did. It is a common human failing not to look ahead, but it may be worth remarking in this connection that not all of the planters as yet had identified themselves completely with the colony. Though most of them undoubtedly expected to live out their lives here, they still thought of themselves as Englishmen living in Virginia, in which inclination they received encouragement by the direct and regular communications maintained through their trade with England. A few of the more fortunate planters broke their stay in America by visits home. William Byrd, at least, sent his children to England for the schooling appropriate to the station he was preparing for them on the River James. Francis Moryson, after

[23] An act of 1667, *ibid.*, 260, had declared that "children that are slaves by birth" should not "by vertue of their baptisms be made ffree," but this left a claim open to such as might be Christian before their arrival in the colony. The act of 1682 removed the basis for a claim even on the ground of conversion prior to importation. See *ibid.*, 490; Helen T. Catterall (ed.), *Judicial Cases concerning American Slavery and the Negro*, I, 60 ff. Ballagh, *History of Slavery in Virginia*, 42 ff., provides a useful discussion, but his emphasis differs somewhat from the author's. As already noted, the question of religion had been settled for Carolina in the Fundamental Constitutions. In Maryland the question was settled by legislation of 1664 and 1671. By the act of 1664 "negroes and other slaves" in the province or to be imported thereafter would serve for life. English women marrying Negro slaves would serve as slaves to the husband's master for the length of the husband's life, and children of the marriage would take the father's status. But by an act of 1681 the children of white servant women by Negroes were considered free. For full discussion, see Brackett, *Negro in Maryland*, 28 ff.

a quarter century as an influential resident of the colony and after completing his duties in connection with the investigation of Bacon's Rebellion, returned home permanently in 1677.

It has become a commonplace to quote extensively from a letter of William Fitzhugh describing in glowing terms of contentment his place on the Potomac in 1686. But it is too frequently overlooked that the letter was written in an effort to effect an advantageous exchange for some establishment in the old country by a man who desired again "to breathe my native air," provided "it could be done with reputation & credit" and without loss of the "true Station and Standing" he had won for himself in the New World.[24]

In a letter of January, 1687, Fitzhugh provides a valuable statement of his reasons for wishing to leave Virginia. "Our estates here depend altogether upon contingency's," he wrote, "and to prepare against that, causes might exceed my Inclinations in worldly affairs, and society that is good & ingenious is very scarce and seldom to be come at except in Books. Good education of children is almost impossible and better be never born than ill-bred. But that which bears the greatest weight with me, for now I look upon myself to be in my declining age, is the want of spirituall helps and comforts, of which this fertile country in everything else, is barren & unfruitfull." [25] Yet, though, on the eve of his death in 1701, he still hoped to get home, he refused to consider surrender of any advantage he had gained by coming to Virginia. That this advantage was not inconsiderable is indicated by a will made in 1700 disposing of over fifty thousand acres of land, fifty-one slaves, and six English servants. A man of many parts who had come to Virginia a few years before Bacon's Rebellion, who as a trained lawyer had worked with other influences of that time to bring about greater conformity in the usages of the colony with the law of England, who had sought refuge from the isolation of colonial life in books, and who, while looking to England as his home, had found in America substantial rewards of industry and shrewdness which bound him to the New

---

[24] The letter, dated April 22, 1686, and addressed to Dr. Ralph Smith in Bristol, may be found in *Virginia Magazine*, I (1893–1894), 395–96. It should be read with other letters there and especially *ibid.*, 396–98. As published by Bruce, *Economic History of Virginia*, II, 243, the opening lines of the letter are omitted.

[25] *Virginia Magazine*, I (1893–1894), 24–25.

World, Fitzhugh may be taken as truly representative of the leading planters in Virginia toward the close of the seventeenth century.[26]

It was an interesting period of transition. The law of inheritance was still democratic, being that of partible descent, under a statute of 1673,[27] and the laws of primogeniture and entail against which Jefferson would war had not yet been enacted. Amusements, whether the occasion be a wedding, a house-raising, an occasional horse race, or even a wake, seem to have been for the most part of that spontaneous and often rowdy variety destined so long to be associated with the free and easy way of the American frontier. And yet men of wealth were becoming increasingly conscious of their position and, if we may judge by Fitzhugh's correspondence, almost painfully conscious of the importance of appearances. In sending instructions for his sister to come over in 1686, he demanded that she come "handsomely & gentelely & well cloathed, with a maid to wait on her" and with her passage paid on the other side "for the credit of it," all which, he explained to the sister, would give "us both credit & reputation." [28] Possessed of land, public office, and the means to import from England whatever else might be required, there was more than one man in Virginia who now prepared to play the part of a gentleman and to play it in the best tradition of the old country.

Returns from the Indian trade continued to provide a substantial part of the payments made by Virginians in London, but already there were indications that leadership in the trade with Southern tribes would pass to Carolina. Not only did Charles Town enjoy the advantage of shorter distances to the hunting grounds of the Catawbas and of the Cherokee, but explorations westward from the town revealed that the mountain barriers which hemmed in more northerly situated provinces gave way in southern Carolina to a terrain offering easy penetration of the interior. During the first years of the colony the energies of the people had been directed

---

[26] *Ibid.*, II (1894–1895), 276–78, for his will, and in addition to this volume, the volumes immediately preceding and following for other correspondence. Louis B. Wright, *The First Gentlemen of Virginia, Intellectual Qualities of the Early Colonial Ruling Class* (San Marino, 1940) contains a short biography of Fitzhugh as a representative gentleman of early Virginia.

[27] Hening, *Statutes*, II, 303. [28] *Virginia Magazine*, I (1893–1894), 391–93.

largely to the burdensome tasks of initial settlement. Those who undertook trading ventures found themselves in competition with efforts by the proprietors to monopolize the trade through their own agents, of whom Dr. Henry Woodward was the chief and the most colorful. Moreover, in an area where the natives had long been subject to the influence of the Spaniard in Florida, it took time to work out a settled policy for dealing with the several tribes. Open war with the neighboring Westo Indians early in the 1680's brought a serious interruption of trade. Fortunately, their resistance was soon broken, and other natives along the Savannah River then were persuaded to assist rather than obstruct the development of a trade with the western tribes. By 1689 the strong hand of Shaftesbury, who had died in 1683 as a political exile, no longer guided proprietary policy, and control of the trade had passed into the hands of the planters.[29] Its rapid development over the next quarter century would provide much of Charles Town's growing wealth.

As the pack-horse of the Carolina trader plodded westward, French explorers moved by boat down the Mississippi. They had come by way of the St. Lawrence River and the Great Lakes to the Illinois country, whence, through the enterprise of La Salle, they had extended their explorations southward to the mouth of the Mississippi by 1682.[30] La Salle named his new discovery Louisiana in honor of Louis XIV, and by other action undertook to assure a prompt exploitation of the discovery. But such were the delays in the development of French interests on the lower Mississippi that it will be enough here merely to note that in the coming contest between England and France for possession of the North American continent Louisiana would be pitted against Carolina.

Of more immediate significance was the clash between Carolina and Florida in which the representatives of English and Spanish imperialism renewed an ancient fight. One of the more interesting features of that renewal lies in the fact that it coincided almost exactly with the successful negotiation of a treaty between the two powers for settlement of long-standing differences in America. By

[29] See especially, Crane, *Southern Frontier, 1670–1732*.
[30] Clarence W. Alvord, *The Illinois Country, 1673–1818* (Chicago, 1922), provides an authoritative study of the background of this achievement.

the Treaty of Madrid in 1670 it was agreed that both states thereafter would abstain from reliance upon piracy as an agency of national policy, and that the hitherto disputed doctrine of effective occupation would be accepted as the test of a valid title to New World lands. More specifically, it was stipulated that England's claims along the coast of North America would be recognized as far south as Port Royal—this being a concession by the hardpressed Spanish government apparently made in the hope that England's southward expansion might be stopped at a line roughly approximating the northward extension of the Florida missions. The treaty marks an important turning point in American history, for the way was now clear for other agreements extending the peace of Europe "beyond the line" to America.[31] The buccaneer as an instrument of national policy would soon disappear, and men would be hanged as pirates for deeds their governments formerly had been delighted to honor.

But a phrase can be misleading, and to say that the peace of Europe had been extended to America by the later years of the seventeenth century is merely to say that the treaties through which European states sought a settlement of their other differences now included provisions seeking to settle their disputes in the New World as well. That agreements reached would not in every case survive the pressure of an intense and developing rivalry was demonstrated at the very outset by the fate which overtook the provision in the Treaty of Madrid regarding the southern boundary of Carolina. In the view of the Carolinians, that boundary extended down almost to St. Augustine, specifically to the twenty-ninth degree fixed in the second proprietary charter. For justification of this attitude, they had only to point to the prompt effort, happily abortive, made by the garrison at St. Augustine to destroy the infant settlement on the Ashley.

In Florida the new English settlement could be viewed only as a threat to St. Augustine and to the security of the Bahama channel upon which the homeward-bound fleets of Spain depended. As early as 1668, when the English pirate Robert Searles attacked St. Augustine, plans had been under consideration for the construc-

[31] See especially, the concluding pages of Newton, *European Nations in the West Indies.*

tion (in lieu of an old wooden fort) of strong fortifications of stone. By 1672 the garrison had been strengthened and a beginning made on the Castillo de San Marcos. Completed by 1687, insofar as any fortification may be said to be finished, this massive structure of stone, with its surrounding moat and fifty pieces of artillery, stood guard, with the similar fortifications of Havana, for the security of one of the empire's basic lines of communication.[32] Outside St. Augustine the Franciscan friar was engaged in a losing contest with the Carolina trader. But if he was forced to fall back, he fell back on the strength of one of the major fortifications in colonial America. Three quarters of a century would pass before the Protestant intruders had placed a period to his missionary endeavors among the Southern Indians.

Port Royal, site of the first Protestant challenge to Catholic interests in America, remained a special bone of contention. Known among the Spaniards as Santa Elena, in 1684 it briefly became Stuart's Town, when a group of Scottish Presbyterians settled there by agreement with the Carolina proprietors. Unfortunately, the English and the Scots had not yet entered into a partnership as empire builders, and jealousies, arising partly from a contest for control of the Indian trade, soon divided the inhabitants of Stuart's Town and Charles Town. In 1686, the Spaniards from St. Augustine wiped out the Scottish settlement.[33]

Northward along the Carolina coast from Charles Town, and well past Cape Fear, one came at last to Roanoke Island and the uncertain entrances to Albemarle Sound, where a community of perhaps three thousand colonists presented to men of the late seventeenth century a more perplexing problem of identification than any other along the Southeastern coast. St. Augustine was Spanish; Stuart's Town had been Scottish; and Charles Town was English; but Albemarle County was American, and thus possessed qualities better understood today than in that day. For practical purposes shut off from direct sea communications with Europe by the shifting sand bars of her coast, Albemarle was closer to Virginia in origin than to the rest of Carolina but separated even from the

[32] Verne E. Chatelain, *The Defenses of Spanish Florida, 1565 to 1763*, pp. 62–75.
[33] George P. Insh, *Scottish Colonial Schemes, 1620–1686*, pp. 186–211; Crane, *Southern Frontier*, 28 n.

older colony by difficult country which included the Dismal Swamp. Albemarle County was in fact a coastal backwoods that served as a haven for the sort of people who in later years would find their way, for good and sufficient reasons, to Kentucky, Tennessee, and Texas. Among those finding refuge there were a good many Quakers, or persons, at any rate, whose religious ideas were irregular enough to win for them that designation.[34]

For the most part, the settlers lived as small subsistence farmers. Much of the area was given over to swamp and marsh, requiring for clearance and drainage a far heavier investment of labor than could be afforded. Settlement tended to be scattered but nowhere far removed from the waterways upon which men depended, as in Virginia, for transportation and communication.[35] Denied the right after 1679 to export their tobacco through Virginia, the inhabitants depended for the marketing of an annual crop of approximately one million pounds upon New England merchants, whose shallow-draft vessels provided the chief means of communication with the outside world.[36] The penny plantation duty imposed by Parliament in 1673 on trade between the colonies thus bore with special weight on the settlers of upper Carolina. Or, to speak more exactly, the duty would have weighed heavily had the Carolinians been in any way inclined to pay it. They were a stubborn lot, described by the proprietors in the year of Bacon's Rebellion "as a people that neither understood your own nor regarded our Interest," [37] and when in the following year Thomas Miller undertook to combine the functions of governor and collector he met rebellion.

The record is incomplete. Miller, who himself a few years earlier had faced charges of blasphemy and treason before Berkeley at Jamestown, seems obviously to have been ill-fitted for the job. Shaftesbury in England would intervene to save John Culpeper, one of the rebel leaders, from the penalties of treason. The general poverty of the community, the influence of disaffected sentiment in

---

[34] Andrews, *Colonial Period of American History*, III, 246–60; and for record of early Quaker missionary effort with comment on the physical difficulties of the country, Saunders (ed.), *Colonial Records of North Carolina*, I, 215–18.

[35] F. W. Clouts, "Travel and Transportation in Colonial North Carolina," in *North Carolina Historical Review* (Raleigh), III (1926), 16–35.

[36] Beer, *Old Colonial System*, II, 194–200.

[37] Saunders (ed.), *Colonial Records of North Carolina*, I, 228.

neighboring Virginia, and the encouragement given the rebels by some of the New England merchants must all be considered.[38] But when that is done, it is still possible to speak of the rebellion with assurance only as a further indication of the widespread discontent existing at that time in the colonies.

Thereafter, the North Carolinians, as later they would be known, seem largely to have gone their own way. The King's ministers faced more important problems in America than any raised by Albemarle. Though that county probably remained in 1689 the larger of the Carolina settlements, it held for the proprietors no such promise as did Charles Town. For a while yet the Fundamental Constitutions of Carolina would leave some mark on the political structure of the northern settlement. That community, however, from the first had been close in that respect to Virginia, and, lacking any such focal point of life as Charles Town was destined to provide in the south, North Carolina would follow in its institutional development a pattern already made familiar in Virginia and Maryland. Indeed, by 1689 the precinct court foretold in its composition and functions the key position that would be held in eighteenth-century North Carolina by the justice of the peace and the county court.[39]

If the record of events in upper Carolina remains uncertain, it is clear enough in Maryland. Charles Calvert, after more than a decade as governor of the province, had succeeded to the proprietorship in 1675 as the third Lord Baltimore. A man of decent sentiments and personally likable, he held ideas nonetheless absolute and inelastic on the subject of proprietary authority. As noted in an earlier chapter,[40] these ideas already had clashed with an independent spirit fostered among the planters in the Assembly by a rapid development of local self-government. The continuing contest between the proprietor and the representative element of the Assembly would be characterized, generally speaking, by restraint on both sides, but the issues were fundamental and the division deep rooted.

The proprietor called to his support doctrines of government as

[38] Andrews (ed.), *Narratives of the Insurrections*, 145–64.

[39] Julian P. Boyd, "The County Court in Colonial North Carolina" (M. A. thesis, Duke University, 1926).

[40] See above, pp. 301–309.

absolute as any which then were being advanced in justification of the last effort of the Stuarts to reassert the independent powers of the English crown. Members of the Assembly, for their part, insisted upon rights and privileges in keeping with the growth of parliamentary authority at home. Thus the issues at stake in Maryland reflected fundamental questions which in England moved toward a final settlement in the Glorious Revolution of 1688.

Other parallels are also worthy of note. In both places popular unrest at times burst out in the form of violent and even hysterical protest. Discontent in the colony fed on many things—the low price of tobacco, the proprietor's decision in 1670 to limit the franchise to freeholders only, his reduction of the number of deputies in 1676 from four to two from each county, trouble with the Indians, and the neighborhood of "Baconist" Virginia were among the more important. But discontent fed, too, on garbled reports of developments at home.[41] At a time when many Englishmen had been led to attribute the great fire of London to a Catholic conspiracy, and had accepted the remarkable fictions of Titus Oates as fact, the Protestant majority in Maryland found another cause for unrest in the Catholic faith of the proprietor and of some of the more prominent planters who sat in the council. To many persons the Catholics seemed to have an influence in government out of proportion to their numbers, and disputes between the upper and the lower houses easily took on the aspect of an ancient contest between Catholicism and Protestantism.

The first outburst had come in the so-called Davyes-Pate uprising of September, 1676, in the very month that Bacon burned Jamestown. Under the leadership of William Davyes and John Pate, the trouble began on Sunday, September 3, in a gathering in Calvert County of some sixty persons for protest over certain questions of taxation, the franchise, and the requirement of a special oath of fidelity to the proprietor. One suspects that the affair was little more than a Sunday-afternoon rebellion, but the government took it seriously enough to apprehend and hang its two leaders. In their place as leaders of popular protest stepped none other than Josias

---

[41] Andrews' chapter, "Fall of the Proprietary in Maryland," in *Colonial Period of American History*, II, 325–79, supersedes all earlier accounts and has been used as the basis of the following discussion.

Fendall, who for his mistakes in 1660 had been pardoned on conditions which barred him from holding any office thereafter, but who in 1677 nevertheless was returned a deputy to the Assembly for Charles County. Denied a right to sit, he continued to stir up popular protest until banished in 1681 after another "rebellion." In Charles County there resided also John Coode, a popular leader of debatable character who was destined to play a prominent role in the historic developments of 1689. The early disturbances can hardly be accepted as a serious threat to the proprietor's position, but they unquestionably reflected a potentially dangerous situation.

That situation acquired new elements of danger after 1684, when Lord Baltimore found it necessary, as had his father before him, to defend his claims before the government in England. The recent grant of Pennsylvania to William Penn had displayed a fine though not unfamiliar disregard for the boundaries formerly granted to the Calvert family in Maryland. Consequently, it had given rise to a boundary dispute that would be ended only on the eve of the American Revolution when Mason and Dixon ran the most famous of those surveyors' lines which have so largely shaped the course of American history. But there was more at stake than the dispute with Penn. The Lords of Trade were approaching the peak of their influence on imperial policy, and they had given unmistakable evidence of their distaste for the kind of independent proprietary authority Lord Baltimore exercised in Maryland. Accordingly, Lord Baltimore took ship for England, whence, as events proved, he would never return to the province.

The colony had become subject once again to an absentee proprietorship, with all its disadvantages. In Baltimore's absence, George Talbot, nephew and acting governor, murdered a royal collector of the customs, and fleeing from justice, left the colony without a resident head except insofar as a council of mediocre men proved able to supply the deficiency. When Baltimore finally gave up hope of an early return from England, where the Lords of Trade pressed him for information on many matters pertaining to his government and even had considered extending the Dominion of New England southward to include Maryland, he made the mistake of sending over William Joseph to act as his deputy in the capacity of president of the council. That the choice had been unfortunate was quickly demonstrated as Joseph for the first time met the Assembly at St. Mary's on November 14, 1688.[42]

Nine days before, on Guy Fawkes Day, William of Orange had landed in England to assist the Protestant subjects of the Catholic James II in the re-establishment of their liberties. This development could not be known immediately in Maryland, but it will serve here to emphasize the incongruity of the note Joseph struck as in an opening address to the Assembly he declared: "there is no power but of God and the Power by which we are Assembled here is undoubtedly Derived from God, to the King, and from the King to his Excellency the Lord Proprietary and from his said Lordship to Us." [43] In a much earlier day that doctrine had proved useful in the English world, but by 1688 it was like Baltimore's feudal concepts of society, outmoded and nowhere more so than in America. The impatient mood in which Joseph's words left the deputies found prompt expression in a protracted quarrel over his demand that members of the lower house take an oath of fidelity to the proprietor. It was an old requirement that had led more than one man in years past to speak feelingly of his allegiance to the King, and only after a two-day prorogation did the deputies cool off and take the oath on November 19. The Assembly then sat until December 8, when it was prorogued to meet again in April, 1689.

In advance of that date, news had reached Maryland of the succession of William and Mary to the English throne, and "jealousies" had been stirred in the minds of the Protestants over the council's failure to proclaim the newly established rulers.[44] The council then had a Catholic majority, including those who openly expressed Jacobite sentiment, and further fuel was added to the fire by the recollection that Joseph during the preceding fall had demanded thankful observance of the birth of a Catholic heir to

[42] See *Archives of Maryland*, XIII (1894), 147–227, for the proceedings of this Assembly.

[43] *Ibid.*, 148.

[44] With Andrews' "Fall of the Proprietary in Maryland," in *Colonial Period of American History*, II, 325–79, and reprint of *The Declaration of the Reasons and Motives For the Present Appearing in Arms of Their Majesties Protestant Subjects In the Province of Maryland* (1689), in Andrews (ed.) *Narratives of the Insurrections*, 305–14, one should read Beverly McAnear (ed.), "Mariland's Grevances Wiy The Have Taken Op Arms," in *Journal of Southern History*, VIII (1942), 392–409.

James II. At the direction of the Privy Council, Baltimore had drafted instructions on February 27 for the proclamation of William and Mary's accession, but his courier died before leaving England and the instructions seem not to have been forwarded. And so in the absence of official instruction and with only imperfect reporting of distant events, the colony was swept by many disturbing rumors: England had got itself a Dutch king and all Catholics would be killed; French armies were going to the rescue of James II, and the French in Canada were conniving with the Indians for destruction of all Protestants in America. So ran the rumors.

A report that the Maryland Indians were abandoning their towns and cutting their corn, sure sign that they would go on the warpath, brought 150 armed men from Calvert County to make their demands of the council. On assurances given and with the prospect of an early meeting of the Assembly, they disbanded. Prorogation of the Assembly before its meeting in April stirred new fears, though Joseph and his associates at a subsequent meeting of the provincial court seem to have given assurances sufficient to keep the peace until July.[45] But there were complaints of inefficiency and charges of corruption against those who dominated the provincial government, and the conviction was growing that failure to proclaim the new Protestant succession was attributable to deliberate suppression of instructions. When word spread that the Catholics were fortifying the Statehouse at St. Mary's, Coode led approximately 250 men against the colony's seat of government to demand possession of all arms and records. Then, having gained an easy surrender of the Statehouse, the Protestants marched again to take the surrender on August 1 of Joseph and other members of the council at Mattapany.

Formed into a Protestant Association, the insurgents called the Assembly into session on August 22 to make provision for an interim government and to petition the King to take over the province. In support of that petition, Coode went himself to England, where for several years the Lords of Trade for their own reasons had considered the very action now proposed. Baltimore succeeded in delaying the decision, but in 1691 the government of Maryland

[45] McAnear (ed.), "Mariland's Grevances Wiy The Have Taken Op Arms," *loc. cit.*, 394.

would pass to the crown without prejudice to the proprietor's right in the soil.

Over all the Chesapeake area, oldest center of English settlement in America, writs now ran in the name of the King, and of a king, moreover, whose powers had been recently hedged about with new safeguards for the liberty of his subjects. Not only did the colonist find assurance in Parliament's recently enacted Bill of Rights, but there were men in America, some of them in Maryland, who could look back on the events of 1689 with a feeling that they too had played a part in establishing within the King's dominions those parliamentary and common-law rights which made of the English Revolution indeed a glorious one.[46] Even in the colonies which staged no revolution of their own in 1689, there were many who could review the preceding years of discontent and protest with the satisfaction of having themselves taken a stand for the great principles now given a central position in the English constitution. It is the sense men thus had of sharing the glory and the benefit of England's Revolution which explains the special significance in American history of the year 1689.

[46] The people of Massachusetts, Connecticut, and Rhode Island had seized the opportunity to throw off limitations imposed on their rights of self-government through the Dominion of New England, and New York had staged a revolution of its own under the leadership of Jacob Leisler.

Att a Court holden for the County of Yorke the 24th of September 1646

Present Mr John Chew   Capt Wm Taylor
         Capt John Chisman   Capt Ralph Wormley
         Mr Wm Pryor   Mr. Row. Burnham

Vpon the complainte of Ann Quile to the Court of the vnsufferable abuses shee hath receiued from her husband Richard Quile wch Is in such secrett manner that It is not fitt to be discust in the Court Publiquely The Court doth therefore order that Mrs Eliz. Hopkins Mrs Margarett Deacon & Mrs Ellnor Coming shall forthwith serch the sd Ann Quile and to make report in what case they finde her that the Court may proceed further in the sd Complaint as they shall [see] cause.

The Court doth order that a Carpenter shall be forth agreed wth to make a howse of office in the prison by cutting away on of the studds of the sd prison and makeing a strong frame wch is to be fetted out of the sd Prison as alsoe to mend the flouer & & weather boarding & Daubing of the sd Prison and that what he shalbe agreed with for doeing of the same to be raysed at the Laying of the Leuey for the County

The Court doth order that there be fower honest men appoynted by Capt Ralph Wormeley to veiwe the marke of a cowe wch is in the possession of Nicholas Clarke and claimed by Mr John Chewe and that the[y] take speciall Notice of the sd marke whether it hath benn altered or defaced by Doggs or otherwise and that they make report thereof to the next Court holden the 26th of october next whereby It may be certeynely knowne whoe the sd Cowe belongs to

The Court doth order that Richard Watkins shall according to his owne agreement made with the Court build a sufficient howse of office to the Prison in manner followeing to say—to cutt away one of the studds of the sd Prison and to make a strong frame wch is to be fetted out from the place from wch the studd is taken and alsoe to repaire and sufficiently to mend the floore and weather bording of the sd Prison and alsoe to daubbe the sd Prison wch is to be done at his owne Charge Meales onely to be found him all wch is forthwith to be done by the sd Watkins for wch sd worke the sd Watkins to receiue the sume of three hundred pownds of tobacco & caske out of the leuey to be raysd for the County

CRITICAL ESSAY ON AUTHORITIES

T HE following essay is intended to indicate, with more evalua-
tion than the footnote citations can provide, the major sources,
both primary and secondary, from which the foregoing study
has been drawn. It does not list all of the works consulted but merely
those found useful for the particular purposes of the author. A complete
bibliography of the Southern colonies in the seventeenth century would
greatly exceed the limits imposed by considerations of space.

PRIMARY MATERIALS

The student of the Southern colonies is fortunate in having at hand
in any reasonably well-equipped library published collections of much
of the more fundamental materials with which he must deal. Except
for South Carolina and Florida, each of the Southern states whose history extends back beyond 1689 has made substantial progress toward
comprehensive publication of its provincial records. First place in this
field of historical activity belongs to Maryland. The *Archives of Maryland* (Baltimore, 1883–), edited in turn by Clayton C. Hall, Bernard C.
Steiner, J. Hall Pleasants, and Raphael Semmes, has passed well beyond the sixty-volume mark. This work provides so complete a reproduction of the legislative, judicial, and administrative action of the
provincial government in the seventeenth century as to leave little occasion for one to look elsewhere for the fundamental records of the
colony's early development.

Next to the *Archives of Maryland* in comprehensiveness of coverage
stand the *Colonial Records of North Carolina,* 10 vols. (Raleigh, 1886–
1890), edited by William L. Saunders. If the history of that colony in
the seventeenth century remains incomplete, the result cannot be
charged to a failure of the state and its people to appreciate the importance of preserving in published form that part of the record which

417

has survived the ravages of time. Indeed, the *Colonial Records of North Carolina* not only assist the student in a study of that community but also help in overcoming the difficulties arising from the strange indifference of South Carolina to a systematic study of its own colorful history. Fortunately for the purposes of this study, the *Collections of the South Carolina Historical Society*, 5 vols. (Charleston, 1857–1897), contain in the fifth volume the immensely valuable papers of the Earl of Shaftesbury pertaining to his colonial interests. Fortunately, too, the devoted labors of Alexander S. Salley, Jr., have overcome the handicap of obviously limited funds to publish under the imprint of the South Carolina Historical Commission and under his own editorship the *Journal of the Grand Council of South Carolina, August 25, 1671– June 24, 1680* (Columbia, 1907); *Warrants for Lands in South Carolina, 1672–1679* (Columbia, 1910); and *Warrants for Lands in South Carolina, 1680–1692* (Columbia, 1911).

The efforts of Virginia to make its records available to scholars have been more successful than those of South Carolina and at the same time less systematic than have been the publication programs of North Carolina and Maryland. William W. Hening, in his *The Statutes at Large; Being a Collection of All the Laws of Virginia, from the First Session of the Legislature, in the Year 1619*, 13 vols. (Richmond, Philadelphia, 1819–1823), made an excellent beginning. Not only did he bring together for the convenient reference of students one of the more fundamental records of Virginia's history but he displayed, if the conclusions of modern scholarship be accepted as the test, first-rate historical and editorial judgment. Hening completed his task just as the great dispute over slavery began, and until that question had been settled and the consequences of its submission to the arbitrament of arms surmounted, little more would be done to follow up his work. In the present century the late Henry R. McIlwaine has edited the *Journals of the House of Burgesses of Virginia, 1619–1658/59* (Richmond, 1915); *Journals of the House of Burgesses of Virginia, 1659/60–1693* (Richmond, 1914); *Minutes of the Council and General Court of Colonial Virginia, 1622–1632, 1670–1676* (Richmond, 1924); and *Executive Journals of the Council of Colonial Virginia, Vol. I, June 11, 1680– June 22, 1699* (Richmond, 1925).

Meanwhile, Lyon Gardiner Tyler, whose name testified to his descent on the maternal side from a distinguished Northern family but who gave his own loyalty unreservedly to the South of his father's family, had founded the well-known *William and Mary College Quarterly* (Richmond, Williamsburg, 1892–). Tyler established a policy of publishing many excerpts from the original record, a policy subsequently followed and improved upon by Earl G. Swem as editor of the second series. It could be wished that instead some more systematic program of publication could have been followed, but in the absence of such a program the files of the *Quarterly* remain a source of major importance that must be mined by all serious students of Virginia's early history. Similarly useful are the files of the *Virginia Magazine of History and Biography* (Richmond, 1893-). Swem's *Virginia Historical Index*, 2 vols. (Roanoke, 1934), provides a most useful tool for the student in its coverage of Hening's *Statutes; Virginia Magazine of History and Biography; William and Mary College Quarterly; Tyler's Quarterly Historical and Genealogical Magazine* (Richmond, 1920-); *Virginia Historical Register and Literary Adviser*, 6 vols. (Richmond, 1848-1853); *Lower Norfolk County Virginia Antiquary*, 5 vols. (Baltimore, 1895-1906); and the calendar of Virginia state papers in the capitol at Richmond.

For the earlier period of Virginia's founding, Alexander Brown in *The Genesis of the United States*, 2 vols. (Boston, 1890); Edward Arber and Arthur G. Bradley as editors of the *Travels and Works of Captain John Smith*, 2 vols. (Edinburgh, 1910); and Susan M. Kingsbury in her monumental edition of *The Records of The Virginia Company of London*, 4 vols. (Washington, 1906-1935), have combined to bring together most of the surviving records of England's first permanent settlement in America. Especially valuable are the first two volumes of Miss Kingsbury's work, which contain the minutes of the Virginia Company from April 28, 1619, to June 7, 1624. The third and fourth volumes include documents, falling within the period of the company's existence, found in the John Smyth of Nibley Papers, in the New York Public Library, which provide a uniquely valuable record of Berkeley Hundred, one of the subordinate ventures upon which the company so largely depended through its last years. Not included, however, are the important papers pertaining to the importation of Virginia's tobacco into England, previously published as "Lord Sackville's Papers respecting Virginia, 1613-1631," in *American Historical Review* (New York, 1895-), XXVII (1921-1922), 493-538, 738-65.

It is also necessary to turn elsewhere for several promotional tracts which, in the absence of a more complete record for the years prior to 1619, assume unusual importance as sources of the colony's early history. One has repeated occasion to consult the compilation of Peter Force, *Tracts and Other Papers Relating Principally to the Origin, Settlement and Progress of the Colonies in North America*, 4 vols.

(Washington, 1836–1846). Tracts of special importance are [Robert Johnson], *Nova Britannia: Offering Most Excellent fruites by Planting in Virginia* (London, 1609); Robert Gray, *A Good Speed to Virginia* (London, 1609); William Symonds, *Virginia. A Sermon Preached at White-Chappel* (London, 1609); *Virginia richly valued, By the description of the maine land of Florida, her next neighbour: out of the foure yeeres continuall trauell and discouerie . . . of Don Ferdinando de Soto . . . Written by a Portugall gentleman of Eluas . . . and translated . . . by Richard Haklvyt* (London, 1609); *A True and Sincere declaration of the purpose and ends of the Plantation begun in Virginia* (London, 1610); [Robert Johnson], *The New Life of Virginea: . . . Being the Second part of Noua Britannia* (London, 1612); Alexander Whitaker, *Good Newes from Virginia* (London, 1613); Ralph Hamor, *A Trve Discovrse of the Present Estate of Virginia* (London, 1615); and *A Briefe Declaration . . . of a Diuision to be now made, of some part of those Lands in our actuall possession, as well to all such as haue aduentured their monyes, as also to those that are Planters there,* published by the Virginia Council in 1616 and reproduced by the Massachusetts Historical Society as No. 11 in its Americana Series of photographic reproductions. No less important for the later years is *A Declaration of the State of the Colony and Affaires in Virginia* (London, 1620), reprinted in Kingsbury (ed.), *Records of The Virginia Company,* III, 307–65.

All students of Virginia's early history should read Secretary William Strachey's *The Historie of Travaile into Virginia Britannia,* published for the first time by the Hakluyt Society (London, 1849). They will find it helpful to run through *The True Travels, Adventures, & Observations of Captaine John Smith,* with an Introduction by John G. Fletcher and a Bibliographical Note by Lawrence C. Wroth (New York, 1930). Occasional notes of value will be found by reference to Thomas Birch, *The Court and Times of James the First,* 2 vols. (London, 1849); and Samuel Purchas, *Hakluytus Posthumus, or Purchas His Pilgrimes* (Glasgow, 1905–1907). The documents quoted by Irene A. Wright, "Spanish Policy toward Virginia, 1606–1612," in *American Historical Review,* XXV (1919–1920), 448–79, throw a helpful light on the subject.

So closely interwoven are the early stories of the Virginia and Bermuda colonies that no one can safely ignore Sir John H. Lefroy's *Memorials of the Discovery and Early Settlement of the Bermudas or Somers Islands, 1516–1685,* 2 vols. (London, 1877–1879). Every student of early American history should read [Nathaniel Butler], *Historye of the Bermudaes* (London, 1882), perhaps the most delightful contemporary narrative of an original settlement. The absence in the extant records of Virginia of any substantial body of personal correspondence between the colonists and their patrons in England finds compensation in the Manchester Papers in the Public Record Office at London, where there will be found many letters sent to Sir Nathaniel Rich and Robert Rich, second Earl of Warwick, by their correspondents in Bermuda. *The Journal of Richard Norwood, Surveyor of Bermuda,* with introductions by Wesley Frank Craven and Walter B. Hayward (New York, 1945), presents the personal record of a young man who in 1613 sought his fortune in America.

For an understanding of the earlier Roanoke Island ventures of Sir Walter Raleigh, the student continues to depend chiefly upon the record compiled by Richard Hakluyt in *The Third and Last Volume of the Voyages, Navigations, Traffiques, and Discoveries of the English Nation . . . performed within and before the time of these hundred yeeres, to all parts of the Newfound World of America* (London, 1600), a work usually consulted in the complete edition of Hakluyt's *Voyages,* issued as *Hakluyt Society Publications, Extra Series,* by MacLehose and Sons in 12 vols. (Glasgow, 1903–1905). Only a few fragments, as in *Transactions and Collections of the American Antiquarian Society* (Worcester, 1820–1911), IV (1860), 8–18, have been added to the record left by Hakluyt. However, Eva G. R. Taylor in her collection of the fugitive fragments of *The Original Writings & Correspondence of the Two Richard Hakluyts,* 2 vols. (London, 1935), has contributed in a major way to an understanding of the developing interest in North America which produced the Roanoke experiment. Included in this collection is "A Particular Discourse, concerning the great necessity and manifold commodities that are likely to grow to this Realm of England by the Western Discoveries lately attempted, written in the year 1584 by Richard Hakluyt of Oxford." Commonly cited as "The Discourse on the Western Planting" and long recognized as one of the more fundamental documents in the background of American history, it was first printed by the Maine Historical Society in its *Collections,* 2d ser., II (Cambridge, Mass., 1877).

Special mention is due Thomas Hariot's *A Briefe and True Report of the New Found Land of Virginia* (London, 1588), which ranks not merely as a major collector's item but as one of the more influential documents in early American history. The William L. Clements Library has issued in *A Brief Account of Ralegh's Roanoke Colony of 1585, being a Guide to an Exhibition* (Ann Arbor, 1935), a brochure offering convenient reference to pertinent bibliographical information regarding Hariot's famous *Report*. Laurence Binyon's *Catalogue of Drawings by British Artists . . . in the Department of Prints . . . in the British Museum* (London, 1907), has provided a guide to another famous survival of Raleigh's first colony—the paintings of John White. Some of these paintings have been reproduced in the *Thirteenth Annual Volume of the Walpole Society* (Oxford, 1925). They have been more recently and more fully reproduced in Stefan Lorant's *The New World; The First Pictures of America, Made by John White and Jacques Le Moyne and Engraved by Theodore De Bry, with Contemporary Narratives of the Huguenot Settlement in Florida, 1562–1565, and the Virginia Colony, 1585–1590* (New York, 1946); but for sharp criticism of this work see Samuel E. Morison in *William and Mary Quarterly*, 3d ser., IV (1947), 395–402; and Julian P. Boyd in *American Historical Review*, LIII (1947–1948), 111–15.

David B. Quinn of the University College of Swansea has brought together for the Hakluyt Society an extremely fragmentary record in *The Voyages and Colonising Enterprises of Sir Humphrey Gilbert*, 2 vols. (London, 1940). More than that, he has prefaced the record with a distinguished Foreword which supplants all other studies of Gilbert's colonizing ventures. Especially important for the purposes of this study has been the reproduction, *ibid.*, II, 351–64, of Christopher Carleill's "Briefe and Summary Discourse upon the Intended Voyage to the Hithermost Parts of America." In this collection, too, one can most conveniently consult Sir George Peckham's *A True Reporte of the Late Discoueries and Possession, Taken in the Right of the Crowne of Englande, of the Newfound Landes: By that Valiaunt and Worthye Gentleman, Sir Humfrey Gilbert Knight* (London, 1583). Another important promotional effort is found in Richard Hakluyt's *Divers Voyages touching the Discovery of America and the Islands Adjacent* (London, 1582).

Older even than Sir Humphrey Gilbert's hopeful efforts were the French and Spanish ventures which wrote the first chapters in the history of Florida. Jeannette T. Connor, as editor and translator, took an important step toward the publication of the basic records of Florida in her *Pedro Menendez de Aviles, Adelantado, Governor and Captain General of Florida, Memorial by Gonzales Solis de Meras* (De Land, 1923). To this was added Jean Ribaut, *The Whole & True Discouerye of Terra Florida; a facsimile reprint of the London edition of 1563, together with a transcript of an English version in the British Museum with notes by H. M. Biggar and a biography by Jeannette Thurber Connor* (De Land, 1927); and Jeannette T. Connor (ed.), *Colonial Records of Spanish Florida, 1570–1580*, 2 vols. (De Land, 1925–1930).

Henry P. Biggar's "Jean Ribaut's Discoverye of Terra Florida" may be consulted in the *English Historical Review* (London, 1886-), XXXII (1917), 253–70. Irene A. Wright (ed.), *Spanish Documents Concerning English Voyages to the Caribbean, 1527–1568* (London, 1929), provides useful information on the background of the story. Appropriately, Herbert E. Bolton's edition of *Arredondo's Historical Proof of Spain's Title to Georgia* (Berkeley, 1925), has contributed heavily to an understanding of this significant chapter in the history of European rivalry in America. Edward Arber (ed.), *The First Three English Books on America* (Birmingham, 1885), testifies to the importance in the background of English settlement of Spain's previous experience.

Records of the English government for the period covered by this study are not complete, but those surviving have for the most part been calendared. Of occasional use has been the *Calendar of State Papers, Colonial Series, 1574–1660*, edited by W. Noël Sainsbury (London, 1860). Use has been made also of the fuller calendar of many of the papers pertaining especially to Virginia provided in the earlier volumes of the *Virginia Magazine of History and Biography*. A check in Grace G. Griffin's *A Guide to Manuscripts relating to American History in British Depositories Reproduced for The Division of Manuscripts of the Library of Congress* (Washington, 1946), has indicated that most of the official documents copied for the period of this study have either been reproduced elsewhere or fall in areas of study well covered by secondary accounts. In general, the author has followed a practice, enforced by considerations of time in a study of this scope, of going into the original sources in search of the answer only to problems which seemed insufficiently answered in the works of other scholars. The several colonial charters are most conveniently consulted in Francis N. Thorpe (comp.), *The Federal and State Constitutions, Colonial Charters, and Other Organic Laws*, 7 vols. (Washington, 1909). An occasional useful reference is Thomas Rymer, *Foedera*, 20 vols. (2d ed., London, 1726–1735).

The work of English colonization was carried on so largely by agencies outside the government that for this period of initial settlement greater importance attaches to the records of the individual provinces or to such a series as the *Original Narratives of Early American History*, edited by the late J. Franklin Jameson. Especially useful in this series have been Clayton C. Hall (ed.), *Narratives of Early Maryland, 1633–1684* (New York, 1910); Alexander S. Salley, Jr. (ed.), *Narratives of Early Carolina, 1650–1708* (New York, 1911); and Charles M. Andrews (ed.), *Narratives of the Insurrections, 1675–1690* (New York, 1915). The fact that so many of the items included in these volumes were of a promotional nature in no way detracts from their importance for the historian, for there are few things more fundamental to an understanding of the settlement of America than the promotional side of the story.

Among the tracts and pamphlets not previously mentioned, most of them promotional in character, which have been used are [Arthur Wodenoth], *A Short Collection of the Most Remarkable Passages from the originall to the dissolution of the Virginia Company* (London, 1651); William Bullock, *Virginia impartially examined, and left to publick view. . . . Under which title, is comprehended the degrees from 34 to 39, wherein lyes the rich and healthfull countries of Roanock, the now plantations of Virginia and Maryland* (London, 1649); *A Perfect Description of Virginia* . . . (London, 1649), in Force (comp.), *Tracts*, II, No. 8; *Virginia: More especially the South part thereof, Richly and truly valued: viz. The fertile Carolana, and no lesse excellent Isle of Roanoak. . . . The second Edition, with Addition of the Discovery of Silkworms, with their benefit. . . . By E. W. Gent.* (London, 1650), *ibid.*, III, No. 11; *The Reformed Virginian Silk-Worm, or, a Rare and New Discovery of a speedy way . . . found out by a young lady in England . . . in May. Anno 1652. For the feeding of Silk-worms in the Woods, on the Mulberry-Tree-leaves in Virginia* . . . (London, 1655), *ibid.*, No. 13; *The Lord Baltemore's Case* (London, 1653), in Hall (ed.), *Narratives of Early Maryland*, 167–80; *Virginia and Maryland, or The Lord Baltamore's printed CASE, uncased and answered* (London, 1655), *ibid.*, 187–230; *Babylon's Fall in Maryland: a Fair Warning to Lord Baltamore* . . . (London, 1655), *ibid.*, 235–46; *A Just and Cleere Refutation of a False and Scandalous Pamphlet Entituled Babylons Fall in Maryland* . . . (London, 1655), *ibid.*, 254–75; John Hammond, *Leah and Rachel, or, the Two Fruitfull Sisters Virginia and Mary-land: Their Present Condition, Impartially stated and related* (London, 1656), *ibid.*, 281–308; Roger Heamans, *An additional brief Narrative* . . . (London, 1655), in *Maryland Historical Magazine*, IV (1909), 140–53; John Hammond, *Hammond vs. Heamans* (London, n.d.), *ibid.*, 236–51; William Hilton, *A Relation of a Discovery lately made on the Coast of Florida* . . . (London, 1664), in Salley (ed.), *Narratives of Early Carolina*, 37–61; Robert Horne(?), *A Brief Description of the Province of Carolina, on the Coasts of Floreda, and more perticularly of a New Plantation begun by the English at Cape Feare, on that River now by them called Charles-River, the 29th of May, 1664* (London, 1666), *ibid.*, 66–73; Samuel Wilson, *An Account of the Province of Carolina, in America: together with an Abstract of the Patent, and several other Necessary and Useful Particulars, to such as have thoughts of transporting themselves thither*

(London, 1682), *ibid.*, 164–76; and Thomas Ashe, *Carolina; or a Description of the Present State of that Country, and the Natural Excellencies therof, viz., the Healthfulness of the Air, Pleasantness of the Place, Advantage and Usefulness of those Rich Commodities there plentifully abounding, which much encrease and flourish by the Industry of the Planters that daily enlarge that Colony* (London, 1682), *ibid.*, 138–59.

Compilations of general value are Elizabeth Donnan (ed.), *Documents Illustrative of the History of the Slave Trade to America*, 4 vols. (Washington, 1930–1935); Helen T. Catterall (ed.), *Judicial Cases concerning American Slavery and the Negro*, 5 vols. (Washington, 1926–1937); and Leo F. Stock (ed.), *Proceedings and Debates of the British Parliaments respecting North America*, 5 vols. published (Washington, 1924–). Of special interest is Vincent T. Harlow (ed.), *The Voyages of Captain William Jackson (1642-1645)*, in *Camden Miscellany*, XIII, No. 4 (London, 1923). Robert Beverley's delightful and informative *The History and Present State of Virginia* (London, 1705), edited by Louis B. Wright for the Institute of Early American History and Culture at Williamsburg (Chapel Hill, 1947); and Henry Hartwell, James Blair, and Edward Chilton, *The Present State of Virginia, and the College,* edited by Hunter D. Farish (Williamsburg, 1940), offer valuable testimony by men who wrote only a short time after the period to which this present volume is devoted. Similarly useful has been John S. Bassett's edition of *The Writings of 'Colonel William Byrd of Westover in Virginia Esq*' (New York, 1901). On the revolution of 1689 in Maryland, *The Declaration of the Reasons and Motives For the Present Appearing in Arms of Their Majesties Protestant Subjects In the Province of Maryland* (London, 1689), reprinted in Andrews (ed.), *Narratives of the Insurrections*, 305–14, is most usefully supplemented by Beverley McAnear (ed.), "Mariland's Grevances Wiy The Have Taken Op Arms," in the *Journal of Southern History* (Baton Rouge, Nashville, 1935–), VIII (1942), 392–409.

Of the unpublished sources for early Southern history the most important are the county records, a source as yet by no means fully exploited. The records which have survived for the period of the seventeenth century are naturally more fragmentary than those for later years, but they nevertheless constitute a body of information of such bulk as to make it impossible for the author of this study to undertake anything approaching a comprehensive coverage. As a compromise the author spent the better part of a month reading through the records of York County, Virginia, from 1634 to 1689, in the hope not so much of acquiring information for purposes of citation as of gaining a feeling for the institution of the county court. This effort was supplemented by a few days devoted to a perusal of the records of other counties in the photostatic copies of the Virginia State Library at Richmond. Use has also been made of the numerous excerpts from county records published in the *Virginia Magazine of History and Biography*, the *William and Mary College Quarterly*, and the *Lower Norfolk County Virginia Antiquary*.

Happily, Volumes LIII and LIV of the *Archives of Maryland*, Court Series 6 and 7, provide ready reference for all students to the *Proceedings of the County Court of Charles County, 1658–1666, and Manor Court of St. Clement's Manor, 1659–1672* (Baltimore, 1936); and to *Proceedings of the County Courts of Kent (1648–1676), Talbot (1662–1674), and Somerset (1665–1668) Counties* (Baltimore, 1937). Happily, too, the editors of these volumes, J. Hall Pleasants and Louis Dow Scisco, have supplied in a lengthy foreword to Volume LIII an authoritative discussion of the origins and early development of the county court in Maryland. It is hoped that the appropriate authorities in Virginia and North Carolina will see fit to render a comparable service to scholarly interests by publishing representative selections from the county records of those states.

SECONDARY STUDIES

When one surveys the secondary literature covering the Southern colonies in the seventeenth century, it is readily apparent that historians of the South have been chiefly interested of recent years in later periods. There have been exceptions, the chief of them being Thomas J. Wertenbaker, whose *Patrician and Plebeian in Virginia; or, The Origin and Development of the Social Classes of the Old Dominion* (Charlottesville, 1910); *Virginia under the Stuarts, 1607–1688* (Princeton, 1914); *The Planters of Colonial Virginia* (Princeton, 1922); *Torchbearer of the Revolution, The Story of Bacon's Rebellion and Its Leader* (Princeton, 1940); and *The Old South; The Founding of American Civilization* (New York, 1942), have done much to keep fresh the interpretation of the earlier chapters of Southern history. Other exceptions which may be noted here are Wesley Frank Craven, *Dissolution of the Virginia Company* (New York, 1932); Louis B. Wright, *The First Gentlemen of Virginia* (San Marino, 1940); and Susie M. Ames, *Studies of the Virginia Eastern Shore in the Seventeenth Century* (Richmond, 1940), this last a study testifying to the wealth of material to be drawn from the county records. Ulrich B. Phillips carried his study of *American Negro Slavery* (New York, 1918) back to its origins, as did Avery O. Craven in a study of *Soil Exhaustion as a Factor in the Agricultural History of Virginia and Maryland, 1606–1860* (Urbana, 1926). Lewis C. Gray's *History of Agriculture in the Southern United States to 1860*, 2 vols. (Washington, 1933), brings together detailed information on the seventeenth century of great value to all students. But in general the historians of the South through the very years of their most fruitful activity have been content, and this is nowhere more apparent than in the field of monographic literature, to leave the story of the earliest years where Bruce, Mereness, and McCrady left it a half century ago.

The modern student finds, of course, much that is helpful in Philip A. Bruce's *Economic History of Virginia in the Seventeenth Century*, 2 vols. (New York, 1895); his *Institutional History of Virginia in the Seventeenth Century*, 2 vols. (New York, 1910); Newton D. Mereness, *Maryland 'as a Proprietary Province* (New York, 1901); and Edward McCrady, *The History of South Carolina under the Proprietary Government, 1670–1719* (New York, 1897). But these men wrote for a different age and one whose interests differed from our own.

Fortunately, the late Charles M. Andrews, *The Colonial Period of American History*, 4 vols. (New Haven, 1934–1938), brings new light and understanding to a study of all the North American colonies. However, there was only so much that Professor Andrews could do in a lifetime, and one is led at times to suspect that his interest tended to flag once he got the settlers across the Atlantic. His work is a study principally of origins, more particularly of the English origins of settlement, and though Andrews thus places the beginnings of the American story in a context that is fundamental to any true understanding of its subsequent development, it is necessary to look elsewhere for the growth of a peculiarly American society. Herbert L. Osgood, *The American Colonies in the Seventeenth Century*, 3 vols. (New York, 1904–1907), continues to be occasionally useful. Even more helpful are studies which break away from the provincial pattern of treatment to examine some phase of the common experience of all the colonies, as in Richard B. Morris, *Studies in the History of American Law, with Special Reference to the Seventeenth and Eighteenth Centuries* (New York, 1930); his *Government and Labor in Early America* (New York, 1946); Abbot E. Smith, *Colonists in Bondage: White Servitude and Convict Labor in America, 1607–1776*, published for the Institute of Early American History and Culture at Williamsburg, Virginia (Chapel Hill, 1947); and Edgar A. J. Johnson, *American Economic Thought in the Seventeenth*

Century (London, 1932). Similarly useful is Marcus W. Jernegan, *Laboring and Dependent Classes in Colonial America, 1607–1783* (Chicago, 1931).

In addition to Andrews' work, the following studies help to fill in pertinent detail on the English background: George M. Trevelyan, *England under the Stuarts* (London, 1904; 12th ed., 1925); Wilbur K. Jordan, *The Development of Religious Toleration in England from the Convention of the Long Parliament to the Restoration, 1640–1660* (London, 1938); Ephraim Lipson, *The Economic History of England*, 3 vols. (London, 1915–1931); James E. Gillespie, *The Influence of Oversea Expansion on England to 1700* (New York, 1920); and George N. Clark, *The Later Stuarts, 1660–1714* (Oxford, 1934). The development of British Imperial policy is ably covered in George L. Beer's *The Origins of the British Colonial System, 1578–1660* (New York, 1908), and *The Old Colonial System, 1660–1754; Part I, The Establishment of the System, 1660–1688* (New York, 1912); Lawrence A. Harper, *The English Navigation Laws; A Seventeenth-Century Experiment in Social Engineering* (New York, 1939); Charles M. Andrews, *British Committees, Commissions, and Councils of Trade and Plantations, 1622–1675* (Baltimore, 1908); his *The Colonial Background of the American Revolution* (New Haven, 1924); and the fourth and final volume of his *Colonial Period of American History*. Mention should also be made in this connection of Viola F. Barnes, *The Dominion of New England* (New Haven, 1923).

English scholars in the period preceding the recent war largely rewrote the history of maritime enterprise and adventure in sixteenth-century England. No student of the American colonies can safely ignore the conclusions reached in a distinguished list of studies: James A. Williamson, *Maritime Enterprise, 1485–1558* (Oxford, 1913); his *Sir John Hawkins, The Time and the Man* (Oxford, 1927); and his *The Age of Drake* (London, 1938); Arthur P. Newton, *The European Nations in the West Indies, 1493–1688* (London, 1933); Sir William Foster, *England's Quest of Eastern Trade* (London, 1933); Eva G. R. Taylor, *Tudor Geography, 1485–1583* (London, 1930); and John W. Blake, *European Beginnings in West Africa, 1454–1578* (London, 1937). To these should be added the previously mentioned Foreword by David B. Quinn to *The Voyages and Colonising Enterprises of Sir Humphrey Gilbert;* Quinn's *Raleigh and the British Empire* (London, 1947); and Eva G. R. Taylor's Foreword to *The Original Writings & Correspondence of the Two Richard Hakluyts.* Lesser items are Eva G. R. Taylor, "The Missing Draft Project of Drake's Voyage of 1577–80," in

Geographical Journal (London, 1893–), LXXV (1930), 46–47; and, by the same author, "More Light on Drake," in *Mariner's Mirror* (London, 1911–), XVI (1930), 134–51. James A. Williamson, "The Exploration of the Pacific," in *Cambridge History of the British Empire*, VII, Pt. I, *Australia* (Cambridge, 1933), 24–53, assists American students to understand the place in their own story of the repeated quest of the South Seas. In connection with these significant products of English scholarship, it is pleasant to list an outstanding work by an American scholar, George B. Parks, *Richard Hakluyt and the English Voyages* (New York, 1928).

British students have also contributed heavily to a better understanding of colonization in the seventeenth century through such studies as Arthur P. Newton, *The Colonising Activities of the English Puritans* (New Haven, 1914); Vincent T. Harlow, *A History of Barbados, 1625–1685* (Oxford, 1926); James A. Williamson, *English Colonies in Guiana and on the Amazon, 1604–1668* (Oxford, 1923); George P. Insh, *Scottish Colonial Schemes, 1620–1686* (Glasgow, 1922); Theodore W. Moody, *The Londonderry Plantation, 1609–41; The City of London and the Plantation in Ulster* (Belfast, 1939); James A. Williamson, *The Caribbee Islands under the Proprietary Patents* (London, 1926); and Charles S. S. Higham, *The Development of the Leeward Islands under the Restoration, 1660–1688* (Cambridge, 1921). Helpful even to an understanding of the problems of seventeenth-century colonization is such a study of a later chapter in the empire's history as Johannes S. Marais, *Colonisation of New Zealand* (London, 1927). The *Cambridge History of the British Empire*, I, *The Old Empire from the Beginnings to 1783* (Cambridge, 1929), has provided useful material for the present study, especially in Arthur P. Newton's chapter on "The Great Emigration, 1618–1648," pp. 136–82.

On the broader subject of Europe's interest in the New World, Samuel E. Morison's *Admiral of the Ocean Sea; A Life of Christopher Columbus* (Boston, 1942), provides a distinguished introduction. J. Bartlet Brebner, *The Explorers of North America, 1492–1806* (New York, 1933); Edward G. Bourne, *Spain in America, 1450–1580* (New York, 1904); John N. L. Baker, *A History of Geographical Discovery and Exploration* (London, 1931); Herbert E. Bolton and Thomas M. Marshall, *The Colonization of North America, 1492–1783* (New York, 1920); Frederick W. Hodge and Theodore H. Lewis, *Spanish Explorers in the Southern United States, 1528–1543* (New York, 1907); and Clarence H. Haring, *Trade and Navigation between Spain and the Indies in the Time of the Hapsburgs* (Cambridge, Mass., 1918), have proved useful.

Woodbury Lowery, *The Spanish Settlements within the Present Limits of the United States, 1513–1561* (New York, 1901); and his *The Spanish Settlements within the Present Limits of the United States. Florida, 1562–1574* (New York, 1905), offer a detailed and frequently entertaining introduction to the history of Florida. Study of that area owes much to Herbert E. Bolton, whose "Defensive Spanish Expansion and the Significance of the Borderlands" may be read with profit in *The Trans-Mississippi West, Papers Read at a Conference Held at the University of Colorado* (Boulder, 1930). John T. Lanning's *The Spanish Missions of Georgia* (Chapel Hill, 1935); Maynard Geiger, *The Franciscan Conquest of Florida (1573–1618)* (Washington, 1937); and, by the same author, *Biographical Dictionary of the Franciscans in Spanish Florida and Cuba (1528–1841)* (Paterson, N. J., 1940), are important works. Michael Kenny, *The Romance of the Floridas; the Finding and the Founding* (New York, 1934), is largely uncritical in its account of Jesuit activity. Mary Ross, "French Intrusions and Indian Uprisings in Georgia and South Carolina (1577–1580)," in *Georgia Historical Quarterly* (Savannah, 1917–), VII (1923), 251–81; Mary Ross, "The French on the Savannah, 1605," *ibid.*, VIII (1924), 167–94; and James G. Johnson, "The Yamassee Revolt of 1597 and the Destruction of the Georgia Missions," *ibid.*, VII (1923), 44–53, are most helpful contributions. Especially useful is Verne E. Chatelain, *The Defenses of Spanish Florida, 1565 to 1763* (Washington, 1941).

Randolph G. Adams, "An Effort to Identify John White," in *American Historical Review*, XLI (1935–1936), 87–91, and W. J. Holland, "The First Picture of an American Butterfly," in *Scientific Monthly* (Lancaster and New York), XXIX (1929), 45–52, come close to a positive identification of White the painter as the governor of Raleigh's lost colony of 1587. Matthew P. Andrews in *The Soul of a Nation: The Founding of Virginia and the Projection of New England* (New York, 1943), provides a readable narrative of the early years of English adventure, but its interpretation at times disagrees with the findings of modern scholarship. Walter F. Prince, "The First Criminal Code of Virginia," in American Historical Association, *Annual Report*, 1898 (Washington, 1899), I, 311–63, remains the authority on the so-called Dale's Code. Henry C. Forman, *Jamestown and St. Mary's, Buried Cities of Romance* (Baltimore, 1938), incorporating some of the results of modern archaeological investigation, represents an interesting attempt to reconstruct the original settlements in Virginia and Maryland. Wesley Frank Craven, *An Introduction to the History of Bermuda* (Williamsburg, 1938), is a study of the Bermuda colony from its founding in 1612 to the dissolution of the Virginia Company in 1624, years through which developments in Bermuda are of fundamental importance to an understanding of Virginia's history. A more extended discussion is available in Henry Wilkinson, *The Adventurers of Bermuda; A History of the Island from Its Discovery until the Dissolution of the Somers Island Company in 1684* (London, 1933). William R. Scott, *The Constitution and Finance of English, Scottish and Irish Joint-Stock Companies to 1720,* 3 vols. (Cambridge, 1910–1912), continues to serve as a valuable reference work. Also useful for their liberal quotations from the sources are Edward D. Neill's *Memoir of Rev. Patrick Copeland, Rector Elect of the First Projected College in the United States* (New York, 1871); and his *Virginia Carolorum* (Albany, 1886). Alexander Brown, *The First Republic in America* (Boston, 1898), has little value.

Cyrus H. Karraker, *The Seventeenth-Century Sheriff; A Comparative Study of the Sheriff in England and the Chesapeake Colonies, 1607– 1689* (Philadelphia, 1930), is a most helpful study of local government. Morgan P. Robinson, "Virginia Counties: Those Resulting from Virginia Legislation," in *Bulletin of the Virginia State Library* (Richmond), IX (1916), like Edward B. Mathews, *The Counties of Maryland, their Origin, Boundaries and Election Districts,* being *Maryland Geological Survey. . . . Special Publication,* Vol. IV, Pt. V (Baltimore, 1907), is a fundamental source of information for all students of government in seventeenth-century America. Of additional help is Susie M. Ames, "The Reunion of Two Virginia Counties," in *Journal of Southern History,* VIII (1942), 536–48. Oliver P. Chitwood, *Justice in Colonial Virginia* (Baltimore, 1905), and Arthur P. Scott, *Criminal Law in Colonial Virginia* (Chicago, 1930), are useful studies.

In the long bibliography of Maryland's early history the author of this present study has drawn upon the following: Gaillard T. Lapsley, *The County Palatine of Durham; A Study in Constitutional History* (New York, 1900); John L. Bozman, *The History of Maryland, from Its First Settlement, in 1633, to the Restoration, in 1660* (Baltimore, 1837); John T. Scharf, *History of Maryland, from the Earliest Period to the Present Day,* 3 vols. (Baltimore, 1879); William H. Browne, *Maryland; The History of a Palatinate* (Boston, 1884); Clayton C. Hall, *The Lords Baltimore and the Maryland Palatinate* (Baltimore, 1902); Bernard C. Steiner, *Beginnings of Maryland, 1631–1639* (Baltimore, 1903); Bernard C. Steiner, *Maryland during the English Civil Wars,* 2 vols. (Baltimore, 1906–1907); Bernard C. Steiner, *Maryland under the Commonwealth; A Chronicle of the Years 1649–1658* (Baltimore, 1911); Raphael

Semmes, *Crime and Punishment in Early Maryland* (Baltimore, 1938); Donnell M. Owings, "Private Manors: An Edited List," in *Maryland Historical Magazine* (Baltimore, 1906–), XXXIII (1938), 307–34; and Annie L. Sioussat, *Old Manors in the Colony of Maryland*, 2 vols. (Baltimore, 1911–1913). Decidedly the best discussion of Maryland's history is that of Charles M. Andrews in *The Colonial Period of American History*, II, 274–379. Vertrees J. Wyckoff contributes valuable information on "The Sizes of Plantations in Seventeenth-Century Maryland," in *Maryland Historical Magazine*, XXXII (1937), 331–39.

Helpful is Bradley T. Johnson, *The Foundation of Maryland and the Origin of the Act concerning Religion of April 21, 1649* (Baltimore, 1883); as are also John G. Shea, *History of the Catholic Missions among the Indian Tribes of the United States, 1529–1854* (New York, 1899); and his *A History of the Catholic Church within the Limits of the United States*, 4 vols. (New York, 1886–1892). Pertinent to the subject of religious freedom is the distinguished study of Rufus M. Jones, *The Quakers in the American Colonies* (London, 1911). John B. C. Nicklin presents helpful information on "Immigration between Virginia and Maryland in the Seventeenth Century," in *William and Mary College Quarterly*, 2d ser., XVIII (1938), 440–46. Louis N. Whealton studied *The Maryland and Virginia Boundary Controversy (1668–1894)* (Baltimore, 1904).

On the fundamentally important subject of agricultural experimentation and development, one should consult, in addition to Gray's previously listed study, Jerome E. Brooks, *Tobacco, Its History Illustrated by the Books, Manuscripts and Engravings in the Library of George Arents, Jr.*, 2 vols. (New York, 1937–1938); Donald D. Brand, "The Origin and Early Distribution of New World Cultivated Plants," in *Agricultural History* (Chicago, Baltimore, 1927–), XIII (1939), 109–17; Charles M. MacInnes, *The Early English Tobacco Trade* (London, 1926); and Alexander S. Salley, Jr., *The Introduction of Rice Culture into South Carolina*, Historical Commission of South Carolina *Bulletin*, No. 6 (Columbia, 1919). Richard H. Shryock has raised some fundamental questions regarding agricultural methods in "British versus German Traditions in Colonial Agriculture," in *Mississippi Valley Historical Review* (Cedar Rapids, 1914–), XXVI (1939–1940), 39–54. In connection with these questions it is helpful to read a Department of Agriculture study by Walter M. Kollmorgen, *The German-Swiss in Franklin County, Tennessee, A Study of the Significance of Cultural Considerations in Farming Enterprises* (Washington, 1940).

James C. Ballagh, *A History of Slavery in Virginia* (Baltimore, 1902);

John H. Russell, *The Free Negro in Virginia, 1619–1865* (Baltimore, 1913); and Jeffrey R. Brackett, *The Negro in Maryland; A Study of the Institution of Slavery* (Baltimore, 1889), all emphasize the legal aspect of the subject. There is need for a study of the economics of slavery in early America. Almon W. Lauber, *Indian Slavery in Colonial Times within the Present Limits of the United States* (New York, 1913), is the standard authority.

Verner W. Crane, *The Southern Frontier, 1670–1732* (Durham, 1928), is a study of special significance, as is also Clarence W. Alvord and Lee Bidgood, *The First Explorations of the Trans-Allegheny Region by the Virginians, 1650–1674* (Cleveland, 1912). Clarence W. Alvord, *The Illinois Country, 1673–1818* (Springfield, 1920), offers sure guidance on the beginnings of French exploration of the lower Mississippi.

Louise F. Brown, *The First Earl of Shaftesbury* (New York, 1933), is a valuable study of one of the major figures in the colonization of America. David D. Wallace, *The History of South Carolina*, 4 vols. (New York, 1934), is a recent survey of the full story. Julian P. Boyd, "The County Court in Colonial North America" (M. A. thesis, Duke University, 1926), naturally is useful chiefly for the eighteenth century rather than the period to which this volume is devoted. F. W. Clouts, "Travel and Transportation in Colonial North Carolina," in *North Carolina Historical Review* (Raleigh, 1924–), III (1926), 16–35, contains helpful information. Evarts B. Greene and Virginia D. Harrington have most helpfully compiled the available information on *American Population before the Federal Census of 1790* (New York, 1932).

SUPPLEMENT TO
CRITICAL ESSAY ON AUTHORITIES

ALTHOUGH the colonial period of American history has been a gratifyingly active field of study in recent years, the Southern colonies in the seventeenth century have received less attention than have other parts of the story. The following list of works (all but a few of them published since this volume went to press more than two decades ago) will emphasize the point. It is a relatively thin listing, except for studies relating to the background of English settlement in America, an area in which English historians share certain interests with American scholars, and for that part of the literature which reflects a growing interest in anything pertaining to the history of the Negro in America.

Reference to Clarence L. Ver Steeg, "Historians and the Southern Colonies," in Ray Allen Billington (ed.), *The Reinterpretation of Early American History: Essays in Honor of John Edwin Pomfret* (San Marino, 1966), 81–99, or to Hugh F. Rankin, "The Colonial South," in Arthur S. Link and Rembert W. Patrick (eds.), *Writing Southern History: Essays in Historiography in Honor of Fletcher M. Green* (Baton Rouge, 1965), 3–37, will suggest that the explanation lies partly in the greater interest students recently have found in the eighteenth-century period of Southern colonial history. Thus, the most important of recent studies of the legislative assembly has been Jack P. Greene, *The Quest for Power: The Lower Houses of Assembly in the Southern Royal Colonies, 1689–1776* (Chapel Hill, 1963). Its introductory pages provide a helpful summary of earlier developments, and one, incidentally, that is not exclusively restricted to the Southern colonies. But no fresh examination of the region's legislative institutions in the seventeenth century has been made except for that found in Michael G. Kammen, "The Origins of Representative Government

435

in British North America: An Interpretive Inquiry," a study prepared for the International Commission for the History of Representative and Parliamentary Institutions (1968), and the much briefer and even more interpretive remarks by the present writer before the Virginia Historical Society on the occasion of its celebration of the 350th anniversary of the first representative assembly (*Virginia Magazine of History and Biography,* LXXVII [1969], 131–45).

A number of general studies carry information of importance to students of the Southern colonies in the seventeenth century. In *The Colonies in Transition, 1660–1713* (New York, 1968), a volume in the New American Nation Series, I have given renewed attention to the story for the period after the Restoration of 1660, with some revision of opinions expressed in the present study. Marshall Harris, *Origin of the Land Tenure System in the United States* (Ames, Iowa, 1953), carries useful detail. Joseph Henry Smith, *Appeals to the Privy Council from the American Plantations* (New York, 1950), is a definitive study. Richard Pares, *Merchants and Planters,* Supplement 4 of the *Economic History Review* (Cambridge, England, 1960), is helpfully suggestive. The earlier pages of Thomas C. Barrow, *Trade and Empire: The British Customs Service in Colonial America, 1660–1775* (Cambridge, 1967), trace the beginnings of a customs service which started in the staple-producing colonies. Bernard Bailyn, *Education in the Forming of American Society: Needs and Opportunities for Study* (Chapel Hill, 1960), carries a very useful bibliography in addition to a suggestive interpretive essay. Max Savelle, *The Origins of American Diplomacy: The International History of Anglo-America, 1492–1763* (New York, 1967), offers sure guidance on a significant aspect of European expansion in the New World. Louis B. Wright, *The Cultural Life of the American Colonies* (New York, 1957), written by an especially well-informed student of life and culture in the Southern colonies, includes a helpful bibliography.

Other general studies have a particular, if not necessarily exclusive, focus on the Southern geographical region. Among them are Edgar W. Knight (ed.), *A Documentary History of Education in the South before 1860,* 5 vols. (Chapel Hill, 1949–1953), of which Volume I is pertinent for this period; Babette M. Levy, "Early Puritanism in the Southern and Island Colonies," in *Proceedings of the American Antiquarian Society,* New Series, LXX (Worcester, 1961), 69–348; Henry Chandlee Forman, *The Architecture of the Old South: The Medieval Style, 1585–1850* (Cambridge, Mass., 1948); William P. Cumming,

The Southeast in Early Maps, with an Annotated Check List of Printed and Manuscript Regional and Local Maps of Southeastern North America during the Colonial Period (Princeton, 1958) ; Arthur P. Middleton, *Tobacco Coast: A Maritime History of Chesapeake Bay in the Colonial Era* (Newport News, Va., 1953) ; and Stephen P. Dorsey, *Early English Churches in America, 1607–1807* (New York, 1952). William P. Cumming (ed.), *The Discoveries of John Lederer* (Charlottesville, 1958), reestablishes Lederer's reputation as an explorer of some importance. John A. Caruso, *The Southern Frontier* (Indianapolis, 1963), is more a history of Florida than of anything else, and this is especially true of the earlier part of the book. J. Leitch Wright, Jr., "Spanish Reaction to Carolina," in *North Carolina Historical Review*, XLI (1964), 464–76, covers the period extending from 1629 to the end of the century.

In the category of general studies, the single most important study remains Abbot Emerson Smith, *Colonists in Bondage: White Servitude and Convict Labor in America, 1607–1776* (Chapel Hill, 1947), for its comprehensive coverage of the servant trade upon which the Southern colonists heavily depended for the recruitment of their labor force until the end of the seventeenth century. Jacob M. Price's comparably authoritative studies of the tobacco trade deal mainly with the period following 1689, but students of the earlier period will find help in his *Tobacco Adventure to Russia: Enterprise, Politics, and Diplomacy in the Quest for a Northern Market for English Colonial Tobacco, 1676–1722*, in *Transactions of the American Philosophical Society*, New Series, LI, Pt. 1 (1961). Price is also responsible for the statistical tables on the tobacco trade appearing in *Historical Statistics of the United States* (Washington, 1960), but statistics on this trade for the period under consideration here remain very limited. Neville Williams, "England's Tobacco Trade in the Reign of Charles I," in *Virginia Magazine of History and Biography*, LXV (1957), 403–49, draws useful data from customs records. Joseph C. Robert, *The Story of Tobacco in America* (New York, 1949), and Jerome E. Brooks, *The Mighty Leaf: Tobacco Through the Centuries* (Boston, 1952), are general accounts.

Except for Maryland, each of the Southern states which trace their origins to the seventeenth century has received an authoritative review of its early history in one or more of the following works: Richard L. Morton, *Colonial Virginia*, 2 vols. (Chapel Hill, 1960) ; Hugh T. Lefler and Albert R. Newsome, *The History of a Southern State: North Carolina* (Chapel Hill, 1954; rev. ed., 1963) ; David D. Wallace, *South*

Carolina: A Short History, 1520–1948 (Chapel Hill, 1951) ; and M. Eugene Sirmans, *Colonial South Carolina: A Political History, 1663–1763* (Chapel Hill, 1966) .

Relatively few additions have been made in recent years to the published records of the Southern colonies for this period. Fortunately, the Maryland Historical Society, which established an early lead for that state in the publication of its provincial records, has devoted the latest volumes in the *Archives of Maryland* to the *Proceedings of the Provincial Court of Maryland* (Baltimore, 1952–1964) . These six volumes embrace the years 1671–1683 and extend the Court Series to a total of fifteen volumes. Three earlier volumes in that series made readily available to scholars the proceedings of several seventeenth-century county courts, and all those who have found these proceedings particularly valuable have welcomed the recent guide and inventory provided by Morris L. Radoff, Gust Skordas, and Phebe R. Jacobsen in *The County Courthouses and Records of Maryland,* published in two parts (Annapolis, 1960, 1963) . Of comparable value, especially at a time of awakening interest among historians in vital statistics, are Phebe R. Jacobsen, *Quaker Records in Maryland* (Annapolis, 1966) , and Gust Skordas, *The Early Settlers of Maryland: An Index to Names of Immigrants Compiled from Records of Land Patents, 1633–1680, in the Hall of Records, Annapolis, Maryland* (Baltimore, 1968) .

North Carolina, which also had been a leader among the Southern states in the publication of its provincial records, elected to observe the three hundredth anniversary of the proprietary charter of 1663 by launching a new series of *The Colonial Records of North Carolina* (the original series, edited by William L. Saunders, was published late in the last century) . Mattie Erma Edwards Parker has edited the initial volume of the new series, *North Carolina Charters and Constitutions, 1578–1698* (Raleigh, 1963) . The volume provides a ready reference to all the royal charters having relevance for the history of the Carolina region, from those of Gilbert and Raleigh to the second proprietary charter of 1665 and including the three Virginia charters. Included also are the "Concessions and Agreement" of 1665, but the greatest value of the volume lies in the six different versions and revisions of the "Fundamental Constitutions of Carolina," dating from 1669 to 1698, which are printed there. Too often historians, depending upon Saunders, have discussed the document without due regard for the successive revisions made by the proprietors. The second volume in the new series, under the same editorship, *North Carolina Higher-Court Records, 1670–1696* (Raleigh, 1968) , promises to be still more useful. So scarce is the documentation for the earliest years of the state's history that William S. Powell (ed.), *Ye Countie of Albemarle in Carolina: A Collection of Documents, 1664–1675* (Raleigh, 1958), is an especially welcome addition to the record. The twenty-eight documents, relating chiefly to the activities of the Carteret family and particularly Peter Carteret, came by bequest into the possession of the North Carolina Department of Archives in 1956. Welcome too are Powell's "Carolina in the Seventeenth Century: An Annotated Bibliography of Contemporary Publications," in *North Carolina Historical Review,* XLI (1964), 74–104, and his *Proprietors of Carolina* (Raleigh, 1963), for the brief biographies not only of the original proprietors but of those who succeeded them, and for the "genealogical" chart which provides a quick reference for the descent of rights in the proprietorship. Mention should also be made of his "Roanoke Colonists and Explorers: An Attempt at Identification," in *North Carolina Historical Review,* XXXIV (1957), 202–26. Hugh Lefler has contributed an interesting item in "A Description of 'Carolana' by a 'Well-Willer,' 1649," *ibid.,* XXXII (1955), 102–105. Mary Lindsay Thornton has compiled a helpful *Bibliography of North Carolina, 1589–1956* (Chapel Hill, 1958).

As Jack P. Greene has suggested in his useful summary of "The Publication of the Official Records of the Southern Colonies," in *William and Mary Quarterly,* 3d. ser., XIV (1957), 268–80, the most important of recent programs for the publication of provincial records is that instituted by the Historical Commission of South Carolina under the able leadership of the late J. H. Easterby. But the publications so far issued under the new program have been of eighteenth-century records —and quite rightly so, in view of the records for the earlier period Alexander S. Salley, Jr., managed to get into print. The chief item requiring mention here is a volume in the American Legal Records Series: Anne King Gregorie (ed.), *Records of the Court of Chancery of South Carolina, 1671–1770* (Washington, 1950). Easterby compiled and the Historical Commission of South Carolina published a *Guide to the Study and Reading of South Carolina History: A General Classified Bibliography* (Columbia, 1950).

Virginia's celebration of the 350th anniversary of the founding of the Jamestown settlement won special distinction from the launching in 1955 of the Virginia Colonial Records Project, a cooperative venture involving a number of the state's institutions for survey and microfilm reproduction of manuscript sources for the colony's history in overseas depositories, especially those in Great Britain. The survey became immediately useful to scholars as it progressed through systematic reports

439

that were placed on file in the state library, in the library of the University of Virginia, and in the research department of Colonial Williamsburg, and that were reproduced and distributed to other libraries and to interested scholars. Julian P. Boyd, "A New Guide to the Indispensable Sources of Virginia History," in *William and Mary Quarterly*, 3d. ser., XV (1958), 3–13, has described the origin and early development of the project, which was continued into the 1960's. The microfilm, on deposit with the Alderman Library of the University of Virginia, has greatly enriched the sources available in this country for the study of Virginia's history from 1580 to 1780. The only comparable project of microfilm publication is that executed by W. S. Jenkins under joint sponsorship of the Library of Congress and the University of North Carolina for reproduction of the early state records. See his *Guide to the Microfilm Collection of Early State Records* and its *Supplement* (Washington, 1950, 1951).

Another contribution to the observances of 1957 was the publication by the Virginia 350th Anniversary Celebration Corporation at Williamsburg of a series of twenty-three historical booklets on seventeenth-century Virginia, addressed more to the general reader than to the scholar but written by a variety of specialists under the general editorship of Earl G. Swem, former editor of the *William and Mary Quarterly* and compiler of the *Virginia Historical Index*. Number 1 in the series was *A Selected Bibliography of Virginia, 1607–1699* by Swem, John M. Jennings, and James A. Servies. Edmund S. Morgan has a discriminating review of the series in *William and Mary Quarterly*, 3d. ser., XV (1958), 287–93.

More recently, and in recognition of the 350th anniversary of the first representative assembly, the Jamestown Foundation has issued, under the editorship of William J. Van Schreeven and George H. Reese, *Proceedings of the General Assembly of Virginia, July 30–August 4, 1619, Written and Sent from Virginia to England by Mr. John Pory, Speaker of the First Representative Assembly in the New World* (Jamestown, 1969). Pory's account of the proceedings of that assembly is, of course, one of the more familiar of the fundamental documents of American history. What lends peculiar importance to this publication, where the original is reproduced in facsimile with each of its pages matched on a facing page to a fresh transcription by Reese, is the unmistakable evidence it carries of a dependence by American historians for more than a century now upon imperfect transcriptions of the document. I have commented upon some of the imperfections in former transcriptions in the *Virginia Magazine of History and Biography*, LXXVII (1969), 477–79.

Susie M. Ames (ed.), *County Court Records of Accomack–Northampton, Virginia, 1632–1640* (Washington, 1954), is an important addition to the American Legal Records Series published under the sponsorship of the American Historical Association. Of comparable importance for students of Virginia's history is *William Fitzhugh and His Chesapeake World, 1676–1701: The Fitzhugh Letters and Other Documents,* edited with a lengthy introduction by Richard Beale Davis and published for the Virginia Historical Society (Chapel Hill, 1963). Although many of the documents in this volume have been available through their publication in the *Virginia Magazine of History and Biography* in the last century, this earlier publication depended upon very imperfect transcriptions. *The Reverend John Clayton, A Parson with a Scientific Mind: His Scientific Writings and Other Related Papers,* edited by Edmund Berkeley and Dorothy Smith Berkeley for the Virginia Historical Society (Charlottesville, 1965), carries a biographical sketch which serves to clear up some of the problems of identification, both of the man and of his writings, that have plagued earlier scholars.

In 1964 the Association for the Preservation of Virginia Antiquities inaugurated a series of *Jamestown Documents* with the publication of *A Voyage to Virginia in 1609: Two Narratives—Strachey's "True Reportory" and Jourdain's "Discovery of the Bermudas,"* edited by Louis B. Wright and published by the University Press of Virginia at Charlottesville. Two additions have been made to the series: George Percy, *Observations Gathered Out of "A Discourse of the Plantation of the Southern Colony in Virginia by the English, 1606,"* ed. David B. Quinn (1967), and *For the Colony in Virginia Britannia. Lawes Divine, Morall and Martiall, etc., Compiled by William Strachey,* ed. David H. Flaherty (1969). All are paperbacks.

The earlier years of European adventure and rivalry in North America continue to claim the attention of scholars, and notably so in the editing and publication of documentary sources. The most important single publication in this area has been Paul Hulton and David Beers Quinn, *The American Drawings of John White, 1577–1590, with Drawings of European and Oriental Subjects,* 2 vols. (London and Chapel Hill, 1964). In this handsome set, John White's famous paintings receive the quality of reproduction they deserve, both for their artistic merit and their historical significance.

David Quinn had previously added to his two volumes on the voyages of Sir Humphrey Gilbert *The Roanoke Voyages, 1584–1590: Documents to Illustrate the English Voyages to North America under the Patent Granted to Sir Walter Raleigh in 1584,* 2 vols. (London,

1955). The subtitle could be viewed as misleading, for these volumes do much more than illustrate. Actually, they bring together in one place, with meticulous editing and a detailed commentary on White's paintings as historical documents, what must be virtually the full surviving record of Raleigh's ventures to Roanoke Island. Quinn's essay on "The Failure of Raleigh's American Colonies," in H. A. Cronne, T. W. Moody, and D. B. Quinn (eds.), *Essays in British and Irish History in Honour of James Eadie Todd* (London, 1949), continues to have importance. Perhaps nowhere will the American student (who rarely if ever is so well versed in Irish history as is Quinn) find more helpful guidance on the connection between developments in Ireland and the beginnings of colonization in America than Quinn provides in his relatively brief *Raleigh and the British Empire* (New York, 1949), unless it be in his more recent work *The Elizabethans and the Irish* (Ithaca, 1966). Quinn is also the author, with Raleigh Ashlin Skelton, of an informative introduction to the facsimile republication for the Hakluyt Society of the first edition of Hakluyt's *Voyages,* 2 vols. (Cambridge, England, 1965), which includes a provisional check-list of surviving copies of the original. Mention should be made, also, of Quinn, "The First Pilgrims," in *William and Mary Quarterly,* 3d. ser., XXIII (1966), 359–90, which recounts an abortive effort of 1597 to employ English Separatists for the purposes of colonization in North America.

Irene A. Wright drew again most helpfully upon the Spanish archives for her *Further English Voyages to Spanish America, 1583–1594: Documents from the Archives of the Indies . . . Illustrating English Voyages to the Caribbean, the Spanish Main, Florida, and Virginia* (London, 1951). Kenneth R. Andrews edited for the Hakluyt Society a valuable collection of documents in *English Privateering Voyages to the West Indies, 1588–1595* (Cambridge, England, 1959). His study of *Elizabethan Privateering: English Privateering during the Spanish War, 1585–1603* (Cambridge, England, 1964), followed, and more recently he has contributed *Drake's Voyages: A Re-assessment of Their Place in Elizabethan Maritime Expansion* (New York, 1968), a work which calls into question some of the assumptions made popular by E. G. R. Taylor and James A. Williamson. Mention should be made also of Andrews, "The Aims of Drake's Expedition of 1577–1580," in *American Historical Review,* LXXIII (1968), 724–41, and "Christopher Newport of Limehouse, Mariner," in *William and Mary Quarterly,* 3d. ser., XI (1954), 28–41.

A Notable History Containing Four Voyages Made by Certain

French Captains Unto Florida (Farnham, England and Larchmont, N.Y., 1964), a facsimile edition of Hakluyt's translation that was published at London in 1587, gains its special value from the inclusion of Thomas R. Adams' survey of "Sixteenth-Century Printed French Accounts of the Attempt to Establish a French Colony in Florida." *Pedro Menendez de Aviles, Founder of Florida, Written by Bartolome Barrientos* (Gainesville, 1965), presents an English translation by Anthony Kerrigan of the original biography of 1567 and includes a facsimile reproduction of the only previous edition, that published in Mexico in 1902. Clifford M. Lewis and Albert J. Loomie, *The Spanish Jesuit Mission in Virginia, 1570–1572* (Chapel Hill, 1953), combines documents with extended editorial comment in support of the view that Jesuit missionary efforts at that time extended as far north as the Chesapeake. Charles W. Arnade, *Florida on Trial, 1593–1602* (Coral Gables, 1959), covers briefly and helpfully a very troubled period in the history of the Spanish colony. In the New American Nation Series, Charles Gibson, *Spain in America* (New York, 1966), surveys authoritatively the colonial period of Spanish–American history and includes an up-to-date bibliography.

The Hakluyt Society has put into print for a second time William Strachey, *The Historie of Travell into Virginia Britania (1612)*, edited by Louis B. Wright and Virginia Freund (London, 1953), this time from the Percy copy of the original manuscript that belongs to the Princeton University Library and that is believed to be the most accurate of the three copies known to have survived. S. G. Culliford, *William Strachey, 1572–1621* (Charlottesville, 1965), is a helpful biography of a man about whom our knowledge is very limited. More recently, the Hakluyt Society has added to its publications of documents fundamental to an understanding of the beginnings of English colonization in the New World, Philip L. Barbour (ed.), *The Jamestown Voyages under the First Charter, 1606–1609*, 2 vols. (Cambridge, England, 1969). Louis B. Wright has brought together a representative selection of documents in *The Elizabethans' America: A Collection of Early Reports by Englishmen on the New World* (Cambridge, Mass., 1965).

In editing *The Jamestown Voyages*, Philip L. Barbour has drawn upon the extensive knowledge he acquired in writing *The Three Worlds of Captain John Smith* (Boston, 1964), which is the best-informed and most judicious biography we have or are likely to have for some time to come. Bradford Smith, *Captain John Smith: His Life and Legend* (Philadelphia, 1953), is much less satisfying, but nonetheless a significant expression of the continuing inclination among modern students to rescue the captain's reputation from the more serious charges of infidelity to the truth that had been brought against him in the nineteenth century. Bradford Smith enlisted the assistance of Dr. Laura Polanyi Striker, formerly of the University of Budapest, for reexamination of John Smith's account in the *True Travels* of his remarkable adventures in Eastern Europe, and she contributed to the biography an appendix on "Captain John Smith's Hungary and Transylvania." This called into question especially the authority with which another Hungarian historian, Lewis L. Kropf, had helped to persuade American students to dismiss that part of the *True Travels* as romance rather than history. She returned to the issue in "The Hungarian Historian, Lewis L. Kropf, on Captain John Smith's *True Travels:* A Reappraisal," in *Virginia Magazine of History and Biography,* LXVI (1958), 23–43. She also translated and published, for the Virginia Historical Society, *The Life of John Smith, English Soldier,* written by Henry Wharton in 1685 (Chapel Hill, 1957), and has prefaced the history with an essay on "Captain John Smith in Seventeenth-Century Literature." In addition, she served as translator of a paper by J. Franz Pichler (archivist of the Central Archive of Styria, Graz, Austria), "Captain John Smith in the Light of Styrian Sources," in *Virginia Magazine of History and Biography,* LXV (1957), 332–54.

The prominence of some of the men who took a lead in early colonizing ventures, as well as the representative character of those who lent their support to these adventures, has both enlarged and enriched the literature that is available for students of Virginia's early history. Thus, Theodore K. Rabb has been led by way of an initial interest in the career of Sir Edwin Sandys to undertake the quantitative study published as *Enterprise and Empire: Merchant and Gentry Investment in the Expansion of England, 1575–1630* (Cambridge, Mass., 1967). Some Americans who turned to A. L. Rowse, *The Expansion of Elizabethan England* (London, 1955), may have been disappointed in the space specifically devoted to the first colonizing ventures (a subject on which the author could speak with authority by virtue of his earlier study of Sir Richard Grenville), but they found the book a rewarding study of the broad context in which those ventures developed and have welcomed the evidence of a growing interest in the American scene that is found in Rowse, *The Elizabethans and America* (New York, 1959). His *Shakespeare's Southampton, Patron of Virginia* (London, 1965), a biography of the man who served as the last governor of the Virginia Company, has more importance for historians of America than does *Sir Walter Raleigh: His Family and Private Life* (New York, 1962), which was published in England as *Raleigh and the Throckmortons*. No student undertaking to reexamine the difficult last years of the Virginia Company can safely overlook R. H. Tawney, *Business and Politics under James I: Lionel Cranfield as Merchant and Minister* (Cambridge, England, 1958).

It would be impossible to list here all the significant studies of English society which in recent years have called into question many assumptions that have guided American students in their interpretation of the England from which the early settlers so largely came. For example, Lawrence Stone, *The Crisis of the Aristocracy, 1558–1641* (Oxford, 1965), is full of information that is often pertinent to the special interests of the American colonial historian. A briefer and more general study is Peter Laslett, *The World We Have Lost* (London, 1965), an interpretation of pre-industrial society in England that provides for the American student possibly the best available introduction to an especially active and important field of current historical investigation. Among American students, no doubt, Laslett is best known for his earlier edition of John Locke, *Two Treatises of Government* (Cambridge, England, 1960), which carries an introduction that should be checked by any student concerned with the question of Locke's influence in the writing of the "Fundamental Constitutions of Carolina." More important for students of Southern history is Laslett's introduction to *Patriarcha and Other Political Works of Sir Robert Filmer* (Oxford, 1949), where he discusses with sympathetic understanding the patriarchal concepts of society and government that found certainly some rootage in the plantation colonies. In this connection, and of particular interest for students of Virginia's history, reference should be added to his "Sir Robert Filmer: The Man *versus* the Whig Myth," in *William and Mary Quarterly*, 3d. ser., V (1948), 523–46, and "The Gentry of Kent in 1640," in *Cambridge Historical Journal*, IX (1947–1949), 148–64. In this connection, notice should be taken of Peter Walne (ed.), "'Henry Filmer of Mulberry Island, Gentleman': A Collection of Letters from Virginia, 1653–1671," in *Virginia Magazine of History and Biography*, LXVIII (1960), 408–28.

Special mention must be made of two works written by American scholars for the specific purpose of enlightening the American student on the English background of his own history. The first is Wallace Notestein, *The English People on the Eve of Colonization, 1603–1630* (New York, 1954), a volume in the New American Nation Series by

445

an eminent authority on the institutional and social history of seventeenth-century England. The other is Carl Bridenbaugh, *Vexed and Troubled Englishmen, 1590–1642* (New York, 1968), the initial volume in a series of social histories by the author to be published under the general title *The Beginnings of the American People.*

Among the writings on the earlier years of the Virginia colony special interest attaches to Perry Miller's two articles on "The Religious Impulse in the Founding of Virginia," in *William and Mary Quarterly,* 3d. ser., V (1948), 492–522, and VI (1949), 24–41, and particularly for the informed guidance they give on the problem of interpreting the oft-repeated professions of a high religious purpose by those participating in the enterprise. Harry C. Porter, "Alexander Whitaker: Cambridge Apostle to Virginia," *ibid.,* XIV (1957), 317–43, has added substantially to our knowledge of one of the colony's first ministers. Richard Beale Davis, *George Sandys, Poet-Adventurer: A Study in Anglo-American Culture in the Seventeenth Century* (London and New York, 1955), is a detailed discussion not only of the poet but also of the adventurer as a resident official in the colony during the company's later years. At times the interpretation of men and developments runs counter to some of the views that have been expressed by the present writer.

Warner F. Gookin and Philip L. Barbour, *Bartholomew Gosnold, Discoverer and Planter: New England—1602, Virginia—1607* (Hamden, Conn., 1963), has thrown a helpful light upon a man who obviously played an important part in the founding of the Virginia colony but about whom very little had hitherto been known. Many interstices in Virginia's early history have been helpfully filled by such essays as Darrett B. Rutman, "The Virginia Company and Its Military Regime," in Rutman (ed.), *The Old Dominion: Essays for Thomas Perkins Abernethy* (Charlottesville, 1964), and David B. Quinn, "Advice for Investors in Virginia, Bermuda, and Newfoundland, 1611," in *William and Mary Quarterly,* 3d. ser., XXIII (1966), 136–45. Also helpful are the following articles in the *Virginia Magazine of History and Biography:* Charles E. Hatch, Jr., "Mulberry Trees and Silkworms: Sericulture in Early Virginia," LXV (1957), 2–61; Martha W. Hiden, "A Voyage of Fishing and Discovery, 1609," *ibid.,* 62–66; Terence H. O'Brien, "The London Livery Companies and the Virginia Company," LXVIII (1960), 137–55; Robert C. Johnson, "The 'Running Lotteries' of the Virginia Company, *ibid.,* 156–65; "The Lotteries of the Virginia Company, 1612–1621," LXXIV (1966), 259–92; Peter Walne, "The 'Running Lottery' of the Virginia Company in Reading, 1619, and in Chester, 1616," LXX (1962), 30–34; Charles E. Hatch, Jr., and Thurlow Gates Gregory, "The First American Blast Furnace, 1619–1622," *ibid.*, 259–96. Gillian T. Cell, "The Newfoundland Company: A Study of Subscribers to a Colonizing Venture," in *William and Mary Quarterly*, 3d. ser., XXII (1965), 611–25, does not bear directly on the history of Virginia but is nonetheless important for students of its history.

John L. Cotter and J. Paul Hudson, *New Discoveries at Jamestown* (Washington, 1957), reports results of continuing archaeological investigations on the Jamestown site. Ivor Noel Hume, *Here Lies Virginia: An Archaeologist's View of Colonial Life and History* (New York, 1963), is by a member of the staff of Colonial Williamsburg.

An interesting item is John Parker, *Van Meteren's Virginia, 1607–1612* (Minneapolis, 1961), which incorporates the views of the Virginia adventure recorded by the Dutch historian Emanuel van Meteren, who for much of this time was resident in London. More recently Parker has published *Books to Build an Empire: A Bibliographical History of English Overseas Interests to 1620* (Amsterdam, 1965).

Nancy O. Lurie, "Indian Cultural Adjustment to European Civilization," in James M. Smith (ed.), *Seventeenth-Century America: Essays in Colonial History* (Chapel Hill, 1959), is largely concerned with Virginia's Indians and was written by an anthropologist. William S. Powell, "Aftermath of the Massacre: The First Indian War, 1622–1632," in *Virginia Magazine of History and Biography*, LXVI (1958), 44–75, carries a title that is self-explanatory. W. Stitt Robinson, "Tributary Indians in Colonial Virginia," *ibid.*, LXVII (1959), 49–64, traces the development of a tributary status as a feature of policy from 1609 into the eighteenth century. Robinson had earlier published a useful survey of "Indian Education and Missions in Colonial Virginia," in *Journal of Southern History*, XVIII (1952), 152–68. William N. Fenton and others, *American Indian and White Relations to 1830: Needs and Opportunities for Study* (Chapel Hill, 1957), in addition to a suggestive essay by an eminent ethnologist, contains a very useful bibliography for all students of this tragic phase of American history.

Among the additional essays included in Smith's *Seventeenth-Century America* are three which bear exclusively or chiefly upon Virginia's history. Bernard Bailyn, "Politics and Social Structure in Virginia," is notable for the influence it has exerted upon the interpretation of the socio-political history of other colonies as well as of Virginia. Mildred Campbell, "Social Origins of Some Early Americans," draws most helpfully upon her extensive researches in England for a discus-

447

sion of those who migrated to America, and especially those taking ship for the Chesapeake under some form of indenture. William H. Seiler's informative "The Anglican Parish Vestry in Virginia" supplemented several of his earlier publications on the institutional history of Virginia's church: "The Church of England as the Established Church in Seventeenth-Century Virginia," in *Journal of Southern History*, XV (1949), 478–508; "The Anglican Parish Vestry in Colonial Virginia," *ibid.*, XXII (1956), 325–29; and "Land Processioning in Colonial Virginia," in *William and Mary Quarterly*, 3d. ser., VI (1949), 416–36.

George M. Brydon, *Virginia's Mother Church and the Political Conditions under Which It Grew*, 2 vols. (Richmond, 1947–1952), is at times defensive in tone but comprehensive and full of useful information. Because of the importance of the subject for the development of the Anglican Church in America, mention should be made of Edward F. Carpenter, *The Protestant Bishop, Being the Life of Henry Compton, 1632–1713, Bishop of London* (London, 1956).

Except for an occasional piece, such as J. Mills Thornton, III, "The Thrusting Out of Governor Harvey: A Seventeenth-Century Rebellion," in *Virginia Magazine of History and Biography*, LXXVI (1968), 11–26, or Robert C. Johnson, "Virginia in 1632," *ibid.*, LXV (1957), 458–66, the political history of Virginia after 1624 has received little attention until the era highlighted by Bacon's Rebellion is reached. Bailyn's previously cited essay on "Society and Politics" was a significant contribution to discussion of that difficult historical problem. Wilcomb E. Washburn, *The Governor and the Rebel: A History of Bacon's Rebellion in Virginia* (Chapel Hill, 1957), is the single most important monographic publication on seventeenth-century Virginia to appear in the last two decades. Written as a sympathetic interpretation of Governor Berkeley's role in the rebellion, it takes sharp issue with the interpretation presented by the late Professor Thomas J. Wertenbaker in his *Torchbearer of the Revolution*. It hardly can be described, however, as having closed the debate, as one can readily see by turning to the pertinent passages in Richard L. Morton's *Colonial Virginia*.

Wilcomb E. Washburn, "Governor Berkeley and King Philip's War," in *New England Quarterly*, XXX (1957), 363–77, has a special interest. In "The Effect of Bacon's Rebellion on Government in England and Virginia," in *United States National Museum Bulletin* 225 (Washington, 1962), 137–52, he considers some of the consequences of the rebellion, a subject to which John C. Rainbolt has helpfully turned in "A New Look at Stuart 'Tyranny': The Crown's Attack on the Virginia Assembly, 1676–1689," in *Virginia Magazine of History and*

Biography, LXXV (1967), 387–406. Sister Joan de Lourdes Leonard, "Operation Checkmate: The Birth and Death of a Virginia Blueprint for Progress," in *William and Mary Quarterly,* XXIV (1967), 44–74, is concerned with the years immediately preceding the rebellion.

John C. Rainbolt, "The Absence of Towns in Seventeenth Century Virginia," in *Journal of Southern History,* XXV (1969), 343–60, is of more general interest. Edward M. Riley touched upon one aspect of the same subject in "The Town Acts of Colonial Virginia," *ibid.,* XVI (1950), 306–23. Neville Williams, "The Tribulations of John Bland, Merchant: London, Seville, Jamestown, Tangier, 1643–1680," in *Virginia Magazine of History and Biography,* LXXII (1964), 19–41, has importance for students of both the political and social history of the time, as does John L. Blair, "The Rise of the Burwells," *ibid.,* 304–29. Ludwell Lee Montague, "Richard Lee, the Emigrant, 1613(?)–1664," *ibid.,* LXII (1954), 3–49, clarifies some questions regarding the founder of one of Virginia's great families. Clifford Dowdey, *The Great Plantation: A Profile of Berkeley Hundred and Plantation Virginia, from Jamestown to Appomattox* (New York, 1957), provides information on the early history of the Harrison family.

Donnell M. Owings, *His Lordship's Patronage: Offices of Profit in Colonial Maryland* (Baltimore, 1953), is virtually unique in its effort to establish the actual worth of the patronage dispensed by the governing authority of a North American colony. Of further assistance in understanding the political difficulties which reached their climax in 1689 are John A. Kinnaman, "The Public Levy in Colonial Maryland to 1689," in *Maryland Historical Magazine,* LV (1960), 253–74, and especially Michael G. Kammen, "The Causes of the Maryland Revolution of 1689," *ibid.,* 293–333.

Social and economic studies of seventeenth-century Maryland include Manfred Jonas, "Wages in Colonial Maryland," in *Maryland Historical Magazine,* LI (1956), 27–38; Erich Isaac's two-part study of the settlement on Kent Island, *ibid.,* LII (1957), 93–119, 210–32; Arthur E. Karinen, "Maryland Population, 1631–1730," *ibid.,* LIV (1959), 365–407, and his "Numerical and Distributional Aspects of Maryland Population, 1631–1840," *ibid.,* LX (1965), 139–59; Kenneth L. Carroll, "Maryland Quakers in the Seventeenth Century," *ibid.,* XLVII (1952), 297–313, and also his "Talbot County Quakerism in the Colonial Period," *ibid.,* LIII (1958), 326–70; and William A. Reavis, "The Maryland Gentry and Social Mobility, 1637–1676," in *William and Mary Quarterly,* 3d. ser., XIV (1957), 418–28.

On the question of the Negro and his role in the newly emerging

449

society, recent scholarship—at any rate, until very recently—has been essentially interpretive in character. Thus, Frank Tannenbaum, *Slave and Citizen: The Negro in the Americas* (New York, 1947), invited attention to the possibilities for comparative study of the institution of slavery in Latin America and in the English colonies of North America, with suggestions that the latter had a harsher form of slavery. The most recent attempt to compare the institution in these two regions is that of Herbert S. Klein, a specialist in Latin American history, in his *Slavery in the Americas: A Comparative Study of Virginia and Cuba* (Chicago, 1967). Oscar Handlin and Mary F. Handlin, "Origins of the Southern Labor System," in *William and Mary Quarterly*, 3d. ser., VII (1950), 199–222, has been as significant as was the work of Tannenbaum for the stimulation it gave to fresh discussion of fundamental issues. A vigorous rejoinder by Carl N. Degler in *Out of Our Past: The Forces that Shaped Modern America* (New York, 1959), and in *Comparative Studies in Society and History,* II (1959–1960), 49–66, 488–95, has served to sharpen discussion of how early the Negro's status in the country became that of a slave. That question, as with other issues relating to the origins of slavery in America, was by no means new, and Stanley M. Elkins has provided a helpful historiographical introduction to his *Slavery: A Problem in American Institutional and Intellectual Life* (Chicago, 1959), which argues that the enslavement of the Negro in North America became so complete as to lend the institution a unique quality. Winthrop D. Jordan, "Modern Tensions and the Origins of American Slavery," in *Journal of Southern History,* XXVIII (1962), 18–30, provides substantive evidence on the issues in debate as well as historiographical comment. Another important item is Arnold A. Sio, "Interpretations of Slavery: The Slave Status in the Americas," in *Comparative Studies in Society and History,* VII (1964–1965), 289–308, which calls into question what has come to be known as the Tannenbaum–Elkins thesis.

Overshadowing all other works pertaining to the subject of slavery in colonial America are two books of recent date. David Brion Davis, *The Problem of Slavery in Western Culture* (Ithaca, 1966), is primarily concerned with the historical and cultural background of the later antislavery movement, but it is also a contribution of the highest quality to the discussion of slavery in colonial America and of such questions as the special severity that has been attributed to the institution as it developed in British America. The other study is Winthrop D. Jordan, *White Over Black: American Attitudes toward the Negro, 1550–1812* (Chapel Hill, 1968). As the subtitle indicates, this is a study of the white man's attitude toward the Negro from the first important contacts by English voyagers with the western coast of Africa to a time well past the American Revolution. It is a very full and informative book, and has an obvious pertinence to the question of how far the present-day prejudice against the Negro is attributable to his previous condition of servitude.

A third study of recent date, and of importance for students of slavery in colonial America, is Kenneth G. Davies, *The Royal African Company* (London, 1957). This covers the quarter-century of the company's trade that preceded the termination of its monopoly by action of Parliament in 1698. Based upon the surviving records of the corporation, the book reveals that probably nine of ten Negroes transported from Africa to British America by the company during these years were landed in the West Indies rather than in the continental colonies, a revelation that helps to explain the limited use of Negro labor on the mainland before the end of the seventeenth century. The findings of Davies thus become somewhat negative for the purposes of the student primarily concerned with the migration of Africans into the Southern colonies before 1689, and the same can be said of other and more general studies of the slave trade which might be mentioned here.

The latest of such studies, however, requires special mention. It is Philip D. Curtin, *The Atlantic Slave Trade: A Census* (Madison, 1969), which presents the first sophisticated analysis of surviving statistical evidence as to the size and flow of the Atlantic slave trade over the course of some five centuries. The results are often startling when viewed in the light of previous assumptions, including the assumption that a peculiarly harsh form of slavery took root in British North America.

Indications that many of the Negroes who reached the mainland in the seventeenth century came from the West Indies lends interest to such essays as A. P. Thornton, "The Organization of the Slave Trade in the English West Indies, 1660–1685," in *William and Mary Quarterly*, 3d. ser., XII (1955), 399–409; Winthrop D. Jordan, "The Influence of the West Indies on the Origins of New England Slavery," *ibid.*, XVIII (1961), 243–50; and Richard S. Dunn, "The Barbados Census of 1680: Profile of the Richest Colony in English America," *ibid.*, XXVI (1969), 3–30.

Of more direct concern to readers of the present volume are James H. Brewer, "Negro Property Owners in Seventeenth Century Virginia," in *William and Mary Quarterly*, 3d. ser., XII (1955), 575–80; Winthrop D. Jordan, "American Chiaroscuro: The Status and Definition of Mulattoes in the British Colonies," *ibid.,* XIX (1962), 183–200; and M. Eugene Sirmans, "The Legal Status of the Slave in South Carolina, 1670–1740," in *Journal of Southern History,* XXVIII (1962), 462–73. Benjamin Quarles, "The Colonial Militia and Negro Manpower," in *Mississippi Valley Historical Review,* XLV (1958–1959), 643–52, deals largely, though not exclusively, with the eighteenth-century period.

John Hope Franklin, *From Slavery to Freedom: A History of American Negroes* (New York, 1950), remains the standard work, but it has been supplemented by August Meier and Elliott M. Rudwick, *From Plantation to Ghetto: An Interpretive History of American Negroes* (New York, 1966), the best brief survey in the literature.

INDEX

INDEX